GUERNICA!

GUERNICA!

GUERNICA!
GUERNICA!

•

*A Study
of Journalism,
Diplomacy, Propaganda,
and History*

•

HERBERT RUTLEDGE
SOUTHWORTH

UNIVERSITY OF CALIFORNIA PRESS
BERKELEY, LOS ANGELES, LONDON

157700

University of California Press
Berkeley and Los Angeles, California

University of California Press, Ltd.
London, England

ISBN: 0-520-02830-9
Library of Congress Catalog Card Number: 74-82850
Copyright © 1977 by The Regents of the University of California
Designed by Kadi Karist Tint

Printed in the United States of America

This book is dedicated to the journalists, men and women, in Bilbao and on the Spanish-French frontier, who gave to the world the news of the destruction of Guernica; and especially to George Lowther Steer, to Noel Monks, to Christopher Holme, and to Mathieu Corman; and also especially to Jean Richard and to Canon Alberto de Onaindia, who broke the wall of silence constructed in France to keep out the news about Guernica.

Contents

Foreword

THE VALUE OF A "NAIVE" RETURN TO TEXTUAL CRITICISM

When asked not "how one writes history" but "how one does history," I am tempted to answer, somewhat jocularly, but with the intention of being enlightening: is there much difference between "doing history" and "doing art?" History has its classic and its baroque styles, its impressionistic and its abstract works, its cubists, as well as its fauves, hacks, and engagés, weekend scholars as well as professionals. And in history as in art only talent distinguishes between those who can uncover a whole universe in a few lines and those who will never uncover anything. To explain why Herbert Southworth's historical method so enchants me I can do no better than to compare him with the so-called naive artists.

Let me be clearly understood: that is the greatest compliment I can give. Beyond all snobbism, all fashion, I have not only loved but admired the "Naive" school of painting for its purifying role among the modern imbroglio. Naturally I speak of the true "Naifs," those whose every touch is sincerity itself, each reworking a scruple, each emphasis a necessity, each hesitation a search for certainty.

I am told such a search is chimerical and that history is an artificial construction just as a painting is not a photograph. But every passionate quest for a concrete truth is in effect a spontaneous critique of false constructions, of fake compositions. The true naif never has the ambition to achieve reality. On the contrary, he begins with the images imposed upon the public by bad painters and photographers, and because he cannot accept these images, he draws nearer—and draws us along with him—to the inaccessible "truth." Southworth proceeds in a similar manner for the event, by proceeding to a critique of its image.

THE RETURN OF THE EVENT

Much has been said against the event. I do not wish to repudiate my own adherence to the effective criticism—already three-quarters of a century old—brought against history reduced to the event, such as positivists had conceived it. Paradoxically, however, the period of this criticism has coincided, through the accession to information of growing masses, with a metamorphosis of the event—a new dimension of the event that is now capable of becoming "monstrous." And this even before the bewitchment of television, as soon as the printed media were able to relay, immediately and with awareness, the "news." For each event, then, has posed a political problem: is it to be revealed or should it be suppressed?

It is striking to be able to use almost word for word Pierre Nora's enumeration of the phases of the Dreyfus case in order to describe the themes of Southworth's *Guernica! Guernica!*: "Initial rumors; the exploitation of silence; the persistent paralysis of official information; hints of compromise within the spheres of power; the affront to great principles; dichotomy of the world into good and evil people; augmented suspense through false documents and a series of leaks; appeal to public opinion through open letters and manifestoes; the mediating function of 'intellectuals' between the public and the event."

In this sense Southworth's work, easily mistaken as a classic study of documentary evidence, will be shown to be, in some future historiography, as one of the first and best responses to Pierre Nora's call: "Today, when the whole of historiography has based its modernity upon the obliteration of the event, the denial of its importance, and its dissolution, the event returns—a different event—and with it, perhaps, the potential for a purely contemporary history."[1]

With Southworth we are plunged into contemporaneity. Forty years have not yet gone by since Guernica was destroyed. At least 6,000, perhaps 10,000 individuals felt the destruction in their flesh, their belongings, in any way through several hours of anguish. And yet, even today, even in far away American universities, the evidence is suspect because a press staff in a military headquarters, on the evening of April 27, 1937, twenty-four hours late and with error in the date, dared to deny the event. Thus, the case is not one of an event becoming a problem but of the problem itself taking the place of the event: why is a local but widely witnessed incident blown up, deflated, reconstituted, distorted, and reborn into two contradictory images, passionately argued throughout the entire world? It is because there are symbolic events.

THE ADVENT OF THE SYMBOLIC EVENT

From the very first day Guernica became a symbolic event, owing to its unexpected repercussions.

Durango had suffered before Guernica, other villages had been razed to the ground, and there had been protests; corpses had been counted. Yet the world had barely reacted. No one thought of denying these events. Thus, after Guernica, the representatives of Germany, Italy, and Portugal easily proclaimed, and had their colleagues proclaim in turn, at the Non-Intervention Committee that the bombing of open cities, however regrettable, was not the first atrocity in this nine-month-old war. But what they did not say, what they could not say, was that they had insisted (and succeeded in obtaining) that the word *Guernica* never be uttered, not only in the motion voted upon but even in the discussion of the motion. South-worth details this stupefying episode in diplomatic history. In a few days the very name of Guernica had become a more burning subject than the flames of its conflagration.

And this is indeed the first distinctive aspect of a symbolic event.

If it bears heavy human responsibilities, and once the controversy is started from below, the unavowable can no longer be admitted from on high nor the confession be demanded without a dramatic rupture. Disquiet then becomes cynicism, and prudence becomes cowardice. Could a "non-intervention committee" utter the name of a town bombed by Germans and partially occupied by Italians? This prelude to Munich, as viewed by the Powers, is frightening in its simplicity.

It is less simple to establish how one had proceeded from intention to the event, from the event to the news, and from the news to myths and to silences. It is through this labyrinth, full of logical constructions of the collective imagination—bright spots as well as dead ends—that Southworth offers to guide us. He hides no zone of doubt, no hole in the documentation, no area where hypothesis replaces certainty. He fustigates only those propositions that go against the evidence in the service of an undeniable initial lie.

The most difficult problem lies at the origins of the event: intentions, decisions, where these were elaborated. Charles Morazé once demonstrated that the documentary evidence behind a decision is all the more likely to be destroyed the more important the political significance of that decision becomes. The same is true of course of military decisions. Can one picture a headquarters carefully preserving orders whose very existence are denied, directed at a body of troops that is not supposed to exist? It is true that all parties soon agreed that the bombing had taken place, only to minimize its importance by discovering a tactical justification for it. The order, then, could be exhibited. But only reports written after the event were furnished. The quest for the objective document, at the sources for the event, is often illusory.

Southworth offers only reasonable conjectures on this point, none favorable to the dramatized versions. Mola, in order to hasten the fall of Bilbao and avoid another Madrid, needed (as his campaign shows and his threats emphasized) intensive bombings of the Basque communication network. His instrument was the Condor Legion. It was under his command, and he was thus responsible for its actions. Technically, it was autonomous. Was Mola aware of its strength? Was the Legion itself aware of its own effectiveness? In fact, they were experimenting. Although bombing Guernica for more than three hours, alternating explosive bombs, incendiaries, and strafing, the Legion did not destroy the bridge and the munitions plant on the edge of town: an annoying detail for the tactical justification. It did not touch the "Casa de Juntas" or the tree of Guernica: an annoying detail for the symbolic version, particularly one that claimed that the fire was a provocation started on the ground (it is easy to make mistakes from the sky).

Thus, another lesson for the historian: the concrete event does not bend to either the logic of avowed intentions or to that of attributed intentions. The event does not of itself clarify the aim it carries out.

If the event is sufficiently significant, however, and touches some sensitive points, then, once broadcast by the mass media, it can set in motion psychological responses on an unpredictable level. The responsible parties must then deny, equivocate, reverse roles. This is still being done in the case of Guernica. In 1937, in order for the wave of indignation to surface, and in order that an ambiguity be opposed to it, it was necessary that the event assume an amplitude that transcended it, by its meaning in the group structures and in the class structures, in their ideological makeup, and in the terrible conjuncture of that springtime. Since then one can measure the continuity of the conflicts and their varying intensity by the softening or hardening of the Franco version of the Guernica affair. One of the great merits of Southworth's work is to have opened this theme: the relationship, up to our own time, between official history and a political drama, between the renewed sharpness of the Basque problem and the bad conscience remaining from an incident.

GUERNICA: THE COMPLEXITY OF THE SYMBOL
AND THE LOGIC OF THE IMAGES

The Guernica event transcends Spain. As an assault against a national shrine, it is also, on the world scale, the revelation of a danger. It is both Reims and Hiroshima. The two symbols complement each other without being confused.

"Guernica: holy city of the Basques," say the guidebooks. The word *holy* may surprise, but it is proper for a community anchored in the "immemorial" and which still feels religious sentiments. The word *holy* is present in the "Gernikako arbolo," the hymn of Carlist origin, but sung by all Basques as a popular song. Of course, the distance is great from the "liberties" sworn to under the tree of Guernica by the lords of Vizcaya to national freedom in the modern sense. Yet the symbolism of Guernica, precisely because it was revived in the nineteenth century, took its place in its ideology. The duality community-liberty retained its emotional weight: the proof is that people still die in 1970 in its name—"Euzkadi ta Askatasuna." In a war carried on in the name of Basque liberties, the word *Gernika* touched the very deepest chord. To tax with hypocrisy, or to suspect a scenario behind the tears of those who told newspapermen "Guernica burns," or behind the religious tone of President Aguirre calling upon world conscience, is even more absurd than it is in bad taste. The Guernica operation had a painful and contradictory effect on the Basques: it broke their morale, while binding them to fight to the end.

Was this effect purposely sought? Can one, following Aguirre, accuse "the Germans in the service of the Spanish rebels" of wanting to wound the Basques in their very soul by attacking their sanctuary? It is hard to conceive of the Condor Legion realizing this was the meaning of their objective, or of receiving instructions to that effect. Was the attack deliberate? All evidence points to it: the vocabulary and the terroristic practices of the generals, the passionate centralization of their doctrine, the denunciation of separatism by the Falange as a "sin that cannot be forgiven." The event seemed to echo only too well a publicly avowed hatred to be merely an accident.

Thus it was not enough for the Franco government, faced with a bombing of such dimensions as to affect the entire world, and whose objective could shock its own supporters in the Carlist sector, to state: "We did not wish to do this." It preferred to say: "We did not do it." But it erred by twenty-four hours in its justification. Yet, within its own camp, its credibility was hardly weakened. Another lesson—an existential adhesion needs coherence: the "reds," in their retreat, had burned Irún, Eibar (and even Moscow in 1812: the argument was made!), therefore they had burned Guernica. Those who did not wish to express their indignation—ambassadors, ministers, the moderate press—were eager, outside of Spain, to grant the Franco government the benefit of the doubt. The most anxious to prove, to demonstrate, were the Anglo-Saxon Catholic circles, to whom Southworth devotes deserved attention. Bothered by the event, they discriminated between men: good versus bad, God against the Devil. But who is closer to God than the Basque people? A fault appears within the logic of the myth. How is one to believe that among God's enemies victims pray, priests bless, or even that Canon Onaindia, a witness shouting in anguish, is truly a canon? The relentless denials and the disqualifications of witnesses, surprise by their violence. In high circles, the campaign was organized. On lower levels, there most probably was sincerity in the belief. A veteran of 1914 can honestly ignore a new aerial technique; an honest parish priest can think it impossible that pilots might enjoy shooting at fugitives and at sheep. Those people think with their leaders. And they did not live through 1940.

Those who did, know better. I retreated through Villers-en-Argonne in flames, after a bombing with incendiaries. I did not set the fire myself! And a Spaniard, a member of a "worker's regiment," retreating along with me, declared: "Ahora os toca a vostros" ("now, it's your turn").

Guernica was the key to the realization that the Spanish conflict might prefigure further conflicts to come. This realization was massive in England, much more attenuated in France. Southworth explains why: In France, the news of Guernica was voluntarily blocked, while in England there was a traditional interest in Bilbao coupled with a denser journalistic network. By April 28, the English press lucidly predicted Coventry.

It is true that political logic immediately transcends concrete information. Prieto, Perí, Pertinax, the English labourites pointed to one responsible party: Göring. This was an oversimplification. Yet it serves today to free the Franco government of any responsibility. Southworth shows that the hypothesis of an order issued by Berlin is in no way supportable. Göring is supposed to have said to officious inquirers in Nuremberg (the question was never asked during the official trial) "Guernica? We had to gain experience somehow." This only confirms one fact, that the Condor Legion was indeed experimenting. But let us not forget—under Spanish orders, in a civil war. The "accidental" aspect resulted from the intensity of the bombing, the violence of the fire, and the fact that only the inhabited town was hit, and not the military objectives, or the symbolic quarter. It is probable that there were recriminations, even some violent scenes, and possibly some sanctions were taken. But this is easier to imagine than to document. Yet the telegrams specifying the common version to be upheld, and the refusal to allow an international inquiry are in our hands. The final word probably was uttered by Jaime del Burgo: "What rotten help they gave us!" But, after all, their help was requested.

It is somewhat artificial, or calculating, to dismiss, as has been done recently, both Guernica mythologies: one based on an idyllic, conventional view of the Basque city, and on an exaggeration of the catastrophe; the other on a lie conceived in panic, because of the very innocence of the responsible parties. There is myth on both sides, in the sense that on each side an existential logic prevails. But is it unimportant to note that one image is constructed upon a conscious lie, while the other is based upon a reality perceived as a symbol and a symptom: a symbol of the broken. Basque people; a symptom of a sickness that gave us Coventry, Dresden, Hiroshima, and Hanoi? It has been fashionable for some time to "demythify" both "memories" left over from the Spanish conflict. Some say that without Picasso Guernica would not be Guernica. Picasso answered that point himself: "Did you make Guernica?" he was asked by a German officer. "No, you did." The answer, according to Vicente Talón, is itself part of the myth. Its authenticity is not important; it demythifies the demythification.

There are many ways to handle a myth. One consists in building a new one. Others consist in concentrating only on the psychosociological fact—that is, on the acceptance of the myth as the sign of belonging to a group, a class, that secretes an ideology. Perhaps this is the most important aspect for the historian. Yet the latter cannot ignore, at the birth of this acceptance, the original propositions. Southworth has made it his specialty to research, around the most controversial episodes of the

Franco "crusade," the organization of silences, of denials, of affirmations, of transmissions, of repetitions, that impose doubts and negations, beliefs and attitudes. He has brought the problem of "myth" to the level of information, of directed information, of "disinformation."

INFORMATION: ITS MECHANISMS AND ITS MYSTERIES

Southworth places a primordial importance to the "first news," the initial manner in which the event, or the imaginary affirmation, is presented. Then he follows step by step, in strict chronological order, the transmission, denials, distortion of this "news" item. This is classical scholarship, although rarely pushed to so deep a level as in *GUERNICA! GUERNICA!* A comparison only brings forth the weaknesses of earlier works in this field. The reader, at first surprised, quickly discovers that although Franco, Mola, Göring, or Sperrle cannot be dismissed at the origin of the drama. Bolín, Steer, Onaindia, and Botto, are just as important as historical personalities, since they were responsible for the repercussion that followed the event—that is, for its new dimension.

Thus, since the problem is essentially that of this repercussion, it is essential to know, in order to illuminate the problem, that Bolín, the author of the absurd denial, was bound to Franco since before the insurrection, that Steer, a passionate and the adventurous reporter, still had the full confidence of the *Times*, that Canon Onaindia was heard by only very narrow French circles, that Botto, who managed to have Havas distribute the Bolín denial, was a venal character who ended with the collaborationist "Radio-Paris," despised by everyone, and that Captain Aguilera, who acted as a guide for foreign journalists on the Franco front, confided to them that he regretted the loss of those hallowed times when pestilence, thanks to the absence of sewers, decimated the always-too-numerous lower classes. This world of the news media deserves to be thus unveiled, since it has become one of the great historical agents.

The connection between information and power is no less important. Southworth shows how the French foreign ministry controlled, through the Agence Havas, the diffusion of news, and also how this diffusion, within the agency itself, was operating according to the wishes of this or that manipulator. We can see in some high functionaries, in Yvon Delbos himself, the relief felt when the Havas dispatch cast some doubt upon the English version of Guernica. And this despite the triumphal acceptance accorded it by Berlin.

It is worth asking, however, whether the ministries relied solely upon the press agencies for their information. Still, the French and the British ambassadors, both frankly pro-Franco, lived in Hendaye and received their information from Irún. Sir Anthony Eden, more tortured, had in his hands the Stevenson report from the Bilbao consulate, which left no possible doubt on the Guernica affair. He kept it hidden, for fear of unleashing the opposition of the Labour party and of compromising "nonintervention." This too must be known.

Finally, as far as the current use of archival sources is concerned, it is both sad and comical to hear through Southworth how the French archives carefully preserve the secrecy of the records from the Non-Intervention Committee that are freely available in London; or how an official Spanish historical office recently announced as a sensational revelation the existence of a new report on Guernica—that had been published in English in 1938, although it is true that no one had ever dared to publish it in Spain. In order to be blind to the contradictions, one had to be a good English or American Catholic, solidly anchored in one's vision of Spain. Southworth has been aware of this for a long time.

SOUTHWORTH, OR PASSIONATE OBJECTIVITY

GUERNICA! GUERNICA! will anger some people. Southworth has already been called, by those whom he has not treated gently, an "anti-Spanish propagandist." Few foreigners, however, have loved Spain as much as he. He simply believes that the best way to love a country is to try to understand its history.

Can one be objective in writing contemporary history? I have long ago stated my views on this. The historian is part and parcel of his work, and his own time is ever present within himself. Differences among historians are to be found in their attitudes. There is the dishonest attitude: to call oneself objective, while knowing oneself to be partisan; there is the blind attitude: to be partisan while believing oneself to be objective; and then there is the attitude of clarity: to state one's position, while believing firmly that thorough analysis is the best way to buttress that position. It is pejorative to say of a work of history that it is a plea for a cause. Yet a good plea made by a good lawyer and for a worthy cause can become a model to the historian.

Southworth, however, and with a very personal style, has adopted a solution that at the same time safeguards and exposes. He has been careful not to be a propagandist. He has preferred to be a polemicist, and that is often less easily forgiven. He has never hidden his point of view, that of Republican Spain. He has not taken on the task of defending or exalting it. He has attacked the theses of its enemies, not the ideological theses, known and understood by him, but the factual affirmations, the presentations of events, the organized silences, the systematic distortions. When he is passionate, it is not against partisan blindness, but against the lie that supports it. Southworth believes in the value of information, but he knows its pitfalls. And he will not allow a compromise between half-truths and half-lies to pass as history.

He is not, in any case, an amateur, a weekend historian. He began in the world's temple to bibliography, the Library of Congress. He has remained, by vocation, a collector and a bibliographer. He gathered together one of the greatest collections of documents on the Spanish Civil War, now in the library of the University of California, San Diego. He has practical experience in the news media, something most historians lack. And all this results in a work whose origin is in bibliography and textual criticism, and opens up onto a new vision of the event as transformed by news—that is, history in the grand manner. I should like to terminate this foreword by saying why I have particularly appreciated Southworth's work on Guernica, and why I have desired for him the sanction of the university.

At the International Congress on Historical Sciences in Moscow in 1970, I overheard, on a tourist bus, a Spanish university professor loudly proclaim that recent historical research, especially in the United States, had finally established definitively that Guernica had been burned by the red "dinamiteros," by the fleeing militiamen.

I must admit that in 1939 I had believed such an opinion could come only from the pen of a Bardèche or of a Brasillach. I was wrong. I did not realize the power of an official denial upon those who are inconvenienced by the impact of an event upon the vision they want to have of things. Here we were, in 1970, at a convention of historians, faced with yet another form of that informatory terrorism: "the latest research proves . . ." I made a vow to find out for myself.

I hardly expected to be so soon faced with an exhaustive, irrefutable analysis of the phenomenon "event-information," leading us through the Guernica affair from the first Steer dispatch to the latest book by Talón and to the rediscovery of Bolín by Professor Jeffrey Hart of Dartmouth College. I now know that there are two "memories" of any Spanish event. But this does not mean that the lie is as strong as the truth.

Pierre Vilar

Preface

I have wanted to write this book for many years—I can almost say since 1937. A more definite intention took form in 1942, when for a few months I took a postgraduate course at Columbia University with Professor José Antonio de Aguirre, then president of the Basque Republic in Exile. I was his only student, and we spent our time talking about the Spanish Civil War. He had only recently escaped from Nazi Germany, where, had his true identity been discovered, he would certainly have been delivered to Franco and to a firing squad, as had been Luis Companys, the president of the Generalitat of Catalonia.

But the first lines of this present work were written as part of a revision, undertaken in 1967, of my first book on the Spanish Civil War, *El mito de la cruzada de Franco*. While working on the chapter entitled "Los católicos en favor de la España nacional," I became aware that what I had written about Guernica had already been said many times, and that thirty years after the tragedy it should be possible to find something new to say about the subject. I decided to add a few paragraphs, or even a few pages. Today, some years later, these few pages have become a few hundred.

The purpose of my initial investigation was to find the answers to two questions: How was Guernica destroyed? By whom was Guernica destroyed?

Later, I added to this double interrogation a third: Why was Guernica destroyed?

It was some time later, in the course of my research, that I understood that, in view of the number and diversity of the commentaries on Guernica written during the controversy that followed the disaster, I should have to make an effort to explain the polemic, its beginnings, its characteristics, its surprising vitality.

From the first moments of my research on Guernica, it became evident that the sources of the news about the tragedy were to be found in the press dispatches sent from Bilbao within the twenty-four hours that followed the destruction of Guernica, this destruction, according to these reports, having taken place during the late afternoon of April 26, 1937.

In normal circumstances, these news reports would have been enough to establish the facts. But the press telegrams from Bilbao were immediately disputed, their good faith denied by the military rebels fighting against the Basque forces allied with the Spanish Republic. Less than seventy-two hours after the destruction (always according to the times set by the first news dispatches from Bilbao), the ruined town fell into the hands of the Nationalist forces, and a new series of dispatches were sent, from Vitoria, to newspapers all over the world.

Two new problems arose from the preliminary examination of these sources:

1. The news from Bilbao was an almost exclusive scoop by the English press. In France the news from Bilbao was handled in an inexplicable, unprofessional manner by the Havas Agency. How did this happen?

2. The news cabled from Vitoria to France was in open contradiction to what had been telegraphed from Bilbao a few days earlier; even the press dispatches sent from Vitoria to England seemed to cast a doubt on the earlier messages.

Were certain journalists lying? And, if they were, why?

It was doubtless possible to find out how, by whom, and why Guernica had been destroyed, while leaving to one side the unresolved questions of the contradictory news dispatches and of the strange behavior of the Havas Agency; but the acceptance of this compromise would have resulted in an incomplete, unsatisfactory account. The sole justification of a new inquest on Guernica was that the problems raised by the controversy be resolved, and not that the dispute be enflamed anew.

An explanation of these new problems would necessarily mean an investigation into what lay behind the printed dispatch. This would require a study of the personality of the correspondent, of the circumstances under which he wrote his message, of the nature of the censorship exercised by the Spanish press officers, of the mechanical means by which his report had been sent out of Spain, of the time involved in transmission, of the political prejudices of his press agency or of his newspaper editor (or owner), and even of the possible pressures employed by an unavowed censorship in the country that received his dispatch.

But how could such an inquiry be carried out after the passing of so many years? Not only were the materials involved ephemeral in nature—press dispatches to which no one could have thought of assigning more than a temporary value—but the personalities behind the telegrams were themselves shadowy and indistinct. The two cablegrams sent from Vitoria which seemed most to impugn the truthfulness of the news received from Bilbao—the one published in the *Times* and that distributed by the Havas Agency—were both unsigned.

The press officer in charge of relations with the foreign journalists in the Rebel zone at the time of the destruction of Guernica was Luis Bolín. He had written that the *Times* report from Vitoria had been written by H. A. R. Philby, known to have been at the time a Soviet spy. Philby was still alive but was living in the Soviet Union. At any rate, the pro-Rebel content of his press dispatches could easily be explained as forming part of his espionage cover.

The circumstances surrounding the unsigned dispatch of the Havas Agency seemed still more obscure. It was this same agency that had been so slow and so niggardly of details when the first news had come out concerning Guernica from the Basque side. Moreover, the Havas Agency had been suppressed as a news service at the end of World War II because of its collaboration with the Vichy government, and all inquiries about any papers left by the defunct service received the answer that all the documents of the agency has been pounded up for wood pulp during the German occupation of France.

An obsession with this, doubtless minor, problem, kept my research on the principal themes from advancing. Then, when I was beginning to feel that all progress was impossible, I discovered one day in a Montreal bookshop a book on the Philby case, and in it I found a reference suggesting that it was not Philby but, rather, James Holburn who had telegraphed the message about Guernica from Vitoria for the *Times*. A look at *Who's Who* gave me Holburn's address, and a few weeks later I was talking with him in London. A part of the mystery was cleared up. At the same time I found in the Public Record Office at London a considerable number of significant English diplomatic documents dealing with different phases of the Guernica problem; one of these furnished me the beginning of an explanation of the Havas cablegram from Vitoria. It was, however, only a partial explanation. The papers of the Non-Intervention Committee were also available in the Public Record Office, their silences on Guernica filled with surprise and interest; these papers, supplemented with information from other sources, permitted the inclusion of a chapter on Guernica in the diplomatic history of its time.

The cryptic references to the Havas telegram found in the English archives encouraged me to try, once again, to find the missing dossiers of the Havas Agency. I had been, some years before, Administrateur-Délégué of a commercial broadcasting company in Tangier, Morocco. The company had subscribed to the news services of l'Agence France-Presse (AFP), successor to the suppressed Havas Agency. I had had, at that time, the pleasure of meeting and talking with Jean Marin, director of AFP. Although I had been assured by persons in the France-Presse agency that all the Havas papers had been destroyed, I decided to make a last effort by writing directly to Jean Marin. A few days later I received a telephone call informing me that I might find some Havas papers at the French National Archives in Paris. At the National Archives I was told that some Havas papers were in fact on deposit there, but that a permit from AFP was needed before consulting them. Finally, armed with this permit, I was able to open the dossiers that, in all probability, constitute the most important collection now known to exist of material relating to the foreign press coverage of the Spanish Civil War. One of the folders was entitled "Affaire, 'destruction de Guernica.' "

I now possessed, with Holburn's testimony and with the Havas files, a possible explanation of the contradiction existing between the press cablegrams sent from Bilbao and those sent a few days later from Vitoria. With these documents, I also had a plausible interpretation of the highly unprofessional manner in which the Havas Agency had acted in handling the news from Guernica. This new information removed certain psychological blocks that could interfere with the pursuit of the main work; it also permitted these problems to be viewed from a fresh outlook.

This work divided itself naturally into two parts chronologically: "The Event" and "The Controversy."

I have arbitrarily fixed the date for the ending of "The Event" around May 6, a little more than a week after the occupation of Guernica by the Insurgents. It could be maintained that "The Controversy" began with the first denials of "The Event" from Salamanca, and that the press reports of "The Event" continued beyond May 6. But the significant phase of "The Controversy" began after May 6, and the basic newspaper dispatches were written before this date. Thanks to the details gleaned from the considerable library formed by the published memoirs of newspapermen and newspaperwomen who had worked in Spain during the civil war, and to the information received from their colleagues who had not yet committed to print their experiences, plus the rich contribution of the Havas dossiers, I was able to construct an indispensable chapter on "The Working Conditions of the Foreign Press in the Nationalist Zone." The first part of the work, "The Event," was then built up in this manner: 1. The News from Bilbao; 2. Riposte from Salamanca; 3. Parenthesis on the Working Conditions of the Foreign Press in the Nationalist Zone; 4. The News from Vitoria.

In studying the elements of "The Controversy"—during the last two years of the Civil War, which followed the destruction of Guernica—I could see a profound difference between the nature of the polemic that developed in England (and in the United States) and the nature of the polemic that took place in France. In England, the discussion grew between, on the one hand, the feverish partisans of the Catholic minority and their Tory accomplices, and on the other hand, the English Labourites and the left in general, supported by Protestant spokesmen. In France, the debate raged between the politically conservative wing of the Roman Catholic Church and the more socially troubled elements of that same church.

The declarations and the documents concerning Guernica, considered vital to the controversy in the one country, were often ignored in the other. The disputants did not have the same public. A significant piece of testimony produced in England could be unknown in France, as for example, the editorial in the *Times* on May 5,

1937. Father Onaindia's report of what he had seen in Guernica, the very basis of the controversy in France, was paid scant attention in England. It was therefore relatively easy and certainly necessary to divide into two parts the narrative concerning the public controversy during the civil war. The sources for these two parts were public: newspaper dispatches, magazine articles, pamphlets and a few books.

Then came the private controversy, politely carried on among the members of the diplomatic corps in post at London, seat of the Non-Intervention Committee. The papers of this committee and the English diplomatic documents—information kept secret for many years—formed the kernel of this chapter; the published Protuguese diplomatic documents and the world press in general were also useful. This chapter could not have been written, or even imagined, if the rule prohibiting the use of official diplomatic papers until fifty years after the date of their composition, now in force in France, had been applied in England. It is probably for this reason that French diplomatic documentation has been of little help for this chapter, or for this work in general. Even the copies of the Non-Intervention Committee papers held in France are forbidden to researchers and are kept under key, although the same papers can be freely consulted and copied in England. With this diplomatic chapter, the controversy has been carried to the end of the Spanish Civil War.

The last part on the controversy was at first conceived in two sections: "The Public Controversy in Spain, 1939-1975," and "The Public Controversy outside Spain, 1939-1975." But this formula involved numerous repetitions, and, moreover, it soon became evident that despite the Spanish censorship—floating, capricious, and undecided—there was considerable interplay between what was published in London, Paris, and New York and what was eventually published in Madrid and Barcelona. Finally, it was decided to class this material chronologically, whatever its country of origin. The changed nature of the controversy was apparent here in the fact that most of the new material on Guernica came out in book form, thus reversing the basic nature of the polemical documentation used during the war years.

This chapter developed in a more complicated and more detailed manner than had been foreseen in the initial project. The destruction of Guernica took place more than thirty-five years ago; "The Event" could be treated as an event of 1937, but "The Controversy" frequently came from today's newspaper. More than half of this long chapter deals with books and articles written since 1967—that is, since the present work was begun. It is worth noting that articles and book reviews that I published during the time of my research have provoked, in their turn, new documentation on Guernica. Such is the nature of research on a subject that feeds on polemic. The mere knowledge that the destruction of Guernica was the object of research outside Spain forced the Neo-Franquista historians to adopt positions that, curiously enough, unbeknownst to their authors, clarified certain aspects of problems that had remained in obscurity up to now.

Once the documentation of "The Event" and "The Controversy" had been examined in detail, there was left but to draw the conclusions. This has been done in the following manner:

1. The Problems of Steer, Holburn, Botto, and the Havas Agency. The solutions proposed have been found in the *Archives of The Times*, in the Havas files, and through interviews with survivors of that period of journalism.

2. The Dead and the Dying. The relationship between this feature of the tragedy and the controversy—the curious manner in which the subject disappeared from the arguments of writers and orators defending the Spanish Rebel position—determined my giving this matter an independent treatment. The sources are generally those used in the studies of the controversy.

3. How was Guernica destroyed? By whom? Why? These basic questions, laid down at the beginning of the research, here find their answers: by documentary proofs, or by an attempt at a convincing hypothesis, if the documents do not allow a conclusive response.

4. The Reasons for the Existence and the Persistence of the Controversy. The argumentation advanced here involves one of the principal problems of the Spanish Civil War—the moral justification for the war given by the Spanish Insurgents to the Spanish people and to the rest of the world.

This work, undertaken as a study of a single event of the Spanish Civil War, has been, under the pressure of documents discovered and facts unearthed, amplified to the point of becoming at times a general inquiry into journalism in wartime, an investigation into the manipulation of news by governments, an examination of the methods by which diplomatic prestidigitation makes problems disappear, an observation of the realities and unrealities of propaganda. These additions have considerably lengthened the manuscript. It is my hope that they have added to its interest.

Acknowledgments

I owe a considerable debt to the many friends who, knowing that I was working on the subject of the destruction of Guernica, have during many years forwarded to me information and documentation. Melvin Voigt, head librarian of the University of California, San Diego, has been especially generous. I am grateful to Victor Berch, Special Collections Librarian at Brandeis University, for his ever present aid. Professor Robert H. Whealey, of the department of history at Ohio University, lent me a helping hand and guided me through the labyrinth of English and German documents. Luis Portillo has assisted me in research on English newspapers. James B. Childs, now retired from the Library of Congress, has kept me abreast of American newspaper commentary on Guernica. Marianne Bruhl has given freely of her time to find documents and articles for me.

I am also obliged to Spanish friends in Spain, who will not be named, especially to Señor A. M., for aid they have furnished for my research. I thank all those who have kindly replied to my inquiries, either in person or by letter; their names appear in the text and in the footnotes. I especially thank, for their support and encouragement, the president of the government of Euzkadi in Exile, Jesús María de Leizaola, and the former minister of the Spanish Republic, Manuel de Irujo. I am grateful to Canon Alberto de Onaindia, who has afforded me, on several occasions, proof of the interest he bore for my investigations.

I wish to express here my gratitude to the following persons for the encouragement and suggestions they have proffered me during the course of this work:

Professor Gabriel Jackson, of the University of California, San Diego; Professor William B. Watson, of the Massachusetts Institute of Technology; Professor Paul Preston, of the University of Reading; Professor Charles V. Aubrun, of the University of Nice; Professor Clara Lida, of Wesleyan University; Professor David Wingeate Pike, of the American College in Paris; Professor Iris Zavala, of the State University of New York, Stony Brook; Professor Pierre Dussauge, of the University of Bordeaux; Juan García Durán, of the Fondren Library, Rice University; and José Martínez Guerricabeitia, of Editions Ruedo Ibérico.

I want to thank The Regents of the University of California, and Dean Roy Harvey Pearce, of the University of California, San Diego, for the chance to spend some months in La Jolla, where the finishing touches were given to this manuscript. The Faculty Senate Committees aided financially in the preparation of the manuscript, for which I hereby thank them.

A special expression of gratitude is here expressed to Professor Pierre Vilar, of the University of Paris I (Panthéon-Sorbonne), who has counseled me with great understanding throughout the many months of research and writing.

My wife Suzanne merits particularly of my gratitude for her aid, encouragement, and patience, without which I should never have arrived at the final page.

H. R. S.

Château de Roche, Concrémiers, Indre, France
Department of History, University of California, San Diego, California
March 1974

GUERNICA!
GUERNICA!

A Preliminary Note

The Spanish Basque provinces in 1937 (and today) were three in number: Guipúzcoa (capital, San Sebastían), a maritime province on the French border; Vizcaya or Biscay (capital, Bilbao), also on the sea and west of Gúipuzcoa; and Álava (capital, Vitoria), an inland province, south of the other two and west of Navarre. (Navarre is often considered part of the Basque country; this is a proposition subject to discussion.) Álava is territorially the largest, but the maritime provinces are more heavily populated. The people are engaged principally in agriculture and, along the coast, in fishing. The leading city, in 1937 and now, Bilbao, was and is, an industrial center, noted for iron production and for its busy port. Bilbao was also in 1937, as today, a banking center, with three of the great national banks having their headquarters there.

During the Carlist wars of the past century, the Basque provinces vigorously upheld Don Carlos, whose movement, dominated by the clergy, was politically reactionary. The Basque position had been adopted in part in order to defend the *fueros,* or local privileges, which permitted the Basques to maintain a certain independence from the central power in Madrid. These privileges were greatly diminished during the early nineteenth century. In 1876 a system called *conciertos económicos* was established; the Basque provinces paid a tribute to Madrid, but they had a certain liberty as to how these sums were obtained. Consequently, the tax system in the Basque provinces was not always the same as in the rest of Spain.

In spite of the concessions obtained through the conciertos económicos, nostalgia for the lost fueros was widespread throughout the Basque country. At the end of the nineteenth century, the idea of Basque nationalism, founded on the defense of regional privileges, was advanced by Sabino Arana y Goiri, and the Basque Nationalist party (PNV) was founded. This party pleaded for a free Basque state, but it was essentially a clerically dominated movement that placed the maintenance of the Catholic faith before its nationalist objectives. It had varying electoral successes during the first three decades of the present century.

General Primo de Rivera abandoned his dictatorial powers in 1930. There then began in Spain a campaign of agitation in favor of a republic. The members of the PNV, belonging to the middle classes and the bourgeoisie, were not hostile to a republic any more than they were opposed to a monarchy. They were against the hegemony of Madrid and Castile. The political debate in the Basque provinces became triangular between the conservative monarchist parties, the Socialists and the Republicans, and the Basque Nationalists. During the municipal elections of April 12, 1931, which brought about the fall of the monarchy, the Republican and Socialist groups formed a common front in the Basque country, and carried Bilbao and San Sebastián and the surrounding regions. Vitoria also voted Republican. However, the PNV fared better than did the monarchists in Bilbao. Eibar, an industrial town in Guipúzcoa, was the first in Spain to proclaim the Republic.

The question of regional autonomy was in the forefront of the political scene. On August 17, 1930, a private meeting had been held in San Sebastián among political leaders of the Republican groups, with the Bilbao Socialist Indalecio Prieto attending on his own behalf, to decide on overthrowing the monarchy and setting up a republic in Spain. There were also present members of the autonomy movements of Catalonia and of Galicia, and a clear decision was taken to grant an autonomy statute to Catalonia when the Republic was established.

The Basque Nationalists were fully aware of the possibility of obtaining autonomy concessions from the Republic. At the same time, they feared having to endorse the avowed anticlericalism of the Republican leaders. The nonmomarchist Catholics of the three Basque provinces and of Navarre formed an alliance called the Basco-Navarese Bloc, and a draft project for a Basque and Navarese autonomy statute was approved by 427 municipalities—chiefly rural—of the region. The Basco-Navarese Bloc campaigned in the 1931 elections for the Constituent Cortes, on the one hand, against the monarchists and, on the other hand, against the Republicans and the left.

The bloc won one seat in Álava, four in Guipúzcoa, two in Bilbao, three in Vizcaya province, and five in Navarre—a very respectable result. The new head of the PNV, a young lawyer named José Antonio de Aguirre, won two seats, one of which was in Navarre.

The Basco-Navarese Bloc was then tempted to become Republican, in order to realize its autonomist objectives, but when, later in 1931, the debate in the Cortes took place concerning Article 26 of the proposed constitution—an article that established the separation of Church and State—the Basco-Navarese took up a firm position against the Republicans. This did not mean that the Basques were satisfied with the Catholic Church in 1931. The PNV program demanded that the Basque provinces negotiate directly with the Holy See, and that a change be effected in the rule that permitted the Basques to approach the Pope only through the intermediary of the Spanish primate, the cardinal archbishop of Toledo. Moreover, there was no bishop in either San Sebastían or Bilbao, although the latter was one of the largest cities in Spain. Ecclesiastically, the Basques were dependent on the bishop of Vitoria. There was no Basque cardinal.

In 1932, when the municipalities of the three Basque provinces and Navarre voted on a statute of autonomy, profound differences appeared. The seabound provinces, Vizcaya and Guipúzcoa, voted overwhelmingly for the statute. Álava gave a feeble majority for autonomy, and Navarre voted no. In September of this same year, the Basque nationalist deputies voted for a Catalan autonomy statute.

Navarese opposition to autonomy (to the Republic?) pushed the Basques toward an independent operation. Work was begun on a plan for Basque autonomy, and on November 9, 1933, a nonofficial "referendum" on a draft project was voted on in the three Basque provinces. Navarre was not included in the voting. Guipúzcoa and Vizcaya balloted in favor of the proposition by more than 88 percent of the registered voters; Álava voted favorably, but by only 46.40 percent of those eligible to vote. Significantly, the bishop of Vitoria, when asked to state whether or not believers could vote for the measure, replied affirmatively. Early on the voting day, he had the announcement made that he himself had voted for the measure.

This plan, however, had to be discarded, for on November 19 Spain again voted to elect deputies to the Cortes, and the conservative right triumphed over the disunited Republican and left parties. The Traditionalists (Carlists) refused to campaign with the Basque Nationalists on a program including the draft project of autonomy. In the three Basque provinces, the PNV elected twelve deputies, of whom one was from Álava. But the majority of the seats in this latter province was won by the right. Bilbao, which, as a large city, formed an electoral district by itself, gave a majority to the PNV, but the minority representation was won by the left (Manuel Azaña, Republican leader, and Indalecio Prieto, Socialist chief in the Basque country).

The Basque Nationalists continued to be torn between their religious sentiments, which were under attack from the left, and their aspirations for autonomy, which were repulsive to the right. On June 12, 1934, when the contitutionality of the Catalan law granting the leaseholders of vineyards (*rabassaires*) the right to purchase these lands was being discussed in the Cortes, the Catalan left (*Esquerra*) abandoned the assembly as a sign of protestation. The Basque Nationalists followed them in a gesture of solidarity. Later, during the summer of 1934, the Basques lowered the tax on wine, contrary to instructions from Madrid; in the discussion that followed, the Basque position was upheld by the Catalan Nationalists. During the summer, there was considerable agitation in the Basque country. The Bilbao city government decided to honor the hero of Catalan autonomy, Macià, who had just died, by giving his name to a street in the capital previously called Avenida de España. The civil governor, nominated by Madrid, forebade the public ceremony intended to celebrate the event. On this occasion, the Catalan left supported the actions of the Basque Nationalists. On September 2, a joint meeting of Basque and Catalan parliamentarians was organized at Zumárraga. This time again the civil governor prohibited the reunion, and only the deputies were allowed to enter the meeting place.

The Basque Nationalists apparently did not play a role in the general strike that took place in the two Basque maritime provinces during the October 1934 uprising, although certain elements of the Basque Workers' Solidarity (*Solidaridad de Obreros Vascos*), the Basque Nationalist trade union, participated in the strike in some places. There is no proof that the PNV took part in any action at this time. The Basque Nationalists voted with the Lerroux-Gil Robles government when they were assured that some imprisoned Basques would be freed. But the Basque member of the Commission on Parliamentary Immunity consistently voted against a project to deliver a deputy of the left to the vengeful justice of the center-right government.

During the "two black years" (*bienio negro*)—1934 and 1935—the Basque Nationalists were forced to leave in suspension their hopes for autonomy. Then came the dissolution of the Cortes and new elections on February 16, 1936. The Spanish electoral system was conceived to guarantee a majority strong enough to govern; it gave most of the seats in a district to a majority however feeble; at the same time, unless this majority was overwhelming, the minority was assured of some seats. If no electoral list had 40 percent of the vote, there was a second balloting. Each province formed an electoral district. In addition, the eight most important cities (of which one was Bilbao) constituted independent electoral districts. There were thus in the Basque country, with three provinces and the city of Bilbao, four electoral circumscriptions. The Basque Nationalists fought alone, against the Popular Front of Republican and left parties, and against the clerical-monarchist right, with the slogan "For Christian civilization, for the freedom of the fatherland [Euzkadi] and for social justice."

There were sixty electoral districts in Spain; in 1936, there were only five districts in which a majority did not gather 40 percent of the vote, and in which, consequently, there were runoff elections. Three of these five districts were in the Basque country, where only in the city of Bilbao was there a definite result on the first ballot. The left won in Bilbao, upsetting the results of 1933, when the PNV had taken a majority of the seats. In the runoff elections, the PNV won four seats in Guipúzcoa and three in Vizcaya, which, with the two seats won as the Bilbao minority, gave it a total of nine deputies, three less than in 1933. The PNV did not elect a single representative in Álava province, where the right and the left shared the two seats. In Navarre the right took all seven seats, but in the two maritime provinces no candidate of the right was elected.

In fact, the right withdrew from the runoff elections when the bishop of Vitoria made a declaration that could be interpreted as favorable to the Basque Nationalists.

The Basque Nationalists were from then on ineluctably drawn toward the Popular Front, albeit without enthusiasm. Of their three objectives, expressed in the electoral slogan, two at least—autonomy and social justice—found therein a chance to progress. The draft project for Basque autonomy, submitted to plebiscite just before the 1933 elections, was now disinterred and presented to the Cortes, with the approval of all the Basque deputies, from the Communist to the Nationalists. But other more pressing problems kept this project from being acted on before the civil war broke out in the Peninsula on July 18, 1936.

In the provinces of Vizcaya and Guipúzcoa, the working class was well organized and politically disciplined. The military revolt was badly prepared. Guipúzcoa was one of the rare provinces where the Republican authorities gave arms to the workers. Only on July 21 did some elements of the armed forces in San Sebastián attempt an uprising. They were soon driven back to their barracks and to a few other buildings by a column of armed workers from Eibar and by some groups of the military who stood by the Republic. After three days of fighting, the Insurgents surrendered. In Bilbao, the chief of the armed forces, Lieutenant Colonel Vidal, took the side of the Republic; some arms were given to the people; miners and other workers converged on the capital. The military did not dare to revolt and there was little or no fighting in Bilbao in July 1936.

What was the position of the Basque Nationalists during these events? Documents and testimony indicate that from the first moments of the military revolt the Basque Nationalists chose the Republic. Around noon on July 18, the San Sebastián radio station broadcast a message asking the armed forces and the citizens to come to the aid of the legal government. This message was written by two Basque deputies, Manuel de Irujo and José Mariá de Lasarte. A solemn declaration of adherence to the cause of the Republic was broadcast from Radio Bilbao on the evening of July 19 in the name of the Basque Nationalist party. This statement was published in the press the next day:

> In view of the events that are taking place in the Spanish state and that could have a direct and sorrowful repercussion on Euzkadi and its destiny, the Basque Nationalist Party declares—aside from all that to which it is bound by its ideology and which it solemnly ratifies today—that faced with the struggle between the citizens and fascism, between the Republic and the Monarchy, its principles place it inevitably on the side of the citizens and of the Republic, in agreement with the republican and democratic regime that was one of the distinctive characteristics of our people during centuries of liberty.[1]

It is at times alleged that the Basque Nationalists hesitated in their manifestations of loyalty to the Republic during the first days of the insurrection. This was perhaps true, and for the person who believes in the reality of the class struggle, it is difficult to conceive how it could have been otherwise. The PNV was not a party of the working classes. Its political base was among the middle classes, the small landholders, the members of the liberal professions. The rich men of the Basque country were generally monarchists. What is important is that this party, whose first allegiance went to its Church, took a position at the side of those who were openly opposed to that Church; that this party, which by its fidelities of class was neither socially nor politically revolutionary, took a position at the side of those openly declared for the revolution. Did the PNV take this position because of the problem of autonomy? Perhaps, but it would be unjust not to see also in its behavior a profound movement in favor of a democratic conception of life. If the Basque Nationalists had taken the side of the Insurgents, the military situation in the two maritime provinces would in all likelihood have been quite other than what it was. The PNV was the only Catholic party that supported the Republic in its difficult moments, and it is significant that in consequence the position of the Catholic Church in the two maritime Basque provinces was quite different from that in the other regions under Republican control.

The province of Guipúzcoa had the advantage of a common frontier with France, but, contrary to what one could normally expect in such circumstances, little military aid crossed the border to assist the Basques. In addition, from the beginning of the rebellion, an insurgent contingent held a position at Oyarzun, halfway between San Sebastián and Irún, but a few kilometers south of the principal road connecting the two towns. From this base, the Rebels began an advance toward Irún in the last days of August. Irún fell on September 3 after having been in great part burned by its defenders—not by the Basque Nationalists but very probably by anarchists. According to the logic of warfare, whoever did burn the town was right in doing so. The fall of Irún was a tragic loss for the Basques; they now had but one access to the outside world: the sea. The Rebel victory was won with the aid of Italian aircraft, with the help of foreign troops (Moroccans), and with elements of the Foreign Legion. These troops had been brought from Africa to Spain in German planes. No such help for the Basques crossed the French frontier, only a few kilometers from Irún. Ten days later San Sebastián surrendered without fighting, and the Basque troops withdrew almost to the limits of Vizcaya province. The troops of insurgent General Emilio Mola did not pursue them, and the Basque front remained relatively calm for more than six months.

Civilian authority in that part of the Basque country still in Republican hands fell almost completely into the power of the Basque Nationalists. On October 1, the Republic granted a statute of autonomy to the Basques, and a government was formed. On October 7, Aguirre was named president. The most important ministries were entrusted to Basque Nationalists, but most of the parties that formed the Popular Front were represented in the government. Life in Vizcaya province, viewed from the outside, was probably more similar to what it had been before the civil war than was life at the same time elsewhere in Spain. "There was no social revolution in Bilbao," wrote George Steer.[2]

The advance of the Army of Africa, across Andalusia to Toledo and the gates of Madrid, was stopped early in November. Málaga fell in January 1937 to a Rebel attack strongly supported by Italian infantry. A Nationalist offensive sought to encircle Madrid by an assault along the Jarama River; it failed in February. Another effort to take Madrid commenced north of Guadalajara at the beginning of March; it ended with the ignominious rout of Italian Fascist soldiers. The initiative, held throughout this period by the Insurgents, was now turned toward the Basque front.

On March 31, General Emilio Mola launched his campaign to end the war in the Basque country and to take Bilbao. His army was composed not only of soldiers of the Foreign Legion, of Moroccans, of Italian infantrymen, of new German armament, of Italian planes and pilots, but also of the men and aircraft of the German Condor Legion. The Basques who opposed this diversified military machine were badly armed and particularly weak in the air. It was difficult for the Republic to send them aircraft, either by air or by sea; and even if the planes did arrive, the necessary servicing installations and airfields were lacking in the hilly country.

On the first day of the offensive, Durango was heavily bombed. From the east and from Álava province to the south, the Nationalist attack was launched. The Rebels proclaimed a sea blockade of the Basque coast. Food became scarce in Bilbao. The Baldwin government in England tried to persuade British merchant ships not to attempt to enter the port of Bilbao. The ineffectiveness of the blockade was demonstrated when several English cargo ships made normal entries into Bilbao harbor. Rain slowed down Mola's first offensive, but the attacks began again on April 20 with a general advance all along the front.

In the path of this Rebel advance on Bilbao lay the town of Guernica, about five miles from the sea, near the Mundaca Estuary on the Bay of Biscay. Between Guernica and Bilbao were twenty miles of rough terrain. Guernica was an old town, typically Basque, situated in a valley and surrounded by low hills. The town had some light industry, but was chiefly a farming center. The distinctive character of Guernica derived from La Casa de Juntas, the town hall, and in front of it two oak trees, one of which was dead. It was here that, traditionally in the past, the Spanish monarchs came to swear to respect the Basque privileges or fueros in return for Basque allegiance to Spain. It was here that Aguirre took his oath as president of the Autonomous Basque Republic.[3]

BOOK I

•

THE EVENT

1

The News from Bilbao

The story of the destruction of the small Basque town of Guernica, late in the day of April 26, 1937, is based, in the first stages of its development, on newspaper dispatches owing entirely to the initiative of press correspondents. It can be said that without the presence of foreign correspondents and Spanish representatives of the foreign press in Bilbao on the night of April 26, there would not have been the event of Guernica as we know it today. The successive phases of the story were also in large part determined by the press. The newspaper articles that influenced the evolution of the Guernica story can be divided into three categories:

1. The bulletins reporting the bombing of Guernica sent out from Bilbao by foreign correspondents or by local representatives of the foreign press, based on their observations and on statements by Basque leaders, or from journalistic listening posts in France on the Basque frontier, roughly from April 27 to 29, while the ruined town was still in the hands of the government, and subsequent follow-up stories such as interviews with captured German pilots or with refugees from Guernica, written in Bilbao, at the frontier, or in France;

2. The reports, communiqués, and declarations published in the Spanish Nationalist press, and eventually in other countries, as an immediate reaction to the printing of the news of the bombing in the foreign press and to statements of Basque officials in Bilbao; and

3. The messages of the foreign journalists who visited Guernica after its capture by the Nationalists on April 29, forwarded between that date and May 6.

These three series of news stories and official statements constitute the first phase of the Guernica incident and establish the foundation for the consequent controversy.

The first news of the burning of Guernica reached Bilbao, the seat of the Basque government, around ten o'clock on the night of April 26.[1] There were at this time in Bilbao four foreign professional correspondents: three British men and one Belgian.[2] There was not one Frenchman. It is remarkable that there were so few, in view of the importance of the fighting going on and of the large number of foreign newspapermen then elsewhere in Spain, on both sides. The Basque front was a primary news source for the reporters working with the Nationalists, because this front was unified and interior displacements were possible—from Salamanca and Burgos, where political news might be found, to Vitoria, field headquarters of General Emilio Mola, who was directing the campaign against Bilbao. The Basque front was a secondary news source for the men assigned to the Republican side, because it was cut off from land communications with the rest of Republican Spain—except for neighboring Santander—and it was in the rest of Republican Spain—in Valencia and in Barcelona—that the important political news on the Republican side was thought to be found. There was even an element of danger in merely approaching the Basque front, for the Nationalists claimed to have the port of Bilbao under blockade, and the daily airplane from Biarritz to Bilbao was in constant danger of being shot down.[3] These explanations of the foreign press situation in Bilbao are logical, but they are not entirely convincing as a justification for the absence of any French newsman as an observer of the fighting raging on France's frontier.

The four foreign professional correspondents in Bilbao on the night of April 26 were George Lowther Steer, of the *Times* of London;[4] Noel Monks, of the *Daily Express,* London;[5] Christopher Holme, of Reuters news agency, London;[6] all three British; and Mathieu Corman, Belgian correspondent of *Ce Soir,* a newly founded Paris afternoon daily.[7] There were also five other persons, presumably British, or at least in communication with the English press, probably part-time or occasional journalists, who cabled news from Bilbao to England at the time of the Guernica disaster.[8]

In addition to these foreigners or presumed foreigners, there were four other correspondents who cabled information to the three American news agencies and to the French Havas Agency. The Havas man was Fernando Fernández-Fontecha;[9] the representative of the United Press (UP) was Emilio Herrero.[10] There was certainly a reporter for the Associated Press (AP) and perhaps one for the Universal News Service, but they have not been identified. They were almost certainly Spaniards.

The preponderance of English men and women among the reporters for the foreign press—a group composed, according to these investigations, of eight British men or women, one Belgian and four Spaniards—was significant in the development of the Guernica story.

It is also worth emphasizing that, of the four foreign professional correspondents in Bilbao on April 26, and of the three newspapers and one news agency they represented, only one reporter, Mathieu Corman, and one news organ, his paper *Ce Soir*,[11] could be considered left of center politically. The three Englishmen might be said to have had a "liberal" reaction to the war in the Basque country, but their employers were firmly in the conservative camp. The presence of this English majority among the correspondents strongly conditioned the development of the Guernica news story, but the initial presence of the English reporters was determined more by the centuries-old economic ties between London and Bilbao, by the sympathies of an island people for the freedom-of-shipping issues personified by the English skippers whose defiance of the Nationalist blockade of Bilbao was being heavily publicized in the English press,[12] than by any emotional kinship with the Republican cause.

When the four foreign professional newsmen in Bilbao heard that Guernica was in flames, they drove as quickly as possible the thirty kilometers to the burning town; each observed the conflagration, talked with survivors, and filed his story when he returned to Bilbao on April 27.[13] The national composition of the foreign press corps in Bilbao, and those interests that had placed English correspondents, rather than Frenchmen or Americans, in Bilbao ensured that the news of the destruction of the Basque town would be widely publicized in all sectors of the English press.

The first reports on Guernica appeared in England on the afternoon of April 27—they were too late for the morning papers—one in the *Star*,[14] and that of Reuters in the *News Chronicle*,[15] the *Evening News*,[16] and the *Evening Standard*.[17] On the following morning, not only was Steer's cable printed in the *Times* and Noel Monks's in the *Daily Express*[18] and a rewrite of Reuters in the *Glasgow Herald*,[19] in the *Manchester Guardian*,[20] and in the *Daily Herald* (which also had another, exclusive but unsigned, story from Bilbao),[21] and Elizabeth Wilkinson's cable in the *Daily Worker*,[22] but such normally pro-Franco newspapers as the *Morning Post*,[23] the *Daily Mail*,[24] and the *Daily Telegraph*[25] gave accounts of the disaster.

Steer's first story on Guernica in the *Times*, which also appeared the same day in the *New York Times*,[26] because of the politically conservative and journalistically prestigious position of the two newspapers—each considered the leading journal in its country—was the most talked about all over the world. This dispatch, certainly one of the most significant reports of the Spanish Civil War, was subdued in tone, unsensational, and certainly did not exaggerate either the material damage or the number of victims. This is the basic document in establishing world public opinion about the destruction of Guernica. It is quoted in full as it appeared in the *Times:*

THE TRAGEDY OF GUERNICA
TOWN DESTROYED IN AIR ATTACK
EYE-WITNESSES'S ACCOUNT
From our Special Correspondent. Bilbao, April 27

Guernica, the most ancient town of the Basques and the center of their cultural tradition, was completely destroyed yesterday afternoon by insurgent air raiders. The bombardment of this open town far behind the lines occupied precisely three hours and a quarter, during which a powerful fleet of airplanes consisting of three German types, Junkers and Heinkel bombers and Heinkel fighters, did not cease unloading on the town bombs weighing from 1,000 lbs. downwards and, it is calculated, more than 3,000 two-pounder aluminum incendiary projectiles. The fighters, meanwhile, plunged low from above the center of the town to machine-gun those of the civilian population who had taken refuge in the fields.

The whole of Guernica was soon in flames except the historic Casa de Juntas with its rich archives of the Basque race, where the ancient Basque Parliament used to sit. The famous oak of Guernica, the dried old stump of 600 years and the young new shoots of this century, were also untouched. Here the kings of Spain used to take the oath to respect the democratic rights (*fueros*) of Vizcaya and in return received a promise of allegiance as suzerains with the democratic title of *Senõr,* not *Rey* [de] Vizcaya. The noble parish church of Santa María was also undamaged except for the beautiful chapter house, which was struck by an incendiary bomb.

At 2 a.m. to-day when I visited the town the whole of it was a horrible sight, flaming from end to end. The reflection of the flames could be seen in the clouds of smoke above the mountains from 10 miles away. Throughout the night houses were falling until the streets became long heaps of red impenetrable débris. Many of the civilian survivors took the long trek from Guernica to Bilbao in antique solid-wheeled Basque farm carts drawn by oxen. Carts piled high with such household possessions as could be saved from the conflagration clogged the roads all night. Other survivors were evacuated in Government lorries, but many were forced to remain round the burning town lying on mattresses or looking for lost relatives and children, while units of the fire brigades and the Basque motorized police under the personal direction of the Minister of the Interior, Señor Monzón, and his wife continued rescue work till dawn.

In the form of its execution and the scale of the destruction it wrought, no less than in the selection of its objective, the raid on Guernica is unparalleled in military history. Guernica was not a military objective. A factory producing war material lay outside the town and was untouched. So were two barracks some distance from the town. The town lay far behind the lines. The object of the bombardment was seemingly the demoralization of the civil population and the destruction of the cradle of the Basque race. Every fact bears out this appreciation, beginning with the day when the deed was done.

Monday was the customary market day in Guernica for the country round. At 4:30 p.m., when the market was full and peasants were still coming in, the church bell rang the alarm for approaching airplanes, and the population sought refuge in cellars and in the dugouts prepared following the bombing of the civilian population of Durango on March 31st, which opened General Mola's offensive in the north. The people are said to have shown a good spirit. A Catholic priest took charge and perfect order was maintained.

Five minutes later a single German bomber appeared, circled over the town at a low altitude, and then dropped six heavy bombs, apparently aiming for the station. The bombs with a shower of grenades fell on a former institute and on houses and streets surrounding it. The airplane then went away. In another five minutes came a second bomber, which threw the same number of bombs into the middle of the town. About a quarter of an hour later three Junkers arrived to continue the work of demolition, and thenceforward the bombing grew in intensity and was continuous, ceasing only with the approach of dusk at 7:45. The whole town of 7000 inhabitants, plus 3000 refugees, was slowly and systematically pounded to pieces. Over a radius of five miles round a detail of the raiders' technique was to bomb separate *caseríos*, or farmhouses. In the night these burned like little candles in the hills. All the villages around were bombed with the same intensity as the town itself, and at Múgica, a little group of houses at the head of the Guernica inlet, the population was machine-gunned for fifteen minutes.

It is impossible to state yet the number of victims. In the Bilbao Press this morning they were reported as "fortunately small," but it is feared that this was an understatement in order not to alarm the large refugee population of Bilbao. In the hospital of Josefinas, which was one of the first places bombed, all the forty-two wounded militiamen it sheltered were killed outright. In a street leading downhill from the Casa de Juntas I saw a place where fifty people, nearly all women and children, are said to have been trapped in an air raid refuge under a mass of burning wreckage. Many were killed in the fields, and altogether the deaths may run into hundreds. An elderly priest named Arronategui was killed by a bomb while rescuing children from a burning house.

The tactics of the bombers, which may be of interest to students of the new military science, were as follows: First, small parties of airplanes threw heavy bombs and hand grenades all over the town, choosing area after area in orderly fashion. Next came fighting machines which swooped low to machine-gun those who ran in panic from dugouts, some of which had already been penetrated by 1000 lb. bombs, which make a hole 25 ft. deep. Many of these people were killed as they ran. A large herd of sheep being brought in to the market was also wiped out. The object of this move was apparently to drive the population underground again, for next as many as 12 bombers appeared at a time dropping heavy and incendiary bombs upon the ruins. The rhythm of this bombing of an open town was, therefore, a logical one: first, hand grenades and heavy bombs to stampede the population, then machine-gunning to drive them below, next heavy and incendiary bombs to wreck the houses and burn them on top of their victims.

The only counter-measures the Basques could employ, for they do not possess sufficient airplanes to face the insurgent fleet, were those provided by the heroism of the Basque clergy. These blessed and prayed for the kneeling crowds—Socialists, Anarchists, and Communists, as well as the declared faithful—in the crumbling dugouts.

When I entered Guernica after midnight houses were crashing on either side, and it was utterly impossible even for firemen to enter the center of the town. The hospitals of Josefinas and Convento de Santa Clara were glowing heaps of embers, all the churches except that of Santa Maria were destroyed, and the few houses which still stood were doomed. When I revisited Guernica this afternoon most of the town was still burning and new fires had broken out. About 30 dead were laid out in a ruined hospital.

The effect here of the bombardment of Guernica, the Basque's holy city, has been profound, and has led President Aguirre to issue the following statement in this morning's Basque Press:

"The German airmen in the service of the Spanish rebels have bombarded Guernica, burning the historic town which is held in such veneration by all Basques. They have sought to wound us in the most sensitive of our patriotic sentiments, once more making it entirely clear what Euzkadi may expect of those who do not hestitate to destroy us down to the very sanctuary which records the centuries of our liberty and our democracy.

"Before this outrage all we Basques must react with violence, swearing from the bottom of our hearts to defend the principles of our people with unheard of stubbornness and heroism if the case requires it. We cannot hide the gravity of the moment; but victory can never be won by the invader if, raising our spirits to heights of strength and determination, we steel ourselves to his defeat.

"The enemy has advanced in many parts elsewhere to be driven out of them afterwards. I do not hesitate to affirm that here the same thing will happen. May today's outrage be one spur more to do it with all speed."[27]

The general chronology of the air attack presented by Steer was the same as that dispatched then or later by all the other correspondents—whether datelined from Guernica, Bilbao, the frontier, or France—who had heard or were to hear the same account from survivors. Noel Monks sent a second story of Guernica, which appeared on April 29,[28] and he repeated his facts when he came back to London a few days later.[29] Holme cabled a confirmation of his account on April 29.[30] Steer, for his part, sent reaffirmations of his original cablegram and they were published in the *Times* on April 29[31] and 30[32] and on May 6.[33]

After the first dispatches about the burning of Guernica went out from Bilbao on the morning of April 27, a number of statements by Basque government officials and by witnesses of the bombardment kept the story alive for days. On the morning of April 27, President Aguirre issued a declaration[34] that was widely reproduced—it formed the final part of Steer's first message. Aguirre made another declaration on April 29.[35] Both provided angry reactions from the Nationalist press and radio. This reaction will be discussed in the following chapter. A few days later, a new eyewitness came forward, a canon of the cathedral of Valladolid, Father Alberto de Onaindia, and his testimony was published not only in the French, American, and British press but all over the world. Father Onaindia's statements and interviews, among the most significant on the subject of Guernica, will be treated also in a later chapter.[36] On May 4 the Basque Minister of Justice de Leizaola and prominent citizens of Guernica spoke on the Bilbao radio in a special program intended as a reply to the Nationalist radio; their statements were widely publicized in the world press.[37]

News dispatches from Bilbao dwelt again, from time to time, on Guernica before the Basque capital fell to Franco on June 21, 1937. The most important were probably those dealing with Hans Joachim Wandel, a twenty-five-year-old German pilot shot down in a German Heinkel 51 airplane, by a Basque machine gunner, on May 13 and taken prisoner. "His diary," wrote Steer in a dispatch to the *Times,*

> shows the word "Guernica" on April 26, the day when the town was destroyed. Wandel admitted that Guernica had been bombed, but said that he, as pilot of a pursuit plane, did not take part. He had accompanied German bombers on other expeditions when they destroyed Basque pinewoods with incendiary bombs, which, he said, were highly efficient.

The visible effort of Steer to convince his public that German pilots were really fighting with the Franco forces gives his text a semblance of unreality. This is an uncontested fact today, but in May 1937, although it had been frequently told to newspaper readers all over the world, it was simply not admitted officially in London, Paris, or Washington. Wandel was in fact the tenth member of an airplane crew shot down or captured on the ground on the Basque front since the beginning of the year—all "without single exception carried German papers."[38] On April 18 a German pilot named Hans Sabotka had been shot down in a Heinkel 111 over Bilbao. He and his two crew members were dead when the Basques arrived at the débris.[39] Previously the Basques had captured an automobile on ground reconnaissance with four members of the German air forces fighting in Spain. Two of these men, Walther Keinzle and Gottfried Schulze-Blanck, were tried and found guilty of "rebellion and murder" before a courtmartial in Bilbao on May 20.[40]

The American press—with the exception of the *New York Times*—received its first news about Guernica through the American press services: the Associated Press, the United Press, and the Universal News Service. The news came either from their correspondents in Bilbao or from their offices set up on the French-Spanish frontier at Hendaye. All three of these agencies immediately reported the bombing of Guernica, even the Universal News Service, which belonged to the Hearst newspaper chain, a strong editorial supporter of the Nationalists. New York had a five-hour news lead on London and Paris; Chicago, a six-hour lead. The *Chicago Daily Tribune*—also a backer of Franco—on the morning of April 27 gave an AP flash on the bombardment, datelined Guernica, in its final edition, thus being one of the first morning newspapers of that date to inform its readers of the event.[41] All three American press agencies sent out a detailed story about Guernica in time for the afternoon newspapers of April 27. The Associated Press sent out not only an expanded version of the cablegram from Guernica mentioned above[42] but also another article from Hendaye, which was based "on advices reaching the frontier," and told of raids in which "insurgent planes killed more than 800 civilians."[43] The *Chicago Daily News,* on the afternoon of April 27, published a UP dispatch from Hendaye, written equally on "advices reaching the frontier."[44]

American agency reports were widely published all over the two American continents on the following morning. One of these stories, that in the *New York American,* a Hearst newspaper, was datelined from Vitoria, in the Rebel zone, and read in part:

> . . . insurgent air armadas rained fire and explosives over six villages near Bilbao today in raids which killed an estimated 900 men, women and children and made thousands homeless. . . . Leaving Guernica and numerous surrounding towns a blazing mass of ruins, the insurgent aviators bombed Bilbao itself for thirty-five minutes. . . . Details of Guernica's bloody desolation reaching Vitoria tonight told a ghastly story of slaughter which even included the machine-gunning of flocks of terror-stricken sheep. . . . Everything lay in ruins. Mola's planes attacked the city in groups of seven, hand-grenading its houses at first, then machine-gunning them as hundreds fled to shelters. Basque radio broadcasts described the casualties as "uncountable" with literally hundreds of Guernica's inhabitants roasted alive or torn to pieces by flying steel and drilling machine-gun bullets. . . . Air observers said that Guernica was being entirely evacuated, its people as well as its demoralized defense troops crowding the roads to Bilbao.[45]

This long article also contained other material attributed to the Bilbao radio, including details of the atrocities committed by the Nationalist pilots and parts of Aguirre's declaration. It is not possible that all of this dispatch was actually sent from Vitoria and passed through the Rebel censorship; but other parts, especially most of the text cited above, could and doubtless did come from Vitoria late on April 26, before it was clearly understood in Mola's headquarters what had happened in Guernica and what would be world public opinion reaction to what had happened. Certain phrases of the above message could not have been sent from Bilbao, or cabled from the frontier, or have been written in a New York office. The most likely hypothesis is that the Universal News Service received at least two cablegrams, one from Vitoria and one from Bilbao; these were probably combined into one news story by a careless editor, either at the Universal Service office or at the newspaper itself.

Many morning newspapers on April 28 (*New York Herald Tribune,* New York *Daily News,* the *Washington Post, La Prensa* of Buenos Aires, *Correio da Manhã* of Rio de Janeiro) carried a UP dispatch from Hendaye, telling of the destruction of

Guernica and of the bombing of five other Basque towns "within the 75 mile crescent-shaped line of the Rebel attack on Guernica . . . according to frontier dispatches."[46] The conservative *Daily News* headline read: "REBELS' NAZI ACES DESTROY CITY, KILL 800."[47] The UP also sent from Bilbao to South America a long, moving, eyewitness account of the events in Guernica on the night of April 26.[48] The AP sent out a new story on Guernica from Bilbao, quoting Basque officials at length on the air raid.[49]

The only United States correspondent sent into Bilbao immediately after the news of the disaster in Guernica was James M. Minifie, of the *New York Herald Tribune*. Guernica was in Rebel hands when he got to Bilbao, but he did talk with survivors among the refugees in the Basque capital. In a cablegram sent from Bilbao on May 5, he reported the statements made on the radio the night before by Minister of Justice Leizaola, by Mayor Labauria of Guernica, and by a Guernica priest Arronategui, and continued:

> Their accounts [those of Leizaola, Labauría, and Arronategui] tallied with eye-witness narratives obtained by this correspondent today from people with American connections about whose reliability there can be no question. . . . One girl, whose father is known to this correspondent, ran to the window when the first plane appeared, exclaiming, "Look, Mother, how pretty it is." When the plane dropped bombs, mother and daughter fled to a refuge. . . . They huddled for three and a half hours in their refuge, expecting the end at any moment. . . . Another man, who watched the destruction of the city from a neighboring hilltop, said he had counted as many as 26 planes at one time. "They came very low, bombing and machine-gunning," he related. "From 4.30 to 7.45, it went on. The boom of the explosions and the rat-tat-tat of machine-guns was terrible. Smoke poured out of Guernica. They dropped incendiary bombs, which burned very large with a bright yellow flame. Everything was burned, and the escaping people were machine-gunned. I watched from the hilltop until 11 p.m. You could feel the heat two kilometers (1.2 miles) away. I don't like the Reds! My sentiments go the other way. But for the other side to say that Reds burned Guernica is a horrible lie. I was there. I saw it, I tell you, with my own eyes."[50]

The English and American daily press, whether it editorially favored one side or the other in the Spanish Civil War, reported, usually in detail, as we have seen, the news of the destruction of Guernica with hardly a questioning voice. Press reaction in France was significantly different; news about Guernica was less abundantly printed and, above all, appeared more slowly.[51] No newspaper reader in England or the United States (or for that matter, Canada or Argentina) was unaware of the news of the bombing by the morning of April 28, 1937. Many important French newspapers waited until the morning of April 29, fully thirty-six hours after the news was first published in Paris and elsewhere, even to mention the name of Guernica. Others waited until April 30 to bring the event before the eyes of their readers. But not only did the French press give a delayed and incomplete coverage of the destruction of Guernica; oftentimes the news printed in Paris of this event that took place a short distance from the French frontier constituted a reprinting or a condensation of London's news and London's reactions.

What was the reason? The French daily press was highly political, much more so than that of England or the United States. Many Paris dailies were published for opinion rather than for information. A French critic of the press wrote shortly after the end of World War II:

> The press of 1939 was divided into two categories, corresponding to the conceptions of the role of the newspaper with its reader: the news press and the political press. The first sought—and in any case claimed—neutrality and political objectivity; for the company to which the newspaper belonged, it was a commercial affair that should, above all, please the public and bring in profits. The second category made the newspaper an organ of a political party; its *raison d'être* was to keep the followers of the political leaders in suspense and to defend the ideals upheld by the party. Profits were secondary.[52]

But did a political control over a part of the French press in itself explain the poor coverage given by French daily newspapers to the news from Guernica? The answer is no. There was another and overriding reason for what was, from the point of view of news reporting, an abnormal situation. The press in France reported on Guernica inadequately and slowly because it had little or nothing to print about Guernica. As already mentioned, only one French newspaper, *Ce Soir,* a leftist, Communist-oriented journal, not yet two months old, had a reporter in Bilbao on April 26, and he was a Belgian. The rest of the French press depended for its daily news from the Republican side of the Basque front on the Agence Havas, the only French news service of any importance and one of the great news agencies of the world. Havas did have a reporter in Bilbao on April 26, the Spaniard Fontecha already mentioned; he himself had just arrived in the Basque capital, coming from Valencia. Thus, the great French news agency had no reporter of French nationality on the scene in Guernica on the night of April 26.

It is true that the situation in the Basque country held a more fundamental economic interest for the English than for the French, but the Spanish Basque country was on the French frontier, not on the English, and it is difficult today in the light of hindsight to understand why the French press was paying so little attention to the Bilbao side of the struggle. The French press had little or nothing to print about the destruction of Guernica on April 27 and the following days because the Agence Havas sent the papers little or nothing to print about the destruction of Guernica. This failure by Havas, this lack of any organized source of information about the destruction of Guernica for the French press, obliges us to take a more detailed look at French newspapers than was necessary for the press of England and the United States, where the press services distributed the news of the destruction of Guernica in detail and quickly.

Ce Soir broke the Guernica story in Paris on the afternoon of April 27 with a short cablegram from Corman, announcing that eight hundred persons had been killed in the bombardment of a Basque town called "Quirnica." Although the story itself was on an inside page, the news was headlined on page one.[53] There was one other reference to Guernica in the French press on the afternoon of April 27; this was on the third page of the mass-circulation newspaper *Paris Soir*, and told of a thousand incendiary bombs being dropped on the town, with 800 dead. But the news was in a dispatch datelined Madrid and was not the principal story of the day on the war in Spain; nor was the news about Guernica the chief element of the dispatch. No source was given for the news. This brief reference to Guernica was being sold on the streets of Paris at an hour when the press across the Channel was unanimously headlining the air attack.

What, then, had happened to Fontecha, the Havas man in Bilbao? Did he rush out to Guernica that night of April 26, as did the foreign professional correspondents? There is nothing in any dispatch to indicate either that he did or that he did not. But he was lodged in Bilbao at the Hotel Torrontegui, where Steer, Holme, and the others were dining when they heard the first news about the fire raging in Guernica.[54] The first telegram from Bilbao, or anywhere else in the Basque country, concerning Guernica, attributed to Havas, appeared only on the morning of April 28. The text, as published in at least five newspapers, four in Paris and one in Buenos Aires, is as follows:

> The bombing of Guernica which lasted eight hours, took place particularly while the market was in progress. The enemy dropped more than a thousand incendiary bombs. The convent of Santa Clara, transformed into an emergency hospital, was destroyed, as was the church Saint-Jean-de-Sainte-Marie and many houses. The airplanes came as low as forty yards from the ground to machine-gun the population. The fires continue all over the town. The number of victims is unknown, but it is stated that they are mainly women and children.[55]

This dispatch must be judged by the standards of the newspaper profession. It concerned one of the most violently discussed events of the Spanish Civil War, and it was issued to clients by a highly competitive news agency. Viewed from this angle, the report is woefully deficient. What would have been the reaction of a Paris newspaper editor who found in these lines on his teletype his first news of Guernica? What bombing? When? Where was Guernica? As a news story the Havas account is inexplicable, unreasonable.

The first AP cablegram about Guernica was shorter than the Havas report, but it contained all the essential information, which the Havas story lacked. Moreover, the original AP dispatch, published in Chicago on the morning of April 27, was a "flash"; that afternoon the AP had a much more complete follow-up story in print. By the time the Havas article was on the wires, the four competitors of Havas for the world news market, AP, UP, Universal News, and Reuters, all had much longer and more informative messages about Guernica in print.

Even before Havas sent out its trifling account of the destruction of Guernica, not only did the UP and AP have already in print articles more informative than the Havas account but these articles had been sent from France itself. The Havas report reads like a fragment from a much longer article or as simply a follow-up story, and this may well have been the case. It lacks the ring of urgency found in the correspondence of all the others who reported on Guernica on April 27, whether they were in Bilbao, in Vitoria, or on the frontier. It might be objected that the Havas agency did in fact send out a more complete account and that individual newspapers altered the text, but it is highly improbable that an editor in Buenos Aires and four editors in Paris would all change text in the same manner. We can therefore conclude that the text given above was the only one distributed by the Havas Agency on April 27 concerning the disaster at Guernica.

This Havas report was not only lacking in facts but also was late in getting distributed. This factor adds to our puzzlement, for Havas, backed by the Quai d'Orsay, was engaged in a press war with the American agencies AP and UP for the South American market, and what counted in Latin America at that moment was the latest news on the Spanish Civil War.[56] We have seen that Reuters had a message in the English press on the afternoon of April 27, as did the American agencies in North America. Both the AP and the UP beat Havas in Latin America with news about Guernica. *La Nación* of Buenos Aires did lead off its page-one treatment of the Guernica story with the short Havas account, but it followed it with an AP report from Guernica, another AP report from Hendaye, and then with extracts from Steer's account in that morning's *Times*.[57] It was in the three latter dispatches that the readers of *La Nación* found the facts about the destruction of Guernica, facts that were missing from the Havas telegram.

Correio da Manhã of Rio de Janeiro, which subscribed to both the Havas and UP services, on the morning of April 28 gave a three-column page-one headline to the disaster at Guernica, featuring three cablegrams from the UP, one from Bilbao, one from Hendaye (unsigned), and one from Hendaye, signed by "Harison-Laroche" [sic], who held down this frontier post for UP. Any single one of these UP dispatches was twice as complete and informative as the Havas one, which the *Correio da Manhã* did not even bother to print.[58]

In other parts of the world where the Havas agency was in competition with Reuters, Havas was roundly beaten on the news about Guernica. The Stockholm *Aftonbladet*, which used both Havas and Reuters services, printed Reuters dispatch on Guernica on the afternoon of April 27 but nothing from Havas.[59] In Holland, the *Nieuwe Rotterdamsche Courant* published Steer's *Times* story, followed by Reuters; it published other stories that day from Havas about Spain but nothing about Guernica.[60] In Canada, where the Havas service was distributed by the Canadian Press Agency, Havas was roundly outdistanced by the American services or by Reuters.[61]

European newspapers in the French orbit, dependent on Havas for their general world news, such as the *Journal de Genève*,[62] *La Métropole* of Antwerp,[63] *La*

Libre Belgique,[64] and *L'Indépendance Belge*[65] (both of Brussels), were all without news of Guernica on the morning of April 28. Ordinarily, Havas did not like to be beaten on important news by the other agencies. When, a few weeks earlier, the newspapers in Rome were publishing fresher Nationalist news about the battle of Guadalajara than Havas was receiving from its men in the Rebel zone, Paris telegraphed and wrote to its correspondents of its displeasure.[66] There is nothing in the Havas files to indicate a similar discontent over the quality or the quantity of the news received from Bilbao on Guernica.

Who was responsible for the inadequacy of the Havas news about Guernica and for the delay in transmission? Perhaps it was simply the fault of Fontecha, but he was an experienced journalist and had been with the agency since before the civil war. A dispatch that he sent a few days later, also involving Guernica, is a model of concise reporting. His pro-Republican sympathies were also never in doubt.[67] It is therefore difficult to believe that all the information Fontecha sent from Bilbao on April 27 about the bombardment of Guernica was contained in the incomplete, inaccurate, and skimpy account distributed by Havas. An explanation might be that Fontecha did send much longer, more detailed, more urgent messages, and that the length, the details, and the urgency were edited out in Paris. Why? It is also worth noting that whereas many essential facts are simply missing from the Havas cablegram, one basic fact—the duration of the bombardment—is, according to everyone else, completely wrong.[68]

It is true that Fontecha sent his cables in Spanish and that translation took time in Paris, but how much time would be needed to translate the short note that Havas did send out? The Havas editors in Paris may, of course, have simply underestimated the importance of the news from Guernica, but they were experienced men too, and certainly by the afternoon of April 27 they were well aware of the sensation that the news from Guernica was causing in London. Havas's connections with the Guernica story were also complicated by the fact that Fontecha was a Spaniard. American news agencies tended to believe the testimony of Americans; British agencies had faith in British eyewitnesses; Havas trusted Frenchmen. All were inclined to think that Spanish correspondents were unobjective about the war (which was probably true) and that foreign correspondents were highly objective in their reporting (which was certainly not true). At any rate, if the Havas agency had been represented in Bilbao by a Frenchman on April 26, it is just possible that the treatment of the Guernica story in the French press might have been different.

The two Paris newspapers that did print the Havas dispatch concerning Guernica on the morning of April 28 were *L'Humanité,* organ of the French Communist party, and *L'Oeuvre,* the Paris spokesman of the Radical-Socialists. *L'Humanité* reported the attack with huge headlines on page one: "MOST HORRIBLE BOMB-ING OF SPANISH WAR. THOUSAND INCENDIARY BOMBS DROPPED BY HITLER'S AND MUSSOLINI'S PLANES REDUCE TOWN OF GUERNICA TO ASHES."

The newspaper also printed on page one a long denunciatory editorial signed by the paper's foreign affairs expert, the deputy Gabriel Péri.[69] But the Communist newspaper had another source for news about Guernica than the Havas Agency, and it was on this other source and not on the Havas report that it based its headlines and its news story. This other news bulletin, much longer and more detailed, came from L'Agence Espagne, a news agency set up in Paris by the Republican government to distribute its side of the news, governmental declarations in their entirety, and background articles on the efforts of the Republic in such fields as culture and social progress.[70] The daily of the Socialist party, *Le Populaire*,[71] and a paper of "grande information," *Le Petit Journal*,[72] also used the bulletin issued by L'Agence Espagne, but neither identified the origin of its information.

Only one of these papers referred to the article by Corman in *Ce Soir* the previous afternoon, the original headlined story in France about Guernica; this was *L'Ouevre*, which also published the short dispatch from Havas, under a page-three headline: "800 BODIES OF WOMEN AND CHILDREN IN GUERNICA'S RUINS."[73]

The paucity of news from Havas about Guernica on the morning of April 28 led at least two other Parisian morning newspapers to rely on their London offices for the story. The conservative *Le Matin*[74] and the mass-circulation paper *Le Petit Parisien*[75] both reported on Guernica as had London. *L'Echo de Paris*, a staunch supporter of the Franco cause, told of the bombing in an article bearing neither date nor source, but which doubtless came from a reporter inside Spain:

> Numerous military objectives have been bombed by Nationalist pilots, particularly the town of Guernica, cradle of Basque separatism. . . . At Guernica, the Reds had established important deposits of military supplies, which have been destroyed.[76]

Another mass-circulation Paris newspaper, *Le Journal*, published its first news about Guernica on the morning of April 28, in the form of a Havas telegram, but it was not the dispatch from Bilbao. It was a denial of the bombing from Salamanca.[77]

That afternoon the sensation-loving *Paris-Soir* published, on an inside page, the first of Noel Monks's dispatches, under his signature, as it had appeared that morning in London.[78] *Ce Soir* gave its readers more details from Corman, including: "The number of victims in Guernica is higher than previously stated."[79] In contrast to these firsthand, on-the-spot stories, *Le Temps* informed its readers for the first time of Guernica with three reports: Aguirre's accusation, from Bilbao; the reaction in London and in the English press; and a denial of Nationalist responsibility, from Salamanca.[80] These three stories, though no source was given, in fact came from Havas. The thoughtful reader of *Le Temps* might have found the geographical setting of this strong, twenty-four-hour-old reaction to news about an incident in Spain of which he, a Frenchman, was just learning, a bit unsettling. The dispatch, from the Havas man in London, read in part:

English newspapers express a lively indignation over the bombing of Guer-. nica. The *Times* and, on the other hand, the organs of the Opposition, dedicate editorials of high quality to the subject, while the conservative newspapers, generally favorable to the cause of General Franco, limit themselves to reproducing the agency dispatches describing the systematic destruction of the old town.

Our thoughtful reader might have asked himself: how was this reaction possible in London and not in Paris? What were these "agency dispatches describing the systematic destruction of the old town," available for reading in London and not in Paris?

Nevertheless, Havas could have been said to have offered its clients a sufficient coverage for the second day of the news story on Guernica *if it had given them the complete account the first day.* Havas had given its customers nothing about Guernica for the afternoon papers of April 27, and since what it sent out later for the morning papers of April 28 was incomplete and incorrect, a journalist might wonder why the agency did not offer its subscribers for the afternoon of April 28, as did, for example, *Paris-Soir,* a full though tardy relation of the news about Guernica. By the afternoon of April 28 the impact of the terrifying news about Guernica had to some extent been blunted, in France and wherever else the press depended on Havas, by the French agency's handling of the first news bulletin.

This blunted impact was still evident on the morning of April 29—thirty-six hours after the first news of Guernica was published in Paris and elsewhere in the Western world. On this morning, eight daily newspapers in Paris mentioned Guernica for the first time. These were of all political tendencies: monarchist Catholic *L'Action Française,* the reactionary Catholic *Le Jour,* and the conservative Catholic *Le Figaro,* the neutral and conservative *Journal des Débats,* the neutral *L'Excelsior,* the official Catholic organ *La Croix,* edited by the Reverend Father Merklen, the Christian Democratic *L'Aube* of Francisque Gay and Georges Bidault, and the independent *L'Ordre* of Emile Buré. The first five of these newspapers, in mentioning the affair of Guernica for the first time on the morning of April 29, did not give the news of the destruction but simply various *reactions* to the news. *L'Action Française* stated: "All the press, red, rosy, Freemason, or Puritan of two hemispheres has been uttering cries of horror since yesterday [April 27]," and concluded that, if the town had been really bombed, "war is war."[81] Léon Bailby's rabidly pro-Franco *Le Jour* simply selected from the Havas bulletins the report of a debate in the Commons and the denial from Salamanca, both dealing with an incident of which the newspaper's readers knew nothing.[82] *Le Figaro* buried the three Havas telegrams published by *Le Temps* the previous afternoon into second place among the Spanish war bulletins of the day on page three.[83] The *Journal des Débats* chose the same three news items as did *Le Figaro.*[84] *L'Excelsior* printed a Havas report from Valencia, containing the accusation by the Basque delegation of German responsibility for the bombing.[85]

Three other newspapers, as indicated above, spoke of Guernica for the first time on the morning of April 29—not as the others did on that morning (printing the second chapter without the first) but by printing the news of the event itself and not simply the reactions to the unmentioned event. The conservative official spokesman of the French Catholic Church *La Croix* informed its readers of the attack on Guernica, belatedly but effectively, with news from Bilbao and quotations from Steer's original story in the *Times*.[86] *L'Aube*, long friendly to the Basque cause, accused the Germans of the raid on Guernica and also quoted the *Times*, in an article signed by Jean Richard, entitled "Guernica, Martyr City."[87] *L'Ordre* denounced the attack on its front page and gave its public extensive information about the event in an article on an inside page, which included Aguirre's accusation, the first short Havas dispatch, the denial from Salamanca, and the reaction in the House of Commons. In a box in the upper left-hand corner of page one was printed: "Who said that the German airforce was worthless? It has just killed a thousand women and children in Guernica."[88] On the following day the newspaper noted: "The bombing of Guernica causes horror in England. All the English press stigmatizes this act."[89]

Paris-Midi, a newspaper of general information, also waited until April 29 to speak of Guernica, and did so with an article from its own London office. "WHO IS RESPONSIBLE FOR SANGUINARY BOMBING OF GUERNICA?" asked the journal in the headlines of a long article.

"The terrible bombings that have just destroyed Guernica . . . have provoked throughout England an emotion impossible to convey," wrote Georges Morel, the daily's London correspondent, who declared, after telling of the interventions in the House of Commons: "Of all the crimes which have sullied this sanguinary struggle, the destruction of Guernica and the annihilation of its population remains the most hateful." Morel continued with quotations from Steer in the *Times*, and answered the question posed by the headline to his article: "One must admit that these precisions leave hardly a doubt as to the reality of the bombings and as to the nationality of those who did the bombing."[90]

Still another Paris newspaper of "grande information," *L'Intransigeant*, waited until April 30 to print the news about Guernica, and then did so, as many of its colleagues had, with a dispatch from its correspondent in London:

> The massacre of the civilian population of Guernica has produced a veritable feeling of horror in England. It is not only the labor unions and the socialist organizations who have officially denounced "this monstrous crime"; in the Parliament, members belonging to all the parties have anxiously interrogated the Foreign Minister and demanded an enquiry.[91]

Another source of information about Guernica for the French press came from interviews with refugees from the devasted town, not only in Bilbao but also in France itself. The Havas man in Bilbao, Fernando Fontecha, on April 29 sent a moving account of the experiences of a woman named Maria Goitia who had survived the bombing.[92] This report was the most widely printed of all those sent by Havas from Bilbao concerning Guernica, and was published not only in France but also in Canada, Switzerland, Scotland, and Morocco.[93] Some days later, Paul Vaillant-Couturier, one of the chief editors of *L'Humanite*, sent from Bilbao an interview with several survivors of the Guernica disaster.[94] On May 6, the ship *La Habana* arrived at La Pallice from Bilbao; among the passengers were eyewitnesses of the air raid. A reporter for *Le Petit Journal* wrote:

> Three young girls and their mother paint for us a picture of their terror during the three-hour-long bombardment, the collapse and burning of their dwelling, and then their bewildered flight along the road to Bilbao, while the German airplanes fired at them with machine guns.

But the prize witness was the Cuban newspaperman Martin Arrisbaya, an editor of *El Pais* of Havana who was in Guernica on April 26:

> At five o'clock, we were passing in the Rentería quarter, when an airplane came over our heads and dropped nine bombs on the Rentería bridge. The bridge was not destroyed, and immediately afterwards a crowd gathered to view the damage done by the projectile. It was market day and there were many peasants in town. At that moment, some twenty airplanes appeared in the sky. . . . The peasants fled along the road, where they were followed by the airplanes which flew low, machine-gunning them. . . . Everyone seemed to have lost his head and fled into the countryside. But there in the open the people were pursued by the aerial machine guns.[95]

After this review of the Paris press treatment of the news about Guernica, it is worthwhile to turn our attention to how the same matter was treated by three newspapers in the southwest of France, where the civil war impassioned many readers: *La Dépêche* of Toulouse, *La France de Bordeaux et du Sud-Ouest* of Bordeaux, and *La Petite Gironde,* also of Bordeaux. *La Dépêche,* an outspoken partisan of the Spanish Republic, informed its readers on the morning of April 28, of the destruction of Guernica with a headline on the front page and the short Havas report buried on page 4. It gave absolutely no other information on the event.[96] On the following day, after an account of the fighting in the Basque country, the newspaper stated: "It is from London that we have up to now received the principal details of this act of war, which is in reality not so much an air battle as a veritable crime." The article then went on to quote the *Times* and Steer's message. Also on April 29, the newspaper printed a dispatch from Bilbao giving the details of the air attack lacking in the Havas story, but no source was given.[97]

The second of these southwestern French newspapers, *La France*, a journal of "grande information radicalisante," partisan of the Spanish Republic, like *La Dépêche,* did not publish a word about Guernica in its edition of April 28. It was only on the following day that it announced the air raid with headlines on page one and three articles (from Havas) about Guernica—one from Valencia, one from

London, and one from Salamanca.[98] *La Petite Gironde,* unlike the other two newspapers in this part of France, was neutral in its politics. It first mentioned the destruction of Guernica in a short report, datelined Bilbao, on April 28; this is not the Havas report, nor is it the unidentified message published by *La Dépêche,* on April 29, but, again, no source is given.[99]

Most of the newspapers in this part of France, like the Havas Agency in Paris itself, maintained a service for listening to the Spanish radios on both sides. It was probably in this way that *La Dépêche* and *La Petite Gironde* received their news about Guernica apart from the short note sent by Havas. The paradox of this situation lies in the fact that a short distance away from Toulouse and Bordeaux, in Hendaye, the American press agencies AP and UP and the English agency Reuters were sending to North America, where interest in the Spanish Civil War was much less than in the southwest of France, much more information about the destruction of Guernica than was available to the French newspapers of the region.

The tardy, and often incomplete, news of Guernica printed in the French press, even by newspapers favorable to the Republican cause, might lead one to wonder if Edgar Ansel Mowrer, the distinguished American correspondent then in Paris, really had his finger on the pulse of French public opinion when he wrote in the *Chicago Daily News* on April 29 that the destruction of the town "has aroused French sentiments hostile to the Rebels to a pitch far beyond anything witnessed." [100] And just where in the French press did the editors of *La France de Bordeaux et du Sud-Ouest* find "the unanimous feeling of reprobation" that they thought to have discovered on the morning of April 29 "in the English press as well as in the French press"?[101] And when *L'Oeuvre* stated in a page-one headline on April 30, "WORLD OPINION ROUSED TO INDIGNATION BY SAVAGE DESTRUCTION OF GUER-NICA,"[102] some readers in Paris might well have asked themselves if what was true for the world was really true for France.[103]

In fact, as we have seen, the news about Guernica did get printed little by little, in the French press. In judging these newspapers, we must weigh what was printed about Guernica with the counterweight of what was available for printing. The chief source of news—foreign or domestic—for the French press was the Havas Agency. The foreign news agencies rarely sold their services in France.[104] The copy that Havas offered its subscribers on the destruction of Guernica was, by all the laws and norms of modern journalism, astonishingly inadequate. The other four worldwide news agencies, three American and one British, far surpassed the Havas Agency in coverage of the incident.

Faced with Havas's deficiency, the French newspaper editors had to improvise, each according to his own resources, as we have seen. *Ce Soir* printed the news from Guernica on the afternoon of April 27, because it had its own man in Bilbao. On the morning of April 28, *Le Matin* and *Le Petit Parisien* got the story from their own London bureaus; *L'Humanité, Le Populaire,* and *Le Petit Journal* used bulletins from *L'Agence Espagne. L'Oeuvre* rewrote Corman's dispatch to *Ce Soir.* That afternoon, *Paris-Soir* used a London source, and *Ce Soir* published another bulletin from Corman. On the following day, *La Croix* and *L'Aube* reprinted extracts from the *Times. Paris-Midi* received a cablegram from its man in London, and *Paris-Soir* again printed what Noel Monks had sent his paper in London. On April 30, *L'Intransigeant* published an article on Guernica from its London office. Newspapers in the southwest of France made up for Havas's inadequacy by listening to the Spanish radio. Thus, the French newspapers that did print the story of Guernica had to make a special effort that the press in England, the United States, Canada, or South America did not have to make.

If the news about Guernica was not printed as completely and as rapidly in France as elsewhere (in the countries where such news could be printed), it was not the fault of the newspaper editors, except in such extreme cases as *L'Echo de Paris, Le Jour, Le Journal, Le Figaro,* and *L'Action Française,* which never did publish the first news about the destruction of Guernica, even when it became available; it was the fault of a news agency that, possessing a monopoly of news distribution in France,[105] sent out but a trifling note on one of the most important news stories of the Spanish Civil War. This unexplained breakdown of the French news distribution had one curious result, as has been shown, in that most of the news printed in France immediately after April 26 concerning the actual destruction of Guernica came through British sources, chiefly from the *Times.*

By noon of April 29, 1937, when the first troops of General Mola, in considerable part Italians, moved into the smoldering ruins of Guernica, in France, as elsewhere in the Western world, most newspaper readers were aware of the destruction of the Basque town. This knowledge, even when it came secondhand from London, had its origin in the messages furnished by the correspondents in Bilbao or on the frontier. What credence can be given to their dispatches? Of the four foreign professional correspondents in Bilbao on April 26, Steer, Corman, and Monks, as already noted, later repeated their original declarations in book form. The fourth, who did not write a book, Holme of Reuters, later reaffirmed the contents of his newspaper dispatches in a letter written in 1968.[106] All the other messages cited—those published in the *Star,* in the *Daily Worker,* in the *News Chronicle,* in the *Daily Telegraph* and in the *Daily Herald;* those of the Spaniards in Bilbao, Fontecha of Havas, Herrero of the UP, and the unnamed correspondents of the AP and Universal News, that of Minifie of the *New York Herald Tribune;* those printed in France by reporters stationed on the frontier—all confirmed the messages of the four foreign professional correspondents in Bilbao. It is therefore difficult to pretend that the original cablegrams of the correspondents resulted from any pressure or constraint from the Basque authorities in April 1937.

As for the press censorship in Bilbao, it sinned rather on the side of carelessness. On May 29, a British diplomat in Geneva informed his government that Steer had told him:

"The military censorship at Bilbao is extremely lax." Steer had often seen messages from foreign correspondents passed through the censorship which seemed to him to give information of considerable value to the insurgents.[107]

This state of affairs was later confirmed by Monks in his book: "I drove back to Bilbao and had to waken the cable operator. . . . Censorship had been lifted completely. The man who sent my dispatch couldn't read English."[108]

Not only were all the correspondents, professional or occasional, foreign or Spanish, in Bilbao, on the frontier in Hendaye, or elsewhere in France, in agreement on the main facts of what had happened in Guernica but also their sources were in agreement. More than a hundred survivors of the Guernica holocaust had told the journalists that Guernica was indeed bombed on April 26, for more than three hours, by airplanes that dropped explosive and incendiary bombs, that the inhabitants were mercilessly pursued in the fields and along the roads by machine-gunning airplane crews, that the town had been set on fire and burned to the ground by the bombing. These witnesses and their interlocutors between them had compiled an impressive dossier. But it was to be denied and challenged.

2

Riposte from Salamanca

Within forty-eight hours of the first news of the air attack on Guernica, a widespread feeling of anger and resentment against those believed responsible for the act became manifest in all parts of the world except in the Fascist countries. In view of the damage done and the people killed since then by aerial bombardment, this reaction may today seem the exaggeration of a more primitive age, and indeed pro-Nationalist apologists today talk of the subsequent and more murderous bombings of Rotterdam, Coventry, Dresden, and Hiroshima as somehow excusing the previous destruction of Guernica.[1] But in 1937, people were not yet hardened to such spectacles, and it is because Guernica was in a way the beginning of the tragic and unfinished tale of slaughter from the air that it was then and remains today a symbol of such crimes.

The symbolism of Guernica was immediately realized by Pablo Picasso when he painted his huge canvas,[2] by Paul Éluard when he wrote his poem,[3] and by Herman Kesten when he wrote his novel.[4] It was felt by Luigi Sturzo when he wrote a few weeks after the event:

> Meanwhile, in the newspapers of Germany and France known for their "national" feelings, we read the opinion that the bombing of open towns cannot be prevented, if such an act responds to the demands of war, if the locality is strategic, if it is feared that arms may be stocked there, if . . . It is for this reason that Guernica constitutes an historic event: in the past such bombardments were tolerated because they were not too prominently in

view. From now on, the history of future wars, in speaking of aerial bomb-ings, will refer to Guernica as now one refers to the *Lusitania,* in speaking of torpedoing by submarines.[5]

This world wide eruption of indignation caused by the original news stories of the destruction of Guernica provoked the second group of newspaper dispatches forming the Guernica series. These were based on the reaction of the spokesmen of the military junta in Salamanca and began with a hastily improvised, blustering all-inclusive denial, founded chiefly on the claim that bad weather had prevented the Nationalist air force from flying on the day of the alleged bombing. Commen-taries on the news of the destruction of Guernica inside Nationalist Spain—reactions to the news from Bilbao being printed in London and New York and to the accusations being made in Bilbao by President Aguirre—began about twenty-four hours after the end of the bombing attack, if we accept the time schedule set up by the news from Bilbao. At nine o'clock on the evening of April 27, "Radio Requeté" declared:

> The news published by the ridiculous president of the Republic of Euzkadi concerning the fires provoked by the bombs of our airplanes at Guernica are completely false. Our aviators have received no orders to bomb this town. The incendiarists are those who, last summer, burned Irún, and yesterday, Eibar. Unable to hold back our troops, the Reds have destroyed everything. They accuse the Nationals of deeds which are but the realization of their own criminal intentions.[6]

That same night, *Radio Nacional* at Salamanca, aired a virulent diatribe entitled "Lies, Lies, Lies." This was, apparently, a reply not so much to the dispatches being printed in London as to the impassioned declaration by Aguirre, issued during the morning of April 27, accusing the Germans flying for Franco of the attack on Guernica.[7] The Salamanca statement denied the allegation:

> Aguirre lies! He lies basely. In the first place, there is no German or foreign air force in National Spain. There is a Spanish air force, a noble, heroic Spanish air force, which constantly fights against Red planes, Russian and French, piloted by foreigners. In the second place, we did not burn Guernica. Franco's Spain does not set fires. The incendiary torch is the monopoly of the arsonists of Irún, of those who set fire to Eibar, of those who tried to burn alive the defenders of the Alcázar of Toledo.

At the end of the discourse, a new element was introduced:

> In these moments news arrives from the Biscay front which shows the falseness of Aguirre's speech. Our planes, because of the bad weather, have not been able to fly today and consequently could hardly have bombed Guernica.[8]

These same themes were used that night by General Gonzalo Queipo de Llano, who had established a reputation at the microphone of Radio Sevilla. He declared that the charges of the "*canalla* Aguirre" were false, "because the *siri miri*—characteristic wind of the region—prohibited all air activity." He also suggested that Guernica was probably set on fire by the Basques.[9]

There were thus established in these statements of April 27 the two essential positions held by the Nationalists concerning the destruction of Guernica during the first days following the disaster:

1. Guernica had been set on fire and destroyed by incendiarism from the ground, and the proof invoked was the manner in which, according to the Nationalists, Irún and Eibar had previously been burned.

2. Bad weather had kept the Nationalist planes from the air, and they therefore could not be held responsible for the consequences of any bombing at that time.

Who was responsible for this propaganda line? It has been written that Franco himself prepared the statement called "Lies, Lies, Lies."[10] George Steer wrote that the communiqué was produced by Vicente Gay.[11] But Gay, a former professor at the University of Valladolid, had been replaced as head of the Delegation of Press and Propaganda on April 15 by Manuel Arias Paz, a major in the corps of engineers.[12] The delegation had been established on January 14, 1937.[13] Its functions were different from, though sometimes overlapping, those of the military censorship, headed at the central office in Salamanca by Luis Bolín. The delegation's authority covered what was printed and broadcast inside Spain; Bolín's office controlled what was transmitted from Spain to the outside world by representatives of the foreign press. The evidence available today seems to indicate that it was neither Gay nor his successor but Bolín who prepared for Franco the first alibi for the Nationalist air force in the Guernica affair. In a 1967 publication on which the Spanish Ministry of Information collaborated, Bolín is said to "have divulged the first version of the anti-myth of Guernica."[14]

Let us now look for a moment at the two positions set up in Bolín's "anti-myth." First of all, let us study the accusations against the Basques or other Republican forces based on analogies with the burning of Irún and Eibar. There is no doubt that Irún was set on fire by anarchists or other elements of the Republican forces. This fact was duly chronicled in the press at the time, and no attempt was ever made to cover up the act, legitimate in time of war. The destruction of Eibar is another story. The town fell on April 26, the very day Guernica was set on fire. When the Nationalists entered the town, they found it in flames, and according to press reports the town was at least three-quarters destroyed.[15] But who set Eibar aflame? Or that part of it not already destroyed? Steer, who seems generally well informed, claimed that Eibar had been fire-bombed late on April 25, the day before its capture, in a preliminary to the bombing of Guernica.[16] That Eibar was indeed bombed that day and that the bombing set fires can be shown by press dispatches passed through the Nationalist censorship.[17] But

. whether Eibar was set on fire by incendiary bombs or by retreating Republicans at the moment of their evacuating the town is not the central question here. Does the fact that Irún was set on fire by incendiarists from the ground, as it was being evacuated, have anything in common with the destruction of Guernica? Does the fact that the ruins of Eibar may have been set on fire by troops who were abandoning this already heavily bombed town have anything in common with the destruction of Guernica?[18] The answer is no. There is a fundamental difference between the destruction of Guernica and the destruction of both Irún and Eibar, and this difference does not appear in the Nationalist statements and communiqués.

Irún was burned upon evacuation by elements of a retreating army. Eibar, or what was left of it, was burned at the moment of its evacuation. Neither in the case of Irún, admittedly set on fire from the ground, nor in that of Eibar, where incendiarism by the Basques has certainly not been proved, has it ever been alleged by the Nationalist accusers that lives were lost in the subsequent conflagrations. The essential element of the Guernica story should not be that the buildings were destroyed but that hundreds of lives were lost during the holocaust, and on this crucial point neither the spokesmen in Salamanca nor the radio orator in Seville said a single word. It is of significance to note that a person who confined his reading to the Nationalist press of the epoch would have remained blissfully unaware that any lives at all were lost in the tragedy. The destruction of property to prevent its being used by the enemy is an admitted part of warfare,[19] and the fact that men with Republican sympathies set fire to unoccupied buildings in Irún constitutes no proof that such men would necessarily have set fire to occupied buildings in Guernica.

The second defense line set up by Nationalist spokesmen on the evening of April 27 was to the effect that bad weather kept their planes from flying on that day, and that Guernica could therefore not have been destroyed by their planes or presumably by any others. But the Salamanca communiqué made clear that the speaker was referring to April 27 and not April 26, the date on which Guernica was, according to all reports, set on fire. In fact, bad weather did occur on April 27. A communiqué from Franco's headquarters announced that on noon of that day, "The regional siri miri set in. This phenomenon cut all visibility for artillery and aviation to the point where the latter could not fly."[20] It was doubtless this military report that inspired the spokesmen in Salamanca, but it is difficult to believe that on the evening of April 27 Bolín and the other Nationalist press officers were unaware that President Aguirre that morning, and a great part of the press of the Western world that afternoon, were talking of a bombing and a conflagration that had already taken place—on the previous afternoon—as was logical unless the newspapers and the president were prophesying rather than reporting.

It is of secondary importance to note that the Salamanca spokesman, before invoking the element of bad weather to prove his case, had simply denied that there was any "German or foreign air force in National Spain." Strange as it may seem today, this lie was part of the make-believe world of European diplomacy at that moment. If Salamanca had admitted that organized units of the German air force were in Spain, the English and French governments would have had to take some action. Unable or unwilling to take that action, these governments and everybody else preferred to maintain the fiction that the Germans and Italians in Spain—if such there were—were "volunteers."

The Salamanca communiqué of April 27, or the essential parts of it, was widely distributed by most of the press agencies, including Havas.[21]

On April 28, the official communiqué from Franco's headquarters mentioned Guernica.

> Basque fugitives who come to meet our columns tell in frightened tones of the tragedies of towns like Guernica, burned and almost completely destroyed in fires deliberately set by the Reds,[22] when our troops were still more than 15 kilometers away.[23] The slanderous maneuvers of the Basco-Soviet leaders, who, after destroying their best cities by fire, attempt to blame the National air force for these acts of barbarism, have provoked a boundless indignation among the National troops. Guernica did not, at any moment, constitute a military objective for the National air force, which attacks only military objectives during the fighting and military-industrial objectives in the enemy rear guard. This falsehood coincides with the fact that the National air force has been unable to fly during these last few days because of the fog and drizzle everywhere.[24]

That same night of April 28, Queipo de Llano returned to the subject, saying that positive proof that Guernica was not destroyed by air bombardment could be found in "data that we possess" showing that "the fire came from below upward and from inside outward," and that "the holes in the roofs characteristic of a bombing by airplanes could not be seen in the houses." The general also repeated that "our airplanes did not fly on April 26, the date referred to in their dispatches, for on that day the rain and the lack of visibility caused by the storm kept our planes grounded." He said that such a bombing would have been an "act of treachery," and concluded: "This task was carried out by Asturian dynamiters, employed by the Marxists, in order afterward to attribute the crime to us."[25]

Later that night (at two in the morning of April 29) Salamanca issued another long harangue on Guernica:

> Guernica was destroyed by fire and gasoline. It was set on fire and converted into ruins by the Red hordes at the criminal service of Aguirre. . . . The fire took place yesterday [obviously the author means by "yesterday" April 27], and Aguirre uttered the infamous lie—because he is a common delinquent—of attributing the crime to the noble and heroic air force of our National army. We can prove, at whatever moment, that the National air force did not fly yesterday, because of the fog, neither over Guernica, nor over any other point of the Basque front. Today the National air force did fly over Guernica. It flew and took photographs of the burning of Guernica, which seems almost totally destroyed. Aguirre . . . has prepared . . . the de-

struction of Guernica in order to blame it on the adversary and provoke a
feeling of indignation among the Basques, defeated and demoralized. . . . We
have said that our air force could not have caused this destruction, because
our planes did not leave the ground yesterday, but, in addition, there are
witnesses of the burning of Guernica by the Reds, witnesses of their work
with the incendiary torch and gasoline. This town will soon be in our hands.
We invite all the world to come there with us, to contemplate the ruins. There
we shall prove in a manner beyond doubt, before the foreign journalists, that
the destruction of Guernica could not have been caused by incendiary bombs,
that its destructión was the work of those who burned Irún and Eibar. . . .[26]

Thus, still on the night of April 28-29, the official position of the Spanish
Nationalists was that Guernica had been deliberately set on fire by the Basques, and
that the Nationalist air force could not be held responsible because their planes had
not been able to take to the air on the day of the supposed bombing. True, there
was not always agreement as to the date when the planes had *not* flown. It is
difficult today to believe that forty-eight hours after the incident the heads of the
press and propaganda services in Salamanca could be ignorant of what had really
happened, and of what was being published in London, Paris, and New York. It
can also be emphasized that at this time the official Nationalist position was that
Mola's troops were fifteen kilometers from Guernica when it was set on fire, that
the town was not a military objective, and that witnesses were on hand to testify as
to the hands that held the torches and poured the gasoline.

This statement, or some other declaration issued at Salamanca on April 28, was
curiously interpreted by a Reuters correspondent at Saint-Jean-de-Luz, and subsequently led to speculation that Franco's stand might be a subtle way of accusing
the Germans of the raid. According to this dispatch,

> Insurgent headquarters at Salamanca yesterday formally and officially denied
> all knowledge of the raid on Guernica. They did not deny that the raid
> occurred, but declared in the most positive way that they had no part in it.[27]

Around midday on April 29, the Rebels entered Guernica, and this event gave a
fresh impetus to Nationalist-inspired statements about Guernica. That night the
Radio General returned to the attack, using as his target the *Daily Express,* which
had sent him some questions to answer on the subject of Guernica. He again stated
that the Nationalist air force had not flown on April 26 because of the siri-miri. He
explained that if the Reuters correspondent had written that he had picked up
unexploded bombs with German markings, it was because he had been bought with
"stolen gold."[28] He insisted: "Guernica was not a military objective. . . . Moreover
the fire started there was not caused by aerial bombs but by explosives, as will be
shown at the proper time." To explain why the Basques had destroyed their own
town and killed their own people, Queipo de Llano referred to Marxist influences
and to the fact that Guernica "was occupied by battalions of Asturian miners,
people who handle dynamite with skill and who have no scruples in destroying

anything that bothers them, as they showed in Eibar." At any rate, he concluded, the destruction of Guernica was not the work of the air force, because no planes of either side could have flown the day Guernica was destroyed.[29]

On April 30, in celebration of the capture of Guernica, an article appeared in the Nationalist press under the heading "The Burning of Guernica." The style indicates that it came from the same pen that forty-eight hours earlier had written the article entitled "Lies, Lies, Lies."

> Guernica is now in the hands of the National army. Rather, there is in the hands of the National army what remained of Guernica, the town which the Red hordes, in a sinister conspiracy with the separatists of Aguirre, have converted into ruins. As Irún, as Lequeitio, Guernica has suffered the apocalyptic storm of those who, on fleeing—these are the precise orders of Moscow—leave fire and misery in the wake of their madness. . . . Guernica has been destroyed by the Reds at the service of the Basque separatists. This is already proved and the proof will be better still with the declarations of those who witnessed in Guernica itself the burning of the town, consciously planned, on the 27th *[sic]*, by those getting ready to flee. Not one of our planes flew that day over Biscay. But there is still more. Today, the correspondents who live and work in our zone were invited to enter Guernica with the occupying troops, to speak freely with the inhabitants, to ascertain the truth of the stupid and repugnant lie of Aguirre.[30]

There are two important features to this declaration:

1. The publicized invitation of the Nationalist authorities to the foreign correspondents accredited to Franco's headquarters signaled a new series of dispatches from the Rebel zone concerning the destruction of Guernica as viewed by the newspapermen who came in with the Nationalist forces.

2. Here for the first time we see perhaps a logical explanation for the repeated Nationalist insistence that the destruction of Guernica took place not on Monday, April 26 but on Tuesday, April 27, "carried out . . . by those getting ready to flee." This flight was more credible on the 27th than on the 26th, as it would have been more credible on the 28th than on the 27th, or more credible still on the 29th, when it really took place, than on the 28th.

Abruptly, on May 2, drastic changes in the Rebel explanation of the disaster in Guernica began to appear. "It is possible," read a new communiqué, "that a few bombs fell upon Guernica during days when our airplanes were operating against objectives of military importance." This revealing statement, sent out from Salamanca by Reuters through the Nationalist censorship, was found in the complete text of the communiqué published in the *Times* and other newspapers,[31] but these words do not appear in the domestic version published in the press of Rebel Spain.[32] The siri-miri, which was supposed to have grounded the Nationalist air force on the day of Guernica's ruin, now rose and disappeared forever, at least from Salamanca's vocabulary. Guernica, which had been declared but a few hours earlier to have been at the time of its destruction a nonmilitary objective, fifteen kilometers from the front, was now a military objective but six kilometers "from the first line of combat" when it was "destroyed."[33] The town was now said to be

> an important crossroads filled with troops retiring towards other defenses. At Guernica an important factory has been manufacturing arms and munitions for nine months. It would not have been surprising if the National airplanes had marked Guernica as an objective. The laws of war allowed it, the rights of the people notwithstanding. It was a classical military objective with an importance that thoroughly justified a bombing. Yet it was not bombed. The destruction of Guernica was the work of . . . incendiary dynamiters.

This document constituted not only a flagrant contradiction of what had been said before by the Nationalist authorities but also contained its own internal contradictions. It was now declared in one sentence that bombs may indeed have been dropped on the town, while in another it was flatly stated that the town had not been bombed at all. The date of the possible bomb dropping was left vague. In reality, bombs were dropped on Guernica on but one occasion, and that was on April 26. This point was, surprisingly enough, made abundantly clear in *Guernica: The Official Report*, prepared by the Nationalists themselves a few months after the destruction of the town.[34] Now on May 2, in spite of what had been said by Queipo de Llano over Radio Sevilla, and in spite of the affirmations made in the official war communiqué of April 28, Guernica was decreed to have been a military objective; logically, Guernica's distance from the battle lines at the moment of its destruction was shortened from fifteen kilometers to six.

The exact motives for these changes of position by the Nationalist authorities are unknown, but an analysis of the changes can suggest some reasons for the new communiqué. A bombing, though of indefinite date, was now admitted, perhaps because bomb holes were visible in Guernica. And the reason for this bombing? Or for these bombings? A valid military reason had to be found, and thus Guernica achieved a status it had been denied up to now: that of a military objective. And this new "military objective" was brought much closer to the front lines. Why? Perhaps because it was seen that—as was probably the case with the communiqué of May 30—in order to render credible the story of Guernica's being destroyed by arsonists working on the ground, in order to render credible a comparison of the destruction of Guernica with that of Irún, or even with that of Eibar, the destruction of Guernica had to brought into a time schedule more compatible with the act of evacuation.

This new communiqué, while stressing the importance of Guernica as a "military objective," failed to point out that none of the positions which could be called "military objectives" in Guernica was destroyed by the bombing or by the fires, whether these latter were started by the bombing or by incendiarists. The installations most logically classed as "military objectives" were the railway tracks, the workshops alongside the tracks converted into arms factories, and the convents turned into barracks. None of these was harmed during the disaster, according to Nationalist sources.[35]

One could raise the question of what interest had the Nationalists in destroying the military installations that might have fallen into their hands in a few days. On the other hand, had the Basques destroyed Guernica, these military installations, rather than the residences, would have been their prime targets. Irún was destroyed to keep the Nationalists from profiting from its capture. If the Basques did burn parts of Eibar upon evacuation, they destroyed, according to Rebel sources, military installations.[36] But none of the so-called objectives in Guernica was touched in the bombing raid or in the fires.

This newly revised position of the Rebels admitted and justified *certain* bomb drops on Guernica, but denied any Nationalist responsibility for the actions that led to the destruction of the town. Moreover, unlike the previous statements from Salamanca, this time no specific denial of a bombing on April 26 was given, nor was any mention made of bad weather on the day of the supposed bombing. The Nationalist withdrawal on these specific points from the earlier declarations on Guernica may have been caused by two facts that the propaganda people at Salamanca had failed to realize on April 27. These were, first, the fact that the Nationalist censorship had passed on April 26, for publication outside Spain, numerous telegrams that testified to the activity of Nationalist planes on that very day, even, as we have already seen in the previous chapter, to the actual bombing of Guernica on that day. Second, correspondents with the Basque forces had filed cables late on April 26, when they had come back from their day in the field, and before they knew that Guernica had been attacked, which told of seeing planes in the air that day near Guernica, which even told of their being attacked themselves by these planes.

Let us look at the first of these two situations. Pembroke Stephens, "Special Correspondent" with the Nationalists for the conservative *Daily Telegraph,* cabled from "Eibar, Bilbao Front, Monday 26," a long dispatch that ended as follows: "The crash of artillery and roar of passing bombing planes overhead told me that the battle was still in progress."[37] This dispatch was published in the morning newspaper on April 27. It could not have been sent before April 26, because the Nationalists did not enter Eibar before the morning of that day; and if sent later, it could not have been printed in the *Daily Telegraph* on the morning of April 27. Stephens therefore referred to air activity on April 26.

Another conservative English newspaper, the *Morning Post,* carried a dispatch headed "From Our Special Correspondent, Vergara (Bilbao Front), April 27," from which the following sentence is extracted: "In the last three days the Bilbao forces have been subjected to an aerial and artillery bombardment without parallel in this war."[38] However the reader looks at this statement, the day of April 26 falls within the three-day limit.

An Italian reporter, Ricardo Andreotti, sent a message from Saint-Jean-de-Luz, on the night of April 26, that the Nationalist air force had been active that day, and for "humanitarian reasons" did not attack the fugitives on the roads leading to Bilbao.[39]

Still another pro-Nationalist newspaper, the *New York American,* printed a Universal service cablegram from Vitoria, dated April 26:

> Vitoria tonight was overflowing with wounded. . . . Bombs dropped by insurgent airplanes almost destroyed the mountain villages of Arbácegui, Guerricaiz and Bolívar. Observation planes came back to insurgent military airports with reports that government troops were in headlong flight behind Durango.[40]

L'Echo de Paris, equally pro-Franco, published on April 27 an unidentified report stating in part: "The Franco air force flew over Bilbao and dropped leaflets to inform the civil population of the capture of Durango and Eibar."[41] Since the Nationalist troops did not enter Eibar until the morning of April 26, this dispatch was certainly written on April 26.

In addition to these four reports published in pro-Nationalist newspapers in England, the United States, Italy, and France, we have at least three dispatches from the UP confirming air attacks on the Bilbao front on April 26. Jean de Gandt, of the UP, who entered Elgueta on April 26, reported:

> In Elgueta there is not a single house undamaged; all were hit by grenades, aerial bombings or completely destroyed by projectiles. . . . We had to pass over mountains of rubble to reach the part of the church still standing, where we found a soldier playing the organ, while the cannons and airplanes thundered above us.[42]

Hérisson-Laroche also reported on April 26:

> The German tri-motored bombers collaborated effectively with the Rebel forces in an attack against the governmental positions of the Ermita de San Miguel del Campo, situated on high ground, behind Monte Campanzar.[43]

Another UP dispatch, by Ralph Heinzen, head of the Paris office, dated April 26, stated:

> The principal column of Mola's army advanced last night up to three kilometers of Durango and at dawn today began to attack the town with artillery, while the revolutionary [Nationalist] air force cooperated effectively in a combined attack.[44]

These dispatches were all written for the South American morning newspapers of April 27; they were written late on April 26—because of the time lag—and certainly referred to Rebel air activity on April 26.

In addition to the above evidence of Rebel air activity on April 26, most of which was passed through the Nationalist censorship, published in England, Italy,

France, the United States, Argentina, and Brazil, there are at least three news stories, all published in the foreign press, all passed through the Rebel censorship, which report not only air activity on April 26 but the actual bombing of Guernica. The account of the bombing of Guernica, as given in detail in the *New York American* on April 28 and more succinctly in *L'Echo de Paris* the same day, have been commented on in the previous chapter. Perhaps even more significant is the telegram published also on April 28, in *Il Messagero* of Rome. It read, in part:

> The national air force today continued to participate intensely in the battle, bombarding heavily Arbacegui and Guerricaiz, where the enemy attempted to reorganize its defense, and especially Guernica . . . the strategic importance of which can be seen by a single glance at the map. For a long time the national squadrons flew over the town and the neighboring fortifications, dropping a great amount of explosives.

This dispatch was sent from Durango, dated "27 notte" and signed by D. Larocca. This message may have been delayed in transmission, for we know that Arbacegui and Guerricaiz were both bombed on April 26, and if Guernica was bombed at all, it was also done on April 26, not on April 27. The editor may have arranged the date; he was not very alert that day, for on the same page, in a neighboring column, he printed another report, from San Sebastián, signed by Ricardo Andreotti, also dated April 27, stating correctly that a Nationalist communiqué from General Headquarters had denied the "Marxist" charges concerning Guernica and had affirmed "that Nationalist airplanes had never flown over this locality [Guernica] ."[45]

The press in Nationalist Spain on the morning of April 27 also published articles mentioning air activity on the previous day. The "Special Correspondent of the Office of Press and Propaganda of the Headquarters of the Generalísimo" told of the gallantry of the Rebel aviators who refrained from attacking the fleeing Basque troops, for women and children were also on the roads.[46] This touching theme was also reported by José Goñi in *ABC* of Seville:

> Through Durango, towards Bilbao, fled thousands of Red separatists. The air force could not attack them, for they were accompanied by women and children. To have machine-gunned them would have been to kill innocent people.[47]

Fernando Ors, correspondent for the *Heraldo de Aragón*, wrote from Vergara on Monday that Nationalist planes were active on Monday on the road from Eibar toward Bilbao.[48]

Another confirmation of air activity on April 26 can be found in the Nationalist press of April 28. The official military communiqué of April 27 reported: "The weather has not permitted any air activity by our air force in Vizcaya."[49] No such statement was included in the communiqué of April 26. The "Special Correspondent of the Headquarters of the Generalísimo," in the article he prepared for the

Salamanca radio on the night of April 27, emphasized the presence of "the low-hanging clouds that at noon produced the regional siri-miri."[50] On April 29 the *Times* published a dispatch from "Our Special Correspondent on the Franco-Spanish Frontier," dated April 28, stating that "a recurrence of bad weather on the Bilbao front hampered the Nationalist offensive yesterday [April 27] and today, bombing operations by aircraft having to be suspended."[51] It is beyond discussion that the siri-miri began on April 27 and not on April 26.

There is thus considerable evidence, passed by the Nationalist censorship, both for the Nationalist and foreign press, before the controversy over Guernica began, to show that, contrary to the official position of the Nationalist spokesmen in Salamanca, there was no meteorological hindrance to flying in the Basque country on April 26, and that there was indeed considerable air activity on that day. There is also evidence presented by the journalists who were on the other side of the battle line. Corman, Holme, Monks, and Steer were out on the afternoon of April 26, and not only saw airplanes flying from the direction of Guernica but were themselves attacked by these fighter planes. Corman cabled from Bilbao, evidently before he sent off his cable on Guernica, as follows:

> Hidden in a shell hole with the correspondents of *The Times* and Reuters Agency, I was able to watch that infernal bombing. We were fired on for twenty minutes by seven fighter planes at Guerricaiz. Shortly thereafter, this small village was destroyed by some sixty bombs, incendiary and explosive, which were dropped in a few short moments. However, this village presents no military character and is 25 kilometers from the front. . . . Two aged priests, their soutanes soiled by the dirt thrown by the explosions, were weeping in the ruins under which the inhabitants are now buried.[52]

The *Manchester Guardian* published a similar story on April 27. It was attributed to "Press Association. Foreign Special Correspondent," datelined "Bilbao, April 26," and was beyond any doubt based on a dispatch from Holme.[53] Noel Monks told the same story, although published twenty-four hours after his first cablegram on Guernica,[54] and he repeated the story later in his newspaper on his return to England.[55] George Steer sent out a factual account of the bombings on April 26; it was published in the *New York Times* on April 27, but not in the *Times*.[56] Steer later confirmed the happening in his book on the war in the Basque country,[57] as did Corman[58] and Monks.[59]

We can now see that there was in print in the newspapers of London, New York, Paris, and elsewhere, including the Nationalist zone of Spain, a far from negligible amount of evidence to prove that the Rebels had not told the truth when they said that no airplanes had taken to the air on April 26, and this evidence doubtless influenced newspaper editors, especially in England, in determining who was telling the truth about Guernica.

The contradictions and differences between the two positions—that of the Basques at Bilbao and the foreign correspondents working there on one side, and the Nationalists in Salamanca on the other—concerning the date of the destruction of Guernica and the responsibilities for that destruction are of fundamental importance in this study, but there exists another enormous difference between the two positions: the position in Bilbao—that of the Basques and of the foreign correspondents there—was that a large number of persons had been killed in the course of the catastrophe; rarely in the Nationalist press was there even a suggestion that lives had been lost.

3

Parenthesis on the Working Conditions of the Foreign Press in the Nationalist Zone

The occupation of the ruined town of Guernica around midday on April 29 by General Emilio Mola's forces marked the beginning of a new series of newspaper reports on the nature and causes of the catastrophe, this time from the portable typewriters of the foreign correspondents with the Nationalist armies. Before we examine what they wrote, it will be instructive to investigate the conditions under which they worked. In April 1937 the foreign reporters in the Nationalist zone were accredited by a press office in Salamanca, operating from Franco's headquarters; their dispatches were censored by this office or by its representatives nearer the front. For the Guernica telegrams, the nearest press office was in Vitoria; the nearest cable head in Vigo.[1] A telegram censored in Vitoria might be held up and further censored enroute to Vigo.[2] Sometimes censored messages were sent by courier across the French frontier to gain time.[3]

The Salamanca press office was directed by Luis Bolín, "Head of the Press Offices Accredited to the Headquarters of the Generalísimo."[4] Bolín's personality and his political convictions played a preponderant role in the development of the Guernica story, as already indicated. He had been, before the war, a journalist in London, working for the Madrid monarchist daily *ABC*.[5] His tasks were perhaps more political than journalistic. In 1933 he collaborated on an anti-Republican book entitled *The Spanish Republic*, accredited to "Anonymous" and published in both London and Madrid.[6] More important for his career, Bolín, because of the political activities that went with his newspaper job, became one of the key conspirators involved in arranging and carrying out the plans for the airplane trip that was to end with bringing General Franco from the Canaries to Morocco in the first days of the civil war.[7] He had also been instrumental in securing the first airplanes sent by Fascist Italy to help Franco. Bolín flew from Italy to Morocco with the Italian planes on July 30,[8] and then went to Seville, where he continued "attached to my Italian friends as Liaison officer with General Queipo's staff."[9] At the same time Bolín occupied himself with press censorship. Arthur Koestler considered Bolin to be "the Rebel press chief" in Seville when he was there early in September 1936.[10] Bolín was already having his troubles with the foreign journalists, and the foreign journalists their troubles with Bolín. Koestler wrote:

> In the vestibule of the Hotel Madrid I found several French journalists. . . . They too did not appear to be exactly cheerful. Grand of the Havas Agency was there. René Brut, the "Pathé Gazette" man, one or two others. Antoine of "L'Intransigeant" was not amongst them. It was he whom the police had fetched out of bed at three o'clock that morning. . . . On the day of my departure I learned that the Frenchmen were under a sort of collective house arrest, as it were. The Rebel press chief, Captain Bolín . . . was in a towering rage with them because news had trickled through into the French press of the horrible massacre at Badajoz. He had declared on the morning of my arrival and after Antoine's arrest that they might not visit the front in future except in organized parties under military supervision. . . . Three days later Brut was arrested. He was kept in prison for three weeks; Bolín personally threatened to shoot him, because he had filmed the blood-bath of Badajoz.[11] Jean d'Esme too was arrested.[12]

Bolín was with General Varela and the Army of Africa that advanced on Toledo in late September. He was in charge of the foreign journalists who were waiting in Talavera de la Reina for permission to enter Toledo.[13] Bolín wrote later that he himself gave to the foreign reporters waiting in Talavera the story of the telephone conversation between Colonel Moscardó, defender of the Alcázar, and his son, a prisoner of the Republicans.[14] Another Nationalist newsman, Joaquín Arrarás, has, however, stated that it was he who brought this information to the foreign press.[15] In any case, the story as told then by the foreign press (and as perpetuated since then by pro-Nationalist writers) was basically false, and does honor to Bolín the propagandist rather than Bolín the journalist.[16]

When Franco began taking over the political command in the Nationalist zone and moved to Salamanca, Bolín appeared on the scene as chief of the press services at Nationalist headquarters.[17] It was, it now seems, not so much Bolín's journalistic capacities, or his abilities for dealing with his colleagues of the newspaper world and their problems, as his participation in the dangerous activities involved in getting Franco from the Canaries to Morocco, which gained him his position in Salamanca.[18] Bolín was soon detested by the foreign newsmen, even by those who personally sided with the Nationalist cause. This was perhaps the first time in his life that Bolín had had the chance to push other people around. He liked to let the foreign correspondents know that he could have them shot if he wished to do so.

Several incidents reveal Bolín's methods. On October 26, 1936, at the moment of the advance on Madrid, two reporters accredited to the Republican government in Madrid, Denis Weaver, of the London *News Chronicle*, and James M. Minifie, of the *New York Herald Tribune*, went out in a military car to visit the front; the chauffeur took a wrong turning, and they were all captured. The chauffeur and the guide were shot, and the two correspondents were brought to Salamanca. There they found another reporter, Henry T. Gorrell, of the UP, who had undergone a similar experience. Each of the three men was received singly by Bolín for interrogation. "It was clear from the start that he [Bolín] did not like me," wrote Weaver. When Bolín saw Weaver's passes for the front signed by the Republican authorities, he warned the reporter: "You could be hanged out of hand for having these papers in your pocket." After four days of detention and further threats, the three newspapermen were allowed to enter France.[19]

In January 1937 Bolín engaged in a quarrel with the UP and the Havas Agency over certain dispatches distributed by these press services five months earlier, concerning the massacre of Badajoz in August 1936. These cablegrams were in reality sent from Portugal, but one of them was distributed with the name of Reynolds Packard, who was at that time in Rebel Spain, but had not gone to Badajoz. A letter, in the *Manchester Guardian*, of January 19, 1937[20] on the Badajoz massacre, referred to the UP dispatch, published in the Paris edition of the *New York Herald Tribune*, on August 16, 1936, under the name of Packard. This letter was brought to Bolín's attention.[21] Packard was the chief UP man in Nationalist Spain at that time,[22] and he made an easy target for Bolín, who demanded an explanation from him. At the same time Bolín asked d'Hospital, the Havas man, to explain certain Havas telegrams about Badajoz published in *Le Populaire* of Paris on August 16 and 17, 1936. Packard sent a panicky cablegram to Webb Miller, European head of the UP, stationed in London:

> I have been summoned to Salamanca. . . . Captain Bolín representing the Nationalist military press authorities, demands that you inform *Manchester Guardian* that I never wrote such articles. . . . I frankly think that in view of the seriousness of this situation you might investigate this message thoroughly and exonerate me in the eyes of the Nationalist government. . . . I must emphasize that the Nationalist government is taking a serious attitude with regard to this message.[23]

The UP did not reply by telling the truth—that the cablegram in question came from the agency's Lisbon office, that the UP had sent out numerous other reports about Badajoz from the same source,[24] and that the agency considered the contents of the dispatch correct; instead, it answered obliquely, saying that the story had been "erroneously published" under Packard's name.[25] This was the truth, but it was not the whole truth. This shabby excuse, however, satisfied both the UP and Bolín.

Havas also answered with a part of the truth. It did not deny the dispatches it had distributed. It identified the author Marcel Dany as "an occasional war correspondent." In reality, he was the chief of Havas's Lisbon office.[26] Neither the UP nor Havas seized on this excellent opportunity to stand up and defend its reporters and their reporting as well as the much vaunted freedom of the press. They knuckled under to Bolín. The reason is not difficult to find. There was intense rivalry among Havas, the Associated Press, and the United Press for the Latin American market on Spanish Civil War news. Most of the news sent out of Spain by these three agencies was printed, not in France or the United States, but in Argentina, in Brazil, in Mexico, and in other countries with Spanish- or Peninsular-speaking or -descended populations.[27]

On February 8, 1937, Bolín, whose family came from Málaga, was present for the entry of the Italian and Spanish troops into the town. He personally supervised the "capture" of Arthur Koestler in Sir Peter Chalmers Mitchell's house. Bolín and another officer held pistols on Koestler, while a third tied his hands behind his back with wire. Koestler was sentenced to death but then freed in a prisoner exchange.[28]

Derogatory remarks concerning Bolin by journalist friends of the Rebels began to be published in England shortly after the Guernica incident. No other English war correspondent protested his pro-Nationalist sentiments more fervently than did Harold G. Cardozo, "Special Correspondent" of the *Daily Mail*.[29] Yet he did not like Bolín. He did not abuse him by name, but his target is unmistakable. "The Press and Propaganda department of Salamanca," he wrote, was "rarely well advised." He went on,

> It is seldom that the Press department of any government acts with consistent wisdom, but the inconsistency of the one set up at Salamanca by the Nationalist Government must have created somewhat of a record.

Cardozo was a strident critic of the Franco censorship:

> Our cables took, according to circumstances, often fifteen to twenty hours, never less than four or five. . . . They [the censors] were not the principal culprits. It was the Central Press Office [Bolín] which issued such strange rulings at such strange times, and gave them to some censors' offices and forgot to give them to others. . . . It is not for me to say who was responsible for such faulty arrangements, but the errors of the organization were well known in Spain.[30]

Another highly experienced reporter, Francis McCullagh, ideologically sympathetic to the Rebel cause, in a 1937 book issued by the official English publishers to the Vatican,[31] drew an unflattering portrait of Bolín, as a man and as a journalist, under the pseudonym of "Señor Capitán Don Luis Bustamente de Torquemada." This person was, wrote McCullagh, a powerfully built man dressed as an officer of the Foreign Legion, with Sam Browne belt, riding breeches, and high boots. He strides . . . with the ruthlessness of the German Kaiser when he was still on his throne, and on his powerful clean-shaven face rests a scowl, worthy of Mussolini when he heard of the imposition of sanctions.[32]

McCullagh placed Sir Percival Phillips, of the highly conservative *Daily Telegraph*, on the witness stand, against "Bustamente" (Bolín) and his organization. Both Sir Percival and his newspaper were Franco supporters. "Neither a soldier nor a journalist," the witness said of Bolín.

He dabbled in journalism in London. . . . I asked the *Daily Mail* man why they refused his articles and he said . . . "because they were damned rubbish." . . . He has made himself hated like poison by the English and American correspondents. . . . Spanish officers, as a rule, dislike newspaper correspondents. Some of them, indeed, have told me so openly. . . . We have never seen a village taken, so that, though we find some villages absolutely empty, we cannot tell for certain whether the villagers were slaughtered or not by the Moors. . . . There are press bureaux in Ávila, Talavera and Toledo. The men in charge of them are young grandees or diplomats, amiable weaklings for the most part, ruled by "Bustamente" with a rod of iron.[33]

Another reporter for the conservative press who had unpleasant experiences with Bolín was Noel Monks, of the *Daily Express*. Bolín, wrote Monks, despite his appearances,

had a cruel streak in him. Whenever he saw a pathetic pile of freshly executed "reds," their hands tied behind their backs—usually behind a farmhouse in every newly taken village—he used to spit on them and say "Vermin." Some of them were mere boys in their teens who couldn't possibly have had an appreciation of what was going on.[34]

Monks was expelled from Nationalist Spain in April 1937, just before he was sent to Bilbao.

"We have nothing against you, Senor Monks," I was told at Salamanca. "If we had we would have shot you. But your paper is 'red' and the generalissimo says you have to go."[35]

It would be unfair to say that all writers and newspaper people who visited Rebel Spain gave a bad report on Bolín. The American newspaperman from the Philippines, F. Theo Rogers, wrote: ". . . Pleasant hours were spent with Major Bollins [sic] . . . now press officer for General Franco. Major Bollins speaks several languages well and his English is of impeccable fluency."[36]

Nigel Tangye, an aviation writer, reported that Bolín "was good to me, and has given me a *carte blanche* pass for myself and a camera all over Spain, including the

Fronts, which is a rare privilege."[37] Cecil Gerahty wrote of Bolin as "my friend." But neither Rogers nor Tangye—nor even Gerahty[38] —was a working reporter, with a daily deadline, while in Spain. There were also other visitors who knew Bolín and certainly saw him while they were in Spain, such as Douglas Jerrold, the Marqués del Moral, and others, but who curiously enough failed to mention his name in their subsequent articles.

Like other chapters of the war history behind Franco's lines, that of Bolín, his organization, his press officers, and the relations of all these with the foreign press has so far been told only in snippets by foreign correspondents in their books. Bolín himself sedulously avoids telling the story in his own memoirs. In all truth, Bolín was rarely available to the working reporters, who usually traveled in the field with the press officers. Two of these—Captain Aguilera, a Spanish grandee, Count of Alba de Yeltes; and Pablo Merry del Val, "one of the sons of the ex-ambassador of the monarchy in London and nephew of the cardinal who was Secretary of State to Pius X,"[39] —adequately give a basis for Sir Percival's description of Bolín's recruiting sector. Another press officer, Major Lámbarri, who probably arrived after Sir Percival's description of the press officers was made, worked in peacetime as an artist for *Vogue.*[40]

Two press officers, Aguilera and Rosales, were involved in the reporting on Guernica. Aguilera was the escort of the foreign newsmen on the Basque Nationalist front at the time of the capture of Guernica. He spoke excellent English; his mother was a Scotswoman named Munro.[41] He had been at Stonyhurst;[42] he had fought in the Moroccan campaigns,[43] and he had been military attaché in Berlin.[44] "Aguilera was one of the bravest men I have ever seen," wrote an American correspondent who was, however, aghast at his political ideas, which the press officer never tired of propounding to his charges.[45]

Aguilera was usually praised by those who sympathized with the Nationalists and condemned by those who favored the Rebublicans. Peter Kemp, a young Englishman of good family who fought with the Rebels, wrote of Aguilera:

> he told a distinguished English visitor that on the day the Civil War broke out he lined up the laborers on his estate, selected six of them and shot them in front of the others—"*Pour encourager les autres,* you understand."[46]

Kemp's book was published in 1957, and some time later Aguilera

> took out a writ against Peter Kemp for recording the incident. . . . The story was thereupon withdrawn by Kemp, although this did little good since the book was already out of print before Aguilera took action.[47]

Whether the incident actually took place or not, there is little doubt that Aguilera did tell the story, for Jean d'Hospital, who was the Havas man in the Nationalist zone for the greater part of the civil war, and did not know Kemp's book, told it to an interviewer in 1968, saying that Aguilera had told the story to him.[48] D'Hospital thought that Aguilera was possibly telling the story to boast of his large estates. The fact that Kemp repeated the story in good faith does demonstrate how an English sympathizer of the Nationalist cause could nevertheless believe its representatives capable of cold-blooded savagery.

An American correspondent, John T. Whitaker, was appalled by Aguilera's talk, and quoted the press officer as saying to him:

> We have got to kill and kill and kill, you understand. . . . It's our program . . . to exterminate one third of the male population of Spain. That will purge the country and we will be rid of the proletariat.

Whitaker cited Aguilera at some length

> because his social and political ideas were typical. I heard his own ideas voiced by scores and hundreds of others on the Franco side.

The American correspondent summed up Aguilera's basic program as being "the destruction of the proletariat and an ultimate war against the democracies."[49]

Edmond Taylor, of the *Chicago Daily Tribune*, found Aguilera remarkable but frightening. He resumed the press officer's point of view on dealing with prisoners as follows:

> In the matter of killing, Aguilera adhered to the idealistic Spanish point of view. . . . At or near the front, and even in Burgos in those days, there was little hypocrisy about prisoners: they were worth taking because you could question them and it saved ammunition, but not worth keeping, so they were not kept.[50]

Virginia Cowles knew Aguilera in Santander in September 1937. He was furious.

> "Why did they [the Reds] have to put ideas into people's heads?" he asked. "Everyone knows that people are fools and much better off told what to do than trying to run themselves. Hell is too good for the Reds."

On one occasion, when Aguilera saw Republican prisoners doing road work, he remarked: "If we didn't need roads, I would like to borrow a rifle and pick off a couple." Miss Cowles fell into his bad graces when she pointed out that if the Republicans had blown up a bridge, it was to "hold up the advance." Aguilera gave her "a hostile look" and said, "You talk like a Red."[51] The press officer got his petty revenge by holding up Miss Cowles's exit permit, and she finally crossed into France in a diplomatic car without the authorization.[52]

However, the English Catholic writer and fledgling journalist Arnold Lunn found Aguilera "not only a soldier but a scholar" and greatly liked by the journalists.[53] Sefton Delmer was expelled from Nationalist Spain by Aguilera, but he forgave the press officer and wrote: "I shall always have the warmest affection [for Aguilera]."[54] Even Cardozo thought him trying.[55] Cecil Gerahty found him amusing and helped him in a bit of "official" looting.[56]

H. R. Knickerbocker of the Universal Service, generally favorable to the Franco side of the conflict, considered Aguilera—in 1936—to be "the best press officer it has ever been my pleasure to meet."[57] This judgment changed early in April 1937, when Knickerbocker was stopped at the French frontier with Spain and told that "he cannot continue his journey to Spain."[58] Knickerbocker did get into Spain again; he was arrested and spent thirty-six hours in a Spanish Nationalist prison a few days before Guernica was destroyed. "Denunciation by persons unknown had brought about my arrest," he wrote when he got back to London.

> Now by accident of war, I was given a glimpse—more than a glimpse—of the terror from the inside. . . . During 17 years' work as a journalist at home and in every European land, I had been shown many jails in many countries, but never one equal to this.[59]

Knickerbocker took his revenge on Aguilera. A few days after his release from prison, he cabled to New York from London a reply to the question: "What sort of society would Insurgent General Francisco Franco establish if he won the civil war?" Knickerbocker's answer was to give a "verbatim report" of the anti-democratic, antiorganized labor, antiwomen's rights, antipublic education, anti-Semitic opinions of one "Major Sánchez," a pseudonym that all the journalists who had been or were in Nationalist Spain quickly identified as Captain Aguilera. The interview ended:

> On the fate of "reds" if his side wins, Sánchez was eloquent:
> "We are going to shoot 50,000 in Madrid. And no matter where Azaña and Largo Caballero (the Premier) and all that crowd try to escape, we'll catch them and kill every last man, if it takes years of tracking them throughout the world."[60]

Charles Foltz, Jr., of the AP, heard pretty much the same speech from Aguilera as had Knickerbocker.[61]

Even before Knickerbocker, F. A. Rice, correspondent of the *Morning Post,* found out in September 1936 that Aguilera could be as harsh with the conservative press as with that suspected of being left. Rice, thinking the Stonyhurst background of Aguilera would interest his English readers, had described him, without giving his name: "I can see him a prefect at Stonyhurst, greatly respected and not very popular." These phrases were judged by Aguilera as not indicating "a wholly respectful attitude," and the correspondent was given the choice either of remaining in Spain, without the right to cross the frontier unless he had special permission, or of leaving Spain at once. Rice chose the latter alternative.[62]

Still another press officer played a role in the development of the Guernica story, Captain Rosales. He was an intellectual carbon copy of Aguilera—or Aguilera of him.

> Rosales is explaining that the masses cannot be taught; that they need a touch of the whip for they are like dogs and will mind only the whip. There is no understanding in such people, for they must be got in hand. Held in hand where they belong. Captain Rosales explains it ethnologically . . . an influx of strains inimical to Spain through the industrial cities of the coast; of this taint in her bloodstream Spain must cleanse herself. She is purifying herself and

will rise up from this trial new and strong. The streets of Madrid will run red with blood, but after—after—there will be no unemployment problem.[63]

Virginia Cowles described Rosalles as "a Barcelona millionaire, who spoke English fluently."[64] She met him for the first time in August 1937 and believed that he had just begun his work as a press officer, but Frances Davis had known him in Burgos during the first weeks of the war.[65]

Not only were the individual correspondents harassed and threatened by the press officers in Nationalist Spain; news agencies were also made to feel the weight of Señor Bolín's displeasure. The French news service Agence Havas was perhaps treated by the Salamanca press office worse than were the other internationally known non-Fascist press agencies. Material found in their archives is highly informative concerning the conditions under which the correspondents were working. Havas doubtless suffered from its known close connections with the French government, which was for the moment the *Front Populaire*.

The first man sent to Nationalist Spain by Havas was Jean d'Hospital, who, with one absence of two months, managed to stay throughout the war.[66] His colleagues were less fortunate; of six collaborators whom d'Hospital had at various times during the civil war, at least two spent time in prison, of whom one was threatened with execution. Albert Grand was sent to Seville early in the war,[67] as noted in the earlier quotation from Koestler, and then came north to join d'Hospital near Franco's headquarters. The correspondents stationed in Rebel Spain frequently crossed the border into France to relax and breathe a different air. Nerves were frayed by the endless cycle of killings.[68] Grand profited from one of these quick visits to the French side of the frontier on September 30, 1936, to telephone to Havas's Paris offices, where his interlocutor took notes as follows:

> Mr. Grand explained the difficulties to which Mr. d'Hospital and he were exposed, difficulties due to their being Frenchmen. Everywhere ill will, incessant affronts; all the favors go to the Germans and Italians, principally to the first-named, who are the real masters here. . . . Moreover, one should not think that just any war correspondent can witness the entry of the conquerors into a town, for the good reason that all the journalists are kept away when they proceed to the executions which inevitably follow a victory. Mr. Grand affirms that he saw near Toledo, on a two-kilometer stretch, 3000 bodies.[69]

On October 30 Havas sent in a third reporter, Ramon de Alderete, but the press office decreed that three men were too many for Havas, and Alderete, the last man in, had to leave, having been in Spain for barely two weeks.[70]

A few days after Alderete had been asked to leave, the Rebel authorities threw Grand in jail for two days; he was then expelled for obscure reasons[71] from Spain.[72] A man named Gés was proposed to take Grand's place, but the press

office in Salamanca turned him down.[73] Finally, Henri Malet-Dauban was accepted
as a Havas correspondent by the Rebel authorities in December.[74] Malet-Dauban
knew Spain well, spoke Spanish, and was widely introduced into Spanish Catholic
circles.[75]

On December 23 d'Hospital wrote to Paris that his new colleague "is well
regarded at General Headquarters."[76] In January, however, despite, or because of,
his friends and acquaintances, Malet-Dauban was put in prison and kept in solitary
confinement.[77] D'Hospital himself found the frontier closed, and he kept Paris
informed about his imprisoned colleague through the kindnesses of other correspondents who left the Rebel zone for France. Despite the imprecision of the
charges against Malet-Dauban,[78] such was the atmosphere of brooding terror in the
Nationalist territory, that many right-wing sympathizers friendly with the correspondent believed him likely to be executed—even already executed[79]—and
d'Hospital envisaged the possibility that his colleague might be shot.[80]

D'Hospital was thus again with no one to help him, whereas his agency's
competitors frequently had a staff of at least three persons.[81] D'Hospital needed a
rest, and Havas offered the position of "envoyé spécial" to an editor in Paris named
Georges Botto.[82] Botto was a veteran of the World War I of rightist sympathies,
and he apparently had little trouble getting his *laissez-passer* from the Franco press
office. He possessed no previous experience as a foreign correspondent. Botto
reached Ávila, where d'Hospital had set up his offices at the time, on February 12,
1937.[83] Malet-Dauban continued in durance vile, but d'Hospital had received some
assurances concerning him from the Rebel authorities. "Malet is in prison charged
with espionage," he wrote to Havas on March 5. "I have only a vague idea of the
charges against him. . . . I have been assured that nothing grave will happen to
him."[84]

Despite the discontent expressed by certain correspondents concerning the
conditions of work and the censorship rules in the Republican zone,[85] relations
between the foreign reporters and the Republican authorities were much closer
than those between the foreign pressmen and the Nationalists. The majority of the
Spanish intellectuals were loyal to the Republic. Men in the Spanish government
like Álvarez del Vayo, Prieto, Zugazagoitia, and others were former newspapermen
themselves and sympathized with the problems of the press. But the military minds
governing the Nationalist zone were instinctively opposed to the press in any form
and to writers in general. A Spanish newspaperman of Falangist sympathies has
written of this spirit among the Spanish military during the Civil War: "There
existed, from the beginning, a suspicious military attitude, mistrustful and at times
hostile towards the press."[86]

Sir Percival Phillips, after some months in Rebel territory, concluded: "Spanish
officers, as a rule, dislike newspaper correspondents. Some of them, indeed, have
told me so openly. One of them added that all the generals begged the *Generalísimo* to exclude correspondents from the country till the war was over."[87]

The same observer found the situation in Republican Spain quite different:

on the other [Republican] side, correspondents are treated much better. I have met dozens of fellows who are in Barcelona and Madrid, and they told me that though there was hopeless confusion, they were always treated like brothers. . . . No need to wait three hours for an audience, and then be told that you must come again tomorrow: you just blow in through the open door of the office, and help yourself to a drink or a cigar if the censor is busy. . . . The humility and *camaraderie* of those Red censors is so flattering and so touching that some Englishmen have actually dropped well-paid newspaper work in order to help them out.[88]

Cardozo was of the same opinion:

Red propaganda was being better and more speedily handled. . . . Cables containing Red propaganda, from Madrid or Valencia, were transmitted with a fairly lenient censorship and with a minimum of delay.[89]

This situation was confirmed by the Havas Agency, which wrote to d'Hospital on March 12, 1937, about

the numerous complaints we have received from our subscribers and foreign customers concerning the scantiness of our service from the Nationalist side compared with the volume of our news from the governmental front.[90]

On March 18, 1937, another reporter who had just left Salamanca, André de Hoornaert, informed Havas in Paris of the trials and tribulations of the agency's two men in Nationalist Spain:

The conditions of life are satisfactory: good lodging and a good table. . . . The conditions of work are absolutely deplorable, at least for our [Havas's] representatives.

Of all the French correspondents, those of Havas were the most unfavorably treated.[91]

D'Hospital wanted to take a rest from the war zone. An accident late in February had left him with two or more ribs fractured.[92] But Havas needed at least two men in the Rebel zone to do the necessary work.[93] The name of Jore was submitted on March 25, but the candidate himself withdrew his name a few days later.[94] Then Havas asked Bolín to accept Axel de Holstein as a correspondent.[95] Although there was no immediate reply from Salamanca, d'Hospital entered France and was in Paris on April 22; he did not return to Spain until July 1.[96] During his absence, the Malet-Dauban problem was solved by the Basque government, who accepted the Frenchman on a prisoner exchange. Malet-Dauban was in Hendaye on May 31.[97] Georges Botto was thus the only active Havas correspondent in the Nationalist zone at the time of the Guernica incident. On May 6 he sent a message to Havas that the nomination of Axel de Holstein was refused.[98] No replacement for d'Hospital arrived until June, at which time Jacques Barré, of Havas's Rome bureau, came to Ávila. Perhaps the Havas people in Paris thought that a man who knew Fascist Italy would have no trouble in Nationalist Spain, but Barré's stay in Spain was remarkably short. On June 21 he wrote to Paris:

> . . . for no reason at all I was insulted [at Vitoria] by an officer of the press office, not merely for my quality as a journalist but also as a French officer. One could attribute this to a moment of bad humor in an ill-bred person, but this very morning with clearly declared hostility the same officer recommenced his insults.

Barré asked to be allowed to return to Italy, and on July 1 he reentered France.[99]

The background and personalities of the men who controlled the war news going out of the Nationalist zone at the time of the destruction of Guernica have been limned in as great detail as possible, for not only did Bolín play a crucial role in the general supervision of the news dispatches, but Aguilera and then Rosales in the field sought to control the contents of these cablegrams.

Bolín had, it must be admitted, a grave problem on his hands in dealing with the foreign correspondents. He could more or less trust the Germans and the Italians, but not always the French, the English, the Americans, or even the Portuguese, as he had found in the case of Marios Neves, who had accompanied the UP and Havas reporters into Badajoz. [100] But at the same time, Bolín knew that he could not do without the foreign reporters. He tried to screen them, keep out the liberals and leftists. John Whitaker explained that Bolín's office ". . . let in no correspondents unless it felt certain they were fascists. They let me in because the Italians during the Ethiopian war had decorated me with the *Croce di guerra*. [101] Nazi recommendations were also useful to the reporter who wanted to visit the Nationalist zone, as the English aviation writer Nigel Tangye found out. He was, as he himself noted, "sympathetic towards the New Germany" and the air attaché of the German embassy in London gave him a luncheon at the Ritz before he left for Spain and "rendered me considerable assistence." [102] In Salamanca, Tangye was told by Bolín: "If only all applicants for passes came with so many letters of introduction and recommendations as you, my duties would be very much easier."[103]

Once the reporter was allowed into the country, Bolín and his subordinates ruled him with threat and bluster. Whitaker told of being awakened one night by Aguilera and a Gestapo officer.

> "Look here" said Aguilera, in his hoarse voice. "You are not to go to the front any more except on escorted tours. We've arranged your case. The next time you're unescorted at the front, we'll shoot you. We'll say that you were a casualty to enemy action. Do you understand?"[104]

Nor did the correspondent know when he had handed in his telegrams whether they would really be sent. McCullagh told of his own disappointment, on returning to London, to see how his stories had been mutilated or even suppressed entirely.[105] Again, Bolín craftily used blackmail on the correspondents. The news agencies and to some extent the big newspapers had to have somebody on both sides of the conflict. It was, for almost three years, one of the big news stories of each day. In January 1937, during the brouhaha over the dispatches concerning the massacre in Badajoz, as already related, Bolín let the United Press and Havas know that they risked not only having their representatives expelled but not having any replacement admitted.[106]

Certain subjects were strictly taboo in the cabled messages—for instance, any mention of the presence of foreign troops with Franco's army.[107] Noel Monks noted:

> We were never allowed to mention that Italians or Germans were even in Spain by the censors, so the only thing to do was drive to the frontier and write about them from France, making sure that our offices wouldn't use our names under them.

Monks crossed the frontier in March 1937 and telephoned a story to London about Italian troops with Franco; the report was inadvertently published under Monks's name. Unaware of this development, he went back into Nationalist Spain and was arrested in Seville.

> Captain Bolín's handsome face was black with anger when the police handed me over to him. "You've put your feet into it now, Monks," he said in that perfect English of his. "Evading censorship is equivalent to spying—and spies get short shrift in this country."

Monks was brought before Franco, whose

> stubby fist banged down on the *Daily Express* as he gabbled violently in Spanish. I looked at Captain Bolín who said: "General Franco says you will be shot for this." ... Franco was going on again and Luis Bolín moved towards me: "Come on, Monks; the firing squad for you."

Monks was not shot but expelled.[108]

The *Daily Express* man then explained a situation that must have troubled many a correspondent with the Rebels and should have troubled their editors and home offices.

> I did feel, though, that I had broken the rules as far as Franco was concerned, and that he and Bolín had every right to be angry with me. But I'd been sent to report a war, and to write about the Spanish civil war without being able to mention Italians and Germans was making oneself a party to Franco's hoodwinking the world into believing that his revolt against the democratic government of Spain was an all-Spanish affair, opposed to a gang of Moscow-

led thugs. So I was one of a long line of foreign correspondents, mainly British and American, who found themselves in trouble with the Franco authorities.[109]

The problem exposed by Noel Monks is pertinent to the story of the destruction of Guernica. The reporters with the Nationalist army knew of the presence of Germans and Italians in considerable numbers with the Franco armed forces, but they also knew that if they reported what they saw it would not pass the censorship. Nor was the correspondent free to talk or write once he had left the Nationalist zone; if he did write or talk, he could never return; if he worked for a newspaper, it might be penalized; if he worked for a news agency, his agency could find itself barred from Nationalist Spain. There was also always the second thought that the reporters who remained in the Nationalist zone might pay for the "indiscretions" of the man who had crossed the border. Arthur Koestler wrote that when Antoine of *L'Intransigeant* was released from imprisonment in Seville, his newspaper printed not a word about the arrest or its consequences. "Newspapers do not publish accounts of such adventures; they are afraid that if they do so the rebels will refuse to allow any more of their correspondents into rebel territory." When stories of the imprisonment of Rene Brut and Jean d'Esme were printed in France, these were denied "for the sake of their colleagues, who were still in Bolín's hands."[110]

Certain formulas were used to hide the truth. Nobody ever saw a German pilot; the word was "technician."[111] This was the word used by Arnold Lunn,[112] by Douglas Jerrold,[113] by the marqués del Moral,[114] by C. G. Grey,[115] by Sir Arnold Wilson,[116] by General Sir Walter Maxwell-Scott,[117] by Nigel Tangye,[118] by the French right-wing journalist Alline,[119] and by others. The men in Salamanca were offended not only by the reports of the bombing of Guernica but by that other offense—the attribution of the bombing to German pilots in German planes dropping German bombs. There were no German pilots, or German planes, or German bombs in Spain. This same censorship explained the fact that only Italian journalists reported from Rebel Spain the presence of Italian troops in the vanguard of those who entered Guernica on April 29.[120]

McCullagh, who was emotionally on Franco's side, said:

> The inference was that even here, in London, I am still under the authority of Captain Bustamente [Bolín] ! What he meant was that, as I held a permit to return to Nationalist Spain, I was still subject to his jurisdiction, and would forfeit that permit if I disobeyed his orders. Such is Captain Bustamente's view of his position, and of the position of the foreign correspondents accredited to Nationalist Spain. . . . There are, today, in London, English journalists, home on holiday from Franco's army, who dare not open their lips on certain subjects.[121]

These working conditions made possible the fact that of the four professional foreign correspondents in Bilbao at the moment of the destruction of Guernica, two had been expelled from Rebel Spain.[122] It was also against this background, in this atmosphere of daily inquietude, if not of actual terror, that those journalists who continued to work in the Nationalist zone sent out their messages concerning the catastrophe at Guernica, and in order to read these messages correctly, the reader should keep constantly in mind and view the picture drawn of that background.

4

The News from Vitoria

According to the press dispatches from Bilbao discussed in chapter 1, the bombing of Guernica began around four-thirty on Monday afternoon, April 26, 1937. Less than three days later, shortly before noon on Thursday, April 29, the first Nationalist units, Italians in large part, entered the town.[1] This action marked the beginning of a new series of newspaper reports, this time from the foreign newsmen who were accompanying the Rebel forces on the Basque front. These men were many, unlike the small group of correspondents in Bilbao, and it is much more difficult to establish their identities. However, a list of names can be drawn up, and a timetable established, for the war correspondents known to have gone into Guernica on April 29 and the immediately succeeding days, and to have written of what they saw.

April 29, noon. Georges Berniard, reporter-photographer of *La Petite Gironde*, of Bordeaux[2]; and three Italians: Renzo Segàla, of *Corriere della Sera* of Milan; Sandro Sandri, of *La Stampa*, of Turin; and Mario Franzetti, of *La Tribuna*, of Rome. Another Italian came into Guernica, either with the first three or shortly thereafter—Piero Saporiti, of the Stefani agency. All four Italians sent out reports on the capture of Guernica.[3] There were also present an English reporter, Pembroke Stephens, of the London *Daily Telegraph*,[4] whose newspaper the following day published a noncommittal report; an unidentified reporter from Agence Radio, who sent out a short notice; and an anonymous man from the German DNB service, who filed a short message.[5]

April 29, 4 P.M. Five French journalists: Georges Botto, of Agence Havas; Max Massot, of *Le Journal,*[6] of Paris; Jacques Mévil, of *Le Petit Marseillais,*[7] of Marseilles; Raymond Méjat, of Metro Newsreels,[8] of Paris; "Jean Dourec," of *L'Action Française,*[9] of Paris; all chaperoned by Captain Aguilera. Botto and Massot each sent a dispatch telling of the capture of Guernica.

May 1. Richard G. Massock, of the Associated Press, and an unidentified reporter for the United Press; Botto, Massot, Mévil, and Pierre Héricourt, of *L'Action Française.*[10] This was an organized tour arranged by the Nationalist press office.

May 3. James G. Holburn, of the *Times,* and William P. Carney, of the *New York Times.*

There may well have been other reporters who went into Guernica during the first days of the Nationalist occupation—East Europeans, Scandinavians, Latin Americans, Swiss—but if so, the research done for this study has not discovered their work. Nor do we have the background for all the articles known to have been written at this time. Some of the correspondents who went into Guernica with the Rebels are now dead; others have disappeared, and some are disinclined to talk. Original telegrams have been destroyed, memories have weakened, and some archives are still closed. But the main story can be woven together now, and we may never know more about these dispatches than what is told here, unless there is revealing material in the Spanish Nationalist archives.

The first reporter in Guernica, when it was in Rebel hands, was Georges Berniard, who had come to do a photoreportage from the Republican side. Berniard had earlier in the war covered the Toledo, Oviedo, and San Sebastián fronts with the Nationalists. When the news of the destruction of Guernica reached Bordeaux, his newspaper, *La Petite Gironde,* ordered him to the Basque front to photograph the ruins of the town. Berniard, as he himself later told the story, left Biarritz early in the morning of April 29 for Bilbao by airplane. He waited a couple of hours in Bilbao to arrange his permits, then left for Guernica, thirty kilometers distant, at ten forty-five, in a Basque government car with a chauffeur and a guide. He passed many refugees fleeing in the direction of Bilbao, but saw few soldiers.[11] On entering the town, he saw neither soldiers nor sentinels.

"At the first street corner, two, four, then twenty rifles were aimed at us," he later wrote. Berniard was taken prisoner, suspected of espionage. The French reporter-photographer was in the following days to know from personal experiences almost all the misfortunes of a journalist fallen afoul of Nationalist regulations. There are four accounts of his adventures: first, the short, succinct account he sent to his newspaper within twenty-four hours of his capture;[12] second, the articles he wrote later in Bordeaux after his release, in which he expressed himself more freely;[13] third, the story related a year later by the Italian journalist Renzo Segàla in a book on his experiences during the Spanish Civil War;[14] and, finally, Berniard's conversation with Pierre Dussauge, professor at the University of Bordeaux, in 1961.

When Berniard and his Basque guide, a poet named Urquiaga, were first taken into custody, an officer asked:

"What is this rabble?"

"They are communists who claim to be journalists," was the answer.

Then turning toward the Palace, he called the "guinea pig" and said to him: "Take care of them, you know what to do." I understood. . . . Now I knew who was to execute us: the "guinea pig."

Here is what we call a "guinea pig."

When, during an offensive, a village has been abandoned, the victors take precautions before entering. In spite of the certainty of a more or less general retreat, they nevertheless fear an ambush. A volunteer goes in, then, first, protected by a handful of men who follow far behind him, and makes known his presence by all kinds of noises. This volunteer is the "guinea pig." If nothing moves, the road is clear and the troops enter, flag flying in the wind; but if the enemy is still in the village, then the "guinea pig" is killed, or rather the enemy fires on him, which, in Spain, is not the same thing. In exchange for his bravado, the hero is rewarded; he will have a large part of the booty, he will kill the first prisoners. That is the reason the "guinea pig" was ordered to "take care of us."

With a fearful laugh he sized us up from head to foot. I could not see myself, fortunately, but Urquiaga was pale green. He extended his trembling hands to be tied. A noncommissioned officer came towards me. He had seen my Leica shining like a new penny. It would be his now. The "guinea pig" drew near me with his rope: it was my turn to put out my hands. It seems impossible for me to tell of the next few seconds. Deprived of the slightest reflex, I felt my legs giving way when suddenly I felt a rush of blood to my head. I recalled then how inexhaustible is the desire to live. It was due to this instinctive reaction that I did not lose consciousness, that, on the contrary, I jumped back and literally stopped the executioner by crying out: "You do not have the right. I am a French journalist!" The soldiers around me had a moment of hesitation. Alone, the "guinea pig" sought his rifle, which he had slung over his shoulder to have his hands free to tie us up. The officer who had called the "guinea pig" gave a brief order. Everybody drew back. He came toward me and said in poor French: "Just the person I'm looking for. First, you are going to sign an attestation affirming that the Basque Palace was respected by the Nationalist Air Force."[15]

Berniard then asked to be allowed to inspect the site, after which he made a rough draft of an attestation; then he wrote a corrected copy, which he gave to the officer. But, "The 'guinea pig' is still there. I belong to him, and he does not want to lose me."

At this critical moment, Berniard saw a young lieutenant, whom he thought to have seen months earlier in Toledo. Berniard called out: "I am a Frenchman." This lieutenant, named Pedro Sanz,

understands my distress, and, in turn, cries out, as if to halt the irreparable: "Just a moment." Ah, just a "moment. . . ." For a long time I could hear the sound in my mind! . . . It was he who saved me! [16]

While in the charge of this lieutenant, Berniard

> finally found a friendly face, a colleague, with whom I had often visited the
> fronts of Madrid, Oviedo and San Sebastián. This amiable brother-reporter
> affirmed that, in spite of appearances, I was not a spy. [17]

Berniard never identified this new savior, and, in fact, in his later accounts did not
even mention the incident. The reporter was Sandro Sandri, an Italian journalist,
and the details of their encounter are given in the book of another Italian newsman,
Renzo Segàla. Segàla saw the Frenchman with two Spanish soldiers. Small and
heavyset, with a large camera around his neck, "he was pale as a cadaver, and
waved in his right hand a small brown book, which we recognized as a French
passport." Berniard claimed to recognize Sandri, who was with Segàla, and appealed
to his Italian colleague to confirm his status of journalist. Sandri acceded to the
demand, although, according to Segàla, he did not remember Berniard at all.
Berniard was explaining with great animation how he had come to Bilbao, then to
Guernica, when he was interrupted by a Spanish officer, who posed the important
question: "Why did you want to photograph the ruins of Guernica?" Berniard
understood the significance of the question, and

> does not know how to reply; he gives another imploring look to Sandri.
> Sandri, for the second time, intervenes to help his colleague. "His news-
> paper," he observes, "has given him orders to come here. We journalists are
> like you soldiers. . . . We must obey, go where we are sent. In any case I
> vouch for him." [18]

The Italian correspondents—Sandri, Franzetti, and Segàla—informed Berniard
that Captain Aguilera would be along soon with some French colleagues. [19] But this
news did not end Berniard's worries. He had on his person highly incriminating
papers, not found in the cursory search made when he was first taken prisoner.
Berniard had been given extremely warm letters of recommendation to the Bilbao
government by some Basque refugees he had met in Bayonne on the night of April
28. These letters had opened doors for him in Bilbao and greatly facilitated his
ill-fated trip to Guernica. When he was given a sandwich to eat, doubtless heavy
with bread, he managed to slip the papers into the sandwich and chew them up and
swallow them. He had also up to this point been able to keep possession of his
camera, loaded with the film he had taken that morning in Bilbao. The films when
developed could be incriminating to Berniard; but he also had no desire for these
scenes of life in Bilbao to fall into the hands of his captors. While playing with his
camera on the bridge over a small stream, he found a way to drop the film into the
water. This was luck and ill luck. His camera was taken from him a few minutes
later as a trophy of war, and when it was found empty of film, he was again accused
of being a spy and not a real press photographer. [20]

At four o'clock Aguilera arrived with four French protégés: Botto, Massot,
Mévil, and Méjat. Berniard explained his problem to Aguilera, who "judged the case

extremely grave." Berniard was declared innocent of the charge of espionage, but he was now accused of having violated a Nationalist decree condemning to death any foreign journalist who, having worked on the Franco side of the conflict, was later captured with Republican troops.[21] However, Berniard was now in the hands of Aguilera, the press officer, and he went on to Vitoria with the other newsmen, a journalist—not a full-fledged spy, but still a prisoner.

The editors of *La Petite Gironde* in Bordeaux were soon informed that their reporter had been captured in the fall of Guernica. The news was first heard on the Insurgent radio, which was listened to by all the press in southwest France, and later from a cablegram sent by the Basque government.[22] Berniard today says that his newspaper was first alerted to his plight by a telephone call from an American correspondent.[23] A note in the Havas files confirms a call from Hendaye to Havas in Paris from an unidentified American reporter acting on behalf of Botto.[24] Berniard thought that the call had come from the internationally renowned Knickerbocker, but this was not possible, for that American correspondent, as already mentioned, was then in London, having just been released from a Spanish Nationalist prison. No traces of an American correspondent's having been in Guernica on April 29 have been found. But there was the English newsman Pembroke Stephens of the *Daily Telegraph,* and he probably made the telephone call, but he did not mention the Berniard incident in his cablegram to his newspaper.

Stephens was frequently in the company of the Italian reporters, and the first men of the press in Guernica after Berniard were the three Italians: Sandri, Segála, and Franzetti.[25] Saporiti, also an Italian, and Stephens were either with the first three or came in very shortly thereafter. "I entered Guernica with the Nationalist vanguard one hour after the departure of the Basque forces," Stephens cabled to his newspaper.[26] A short item in *L'Express du Midi* of Toulouse in fact credits the life-saving recognition of Berniard not exclusively to Sandri but to "the special correspondents of *La Stampa* [Sandri], of the Stefani agency [Saporiti] of the *Daily Telegraph* [Stephens], and of the Agence Radio."[27] This latter person has not been identified, and it could have been he who sent the message to Toulouse, just as he sent a message to *Le Journal* of Paris.[28]

Sandri, Segála, Franzetti, and Saporiti were Italian journalists accompanying Italian troops, the *Frecce Neri.*[29] The Italian correspondents worked independently of the Franco press control officers and of the Spanish censorship. Reynolds Packard explained the system a few years later:

> The fascist press officials, who were all in Black Shirt uniform, operated a special courier service for dispatches between the front lines and Saint-Jean-de-Luz, in France. It enabled messages sent by this route to reach the outside world twelve hours before those filed by cable through slower Spanish censorship.[30]

This system permitted the Italian newsmen, who bypassed Bolín's censorship, to get their versions of the news into print more quickly than could their French,

English, or American colleagues, who were obliged to pass their material through regular Spanish channels.[31] One result of this independence enjoyed by the Italian reporters with Italian troops was that their company was sought out by other correspondents, notably by Carney, of the *New York Times,* and Pembroke Stephens, and even on occasion by Packard of the UP, to the chagrin of the Franco press officers.[32] Saporiti later wrote: "I filed my story [on Guernica] crossing the French border by car and phoning from Saint-Jean-de-Luz,"[33] and it is possible that Stephens and the other Italians did the same, and that it was Stephens who called Havas about Berniard.

All four of the Italian correspondents in Guernica reported Berniard's difficulties. The Stefani message, as published in *L'Osservatore Romano,* said that "the explosive advance of the *legionari*" had taken Berniard "by surprise." Sandri and Franzetti told their readers that Berniard reported misery and political discontent in Bilbao, and both were inclined to view Berniard's troubles as more illustrative of Basque disorganization than of Nationalist harshness toward journalists. They thought the Frenchman naïve to have come to Guernica, trusting in the Basques' analysis of the military situation. Segála said little about the French reporter, but drew the conclusion that Bilbao at ten o'clock on the morning of April 29 did not really know where the front line was.[34]

Readers of the Italian press were better informed of Berniard's situation than were those who read the French press on the morning of April 30. *Le Journal,* with a short factual account attributed to Agence Radio, was the only Paris newspaper that mentioned the incident.[35] This did not indicate that Georges Botto, the Havas man who went into Guernica, had been inactive. He had been responsible for the telephone call from Hendaye to Havas in Paris. He sent an urgent message announcing Berniard's capture at 8:10 P.M. from Vitoria, probably on arrival, and then sent another telegram at ten that night.[36] Havas, on receiving the telephone call from Hendaye, telephoned to Lemoine, the chief editor at *La Petite Gironde.* Berniard's newspaper and Havas agreed not to publish anything about Berniard for the moment, in the interest of the captured newsman.[37]

Botto also arranged for Berniard to send a telegram to his newspaper through the Havas facilities, giving a brief résumé of his adventures. This message ended by saying that on arriving at Vitoria, Berniard was brought before a general of Mola's staff, and that "Captain Aguilera pleaded my case so well that a few minutes later I went out a free man and liberated of all worries."[38] This story was not quite true. Berniard's first telegram was published on May 1 on the first page of *La Petite Gironde.* The time of dispatch was indicated at 8 P. M., April 29. The hour at least was false, as Berniard himself wrote a few days later when he was free in France: it was only at ten o'clock that night of April 29 that he was brought before the military authorities in Vitoria. Nor did this interview end his anxieties. At the end he was dryly informed by an officer that he was to be shot at dawn. This may well have been a typical piece of military humor, and a few minutes later Aguilera assured him that he was merely "under house arrest." However, Berniard continued, "I passed, I assure you, a bad night. I was still frightened and also I had difficulty in digesting the paper sandwich."[39]

Georges Berniard today confirms that he spent the night of April 29-30 in fear for his life.[40] He had been placed under Botto's protection in the Havas man's "sumptuous" apartment,[41] but after Botto had gone to sleep Berniard seriously thought of getting hold of a knife, killing the sentinel before the door, and trying to escape. Only the thought of the jeopardy in which he would place Botto restrained him. Méjat, the newsreel photographer, stayed with him throughout the night. It was only on the following morning, Berniard says today, that he actually believed that his life was to be spared.[42] It was therefore in all probability only on the morning of April 30 that the telegram was really dispatched to *La Petite Gironde.*

It was not until two days later, at midnight on Saturday, May 1, that Berniard was told that his "house arrest" was lifted, and it was only on May 2, in the late afternoon when he crossed the international bridge, having been accompanied up to this point by Aguilera, Botto, and other journalists, that he was really free.[43] Berniard wrote nothing about the presence of "Jean Dourec" in these negotiations but "Dourec" maintains today that he brought Berniard to Irún in his automobile. He also affirms that he was largely instrumental in securing Berniard's freedom, intervening with Colonel Ungría of Franco's staff and explaining that the liberation of Berniard would create goodwill for the Nationalist cause.[44] Perhaps Berniard thought it politically unwise for him to mention his relations with the man from *L'Action Française.*

Back in Bordeaux, Berniard wrote a series of three articles for his newspaper, which, because of the passions of the times, pleased few persons, but which were, nevertheless, as the extracts already cited show, informative. He also added some illuminating details about his final liberation. When, at midnight on Saturday, May 1, Captain Aguilera told Berniard that "it was all finished, that I was free," the press officer added:

> "I hope that they will be content back home (by this he meant to speak of my newspaper). You should realize that it is generals Franco, Mola and Solchaga who are responsible for this measure of clemency for you. Say this to your editors, and above all send me copies of the newspapers in which you express your thanks." "I promise to do that, Captain," I replied, having understood. Moreover, if I had not understood, my colleagues would have made things clear to me. They had taken so much trouble to help me. They had guaranteed my behavior. I owed it to them to do whatever was necessary to preserve their peace of mind. *La Petite Gironde,* unhesitatingly, has honored my engagement. I am profoundly grateful to them for doing so.[45]

What was this engagment? It was quite simply the publication in *La Petite Gironde* of an article in which the newspaper made itself the interpreter of Georges Berniard's gratitude to Franco, Mola, and Solchaga "for the courtesy, the humanitarian spirit, and the respect for the laws of warfare to which he bears witness of having benefited in the course of this dramatic incident."[46]

When Berniard entered France, he carried two messages from Georges Botto, which he communicated by telephone to Havas in Paris. The first was for publication and announced the liberation of Berniard and his return to France. The second was a *note de service* that read:

FRENCH FRONTIER BERNIARD HAS JUST ENTERED FRANCE NOT WITHOUT DIFFICULTY PLEASE INSIST STRONGLY WITH PETITE GIRONDE FOR INSERTION FIRST NUMBER TO APPEAR ARTICLE BROUGHT BY BERNIARD AND SEND ME URGENTLY SEVERAL NUMBERS STOP THIS PRIMARY INTEREST ALL REPRESENTATIVES FRENCH PRESS BOTTO.[47]

Berniard now ways that this telegram was dictated by Rebel officers.[48] It can therefore be easily imagined that its publication was one of the conditions of Berniard's release.

There was only too obviously in the telegram of Botto and in the whole experience of Berniard a suggestion of permanent menace hanging over the corps of foreign press representatives, and most especially over the Frenchmen. There was no doubt that Berniard's life had been actually in danger when he was first taken and suspected of being a spy and later when he was accused of having transgressed the Franco decree against a correspondent's leaving Nationalist territory to work in the Republican zone. Berniard certainly thought his life in peril, and so did his colleagues; there was doubtless in the minds of all the Frenchmen the knowledge of Malet-Dauban, still in solitary confinement and probably sentenced to death. Berniard knew that his guide had disappeared, his hands manacled, in the custody of the "guinea pig."[49] The guide was shot shortly thereafter,[50] but it is not clear just when Berniard found this out. Berniard also knew that the two Basque journalists who had left for the front that morning of April 29 in Bilbao before he did, tired of waiting for him and his permits, had also been taken prisoner. "They died courageously, their fists raised in defiance, on the morning of the first of May."[51]

But the correspondents in Guernica on April 29 wrote about things other than the unfortunate Berniard; they wrote about the destruction of the town. Berniard himself, the first foreign pressman in Guernica under the Nationalist occupation, made a fairly thorough examination of the ruins while a prisoner. He waited until May 8 to give his opinion of what he had seen. He had come back to Bordeaux convinced that his colleagues in Vitoria were hostages for his own good behavior. He could easily have been annoyed at the Basques. They had told him in Bilbao that Mola's troops were twenty kilometers from Guernica,[52] and this incredible error in military intelligence could have cost Berniard his life, as it did cost those of his two traveling companions. Nevertheless, what he wrote could not have been entirely satisfying to the press officers in Vitoria. He wrote that the town had been heavily bombed. He qualified this accusation with another against anarchist incendiaries.

When they [the anarchists] start a fire, as I have seen them do in Irún, they deny it. In my opinion they are still lying when they deny having set fire to Guernica, already frightfully mutilated, moreover, by the Nationalist air force.[53]

The charge against the anarchists does not erase that against the Rebel air force, and the fact that a year later Segàla reproached Berniard for this latter charge[54] indicates that this part of his article was the subject of discussion among the reporters with the Nationalists.

There were other postscripts to Berniard's adventures. "The foreign correspondents on the Biscay front," read a dispatch which appeared in *L'Action Française*, probably coming from Havas, although this detail was omitted, "telegraphed General Franco to thank him for the instructions given relative to the freeing of Berniard." The article continued:

Yesterday afternoon [Sunday, May 4?] when General Mola received a visit from the Special Correspondent of the Havas Agency on the Biscay Front, he declared that the decision taken concerning Berniard was perfectly natural, for the enquiry carried out showed that the collaborator of *La Petite Gironde* was merely doing his professional duty and that he was executing the orders received from his superiors.[55]

This report showed a continuing malaise among the foreign correspondents in Vitoria and also perhaps a certain busybodiness on the part of Georges Botto. General Queipo de Llano, in his radio talk on the night of May 7, commented on the kindness and charity shown Berniard, but added that the assertion by the editors of *La Petite Gironde* concerning a Nationalist decree condemning to death any reporter who, having worked on the Franco side, later turned up with the Republicans was "a currish lie characteristic of the Marxists."[56]

Two other Frenchmen, Botto and Massot, reported on the condition of Guernica when it was captured, as did the four Italian correspondents who were there on April 29. Botto telegraphed a press report from Vitoria at ten o'clock on the night of April 29, in which he took a clear pro-Nationalist stand. The whole town of Guernica, he stated, "was set on fire by Reds before departing stop can be compared Fleury hyphen Verdun fire much greater than Irún Eibar."[57] This dispatch was not widely published, and in fact has been found in only one newspaper—in Rio de Janeiro.[58]

On the following day Botto sent a longer dispatch, or perhaps several telegrams describing the ruins, but was noncommittal as to the responsibility for them.

The town offers a desolate aspect. . . . Around the church, the hospital and the parliament building a few houses still stand, almost undamaged. They are the only ones. The rest of the town is a field of rubble. Among the formless ruins rise a few shattered walls. The openings of what were doors and windows are encircled by a black frame, painted by the fire that devoured the wood. . . . Guernica had been evacuated. The few civilians who remained search among the ruins of their houses for the objects which may yet be saved.[59]

Max Massot wrote an article about the capture of Guernica which is difficult to explain, for it appears to be the first one passed through the Franco censorship which admitted that bombs had been dropped on the town by the Rebel air force.

> Before withdrawing . . . the forces of the government set fire to all the buildings of the town, many of which had, moreover, been dynamited by the volunteers of the Asturian battalion which formed part of the garrison. If it is exact that some bombs were dropped on the town by the Nationalist air force, it is also exact beyond any doubt that the burning of Guernica was wrought by the defenders of the town, who have systematically destroyed all the urban conglomeration. One can say that not a single building has escaped the effects of this terrible conflagration.[60]

It is possible that this message did not go through the Franco censorship, that it was telephoned from Saint-Jean-de-Luz or some other place on the frontier in France and datelined San Sebastián, but it seems more probable that Massot went to Vitoria with the other French correspondents on the night of April 29; this is the impression given by Berniard, and it was from Vitoria that Massot sent another message on May 1 or 2.[61]

The dispatches sent out by the Italian journalists who found Berniard a prisoner were unanimous in attributing the destruction of the town to dynamiters and arsonists. Segàla wrote:

> . . . of the seven thousand inhabitants of Guernica not more than thirty or forty remain. This is not surprising, for even those who, as at Eibar, may have wanted to brave the anger of the Reds and remain to await the national troops, have had to flee during the night to save themselves from the flames and from the explosions of the mines which the communists had placed under the houses. Guernica exists no more. The Reds have treated this gay and industrious old town as the mediaeval victors treated a conquered city: not a stone has been left on stone. The wicked crime, committed the other day in Eibar, has been repeated here in full and absolutely irreparable proportions.[62]

A year later Segàla changed his story a bit, calling the troops by their true name of Black Arrows, rather than "Legionaries." The Black Arrows began marching toward Guernica early on the morning of April 29. "A great column of white smoke" was the first sign they saw of the town. "Guernica is still burning." Along the road the soldiers sang "Giovinezza" and "Cara al Sol," the Fascist and Falangist songs. Inhabitants awkwardly gave the Fascist salute. Nor did thirty or forty persons remain in Guernica; now there were only three to greet the victors.

> . . . We are at the gates of Guernica, near a cluster of low houses, the balconies flowering with geraniums. In a doorway stand three women immobile, two young girls pale and disheveled and an old lady of eighty years,

who looked at us with two tired, blind eyes. We learn very soon that they are the only human beings—among the seven thousand of the population—who have remained in Guernica.

Segàla also affirmed—a year after the event—that when he entered Guernica,

we did not know that the international press allied with the different Popular Fronts was already mounting a shocking campaign to uphold the position that Guernica was destroyed by incendiary bombs dropped from Nationalist airplanes. If we had known it, it is probable that, even in the midst of the tragic, apocalyptic *décor,* we would have smiled. If the infamous carnage had in fact been carried out by airplanes, the houses would have appeared split by the explosions, demolished, overturned, but would still have conserved their structure, their lines, and in the streets great holes dug by the explosions would have been visible. Instead, the roads, although still covered by smoking ruins, are intact. And the holes, very deep, open within the perimeter of the house foundations, an unmistakable sign that they are the result of explosions from within the same buildings. Guernica in fact has not only been burned but destroyed by the Reds with tons of dynamite, that dynamite which the Asturian miners handle like masters and which they always carry on their backs, wherever they go, wrapped in thick oiled green-colored paper.[63]

It is extremely difficult to believe that any of the reporters with the Nationalist armies on April 29 was ignorant of what Bilbao had been saying for forty-eight hours about the destruction of Guernica and, equally, of what Salamanca had been replying. Sandro Sandri was certainly well aware of the position of the Bilbao radio, of "the anti-fascist French press," and of Salamanca, for he utilized a great part of his dispatch concerning the capture of Guernica to refute the first two positions and to uphold the third.

The stupid nonsense of the aerial bombardment of Guernica, broadcast from the microphones of the Bilbao radio station and picked up by the antifascist French press, which in these days is spreading the most fantastic news about the event . . . is false. Guernica has never been bombed by the National air force, for the simple reason that it does not constitute a military objective and around it there exist neither trenches nor defenses which could justify the bombardment. Moreover, far heavier aerial bombardments, as for example those of Elgueta, where four Red artillery batteries were placed, did not cause the slaughter [scempio] which the Asturian dynamiters caused in Guernica. . . .

Aerial bombs, falling from on high, destroy a building from the roof to the foundations; here in Guernica, however, the houses have been destroyed by explosions coming from below, which have literally made the houses spring into the air. The tales of the few remaining inhabitants agree in accusing the Asturian dynamiters of the crime; they have explained how it was carried out. The centers of explosion were prepared when the news of the fall of Marquina had barely reached here, and the charges of dynamite were placed in each house, save, through the intercession of the Basque Nationalists, in the churches and near the porch, where rises the tree in the shade of which the ancient lords of the Basque country distributed justice to the people. These centers were linked up by wires, to be set off electrically. Tuesday [*sic*], in the afternoon, the order was given to evacuate the population and hardly had the inhabitants reached the surrounding hills or fled towards Bilbao when the explosions began. An old man, who returned to the town this morning when he saw the red and yellow banner flying from the hillside, told me that he had counted 153 explosions, for the town was blown up by sections, until its complete destruction. The damage done, as can be well imagined, is simply incalculable. Gasoline was thrown on the ruins, and the fearful fire which followed completed the disaster. . . . We walked through the two streets in which the bitter smell of the explosives is still so strong that one seems to breathe sulphur smoke. . . . The Asturian dynamiters, on Tuesday [sic], blew up the houses of the town, one by one, then set fire to the ruins, completing the destruction.[64]

Franzetti's article also placed the destruction of Guernica on Tuesday night. He told of entering with the troops into the town "now deserted by inhabitants and the Red militia." Perhaps ten houses had been spared, because of their poor condition, "from the dynamite and the gasoline of the Asturian battalions." He explained that

at Guernica, as at Eibar, the Asturians have wished to leave the sign of their barbarity, and with an unimaginable zeal did not even wait for the Nationalists to near the town to set it on fire and to pillage it; they began Tuesday night, so that for two consecutive days the fire was master, sparing nothing. Churches, palaces, factories, villas, houses, all were destroyed and of Guernica there remains nothing.[65]

Sandri and Franzetti directly placed the destruction of the town on Tuesday night, and Segàla indirectly fixed the disaster on the same date or later,[66] —that is, twenty-four hours, or even longer, after the time declared by the correspondents in Bilbao. These hours, Tuesday afternoon and night, were of course in accord with the Nationalist position, denying that any of their airplanes had flown on Tuesday afternoon, and the Italians doubtless sought this agreement in their reports. Sandri gave a control date: Guernica was destroyed when the news of the fall of Marquina arrived. Marquina was occupied by the Nationalists on Tuesday, April 27.[67] Segàla, in his newspaper dispatch, blamed the damage done to Guernica on "the Communists." A year later he attributed the destruction to "the Reds" and the "Asturian miners." Sandri fixed the responsibility on "Asturian dynamiters." Franzetti blamed "the Asturian battalions." These words were of course interchangeable in their journalese. Sandri's article is significant in that it was the first newspaper report on Guernica after the Rebel occupation which gave a technical argument to maintain the Nationalist theses. It did no great credit to Sandri's imagination, for he merely repeated what Queipo de Llano had said the previous night. In view of Sandri's knowledge of the two opposed positions concerning

Guernica, it is impossible to believe Segàla's assertion a year later that he knew nothing of the Basque allegations when he entered the ruined town. There is another important fact in Sandri's long, detailed account of how Guernica was destroyed: the population was evacuated before the destruction began. There were therefore no victims. Nor were there victims in the accounts of Segala and Franzetti.

Pembroke Stephens did not see what the Italians saw nor did he hear what they heard.

> Guernica presents an appalling spectacle of desolation. . . . The destruction is even more complete than at Eibar. Here and there a solitary wall of a house rears its gaunt and blackened silhouette against the blue sky. There is little else except wrecked houses blocking practically every street. . . . [He found] a group of excited and distracted women, wearing a queer medley of garments—men's socks and shoes, ill-fitting blouses and skirts and overcoats too big for them who told me that they had lost everything in the fire. Their homes had been destroyed at night. They had to flee in their night-dresses, grabbing clothes as they went from the ruins of other houses that had not fallen a ruin to the flames.

He said the women had not eaten for three days. Stephens thus placed the disaster on Monday, and not on Tuesday, as did the Italians. It would seem probable that Stephens and the Italians talked about what had happened at Guernica, but if they did, the Englishman did not accept the Italian versions. In fact, his readers were apparently given no explanation of what had happened at Guernica. But there was the phrase about the women who "went from the ruins of other houses that had not fallen a ruin to the flames."[68] Were there then houses in ruins from other causes than the fires? Perhaps from explosive bombs? Stephens had his ideas on this subject, but since his job was to keep reporting from the Rebel side, he preferred not to put them in print, as will be seen later.

On May 1 at least five correspondents visited Guernica with Nationalist officers and then wrote dispatches: an unidentified reporter from the United Press; Richard G. Massock, of the Associated Press; Botto, of the Havas Agency; Massot, of *Le Journal*; and Mévil, of *Le Petit Marseillais*.

The UP man took

> advantage of an invitation of the Nationalist general staff . . . to investigate whether or not, as the governmental forces and some organs of information repeatedly affirmed, it is true that the destruction [of Guernica] was due to bombs dropped by Revolutionary [Nationalist] airplanes. Accompanied by an officer, the correspondent walked through practically all the streets and squares and frequently had to turn from his path and follow another lane, because the walls, on collapsing, formed natural barricades fifteen meters high. The officer explained how the buildings whose walls were still standing

showed no signs of having been bombed from the air, but did show signs that their ruins were caused by explosives set off at the base of the walls or nearby. . . .

From a careful examination of many buildings there follows the conclusion that all show signs indicating fire and that the fire came from within. In certain cases the houses seem intact, but the panorama changes when one enters. The officers showed at the same time huge holes which perforated the highway, indicating the places where the governmental forces placed their mines.

The officer who accompanied the UP man, "in order to demonstrate the difference existing between this spectacle and that offered by an aerial bombardment," took the reporter to Durango, "where it was confirmed that many houses had been hit and damaged by the bombs, but none set on fire."[69]

This dispatch began with the phrase: "While the fires were slowly dying in the debris of hundreds of houses," thus indicating that five days after April 26, the date according to the correspondents at Bilbao when the fires began, the flames were still smoldering. In this cablegram, and in others also passed through the Nationalist censorship, the reporter frequently had recourse to such phrases as "the officer explained that" and "the officer showed that"; these circumlocutions can be interpreted as subterfuges to leave the onus of the opinion expressed on the Nationalist officer and not on the correspondent. In fact the reporter offers but one conclusion: that all the buildings examined "show signs indicating fire and that the fire came from within." In this UP dispatch, and in others written on the same day, we find for the first time the suggestion that the truth about the destruction of Guernica can be found in a comparison of Guernica's ruins with those of Durango. This idea, according to the UP man, came from an Insurgent officer.

Richard G. Massock, of the Associated Press, apparently was on the same tour as the UP man.

> Insurgent officers seeking to disprove the Basque charges that [Guernica] was set afire by incendiary bombs from the air, conducted a special tour of the ruins for foreign correspondents today. This inspection failed to disclose any of the usual marks of an aerial bombardment either in the streets or on the walls still standing. . . .
>
> Insurgent officers professed to be afraid Bilbao might be destroyed by fires set by its own defenders as—according to the Insurgent versions—Eibar and Guernica were destroyed. They asserted prisoners had told them that extremists in the Basque ranks had orders to burn towns as they were abandoned in retreat.[70]

The most widely published and the most discussed of the newspaper reports resulting from the May 1 visit of the correspondents to Guernica was that of the Agence Havas, sent in by their man covering Bilbao front—in fact their only man then covering the war with the Nationalist forces—Georges Botto. The cablegram was sent from Vitoria, and was dated on Saturday at 1900 hours—that is, on May 1; but it was distributed only on the following day in Paris and therefore dated May 2 by the agency.[71]

> The officers of General Mola's staff yesterday conducted the foreign journalists to Guernica to permit them to make a thorough visit of the ruins of the town and to let them see for themselves, with their own eyes, that contrary to the news sent out by a government source, the destruction of the town was not the work of the Nationalists.
>
> The foreign journalists have gone all over the town in all directions and have been able to question with complete freedom the few civilians who awaited the arrival of General Franco's troops; they have been able to see for themselves that all the sections of wall still standing bear no trace of bomb splinters and that, on the other hand, all the windows are girdled with traces of flames. The beams of the houses are just finishing burning three [*sic*] days after the occupation.[72]
>
> Nationalist officers have drawn the attention of the journalists to the fact that nowhere does one find signs of bomb splatter and that the absence of traces of projectiles as well as the verifications made elsewhere show that the town was deliberately set on fire. Yesterday, one could still follow the havoc wrought by the fire which must have begun in the south of the town and which, fanned by the breeze, spread to the north.
>
> The attention of the journalists was also called to the fact that the places where the fire did not catch on, especially the houses of reinforced concrete, were drenched with gasoline, and they could see in the interiors signs of flames which must have been caused by kerosene because the smoke has covered the walls with very thick soot.
>
> In spite of meticulous searching, the journalists have found no bomb holes; only a few have been located on the outskirts, particularly near the routes serving the town. Civilians remaining in the town after the departure of the government forces have stated clearly that the "reds" began their evil work Monday evening.
>
> Moreover, the journalists were shown, in the town itself, four craters caused by mines; these have not yet been filled in and are a great bother to traffic.[73]

This report, like those of the American agencies AP and UP, shows that the visit to Guernica on May 1 was an organized tour. Both the Havas report and that of the UP indicated that the town was still burning, at least in some parts, five days after April 26. The Havas dispatch also contained cautious phrases like "Nationalist officers have drawn the attention of the journalists to the fact" and "the attention of the journalists was also called to the fact." This dispatch by Georges Botto is the only one known to have been sent out at this time which makes such a clear reference to gasoline. It is also the first to speak of the presence of a breeze to fan the flames.

The Botto dispatch on Guernica was widely and quickly distributed by the Havas Agency, in contrast with its handling of the first news on Guernica from

Bilbao. It was published not only in France but also in Belgium,[74] Switzerland,[75] Scotland,[76] Morocco,[77] Argentina,[78] Portugal,[79] and doubtless elsewhere. That part of the French press which had reacted slowly or not at all to the news that Guernica had been bombed, welcomed the new Havas telegram. *Le Figaro* gave it a three-column headline: "FOREIGN JOURNALISTS' INQUIRY IN GUERNICA REVEALS THAT TOWN WAS NOT BOMBED. HOUSES HAD BEEN DOUSED WITH GASOLINE AND SET ON FIRE BY GOVERNMENT FORCES."[80]

Botto's story had a great success in another country, where normally Havas dispatches were not printed—Germany. On the night of May 3, Mr. Ravoux, head of the Havas bureau in Berlin telephoned to Paris to say that

> the German press gave heavy publicity to the dispatch of our special correspondent on the Biscay front, concerning the destruction of Guernica. The German press noisily opposes this report to the news published by *The Times*, Reuter and the English press in general, on the destruction of that town. Several provincial editions just received at the moment of this telephone call, published our telegram on the front page with titles like this: "THE LIES OF THE ENGLISH PRESS DENIED BY HAVAS."

The memorandum of this telephone call bore this notation in handwriting: "Nothing in the Paris press. London has not yet noted any reaction in the English Press."[81] Havas did not distribute to its customers any news about the employment of the Botto dispatch by the Nazis to disprove the accounts in the English press concerning Guernica. There was consequently little in the French press on the subject. Eventually, a great deal was published in England about the German attacks on the English press, but the interesting fact that the attacks were inspired by and based on the Havas telegram and other reports in the French press was largely overlooked.[82]

A spillover from the German printings of the Havas dispatch showed up in Franco Spain, where readers of the press learned by courtesy of the DNB how *Le Figaro, Le Jour,* and *L'Echo de Paris* had headlined the Havas article.[83] General Queipo de Llano told his listeners that

> the Marxists continue lying about Guernica, but the truth is becoming known through the visit to Guernica made by a group of journalists who have confirmed what I said on the matter the first day. After visiting the ruins, they have verified that the town was destroyed by fires and not by bombs. These newspapermen have inspected the debris in all directions and have been able to question the inhabitants. They have been able to observe that on the walls still standing there are no traces whatsoever of bombing. The beams are still burning three days after the town was abandoned by the Marxists. Nowhere are there signs of explosions. The journalists have also been able to see that where the fire could not penetrate because of the reinforced concrete construction, there are great pools of gasoline. The only signs of bombing are on the outskirts of the town, notably on the highway. The inhabitants of Guernica

say that the town was burned by the Marxists, who tried to place some mines by digging large holes in the square which have not yet been filled in.

This harangue was obviously based in large part on the Havas-Botto dispatch, with some of the general's own characteristic exaggerations.[84] It is significant that he cited what had appeared in the French press as representing the totality of the conclusions of all the foreign journalists who visited Guernica at the time.

The cablegram from Mévil, sent from Vitoria and dated May 2, like the Havas report, was strikingly similar to that of Botto, though much shorter.

> *The officers on General Mola's staff yesterday conducted the foreign journalists to Guernica to permit them make a thorough visit of the ruins of the town* and to permit them to deny the affirmations of the foreign press according to which Guernica was set on fire by incendiary bombs dropped from Nationalist planes.
>
> In this town, all the inhabitants have stated that the fire was set by the Asturian battalions.
>
> The state of the town where there is no trace of bombardment proves that they are telling the truth. *Nationalist officers have drawn the attention of the journalists to the fact that nowhere does one find signs of bomb splatter, and that the absence of traces of projectiles as well as the verifications made elsewhere show that the town was deliberately set on fire.*

Certain words in the dispatch attributed to Mévil are italicized above. In the original French they constituted thirty-one words in the first paragraph and forty-eight words in the last paragraph. These underlined parts can be found word for word in the dispatch sent out by the Havas Agency man. This similarity can be explained by saying that the Marseilles editor combined Botto's and Mévil's telegrams. The similarities between the printed dispatch of Botto and that of Mévil can be found in Botto's text as corrected in Paris, therefore we can exclude the possibility that the similarities are due to a paper given the journalists by the press officer, indicating the general lines of what would be admitted in their dispatches.[85]

Still another French journalist went into Guernica on May 1. He was Max Massot, who represented the extremely pro-Nationalist *Le Journal.*

> Was Guernica . . . smashed to pieces by the Nationalist air force, as the Bilbao government affirms, or was it burned by the Reds before they were obliged to abandon it?

He had already answered the question a few days before, but he said he now

> deliberately put to one side as suspect the precise and concordant testimonies of the five or six inhabitants heard in Guernica itself, an hour after the occupation, and who, having passed the previous night in terror prowling like smoked-out foxes around their dens in flames, had just followed Franco's soldiers into the town.

Massot "sought to compare the effects produced by an acknowledged, admitted bombing"—that is, the ruins of Durango—"with the chaos of Guernica." He made the same journey as the UP man, a journey suggested by the Nationalist press officers.

> In Durango, which suffered, as a center of military concentration . . . the double effect of bombing by air and by artillery, the small houses were blown away by a single strike, scattered, one might write, by the heavy bombs; pierced, cut up into pieces by the shells. The better built structures fell down, piece by piece. The explosives produced, on the metals, their ordinary effects, that is to say, breakage or torsion, often without harming the paint. The trees are gashed by shrapnel, as with a knife. The walls are riddled with holes of different sizes; the shot has pulverized the parget and cut into the stone. In all, twenty per cent of the houses are destroyed, which represents a long bombardment spread out over several weeks, with at least three hundred points of impact by projectiles of large calibre. Besides it was known that Durango had been evacuated by five-sixths of its inhabitants.

Massot found a quite different picture at Guernica, where

> of five hundred houses more or less, 90% are destroyed. As the first olfactory impression, the persistent odor of burnt wood and wool. Not more than three or four houses are scarred by shot, and one can still see near each one of them a large mine hole intended to cut the road or street at a given point.

The correspondent then advanced a series of "technical" arguments:

> I know all of the fronts of the world war. I have seen holes made by the 42-s in the outskirts of Arras, and I have walked in them. I have seen in this war all of the results of air bombs. I conclude clearly that the five funnel-shaped holes seen in Guernica can have been produced only by mines, for neither of the adversaries in the war possesses a shell or a bomb capable of making them.
> There are also many trees in Guernica. Not one has been gashed. Finally, everywhere there is burnt wood. The beams, the joists, the furniture, all are now but a vision of formless and charred objects. The iron of the balconies has been reddened by fire, tongues of black smoke have, everywhere, slavered out the windows over the pieces of wall still standing.
> The ruins offer this particular contrast of white and black, of plaster and charcoal, which everywhere in the world is the undisputed appanage of fire. One hundred airplanes bombarding for twenty days without stopping could never have realized a "work," which the hand of man has signed with a burning brand, the word "fire."[86]

This dispatch, as favorable to the Nationalist cause as that of Botto—if not more so—was much less influential. It was printed in only one newspaper in Paris, and that one was already well known for its extreme partisanship for Franco. However, Massot's report, like Botto's, was reprinted in Nazi Germany on the day following its Paris publication.[87] It was published in the press of Nationalist Spain,[88] and used by General Queipo de Llano in his radio program.[89] Massot's dispatch is significant for its attempt at a technical analysis of the causes of the ruins. This method—even the same arguments—was later widely used by advocates of the Insurgent theses in the ensuing controversy, as we shall see.

However, Massot was not completely satisfied with his account, or perhaps he felt that it did not sufficiently explain the ruins of Guernica. On May 7, at any rate, he sent still another version of how Guernica was destroyed, despite the fact that it contradicted his previous articles on the same subject. *Le Journal* duly published it.

On Monday morning, a certain airplane without apparent markings, began to circle over Guernica. Gradually it lowered its flight. Suddenly, in the very middle of the great square, one saw a section of "gudaris"—separatist soldiers—spreading out side by side four bed sheets. And, using an extinguished brand, they traced unknown signs on the white of the sheets. From the plane, a parachute supporting a small packet fell among the militiamen. It was the signal.

The soldiery spread out; while some, clapping their hands, chased away the passers-by and ordered them to take shelter, others discharged a truck loaded with gasoline cans. Each man seized his part of the combustible and ran towards a designated place. There with a quick slash, he opened the bottom of the can and began his task of drenching everything with gasoline. Then whistle calls gathered the incendiary troupe, who went towards the arms factory. The manoeuver lasted more than an hour. Then, the phantom airplane reappeared and began to fly at a very low altitude. Suddenly, special bombs, quite light but endowed with enormous incendiary power, began to fall with regularity: the monstrous egg-laying of an anonymous bird of prey which seemed to seek his path in the smoke of the charnel-house. Some projectiles grazed the roof-tops. But, those which hit the target suddenly set on fire a chain of liquid mesh which spread the fire along the walls, in the streets and onto the roofs. This was the only well-conceived maneuver carried out by the Reds during the present campaign in the Basque country.[90]

This new version by Massot is curious indeed. It had not only been passed through the Nationalist censorship but also had been printed in Nationalist Spain six days before Massot's article was printed in France.[91] Yet by espousing the theory that the fires that destroyed Guernica were kindled by incendiary bombs, Massot denied the "technical" arguments he himself had advanced and which ignored the existence of incendiary bombs in the Guernica holocaust. In fact, Massot thoughtlessly rebutted his own position of less than a week before, in which he had said that "one hundred airplanes bombarding for twenty days without stopping" could not have set the fires that destroyed Guernica. He had by now brought the figure down to one airplane and some cans of gasoline. It would have been but a short step from there to a rain of incendiary bombs from fleets of airplanes (without the gasoline) to arrive at the story that had the unanimous support of the foreign correspondents in Bilbao.

There remain eight more journalists (and perhaps still others whose dispatches have not been located) who, accredited to the Nationalist side of the war, visited Guernica in the course of their work and who wrote—or spoke—of what they saw: James Holburn, of the *Times;* William P. Carney, of the *New York Times;* "Jean Dourec" and Pierre Héricourt of *L'Action Française;* Harold G. Cardozo, of the *Daily Mail;* Charles Foltz, Jr., of the Associated Press; Virginia Cowles of the *Sunday Times,* and David Darrah, of the *Chicago Daily Tribune.*

Holburn had come to Spain from his newspaper's Berlin bureau on February 19, 1937,[92] and a few weeks after the Guernica incident returned to Berlin, leaving his post to a new man on the *Times,* Harold A. R. ("Kim") Philby.[93] Holburn's unsigned dispatch was published in the *Times,* in the *New York Times,* and in *La Nación,* of Buenos Aires, on May 5. This is, with the Havas dispatch of Botto, the most widely cited among those concerning Guernica sent out by the correspondents who were assigned to the Nationalist side of the conflict. It read as follows, in the *Times:*

> THE RUINS OF GUERNICA. A RIVAL VIEW. NATIONALISTS TO HOLD INQUIRY. Vitoria, May 4. Public opinion here (with the Nationalist forces) is still disturbed by the allegation abroad that the beautiful Basque town of Guernica was destroyed by incendiary bombs dropped by Nationalist aircraft, and a Commission of civilian engineers has been appointed to investigate the causes of the fire which swept the town. It is feared that the conflagration destroyed much of the evidence of its origin, but it is felt here that enough remains to support the Nationalist contention that incendiaries on the Basque side had more to do with the razing of Guernica than General Franco's aircraft.
>
> A visit to Guernica shows that of the main part of the town consisting of large four and five story buildings, little remains but a few ragged portions of wall. A few public buildings, including that housing the Basque archives, and some villas not in the crowded center, where fire has made a clean sweep, have escaped.
>
> There is nothing to compare with the havoc wrought in Guernica, except in Eibar, 80% of which was destroyed by bombs and fire, and in that part of Irún where the shells of large buildings stand—monuments of proved incendiarism. Durango also is largely demolished, but having escaped fire, gives the impression of a town needing repairs rather than rebuilding.
>
> That Guernica after a week's bombardment by artillery and aircraft should not have shown signs of fire supports the Nationalist contention that aircraft were not responsible for the burning of the town, which was bombed intermittently over a period of three hours. There is the case of the village of Elgueta, which was levelled by bombs and shells but which did not go up in flames, while in Eibar, which had been a target for bombardment since September, there was no fire until the Basques were evacuating the town.

It has been asserted that Guernica was subjected to bombing of exceptional intensity, but the distinctive marks of an aerial bombardment are not
numerous. In Durango explosions blew great pieces of the walls of buildings
out into the streets, exposing the interior of houses, and outside walls were
indented by flying fragments of shells and bombs—there are pieces of shells
and bombs to be found among the wreckage and in the streets, while in the
main square are bomb-holes full of muddy water.

In Guernica, on the other hand, few fragments of bombs have been
recovered, the façades of buildings still standing are unmarked, and the few
craters I inspected were larger than anything hitherto made by a bomb in
Spain. From their positions it is fair inference that these craters were caused
by exploding mines which were unscientifically laid to cut roads.

There was a bomb hole in the roof of a large church, but this church was
one of the buildings not burned. A works foreman in Guernica who witnessed
the air raid said the first few bombs dropped on the Educational Institute and
on two convents on the outskirts of the town. These buildings did not burn.
Lining one of the roads leading into the town is a row of villas. Three or four
have been destroyed by fire but they show no signs of having been touched
by bombs. Next door is one house demolished by a bomb, but untouched by
fire. A local dentist who watched the bombing from a hill outside Guernica
said that when he returned to the town there was only one or two small fires.
Next morning the town had been swept by fire.

In view of these circumstances it is difficult to believe that Guernica was
the target of a bombardment of exceptional intensity or was selected by the
Nationalists for an experiment with incendiary bombs, as alleged by the
Basques.

Residents who survived the bombardment and fire are for the most part
unable to help the investigators much. They say that they were either in
refuges or out in the country when the fire began and were told afterwards
that airplanes were responsible.

In the investigators' opinion it will be difficult to establish exactly how the
fire started.[94]

There are several significant features to Holburn's article. The first is the clear
affirmation that Guernica was "bombed intermittently over a period of three
hours." Another is the citation of the testimony of a survivor who "said the first
few bombs dropped on the Educational Institute and on two convents on the
outskirts of the town. These buildings did not burn." The reporters in Bilbao had
written that the bombing had lasted three hours, and that the first bombs were
explosive and not incendiary. Thus, Holburn's article is a confirmation of the
reports from Bilbao. Holburn, moreover, brought the bombing and the fires into
chronological and proximate order.

A local dentist who watched the bombing from a hill outside Guernica said
that when he returned to the town there was only one or two small fires.
Next morning the town had been swept by fire.

This night in question could not be other than that of April 26-27. Holburn's dispatch, passed through the Franco censorship, removed from the Rebel statement of May 2 its ambiguity as to when Guernica was bombed, restricted the bombing to a single action, and placed the bombing and the fires into a cause-and-effect relationship. Holburn thus in fact confirmed the essential parts of Steer's dispatch a fact that did not escape the attention of the *Times* editors.[95] Also, Holburn informed his editors and his readers that the Guernica people with whom he talked, although refusing to offer their personal opinions about the bombing, were nevertheless unanimous in saying that those witnesses with whom they later talked told them that the aircraft had started the fires. Still another important feature of the article is the last sentence: "In the investigators' opinion it will be difficult to establish exactly how the fire started." (It is true that Holburn also wrote that Guernica did not show "signs of fire," but this contradiction will be dealt with farther on.)

Steer never met Holburn, but he was angered by his colleague's article. Steer later wrote that

> it was mostly a rewrite of a document published for the whole foreign and "nationalist" press at Vitoria, and purporting to be a report by civilian engineers of the causes of the burning of Guernica.[96]

He went on, with searing irony:

> Franco must have been very cross with them. They did their work inadequately. "That Gernika after a week's bombardment by artillery and aircraft, should not have shown signs of fire . . ." they began, feeling their way feebly towards a compromise. Very feebly; for Gernika had never been shelled or bombed before April 26th. But the engineers showed goodwill. They had to explain away some of the holes that could not be covered in time."[97]

Steer was mistaken about the origin or inspiration of his colleague's dispatch. In reality, Holburn made a completely independent investigation of the town, and did not go in with the other reporters.[98] Like all the other correspondents in Spain, on either side, he read his eventually printed copy weeks or months later, if at all. Holburn declared, on reading his Guernica dispatch in January 1969 for the first time since he wrote it in Vitoria:

> Reading the dispatch reminded me that I met a man, in Guernica or Vitoria, who purported to be chairman of a commission of civil engineers appointed by Franco to inquire into the causes of the burning of Guernica. The comparisons with Durango, Eibar, Elgueta and Irún must have been made to me by him, for I never saw Durango, Eibar or Elgueta. His must have been the opinion I quoted that "it will be difficult to establish exactly how the fire started."[99]

It is this last phrase in Holburn's article—that and the fact that he had managed to pass through the Nationalist censorship several confirmations of Steer's original dispatch—that should have held all Steer's attention. After all, he was certainly aware of the difficulties of coping with the Rebel censors. Steer would also have been well advised to read Holburn's article more carefully, especially the section that most irritated him. This has already been given, but it is necessary to quote it again:

> Durango also is largely demolished, but having escaped fire, gives the impression of a town needing repairs rather than rebuilding.
> That Guernica after a week's bombardment by artillery and aircraft should not have shown signs of fire supports the Nationalist contention that aircraft were not responsible for the burning of the town, which was bombed intermittently over a period of three hours.

This last sentence, however carefully read, means nothing. Certainly Holburn knew that Guernica had not been bombed and shelled for a week. What did he mean by writing that Guernica did not show "signs of fire," thus contradicting his own statement that the town had been burned to the ground? Holburn, like all the other correspondents, knew that Durango had been bombed and shelled but not burned, and that Guernica had bombed but not shelled, before its capture, and certainly burned. Did he not, then, more probably cable as follows?

> Durango is also largely demolished, but having escaped fire, gives the impression of a town needing repairs rather than rebuilding. That *Durango* after a week's bombardment by artillery and aircraft should not have shown signs of fire supports the Nationalist contention that aircraft were not responsible for the burning of the town [Guernica], which was bombed intermittently over a period of three hours.

Holburn's original cablegram is no longer available. But by substituting the word "Durango" for the word "Guernica" as the town bombed and shelled for a week and leaving "Guernica" as the word for the town bombed for three hours, we give a factual accuracy to the telegram. That this version was probably what Holburn actually cabled is supported by the fact that it agrees with the Spanish text published in Buenos Aires on the same day that the two identical articles, with the confused paragraph, were published in London and New York.[100] The explanation is that Holburn's original cablegram may have been badly edited in London.

The cablegram based on Carney's visit to Guernica was shorter than that of Holburn, appeared only in the *New York Times,* and even in that newspaper played a secondary role to the article sent by Holburn, for the latter appeared on page one and Carney's story on page 18. The reason the New York newspaper gave precedence to Holburn's report can probably be found in the fact that Holburn's confirmed the bombing, which was news, and Carney simply repeated what had been already written by others. Carney datelined his dispatch "Guernica, May 4." It read:

This writer found most of the destruction here could have been the result
of fires and dynamitings, as the Nationalists claim, because the roofless shells
of many buildings are still standing and huge shells dropped from planes do
not hollow out buildings, leaving their four walls standing.

In the streets, where most of the damage was done, particularly around
two big arms factories, the Talleres de Guernica and the Esperanza Works,
there are no bomb holes in the streets. It is not likely that bombs dropped in
the air raid would all land atop houses or buildings and none fall in the
streets. In many respects Guernica presents the same picture of desolation
that can be seen at Irún and Eibar and in part of Málaga where destruction
by incendiary mobs before these cities were abandoned never has been
questioned.[101]

The significant part of this article is in the first paragraph, because it reveals a
"technical" argument that we shall encounter time and again in studying the
controversy that was to follow immediately after the dispatches of the correspondents who visited Guernica with the Nationalists. Despite the fact that the writer
thought that Guernica had been, at least partly, destroyed by "fires," his reference
to destruction from the air is limited to "huge shells dropped from planes." Carney
had seen them in Madrid.

The destructive power of 400- and 500-pound bombs dropped by the trimotored Insurgent planes almost defies description. When the bombs strike
the earth great thick clouds of yellow, black and red smoke mixed with
stones and brick dust rise several hundred feet. Eights and ten story buildings
are partly or wholly levelled.[102]

The buildings he saw in ruins in Guernica had not all been "levelled," but he did
not ask himself the question whether or not a two-pound incendiary bomb would
"level" a building or simply burn it down.

"Jean Dourec" published an article about the destruction of Guernica in
L'Action Française the day after the royalist newspaper had published the Havas
dispatch of Georges Botto. Dourec said he entered Guernica with the Nationalist
troops and found the town in still-smoking ruins.

Here, all the houses, all the buildings, emptied of their contents, eaten by the
fire, present an aspect of death which testifies to the systematic doggedness in
the art of destruction of which the Reds are past masters. The sacking of the
town by its "own defenders" was followed by dousing all the buildings with
kerosene or gasoline and the use of incendiary bombs, and completed by the
technique of the Asturian dynamiters whom Bilbao called to its aid. These
vandals stuffed the sewers with dynamite and, before taking flight, blew up
everything still standing.[103]

Héricourt published his articles around the middle of May.[104] It is not clear
when Cardozo visited the town, but his report on Guernica appeared only later in

book form.[105] Charles Foltz, Jr., did not record his impressions of Guernica until 1948.[106] Miss Cowles visited Guernica in August 1937, and wrote of her experiences later in that year.[107] All these stories will be considered elsewhere, leaving this chapter reserved for the reports that appeared in print immediately after the capture of the town and that served to fuel the already simmering controversy.

These reports sent through the Spanish Nationalist censorship simply cannot all be true. They contradict one another. Holburn confirmed the bombing; even Massot, in his first version, affirmed the bombing. Others like Botto, Dourec, and Massot (version three) found that gasoline had been used to start the fires. If Sandro Sandri's article is true, then all the others are false. If Massot's third account is true, then all the others, including Massot's first two, are false. One can conclude that the Nationalist authorities, were they charged with controlling information for the Spanish press and radio or for the foreign media, were in the grip of a great bewilderment, that they were too nervous to establish a reasonable account of what had happened at Guernica. There was, however, one element that persisted throughout these reports, a silence concerning the dead of Guernica.

Among all these correspondents, there was only one who saw Guernica under Nationalist auspices and who wrote almost immediately of what he saw, under no direct control of the Insurgent press officers and without passing through any censorship: this was Georges Berniard.[108] He wrote that Guernica had been "frightfully mutilated" by bombing. His protector and host of those days, Georges Botto, had denied the bombing a day or two earlier. Berniard suggested arson of the last hour carried out by "anarchists." Botto threw all the responsibility onto the "Reds" and on gasoline. The two men certainly talked about Guernica while Berniard was confined in Botto's apartment in Vitoria, and after Botto's return from making his second visit to the ruins. Botto had rendered service to Berniard; yet the reporter from Bordeaux was in effect calling his benefactor a liar. This striking contradiction passed unperceived, at least in the Paris offices of the Havas Agency.

BOOK II

•

Part One

•

THE CONTROVERSY
DURING THE
SPANISH CIVIL WAR

1

The Public Controversy in England and the United States

As the war correspondents with Mola's army abandoned Guernica for fresher sources of news, the ruined Basque town became the center of a heated controversy. The dispute raged almost everywhere in the West, where debate was permitted, but its center was in England, with a spillover into the United States and France. The controversy in England and the United States involved, on the one side, the Catholic Church and its conservative allies against the liberals, and the left; in France, the quarrel split the already-weakened Catholic front.

It is perhaps incorrect to call this difference of opinion a controversy or a dispute, for the normal rules of debating were not used. Most of what was said about Guernica in England, the United States, and France after the first month of charge and countercharge came from the partisans of the Rebel side. The Republican position was stated once and for all time by the foreign correspondents in Bilbao and by the Basque government during the first days following the destruction of Guernica. This position did not vary in the days or months or years that followed. It was the Nationalist arguments that were constantly changing. New evidence was presented and new discussions were advanced; a few weeks or months later, these arguments were changed for newer evidence and newer discussions. At times there was a pro-Republican rebuttal, but this rebuttal was always a reaffirmation of the original charges.

The controversy was naturally most virulent in England, where public opinion was from the first most affected by the story of Guernica. The English reaction to the disaster threw the friends of Franco in England into disarray, much in the manner the news of Guernica had acted upon the press and censorship officers in Salamanca. Much later, an English professor, an intellectual sympathizer with the Nationalists, E. Allison Peers, wrote that

> what happened there [at Guernica] or was alleged to have happened, aroused storms of protest in left-wing, and in many neutral, circles; in Great Britain, skillfully exploited by propagandists, it probably did the Nationalists more harm than any other single event of the war.[1]

The reaction of Franco's friends, in the opinion of one of the leading witnesses and the correspondent who bore the brunt of the attack, George Lowther Steer, constituted "some of the most horrible and inconsistent lying heard by Christian ears since Ananais."[2]

Hardly had the fires died down in Guernica before the campaign began. Its visible commander was Douglas Jerrold, an active Catholic editor and publisher, but behind Jerrold was the marquis del Moral,[3] a Britisher by birth with a Spanish title, who had collaborated with Jerrold and Bolín in the 1933 anti-Republican book *The Spanish Republic.*[4] The marquis del Moral, Frederick Ramón de Bertodano y Wilson, was apparently born in Australia but acquired Spanish nationality in 1928. He had served in the British army, including service in the Boer War and in World War I.[5] He was active in pro-Franco propaganda in England from the first day of the rebellion. On August 30, 1936, he sent a handwritten letter to H. J. Seymour in the Foreign Office, enclosing photocopies of what he called "certain secret reports and orders of the Socialist-Communist Headquarters in Spain for the rising projected between 3 May and 29 June but postponed."[6] These "documents" were pronounced forgeries by the Foreign Office.[7] There are indications that the documents may have been given to del Moral by Arthur Loveday, a former president of the British Chamber of Commerce in Barcelona.[8] Del Moral's communication to the Foreign Office marked the first appearance on the English scene, or, insofar as is now known, anywhere outside Spain, of these documents, which were certainly spurious in the sense that they were not at all what del Moral pretended.[9] These documents, or variations of them, were subsequently reprinted in a number of other publications in France, in the United States, in Germany, and elsewhere.[10] The photocopies that were given to the Foreign Office on August 30, 1936, are identical in every detail with the photocopies published in 1937 by the Nazi-controlled Anti-Komintern in Berlin in the publication entitled *Das Rotbuch über Spanien.*[11] It can, therefore, be stated either that del Moral gave the copies to the Anti-Komintern, that he received them from the Anti-Komintern, or that both he and the Anti-Komintern received them from a common source. Del Moral was also in all probability the author of the "Historical Note" published in the Nationalist propaganda booklet *A Preliminary Official Report on the Atrocities Committed in Southern Spain in July and August, 1936, by the Communist Forces of the Madrid Government.* If this authorship is admitted, then del Moral was the man who received the aviation correspondent Nigel Tangye at Spanish Nationalist head-quarters in London in December 1936, just before Tangye left for Spain.[12] He was also sufficiently active behind the scenes of English parliamentary politics a few days before the destruction of Guernica to have recommended, in a letter addressed to Lord Howard of Penrith a change in Tory tactics concerning Spain.[13]

Also busy in the campaign was Brigadier-General Sir Henry Page Croft,[14] a Tory Member of Parliament and a strong Franco partisan.[15] One of the first moves was to have the marquis del Moral go to Spain,[16] talk with Franco about English reaction to the Guernica bombing, visit Guernica, and return ready to defend the Nationalist position. Before he left on his mission on May 8,[17] del Moral was briefed by Sir Henry,[18] and the marquis' subsequent arguments followed in great part what Croft later claimed as his own immediate analysis of the Guernica incident.

In Spain del Moral had "a long interview" with Franco,[19] who gave him "special permission to make this investigation [about Guernica]."[20] It is more than probable that del Moral saw his friend Luis Bolín at the time of this visit, although he did not mention seeing the head of the Salamanca Press Office, nor did Bolín, writing later of the war, mention seeing del Moral during the conflict.[21]

The marquis lost no time when he came back from Spain on May 22. On May 25 he told the Portuguese ambassador in London, Armindo Monteiro, that he had

> insisted with Franco that he issue a new declaration about the bombing of Guernica, which continued to make a great impression on British opinion, and asked that he consent to an enquiry, for this was the opinion of the English friends of Franco. Franco promised to renew the previous statements, however, under other forms. . . . Del Moral insisted strongly with Franco that he should present himself as a humanitarian general, avoiding the destruction of cities. Franco replied that he would do what he could, but unfortunately the Reds fortified themselves in the cities and he could not leave behind him or on his flanks towns occupied by the enemy.

Del Moral also explained to Monteiro what had happened in Guernica. The envoy wrote to Lisbon that the marquis had,

> after visiting Guernica, the firm conviction that the town was not destroyed by airplanes, but by the same hand and by the same process used in Irún.[22]

On May 26 the marquis addressed a select group of Parliament Members in a private gathering in a House of Commons committee room, presided over by Sir Henry Page Croft, on the subject of Spain in general and of Guernica in particular.[23] Essentially, the marquis' argument was based on "technical" considerations. He admitted that Elgueta and Durango were heavily bombed, but he also noted they had not burned. On the other hand, Eibar,

> after some previous bombing and shelling . . . was evacuated by the Red forces [who] burnt and destroyed almost every building in the town. . . . The

fire spread with great rapidity owing to the method adopted and a strong wind.[24]

Guernica, the marquis asserted,

> had during several days preceding the 26th April been bombed and shelled as it was a military objective and the few bomb holes visible were mostly to be seen at the outskirts of the town near the roads.[25]

This last sentence is of interest, for it is the first time, to our knowledge, that anyone involved in the Guernica controversy reported that the town had ever been shelled and bombed before April 26. However, del Moral insisted, these bombings and shellings had not destroyed the town. The destruction happened in this way:

> Most of the population had been evacuated by the Reds to Bilbao, but some of the civilians who had remained insist that the Reds began destroying the town on the Monday night, the 26th April, by spraying the interiors with petrol and setting these on fire by throwing in hand bombs. There was a strong wind blowing which helped the conflagration.[26]

There are two details of significance here: (1) the town was destroyed after evacuation, and (2) the flames were spread by a strong wind.

The marquis insisted that Guernica was a military objective: it was less than four miles from the fighting line when destroyed; an armament factory was "close to the town"; there were two barracks "in the neighborhood"; Guernica was an "important cross roads"; it was "full of troops." He added that it contained "a number of small houses making arms' components and work was carried on by individual workers outside the main factories as at Eibar."[27] To del Moral's way of thinking, any house in Spain could be a military objective. Del Moral also noted that there were "trenches or defensive positions in the immediate neighborhood," but he did not see them personally.[28]

As all the defenders of the Nationalist position on Guernica were to do after him, the marquis attacked George Steer. He found four reasons to dispute Steer's statement that "Guernica was destroyed by an intense bombardment by Nationalist airplanes with heavy bombs and incendiary bombs," reasons "which in justice cannot be ignored by those who sincerely desire to arrive at the truth." These were, first, that "hardly any pieces of bombs" had been found except by Steer;[29] second, the walls in Guernica "except in two instances" were not marked by shrapnel scars, but in Elgueta and Durango they were; third, several electric light bulbs were still in place, unbroken, in the streets. The marquis' fourth objection was that, given the proportion between open spaces and covered spaces in Guernica, a certain proportion of the bombs must have fallen in the open spaces and "must have left some traces." He did not find these traces, although

> the heat created by an incendiary bomb is so intense that even on the hard road traces are apparent but in a garden or field it is obvious that all

vegetation within a considerable area of the fire must be burnt or scorched to such a degree that the traces would remain for weeks or longer.[30]

The marquis assured his listeners that, contrary to Steer's information, Guernica had never been attacked by incendiary bombs, and was not bombed on April 26, either by explosives or incendiaries.

There had been bombing of Guernica during the week before the destruction of it by the retiring Bilbao Reds. The destruction of Guernica was never committed by General Franco.[31]

The marquis also found that Steer's dispatch had been "contradicted" by that of Holburn, although, as we have seen, the message from Vitoria certainly confirmed the bombing of April 26. He further found "a great deal of nonsense" in Steer's first cablegram on the subject of the nonmilitary importance of Guernica,[32] but he forgot to add that for more than a week every message from Salamanca, approved by his friend Luis Bolín, had repeated this "nonsense." In fact, the analysis of the marquis was a denial of Bolín's initial position and supported the later communiqué of May 2: Guernica was near the battlelines, it was a military objective, and it had been bombed but had not been destroyed by Franco's air force.

But Steer was not the only newspaperman to feel the scorn of del Moral. He charged "the British press [with] hostile and mischief making propaganda." He airily dismissed the reports of Noel Monks. "With regard to the statement by Mr. Noel Monks in the *Daily Express* he [del Moral] has not inclined to accept the fact that he [Monks] saw anything at all."[33] In a later article on Guernica, del Moral discounted all the press reports from Bilbao with these words:

The correspondents were not eye-witnesses, the story was based on vague reports, and the deductions were so erroneous as to indicate a partiality in accord with preconceived desires.[34]

The Anglo-Spanish aristocrat, in the course of questions from the floor, got himself awkwardly boxed into a corner.

Mr. Pilkington . . . thought the Marquis' argument fell into two halves, and he wanted to know which was the stronger. First of all he thought the Marquis put forward evidence to prove that Guernica was not in fact destroyed by Franco and the second part went to prove that the strategic importance of Guernica was sufficient to warrant it having been destroyed.[35]

Some of those present probably asked themselves why, if the destruction was warranted by the laws of war, del Moral did not simply admit the act he so vehemently justified. The lecture and the questions avoided the matter no one cared to bring to the floor: the dead. Del Moral justified the destruction of the town, not the slaughter of the inhabitants. He did attack this problem indirectly by saying that he was told in Guernica that "the statement . . . that the fleeing

population was machine-gunned and numbers killed" was "an absolute
fabrication."[36]

Del Moral concluded:

> With the actual results of destruction before one's eyes there is no other
> conclusion but that Guernica, Eibar and Irún were destroyed in an identical
> manner, viz., by fire from the Red forces.[37]

The joining of the three towns is significant. As has been pointed out earlier, the
destruction of Irún and that of Eibar involved, at least in the controversial phase,
no deliberate loss of human life, whoever was responsible. The marquis del Moral
arranged his story so as to have no victims in Guernica either, for, as he repeated
twice—once in his lecture and once in a reply to a question from Admiral Sir
Murray Sueter—"Most of the inhabitants had been evacuated."[38] Yet since he
insisted so strongly that Franco's air force had destroyed such towns as Elgueta and
Durango, why, except for the loss of human life, unadmitted by Franco's partisans,
was it so important to deny the responsibility for the destruction of a town like
Guernica?

At almost the same time that the marquis del Moral was privately informing
Members of Parliament and ambassadors of his views on the destruction of Guernica, Sir Henry Page Croft told publicly of his opinions about the disaster in the
Basque town in a privately printed pamphlet, published in the provinces. These
opinions now seem based on the information brought back from Spain by the
marquis. Croft had told his "friends" before they left for Spain

> that to have reduced Guernica to ashes from the air in such an incredibly
> short time would have necessitated the use of a vast number of incendiary
> bombs; that it was inevitable under any circumstances and the most perfect
> marksmenship [sic], a very large proportion of such bombs, probably at least
> two or three to one would have fallen on either side of the houses in the
> gardens and on the open spaces.

The evidence brought back by these "friends" was clear

> that no sign of incineration apart from the buildings was evident; that no
> foliage, vegetation or trees were burnt, although some of the latter showed
> splits from some form of explosion, but most remarkable of all, the Town
> Hall with archives and the famous tree . . . went absolutely scatheless from
> any sign of fire in spite of the hail of bombs which it is alleged fell in the
> whole town of which they are the center.

Guernica, Croft went on, "was a legitimate military objective, if it was indeed
bombed, but there was no evidence that it was destroyed by incendiary bombs."[39]

Sir Henry compared the dispatches of the two correspondents of the *Times*. He
could not doubt Steer's "good faith," but he did doubt the correctness of his
"evidence."[40] Anyway, the dispatch of the *Times* man from Vitoria "most cer-

tainly discredits the whole story of his Bilbao colleague and most emphatically gives the verdict of non-proved to the charges of Bilbao." Furthermore, the "friends" of Croft who visited Guernica found evidence to confirm that of the *Times* man in Vitoria, "since examination went to show the houses were ignited from the ground."[41] This is an unjustified interpretation of Holburn's dispatch, and Sir Henry had forgotten or chose to ignore the fact that Holburn had cabled that Guernica was indeed bombed.

There were, however, discrepancies between these two early defenders in England of the Nationalist position. Croft did not admit that Guernica had ever been bombed, whereas the marquis del Moral insisted that the town had been both bombed and shelled before April 26. The Anglo-Spanish nobleman also stated twice that Guernica had been evacuated of most of its inhabitants before the destruction was begun. Croft's viewpoint was different. He likewise avoided any direct reference to the victims of the bombing or burning, but he noted that, according to Steer

> it was market day in Guernica and large numbers of civilians were assembled in the streets—surely a grave dereliction of military duty on the part of the local Basque authorities.[42]

He went on to "discount the suggestion that there was a massacre of vast numbers of civilians from machine gun fire." [43] Steer, Monks, Holme, Corman, and others, after talking with survivors had not "suggested" this detail but had emphasized it.

But neither the confidential reports of the marquis del Moral nor the pamphlet of Sir Henry Page Croft, privately printed in the provinces, could greatly influence the mass of English public opinion. This particular task was entrusted to Douglas Jerrold, a militant Catholic, editor of a well-known publishing house busily engaged in printing pro-Franco propaganda,[44] who had proved his loyalty to the Spanish right by collaborating with Bolín and del Moral in their 1933 attack on the Spanish Republic, and his loyalty to the insurrection by helping Bolín secure the airplane that brought Franco from the Canaries to Morocco.[45] He had visited Nationalist Spain in March 1937, in company with Major Yeats-Brown and General J. F. C. Fuller; they "had received a very friendly welcome from the Generalissimo" and "wherever they went they had been treated with courtesy and friendliness."[46] All three of the travelers later wrote of their visit to the Rebel zone: Fuller in a pamphlet,[47] Yeats-Brown in an article[48] and a book,[49] and Jerrold in an article[50] and in his autobiography, then almost completed.[51]

Jerrold now endeavored to bring to public attention, through articles in the English and American press, the same interpretations of the Guernica disaster as those that del Moral had confided to his select group of parliamentarians on May 27. He began with an article published in the London Catholic weekly the *Tablet* early in June,[52] then revised slightly and printed in the pro-Fascist New York monthly the *American Review* shortly thereafter.[53] The *Tablet* article was commented on editorially in another London weekly, the *Spectator*.[54] Jerrold seized on this opportunity for a "Letter to the Editor"[55] and then another one.[56] Steer, considering himself under assault, then revealed himself to be the author of the unsigned Bilbao dispatches in the *Times* and counterattacked.[57]

Jerrold's position was:

> Guernica was bombed in the proper course of the operations against Bilbao, but it was not bombed on the day that it was burned, and it was burned by the retreating Basque (or more probably by the Asturian) troops and not by the Nationalist forces.

The proof he brought forward was composed of interpretations of the dispatches sent by the foreign correspondents with Mola's army, shored up with attacks against the earlier witnessing of Steer, arguments to justify the bombing of the town, and pontifications on the "technical" points involved, as previously elaborated by Croft and del Moral.

"The correspondents of the Havas agency, of the *Times*, and of several other newspapers" Jerrold wrote,

> have affirmed positively that most of the damage which they saw was wrought not by bombing but by deliberate destruction by fires from the ground. The statements are explicit. There were only a few bomb holes, and the walls of the houses in the quarter most completely destroyed bear no marks of bomb splinters. Nor can the damage done by a bomb and that done by dynamiters and incendiaries be confused by any competent observer.[58]

Jerrold exaggerated the number of correspondents testifying for his side. He never in reality brought forward more than two, both of whom were then unidentified: The *Times* man, now known to have been Holburn, and the Havas representative, now identified as Botto. Jerrold may have been misled by Botto's phraseology; his dispatch sometimes read as if it was the report of a group. Thus, later in one of his letters to the *Spectator*, Jerrold declared, "The full report of these journalists was published in the *Temps*, the *Matin*, and other papers."[59] "These journalists" were simply Botto; the *Temps* and the *Matin* published the same report, that of Havas.

As we have seen, the statement of Holburn was not explicit in the sense indicated by Jerrold, and Botto's dispatch, certainly favorable to the Nationalist arguments, was nevertheless hedged about with precautionary phrases that, if carefully read, diminished its explicitness. Holburn's dispatch not only confirmed the bombing of April 26 but ended with this inconclusive "opinion" of the Nationalist experts: "It will be difficult to establish exactly how the fire started." If Holburn is Jerrold's witness, then Guernica was bombed on April 26, the Havas man was wrong, and Jerrold himself was wrong. Jerrold was simply dishonest in thus interpreting the *Times* dispatch from Vitoria—for he certainly knew how to read, if not to reason. He was further dishonest in hiding from his readers the conclusion of the *Times* concerning its reports on Guernica, expressed in an editorial published the same day as Holburn's dispatch and specifically referring to it. This editorial, a reaction to the German campaign against treatment of the Guernica reports in the *Times*, read as follows in the part concerning Guernica:

> Responsibility for the destruction of Guernica and of some hundreds of its civilian population, has not yet been definitely brought home to anyone. But the truth is beginning to emerge. In an official communique from Salamanca, published in the *Times* yesterday, insurgent headquarters had noticeably shifted their ground. The communiqué dismissed the bombardment as "a comparatively minor event" but it did not repeat General Franco's original assertions that, owing to rain and mist, no Nationalist aircraft left the ground on the Northern Front during the afternoon of the bombardment. It did repeat former denials that the town was even bombed at all; but these can hardly have been meant to be taken seriously. This morning comes a dispatch from our Special Correspondent with the insurgent forces (who, it should be remembered, is working, like all correspondents in Spain, under a political and military censorship) in which he describes a visit to the ravaged town. From his observations it does indeed appear possible that some part of the conflagration after the bombardment may have been the work of incendiaries. But for Nationalist headquarters to contend (to quote this message) that "incendiaries on the Basque side had more to do with razing Guernica than General Franco's aircraft" is a very different matter from protesting that no bombs were dropped at all, and that all General Franco's aircraft were on the ground at the time. Moreover, it is now in fact admitted that the bombers were in action "intermittently over a period of three hours" and this figure corresponds with the original account given by our Special Correspondent in Bilbao, which Berlin describes as a fabrication.[60] Independent reports have also established beyond doubt that the aircraft engaged in bombing and machine-gunning the defenseless inhabitants of Guernica were of German make, and several unexploded incendiary bombs have been recovered bearing the stamp of a German factory. The identity and the nationality of the pilots are not yet known; but they can hardly remain a secret for long.[61]

This editorial, certainly one of the important documents for the dossier of the Guernica controversy, was consistently overlooked not only by Jerrold but also by all the other defenders of the Insurgent position who were to discuss the merits and meanings of Steer's and Holburn's dispatches. It is evident that the opinion of the editors of the *Times* concerning these dispatches was of primary interest, for they knew better than anyone else both men, their methods of work, and the conditions under which they were working. Jerrold's ignorance of the *Times* editorial, or his ignoring of it, was inexcusable.[62]

To bolster his arguments, Jerrold not only quoted untruthfully from the correspondents who wrote of the Guernica catastrophe from the Nationalist side but also denigrated, with false statements, the testimony of Steer. The *Times* man was in Bilbao, Jerrold wrote in the *Tablet,* when "he heard accounts of Guernica" and went there "in the small hours of the following morning."[63] This gives the impression that Steer heard some rumors about the bombing and arrived tardily on the scene. In fact, as already shown, he heard the news as soon as it reached Bilbao, and once it was known the town was in flames he went to Guernica as fast as he could.[64]

Jerrold further argued that Steer was wrong about Guernica for "he was eight and a half miles away from Guernica when he 'saw' the airplanes, and he was certainly in Bilbao when he wrote his dispatch."[65] It is not easy to follow Jerrold's reasoning at this point, but he is wrong to suggest that Steer did not "see" the airplanes on the afternoon of April 26. Steer, as noted earlier, had reported this fact in the *Times* on May 6—that is, some days after the bombing, and perhaps Jerrold felt safe in challenging this statement made after the fact. What Jerrold did not know was that Steer had cabled the news of seeing the airplanes on the afternoon of April 26, immediately after the event, and before knowing about Guernica; the *Times* did not publish the cablegram, but the *New York Times* did. As for the fact that Steer wrote his cablegram in Bilbao and not in Guernica itself, it is difficult to know what canon of journalistic practice he violated. Jerrold seems to believe that a reporter's story must be written at the scene of the crime to be valid. Steer probably took some notes, or he may have been capable of retaining facts in his memory for as long as twenty-four hours. In fact, Jerrold is here demonstrating that he, like many other pro-Franco critics and amateur journalists, knew little or nothing about daily journalism.[66]

Jerrold also deliberately misled his readers about the second visit that Steer made to the burning town, on April 27. In the revised version of his *Tablet* article, published in New York, Jerrold added the observation that the *Times* man in Vitoria, unlike Steer, had "visited Guernica after the destruction."[67] Jerrold repeated this misrepresentation in a letter to the *Spectator* on July 2:

> The *Times* correspondent at Bilbao was in Guernica while the town was burning, and vividly describes the flames and heat. Under the conditions prevailing, it was obviously impossible for him to make a full examination. He had been told in Bilbao that a great air-raid had taken place, and he arrived some hours afterwards, and found the town in flames, and since Guernica has been bombed from time to time in the course of earlier operations, there was no reason for him to doubt the authenticity of the story.[68]

He repeated the same statement in his second letter to the *Spectator,* affirming that he did not doubt Steer's "good faith for a moment, but it is difficult to be satisfied that a hurried visit in the middle of the night to a burning town provided an opportunity for such meticulous examination."[69] Jerrold indulgently excused Steer's understandable mistakes; he did not go so far as to call him a liar, but rather treated him as ingenuous and slightly half-witted. However, Steer had clearly stated in his initial report on Guernica that he had come back to the still burning town on the afternoon of April 27, before writing his cablegram.[70] It is difficult to believe that Jerrold did not know that he was here misrepresenting the facts.

The Catholic editor had the ungrateful task of reconciling contradictory facts. He could not deny that Guernica had been bombed at some time, for the Nationalist communiqué of May 3 and Holburn's dispatch, both passed by the Salamanca censorship, were there to confound him. He therefore had to twist the *Times* dispatch and interpret the Rebel communiqué so as to predate the bombings, place them before April 26. He had to insist that Guernica "had been bombed intermittently for several days before it was given up,"[71] but that "it was not bombed on the day that it was burned."[72] There were witnesses other than the foreign correspondents to upset Jerrold's story. "The sorely tried inhabitants of Guernica," he declared, were victims

> of war hysteria. . . . Hearing the explosions and seeing the smoke and flames that accompanied the burning of the town [they] assumed that it had been bombed that day as it had on previous occasions.[73]

Another of Jerrold's problems was to justify these "previous" and "intermittent" bombings carried out "in the proper course of the operations against Bilbao." Guernica, he asserted, "is a strategic position of considerable importance." It "is the center of an important part of the Basque small-arms industry," he wrote, and then stated that it was "a matter of established fact" that Guernica "is surrounded by small arms factories." Furthermore, the mayor of Guernica himself had said the town "was full of troops when it was bombed."[74] Of these arguments, only one was true: Guernica was a strategic position "of considerable importance." But it was not a really important arms-manufacturing center, as was Eibar.[75] Nor did the mayor say that the town was "full of troops when it was bombed." He merely stated that there were "militia in Guernica."[76] There were, as Jerrold insisted, military objectives in and around Guernica—the two small factories mentioned, the highways, the railroad tracks, even the militia barracks—and an attack on them could be justified. But if these were attacked, they were not hit (with the exception of part of the railway station[77] and the wounded in a military hospital),[78] and one can wonder, in view of the poverty of the military objectives actually damaged when compared with the wealth of the projectiles dropped, if the bombardment really sought to attain any of them.

Jerrold sought to uphold his theses by recourse to arguments of a "technical" nature, in general, arguments already advanced before smaller audiences by del Moral.

> I have seen the destruction at Irún, which was admittedly wrought by the same army, under the same leadership, as that which was defending Guernica

he wrote early in June,

> a complete street—the principal street of the town—systematically destroyed, house by house, with only the walls left standing, and the interiors completely gutted by fire. A rain of bombs might, in loose journalistic parlance, "destroy" a whole street in a town, but it would not destroy it *in that way*.

At Guernica, as at Irún, there is hardly a mark in the street. A "rain of bombs" would fall as often in the streets as on the houses and gardens and must leave traces which could not possibly be obliterated. The roadway would be destroyed; the flowers would be withered. . . . People who talk about destruction from the air have no idea of the local effect of a bomb. I have seen, at Málaga and elsewhere, the effect of bombs on a score of houses. A bomb falling from a height will tear its way through a house and explode, leaving half the house standing. That part of the house which it hits, however, will be totally destroyed; the burst will be outward as well as upward and the outside walls will never be left intact. . . .[79]

Jerrold also averred that

to destroy an entire small town . . . not hundreds, but thousands of bombs would be required. The resources for such wholesale destruction are entirely lacking to either side in this war. . . . Such destruction would mean using a month's supply of ammunition for General Franco's entire army, and denuding all fronts of air protection to indulge in an orgy of lunatic folly.[80]

There is an unreal quality to this first article by Jerrold concerning Guernica, for nowhere therein does he mention incendiary bombs; he presents incendiarism from the ground as the sole possible explanation of the fires.

In his first letter to the *Spectator* on the subject of Guernica, Jerrold did not hesitate to use both Holburn and Botto as witnesses for his "technical" interpretations of the causes of the tragedy, attributing to them assertions they never made.

The results of this examination [made by] all the correspondents accompanying the Nationalistic forces . . . reveal an absence of all traces of bombs, whether explosive or incendiary, in the streets and gardens of the town, and also the absence of all damage to grass or flowers, where either exists, in the neighborhood of burnt-out houses.

He considered "these facts . . . plainly and totally inconsistent with the destruction of the town, either by explosive or incendiary bombs." He added:

A third equally plain inconsistency is the survival unbroken of some of the street lamps within a few yards of houses which were alleged to have been destroyed by bombs.[81]

Whatever one may think of the unsupported affirmation of Jerrold that certain "facts" were "inconsistent with the destruction of the town either by explosive or incendiary bombs," it is important to note that, contrary to Jerrold's statement, these "facts" can be found nowhere in the dispatches either of the *Times* man or of the Havas man in Vitoria; they come straight from the confidential talk given by the Marquis del Moral on May 27. The marquis had visited Guernica during the week of May 16-22[82]—that is around three weeks after the destruction of the town. Vegetation in the rainy Basque country could greatly change in the course of three spring weeks.

A few weeks later Jerrold returned to the charge, and again repeated the "technical" arguments of del Moral and Croft and declared that "this material evidence is not consistent with the attribution of the bulk of the damage to the effects of air bombardment." [83] It was, he asserted,

conclusive, not as evidence that Guernica was never bombed, but as evidence that the destruction by fire of the whole town was the work of some other agency. Had there been nothing to guide us as to the nature of that agency, it would remain a mystery, but as Irún and Eibar were admittedly [84] destroyed by incendiaries serving the Basque government . . . there is no mystery at all. The only mystery that exists is the conflict of testimony as to whether some bombs were dropped on Guernica not only prior to the day of its destruction, but on the day of its destruction. I gave my view that this was a case of war hysteria, that the sorely tried inhabitants of Guernica and the neighborhood, hearing the explosions and seeing the smoke and flames that accompanied the burning of the town, assumed that it had been bombed that day as it had on previous occasions.[85]

Jerrold took pride in his "technical" judgments, and again associated them with the conclusions he attributed to Botto and Holburn.

I repeat, however, that the main issue concerns the complete and deliberate destruction of Guernica by fire. . . . That issue must be decided by the technical considerations which I have mentioned, and it was these technical considerations, of course, which led the journalists who entered Guernica with General Franco's forces to the unanimous conclusion that the burning was the work of Basque incendiaries.[86]

The weakness of Jerrold's position is obvious. It falls to pieces if it could be proved that Guernica was bombed on April 26 and not ever bombed before that date. It is curious that he worked himself out on such a limb, for if he had read Holburn's dispatch carefully, he could have seen that the *Times* man, his own witness, contradicted him.

These newspaper dispatches meant certain things to Jerrold and the friends of Nationalist Spain and other things to their adversaries. Holburn wrote that in Guernica "the distinctive marks of an aerial bombardment are not numerous." He observed that

in Durango explosions blew great pieces of the walls of buildings out into the streets, exposing the interior of houses, and outside walls were indented by flying fragments of shells and bombs—there are pieces of shells and bombs to be found among the wreckage and in the streets, while in the main square are bombholes full of muddy water. In Guernica, on the other hand, few fragments of bombs have been recovered, the facades of buildings still standing are unmarked.[87]

The Havas report contained the same description

that all the walls still standing bear no traces of bomb splinters and that, on the contrary, all the windows are girdled by signs of flames. The beams of the houses are just finishing burning, three days after the occupation.[88]

These are observations with which no one could quarrel.[89] The quarrel lay in the meaning of these observations. The difference between the destruction of Durango and that of Guernica was visible, and can today be strikingly confirmed by looking at the photographs in two brochures published in Bilbao immediately after each attack.[90] The photographs in the Durango pamphlet show wood everywhere but not a charred stick. In Guernica the wood was consumed by the flames. Durango was hit by explosive bombs, by artillery, but never by incendiary bombs. If Guernica had been hit by both types of bombs, would not its aspect have logically been radically different from that of Durango? Could not this difference have argued in favor of the incendiary bomb attack as much as it argued, in Jerrold's opinion, against an explosive bomb raid? What did it signify if but "few fragments of bombs" had been discovered? And who really knew how many had in fact been discovered? Fragments of which type of bombs? Steer had written that the planes dropped "bombs weighing from 1000 lbs. downwards and, it is calculated, more than 3000 two-pounder aluminum incendiary projectiles."[91] The two-pound aluminum incendiary bomb did not "tear its way through a house." If it fell on the roof or balcony of a house, it could set it on fire, and frequently did. Did this type of bomb leave "traces of bomb splinters"? Or were such bombs consumed in the flames? What were "the distinctive marks of an aerial bombardment" of a town, carried out in great part by incendiary bombs? No correspondent with Mola's army knew for sure, for he had never seen a bombardment such as the one that, according to the correspondents at Bilbao, destroyed Guernica, unless it was the one at Eibar.

But just as there were differences between the aspects of ruined Durango and ruined Guernica, so were there differences in the reports of the destruction of the two towns of Irún and Eibar and in the reports of the destruction of Guernica. In the latter case, according to the messages from Bilbao, which Jerrold was assiduously attacking, there had been many dead. But nowhere in his writings on Guernica did he mention a single corpse.

Before Jerrold had written his second letter to the *Spectator,* another correspondent who had been with the Nationalists near the Basque front while Guernica was being destroyed, Cecil Gerahty,[92] of the *Daily Mail,* came forward with his testimony. Gerahty had come back from Spain early in May, and had called in at the Foreign Office on May 10, where he was received by Donald Maclean. Gerahty told Maclean that he had been in Marquina, ". . . about 7 or 8 miles from Guernica on the day of the destruction, and was out in the open during the afternoon hours when the bombing is alleged to have taken place." He "neither heard nor felt any bombardment," and believed "from his previous experience" that this was "at least one proof that Guernica was not bombarded on the day in question." Gerahty had brought with him "photographs taken on that day showing extremely misty weather conditions which in his opinion would have prevented any air activity."

Maclean's report continued:

> He then went on to say that the only rebel air bases from which Guernica could have been bombed are Burgos, where the bombers are kept, and Vitoria where the fighters are stationed. At his position at Marquina he would have been bound to have heard them passing over on their way to attack Guernica or on their return journey; he in fact heard nothing. He added that he went to Burgos the next day and saw the bombers still in the same position as he had seen them on the [day] previous to the raid. He was told by acquaintances that the machines had not been able to go up the previous day owing to the bad weather.[93]

This could have been an interesting meeting. Gerahty was "an Irish Catholic who had worked for the *Daily Mail*," and the man who sent him to the Foreign Office thought him "an extremely capable person."[94] Gerahty had been in Spain collecting material for a book on the war, then on the point of appearing.[95] Gerahty was, in Maclean's opinion "obviously committed to the Rebels," and from his talk with him, the Foreign Office man concluded "that he had very good connections with the Insurgents and apparently had direct access to General Franco." Gerahty told Maclean that "he had had a hand in bringing about the recent reorganization of the Salamanca Propaganda Bureau."[96] Maclean was a Soviet sympathizer and later a Soviet spy,[97] yet he wrote, "I do not think that there is any reason to doubt his [Gerahty's] sincerity" about Guernica. The interview cast no credit on Gerahty's capacity as a war front observer or on Maclean's ability as a questioner or an interpreter of answers.

Gerahty's first book on the Spanish Civil War came out in June 1937, and in it he repeated what he had told Maclean about Guernica.[98] Jerrold announced in his second letter to the *Spectator:*

> Mr. Gerahty states that he was in the neighborhood of Guernica on the day when the alleged bombing took place, that he was in a position to see any bombing that had taken place, and that none took place. He is the only Englishman as far as I know, who is in a position to see the bombing that had taken place and he did not see it. [Steer] does not claim to have been any eye-witness of the bombing, but only of its effects. I therefore regard Mr. Gerahty's explicit statements as very strong evidence in support of the view which I have put forward as to the value of the testimony of certain other alleged eye-witnesses.[99]

A copy of the *Spectator* with Jerrold's second letter, in which Steer was obviously attacked, though not by name, fell into Steer's hands, and he revealed himself as the author of the famous dispatch—a fact already known to the readers of the *New York Times,* and doubtless to many persons in England as well. In a reply to Jerrold, published in the *Spectator,* Steer wrote that Jerrold's letter "throws such doubt on my professional competence . . . I feel I must abandon anonymity and warn the author off course."[100]

This polemical letter constitutes an important addendum to Steer's account of the tragedy, and it will be quoted at some length. First, Steer challenged Jerrold's version of the circumstances of his visit to the burning town.

> I did not, as Mr. D. Jerrold alleges, pay a "hurried visit" to Gernika. I was walking in and around Gernika between 11 P.M. and 1 A.M. in the evening of April 26th-27th carrying out the careful enquiries which the situation demanded. In order to make absolutely certain of the facts, I chose not to hurry back to Bilbao and send a story that evening, but to wait until the next afternoon. By that time I had questioned about 20 of the homeless people in Gernika itself, and 80 more in Bilbao next morning. They showed no signs of war-hysteria.[101]

Steer then went into a discussion of the facts, of what he had seen in Guernica, and disputed the "technical" evidence presented by Jerrold. During the two hours he spent in Guernica during the night of April 26, he said, he

> had and used the opportunity for the "meticulous examination" of the new bombholes there. It is not true, as Mr. D. Jerrold states, that there were none in open spaces in Gernika. I saw there immense bombholes in the open space immediately east of the Casa de Juntas; about 40 feet wide and 20 deep, they were of precisely the same kind as that in which I and other correspondents sheltered that afternoon in the village of Arbacegui-Gerrikaiz. The metal fragments were exactly the same type. The bombholes were bombholes, not shellholes. As for the idiotic story about mines, what retreating army in the world mines and destroys roads 15 miles behind the furthest point of its retreat, on the only line of communications with its base, and lays the mines so badly that they go off in the middle of a public square?[102] For the whole assumption at the back of Mr. Jerrold's argument is false. There were *no departing troops going through Gernika on April 26th: the Basque army did not fall back on Gernika until two days later.*[103]

Steer continued to attack the "technical" support for Jerrold's theses:

> As for the gardens in which D. Jerrold will find bombholes, I suggest that he should visit the Hospital on the left of the main road going out of Gernika to Bermeo, opposite the main garage of the town. And the now tumbled buildings of Gernika were plastered with bombholes, including the school buildings and the two churches of Andra Mari and San Juan, when I visited the town. I do not think that either Mr. Jerrold or myself can deny that Gernika was burnt to the ground in a very thorough way. If therefore grass and flowers are, as he alleges, in fine condition, it does not seem to affect the argument in either sense. I may add, however, that the two-pounder thermite bomb dropped in enormous quantities on Gernika does not normally burn vegetation; if it falls on open ground it penetrates up to the fin, and there are no signs of burning on grass, for instance, but a narrow ring of grey ash around the projectile.

Steer also refuted Jerrold's presumption that Guernica had been bombed before April 26, saying that "so far as I know no such claim has ever been made by either side," and concluding:

> The story of earlier bombing was only invented after April 26th as a final line of defense against overwhelming evidence that Gernika had in fact been bombarded.104

Steer then proceeded to analyze the testimony of Gerahty, advanced by Jerrold. Gerahty was in fact calling his colleague a liar. He had written in his book that

> on my return to England I found the papers full of descriptions of Guernica having been bombed to destruction on that very afternoon, the action being described as a crime. Actually, the weather prevented the planes from flying. At the exact hours indicated as being those of the bombardment I was at Marquina, only a few miles from Guernica and where the alleged bombing could easily have been heard had it taken place.105

Steer tore apart the testimony of Cecil Gerahty:

> Finally, after Mr. Jerrold's long distance demolition of "alleged eye-witnesses" such as myself . . . may I be permitted to analyze Mr. Jerrold's fabrication of an eye-witness to his own argument? He cites Mr. Gerahty, author of *The Road to Madrid,* to clinch the matter, but I fear that Mr. Jerrold is incapable of reading black and white. Or perhaps he is over-eager.
> 1) On p. 233 of *The Road to Madrid* Mr. Gerahty leaves Salamanca on a Sunday morning (April 25th) and p. 234, rests the night at Vitoria. P. 234, "Next day," April 26th, he was "unable to visit the Front as rapid movements were going on," and "had to content himself with making closer acquaintance" of Vitoria. He was "not able entirely to forget the war, as a fleet of fifteen bombing planes on their way to attack the enemy . . . passed over the town"; p. 235, "Next morning" Tuesday April 27th., Mr. Gerahty was able to leave Vitoria and visit the Front.
> In other words, Mr. Gerahty was at Vitoria the day Gernika was bombed, 40 miles away across mountains, and he saw the planes flying there. So much for Mr. Gerahty's claims to be an eye-witness of no bombardment.
> 2) Nor does Mr. Gerahty say, as Mr. Jerrold alleges, that he was "in a position to see the bombardment." On p. 242, he says that on Tuesday, April 27th., he was at Marquina "where the alleged bombing could easily have been *heard* had it taken place." As a noisy battleline on April 27th lay between Markina and Gernika, this statement is, to say the least, meaningless; but in consideration of the fact that Gernika was bombed twenty-four hours before, we can let Mr. Gerahty step off the witness-stand with the modest suggestion that, as a correspondent, he should in future be quicker on his own stories. As for Mr. Jerrold, lessons in reading and basic chronology are indicated.106

It might be hoped that this crushing riposte would have brought Jerrold to reflection, but there is no evidence to support the wish. In 1941, when England itself had been, and was being, bombed by some of the same German aviators who had devastated the Basque country, Jerrold could show only that the English friends of Franco had learned nothing during the four years since the destruction of Guernica. He wrote:

> It is nevertheless to be hoped that the Press, which, however innocently, misled the public so grossly over the facts of the Spanish civil war, has learnt its lesson. There is only one weapon against propaganda, and that is ruthless, independent investigation by trained observers. It is necessary to say that the majority of the correspondents sent to Spain were not trained observers. Very few of them knew Spanish. Almost none had any experience of war and none except Harold Cardozo, H. R. Knickerbocker and Carl von Weygend [sic] had any prolonged experience of European politics from the inside.[107]

Jerrold's paragraph reveals a profound ignorance of the journalism of the Spanish Civil War. He did leave Gerahty out of his honors list, but the three men he picked for distinction worked either for Rothermere (Cardozo) or Hearst (Knickerbocker, von Wiegand)—that is, they represented the most sensational and superficial newspapers of the Anglo-American press. Of course, this press was politically reactionary and favorable to Franco, but it is nevertheless strange that the director of a publishing house should have such low taste in journalism.

Steer's explanations had no effect on Jerrold's friends. Arthur Bryant, who had already shown his colors by writing the preface to *The Second and Third Reports on Communist Atrocities* for Jerrold's publishing house, pronounced an opinion on Guernica similar to that of Jerrold. He admitted that the town had been bombed by Nationalist planes, but he added that the town "was subsequently dynamited and fired like many other Spanish towns and villages by the Communist miners from Asturias before they retreated." Moreover, Guernica was clearly a military objective, and the bombing of the town was no more an atrocity than had been the aerial bombing of German towns by the English during the World War I.[108]

Arnold Lunn immediately quoted at length what he called Jerrold's "analysis" of "the legend of Guernica."[109] And thirty years later, Bolín quoted Lunn's quotations from Jerrold, who, he wrote, is "gifted with the technique of sifting evidence" and whose discussion of the "Guernica myth" he called a "scholarly analysis."[110]

Other correspondents hastened to participate in the controversy over Guernica, among them, Harold G. Cardozo, of the *Daily Mail*, who had covered the Spanish Civil War with the Rebel forces from the beginning. He and his newspaper were frantically pro-Nationalist.[111] Cardozo was not among those who went into Guernica when it fell on April 29, nor apparently did he make the organized visit of May 1, but he did go into the town shortly after its capture, at an unspecified date,[112] as he recounted in his book published in 1937. From the first he held strong opinions concerning the Guernica incident. Peter Kemp, an English volunteer with the Franco forces, who knew Cardozo in Spain in May 1937, wrote twenty years later that the *Daily Mail* man was "indignant" at the British reaction to "the story . . . that Guernica, an open town, was destroyed by incendiary bombs dropped by Nationalist aircraft."[113]

Like Jerrold before him, Cardozo admitted that Guernica had been bombed, but he strongly denied that the bombing had caused the burning. "Certainly Guernica had been bombed by Nationalist planes, and many of these were presumably of German or Italian origin and had, perhaps, German or Italian pilots."[114] But, he insisted, "the so-called bombardment" took place the day "when certainly the city was burnt."[115]

The *Daily Mail* correspondent sought to substantiate his arguments with the hearsay testimony of his colleagues in the Nationalist zone and by slighting references to Steer and others who were in Bilbao with the Basques.[116]

> I can record what I actually saw myself and what I heard from British and French correspondents who entered the town before me. First of all, none of them saw the number of dead who would have been lying in the streets and in the highways leading to the town had even one-tenth of the stories told been true. Yet the Nationalists had had no time to fake the situation. The correspondents entered Guernica within a few hours of the first Nationalist patrols. So the hundreds of persons shot down by the machine-gunning planes or killed by the bombing had all disappeared.[117]

The reasoning here is unconvincing. It would seem probable that the strongly Catholic Basques had had time between April 27 and 29 at least to remove the corpses of their dead from the highways. The detailed visits to Guernica made by the correspondents did not take place until May 1—that is forty-eight hours after the Nationalist entry. Certainly during that time the Nationalists did have time to "fake" the situation, if only to fill in bomb holes.

Cardozo added to the information he said he had received from his colleagues some observations of his own, all seemingly intended to show that there was no connection between the bombing and the burning.

> At Guernica [sic] there were bombed houses, crumpled up and in ruins, but they were unscathed by fire. At Guernica there were houses burnt out, their blackened facades outlined against the sky, but they were not pitted by bomb fragments, and the roadway showed no scars. I examined several buildings with great care to establish in my own opinion beyond doubt, as far as this could be possible, the origin of the separate fires which undoubtedly ravaged Guernica and burnt down more than three-quarters of the town. As a result I can state that it seemed to me—I am not an expert—that undoubtedly the fires were entirely apart from the destruction caused by air bombs.

Cardozo does admit that it had been charged that Guernica was hit by incendiary bombs "with slight explosive force. But," he wrote,

> I could not see in these burned-out streets of Guernica a single sign of an incendiary bomb having burst outside the burnt-out houses. None of them had burst in gardens or in the road.[118]

But did the small incendiary bombs "burst" when they fell? Did they leave indelible traces when they landed in a garden or on a highway? Obviously, if Cardozo had seen Steer's reply to Jerrold in the *Spectator,* it had had no effect on his thinking.

Cardozo belittled the dispatches of "the alleged eye-witnesses," who, he said, ". . . were all brought up later, mostly at night, when the city was burning, and were told what had taken place." This is not a loyal account of what had happened at Bilbao and Guernica on the night of April 26-27. All four of the foreign correspondents in Bilbao had seen the airplanes on their way to Guernica on the afternoon of April 26. They went on their own accord to see Guernica in flames—reporters seeking news. "Convenient witnesses were brought forward to confirm these stories," wrote Cardozo, [119] but the dispatches from Bilbao indicate that the pressmen were free to interview anyone they found at hand, in Guernica or in Bilbao. Certainly they interviewed more people of Guernica within forty-eight hours of the disaster then did all the newspapermen and officials who came in later with Franco's army.

Cardozo concluded his comments, with more passion than reason, by writing that Guernica was set on fire

> outside of any pretense of military necessity, by Communists or Anarchists enraged at having to abandon [it] to a hated foe. All else is untrue, all else is the fabrication of a system of propaganda which has lived on lies.[120]

At almost the same time that Cardozo's book was published, the *Sunday Times* printed an unsigned article that dealt in part with Guernica. This article was in reality written by Virginia Cowles, who had visited Guernica in August 1937, in the company of the press officer Captain Rosales, who evidently believed that Guernica had never been bombed. The *Sunday Times* article said:

> We arrived in Guernica to find it a lonely chaos of timber and brick. . . . One old man was standing inside an apartment house that had four sides to it but an interior that was only a sea of bricks. . . . I went up to him and asked if he had been in the town during the destruction. He nodded his head and, when I asked what had happened, waved his arm in the air and declared that the sky had been black with planes. *"Aviones,"* he said: *"Italianos y alemanes."* Rosalles was astonished. "Guernica was burned," he contradicted heatedly. The old man, however, stuck to his point, insisting that after a four-hour bombardment there was little left to burn. Rosalles moved me away. "He's a Red," he explained indignantly.[121]

Later that day, Cowles and the press officer reached fallen Santander.

> Rosalles described our drive along the coast and told them of the incident at Guernica. "The town was full of Reds," he said. "They tried to tell us it was bombed, not burned." The tall staff officer replied: "But, of course, it was bombed. We bombed it and bombed it and bombed it, and *bueno,* why not?"

Rosalles looked astonished, and when we were back in the car again, heading for Bilbao, he said: "I don't think I would write about that if I were you!"[122]

This article was immediately reprinted as part of the controversy,[123] but it was not until 1941, when Cowles republished the article in her book *Looking for Trouble,* that the author could be identified.[124]

Another correspondent who defended the Nationalist position on Guernica was the American Associated Press reporter H. Edward Knoblaugh. He never worked on the Rebel side; he was head of the AP office in Madrid when the civil war broke out and left in 1937 after numerous disputes with the Republican authorities.[125] Like Jerrold and Cardozo, Knoblaugh admitted that Guernica had been bombed, but he denied that the principal damage came from the bombardment. He justified the air attack because Guernica "had an arms factory," and "was used as a Loyalist military base," and was "in the path of Franco's march on Bilbao." He considered the uproar over the destruction of the town totally unjustified, and wrote that the air raid constituted "one of the most fortunate bits of material for the propaganda machine." He added that the bombing of Guernica

> aroused such a wave of indignation abroad that not even the joint statement of disinterested correspondents, testifying that the principal damage had been caused by Anarchist incendiaries and Asturian dynamiters before they evacuated Guernica, carried much weight.[126]

This "joint statement" never existed and was probably a false interpretation of Botto's Havas dispatch. Certainly no single dispatch ever filled Knoblaugh's specifications, and none of his colleagues of the Associated Press with Mola's troops ever cabled a dispatch that in any way justified his declaration. Significantly, the reader of Knoblaugh's ironic paragraph on Guernica would never know that anybody was killed in "one of the most fortunate bits of material for the propaganda machine."

Knoblaugh, although published in England as well as in the United States, carried more weight in his native country, which is probably why, despite the short length of his remarks on Guernica, he was singled out for praise by the Reverend Joseph F. Thorning, Ph.D., professor of sociology at Mount St. Mary's College, Emmitsburg, Maryland, in a vigorous defense of the Rebel doctrine on Guernica.[127] Father Thorning delivered his opinion on December 29, 1937, before the members of the American Catholic Historical Association at its annual meeting held in New York City. Father Thorning's address was a long diatribe against the conduct of the secular press during the Spanish Civil War.[128] On Guernica, he attacked Steer and cited approvingly the Vitoria cablegrams, from the *Times*[129] and the Havas agency. Following the examples of Jerrold, Cardozo, and Knoblaugh, he admitted that the Basque town had been bombed, but denied the importance of the damage done during the air raid. "The damage done by Franco's planes," he stated, "was insignificant in comparison with the havoc perpetrated by gasoline flames kindled by Spanish anarchists in their retreat."[130]

Despite Thorning's insistence that the Nationalists had not destroyed Guernica, he took the precaution of justifying such destruction for military reasons. The main object of the priest's attack was Steer. His dispatch "was at best an inadequate and misleading story," and its author "had been contradicted by the *London Times* correspondent who was with the Nationalist forces."[131]

Father Thorning produced new evidence against Steer. He read a cablegram, doubtless authentic, sent to Steer in Bilbao from the *Times* on May 4: "VIEW OTHER SIDES DISMISSAL YOUR GUERNICA STORY FURTHER JUDICIOUS STATEMENT DESIRABLE." Father Thorning interpreted this request for an amplification of a news story as proof that the *Times* "had reason to suspect the accuracy of the Steer report."[132] But the Catholic spokesman was falsifying the evidence, as had Jerrold before him, by failing to speak of the editorial in the *Times* of May 5, 1937. This statement, as already emphasized, showed that a day after the telegram produced by Thorning had been sent to Steer, the editorial staff of the London newspaper supported Steer's original dispatch.

On the other hand, Thorning told his audience:

> The Havas Agency and a committee of international correspondents who investigated the report positively affirmed that most of the damage they saw was wrought by deliberate destruction by fires from the ground.[133]

Thorning also offéred a "technical" interpretation of the ruins, and cited Jerrold:

> In a case of this kind the outside walls of a bombed house will never be left intact. The pock-marks left on the streets of Guernica due to exploding bombs are relatively few compared to the unmistakable scars inflicted by fire.[134]

The clerical polemicist presented still another "technical" witness, Russell Palmer, described as "a prominent publisher who is both a Protestant and a Mason" and who had "made a special investigation to determine what happened at Guernica." Thorning quoted Palmer's testimony as follows:

> I explored the ruins of Guernica very exhaustively and believe that anyone who does so will come to the same conclusion that I did, viz., that the town was dynamited by retreating Basques. I took a number of photographs of Guernica which showed damage which could not possibly have been effected from the air.[135]

Father Thorning also charged that a photograph in a brochure about Guernica, issued by the Spanish Embassy in Washington, was a "fake." Other photographs in the pamphlet, he wrote, "prove nothing except that the principal damage was done by incendiarism and not by bombs."[136]

Father Thorning was relentless in his denigration of the English correspondent he considered—justly—responsible for the wide publicity given to the destruction of

Guernica, and attributed to him the basest of motives. Noting that the *New York Times* had published three editorials in line with Steer's version of what had happened at Guernica, Thorning concluded that Steer

> knew well enough that the three editorials reflected the attitude of the men who were paying him. If he hadn't suspected where the sympathies of his employers lay before this date, he could easily conclude that in their eyes at least the Guernica incident "si non é vero, é ben trovate."[137]

Father Thorning made one more effort to discredit Steer's report on Guernica. In a footnote to the pamphlet published in 1938, embodying his address to the American Catholic Historical Association, he wrote:

> Following *The Times* (London), which published a repudiation of the original Guernica report (December 14, 1937), *The New York Times* on December 27th acknowledged that Guernica had been destroyed "upon evacuation."[138]

Flimsy is the word for Father Thorning's evidence. Here is the substance of what he called "a repudiation." The *Times* published a long article on aerial warfare in the Spanish Civil War on December 14, 1937, written by Wing Commander James, M.C., M.P. There is in this fairly long article but one oblique reference to Guernica: "The destruction of many places upon evacuation, such as Guernica, is on a different footing, and may be excused as acts of war."[139] This article has not been found in the *New York Times* of the date indicated, but the phrase cited would indicate that Thorning was referring to James's article in both instances. Again we see Father Thorning's strange conception of journalistic practices. The equation of an indirect mention of Guernica in a signed article by a special contributor to a newspaper with an editorial position on Guernica by that newspaper is unjustifiable, although it might appear normal practice to a man accustomed to the *Imprimatur* and *Nihil Obstat* of the Roman Catholic Church.

Another American priest who made an aggressive defense of the Spanish Nationalist propaganda positions, and especially of that on Guernica, was the Jesuit Father Wilfrid Parsons. Shortly after the destruction of the town, he wrote that Guernica "bids fair to take its place as the greatest propaganda hoax (after Badajoz) in the whole merry game of misleading the public." Here is his account of the event:

> The Basques evacuated it [Guernica] , because of a strategic move of Franco's armies. When General Mola moved in, he found it in ruins. These are the facts.

The next day, he went on with that misplaced irony so many of Franco's friends were fond of using,

> the whole world press flared with the lurid story that Hitler's planes had bombed it [Guernica] flat and killed nobody knows how many women and children (never any men). The world apparently believed it. . . . It was certainly exploited to the limit. But another group of foreign newspapermen came in with Franco. What did they find? That Guernica was not blown

down, it was blown up. The very same dynamiting Anarchists who had destroyed Irún had planted mines in the houses and streets, as you might expect, and after soaking the houses with gasoline had set the mines off and departed. This was vouched for by many neutral eye witnesses.[140]

Father Parsons was one of the Church's leading intellectuals in the United States,[141] but his account of the destruction of Guernica and of the newspaper coverage of that event would shame a high-school scholar. His "facts" are simply not facts, as a reading of the *New York Times* from April 28 to May 6—that is, two months before Father Parsons wrote—would have shown him. The "many neutral eye witnesses" of the gasoline-soaked and heavily mined houses of Guernica did not exist when Father Parsons wrote his article, and they do not exist today.

Father Parsons vented his choler and sarcasm, as did his colleagues Thorning, Code, and others, on the press, especially on the *New York Times*. He also attacked the publisher of the *Philadelphia Record*, J. David Stern, for headlining the news of Guernica, "CATHOLIC MARTYRS TO A NEW BARBARISM," and told how Franco's friends in Philadelphia retaliated with an eight-page pamphlet tauntingly entitled *The Philadelphia Record Weeps for Catholic Martyrs*. Father Parsons accepted without question the newspaper stories sent out by some of the foreign correspondents, such as Botto, who went into Guernica with Mola's army, but had few illusions as to their general acceptance. "Did the newspapers accept the truth?" he asked, and answered, "Not noticeably. Guernica is still an atrocity, like Badajoz."[142]

The visit of the marquis del Moral to Spain, and his subsequent return to England to give the opinion of a military expert on the destruction of Guernica, was the beginning of a series. Among the first to follow him, not in making the visit but in giving opinion, was Major General J. F. C. Fuller, who had been with Jerrold and Yeats-Brown in the Nationalist zone before the Guernica incident. Fuller was a prolific writer on military history, and he now offered his opinion on "the alleged bombing . . . which sent France, England and the U.S.A. into hysterics." However, whether or not Guernica was bombed, "it was in every way a legitimate air target," he wrote.

> But what is undoubted is that it [Guernica] was not destroyed by air bombardment, but instead was burned down by order of the Basque Government which, as it set it on fire, attributed its total destruction to Franco's inhumanity.[143]

General Fuller's erstwhile companion, Major Yeats-Brown, went back to Spain in August.[144] On returning, he, perhaps unconsciously, gave the lie to del Moral, Jerrold, and Cardozo, who were claiming that Guernica was *not* bombed at all on April 26. He asserted: "Guernica was bombed, intermittently, for about three and a half hours on the afternoon of April 26."[145] (It is to be noted here that Yeats-Brown used almost word for word the language of Holburn in his Guernica dispatch to the *Times*). Yeats-Brown's affirmation, by a "friend" of the Cause, a man who had traveled with Jerrold himself to Spain a few months earlier, marks a new turning in the ever-changing Nationalist position on Guernica. But Yeats-Brown's declaration about the bombing on April 26 did not keep him from adding that "Guernica was burned chiefly by the Reds," and he gave as proof the fact that

> the whole of one side of a street below the Casa de Juntas is gutted, while the other side stands intact, save for one house which was bombed, but not burned. How could aeroplanes destroy buildings along a straight line of over two hundred yards?[146]

The major justified the bombing by positing the strategic importance of Guernica, "a nodal point in the Red defense," and by giving the bombing force a tactical objective—"a concentration of three thousand Red troops was expected to occur on the 26th." He added, parenthetically: "These troops arrived, in fact, on the 27, and more troops passed through Guernica that day and the next, retiring towards the Iron Belt."[147]

Yeats-Brown illustrates here the compounded confusion existing among the Nationalist sympathizers on the subject of Guernica. Each one contradicts the other in searching for a coherent account that will fit the undeniable facts and still save the honor of the Rebels. By the time Yeats-Brown was writing, it was generally admitted that the fires had begun in Guernica on April 26. Yeats-Brown placed the bombing on the same day. He also accused the Republicans of setting the fires. He then wrote that troops were passing through the town on April 27 and 28. Did he suggest that the Basques set fire to the town while expecting their troops to use it as a point of passage?

A few weeks later, another Englishman of military background, Sir Arnold Wilson, visited Guernica.

> I need only say that no one acquainted, as I am, with the effects of bombardment from the air can doubt that most if not all the material damage was caused by wilful incendiarism—and such is the verdict of the inhabitants.[148]

Wilson was hedging his bets by admitting that some damage might have been done by air bombing.

In October, still another English military figure, this time an aviator and a Member of Parliament, Wing Commander James (whose testimony we have already seen offered by Father Thorning), visited the now famous ruins of Guernica.[149] He spoke in Parliament on his return from Spain, on October 21, 1937:

> The fact is that in that part of the town which I did examine in great detail almost the whole of the destruction was done by simultaneous incendiarism from inside. That, I am afraid, will annoy some people, but I will state my opinion.

When James Maxton, of the ILP, and A. Jenkins, a Labourite, asked him how did he know "that it was not incendiary bombs which brought about the destruction?" he replied, perhaps with conviction, but wide of the point:

> Anybody who has spent part of his life, as I have and other Members of this House, living in towns which were shelled and having seen towns burned, cannot possibly mistake the effect of explosives and burning. You cannot have explosives without a splatter.[150]

James's insistence on splatter is of interest, for it was the absence of such marks which many witnesses (del Moral, Jerrold, and others) had already invoked and which others were later to invoke (Sencourt, Bolín) as proof that the town had not been bombed. But he repeated the idea. "I was surprised," he again told the Commons, "to find the unmistakable splatter of shrapnel in two places."

When another Member of the Opposition, Colonel Wedgwood, continued to question him on incendiary bombs ("Surely the Hon and gallant Gentleman has heard of incendiary bombs?"), James made another admission: "The practice of bombing in the last few months has always been to mix explosive and incendiary bombs. The places I examined bore the marks of the two bombs."

James also told his fellow parliamentarians—perhaps in an effort to explain the "splatter"—that Guernica had been shelled as well as bombed. "Guernica is pretty completely destroyed. Guernica was bombed and Guernica was also shelled."[151] James repeated this statement some weeks later in a letter to a newspaper. "Examination satisfied me," he wrote, "that Guernica was both bombed and shelled." [152] "But," he continued, repeating his allegations in the Commons,

> it was equally clear that by far the greater part, perhaps 95 percent, of the very complete and uniform destruction of certain parts of the place was due to incendiarism, and could have been due to nothing else. The effect of burning is distinct of that of bombing, and it is quite unmistakable.

In this letter, James attempted to answer the questions of the Opposition more directly than he had in the Commons, and went on:

> It is incredible, if incendiary bombs were so extensively used, that there were no signs of any having fallen into the roadways between burnt-out blocks. The principal streets were tarred, and could not have failed to retain the mark, as they did in three places, of high-explosive bombs. I could see no signs that these roads had been renovated.

But was James absolutely certain that the light two-pound aluminum incendiary bombs would leave their indelible mark on a tarred street as did the "high-explosive bombs"? Steer had, months before, explained this difference in his letter to the *Spectator*.

James then drew a curious scene of the battle for Guernica:

The destruction, both by the explosives of the advancing attackers and by the burning of the retiring defenders, conforms to the probabilities of the military operations upon the day in question.

This battle described by James seems mythical today. Of which "day in question" is he writing? Of April 26, when, according to almost everyone by the time of his writing (February 1938), Guernica was burned, and which a defense witness, Yeats-Brown, had shortly before confirmed as the date of the bombing? Or of April 29, the only day when there were "retiring defenders" in Guernica? When James stated, with seeming impartiality, that

the defenders in retreat to the new line upon the high ground to the west of the town, had every reason and military right to destroy it upon leaving,

he was simply not talking about the military situation in Guernica on the night of April 26-27; and that is the night when, according to everybody in 1938, Guernica was in great part destroyed.

Aside from his own expert observation, James also "sought the opinion of an inhabitant . . . a middle-aged priest, who . . . was there upon the day of the destruction." The priest told the investigator

that many airplanes came over, and many bombs were dropped; that the roads were machine-gunned; it was market day and that there were many civilians about as well as troops and transport; that the total casualties were about 100, and that though the town was damaged by the air attack, the final destruction was caused by the retreating militia. He answered frankly and unshakenly under my cross-examination.[153]

This testimony provokes the same queries as the preceding quotation. What did the priest mean by "the final destruction." The mythical battle of James' imagination? By the time the "retreating militia" came through Guernica, the town had been burning for forty-eight hours. What is of significance in this article is the evidence of the slow but steady erosion of the Nationalist positions concerning Guernica. Now in February 1938 one of their own outspoken champions brings up a witness who completely confirmed Steer's telegram from Bilbao, except for the use of incendiary bombs. More damaging still to the Nationalist arguments was the statement of James' priest relative to the "total casualties" of "about 100." Is this not the first time an advocate of the Rebel cause admits casualties in the bombing?

Botto, del Moral, and Jerrold could detect no slightest sign of a bombing. James, months later, found the mark "in three places, of high-explosive bombs." The whole argument was now displaced: Nationalist defenders admitted that Nationalist-German airplanes had bombed Guernica, killing around a hundred persons, but they still insisted on blaming the Basques for the damage to the town. But were not the deaths the nucleus of the drama? This evolution in the pro-Rebel arguments had been so gradual that James himself probably did not fully comprehend the import of his article. There was, of course, the reservation of the "final destruction," but that detail bore within itself its own contradiction, as perhaps the priest realized when he answered "frankly and unshakenly" to the interrogation of the English officer. James will appear again in this story as a witness on Guernica in 1970.

Nor were these all the military witnesses who came forward. Brigadier General Percy R. C. Groves, after a trip to Nationalist Spain, declared that it was impossible that Guernica was destroyed from the air.[154] Still another man of arms—Major General Sir Walter Maxwell-Scott—was, however, more nuanced in his judgment. At a meeting of the Friends of National Spain, he merely pointed out that during World War I there had been an English project to bomb Berlin. "There would have been no outcry from the people of this country if that has been carried out. It was a matter of pure hypocrisy [the outcry over Guernica]."[155] This was in some ways a confirmation of the bombing, and it can be noted that Maxwell-Scott was speaking after James's article had appeared.

Often during the thirties aviators seemed favorable to the Fascist movements, and aviation writers even more so. One of the first authoritative, technical voices to be raised about Guernica was that of C. G. Grey, editor of *The Aeroplane:*

> nothing has quite equalled the stories about Guernica since the 1914 stories about German atrocities in Belgium which were later proved to be wholly inventions.

Grey attempted an ironically humorous style about Guernica and finished in simply bad taste:

> There were the usually harrowing word pictures of the slaughter of thousands of women and children in rather greater numbers than the probable population of the town.[156]

Aside from the fact that there is no basis for his allegations of an exaggerated number of victims in the news reports from Bilbao—Steer was notably restrained on this subject—Grey's statement is of some interest for being one of the rare articles published in defense of the Nationalist theses in which the question of victims is even mentioned. And Grey could do it only in the guise of heavy-handed humor.

Grey, who was frankly pro-Fascist in his political opinions, dismissed the very conception of such a raid by German airplanes.

> I could understand one of these German technical sections sending up a solitary machine, with the latest type of bombs and bomb-sights and dropping the bombs on some Red target—any target would do—just to find out whether the thing was working properly. But we can be sure there is no independent German organization in Spain which could either order an attack on a town, or could have control of enough aeroplanes to carry on an intensive bombing attack such as that described.[157]

Another aviation writer, this time with a military title, Major Al Williams, aviation expert for the Scripps-Howard chain of newspapers, was unabashedly for

Franco. He admitted that Guernica had been bombed "by Franco's men for about four hours on the afternoon of April 28 *[sic]*, 1937." But he justified the attack because

> the Reds, as usual, had set up military establishments such as ammunition dumps, arms factories, etc., right in the middle of the town of Guernica. This was another cute little trick which the Reds had developed to the nth degree, of locating military objectives in the midst of noncombatants.

Williams's statement constitutes the first allegation I know of that there were "arms dumps" in the middle of Guernica. If it were true, it would easily explain the damage done, but there exists no other testimony to confirm Williams's unsupported statement. The arms factory was on the outskirts of the town. As to the damage by the air raid, Williams cited the visits of "several reputable Englishmen" who "one and all" agreed "that the principal damage to the city was not done by air bombs, but by the dynamite and incendiarism of the Reds and anarchists."[158]

Major Williams attacked John Gunther for accusing, in his book *Inside Europe*, the German air force of destroying Guernica. Gunther had cited Steer. Williams had evidently read Thorning. "Later on," the aviator wrote, "it was learned from Mr. Steer's own admission that he was never closer to Guernika than eight miles." "Never" is too definite a word, and if Major Williams had read Steer's articles in the *Times*, he would have known that the correspondent visited the town not only on the night of April 26-27 and again on April 27 but also many other times during the civil war. It was on the afternoon of April 26, when Steer and other correspondents were attacked by German planes, that he "never" visited the town.

Williams said that Holburn's story constituted a "retraction of Mr. Steer's reports," and that "*The Times* itself began to suspect that there was something phony about this incident, making little effort to hide its suspicion by sending" to Steer the cablegram Thorning had produced in 1937. "Later on," Williams continued, "*The Times* was decent enough to publish a repudiation of the story which was reported to have been sent in by Steer."[159] This strangely worded assertion seems to place in doubt even the fact that Steer sent the dispatch to the *Times*, a position for which Williams gives no authority. In reality, the *Times* was more "decent" than Major Williams thought, and no such "repudiation" was ever published.

James Holburn, in his dispatch from Vitoria published in the *Times* on May 5, 1937, had mentioned the constitution by the Nationalist authorities of a "Commission of civilian engineers . . . to investigate the causes of the fire which swept the town"[160] of Guernica. It may well be that this little-publicized commission was named at that time to head off the demands then being expressed in London and Paris and elsewhere for an international enquiry into the destruction of Guernica, an action to which the Germans as well as the Spanish Nationalists were firmly opposed.[161]

This commission, composed of two magistrates and two engineers, ordered "to investigate the facts regarding the bombardment and destruction of the town of Guernica,"[162] apparently waited at least two months to begin work. The earliest interviews are dated July 30, and the report eventually handed in was based on an inspection made only on August 9, 1937[163] —that is, more than a hundred days after the investigation made by the foreign correspondents during the night of April 26-27 and again on the day of April 27.[164]

In addition to the inspection of August 9, the commission interviewed twenty-two witnesses,[165] a surprisingly small number (many fewer than the correspondents from Bilbao had seen on April 26 and 27), on July 30 and 31, on August 8 and 9, and registered another declaration on September 8. The commission finished its work shortly thereafter in that same month of September.[166] There is no evidence that any copy exists in Spanish except in typescript,[167] but an English-language version appeared in London in 1938,[168] published by Jerrold's house, Eyre and Spottiswoode, with a preface by Sir Arnold Wilson, an ardent defender of the Franco cause,[169] whose testimony as a military expert has already been noted. It is, then, only with its publication in England in the spring of 1938, and not at all with its completion in Spain in September of the previous year, that *Guernica: The Official Report* enters into the story of the controversy.

The publication in England consisted of four parts: first, the preface by Wilson; second, the "Report of the Commission"; third, the "Report of Inspection" by the commission; and fourth, the sworn testimony of the witnesses. The last three parts were translated from the Spanish. There was a certain, but not always perfect, consonance among the first three parts; but between the fourth part, that of the witnesses, and the first three, that of the pleaders for the Nationalist cause, there was overt contradiction.

The confusion that reigned in Rebel headquarters during the first days following the burning of Guernica and which gave birth to those early Nationalist statements that were later disavowed by the communiqué of May 2 has been analyzed. It was impossible for the Nationalists to maintain the absurd posture of denying even the flight of an airplane on April 26. They were forced to move to another position. The flurried reaction of the Nationalist Press Office under Bolín did not substitute for the abandoned explanation a complete and coherent one, but, instead, produced a series of overlapping and fragmentary versions, each one in open contradiction to parts of the others.

The erratic progress of this defensive propaganda line, from Bolín to del Moral, through Jerrold and Cardozo, then to Yeats-Brown, to Father Thorning, and his colleague Father Parsons, to James's letter of February 1938, led to the position that Guernica had indeed been bombed on April 26 but that the real damage to the town had been done by arsonists on the ground. In looking back on these strenuously advocated arguments, proposed one day and abandoned on another, it seems incredible that they were proposed by rational persons. The situation arose of course from the lack of any firm policy, from not knowing from one day to the next which explanation was the more politic to uphold. The publication of *Guernica: The Official Report,* more than a year after the destruction of the town, reveals the chaotic condition of Nationalist propaganda. No sane explanation exists for the publication of this report in England in 1938 by Nationalist partisans.

Guernica: The Official Report (excluding Wilson's preface, written in England) was the most detailed, the most informative study produced in Spain during the civil war concerning the destruction of Guernica. The testimony of the twenty-two witnesses is an invaluable source of information about the disaster. Even the "Report of the Commission" and the "Report of Inspection" are of value. Significantly, they make no mention of the official Nationalist communiqués of April 28 and succeeding days; they even openly contradict those official documents by admitting that airplanes were flying over Guernica on April 26. The "Report of the Commission" did try to suggest that perhaps the airplanes did not come from Franco's forces, but this was done by indirection and halfheartedly.[170] The authors of the report reasoned that since the arms manufactory in Guernica had not been destroyed, the Republican militiamen had carried out the destruction.[171] It could more easily be argued that the Republicans—if they were evacuating Guernica, as the report claimed—would have had more interest in burning down an arms factory than private dwellings.

The report also stated that since neither the Parliament House nor the Tree of Guernica was damaged, additional proof was furnished in favor of precise incendiarism from the ground rather than haphazard bombing from the air.[172] But this thesis is also unsound, for the report itself shows that the two supposedly contradictory events did take place: Guernica was admittedly bombed, and the Parliament House and the Tree were untouched. Hence, the two acts were compatible, according to Nationalist sources.

There are, as said above, striking contrasts between the first three parts, analyses and reports of outsiders, and the fourth part, testimonies of the inhabitants. We have seen that certain foreign visitors to Guernica found the natives willing to express with peasant stubbornness their account of what they had seen and heard on April 26. The same characteristics appear in the testimony accompanying *Guernica: The Official Report.* In fact, it is surprising to observe the number of persons who, while appearing politically neutral, nevertheless testify against the official theses. But their declarations are limited to what they saw and heard; they carefully offer no opinions. Thus the witnesses—while insisting that the town was bombed—usually refuse to identify the airplanes over Guernica on April 26.[173]

A municipal employee stated: "That a little later he noticed an airplane, origin of which he did not know."[174] A shopkeeper: "That he did not know the nationality of any of the airplanes in question."[175] A magistrates' clerk: "That he does not know the class or nationality of the airplanes which carried out the bombing."[176] A spinster: "That she does not know their nationality."[177] An assistant priest: "That he does not know the origin and nationality of the airplanes."[178] A lawyer: "That he does not know the origin of the airplanes which carried out the bombing."[179] A baker: "That he does not know the nationality of the planes which did the bombing."[180] A doctor: "That he was . . . unable to see the airplanes which bombed Guernica or their number or their markings."[181] A student: "That he does not know what type of airplanes bombed Guernica." [182] Storeroom manager: "An airplane whose characteristics he is unable to specify." [183] Industrial engineer: "That he does not know what the airplanes were or whence they came." [184] Businessman: "Planes appeared the number of which he cannot, however, specify nor their distinguishing marks." [185] Only one witness sought to be more precise:

> That he also observed another group of four black monoplanes, of a type similar to that which he had on other occasions seen among the Red airplanes. . . . That he had no certain knowledge as to what forces these airplanes belonged, whether Nationalist or Red, although it seemed to him that owing to the number of militiamen and to the fact that Guernica was a military objective, they must have been National planes.[186]

It would seem that after these attestations under oath, it would have been difficult for the Nationalist investigators to express doubt that Guernica was indeed bombed. But the authors of *Guernica: The Official Report*, ignoring in great part the statements of their own witnesses, note simply that around four or four-thirty in the afternoon, an unidentified airplane, or several unidentified airplanes, appeared, and concluded:

> In short, the appearance of the aeroplane or aeroplanes can be taken as a fact, but nothing can be learned about them, nor about what occurred afterwards in relation to them. There also appears to be no doubt that the people, frightened by the presence of the aeroplane and by the noise of its engine or engines, hurried to the shelters. Up to a certain point, this explains the confusion of the evidence, since from inside a shelter nothing can be seen of what happens outside and what is heard is confusing.[187]

This confusion is not borne out by the evidence of the witnesses cited above. Nor was it even accepted by Sir Arnold Wilson, who wrote that there was "universal agreement" that "Guernica was bombed by aeroplanes intermittently between 4:30 and 7 p.m. on April 26."[188]

There were other disputed points on which there is a grave difference between the testimony of the witnesses and the conclusions drawn from this testimony by the commissioners. Were incendiary bombs dropped on Guernica? The "Report of the Commission" read in part on this matter as follows:

> Among the ruins have been found various stabilizers belonging to incendiary aerial bombs, and these have been used as an argument for imputing the origin of the fire to such a cause. But the flaw in this argument is that, at eight o'clock on the night of 26th April, when the townsfolk left the shelters and those who had gone into the country returned, only a few houses were burning and the fire could have been got under control. The fire began when

the townsfolk had taken refuge in the shelters owing to fear of explosions, so that no one saw how it commenced, and it has been impossible to clear up the question of the origin of the above-mentioned stabilizers. . . . Again, a conflagration caused from the air always begins from the top downwards, and there are none such in Guernica.[189]

This quotation poses two problems: (1) the origin of the stabilizers and the fires, and (2) the state of the fires at eight o'clock. Evidence on these points is furnished by several of the commission's witnesses. One, a judge, who was outside Guernica but saw the airplanes, said he was later informed that incendiary bombs were dropped.[190] A municipal employee "saw a bomb burning on a certain piece of ground and he was informed that it was an incendiary bomb."[191] A magistrate's clerk declared that "his own house was burning in the upper story. That according to a neighbor, a bomb had fallen on the balcony . . . of the third story."[192] A spinster: "That she saw them [airplanes] drop bombs, some of which must have been of an incendiary nature . . . she saw some bombs burning on the ground and a circle of ashes around them."[193]

Another witness, a lawyer, left his shelter "about half-past seven on being informed by the gardener that the top story was on fire."[194] A bank clerk stated "that he does know that his own house was set on fire by an incendiary bomb . . . on leaving the shelter he saw that the eaves of his house had begun to burn."[195] A doctor affirmed: "That the building caught fire and that he noticed the flames in the eaves of the roof."[196] The manager of a factory storeroom swore that when he came out of the shelter at the end of the attack, he saw some houses "burning from the roofs." This witness was highly affirmative in his belief that incendiary bombs were the cause of the fires and said "that in his opinion the incendiary bombs which caused the burning of several houses during the bombing were dropped by Red airplanes."[197] A notary testified

> that one of the bombs fell three or four meters in front of the shelter in which he was, and that he noted that it gave forth a flame which did not expire for half an hour, but that it did not explode. That the ashes of the above-mentioned bomb were of an earthy consistency, rather like damp calcium carbide, but that he did not pick any up. That he left the shelter at about a quarter to eight, and that he saw that the roofs of various houses scattered throughout the town were on fire.[198]

A businessman: "That he then saw that the roofs were burning of, at most, one-fourth part of the total number of houses which were eventually destroyed."[199]

We can, without scruple, accept these hostile witnesses, who deny the conclusions of their sponsors, the commissioners. It was an outright lie for the commissioners to state that "no one saw how [the fire] commenced, and it has been impossible to clear up the question of the origin of the . . . stabilizers." The commission's own witnesses swore that the fire was begun by incendiary bombs dropped from airplanes. It was an outright lie for the commissioners to state that there were no fires in Guernica which began "from the top downwards." As shown above, there were numerous witnesses who saw only the roofs of the houses on fire.

The commissioners, having eliminated the incendiary bombs as a cause of fire, advanced a "technical" argument to absolve the Nationalists of blame. They admitted "that it was fire which destroyed these blocks of houses," but insisted that "the walls still standing are proofs that no aerial bombs could have fallen within that huge area of houses destroyed by the fire."[200] This technical reasoning had already been advanced in England by del Moral, Jerrold, and others. It had also been answered, logically, by Steer.

Now let us look at the extent of the fire at eight o'clock on the night of April 26, when, it was generally agreed, the bombing stopped. The "Report" stated: "At eight o'clock on the night of the 26th April, when the townsfolk left the shelters, a certain number of houses began to burn."[201] And, "at eight o'clock on the night of the 26th April . . . only a few houses were burning."[202] Also:

> The undoubted fact is, as can be seen, that at eight o'clock on the night of the 26th April a number of houses in Guernica were burning. . . . All witnesses are in agreement that the houses were few in number and that the fire was not intense.[203]

But it was precisely on these points that the witnesses were not in agreement.

A municipal employee declared that he left the shelter at eight o'clock and "he then noted that about fifty houses were on fire."[204] A magistrates' clerk swore that "on leaving his shelter he observed that a fourth part of the town was on fire."[205] When the bombing was over, a priest affirmed, "less than a fourth part of the buildings which were actually consumed was burning."[206] A librarian stated that "immediately on the conclusion of the bombing [he] noticed that a great part of the buildings of Guernica was aflame."[207] A baker asserted that, sometime after four o'clock, "the center of the town was already a furnace."[208] A businessman told the commission that when he left the shelter at "seven-thirty or seven-forty-five . . . he then saw that the roofs were burning of, at most, one-fourth part of the total number of houses which were eventually destroyed."[209]

The figures sworn to by these various witnesses are concordant. There were 271 houses destroyed in Guernica;[210] a quarter of this number constitutes 67.75 houses. We can therefore say that four of the commission's witnesses declared that at least fifty houses were on fire at eight o'clock. These were not, as the "Report" concluded, "few in number."

Sir Arnold Wilson stated on this subject:

> There is direct and unassailable evidence that, at the very most, only a quarter of the town [75 houses] was on fire at 8 P.M. . . . after the last airplane had disappeared.[211]

But Wilson may have realized that any town in the world, with a quarter of its houses in flames and no fire-fighting equipment, was in dire straits. So, while insisting that "Guernica was destroyed by fire," he added this precautionary phrase: "There was little or no wind to carry the flames from house to house. The fire was therefore not accidental."[212] What Sir Arnold seems to want to prove is that the houses that caught fire after eight o'clock were set on fire by a different agency from those in flame at eight o'clock; it is difficult to follow his reasoning that the fires raging at eight o'clock, as a result of the bombing, were "accidental."

But more than Sir Arnold's reasoning was at fault: if we accept the witnesses that he himself sponsors, they throw the lie in his face. *There was a high wind blowing that night of April 26.* A municipal employee stated under oath that "the wind was blowing" and blamed that wind for the burning of many houses.[213] A shopkeeper swore: "That the house was burnt down, together with the other seven houses in the same block, owing to the assistance given by the wind."[214] A magistrate's clerk attested that "the wind aided the fire to travel."[215] A spinster affirmed: "That some houses were burning, and that on account of the strong wind blowing the fire spread to others."[216] These statements seem conclusive, and there is no rational explanation of why Sir Arnold declared the contrary, with no evidence to support his declaration.

Since the commissioners and Sir Arnold Wilson—neither the ones nor the other—had a consistent explanation for the origin of the fires that destroyed Guernica, they were forced to paste together a contradictory series of explanations. The bombing of Guernica had been admitted by Salamanca on May 2; the fact that Guernica had been burned could not be ignored. Therefore, the problem facing the defenders of the Franco cause was to play down the damage done by the Nationalist-German bombers and to attribute the fires (or the greater part of them) to another agency. This effort at a solution involved several arguments. One was to deny, as shown above, the existence of the incendiary bombs, a position gainsaid by the commission's witnesses. Another argument was, as also shown above, to put into doubt any effective bombing activity. The people of Guernica were in shelters and did not know the origin of the sounds they heard outside. Part of the conclusions of the commission read:

> V. For three hours and a half, and throughout the following night, the inhabitants of Guernica listened to heavy explosions which took place within the town. . . . The explosions heard within the town by the inhabitants of Guernica were the result of dynamite detonated in the sewers and in other parts of the town, in accordance with the Basque Government's prearranged plan.[217]

The commissioners thus conclude that the inhabitants of Guernica went into shelters when they saw the first airplane, and that they did not really know whether or not other aircraft subsequently came over Guernica, and that the explosions heard by the people within the shelters were caused not by bombs ·but by dynamite. The people of Guernica were apparently too feebleminded to realize what was going on. This conclusion of the commission is not only unsupported by any evidence but also decisively undermined by the commission's own witnesses.

A judge, who was in nearby Ajanguiz, affirmed that the airplanes "made their presence known" at twenty minutes to four and "continued to do so until a quarter to eight at intervals of not more than fifteen minutes at the outside."[218] A municipal employee, who went into a shelter, swore that "he heard the sound of various airplanes and various explosions which differed in intensity."[219] A shopkeeper attested that after a plane dropped a bomb near his house in the middle of Guernica, he and his family left town, but from a nearby point he saw that "various other airplanes dropped bombs on Guernica" and said "that about half-past seven the bombing ceased."[220] A magistrate's clerk declared that at five in the afternoon "the alarm signals drove him to shelter," and that he stayed there "until eight o'clock, at which time the bombardment ceased."[221] A spinster said under oath that "about five o'clock groups of airplanes began to arrive, of which she counted first five and afterwards nine. . . . That she saw them drop bombs. . . ."[222] An electrician testified that "on the day of the bombing" he took shelter in a refuge "where he remained during the continuance of the bombing, which lasted from half-past four o'clock until eight."[223] A priest asserted

> that about half-past four in the afternoon he heard the sound of various airplane engines and of explosions. . . . That the bombing lasted until half-past seven or eight o'clock at night.[224]

A librarian, who observed the action some few miles from Guernica, declared:

> That the aeroplane began to drop bombs on Guernica to the number of eight or nine . . . that he also observed another group of four black monoplanes . . . and that he saw that they all dropped bombs over Guernica and machine-gunned the town . . . that the bombing ceased about half-past seven.[225]

A bank clerk left Guernica for the outskirts when the first alarms were given, and "he noted that the aeroplanes dropped bombs upon, or, rather, machine-gunned, the cross-roads." He testified that "the bombing . . . lasted about three and a half hours."[226] A baker, who observed the air attack from outside the town, asserted that "at about four o'clock" he saw planes; "that they made various flights over Guernica, dropping bombs, those of the three-engined planes being of heavy calibre."[227] A doctor declared that, on hearing the noise of an airplane engine, he sought shelter, where he stayed for about an hour; then, thinking the raid was over, he came out; he again heard the sound of engines and again entered a shelter in the church of Santa María, where he remained for two hours and a half;

> that the bombs dropped . . . especially two which fell near the church, caused a terrible shaking and explosion, and that on his departure he saw their effects near the church.[228]

A student related

> that about half-past three in the afternoon he saw an airplane arrive which dropped certain bombs, and that later he heard the noise of the engines of a

squadron. . . . That the bombing continued until half-past eight in the evening, up to which hour the noises of the engines was audible.[229]

A manufacturer and lawyer declared:

That on the commencement of the bombing at four o'clock in the afternoon he saw an airplane which dropped various bombs near the station. That after a short interval another airplane arrived and dropped bombs, and that after this there was a pause in the bombing of about twenty minutes. That later other squadrons of airplanes arrived and dropped bombs which caused heavy explosions.[230]

An industrial engineer, who seemingly did not enter a shelter, said under oath,

That on the 26th of April the bombing started at half-past four in the afternoon . . . and that during it there was an interruption which the witness thought to have been about five minutes, after which it continued till about eight at night.[231]

A notary affirmed that when he heard an airplane motor he took refuge in a cellar

for about three and a half hours, the approximate time during which the bombing continued. . . . That one of the bombs fell three or four meters in front of the shelter where he was.[232]

A businessman declared that he saw an airplane around four o'clock, which dropped "some seven bombs." A quarter of an hour later other planes appeared, and he sought shelter, "from which he did not emerge until seven-thirty or seven-forty-five, at which time the bombardment ceased."[233]

We have now seen that the witnesses brought forward by the Nationalists themselves gave this picture of Guernica on the afternoon of April 26, 1937: bombers overhead from approximately four-thirty to eight o'clock, dropping explosive and incendiary bombs: after the bombing, at least fifty houses in flames, with a strong wind blowing. In spite of this evidence, sponsored by themselves, the authors of the "Report" chose to ignore the many confirmations of the presence of squadrons of airplanes, even of the incendiary bombs, which are not even mentioned in their conclusions. The Nationalist investigators also chose to overlook the numerous witnesses who heard airplane motors while in the shelters, and pretended that the explosions heard in the shelters were, in all probability, not bombs dropped by airplanes but dynamite explosions.[234] In short, that the destruction of Guernica was caused by the Basques themselves.

But why did the Basque militiamen dynamite and burn? An explanation had to be found. Father Onaindia had said that he "had heard" that Guernica was to be evacuated on April 26, and that he had gone to see friends there for that reason.[235] The rumor that apparently prompted Onaindia's trip became, in the arguments of the investigators, an order. "The destruction of Guernica was the climax of the evacuation order issued by the Basque Government for the 26th April," affirmed the commissioners.[236] Guernica was to be evacuated but, beforehand, dynamited and burned; everything had been prepared before the planes came over to destroy Guernica that same day.[237] The "Report" offered no evidence whatsoever—from their own witnesses or from elsewhere—that Guernica was in fact to be evacuated on April 26. There is a strong logical argument against such an assumption: the front was still distant from Guernica. "What retreating army in the world," later exclaimed Steer,

> mines and destroys roads 15 miles behind the furthest point of its retreat, on the only line of communications with its base, and lays the mines so badly that they go off in the middle of a public square? . . . There were *no departing troops going through Gernika on April 26th; the Basque army did not fall back on Gernika until two days later.*[238]

Perhaps the writers of *Guernica: The Official Report* sensed that it was illogical to charge the Basques with the destruction of a town so far behind their own lines, and they extended the period of incendiarism to coincide with the rebel advance:

> For three successive days these militiamen continued to set fires alight and to help them spread; and some of this work was continued later, even after our troops had entered Guernica.[239]

This evidence of the continued breaking out of new fires is confirmed by many of the witnesses.[240] And the commissioners in their "Report" stated, concerning a house that began to burn on April 30, twenty-four hours after the occupation of the town by Nationalist troops:

> Guernica had only just been captured, and certain hostile individuals still remained concealed in various places; these were without doubt the incendiaries in this case.[241]

But if the reader will recall the descriptions of Guernica when it was captured on April 29, he may well doubt that these "hostile individuals" could have found a hiding place in the debris; and if he will further recall the inexorable punishment that awaited any captured Republican (and which was almost meted out to the Frenchman Berniard), he may well ask what would have been the interest of even the most "hostile individuals" to burn down still another house in ruined Guernica, at the certain risk of their own lives?

How then explain these new fires that kept breaking out? There is an explanation, even an authoritative one, of these delayed fires. The English consul in Bilbao, Ralph C. Stevenson, went to Guernica on April 27, and in his report to his ambassador, Sir Henry Chilton, he wrote:

> Many [houses] were still burning and fresh fires were breaking out here and there, the result of incendiary bombs which owing to some fault had not exploded on impact the day before and were doing so, at the time of my visit, under falling beams and masonry.[242]

Almost as if the commissioners themselves did not really believe that with these arguments they had absolved the Nationalist bombers of blame in starting the fires, they now proceeded to build up a secondary line of defense. A new reason for accusing the Basques of the destruction of Guernica was found: "The Red militiamen not only took no steps to check the conflagration, but they prevented the townsfolk from taking steps to that end."[243] Wilson affirmed:

There is widespread and direct evidence of a most (in a legal sense) satisfactory character that from 8 o'clock onwards no effort to extinguish the fire was made or permitted by the militia. At that time less than a quarter of the town was burning. The fire could therefore have been stopped.[244]

But what was the situation in Guernica at eight o'clock when "less than a quarter of the town was burning?" According to Steer, the telephone was put out of commission by the second group of Heinkel 111 light bombers, which came over the town some time before five o'clock that afternoon.[245] It took time to get word to Bilbao and for the fire fighters to get to Guernica. One witness swore that "between ten and eleven at night firemen arrived from Bilbao with three trucks."[246] Some of the witnesses later protested that the firemen did not do all that could have been done to put out the flames,[247] but it is highly probable that by the time the firemen reached Guernica, the flames were beyond control. Guernica was very probably doomed by the time the raid ceased at eight o'clock. The firemen did what they could to save *public property,* with the reduced water pressure available. Steer observed, "A fire brigade with a feeble jet was playing on the chapel of Andra Mari."[248]

Wilson summed up his own contradictory thoughts on the destruction of Guernica, as well as those of the Nationalist commission, when he wrote:

By far the greater part of the destruction worked in Guernica was the deliberate work of the retreating forces, and that part, if any, which was the result of the air raid of the 26th, could have been localized and, in so far as the fires were concerned, substantially mitigated by prompt action on the early evening of the 26th.[249]

Wilson's summary merits these remarks: (1) that there were no "retreating forces" in Guernica on the evening of April 26, but that it is an undeniable fact that Guernica was destroyed at that time; (2) that Wilson admitted that a quarter of the town was on fire at eight o'clock that evening, and so it is difficult to follow him in questioning whether "any" part of the destruction could be attributed to the air raid; (3) that Wilson admitted that fires were possibly started by the air raid. In spite of these contradictions, Wilson went on to charge that the burning of Guernica was the responsibility of the Republican forces, because they did not— undoubtedly could not—put out the fires.[250]

In the heat of the controversy over Guernica, over the extent of the damage done, by explosive aerial bombs or by simple explosives; over the origin of the subsequent fires, incendiary bombs, or arsonists on the ground; over who carried out the bombings and who started the fires, the people who perished in the holocaust were often lost to view. In *Guernica: The Official Report,* the commissioners state: "The number of victims in Guernica on the 26th April did not reach one hundred."[251] There were other references to the victims in the testimony of the various witnesses, but this whole problem of the dead and the dying in Guernica will be studied in a later chapter.

Guernica: The Official Report, if read attentively, especially that basic part that reproduced the testimony of the witnesses, is highly favorable to the position of the Basque government: This was probably realized in Spain, and it was for that reason that the document remained unpublished in its country of origin.

This analysis has shown that the testimony of the inhabitants of Guernica, sponsored by the Nationalist government itself, effectively demolished the arguments of those persons in England and the United States, such as del Moral, Jerrold, Lunn, Cardozo, Thorning, and others, who most outspokenly defended the Nationalist statements concerning Guernica. Why then did Jerrold have *Guernica: The Official Report* published by his own firm of Eyre and Spottiswoode? We can, I think, immediately dismiss any suggestion that Jerrold was secretly a Republican agent. One explanation is that Jerrold read the document but did not seize its meaning. To support this hypothesis, there are other instances in Jerrold's writings on Guernica where his summaries of what others had written are completely false, and Steer, in his reply to Jerrold in the *Spectator* [252] suggested that the Catholic editor did in fact have difficulty in understanding what he read.

And how was Sir Arnold Wilson gulled by the Nationalist document?—for gulled he was. He asserted that "there will be universal agreement" about the findings of the commission.[253] And concerning his own observations, which have been shown to be erroneous, he opined:

> There is not one of the conclusions which I have noted in this preface which would not be held established by any English Court of Law, none which, in the ordinary process of law, an English jury would not hold to be proven.[254]

Wilson, wrote Peter Kemp, "was gifted with truly phenomenal mental . . . powers" and "could memorize a book after reading it through once." Perhaps he was capable of memorizing the testimony of the witnesses in *Guernica: The Official Report* but incapable of understanding testimony that contradicted his prejudices, for Kemp also observed that Wilson was a man of "decided political views [who] could tolerate no opposition, however sincere."[255]

Wilson was not the only pro-Nationalist advocate fooled by *Guernica: The Official Report.* The American Jesuit Father Code charged that Herbert L. Matthews, correspondent with the Republicans for the *New York Times,* had reported

> "the falsehood"—that Guernica had been destroyed by "German aviators"— despite the fact also that Eyre and Spottiswoode of London has published the

findings of a Commission. . . . The English translation [of which] carries the foreword of Sir Arnold Wilson, M.P., and substantiates irrefutably the charge that the retreating Leftist army destroyed the city before the arrival of the Nationalists.[256]

The only possible explanation for this curious statement is that Father Code had perhaps read Wilson's foreword but not the testimony of the witnesses. Two other defenders of the Nationalist cause, William Foss and Cecil Gerahty, placed *Guernica: The Official Report* in evidence, affirming that "The report is manifestly restrained, conscientious and true." Foss and Gerahty denounced the English press for not giving headline importance to the publication of the Nationalist document, which they resumed by a mishmash, combining some of the conclusions of the commissioners with some of those of Wilson. They pretended that this résumé was based on the testimony of "twenty-one eye-witnesses," but, as with Code, it is clear that neither Foss nor Gerahty had read that testimony.[257]

Still another committee of investigation, set up by the Spanish Rebels, gave its opinion on the destruction of Guernica. This group, composed of persons from the University of Valladolid, was established during an extraordinary assembly of the Spanish universities, held in Salamanca on June 15, 1937. Salamanca authorities were visibly preoccupied by the unfavorable press treatment that the Nationalist cause was receiving abroad.

The essential object of this assembly was to find an answer to the false propaganda, spread abroad by the leaders in the Red zone, propaganda which might lead to doubt and perplexity among cultured European centers, and which threatened to create false conceptions, especially with reference to the Basque provinces.[258]

The committee named by the University of Valladolid was composed of the acting dean and two professors of the Faculty of Philosophy and Letters, who visited the Basque provinces and signed all the *actas* concerning the Basque towns, except that of Guernica. Despite the importance of Guernica in the worldwide discussion on the war in the Basque country, the Valladolid committee apparently did not visit the town and made no enquiry into what had happened there. In referring to Guernica, the committee merely reproduced a letter from a professor of the university who was in Guernica when the war broke out and stayed there until April 27, 1937. This professor, in his letter, insisted on the military importance of the town: barracks, troops, arms factory, and so forth. "All Guernica was a military objective," he wrote

On the last Monday of April [26 April] a squadron of airplanes flew over Guernica, over the military objectives already mentioned. Having taken refuge in the ascent to the tower of the Church of Santa María, I heard detonations and gunfire.

When "the danger had passed," he came out and saw "buildings on fire." He left the town at two in the morning, and did not return until the Nationalist entry. At that time he was surprised to see "that the town was destroyed."[259]

Guernica is given proportionately more attention in the basic twelve-page "Report" of the Valladolid commission than in the following 171 pages of *actas*.[260] The argument offered in the "Report" is highly vulnerable. After insisting, as had the author of the *acta*, on the military importance of Guernica, the "Report" stated:

> The thought that the war would be stopped for sentimental reasons could occur only to the Basque leaders. The National advance continued, but not forgetting these sentiments, and although our army destroyed military objects, dispersed military concentrations and put the enemy to flight; they respected the religious center of "Santa María," "La Casa de Juntas,"[261] that historical site which symbolizes all that Guernica represented so far as was humanly possible all objects that had no military importance including. This line of conduct did not suit the premeditated propaganda which the Red leaders proposed to spread abroad. The complete destruction of all that existed in Guernica would have helped them better to play their parts as victims. Once more fire broke out in the town.[262]

There are of course obvious contradictions in this text. While claiming pinpoint precision for the Rebel bombers, who purposely did not hit the Church of Santa María or the Casa de Juntas, it fails to note that neither did they hit any military objectives. And again, if the propaganda position of the Basque government would have been better if the church and the national shrine had been destroyed, and if propaganda had been the objective of the Basque government, why did not the Basques burn down these buildings? As for the insinuation that the Basques had rekindled the flames, the report of the English consul, cited above, is sufficient refutation.

The Report of the Burgos Commissioners on the destruction of Guernica, which contained the testimony of eyewitnesses to the bombing, to the use of incendiary bombs, and to the responsibility of these bombs for the subsequent fires, confirmed in great part the cablegrams from the reporters in Bilbao. Despite the publication of *Guernica: The Official Report* in London, the defenders of the Nationalist cause in England and the United States continued to write as if the essential facts cabled from Bilbao on April 27 and the following days were still in question.

One of the leading partisans of the Franco movement in England was Robert Esmonde Gordon George, formerly a professor at the University of Egypt, who wrote under the name of Robert Sencourt. A Catholic and a monarchist, he had already manifested his interest in Spain by the publication of *Spain's Uncertain Crown*, a history of the monarchy from 1808 to "the disaster of 1931." In 1938 he published *Spain's Ordeal: A Documented Survey of Recent Events*.[263] This strongly pro-Franco book contained twelve pages on the destruction of Guernica, ten of which were given over to a slashing attack on Steer and the other correspondents who found themselves in Bilbao at the moment of the Guernica disaster. He mentioned *Guernica: The Official Report* but briefly.[264]

Sencourt's central thesis was the one that had been adopted in progressive stages by the Nationalist defenders, after abandoning the excessive statements of Bolín, del Moral, Jerrold, and others made during the early weeks of the controversy. Sencourt admitted that Guernica had been bombed by German planes; he admitted that the fleeing population had probably been machine-gunned by German aviators who "lost sight of the nice regulations of international law."[265] But, he insisted, Guernica had been burned by the Basques.

"The buildings at Guernica were destroyed less by bombardment from airplanes than by local incendiaries," Sencourt wrote. "Such, after investigation, was the crushing verdict accepted by *The Times.*"[266] This is an interpretation of Holburn's dispatch.[267] However, Holburn did not write exactly as Sencourt claimed. In fact, a study of Sencourt's pages on Guernica reveals that he suffered from the same infirmity as Jerrold—a congenital incapacity to read plain English. Holburn's report in the *Times* read:

> It is feared that the conflagration destroyed much of the evidence of its origin, but it is felt here that enough remains to support the Nationalist contention that incendiaries on the Basque side had more to do with the razing of Guernica than General Franco's aircraft.

"The crushing verdict accepted by *The Times*" was simply that "here"—that is, at Vitoria, Mola's headquarters—in the Nationalist censorship, "it is felt that enough [evidence] remains to support the Nationalist contention." This was the simple statement that at Nationalist headquarters people were upholding the Nationalist position. This was hardly "crushing" for anybody who knew how to read a newspaper dispatch.

Sencourt further misquoted Holburn in attempting to prove Steer in error concerning the origin of the fire. He wrote: "The regular correspondent of *The Times* [Holburn] considers that: 'It will be difficult to determine how the fire started.' "[268] This was not at all Holburn's consideration. The correspondent of the *Times* had written: "In the investigators' opinion it will be difficult to determine how the fire started." This reference was to an early opinion of one of the members of the Burgos Commission. Again, the man of the *Times* was merely reporting the thoughts of somebody in Vitoria—thoughts that Holburn never claimed as his own—nor was this thinking so favorable to Sencourt's thesis as he was pretending.

Sencourt further bolstered his arguments with another incorrect quotation. " 'The deliberate arson of the town was evident,' wrote the *Echo de Paris* on 3 May."[269] It is unimportant that the above phrase did not appear in *L'Echo de Paris* (Sencourt was not careful about details; it did appear in many other newspapers). It comes from the Georges Botto dispatch to the Havas Agency, but here again Sencourt falsified a quotation. What the Havas Agency distributed, as shown earlier, was:

> The Nationalist officers have drawn the attention of the journalists to the fact that nowhere does one find signs of shrapnel and that the absence of traces of projectiles as well as the verifications made elsewhere show that the deliberate arson of the town was evident.

These were conclusions drawn neither by *L'Echo de Paris* nor by Botto but by Nationalist officers accompanying Botto and other journalists.

After further quotations from the Havas telegram of certain allegations concerning the burning of Guernica, which he erroneously attributed to "a number of foreign journalists," Sencourt observed:

> The statements of the *Echo de Paris* are supported by three distinguished British officers, Sir Arnold Wilson, Brigadier Page-Croft [sic] and Major Yeats-Brown.

But if one reads the entire Havas dispatch, one can find a fundamental contradiction between that account and at least two of the three officers named by Sencourt.

Botto was writing during the first days of the Guernica incident, Croft during the first weeks; both of them denied any bombing at all. Wilson and Yeats-Brown, writing a few months later, were forced to admit the bombing, while limiting its effects. Botto and Wilson were in disagreement over whether or not the wind was blowing on the night of April 26. Botto said it was; Wilson made a strong denial.

The chief military witness sponsored by Sencourt was Wing Commander James, whose testimony has already been analyzed, who equally admitted a bombing denied by Croft. Sencourt declared that James's information gave to the Botto dispatch its "final vindication." This statement is an unpardonable perversion of the facts. The Botto dispatch denied any bombing and mentioned no casualties. James had sponsored a witness who confirmed the bombing, and said "that the total casualties were about 100." Sencourt did not seem to appreciate these differences.[270]

However, Sencourt seemed less intent on proving his arguments by appeals to "technical" evidence and the statements of military experts than by simply destroying Steer's reputation, as a newspaper correspondent and as a man. Like other overexcited partisans of the Rebel cause, Sencourt set himself up as a critic of the newspaper profession without even a competent amateur's knowledge of the métier. It is not out of place here to establish a few ground rules for the evaluation of newspaper reports for this kind of research. Since the invention of the telegraph, anything written outside the home offices and subsequently communicated to a newspaper by other means than a manuscript has been susceptible of errors in transmission.

These dispatches are generally considered as quick summaries of information, rarely as deathless prose. The editor may publish the entire dispatch; he may publish a part of it, or none of it. He may misread the dispatch. He may alter parts of it. He may publish it when received; he may keep it a day or two before deciding to use it. The correspondent in a faraway country may never see his printed article. It is therefore unfair that a research historian not view this newspaper material with a slightly different optic from that used in regarding copy proofread and corrected by an author.

As an example, we have a garbled dispatch of the Spanish Civil War which has not only survived in its mutilated form the initial newspaper printing in 1936[271] but which has since then been reprinted in at least five anthologies.[272] I am referring to Jay Allen's famous dispatch on the Badajoz massacre. It was originally sent from a cable office in Tangier. At one place it reads, as published: "I know there are horrors on the other side aplenty. Almendra Lejo, rightist, was crucified, drenched with gasoline and burned alive." Jay Allen obviously cabled something like the following: "ALMENDRALEJO RIGHTIST CRUCIFIED, . . ." which should have been decoded from the cablese as follows: A rightist of Almendralejo [Andalusian town] was crucified." In another part of this article, Jay Allen referred to the Portuguese correspondent Mario Neves.[273] This name was garbled in transmission, printed in the *Chicago Daily Tribune* as "Mario Pires," and has continued to be spelled that way at least five times subsequently in anthologies. Any news report, technically transmitted by telegraph, telephone, radio, and so on, has a built-in possibility for errors, and this fact should be taken into consideration when judging news dispatches as historical sources.

Sencourt was woefully ignorant of journalistic habits, and he gave his judgments on newspaper reports and reporters as if he were criticizing the printed pages of a book proofread by the author. He blamed Steer for the headline the *Times* placed on his cablegram; "The Tragedy of Guernica: Eyewitness' Account."[274] But Sencourt should have known that the correspondent does not make decisions for the news editor. He might make an occasional suggestion, as perhaps Steer did,[275] but the final decision would be made by the editor in the home office and would depend not only on the nature of the news received from the correspondent but also on the nature of the general news of the day.

Sencourt made still another feeble attack on Steer, in writing:

In *The Times* of 5 May, we read in a telegram dated 4 May that "the Mayor of Guernica, a priest named Arronategui, whose brother died in the bombardment, broadcast from the Bilbao wireless station to-night." We read on 6 May a telegram dated 5 May: "Father Arronategui, a priest of Guernica, also spoke on the wireless last night," but one had read on 28 April that "An elderly priest named Arronategui was killed by a bomb."

Sencourt then declaimed:

Were there then in the town of five thousand people three priests of the same name, one killed, one surviving to broadcast as mayor, one surviving to broadcast not as mayor?[276]

It is obvious that Steer's dispatch would have been more comprehensible for people like Sencourt had it read that "the mayor of Guernica [and] a priest named Arronategui, whose brother died in the bombardment . . ." The triviality of this attack on Steer does not merit this rectification, and attention is given to it here simply to indicate the profound and petty hatred for Steer that existed in English conservative, Catholic circles. Sencourt's attack was worse than trivial; it was intellectually dishonest. In his attack on Steer, Sencourt quoted from the *Times* of May 5 and 6. The "error" was in the newspaper of May 5, but on the following day, in Steer's story, the *Times* printed in brackets the correction.[277] Sencourt quoted from this dispatch in his book;[278] he must therefore have seen the correction, which was moreover hardly necessary, for any person of good faith and modest culture could have understood that the conjunction might have been lacking.

Sencourt also challenged the account of the bombing of Guernica sent by the correspondent of the *Star,* in which one could find a reference to "President Euzkadi." Sencourt remarked: "Now the President's name was Aguirre, not Euzkadi which means Basque."[279] Ergo, the whole account was suspect. What was suspect was Sencourt's knowledge. The cablegram to the *Star* was naturally written in the abbreviated telegraphic style used by correspondents, for words cost money, and doubtless did read "President Euzkadi" instead of "president of Euzkadi," just as "President France" would mean "president of France" and not that the correspondent thought "France" was the name of the president. The editor of the *Star* probably did not understand the word "Euzkadi," which was certainly not in general use before the civil war. It does not mean "Basque" as Sencourt pontifically informed his readers, but "the Basque country." This trivial incident shows carelessness on the part of the editor of the *Star,* ignorance and vindictiveness on the part of Sencourt, but proves nothing concerning the qualifications of the reporter of the *Star* or the veracity of his report.

Sencourt was particularly venomous in his assault on George Steer. "He was not a staff correspondent of *The Times,* but a free-lance journalist who offered it contributions."[280] The *Times* man at Vitoria was "the regular correspondent of *The Times,*" he declared,[281] insinuating that the *Times* man at Bilbao was of a lesser breed. Sencourt, again having reading problems, confused "the regular correspondent of *The Times*" with a mythical "investigator whom *The Times* had sent out to inquire what had really happened."[282] On another page of his book, Sencourt called this person "an authoritative investigator sent later by *The Times* after Mr. Steer's contribution had aroused suspicion." This "investigator" never existed save in Sencourt's malicious imagination. He fitted in well with the attempt to downgrade Steer. According to a footnote in Sencourt's book, he was born of a faulty reading of Holburn's dispatch in the *Times* of May 5, 1937,[283] but it remains extremely difficult to understand how Sencourt arrived at this interpretation. The *Times* had Steer in Bilbao and Holburn in Vitoria; both were good journalists, and both enjoyed the confidence of the London editors. There was no need for the "investigator" and, had he come, knowing Bolín as we do and the distrust with which he viewed the working press, we can doubt that the "investigator" would ever have got to Guernica, and certainly not in time to send a cable that could have been printed on the morning of May 5.[284]

Further doubt on the existence of the spy sent out to control Steer's cablegram was to be found on the editorial page of the *Times* on the same day that Holburn's dispatch was printed. This was the editorial supporting Steer's original dispatch. It is difficult to believe that Sencourt read the news stories about Guernica and failed to see the editorial opinion. However, the historian Sencourt did not inform his readers of this evidence unfavorable to his arguments.

When Sencourt cited Wing Commander James, he concluded: "It is inconceivable that [he] is deliberately lying," and added piously, "nor would one think it of Mr. Steer." How did Sencourt explain Steer's cablegram? Steer was a "gifted, sensitive and imaginative artist, who had deep emotional reasons for writing as a partisan of the Separatists," and who "could not bring to bear the necessary objectivity of judgment on the stories which were told him before and after his arrival in Guernica."[285] Steer, Sencourt went on,

> leaves us open to the suspicion that the German thermite bombs he fingered were placed there to deceive him; for he himself says he had often picked them up elsewhere.

He finally dismissed Steer by writing: "He no longer makes contributions to *The Times;* nor is he in Spain. It had been felt that, already in Ethiopia, he had been unduly partial to the Negus."[286]

Sencourt's aim was to get rid of the troublesome problem of the incendiary bombs, and he asked: "If the flames were burning around midnight with this intensity [described by Steer], how could they have been kindled by peculiarly strong thermite bombs as early as five or six in the preceding afternoon."[287] The obvious answer to this question was that the fires kept spreading. Far from proving the absence of incendiary bombs, as suggested by Sencourt, this continuation of the fires could be used to prove their presence, as explained before in the report of the English consul in Bilbao; the fires were constantly being rekindled by falling masonry and other objects that touched off unignited thermite bombs.

Another pro-Nationalist interpretation of the events of Guernica appeared in England in 1938, some months after the publication of Sencourt's work. It was a collaboration between William Foss and the *Daily Mail* correspondent we have already encountered, Cecil Gerahty, entitled *Spanish Arena*.[288] It carried a foreword by the Duke of Alba, by that time Franco's representative in England. We have seen that Gerahty had close ties with the propaganda offices in Franco Spain, and perhaps this liaison explained the fact that *Spanish Arena* was immediately published in both Fascist Italy and Nazi Germany.[289] Foss and Gerahty did not repeat the mistake Gerahty had made about Guernica in his earlier book. They offered little of the "technical" arguments advanced previously by pro-Nationalist defenders in England, from Jerrold to Sencourt, and contented themselves with strident denials, except for references to *Guernica: The Official Report.*

Despite Gerahty's own credentials as a newspaperman, he and Foss denounced the English press for its handling of the news from Guernica.

> The Guernica story has proved, however, an excellent touch-stone of the good faith of the various English papers. . . . Proof of the falsity was published as early as 2nd or 3rd May in the Press of France and elsewhere abroad. . . . The story of Guernica's "wanton bombing" raised the indignation of Britain. It was untrue in almost every particular.[290]

Foss and Gerahty limited their attacks on Steer to quotations from Arnold Wilson's remarks in the foreword to *Guernica: The Official Report,* perhaps out of respect for the lesson Steer had given to Gerahty in the *Spectator.*

The slanderous innuendoes of Father Thorning and Sencourt against George Steer were continued by another American priest, Father Joseph B. Code, who in a chapter entitled "The Myth of Guernica," in his pamphlet aggressively entitled *The Spanish War and Lying Propaganda,* called Steer's first cablegram about Guernica "a fabricated story" and his report of the bombing a "false atrocity story."[291] Father Code also echoed Thorning's accusation that the *Times* "sent a telegram to Mr. Steer to the effect that it was known that his story was without foundation." The reader can refer back to the telegram quoted by Thorning to see that Code's statement is a complete falsehood. He added that Father Thorning had in his possession the cablegram from Steer to the *Times* in which the correspondent

> asked not only that the dispatch be featured in the news columns, but that editorials should denounce what he described as the destruction of the city by German aviators and the mass murder of its citizens by the forces of Franco.[292]

This copy of Steer's cablegram may well have been genuine, and there is nothing inherently wicked about a correspondent's informing his editor of the special news value of his cablegram, even in a message separated from the news story itself. In this particular case, since Steer's dispatch on Guernica was one of the most important news stories of the Spanish Civil War, Steer merely showed an understanding of his profession when he pointed out to London the significance of his message.

2

The Public Controversy in France

The controversy over the destruction of Guernica assumed a quite different aspect in France from what it did in England and in the United States, but nevertheless in France it resulted, as it did in the other two countries, in a swelling of the current of opinion hostile to the Nationalist cause. In the two Protestant countries, the dispute obliged some conservative political elements to take a stand against the Rebels in Spain, but the Catholic Church, a minority group, presented an almost united front in defense of the Nationalist position on Guernica. In Catholic France, the war in the Basque country (which in its impact on public opinion reached its culminating point in the destruction of Guernica) split the Catholic forces.

How did this happen? Technically, the phenomenon in France repeated the Anglo-American experience: irrefutable testimony, emanating from a source generally associated with the right, convinced a number of people normally sympathetic to conservative causes that the Spanish Nationalists were at fault in Guernica. In England, this phenomenon had been brought about through the testimony of war correspondents of moderate political tendencies, published in a conservative and right-wing press. In France, the actors changed, but the basic formula did not.

There were, we can recall, no French correspondents of any persuasion in Bilbao on April 26; the French correspondents were all on the Nationalist side. This detail—in Popular Front France—was in itself extraordinary. On-the-spot stories about Guernica came from French correspondents only after its capture by the

Nationalists. It was then that the conservative, right-wing and neutral press of France, which in some cases had ignored the news about Guernica for thirty-six hours (or more) longer than had its British colleagues, began publishing stories by French reporters; these were completely favorable to the Nationalist positions. But at the same time and in spite of these widely published news reports, there developed among sectors of French conservatism a strong current of opinion favorable to the Basque cause, a current provoked by the destruction of Guernica.

What caused this sentiment, if it was not inspired by the reports of French correspondents? It was the result of the testimony of a Spanish Basque Catholic priest who by chance found himself in Guernica during the bombardment. His witnessing was the decisive element in changing the viewpoint of a certain section of French public opinion, just as the witnessing of the three British correspondents had been determinant in forming and changing the opinion of a certain part of English and American public opinion. In neither case did the impetus come from the left.

This Spanish Basque priest was Father Alberto de Onaindia. Onaindia was then thirty-four years old, and held the post of canon in the cathedral of Valladolid, but he was working in the Spanish Basque country when the civil war broke out. Learning, on the evening of April 25, that the military situation was worsening, he left Bilbao the next day in an automobile with a friend to find his mother—in Aulestia, near Marquina—and take her and other members of his family from the danger zone.[1] Guernica was on the route he took. It was four-thirty in the afternoon when he and his traveling companion arrived at the entrance to Guernica. Years later he wrote in his memoirs of what followed:

> It was Monday and market day. We were passing near the railroad station when we heard a bomb explosion; it was followed immediately by two others. An airplane which was flying very low dropped its load and left, all in a few seconds. It was Guernica's first war experience. The panic of the first moments shocked the inhabitants and the peasants come in to market. We observed a considerable excitement. We got out of the automobile and tried to find out what was happening and to calm the many women who were growing more nervous and excited. Minutes later other bombs fell near the Convent of the Madres Mercedarias and the people began to leave the streets and to hide in cellars and under shelters. There very soon appeared, as if coming from the sea, some eight heavy planes which dropped many bombs and behind them followed a veritable rain of incendiary bombs. For more than three hours there followed waves of bombers, of airplanes with incendiary bombs and of solitary machines which came down to two hundred meters to machine-gun the poor people who fled in fright. I did not know the mark of the airplanes, because I do not understand about such things.
>
> For a long time we were at the exit of the town toward Munitibar and Marquina. The explosion of the bombs, the fires which were beginning to break out and the harassment of the machine-gunning planes forced us to

take cover under trees, under house entrances, dropping to the ground in the field when we saw a plane approaching. There was no anti-aircraft defense, no defense of any kind, we were encircled and corralled by diabolic forces in pursuit of defenseless inhabitants. Through the streets wandered the animals brought to market, donkeys, pigs, chickens. In the midst of that conflagration we saw people who fled screaming, praying, or gesticulating against the attackers. We finally left the burning town, but when we saw approaching airplanes which would pass over us, we left the automobile and ran to hide under some trees. We sought the protection of a small stone bridge over a nearby stream, while a few meters away three bombs exploded raising a cloud of blinding dust. Someone left the highway and climbed into the wood. When calm returned, we found a woman dead, machine-gunned, and a young *gudari* who had been a victim of the bomb explosion. He had no visible wound, but a great quantity of blood escaped from his mouth and nose. I gave absolution to both of them. We were told the *gudari's* name was Gotzon. All the gutters and ditches were filled with people who wanted to hide or find protection against the cowardly attack of the enemy air force. Providence saved us that day. Many tree branches and a lot of dirt fell on our heads each time that bombs exploded around us. At seven forty-five of that radiant April evening the systematic destruction of our holy town drew to an end. They were German planes sent over Guernica to carry out a trial in totalitarian warfare. It was the first example of this kind of war: first some bombs to alarm the population, then waves of bombers with explosives followed immediately by incendiary bombs and, finally, light planes that machine-gunned the unfortunate people who sought flight to save their lives. I had other bombing experiences later in England during the Second World War. But I never felt so unprotected and so much a defenseless victim as on that April 26 of 1937.

Guernica was burning. We did not perceive many flames during the first two hours because it was day and the smoke was hiding the fires. But when we wished to penetrate into the town, we could not take many steps without feeling ourselves choked by the smoke and the flames which were beginning to consume all the dwellings. Many people were gathered outside the agglomeration of houses. Some were weeping, others were praying and not a few regarded the spectacle petrified with horror and fear. I started out walking to Munitibar.[2]

Father Onaindia had not forgotten the object of his trip. En route, he found transport, which he was able to requisition, by virtue of the documentation he carried.[3] When he reached his mother's home, he found that she had already left, and later that night, by chance, he discovered her, exhausted, sitting by the roadside. In the course of the night, he managed to find most of the rest of his family and bring them into Bilbao. The next morning, April 27, he related his experiences to President Aguirre. Onaindia's story doubtless weighed heavily on the statement that Aguirre released later that morning.

Aguirre asked Onaindia to go at once to Paris to tell of what he had seen. He took the airplane to Biarritz on April 28.[4]

On arriving in France, Father Onaindia gave a number of interviews to the press, of which at least seven different versions have been found.[5] The most widely published account was that sent from Biarritz, by the UP, which appeared on April 30 in important newspapers in such localities as London, New York, Chicago, Montreal, and Buenos Aires.[6] This constituted the first published statement by Father Onaindia; it was sent by an American agency from France; it was not published in France. Once again the Havas Agency was beaten on a news story concerning Guernica, and this time the news originated on French soil. A few days later Father Onaindia wrote to Mgr. Múgica, the exiled bishop of Vitoria, then in Rome, "Thousands of newspapers published my interview."

Father Onaindia took the train to Paris during the night of April 28-29 and, on arriving in the French capital, he "was surrounded by newspapermen asking me whether in fact I had been at Guernica since the military denied the fact." "This calumny," he wrote to Mgr. Múgica, "seemed to me almost worse than the burning of the town: to murder poor innocent people and then attribute to them the most horrible crime of this war."[7]

A reporter from the UP certainly saw Onaindia at that time,[8] but the significant interview granted by Onaindia on his arrival in Paris was to Jean Richard and published in *L'Aube* in the edition dated April 30-May 1.[9]

Did Father Onaindia in Paris see a reporter from the Havas Agency? If he was "surrounded by newspapermen," as he wrote, and as would have normally been the case, it is impossible to believe that there was not a man from Havas in the group. Moreover, Onaindia thought he had been interviewed by someone from Havas, and in a declaration printed in *L'Aube,* on May 6, gave his guarantee to the interview "published by the Havas Agency."[10] Published where? No trace of such an interview has been found in the French metropolitan press. Father Onaindia today thinks he was interviewed in Saint-Jean-de-Luz by Havas, but further questioning reveals that the man he talked with was Hérisson-Laroche, of the UP.[11]

Two copies of an interview with Father Onaindia, attributed to Havas, have been found: one in *La Libre Belgique,* a Catholic newspaper of Brussels, on May 1, 1937,[12] and one in *L'Echo d'Alger,* on May 4, 1937.[13] It is interesting that the Onaindia interview, which in its various versions constituted one of the two most significant newspaper accounts of the Guernica incident, was, if distributed at all in France by Havas, certainly very poorly distributed.[14] It was also tardy, as had been the Havas service on Guernica since the beginning. Pierre-Louis Falaize later wrote: "*L'Aube,* the first in the press, thanks to Jean Richard, placed on the record what is and will remain, a significant document for history."[15] This meant that *L'Aube* knew of no other interview previous to that of Richard.

On April 30, another interview with Onaindia was published in Rotterdam,[16] and the same article appeared, a day later, in a Bordeaux newspaper very favorable to the Spanish Left, *La France de Bordeaux et du Sud-Ouest.*[17] There are similarities between this interview and that published in Brussels and Algiers, but it is definitely a different interview.[18] No source was given. Subsequently, an "unauthorized" interview with Onaindia appeared in the Communist daily *L'Humanité*,[19] and "Víctor Montserrat," a correspondent for *La Croix*, printed still another interview in his book *Le drame d'un peuple incompris*.[20]

An interview with Father Onaindia was published in England on May 3, distributed by the Basque delegation in London.[21] This was a shortened version of the interview already published in Rotterdam and Bordeaux. A longer version of the interview released by the Basque delegation in London was later incorporated into a Basque government propaganda brochure.[22] This suggests that the Rotterdam and Bordeaux newspapers received their copy either from the Basque delegation in Paris or, more probably, from the Republican news service Agence Espagne.[23] This version was the one later referred to by the Nationalist Commission that investigated the destruction of Guernica, to insinuate that Guernica was burned as part of a Basque plan of evacuation.[24] Still another interview with Father Onaindia was published in a Republican propaganda pamphlet, issued in Paris, probably in 1937.[25] Some of these statements were more detailed than others, but the essential part of the story, even passing through different interpreters, never varied.[26]

Havas's failure to give a wide distribution to an interview with Father Onaindia resulted once again in the anomaly that Paris was the only large capital in the Western world with a free press where the readers of the large-circulation newspapers were told nothing about a significant development in the story of the destruction of Guernica. However, this development, if not presented to the great mass of newspaper readers in France, was available to the readers of *L'Aube*, a "journal of ideas and opinions"[27] of Christian Democratic tendencies, and these readers were precisely the persons in France most likely to be influenced by it. One immediate result was that on the same front page of *L'Aube* that held Ondainia's declaration there appeared an article by George Bidault, then one of the paper's editors, under the heading "THE MARTYRDOM OF GUERNICA." After observing that the newspaper had previously denounced "the murders of Madrid and Barcelona, the massacre of Badajoz," Bidault wrote that "faithful to ourselves and above all to our duty, we associate our voice with those raised around the world against the assassins of Guernica." His article terminated:

> For three hours, the German air fleet bombed the defenseless town. For three hours, the German airplanes fired their machine-guns on the women and children in the streets and in the fields. All of this in the name of civilization. And even, for the Crusade, as they say.[28]

For reasons perhaps connected with his projected visit to the Vatican, Onaindia had not been mentioned by name in the interview published in *L'Aube*, although he had been named in the previously published UP interview, and was named in the article attributed to Havas which appeared in Belgium on May 1. *L'Aube* called the person interviewed simply "a Basque priest," but Alberto de Onaindia was more than a country priest. He had for some years been active in Catholic social work in the Basque country, a factor that distinguished Spanish Basque Catholicism from the Catholicism of the rest of Spain. Such work was generally closely associated with Basque Nationalist politics.

After the civil war broke out, Father Onaindia went to France, where he maintained relations between the Basques and the papal nuncio to France, Mgr. Valerio Valeri; he had even gone to Italy on a Spanish Republican passport late in 1936—not a mean feat in itself—and conferred with the undersecretary of state of the Holy See, Mgr. Pizzardo, later Cardinal Pizzardo.[29] He had come back to Bilbao from France on April 24, and "gave a complete report to President Aguirre of our activities abroad."[30]

In Biarritz, en route to Paris, Father Onaindia said that he was "going to try to see the Pope and beg him to intervene." He added:

> The Basque Government at Bilbao has delegated me to ask the Papal Nuncio in Paris for permission to intervene directly with the Pope, in the hope that he can obtain a promise from the Rebels to renounce this war against the civil population. . . . I hope to obtain a passport to go to Rome in the hope that the Vatican's influence will be sufficient to overcome any possible objections of the Italian Government. Furthermore, the Bilbao Government would like for His Holiness to appeal to priests in all the democratic countries of Europe to join in urging protection of Basque women and children from the Rebel aviation.[31]

It seems improbable that Father Onaindia, after making this statement, really expected to get to Rome, or that, once in Rome, he could achieve his aims. Franco had already denied the bombing; the Vatican was on Franco's side, as were the great majority of the "priests in all the democratic countries of Europe."

In Biarritz, Onaindia also sent a telegram and wrote a letter to Mgr. Múgica, the exiled Bishop of Vitoria, then in Rome, and it was probably there that he addressed a message to Cardinal Gomá, "begging him to intervene with his people [the Nationalists] to put a stop to this extermination of a peaceful people."[32]

When Onaindia reached Paris on Thursday he found that the nuncio would be absent until Saturday. He was received by the prelate's secretary. Onaindia described the scene in the letter he later sent to Mgr. Múgica, in Rome:

> I had a violent scene with his [the nuncio's] Auditor; in a high mandarin's voice he told me that I was lying in saying that I came from Guernica. It was the first time we had met. Indignant, I told him that he should be put out of the Nunciature at once, for he was unworthy of that post if he so received a Catholic priest who had come from his parish to report the most horrible tragedies. I showed myself inflexible and he asked my pardon, turning humble and embracing.[33]

On leaving the nuncio's quarters, Onaindia told the press that he expected to see Mgr. Valeri on Saturday and obtain a passport to go to Rome.[34]

After seeing the nuncio on Saturday, Father Onaindia was less sure of his trip to Rome. Nevertheless, he put on a good face before the press. Mgr. Valeri, he said, "wanted me to go to the Vatican to relate in good faith what I saw of the bombing of Guernica, and then visit the Secretary of State, Mgr. Pacelli." The nuncio also

> offered to send a telegram to the Vatican giving the time of my departure from Paris and of my probable arrival in Rome, but the Holy See cannot give me a passport, for these are chiefly limited to pontifical diplomats nor can it guarantee my trip through Italy to Vatican City.[35]

This was in reality very little, and in the letter that Onaindia later sent to Mgr. Múgica he wrote that he insisted on the safe conduct, "because the foreign newspapermen were telling me not to take the risk without precaution." He had asked the nuncio, he told Mgr. Múgica, "if he could not take some steps through the Bishops of Spain to ensure that the war should not be one of extermination but conducted by legal method." The nuncio "recommended ... surrender."[36] Onaindia's trip to the Holy See was put off and never took place. But the Basque emissary hopefully told the press, "I explained in detail to Mgr. Valeri about the bombing of Guernica and I am certain that he believed my words, although he confessed that such deeds seemed to him impossible."[37]

Father Onaindia then went to Belgium, where he was able to speak with the secretary of Cardinal Van Roey in Malines: "I told him what I had seen of the destruction to which Guernica and the Basque country were subjected." Back in Paris, he was again interviewed by the UP, to whom he declared, after speaking of his visit to Malines:

> I cannot go to Rome to see Cardinal Pacelli, unless the Italian authorities give me guarantees that I shall not be harmed. I wrote to my bishop of Vitoria, Mgr. Mateo Múgica, who is in Rome, so that, if I am unable to go to the Italian capital, he may come to Paris. I shall thus give him details on the atrocities committed, so that he may, in turn, make them known to the Secretary of State of the Vatican.[38]

Onaindia's letter to Mgr. Múgica, already cited above, was circulated in Vatican circles, and the British envoy to the Holy See, D. G. Osborne, received a copy from an English Jesuit and forwarded a rough, incomplete translation to London on May 11. This letter contained another account of Guernica by Onaindia, reading in part:

> God brought me at exactly 4.30 on the 26th to Guernica. I was there during the whole of three hours crouching on the ground and taking shelter at last in a hole under the bridge in the company of five communists; close by they were dropping bombs and machine-gunning, three bombs fell within 30 yards of us. ... The scene was Dantesque. Guernica was bombarded furiously with incendiary and ordinary bombs. ... It was two o'clock in the night and at last I got out of town, it was all in flames. We do not know how many people were burned in it.[39]

At the same time there were circulating in Vatican City

> copies of a telegram from the Acting Vicar-General of Vizcaya to the Bishop of Vitoria protesting against the aerial bombardments of Durango and Guer-

nica, and of a letter from the Spanish Provincial of one of the Religious Orders to the Cardinal Secretary of State, defending the Basques as Christians.[40]

Osborne was a Nationalist sympathizer, but he nevertheless observed:

> I imagine that the Vatican may be considerably embarrassed by the campaign against the Basques and the bombing of their towns and villages, for, as the Dean of Valladolid *[sic]* says in his letter, the Basques are a Christian people fighting for their national existence.[41]

Father Onaindia never got to Rome to testify about Guernica, nor did Mgr. Múgica come to Paris to hear Onaindia's recitation, but two other Basque priests, sympathizers with the Bilbao government, did manage to visit Rome to inform the Vatican of what had happened at Guernica. On May 11, a group of twenty-two Basque priests of the Vitoria diocese, at the "respectful request" of President Aguirre, signed a document in Bilbao, addressed to the Pope, and testifying to the aerial bombings suffered by the Basque people. The first signature was that of Ramón Galbarriatu, vicar-general of the Vitoria diocese. The paper was not signed by Father Onaindia, but ten of the signatories were eyewitnesses to bombings in the Basque country, and one, Eusebio de Arrona-tegui, was a witness to the bombing of Guernica. There was quite probably a political reason for the exclusion of Onaindia, but another reason could have been invoked: Father Onaindia belonged technically to the diocese of Valla-dolid, and the signers all belonged to the diocese of Vitoria. Concerning the destruction of Guernica, the document said:

> Similarly on April 26th aircraft in the service of General Franco bombed and machine-gunned horribly the venerated town of Guernica, setting fire to the Church of San Juan, damaging the Church of Sta. María, and reducing to cinders almost all the buildings in the town. They machine-gunned the inhabitants pitilessly when they ran in terror, fleeing from the explosions and fires which surrounded them, causing hundreds of deaths. The airplanes, which flew with impunity almost at ground level, saw perfectly the ruin and casualties which they were causing. Nevertheless they continued to attack in full knowledge of what they were doing.[42]

This document was taken to Rome by two of the Basque priests who had signed it, Agustín de Ysusi, dean of the Bilbao clergy and Pedro de Menchaca, canon of the cathedral of Vitoria and provisional director of the Seminary of Bilbao.[43] How were these two Basque priests, known for their sympathies with the Bilbao government, able to get to Rome? It seems that their trip was facilitated by the Italian consul-general in Bordeaux, and his action was related with certain maneu-vers of Count Ciano, the Italian foreign minister, who had, in the early days of May, ordered the Italian diplomat Marchese de Cavaletti de Sabina to try to get in touch with the Basques and arrange a separate peace. Nothing came of this Italian scheme, but the visas that permitted the two Basque priests to go to Rome were given in an effort to convince the Basques of the good faith of the Fascist government.[44]

When the priests arrived in Rome, Mgr. Múgica tried to arrange an interview with the Pope, through the intervention of Mgr. Pizzardo, who had been Father Onaindia's interlocutor a few months earlier. He was told that an audience with the Pope was unnecessary, for the Pope already had their testimony. Mgr. Múgica then tried to get the Basque priests to be received by the papal Secretary of State Cardinal Pacelli, who was Pizzardo's superior. This démarche seemed also to fail when, at three o'clock one Sunday afternoon, the two priests were summarily convoked and told they would be admitted by Pacelli, provided that they did not tell of the interview or mention the May 11 letter. They were received with scant courtesy, left standing for eight minutes, and when they brought up the subject of the letter they found the interview terminated.[45]

The trip of the Basque priests to Rome had been covered with great secrecy, but when they returned, a bare account of their visit, together with the text of their document, was released to the press by the Basque government delegations in Paris and London.[46] The vicar-general of the Vitoria diocese, Ramón Galbarriatu, in a statement written in June, probably immediately after the fall of Bilbao, reneged on his signature. In this document, entitled "My Question of Conscience," he raised a

> solemn protest against the pressure abusively exercised against myself and other companions of the priesthood, by the so-called provisional government of the Basque Country, forcing us to sign, against our wills, a wretched paper concerning what happened in Durango and Guernica.

He did not name the others forced to sign against their will. Why did he sign? He recalled the reprisals taken in Bilbao and Durango against right-wing sympathizers after those towns had suffered from aerial bombings.

> In view of these facts, my definite refusal to sign the wretched document would have been interpreted by the government and the angry people as approval by the ecclesiastical authorities of the bombings which had made many victims, even priests and nuns.

At this point, the vicar-general seemed to confirm the bombings, and, in fact, he never became precise in stating just what he thought to be false in the May 11 document concerning Durango and Guernica. He did write that some of the church structures in Durango which were bombed either were being or had been used by the Basque military. But he did not deny the bombings, or that priests and nuns had been killed in the course of them. As for Guernica, he declared ambiguously:

> Note also that in Guernica the lovely and unique parochial church was not destroyed or damaged, nor was the Casa de Juntas, nor the Convent of Clarisas; note also that this town . . . has also had for many years an impor-

tant arms factory and was the concentration center for large military forces
of Euzkadi. How could it pretend to be unharmed in the whirlwind of war?
And who, knowing the anarchistic insanity of the Red army on occasions
anterior to Guernica and Durango, and on the later evacuations of Amorebieta, Munguía, Las Arenas and Bilbao, can conceive that there [at Durango
and Guernica] its action did not take, as was normal for it, the form of
destruction and extermination?[47]

This complicated and involved explanation cannot be considered to have constituted a denial of the bombing of Guernica; it could be considered a justification of
the bombing. Perhaps Galbarriatu was under pressure by the Basque government to
sign the May 11 document. In view of the numerous executions already carried out
against Basque priests by the Nationalist forces, of the numerous imprisonments of
Basque priests in course, it can well be believed that Galbarriatu found himself
equally under pressure in Bilbao which was occupied by the Nationalists, and in
fact his recantation did him little service. He was confined in Santo Domingo de la
Calzada and died there a few months later.[48]

There was no public reaction from the Vatican to the Basque letter of May 11.
In fact, the position the Vatican was going to take on Guernica was possibly formed
before that date and certainly before the mission of Ysusi and Menchaca. Father
Onaindia wrote that Cardinal Isidro Gomá y Tomás, primate of Spain, informed the
Holy See that he had personally been in Guernica some days after the destruction
and was able to verify by some short circuits that the Basques had burned Guernica,
and that he later made such a statement publicly before the Pontifical Spanish
College in Rome. [49] This college, doubtless completely in the hands of Nationalist
Spaniards, had decided its position before May 19, and on the basis of the primate's
statements. On that date, the British ambassador, Sir Eric Drummond, cabled
London concerning a report given to the embassy by Macartney, Rome correspondent of the *Times.* According to the diplomatic cablegram, Macartney said that the
Times

> which had gone all out for the Guernica incident, was now beginning to feel a
> little alarmed that it might have been backing the wrong horse. He was
> consequently being bombarded with requests to find out all he could about
> the reports which a Spanish priest was supposed to be bringing to the Pope
> about the details of the incident.

The reference is evidently to Father Onaindia and his projected trip to Rome, but
nowhere in the message does his name appear. Macartney (and the *Times*) were
seemingly unaware that Onaindia was giving all the details about Guernica to any
correspondent in Paris who would listen, but it may be that Macartney ill interpreted, or even exaggerated, the queries from London. Macartney then sent "a
Catholic friend" to the Spanish College in Rome. He found out that the unnamed
priest (Onaindia)

> was a young Basque of well-known Red tendencies; that so far as the Spanish
> College were concerned they were not disposed to believe him, but to place

their faith in the accounts given by the Cardinal Archbishop of . . . Toledo, and that the young Basque priest when he arrived—if he ever did—was not likely to cut much ice at the Vatican.[50]

From the moment that Father Onaindia gave his first interview, a campaign of calumny was unleashed against him by the Catholic partisans of the Nationalist cause. The correspondent of the *New York Times* with the Rebels, William P. Carney, cabled on May 4 that the Insurgents called Onaindia "just an unfrocked young priest." [51] The cathedral chapter in Valladolid, capital of Falangist violence, said at first that Onaindia was unknown and that he was a personage invented by the Basques. [52] When this fiction could no longer be maintained, the chapter adopted another position: Alberto Onaindia was an "impostor," because he had called himself "dean" of the chapter, whereas in reality he was a "canon." Moreover, he was "well known for his separatist ideas" and had been absent from his post for five years.

> Proceedings have been begun against him for rupture of residence and if he has not yet been judged, it is because it is impossible to get in touch with the accused to inform him of the charges. The undersigned metropolitan chapter condemns the unworthy and scandalous conduct of Onaindia and makes known that it has broken with him for all time the bonds of fraternal communion, considering him as morally excluded from the bosom of the chapter.[53]

This statement from the chapter was sent to, among others, General Queipo de Llano, who found it useful as radio talk material, adding the perfectly untrue detail that Father Onaindia "has already been excommunicated by the Holy Father." [54] This reaction from the Valladolid chapter was not provoked by anything published in France but from an item in the English press, where Onaindia was—probably through a translation error—called "dean" instead of "canon,"[55] and it was on this almost invisible thread that was hung the charge of "imposture." What is certain is that in the statements to the French press, where Onaindia was present, he was given no higher title than "canon"; nor did he need a slight hierarchical elevation to reinforce the impact of his relation. In the first story in *L'Aube,* Onaindia was simply called "a priest"; in the UP account, he was a "canon" and "a Catholic dignitary." However, this flimsy pretext provided by an error in the English press permitted Jerrold and Lunn contemptuously to dismiss Onaindia's report. The former observed: "As regards the Dean of Valladolid, the ecclesiastical authorities in Valladolid say that the priest in question is not the Dean."[56] Lunn also wrote: "The excitable story told by the 'Dean' of Valladolid would be more impressive if the ecclesiastical authorities admitted that this gentleman is the Dean." [57] Another English pleader for the Franco cause, J. Alban Fraser, falsely declared:

> But what about the Dean of Valladolid? the reader may ask. Enquiries made there have elicited the reply that there neither is nor has been a Canon of that

name belonging to Valladolid, and that the only cleric of such name known is an unfrocked priest.[58]

Lunn and Jerrold were playing with words. In all decency, they should have said that Father Onaindia never held the rank of dean but he did hold that of canon. Fraser's statement was more mendacious, for the Valladolid chapter, casting Onaindia out, did not deny that he had been a canon; nor was he ever licitly "unfrocked."

A London Catholic weekly, the *Universe*, questioned the honesty of Father Onaindia, basing its charges on the position adopted by the Valladolid chapter.[59] When Luigi Sturzo, then in English exile, read this, he wrote: "The fact that he [Father Onaindia] may be in conflict with the Valladolid chapter on a matter of canon law diminishes in no way the value of his testimony."[60] Father Onaindia wrote an account of the facts to Sturzo. He held the title of canon in the metropolitan chapter of Valladolid cathedral, but for the past five years he had been authorized by his archbishop, Msgr. Gandasegui, also a Basque, and the metropolitan chapter to ask the Holy Roman Congregation for permission to live in Bilbao. He had always ceded his canonical emoluments to the chapter. Father Onaindia added that in consequence his absence from Valladolid was regular and in conformity with canon law. Until the day he made his statement concerning what he had seen in Guernica, he continued, no observation whatsoever had been made to him about his relations with the Valladolid chapter.[61]

Another English Catholic weekly, the *Catholic Herald*, picked up the Onaindia story from *L'Aube*—credited to "Basque Priest"—with certain misgivings. Before mentioning the interview, the *Catholic Herald* asked for assurances from *L'Aube*, which cabled: "We certify that the Basque priest interview is first-hand and we hold his name at your disposal." The English weekly then reprinted extracts from the interview.[62] However, the following week the *Catholic Herald* recanted. The author of the interview, it wrote, was not "as we had thought, an independent Basque priest communicating solely to *L'Aube*, but the same Canon of Valladolid who . . ." The Catholic publication did not openly call Father Onaindia a liar, but elsewhere on the same page it qualified charges that Guernica had been destroyed "by Nationalist bombardments" as "an absolute lie."[63]

Still another English Catholic weekly, the *Catholic Times*, went to battle against Father Onaindia. This publication had first reacted to the news about Guernica by stating that it "was a fool story and a lie at first sight."[64] The following week it carried a front-page article, "BASQUE 'DEAN'S' STORY EXPOSED." Onaindia was "repudiated by his brethren," and his "eyewitness" account of the bombing was "preposterous."[65]

Calummy against Father Onaindia continued from his fellow Catholics. When the civil war broke out, the archbishop of Valladolid, Msgr. Gandasegui, a Basque like his canon Onaindia, was also in the Basque country, where he was undergoing treatment for an incurable prostate condition. Father Onaindia was able to intervene when the prelate was under arrest, and also arranged a safe-conduct for him to leave the Republican zone.[66] When Msgr. Gandasegui died in Valladolid in May, only hours before his native town of Galdácano was bombed as had been Guernica,[67] a French newsman wrote a story entitled, "VICTIM OF RED BARBARITY AND SEPARATIST FOLLY," alleging that the archbishop's death was caused by grief over the uncanonical conduct of his canon, who for this special occasion was momentarily restored to his rank in Nationalist circles.[68] Father Onaindia immediately replied, stating his version of his relations with Msgr. Gandasegui and demanding that his letter be published. The newspaper ignored it.[69] When Father Onaindia took a public position concerning what he had seen in Guernica, he was given the standard treatment reserved for all Spanish priests who sided with the Republic. If they could not be imprisoned or shot, they were slandered and "defrocked."[70]

The truth is that, in spite of the uncharitable treatment given to Father Onaindia by the clerical authorities in Rebel Spain, he remained a priest in good standing and high reputation in the minds of his fellow Basques, of French Catholic laymen, of some French ecclesiastics and of the papal nuncio in France, Msgr. Valerio Valeri. The bishop of Vitoria, Msgr. Múgica, in exile in Rome, wrote of him as follows:

> What has been said and done against Don Alberto de Onaindia is truly unjust. He is not of my diocese but he had labored in the social-worker apostolate efficaciously and admirably. I have not been able to keep quiet. I wrote to Cardinal Pacelli to tell him who Don Alberto de Onaindia was: an exemplary priest of irreproachable conduct. . . . Few persons will have merited as much as he before Our Lord, in this period of war, for the devotion and efficacity which he has always employed, to save from grave dangers, the lives of all sorts of persons of different and contrary ideologies, among them, his Archbishop of Valladolid, and the auxiliary Bishop of Valencia.[71]

Mgr. Múgica gave this opinion freely in Rome and Vatican City. When D. G. Osborne, the British envoy to the Vatican, reported to London on May 11 concerning Onaindia, he stated, quoting "an English Jesuit, who has often supplied me with reliable information" that: "The Bishop of Vitoria has, I am assured, testified as to the integrity and reliability of the Dean [*sic*] of Valladolid."[72]

The interview of Father Onaindia by Jean Richard was probably the most significant article printed in France concerning the destruction of Guernica. It brought before the influential French Catholic intellectual audience the testimony of a priest.[73] This priest was, moreover, in Paris, and he talked with small groups of Catholic intellectuals, telling them with conviction and emotion of what he had actually seen in Guernica. The unending Spanish Civil War, with its almost daily list of atrocities, and the close identification of the Catholic Church with one of the conflicting sides (a side frequently blamed for these atrocities), were posing a problem of conscience for many French Catholics. This problem became more acute with the struggle in the Basque country, where Catholic *Carlistas* from Navarre and militarists espousing the centralizing doctrines of the Castilian hierarchy were killing the more socially minded priests of the Basque country. In February 1937 a group of French Catholic intellectuals had called for an end to the fighting and had thrown onto the Spanish military the responsibility for starting the civil war. This manifesto was signed by Mme. Malaterre-Sellier, Jacques Maritain, Louis Martin-Chauffier, Emmanuel Mounier, Marc Sangnier, Étienne Borne, Francisque Gay, Georges Hoog, Jacques Madaule, Yves Simon, Paul Vignoux, and others. One signature was missing—that of François Mauriac.[74]

Then came the offensive against Bilbao, the bombing of Durango and other Basque towns, and finally the destruction of Guernica. During one meeting with a Catholic group, Father Onaindia was submitted to an intensive grilling about the attack on Guernica by Jacques Maritain, Gabriel Marcel, and Jacques Madaule. "They subjected me to a long and thorough interrogation, studied my statements to see if they could discover an error," the Basque priest later wrote.

> It was almost as if I myself were responsible for the Nazi airforce and the barbarous bombing! But such was the anguish felt by a large part of public opinion that these Catholic personalities, well known and respected in the intellectual world, were making an effort to discover the truth and then proclaim it.[75]

These Catholic groups were extremely cautious. They could, in all conscience, condemn the atrocities of the Nationalists; they could not take the side of the Republic and its Communist allies. Jacques Maritain later wrote: "Not to take the side of Salamanca, is not to take the side of Valencia."[76] At one of the small Catholic gatherings called to hear Father Onaindia, there was present a man, named F. V. Liebermann, who took notes and later published in *L'Humanité* a long account entitled an interview with Onaindia.[77] This publication in a Communist newspaper seemingly shocked some people, and Onaindia received numerous visits and telephone calls and finally sent a rectification to the press. This explanation appeared in *L'Aube* on May 6 and in *La Croix* two days later. "I have never made a statement to the newspaper *L'Humanité*," he wrote (which was technically correct), and added:

> As for the interviews I have given about the destruction of Guernica from the air, I confirm what has been published by the Havas agency. Any other commentaries or evaluations published by the press have been made under the personal responsibilities of the journalists who have signed them.

An exception was, however, made for the article by Jean Richard, published in *L'Aube* on April 29, which "is naturally in accord with the facts."[78] In truth, the interview in *L'Humanité* was as accurate as most such interviews not later corrected by the person interviewed, but if Onaindia had knowingly given an interview to the Communist newspaper, his credibility with the liberal Catholics would have been diminished.

The publication of the interview with Onaindia in *L'Humanité* immediately brought the Basque priest under attack from *L'Action Française*, which had defended the Nationalist position on Guernica, not only with the Havas-Botto dispatch but also with the account of Jean Dourec. On May 6, the monarchist newspaper commented ironically on Father Onaindia's naïvete in granting an interview to the Communist organ.[79] That same day, Charles Maurras, writing from his prison cell under the pseudonym of "Pellisson," asserted on the front page of *L'Action Française* that "the imposture of Guernica is finished." He cited as proof the Havas-Botto dispatch.

> The fable, the twice-odious fable, has been disproved. Guernica was not destroyed by the National air force. The town did not perish under the bombs dropped from the sky. It was devoured by the fires which the Russians methodically set on leaving the town, but (a lovely refinement on the same method) which were attributed to the conquerors.

After tracing the development of the Guernica story to "the liberal press of London" and to the fact that the English were always willing to believe an atrocity story blamed on a Latin people (apparently forgetting that the non-Latin Germans were the chief culprits before the court), he continued:

> After this beginning on the Thames, the socialists on the Seine picked up the story. But this was nothing. A part of our bourgeois press had to follow them. Then the old guard comes in: one Jew, two Jews. . . . Then our Christian Democrats come in. Is there anything more vile? The Jews? No, not the Jews. Our *Pédés* place their hand over their heart. We know how they were severe (they themselves say so) on the horrors of Barcelona and Madrid. They also stigmatize the horrors of Guernica. . . . Unfortunately, forty-eight hours later, we learn that the horrors of Guernica are not at all what one thought, that they are in fact quite the contrary, that their authors are the best friends of *L'Aube*, of Jewry. . . .

A final warning concluded the article:

> It is, therefore, indispensable that all the precautions of the critical spirit, that all the guards of intelligence and reason be alerted and remain ever awakened to fight against this enterprise of falsification.[80]

Another Catholic journal that reacted in high dudgeon on seeing Onaindia's interview in *L'Humanité* was *Le Nouvelliste de Bretagne*, the editor-in-chief of which, Armand Terrière, immediately placed in doubt the very existence of Onaindia.

> They wish then to make us believe that the Nationals are as barbarous as their adversaries. The destruction of Guernica has caused a lot of ink to flow in the Left press. . . . The Canon Alberto de Onaindia, if Canon there be, did he know when he made these confidences that they were intended for the organ of the Soviets?

Terrière concluded that despite Onaindia's affirmations, one could easily admit that

> the anarchists and bolshevists who hate the Basque Catholics while using

them, could easily have, as the Spanish Nationals affirm, set fire to the town and used dynamite, before abandoning it.[81]

Two days later, Terrière reproduced Onaindia's latter to *L'Aube* and Richard's original interview with Onaindia, and summed up:

> It seems that one must conclude from these different testimonies that the unfortunate Basque town was the victim of both the German aviators in the service of the National army and of the bolshevists and anarchists with whom the Bilbao leaders have unfortunately made common cause.[82]

La Croix, the official Catholic daily in France, did not mention the interview with Father Onaindia which had appeared in *L'Aube.* This newspaper had on April 29 adopted the pro-Basque version of events in Guernica; then on May 4, it published the Havas-Botto dispatch, under the heading "WHO DESTROYED GUERNICA?" and answered:

> It is difficult to know what really happened. . . . Also, in some circles, it is said that the two theses are partially exact. That is, that the German airplanes flew over Guernica and dropped some bombs, but that the extremists, allied with the Basque nationalists, took advantage of the circumstances to carry out, in their turn, a work of destruction, exploding the mines that they had probably prepared to burn down the town the day that their adversaries were near, just as they had done at Eibar.[83]

This reasoning was to be followed by Wladimir d'Ormesson in *Le Figaro.*[84] This too convenient fence straddling displeased the Christian Democrats at *L'Aube,* and Jean Richard, two days later, attacked *La Croix* and *Le Figaro,* without, however, naming them.

> Many seek to persuade themselves that the burning of the holy city of the Basques was done by the Basques themselves. In order to spare the suscepti-bilities of exacting friendships, they sustain with guilty candor two opposing theses, without seeking to know the truth.[85]

The most significant result of Father Onaindia's sincerely related testimony was the publication in Paris, on May 8, in at least two Catholic dailies, of a manifesto, signed by numerous Catholic laymen of intellectual eminence, protesting the bombing of Guernica. This document, which gave renewed vigor to the controversy over Guernica, read in part:

> The Spanish civil war has just taken on, in the Basque country, a particularly atrocious appearance. Yesterday, it was the aerial bombardment of Durango. Today by the same method, it is the almost complete destruction of Guer-nica, a town without defense, sanctuary of Basque traditions. Hundreds of non-combatants, of women and children, have perished at Durango, at Guernica and elsewhere. Bilbao, its population swollen by refugees, is men-aced with the same fate. Whatever opinion one may hold concerning the quality of the factions which face each other in Spain, one can not deny that

the Basque people are a Catholic people, that public worship has never been interrupted in the Basque country.

Under these conditions, it is the Catholics, without any distinction of party, who should be the first to raise their voices so that the world may be spared the pitiless massacre of a Christian people. Nothing justifies, nothing excuses, the bombing of open towns such as Guernica. We address an anguished appeal to all men of feeling and good will, in all countries, for an immediate end to the massacre of non-combatants.

The signers were: François Mauriac, of the French Academy, André Bellivier, Charles du Bos, Stanislas Fumet, Hélène Iswolski, Georges Hoog, Olivier Lacombe, Maurice Lacroix, Jacques Madaule, Gabriel Marcel, Jacques Maritain, Emmanuel Mounier, Jean de Pange, Domonico Russo, Boris de Schloezer, Pierre van der Meer de Walcheren, Maurice Merleau-Ponty, Marcel Moré, Claude Bourdet, Claude Leblond, Francisque Gay, Georges Bidault, Jean Leroy, deputé des Vosges, Louis Terrenoire, Jean Richard, Pierre-Henri Simon, Étienne Borne, Luigi Sturzo, and many others.

No Catholic appeal of the Spanish Civil War published in France in condemnation of Nationalist activities had to this time garnered so many and such influential signatures. This was due to the testimony of Father Onaindia, who had himself spoken with heartfelt eloquence to many of the signers, a fact that was underlined in an annex to the document itself:

This present appeal has been published after some of the signatories present in Paris—Mr. Stanislas Fumet, Mrs. Hélène Iswolski, M. Olivier Lacombe, Jacques Madaule, Gabriel Marcel, Jacques Maritain, Pierre van der Meer de Walcheren—have been able to hear, concerning the facts about Guernica, the testimony of the Canon Onaindia y Zuluaga, who was present at the moment of the bombardment. With reservations concerning the conclusions that only an international enquiry could establish, whether or not other elements took part in the destruction, it is evident from this testimony that Guernica, a town without defense, was really bombed unceasingly for three hours and that the airplanes pursued the fleeing people with machine-gun fire.[86]

With this document a significant sector of French public opinion, significant not only in France but internationally, had adopted the version of the destruction of Guernica completely concordant with that given by the British newspaper correspondents who were in Bilbao, and completely opposed to that fostered by Nationalist propagandists and deeply at variance with that published widely in France, Nazi Germany, and elsewhere, distributed by the French news agency, Havas.

L'Osservatore Romano commented immediately on the appeal, news of which it attributed to the Havas Agency. It had apparently not been communicated directly to the Holy See. The Vatican daily insisted that the appeal took no position concerning the conflicting parties of the civil war, and headed the article "Per i non combattenti." However, the Havas article did refer to the "bombing" of Guernica, a town that had been burned by arsonists according to the news previously published in the newspaper. [87] It also noted that the appeal spoke of "important eye witnesses, especially at Guernica," but it did not mention Father Onaindia by name.

> The article said: This iniative should be extended . . . not only to the Basque country, but to all of Spain, wherever the civil population might be in danger and whatever the origins of the menace; yesterday, for example, to Oviedo, today to Valladolid and Saragossa.[88]

On the following day, *L'Action Française* wrote of the appeal and of the reaction of *L'Osservatore Romano,* under the heading: "*L'Osservatore Romano* gives a lesson to MM. Mauriac and Maritain." It noted that the signatories attributed to themselves the title of "Catholics," and then quoted from the previous day's article in the Vatican daily, which it interpreted as a rebuff to the signers of the manifesto. On its own, the monarchist daily added:

> The allegations of the manifesto concerning Guernica are founded on lies. Leaving to one side this detail, it appears clearly from the article in *L'Osservatore Romano* that MM. Mauriac and Maritain are lacking not only in Catholic religious feeling but also in sentiments of humanity.[89]

When Jacques Maritain saw the article in *L'Osservatore Romano* commenting on the appeal of May 8, he addressed a letter to the editor, Count dalla Torre. Parts of this letter were published on the first page of the Vatican daily, some days later. "I am grateful to you for having marked the true character of this document," wrote the French Catholic philosopher. "I can assure you that all those who have signed it protest equally against the bombing of any open town, by anyone." He told the editor about the formation by himself and some friends of the Committee for Civil and Religious Peace in Spain.[90]

> which groups men of very different opinions, and who, wishing to realize a labor free of all political parties, desire to contribute, in so far as it is possible for foreigners to do so, to render less inhuman the consequences of the Spanish war and to hasten the end of this cruel struggle among fellow-citizens.

After the extracts from Maritain, the organ of the Holy See concluded:

> All this shows how false were the assertions of a newspaper which had spoken of lessons given by ourselves to some one who, on the contrary, has seen therein a just commentary, declaring himself in full agreement with it.[91]

La Croix commented twice on the Vatican daily's reaction to Maritain's letter, on each occasion interpreting the reaction as a reprimand to *L'Action Française.*[92]

Another highly criticized Catholic publication, *Sept*—edited by the Dominicans—also participated in its manner in the discussion over the May 8 manifesto.

The text was printed in the weekly on May 14,[93] and two weeks later Francois Mauriac attempted to explain why he had signed the document. His argument, in an article entitled "The Suffering Member," was that the world Catholic community could not let the Catholic Basques think that only the Marxists had come to their aid. "It cannot be permitted that on the day the Basque people awake from their nightmare they can verify that only the mortal enemies of their church have come to succor them."[94]

An early assault on the appeal of May 8 appeared in the extreme right-wing weekly *Je Suis Partout,* edited by Robert Brasillach. This attack on Maritain and his friends had been published originally in Rome, the work of two Spanish Dominicans, Venancio Carro, professor of theology in Rome, and V. Beltrán de Heredia, a Basque professor. Concerning Guernica they wrote:

> Obeying a watchword, the Marxist and Masonic press of England invented the legend of the bombing of Guernica, of its destruction by incendiary bombs, and the same press of France hastened to pick up the news, which was then spread by the Masonic agencies. . . . The group of writers [signers of the May 8 manifesto] did not wait to cover themselves again with ridicule. Their calumny was denied, by eye witnesses and correspondents of the international press, but these facts had no importance. This group apparently had more faith in the Masonic agencies and the Marxist press than all the rectifications of our invincible *caudillo* and fervent Catholic, General Franco, although his position was supported by the testimony of the French correspondents.

In fact, the Spanish priests wrote, "According to the latest news from Spain . . . Guernica was bombed by the miniscule and cowardly airforce of Aguirre."[95]

Shortly thereafter, Carro wrote a longer pamphlet in defense of the Nationalist position on the civil war and included therein several pages about events in the Basque country, written after he had visited Guernica.

> In the Basque country . . . the destructive effects of artillery and aircraft are greatly inferior to, and of a different type from, those produced by dynamite and fire. These latter effects are abundant in Eibar, in Guernica, in Mungúia, in Durango, in Amorebieta, and in Bilbao itself, although in the capital they failed in their calculations, thanks to Divine Providence. . . . The Nationals had no part in all this work of dynamiting and incendiary destruction; they did not provoke them and in more than one instance they were the victims. We saw the terrible ruins of Eibar, the lesser ones of Guernica, Durango, Amorebieta, Mungúia, Galdácano and Bilbao. Everywhere dynamite and fire were the true causes of so much ruin; it was the work of the separatists and Marxists.

He added a new accusation against Aguirre and the Basques. The Casa de Juntas, he wrote, far from being a venerated shrine for the Basques, was in reality being used as a dung heap when the Nationalists arrived.[96]

It is impossible not to stop here for a moment and note how reckless were those priests with their facts. Carro and Beltrán de Heredia, in their near hysteria, had accused the Basque air force of bombing Guernica, a charge few in Spain would have dared make, so well known was the near inexistence of that force. Carro charged the Basques of using the Casa de Juntas for a stable, a charge not made even by the Rebel press after the capture of Guernica. The testimony of Berniard would be sufficient to prove the accusation false. Carro said that Durango had been burned and dynamited at a time when the Nationalist propagandists were insisting that it was the very model of a town battered by shot and shell and bomb. According to press messages passed through the Rebel censorship, Munguía and Eibar were all heavily bombed. Amorebieta was also certainly bombed.[97] The Nationalists never denied the frequent bombings of Bilbao. Some bridges of the town were wrecked at the moment of evacuation by dynamite, but such acts were normal acts of war. Carro's essay was published in Spain in a pamphlet together with the earlier work he had done with Beltrán de Heredia and with still another short essay by the "Professor of Theology Carro," a sarcastic assault on the "Committee for Civil and Religious Peace in Spain."[98]

On June 28, the cathedral chapter of Vitoria had held a meeting to discuss the letter addressed on May 11 to the Pope, signed by certain Basque priests. We have already seen that in June Mgr. Galbarriatu had written a statement on this question, concerning his own signature and his reasons for signing. This paper by the cathedral chapter was doubtless done at almost the same moment. It was addressed to Cardinal Gomá, as a "protest against the lies, forgeries and omissions of a document attributed by the Reds to Basque priests." This document alleged that

> as for certain names given as signatures with the mention "charged with the parish of . . ." it has been verified that the priests in question were absent, having had to hide or flee because of the harassments, imprisonments and killings to which they were exposed.

The identity of these priests was not revealed, although it would seem that there existed no reason for not giving their names. Of more significance is the fact that the document did not either affirm or deny that Guernica had been bombed. The letter declared,

> The chapter does not wish, on any terms, to involve itself in comments on that part of the document touching on the bombing attributed to the National airforce, because it is not the business of priests to judge or take sides in this sort of matters.[99]

This letter was not widely printed in Rebel Spain, perhaps because it was not positive or precise on any point in litigation.[100] It was somehow brought to the attention of the editors of *La Libre Belgique,* who gave it wide publicity on the front page under the title "Epilogue to Guernica," and with a preface that defended the Nationalist position on Guernica; the newspaper in effect turned its back on Father Onaindia. The Belgian Catholic journal wrote:

A bombing raid by German aviators, noisily cried the Reds, who cite the testimony of ecclesiastics [Onaindia] and argue about a letter addressed by the Basque clergy to the Pope. . . . But, immediately, the Nationalist thesis began to assert itself. If there was an aerial bombing, it touched only the outskirts of the town where the Red troops were concentrated. And when, shortly thereafter, the National troops entered Guernica, Salamanca affirmed with photographs as proof, that the tragic fires were caused not by bombs but by anarchists handling sticks of dynamite and cans of gasoline.

The newspaper noted that the Vitoria chapter gave no judgment concerning the facts, but, it added, the letter "took away all value from the famous testimony of the Basque clergy in favor of the Red thesis."[101]

This article in *La Libre Belgique* came to the attention of Robert Brasillach, who used it as a peg on which to make a belated and awkward denunciation of the May 8 manifesto, under the title "THE MANIFESTO OF THE DUPES." More than anything else, Brasillach's article revealed a great confusion in his own mind concerning the controversy over Guernica. "Besides," he wrote,

they [the signers of May 8] made a great deal of noise, in their camp, about certain protestations signed by the chapter of Guernica, protesting against the famous Hitlerian planes which had set the town on fire.

The French polemicist had obviously mixed up the chapter of Valladolid, Father Onaindia, the signatories of the Bilbao letter of May 11, and the chapter of Vitoria. He wrote that the statement of the Vitoria chapter took formal position "against the lies, the forgeries and omissions" contained in the Bilbao letter and asked:

Then, the indignation against the bombing of Guernica . . . all that reposed on a forgery? on imaginary signatures? What are MM Mauriac and Maritain waiting on to go to Saint Jacques de Compostelle?

He drew this moral:

And all this means simply: "they are lying, they are lying by word and by omission," as the Catechism says. . . . One lies also when one becomes the accomplice of liars.[102]

One of the first reactions to the May 8 manifesto came from Juan Estelrich, Spanish Catalan head of the Nationalist propaganda offices in Paris. The manifesto appeared when he was correcting the proofs of a book, *La persécution religieuse en Espagne,* which was to be published anonymously in France. He commented on it in a footnote to the chapter in which he denounced the previous manifesto of the French Catholic intellectuals, published in February. The new appeal, Estelrich noted, "comes again to trouble consciences." The authors of the manifesto used the bombing of Guernica as a pretext,

> though it is already proved that the destruction of the sacred Basque town was caused by the Reds before retreating, thus continuing the uses of the tactic already employed by them, as everyone knows, at Irún and Eibar.

Estelrich then went on to accuse the French Catholics of having ignored the atrocities on the Republican side.[103]

Estelrich's comments were in turn read by Jacques Maritain, one of the signers of the May 8 manifesto—and who had been signaled out for special attention by Estelrich in his book—when he himself was correcting the proofs of a long essay already published in *La Nouvelle Revue Française* of July 1, and then being expanded as the preface to the book by the exiled Spanish Catholic Alfredo Mendizábal, *Aux origines d'une tragédie*.[104] Maritain charged that the "anonymous author [Estelrich] professes faith in all the lies advanced against the Basques, especially in the legend of the destruction of Guernica by the Reds."[105] He had taken a firm position. Guernica had been bombed.

> It is a sacrilege to profane the holy places and the Holy Sacrament, to persecute what had been consecrated to God, to dishonor and torture nuns, to exhume corpses to turn them over to derision, as was done during the dark days which immediately followed the outbreak of the war; and it is a sacrilege to shoot hundreds of men to celebrate the Feast of the Assumption, as was done at Badajoz, or to annihilate under bombs from the air, as was done at Durango—for the holy war hates the believers who do not serve it more ardently than it hates the infidel—the churches and the people in them, and the priests who were celebrating the mysteries; or, as at Guernica, a whole town with its churches and its places of worship, mowing down with machine-guns the poor people in flight.[106]

Someone had written to Maritain "with legitimate indignation" to protest that the Republican air force had dropped bombs on the Church of the Pillar in Saragossa, "which fortunately had not exploded," and the Catholic philosopher observed: "But those who rightly hold this act for an act of vandalism should be the first to reprove wholeheartedly the destruction of Guernica." He continued:

> As for those who are scandalized by the protestation (May 8, 1937) of a certain number of French Catholics against this destruction [Guernica] (where more than a thousand persons were killed), I note also: 1. that these signers reprove all bombings of open towns, by anyone (one recalls that *L'Osservatore Romano* has challenged the lying invention of those who pretended that it had given those signers a "lesson" on this matter). If the Valencia air force destroys one day, according to the principles of total warfare, a town in the white zone as the German air force destroyed Guernica, these persons will not fail to raise their voices in protest.[107]

One of the first to reply to Maritain was Vice Admiral H. Joubert, in a pamphlet sponsored by Les Amis de l'Espagne Nouvelle. Now a reserve officer, Joubert had previously served for three years with the French embassy in Madrid. The vice admiral developed a theological argument, supporting the thesis that Maritain had expressly denied, the one upheld by the R. P. Ignacio G[onzález] Menéndez-Reigada: "that this was a holy war, the most holy known to history." In the course of his argument, the vice admiral examined the war in the Basque country and the destruction of Guernica. One aspect of the situation in France concerning the Spanish Civil War at this moment was revealed by the fact that *Les Amis de l'Espagne Nouvelle* were forced to use to defend the thesis of the "holy war"—not a "holy" man but a "warrior." Joubert challenged the "exactness" of Maritain's "impressive picture." In his opinion, ". . . the assertions of an imaginative person, who was not present at the time, have been disproved by the international verification demanded by General Mola himself." This description of the visits of Botto and the other correspondents was, to say the least, highly exaggerated. Guernica, the naval reserve officer went on, was "in the front line of combat," and "if it unfortunately suffered from a bombing justified by the defensive organization of the Reds, its real destruction was due to the Reds, as Estelrich proved."

Joubert then lamented that in this, as in other cases, the intellectuals' good faith was surprised by "skillful propaganda" and their feelings of pity exploited.[108]

A few months later, Joubert returned to the question of Guernica in greater detail, this time depending in part for his arguments on Douglas Jerrold. In a public lecture, he declared:

Gentlemen, I have visited Durango and Guernica, I have made an enquiry on the spot—I speak Spanish—talked with simple and unforewarned people.

He now admitted the bombing of Guernica.

In Guernica, a staging center near the front, a bombing took place but the importance of the raid and the damage done have been greatly exaggerated.

Since the Tree of Guernica and the Casa de los Fueros had been spared, it was evident "that the bombing was not carried out in hatred of the Basque people." If Guernica was finally destroyed, it was because "the Reds . . . systematically destroyed the town before leaving it." But why did the incendiaries also spare the Tree and the Casa de los Fueros? Here Joubert added a new version: the Basques had defended this part of Guernica against the Red incendiaries. One aspect of the Guernica story preoccupied the vice admiral: how did "such legends" find credit with "so many honest people"? His answer:

. . . because some writers used reports without controlling them, believing in a propaganda of which the Basque priests, obsessed with separation, had made themselves the instruments, even up to the Holy See.

Another answer:

> ... because the Red propaganda is admirably done and does not draw back
> before any lie.[109]

In 1938 Jacques Maritain returned to the subject of Guernica, showing, as
Mauriac had done before him, a fear lest the Catholic Church be judged too harshly
by history for its positions taken during the years of the rise of Fascism and of the
Spanish Civil War. "We are certain," he said,

> and this is what I would have said here to François Mauriac, if our
> friend had not been retained elsewhere, that those who must refute at a
> later time the perverse historians diligently calumniating Catholicism for
> its contacts with the powers of evil, will not be angry to find, when
> they search the archives, some Catholics who raised their voices against
> the destruction of Guernica.[110]

On another occasion he said:

> There is nothing so grave and scandalous as to see, as we have seen for some
> years now in certain countries, the iniquitous and barbarous methods em-
> ployed by men who claim to belong to the Christian order and to Christian
> civilization. The example offered by the airplanes which bombed Guernica
> and Granollers is not a good example; at the same time that they were killing
> children and women they were wounding for a long time to come the human
> conscience.[111]

These statements and the previous manifesto of May 8, as well as the telegram
sent to the Vatican by the French Committee for Civil and Religious Peace in Spain
concerning Guernica, rankled the conservative Spanish Catholics for years after the
end of the fighting. One of them, a priest named Antonio José Gutiérrez, dedicated
almost one hundred pages to an attack on Maritain, Mauriac, and others, an attack
based in part on the alleged Jewish origin of the noted Catholic philosopher.
Gutiérrez's statement of what had happened in Guernica was the standard, often
contradictory, inconclusive version current in Spain for more than thirty years after
the incident: Guernica was but five kilometers from the fighting front; it possessed
an arms factory; it held enemy reserve forces, and was blocking the Nationalist
advance. This argument seemed to justify the destruction of the town by the
Nationalists, but then Gutiérrez added:

> The Nationals had neither interest in, nor profit from, the deliberate destruc-
> tion of the town, of which they were soon to be masters. Nor could they halt
> their advance, or send it by other paths, simply to please their adversaries.
> The criminals were the Reds and their allies who defended a town in the line
> of military advance and systematically destroyed, when they fled, what they
> could not defend, just as they destroyed by flame and dynamite the town of
> Irún.[112]

But, he noted, a "reasonable explanation" of all this had already been given. He did not state where. He did not discuss a bombing; he neither affirmed it nor denied it. What Gutiérrez found impossible to forget was the attitude of Maritain, Mauriac, and the other pro-Basque French Catholics. Gutiérrez found Mauriac to be "a writer completely profane, without competence in moral questions."

That Maritain, "with the conceits and pretensions of a moralist should take the misfortune of Guernica as a pretext for his insensate declamations, was unpardonable." Maritain, he continued,

> ....agitates the affair of Guernica with that tearful accent of his which pretends to be ascetic and remains simply an inadmissible mixture of religion and politics[113]

He stated that Maritain, who was

> so scandalized by the harsh operations of the war zone, never raised his voice against the crimes and bombings carried out far from the front, with no military objectives, by the legitimate government, composed of Basque separatists, Masons and bolshevists. . . . For none of these crimes, multiplied and continuous, was an urgent telegram addressed to the Sovereign Pontiff by the pious members of the "French Committee for Civil and Religious Peace in Spain."[114]

Spanish-speaking Catholics in South America also reacted strongly against the manifesto of May 8 of the French Catholic intellectuals. A representative of Latin American Catholicism, Mgr. Gustave J. Franceschi, of the Argentine Academy of Letters, was visiting in Spain at the time of the destruction of Guernica. His presence in Nationalist Spain was widely chronicled in the press as evidence of the wide support the Rebel cause had in Spanish America.[115] Mgr. Franceschi was editor of the review *Criterio,* and during his journeys throughout Rebel Spain he sent back articles to his magazine. He wrote from Vitoria on May 11, disgusted by "the lies used 'informationally' by eminent politicians." He was referring to Lord Cecil of Chetwood, and to Pierre Cot, French minister of aviation, who had both spoken about air bombing and Guernica to a mass meeting in London on April 30. They had spoken thusly, Franceschi wrote, in spite of the fact that the original charges of the English and French press—that Guernica had been bombed by Nationalist planes—were roundly denied by Franco's headquarters, which announced that bad weather had grounded the planes. The Argentine priest declaimed:

> *I have been in Guernica* not once but twice. . . . The ruins I have seen in Spain, now for almost a month, have taught me to distinguish among the results of aircraft bombing, artillery shelling and burning. When the principal walls are still standing, without holes, while all the interior part of the house is destroyed, not a piece of wood unburnt, and moreover the upper part of

the windows blackened with smoke, and when this scene is repeated exactly in all the houses on both sides of the street, and in several streets, then it is evident that we are in the presence of arson. This is what happened in Guernica, as I can show with the photographs I personally took.

Mgr. Franceschi found incomprehensible the fact that Lord Cecil could invoke the name of the Almighty, that President Aguirre, "who could not fail to know the truth about Guernica and yet was the principal inventor of the lie," could confess and take Communion. "How," he asked, "can they reconcile such demonstrations of religious feeling with the most evident political immorality?"[116]

It was in reply to this article of Mgr. Franceschi, published in *Criterio* on May 27, that Doctor Juan Pascual de Orkoya, an Argentine Basque, wrote to the Catholic editor on June 17 an open letter, later published as a pamphlet under the title *La verdad sobre la destrucción de Gernika.* This analytical work of the first order was the earliest effort made to throw light on the problem of Guernica by studying the evidence found in the newspaper dispatches of the well-nourished press of Buenos Aires. Pascual de Orkoya arrived at this conclusion:

> If we leave to one side our prejudices and allow ourselves to be swayed by reason, we shall have to admit *the destruction of Guernica by the airforce at the service of the Rebels as an historically certain fact.*[117]

Mgr. Franceschi left Spain for France early in June. In Paris he discovered the existence of the Committee for Civil and Religious Peace in Spain, which had just published an appeal signed by Maritain, Mauriac, Mounier, and others. He marveled at "the ingenuousness of these persons of so much talent who, while their own house is smoking, offer to put out the fire in their neighbor's dwelling."[118] He was home in Buenos Aires a few weeks later and there found,

> even in the Catholic camp, a disturbance that was to some extent the echo of the opposing opinions which the attitude of some French Catholic intellectuals, Maritain, Mauriac, Mounier, etc. had produced.[119]

He then immediately wrote a pamphlet in reply, a general defense of the Spanish right since 1931, justifying the military revolt. Concerning Guernica, he asked how was it possible that Maritain and the other French writers,

> who weep tears of blood for the destruction of Guernica, attributed without proof to the Whites, and who raised their voices to protest the loss of houses, do not protest the loss of souls in the Basque country.[120]

In his criticism of the French Catholic intellectuals, Mgr. Franceschi was never as offensive as was the French right-wing press. He was quite frankly bewildered by their attitude and thought he had found the answer in their patriotism. They feared that some day Hitler might be the enemy of France, and Franco the ally of Hitler.

> But this patriotic anxiety of M. Maritain and his colleagues, an anxiety that appears clearly in their writings, may be very respectable from the viewpoint

of French temporal interests, but in no wise can it influence our judgment concerning the Spanish movement seen in the light of Catholic principles.

And he again expressed his bewilderment before

that attitude that reserves all its Christian charity for its enemies and none for its friends, that weeps for the eight hundred—authentic or not—of Guernica, but not for the eight thousand of Málaga. . . .[121]

Another foreign, slightly veiled, attack against Maritain, Mauriac, and other French Catholics because of their position on Guernica, and also against Onaindia, came from the English Catholic Lord Clonmore. Vatican City, he noted, had reported "that after the Guernica affair certain well-known non-Italian theologians had taken a hostile view towards Franco." He said that this "hostile view" was "supposed to have been intensified by the propaganda of a certain Canon who claimed to be a Basque priest." He dismissed Onaindia, who was not named, any more than were the "non-Italian theologians," by adding: "It has since, however, been reported that this Canon has been disowned by the Chapter whom he claims to represent."[122]

L'Action Française was not technically a Catholic newspaper; it was even on the *Index* of the Vatican.[123] However, its editors considered themselves Catholics, and its readers were conservative Catholics. It was but natural, then, that it should be in the forefront of those combating the group around *L'Aube,* and the positions of the *Aube* group concerning the destruction of Guernica. *L'Action Française* was the French newspaper that published the largest number of dispatches concerning Guernica favorable to the pro-Nationalist arguments. We have already seen that it printed the Havas-Botto report and another article signed by Jean Dourec in the days immediately following the capture of Guernica by the Rebel army. After the distribution of the May 8 manifesto, *L'Action Française* not only attacked the manifesto, as already related, but also increased its accounts and analyses of what had happened at Guernica. On May 11 and 19 the monarchist journal published two more reportages on the subject, this time from its chief correspondent in Spain, Pierre Héricourt, who by May 19 had made, he wrote, four trips to the ruined town.[124]

To uphold the Nationalist theses, he advanced three principal arguments:

1. The dissimilarity of appearance between the ruins of Durango and Guernica;

2. The absence of bomb splinters on building walls, and of bomb holes in the streets, of Guernica; and

3. The impossibility of provoking such a rapid and complete destruction by the means at the disposal of the Nationalist air fleet.

"At Durango," he wrote, repeating a theme already used by other correspondents; "it is perfectly clear that National airplanes bombed the town," because "one can see on the walls the characteristic impact of shrapnel. But at Guernica, there is nothing similar."

Héricourt insisted on the almost total absence of bomb holes in the streets. He had found only five large holes in all Guernica, and these, he told his readers, could have been made by mines. "How can we explain," he asked,

> that no bombs fell on the roads which cross the agglomeration in all directions? How can we explain that Franco's flyers could have achieved this *miracle:* strike so carefully at the houses on both sides of a street and be so skillful as to spare completely the roadway?[125]

A week later, he wrote that

> the troops have already done a considerable job of cleaning up. One can now circulate on these roads and streets, cleared of the rubble from the burned houses.[126]

A curious reader might have asked how did Héricourt know, a week earlier, that there were no bomb holes under the rubble? Nor were the streets yet completely disengaged.

The third argument advanced by Héricourt was thinner still:

> But a simple observation would suffice to prove the crime of the Reds: to reduce such a town to ruins in a few hours would have demanded thousands of bombs and a powerful air fleet.

The news stories from Bilbao had told of such an air fleet and of such an amount of bombs. The journalist may have felt the instability of such arguments. If it was so easy to demolish a town like Guernica with sticks of dynamite and cans of gasoline, what was the advantage of a costly air fleet? He sought a rationalization, linking primitive manpower to modern techniques of distribution. In his May 11 article, he wrote that in a first visit to ruined Guernica on May 1, he had smelled gasoline. He now suggested that "the devastation was scientifically organized and . . . the gasoline was poured into canals to make certain that the fire would spread from one group of houses to the other."[127]

This idea apparently grew on Héricourt, and he elaborated on it in his second article. He had found "new and sure proof that the fire was provoked by the Reds." At the inner doorway of a church, he had discovered signs of a pipeline hastily traced by pickax strokes at the edge of the floorboards to channel the gasoline.

> But the wet floorboards did not burn as quickly as the walls which fell down. On cleaning up the debris, the conduit was exposed.

One target of Héricourt's barrage was the bearded editor of *L'Aube*, Francisque Gay, and the correspondent finished his article by writing:

If I still believed in the good faith of Francisque Gay, I would advise him to take his beard for a walk around unfortunate Guernica, ruined by the Christian Communist incendiaries, his friends.[128]

After Héricourt's first article on Guernica, another contributor to *L'Action Française,* J. Delebecque, praised the correspondent's testimony, recalling for the readers that Héricourt had seen service in World War I and therefore knew whereof he wrote. "For all men of good faith, the case has been heard; Guernica was deliberately burned by the Reds before they abandoned the town." Delebecque then took on the *Times,* noting with regret that after publishing Holburn's dispatch, the London newspaper had on the following day printed another cablegram from Bilbao, further sustaining the Basque position.

Paris and London continue to cover with their silent approbation the campaign of lies and calumnies that is going on. . . . However it is difficult to believe that such an attitude, the stubborn refusal to face the evidence, will succeed in the end. . . . You can throw truth into the bottom of a well and drop stones after her, but you cannot kill her. She will reappear, pale and bloody, to put her torturers to shame and confusion.[129]

When other right-wing publications printed opinions on Guernica, *L'Action Française* at times reprinted them. On May 7, André Salmon, who had been a correspondent in Rebel Spain for *Le Petit Parisien,* addressed a letter to two of the editors of Doriot's *L'Emancipation Nationale.* "I saw nothing and know nothing about Guernica," he wrote. "But I have seen Irún break out in flames. I have seen the fire light up, window after window. The horror of the sight is still with me."[130] He was convinced that Guernica had suffered the fate of Irún. Maurras ("Pellisson") quoted these lines in *L'Action Française,* and used them to launch still another attack on *L'Aube,* Francisque Gay, and Georges Bidault. *L'Aube,* he thundered evangelistically, "commits each day the sin against the spirit, which Scripture tells us will not be pardoned."[131]

A year later, L. F. Auphan, making the inaugural trip of Luis Bolín's new tourist service for the devastated war zones, wrote still another version for *L'Action Française* of what had happened at Guernica. This time, a bombing of the town was admitted. A considerable part of Auphan's article was given over to an attack on "the venerable canons of Guernica," a conception that probably constituted a fantasy mélange of Onaindia and the signatories of the appeal of May 8. These "venerable canons," he told his readers, had been responsible for a statement about Guernica that had produced a certain agitation. But when Auphan visited Guernica, he was told: "Here there are no canons and there is no cathedral chapter in Guernica." He found the Casa de Juntas unharmed and the famous tree whole.

The two trees, symbol of Basque liberties, remain standing. The monument around them shows no sign of shrapnel or shell and nevertheless in this letter-manifesto, the famous canons who never existed, pretended that the aviators and artillerymen of Franco had destroyed this sanctuary of faith and tradition.

Having proved to the satisfaction of the editorial staff of *L'Action Française* that Alberto Onaindia, "canon of Guernica," had never existed, he went into the lower town. He found a convent with a hole in the roof. It had been used as a barracks, he reported, and had been consequently spared by the arsonists, as had been the church and the nearby Casa de Juntas, used by the Reds to store munitions. But bombs had fallen on Guernica.

> The Nationals did bomb one sector of Guernica and their bombs hit the target. This was a factory to produce explosives for airplanes; its dilapidated facade, covered with shrapnel splash and holes, stands out singularly among the other ruins. No! Here there is no enigma, for here as elsewhere the instructions given by the Soviet leaders have been scrupulously observed and the Red troops set fire to the town, from which-they were being driven by Franco's troops.[132]

These articles show the editorial confusion that reigned at *L'Action Française* concerning Guernica: at least four different versions of the annihilation of Guernica were presented to the readers in the course of fifteen months.

In France, the debate concerning the devastation of Guernica polarized around the testimony of Father Onaindia, but other elements, notably the Havas-Botto dispatch and the later articles in the *Times,* were also projected into the controversy, and frequently they were all mixed up together. The Havas Agency distributed a summary of Holburn's report of May 5,[133] but it did not send out any information about the editorial in the newspaper of the same date or about Steer's article of May 6.[134] But elsewhere in the world, this editorial was thought important, and was fairly widely published, especially in the *New York Times* and in *La Nación* of Buenos Aires. Steer's article of May 6 was also widely reprinted, except in France. It is difficult today to justify journalistically Havas's distribution of Holburn's article of May 5 (which could be interpreted as favorable to the Rebels if carelessly read in English, and which was completely favorable to the Rebels in the Havas summary) and the nondistribution of Steer's story of the following day (completely favorable to the other side). And it is difficult today to know whether the Havas man in London, Paul-Louis Bret, thought the editorial and Steer's dispatch not worth cabling, or whether he cabled the information and Havas, for unknown reasons, suppressed it. (It is also possible that Havas had simply told Bret not to send anything more on Guernica from London.)[135] The Havas service cannot be consulted today, for the original news dispatches concerning the Spanish conflict, with one sole exception, have been turned into wood pulp.

More disquieting is the fact that the Havas summary of Holburn's dispatch was, to say the least, inadequate. It omitted the essential part of Holburn's report—this was, as already pointed out, that he told his editors and his readers, in a dispatch passed by the Salamanca (Vitoria) censorship, that Guernica "was bombed intermittently over a period of three hours." There were several other references to a bombing in Holburn's story. This was news in France on May 5 for it contradicted everything already published in France from the correspondents on the Rebel side: the Havas-Botto telegram, the first Massot story in *Le Journal,* and Dourec's article in *L'Action Française.* In the Havas resume of Holburn, there is but one indirect reference confirming that Guernica had been bombed. Nor did Holburn's concluding words appear in the Havas summary: "In the investigators' opinion it will be difficult to establish exactly how the fire started." Since the original of this dispatch has also been destroyed, there is no way of knowing if the story printed in France was the exact message sent from London.

The Havas résumé of Holburn's dispatch was invoked on May 9 by a right-wing Lille newspaper, *La Dépêche,* in a virulent attack against "a certain newspaper of Paris which is hardly antireligious," by which it indicated *L'Aube.* Father Onaindia had visited Lille a few days after his arrival in France, summoned by Cardinal Achille Liénart, to whom the Basque priest explained what he had seen in Guernica.[136] He evidently did not visit *La Dépêche,* for the newspaper placed in doubt his very existence. It interpreted the Havas-Botto dispatch as the collective voice of the foreign press corps in Vitoria, pointing out that "General Mola had let the foreign correspondents visit the ruined town" and that their testimony was that "the 'Reds' had destroyed Guernica." He added that "the correspondent of *The Times* [Holburn], although hardly favorable to the Spanish Nationalists, loyally confirmed this fact." But *L'Aube,* despite this evidence, had not printed a word of rectification, and "its unfortunate readers, almost all honest people of good faith, are still ignorant of the truth." As for the Basque priest sponsored by *L'Aube,* "it seems that he has never existed except in the imagination of a demagogic and sectarian writer." The conclusion of the editorialist: "The destruction of Guernica was caused by fires, and, therefore, was done by the Reds."[137]

In reply, *L'Aube* recalled Onaindia's original declarations on April 30, confirmed on May 6, which had had an "international repercussion."

> A whole sector of the French and English press has passionately discussed these declarations or reproduced them. . . . This act has caused an emotion everywhere, people seeing it as a return to the barbarous methods which one thought, after the Great War, would not again appear.

The writer in *L'Aube* remarked that since Father Onaindia had confirmed his identity and repeated his declaration in the Catholic newspaper on May 6, three days before *La Dépêche* had appeared, it could hardly pretend that the priest did not exist. And since the Lille newspaper demanded the truth, here it was: "*La Dépêche* lies." True it was that the *Times* had published a cablegram from its man in Vitoria, "a telegram which is, in fact, in the sense indicated by *La Dépêche,*" but,

L'Aube pointed out, in the same number, the *Times* devoted an editorial to the contents of this telegram.

> Did *La Dépêche* see it? If it did, why did it not point out that *The Times* therein maintained its original version of the smashing of Guernica by German planes of the Rebel army? . . . This article appeared in *The Times* of May 5; *La Dépêche*, in four days, has not had the time to read two articles. Let us rather say that it did not want to read them. And since *La Dépêche* wishes, as we do also, to recognize the perfect loyalty of *The Times* in this affair, why did not *La Dépêche* speak of the new dispatch of *The Times*, published the next day, refuting with supporting proof, all the allegations of General Franco? Why? Because certain newspapers do not seek the truth such as it is, but seek to diffuse an image of the truth, as they desire it to be."138

L'Aube, by first publishing the statement of Onaindia then by reaffirming it, was to prove the most active defender in France of the Republican arguments concerning Guernica. It was not surprising that *L'Aube* was also involved in another skirmish concerning Guernica, fought principally between Léon Bailby, editor of *Le Jour*, and David Scott, head of the *Times* Paris bureau. When Bailby, ardent defender of the Franco cause, received the summary of Holburn's dispatch about Guernica, through the services of the Havas agency, he rushed into print to congratulate the author of the story and the newspaper that had printed it.

> It is known that the Catalan and Valencian anarchists lied to the world when they pretended that Guernica had been atrociously bombed by the foreign aviation in the service of the Nationals,

he wrote, aggressively defining his position, and bemoaned:

> We were shown the German airplanes using their machine-guns to take pot-shots point-blank at women, children and old people fleeing their little town set on fire by aerial bombs. An indelible image of cruelty by Franco and Mola was graven on the spirit of civilized men.

Bailby then invoked the dispatches from the correspondents who entered Guernica after its capture, misinterpreting, as others had done, the opinion of the Havas man for that of the unanimity of the foreign correspondents.

> They verified the fact that the fire, far from falling from the heavens, came from the ground, that the walls black with smoke had been doused with kerosene.

However, Bailby was tormented by one scruple: the articles of the British correspondents.

> How could serious newspapers like *The Times* assure us of having been witnesses of murders carried out by the German aviation at Guernica?

The editor of *Le Jour* had found the answer.

> *The Times has had the courage to recognize its error and to efface the memory of it with a new, better documented statement brought by its correspondent at Vitoria.*

This was followed by a quotation from Holburn, in capital letters:

> IT IS (he says) THE BASQUES WHO ARE RESPONSIBLE FOR THE BURNING OF GUERNICA AS THEY WERE OF THAT OF DURANGO AND EIBAR. IN FACT, IN THESE TOWNS WHICH SUFFERED A CONSIDERABLE BOMBARDMENT DURING THEIR RESISTANCE, FIRES BROKE OUT ONLY AT THE MOMENT OF EVACUATION. THAT IS, THE FUGITIVE REDS SOUGHT AT THE SAME TIME TO LEAVE BEHIND THEM NOTHING BUT ASHES AND TO CHARGE THEIR PURSUERS WITH AN IMAGINARY CRIME.[139]

Bailby's article immediately brought another controversialist into the fray. This was Jean Maze, editor-in-chief of *La Flèche*. His reply to Bailby shows how the inaccurate Havas resume of Holburn, and then the perversion of that résumé by Bailby, all served to falsify the position of the *Times* before the French public. Maze saw the position of the French press more clearly than did many of his colleagues. His article was entitled "How the French press lies . . ." and for him Bailby was "the most hateful pisser of ink in French journalism." To say that Guernica had been burned by the "Reds" was "so grotesque that it took a miserable dupe of the daily farce like Bailby to believe it." There is not, he affirmed,

> in Paris or London, or in Bilbao, a single news agency editor, a single serious journalist—of the Right or of the Left—who would uphold the position that the destruction of Guernica and the massacre of its inhabitants is not due to the airforce at the service of the "national" government.

Nevertheless, there were newspapers in Paris that did maintain the contrary, and

> One must analyze the raw material of the lies of our great press and the different forms which our licensed liars give this material.

The difficulty for Maze was to explain this "raw material," the dispatches of Holburn and Botto. The task would have been much simplified had Maze gone to the English-language original in the *Times* and analyzed that dispatch, with its emphasis on the fact of the bombing, and then have demonstrated the contradiction between the *Times* man, who admitted the bombing, and the Havas man, who denied that bombing. But the Havas résumé did not mention that essential fact. Maze apparently trusted the Havas résumé and even Bailby's deformation of it. He considered that both the *Times* and Havas had said the same thing:

> Each declares that "the journalists" visited Guernica conducted by officers of General Mola's staff. "They" have been able to verify that all the sections of

wall still standing bear no trace of bomb splatter, which proves the evident arson of the town. Nowhere does the Havas correspondent tell us that he has seen "himself," that he has verified "with his own eyes," all this evidence, that he has accompanied the journalists on their visit. One can then believe without risk of being mistaken that the visit was organized solely for the editors of the rags of Seville and Burgos, and that the reports of the correspondents of Havas and of *The Times* were based on a semiofficial report which was given them later.[140]

That is, Maze, believing that Guernica had been bombed by aircraft from the Nationalist side, could explain the telegrams from the correspondents of the *Times* and Havas only by assuming that neither man had really visited the ruined town. Maze was of course ill informed as to the real contents of Holburn's dispatch, but his speculative analysis contains probably the first suggestion that something was incorrect about the Havas-Botto story.

Another journalist in Paris was still more outraged by Bailby's work. When David Scott,[141] head of the *Times* office in Paris read *Le Jour,* he sat down and wrote a letter to Bailby, saying that he could not find in Holburn's dispatch "any declaration corresponding near or far to what you have published in the guise of a quotation from our newspaper," and drawing to Bailby's attention the fact that Holburn "declares at the end of his article that the Insurgent authorities themselves recognize the difficulty of establishing the cause of the fire," Scott pointed out that in the *Times* of May 6 there appeared a new article from the correspondent in Bilbao (Steer), which proved "that *The Times* in no wise abandons its original position." He also adjured Bailby:

> You are certainly aware of the conditions under which the foreign correspondents are obliged to work in that part of Spain where the Insurgents are today masters. For the editor who seeks the truth, this fact could be only one reason more for avoiding all interpretations, and still more any tendentious quotation from the messages of these journalists.

Scott then requested that his letter of rectification be printed in *Le Jour,* in a place of importance equal to Bailby's original article, as provided for in French law.

Bailby paid no heed to Scott's summons. When the English correspondent telephoned to Bailby's office, the French editor was absent. Finally, Scott gave Bailby an ultimatum of twenty-four hours.[142] On the afternoon of May 17, Bailby reacted, publishing his reply to Scott on the front page, under the same headline as his May 6 article: "IT IS THE REDS WHO SET FIRE TO GUERNICA." He admitted receiving a missive from the representative of the *Times,* written in a "discourteous tone." Bailby immediately inflated this argument over the authenticity of a newspaper text into a dispute between France and England, sentimentally recalled the *Times* of Lord Northcliffe, and finally found Scott's attitude a menace to world peace. He then denied that he had quoted the *Times;* he had made a résumé of Holburn's article.

The subaltern, of whom I spoke above, considers this résumé inexact. I am, therefore, going to make him happy and edify our readers by publishing integrally the text of the Havas dispatch, dated: London, May 5, and which has never been contested.

It is not known whether or not Bailby had seen the original text in the *Times*; he wrote that his article of May 6 was based on the Havas summary. But it is immediately clear why, had he seen both Holburn's text and the Havas summary, Bailby preferred to publish the Havas summary rather than the entire article. As already stated, the summary was poorly done and omitted the essential part of Holburn's cablegram. After reprinting this inadequate Havas summary of Holburn's dispatch, Bailby summed up:

> Since then, similar testimony continues to fortify our thesis. *L'Action Française,* whose special correspondent in Spain, Pierre Héricourt, confirms Communist responsibility for the fire, publishes new documents which prove how carefully lying propaganda is being carried on in this affair, even in Catholic circles.[143] It is the Reds who have set fire to Guernica. The audacious counter-verities advanced against this fact will not change anything.[144]

On the morning of May 18, Scott published his letter in the Socialist organ, *Le Populaire.*[145] The dispute continued on the following day, in *L'Aube,* which reproduced not only Scott's letter to Bailby but also extracts from Bailby's article dated the previous day and a sharp reply to the latter by Pierre-Louis Falaize. The article effectively demolished Bailby's arguments, showing that what he had offered as a quotation from the *Times* on May 6 and what he preferred to call a "résumé" of a Havas dispatch on May 18 was neither in the English newspaper nor in the Havas summary nor was it an honest "résumé" of either. It was pure Bailby. Falaize here found himself in a certain quandary; he had previously recognized that the Holburn story in the *Times* was "correctly enough translated by the [Havas] agency."[146] This was, as shown, inexact, but it was impossible for Falaize to reverse his opinion at this point. He was, therefore, reduced to stating that Bailby did not reprint all of the Havas dispatch,[147] that Bailby should have reproduced the Holburn story rather than a Havas summary, and that Bailby's interpretation of the Havas article was "tendentious." Falaize explained Bailby's preference for the Havas summary:

> It is easy to understand M. Bailby's embarrassment: each paragraph of the English [Holburn's] correspondence contains reticent phrases revealing what Mr. Scott called "the conditions under which the foreign correspondents are obliged to work in that part of Spain where the Insurgents are today masters."

Falaize then repeated a curious rumor apparently circulating in Paris newspaper circles: the Havas correspondent (Botto) had sent his message without having really visited Guernica; not only had he not visited Guernica, he had put at the end of his dispatch this sentence, "Please give widest possible publicity to this news." This statement constituted, as had Jean Maze's earlier article in *La Flèche,* a clear suggestion that the Havas-Botto dispatch was completely false.[148]

Needless to say, Bailby's performance did not satisfy Scott, who on the following day addressed still another letter to the editor of *Le Jour:* He wrote:

> I do not ask you to quote *The Times* but I do ask you, if you insist on quoting it, to quote it exactly and not to deform the text. You have preferred to summarize its text while appearing to quote it, at the same time giving it a sense agreeing with your political predilection.

The difficulty for Scott was the same as that experienced by Falaize: to attack Bailby without too openly attacking the Havas agency, which was the source of Bailby's information about Holburn's report. Scott continued:

> Not only have you published an imaginary text disguised as a quotation from *The Times,* but, to make your quotation, you have based your information on an agency text which to start with was but a summary, for the exactitude of which you had no guarantee.

Scott expressed his surprise that the editor of a newspaper like *Le Jour* would content himself with "the version of a cable agency" and had not gone to the source, *The Times* itself, to verify the text. There was in this letter a hardly veiled suggestion that the Havas summary of Holburn's cablegram was inadequate. This new letter by Scott was equally ignored by Bailby, and it appeared a few days later in *L'Aube.*[149]

A polemical position similar to that of Bailby was sustained by the Paris right-wing weekly *Gringoire* directed by Horace Carbuccia. In this publication Raymond Recouly praised Republican propaganda concerning Guernica, which had been developed "with great skill . . . a remarkable understanding of the psychology of Anglo-Saxon sentimentality." But, Recouly went on, the situation had changed when the foreign reporters with Mola went into Guernica. "The results of this investigation are disastrous for *The Times,*" he declared, citing at length the "telegram of the Havas agency, little suspected of partiality towards the Nationals," and attributing, once again, the conclusions of the Havas-Botto dispatch to "the journalists belonging to different nations." The few survivors spoken to by Botto declared "that the Reds had, once again, as at Irún, set fire to the town before evacuating it." Recouly also cited Massot, who "develops this accusation by a series of convincing and luminous proofs." His conclusion was:

> One of two things is true; either these journalists, the special correspondent of the Havas Agency, that of *Le Journal,* all their colleagues, have lied, which is difficult to admit; or, the correspondent of *The Times* [Steer] (who moreover was not present at the supposed bombing, having, as he says, visited

the town only the following morning), if he did not deceive himself, knowingly deceived his readers.150

This is a fair assumption, concerning Botto and Massot, perhaps fairer than Recouly realized.

Recouly wrote again about Guernica the following week. This time he declared that

all the war correspondents accredited to the National Headquarters, having been invited to visit in detail the site [Guernica], have affirmed that the damages were not at all caused by aviation bombs, but by the fire which the governmental troops had, on their departure, set alight.

Once again Botto's conclusions become those of all his colleagues, and once again the beginning of the fires in Guernica is fixed to coincide with its evacuation. The *Gringoire* reporter now discovered "the correspondent of *The Times* with the Nationals [Holburn]," who, he averred,

completely supported the affirmations of his colleagues, recognizing that he had not seen a single bomb hole, but, on the other hand, many evident traces of voluntary incendiarism. *The Times,* whose sympathies go openly to the Reds, published this telegram, which demolished from top to bottom the accusation brought by its other correspondent. Such are the facts, summarized in all sincerity, in full impartiality.151

But as the reader knows, this statement did not constitute "the facts, summarized in all sincerity, in full impartiality." Holburn's dispatch was dishonestly interpreted; the *Times* editorial of May 5 was ignored, and Steer's report of May 6 unmentioned. The limitations on the debate in France about the facts concerning Guernica were in great part due to the manner in which the news about Guernica had been presented to the French public. The debate between Scott and Bailby was between newspapermen, and even they did not know too well the texts involved. The important texts on the English side were: the original news stories from Steer, Monks, and Holme, published on May 27, 28, and subsequent days; Holburn's dispatch of May 5; the *Times* editorial of May 5; and Steer's cablegram of May 6. The original messages from Steer, Monks, and Holme were all known by one means or another in France, usually through the London correspondents of certain newspapers. But Holburn's dispatch was known only through the unsatisfactory Havas summary. The *Times* editorial was unknown. It is difficult to explain how Scott did not know of it; but if he did, it is equally difficult to explain why he did not make a point of it in his dispute with Bailby. *L'Aube* made a reference to the editorial and to Steer's report of May 6, in an article on May 12, but it never did publish a single quotation either from the editorial or from that article of Steer's. Steer's May 6 article did not appear in France until June 1937, when it was published in *Esprit* (see below). Thus, some of the basic elements for the controversy were either never published in France, or published late, or published for a limited audience. The fact that these important papers for the Guernica dossier were either imperfectly known, or completely unknown, in most of France made such writing as that of Recouly possible. But, if they were poorly known or unknown, was it not to some degree the responsibility of the instrument charged with the distribution of news in France, the Havas agency?

One of the signers of the May 8 manifesto, Emmanuel Mounier, founder and editor of *Esprit,* made vigorous use of his monthly magazine to defend the Basque position. In its issue of June 1937 the editors assembled twenty-two pages of documents and arguments concerning the destruction of Guernica, under the heading: "Guernica, or the Technique of the Lie."[152] This article was divided into four parts: (1) "The principles"; (2) "Facts and Testimonies"; (3) "Lies"; (4) "Epilogue." In the first part, the editors of *Esprit* began with Hitler's famous statement of "principles," that "the very enormity of the lie constitutes a factor which favors its acceptance," and commented:

> No doubt exists that each word of this diatribe reveals at the same time a tactic conscientiously followed by the imitators of Hitler in all countries, from the burning of the Reichstag to the bombing of Guernica. In stating the principles, he applies it, for it is always a question of imputing to the enemy the methods and exploits that one has planned or has done oneself. It is true that the political lie becomes an offensive arm of the first order. This matter of Guernica permits a clear establishment of the facts, and by that same act permits the exposure in a particularly convincing manner of all that strategy of lies which, in creating a permanent ambiguity, disorients the consciences of the whole world.

In the section "Facts and Testimonies" were included most of the basic documents then known.[153] But there were two significant omissions: the *Times* editorial of May 5 and the Havas-Botto dispatch. In the section entitled "Lies," there is a résumé of Massot's article in *Le Journal* of May 3; there is a reproduction of his dispatch of May 8, also in *Le Journal;* there is a mention of an article in *Le Jour* of May 3 but no reproduction or résumé of this story.[154] This dispatch, though not identified as such, was the Havas one sent by Botto. If *Esprit* considered Steer's report to be the truth, and Massot's May 8 report a "lie," why then did it not reproduce the Havas dispatch as another example of a "lie"? It was as pro-Rebel as Massot's article, and a thousand times more widely distributed and read. Are we not permitted to think that the Havas-Botto dispatch, with the prestige of the official French agency behind it, was causing a certain malaise in journalistic and political circles in Paris? There were rumors about it; it evidently provoked discussions, but no satisfactory explanation was found. Scott never denounced Botto's dispatch, although this was cited by Bailby (it was not his role); but he also hesitated to make an open accusation of Havas when he found its résumé of Holburn deficient. Maze in *La Flèche* and Falaize later in *L'Aube* suggested involved explanations of the Botto dispatch, which in part exonerated the correspondent and completely exonerated the agency. The most ardent defenders of the Basque cause faltered before a formal accusation of Havas. *L'Aube* never attacked the Havas dispatch of Botto. *Esprit* perhaps compromised; it did not call the Havas correspondent a liar, as it did Massot, but it did reprint Falaize's attempt to explain Botto's dispatch, and in the "Epilogue" it gave Maze's earlier speculation of how Botto (and Holburn) had written their reports. The editors of *Esprit* terminated by noting:

> We do not ask anyone to take the side of the "government" of Madrid, that is neither our role nor the purpose of this documentation. It is even perfectly conceivable that one be hostile to the political formula represented by that government . . . and still not believe that one has the right to conceal certain facts that no conscience can approve. These facts may upset certain judgments of convenience, certain comfortable partisanships; truth is then in its proper place, and perhaps this is for some the sign by which it is recognized.[155]

Another element for the Guernica controversy in France came from Bilbao, and appeared in the French press on May 13. It was the report of a letter, sent by a Spanish Jesuit, Ramón Azuarga, to a religious publication of the Nationalist zone, *El mensajero del corazón de Jesús.* In his missive the Jesuit listed certain "incontestable historical verities," some of which concerned Guernica:

> Rebel planes dropped a considerable number of incendiary bombs on Guernica. At Durango and Guernica, those who could escape from the fire were pursued "like rats" by machine-gunners, to the very cemeteries. . . .

He also noted that "troops burn towns only when the enemy is upon them," pointing out that Moscow was burned when Napoleon was in the city, and that Guernica was some distance from the front when it was set on fire. He added this argument: "History knows no example of combatants bombing or burning their own town, or machine-gunning their own people."[156] This letter was of course never printed by the magazine to which it was addressed, but it was reprinted in propaganda pamphlets.[157]

A number of right-wing French journalists went into Guernica from time to time. In July 1937 René Benjamin visited the ruined town and later wrote in *Candide* of "the methodical burning of the houses," which he called proof of "the gratitude of the Reds towards the people who trusted in them." He found there "ruins, debris . . . and silence. Nobody had come back. Those who lived there have fled in terror and are dying of hunger far away from their homes, among the Reds who led them."[158]

In November the naval officer turned novelist, Claude Farrère, came back from a trip to Nationalist Spain and made a declaration concerning Guernica to the France propaganda weekly in Paris, *Occident,* edited by Joan Estelrich:

> And I add that the conduct of the Reds has been unspeakable. I went to
> Guernica. I have the absolute conviction that all the destruction there was
> done exclusively with dynamite. I know about warfare and it is not possible
> that I might be confused between visible signs of shelling and the material
> proof of attacks by dynamite and fires.[159]

A French journalist, Marcel Sauvage, entered Nationalist Spain in September
1937, and in the course of a trip through the Rebel zone visited Guernica, in the
company of a "French general, a former chief of our general staff." It is difficult to
get a clear idea of what he thought about the devastation at Guernica. He gave the
Basque-Republican version, then the pro-Nationalist version. He noted: "The international military technicians say: *act of war* and recognize that Guernica was
bombed by airplanes and by cannons." He also wrote a cryptic paragraph about the
newspaper coverage of the event:

> A visit to Guernica permits one immediately to appreciate the professional
> conscientiousness of most of the war correspondents, and, on the same plane,
> the value that one can accord to the photographic documents published in
> the newspapers of opinion.[160]

Which correspondents? Which photographs in which newspapers? Is this all
sarcasm?

In his conclusion Sauvage insisted on the bombing: "At any rate, it is evident
that the small town was bombed, then set on fire, a certain part destroyed. Not
completely annihilated." He was also impressed by the irony of the fact that the
only living human beings he found in Guernica were the men and women working
in the arms factories, which had been untouched by the raiders and had been left
intact by the retreating Basques.[161]

The "former chief of our general staff" was undoubtedly General Maurice Duval,
who made frequent visits to the Nationalist war zone and wrote two books on the
military aspects of the fighting. He admitted the bombing of Guernica, and he
justified it for military reasons, but his account of the circumstances of the
bombing differs radically from any other. "These bombings had a military justification," he insisted.

> Guernica was part of a defensive whole. The attacker cannot know in the
> midst of a battle what place is still occupied and what is not. It is legitimate
> on his part to take all the precautions which permit him to spare his own
> troops.

This picture of Guernica being bombed in the midst of a raging battle is so far
from the known facts as advanced by either side that one can wonder who briefed
the general on his visits. He also observed that "it is not reasonable to pretend that
the town was evacuated before the arrival of the enemy."[162]

Eddy Bauer, a French-speaking Swiss university professor with a military background and an avowed Maurassien, went to Rebel Spain as a war correspondent in 1937, and in August visited Guernica.

> Less fortunate than M. François Mauriac, of the French Academy, or M. Jacques Maritain, who have been able to learn the facts some 600 kilometers distant, we have been forced to visit the place itself [Guernica] to form an opinion.

In Guernica, Bauer was guided by an engineer of public works, Olazábal, who had also been one of the witnesses brought before the Nationalist commission. The engineer told Bauer that on April 26 he had seen a squadron of airplanes in the sky over Guernica, and "that the population immediately ran to the shelters and at the same time a violent bombing began." He could not identify the airplanes. During the night, he said, the fires gained in intensity, spreading to the west, the direction from which the wind was blowing. (This strange fact does not appear in his statement before the commission, where he gave, in fact, considerable testimony to the contrary.) In spite of the presence of this witness to the bombing, Bauer concluded, with a contemptuous reference to "the testimony of more or less imaginary canons" (Father Onaindia and the priests who had signed the Bilbao statement of May 11?) that

> the destruction of the unfortunate little town, just as that of Irún on September 4 of last year, must be attributed on the whole to the anarchists, who fought at the side of the Basque Nationalists, and these, with an unqualifiable wickedness, took advantage of the crime of their allies to crush their enemies.[163]

This dean of the faculty of letters and professor of history at the University of Neuchâtel does not present an iota of proof for this conclusion.

The testimony of Father Onaindia and the appeal of May 8, inspired by this testimony, were the targets of the ire and sarcasm of another visitor to Guernica, the count of Saint-Aulaire. This French diplomat with Maurrasian sympathies, who had served in Spain during the monarchy, came to war-torn Spain late in 1937. He characterized the statement of "the phantom-canons . . . denounced by the chapter of the cathedral of Vitoria as a forgery," and expressed wonder that "Catholic intellectuals" should attribute more credit to a forgery than to the letters of the Spanish primate or the encyclicals of the Pope. (Neither Cardinal Gomá nor the Pope had at this time taken a public position on the bombing of Guernica.)

> This forgery had a great advantage. It gave a hearty laugh to Spanish Catholics and, in showing that the signers of the manifesto, in spite of appearances, were not responsible people, consoled them for the profound sorrow which so much injustice had at first caused them.[164]

He wrote that in his presence "a monk in Salamanca compared the signers of the manifesto to the scribes and pharisees who were the worst enemies of Christ."[165]

For Saint-Aulaire, the accusation that the Nationalists had destroyed Guernica by bombing was "at the one time the most vulgar and the most successful of lies."[166] He declared:

> Franco could not completely save Guernica, as he had saved Bilbao, for the Reds had burned it, as was their habit, before evacuating it. It is enough to walk through the ruins to recognize their trade-mark there: all the walls are charred and still smell scorched.

The diplomat then introduced into the literature on Guernica still another commission, one of which no mention has been found elsewhere. "Not without humor," wrote Saint-Aulaire,

> the Nationalists invited an international commission to visit Guernica, a commission headed by an English architect, "specialist in destruction," who learnedly demonstrated what is, obviously, the evidence.[167]

This distorted reference may be vaguely based on the McKinnon Wood visit to Bilbao (see following chapter), but this English specialist never got to Guernica, nor was he ever invited to visit the town by the Nationalists, with or without humor. Nor is it very clear just what Saint-Auliare meant by the "evidence." He mentioned as part of this evidence the fact that the Casa de Juntas, "which was said to have been the principal target of the Nationals," was undamaged. Ergo, the destruction was the work of the Basques. He also brought in an English witness, Wing-Commander James and his letter to the *Daily Telegraph* of February 18, 1938.[168] He then curiously reversed his reasoning by admitting a bombing.

> General Mola, commander of the army of the North, which conquered Guernica, when obliged to bomb military objectives near this sanctuary [Casa de Juntas in Guernica] , gave strict orders to spare it.[169]

A few months after the destruction of Guernica, the defenders of the Nationalist cause in France were as confused about what had really happened in Guernica as were their English counterparts.

But if Franco's friends in France were confused as to the details of what had happened at Guernica, they were not confused as to whom to blame for the damage done. Shortly after the article by Saint-Aulaire appeared in *Je Suis Partout*, the Nationalist propaganda organ *Occident* summed up certain opinions about Guernica:

> Douglas Jerrold, Ed. Bauer, Claude Farrère, Admiral Joubert, *The Times'* correspondent in Vitoria, and finally, the Count of Saint-Aulaire, . . . that is, everybody who has attentively examined the town of Guernica after its liberation, has pronounced the same categorical verdict: Only the fleeing incendiary militiamen sought destruction! These were the same men who filled all of Northern Spain with ashes, ruins and falling walls.[170]

The dispute over Guernica finally stopped in France, as in England, for lack of something new to say. One final opinion appeared in June 1939, on the eve of World War II, in the first general history published on the Spanish Civil War, *Histoire de la guerre d'Espagne,* by two French journalists, Maurice Bardèche and Robert Brasillach. "It was because of Guernica that the antifascist press of England and France launched their most violent manifestos," they wrote, "accusing the German airplanes of destroying the town." The French journalists placed two battalions of Asturian miners and two of Santander militiamen among the twelve defending the town.

> But they opposed no resistance and preferred to abandon their positions, not without having set fire to, and systematically destroyed, the town, which the Nationalists seized without fighting.

The two writers insisted that "a visit to the town was sufficient to realize that it had been above all burnt before evacuation exactly as Irún."[171] This did not rule out a little bit of bombing. The earliest date for their visit to Guernica was July 1938.[172]

In all reasonableness it seems difficult to admit that even if a walk through the ruins—by nonprofessionals in the assessment of war damage, fourteen months after the destruction—could show that the town had been set on fire by arsonists rather than by incendiary bombs dropped from airplanes, this same promenade would also reveal the fact that it had been burned precisely before or after evacuation by the Basques. Would not the ruins have had the same aspect in July 1938 had they been created a few days earlier than April 29?—a few days later?

Brasillach and Bardèche also remarked on the appeal of May 8, which "set fire to the powder, although the destruction of Guernica by airplanes was far from being proved." They did not mention Father Onaindia, but they did mention the document of May 11 which had been presented to the Vatican. The French writers attributed the document to "the chapter of Guernica" and denounced it as a forgery. "The famous chapter of Guernica was a chapter from a serial story," they asserted.[173] This work marked, for the time being, the end of the controversy in France. World War II and the German occupation of France brought newer disputes to the fore.

When France fell to the German advance in June 1940, Father Onaindia became a fugitive in the French Basque country, as did thousands of others. He could not cross into Spain without risking being shot, but by chance he was able to board a Polish destroyer and arrive in England, where he worked for the BBC during World War II. He spoke on the French radio during the years immediately after the Liberation, using the name of "Father Olaso," then entered UNESCO, where he works today,[174] a respected figure in the intellectual world.

3

The Secret
Controversy among
the Diplomats

The first news stories to be published concerning Guernica charged German involvement in the tragedy. The London afternoon papers of April 27 blamed the disaster on "GERMAN WAR PLANES."[1] American journals of the same date spoke of "bombing planes identified as of German manufacture."[2] Steer's dispatch, published in both London and New York on the morning of April 28, described the planes that carried out the bombing as being German. The *Daily News* of New York, a mass circulation newspaper, headlined: "REBELS' NAZI ACES DESTROY CITY, KILL 800."[3] Headlines in the *Washington Post* charged the crime to "PLANES ALLEGEDLY PILOTED BY GERMANS."[4] In spite of the scant news available to the French press on the subject of Guernica and the decision of a large part of that press to ignore the little available, on the morning of April 28, many Parisians—for example, the readers of *Le Petit Parisien*—were informed that Guernica had been wiped out by "GERMAN AIRPLANES OF FRANCO'S ARMY."[5] The *Morning Post* of London, unable to think Franco capable of such an atrocity, did suggest that perhaps the Germans had acted without the Spaniards' knowledge.[6] On the following day a news story in the same newspaper, coming from the French-Spanish frontier, said, "Reports available here suggest that there can be no doubt that German aeroplanes coming from Junta territory destroyed the town [Guernica]."[7]

The accusations against the Germans in the news stories found an echo in the writings of editorialists and commentators. On the morning of April 29, the *New*

York Times editorially denounced "wholesale arson and mass murder, committed by Rebel airplanes of German type Monday afternoon and early evening [which] left . . . Guernica . . . a smoldering ruin." That same day the French political journalist "Pertinax," who enjoyed a wide audience not only in France but also in the English-speaking world, declared to the American public that "well-informed quarters" in Paris thought that the bombing of Guernica had been ordered directly by Göring, who

> intended to give a practical demonstration of what air warfare can achieve and vindicate some of his strategical and tactical conceptions, which hitherto had been challenged at times by the general staff of the German army.[8]

The influential foreign correspondent Edgar Ansel Mowrer, of the *Chicago Daily News,* noted that

> All the stories of German "frightfulness" during the great war are being revived here as it becomes more and more certain that it was new German Heinkel and Junkers airplanes, manned by Germans and equipped with the latest model aluminum incendiary bombs made in Germany that destroyed the unmilitarized town of Guernica.[9]

On April 30 a significant American reaction came from the typewriter of Dorothy Thompson, an American woman commentator on international affairs, who had risen to worldwide prominence through her warnings on the menace of Hitler. She used Steer's dispatch as the basis for an anti-Nationalist article entitled "Women and Children First." She wrote that the bombing of Guernica was carried out by airplanes "reputedly German."[10] On April 30, in Paris, Georges Bidault, writing in *L'Aube,* publicly accused "German airplanes" of destroying the Basque town.

The *New York Times* formally blamed the Germans in an editorial on May 1. "The systematic bombing of the open town of Guernica was perpetrated, according to all available evidence, by German planes manned by German pilots," and insisted that "this climax of cruelty horrifies the world more than any other barbarity of a barbarous war." In London, the *Times* had not indicted the Germans directly in its editorial of April 28, but on May 5 it wrote:

> Independent reports have also established beyond doubt that the aircraft engaged in bombing and machine-gunning the defenceless inhabitants of Guernica were of German make, and several unexploded incendiary bombs have been recovered bearing the stamp of a German factory. The identity and the nationality of the pilots are not yet known but they can hardly remain a secret for long.

The Spanish Republicans, with the Basque government in the fore, and their allies on various international committees and political formations, also sought to bring before public—and governmental—opinion the charges against the Germans.

President Aguirre had made the charge in the first statement on April 27. On the following day he addressed a telegram to Prime Minister Baldwin, to protest Rebel accusations of Basque responsibility for the destruction of Guernica and charged German airplanes with "unprecedented savagery." On April 29, the Basques sent another cablegram to Baldwin, confirming their denials of Salamanca's statements—which, the message noted, were being echoed by the Berlin radio—and ending with an appeal for an on-the-spot investigation of how Guernica had been destroyed. "We are ready to receive all commissions, persons and institutions who desire to investigate on their own account the deeds that have been done on Basque territory." These Basque messages, of subsequent importance, were handed to the British Foreign Office by Spanish Ambassador Pablo de Azćarate.[11]

On April 29, Aguirre cabled to the Anglican dean of Canterbury, Hewlett Johnson, who had earlier in the month of April, visited the much-bombed city of Durango. "Before God and History which will judge us," said Aguirre,

> I declare that, during three hours and a half, German airplanes bombed the defenseless civil population of the historic town of Guernica, which they reduced to ashes, after having pursued women and children with machine-gun fire.[12]

Nor were the Americans and President Roosevelt forgotten in this campaign to arouse public opinion. Late in the afternoon of April 30, Spanish Foreign Minister Julio Álvarez del Vayo called, incognito, on the American ambassador in Paris, William Bullitt, and said that he greatly feared "that the Germans would destroy Bilbao by air attack as they had attacked Guernica."[13] President Roosevelt also received numerous cablegrams from abroad on the subject of Guernica. On April 29 President Companys of Catalonia cabled the American president to call his "attention to this inexpiable crime," carried out by "foreign imperialists."[14] That same day, anti-Fascist groups in Paris telegraphed to Roosevelt to denounce "the crimes committed at Guernica and . . . the systematic and unjustifiable destruction of open towns and massacre of the civilian population by Spanish Rebels and German aeroplanes."[15]

These same official démarches were quite probably made to the French government, but it is difficult today to find traces of them. The Basque delegation in France, headed by Rafael Picavea, seemingly handed notes to the French Foreign Ministry concerning Guernica on April 27 and 28.[16] Early in May, Delbos did receive a delegation composed of the Basque Minister of Industry S. Aznar, Picavea, and a member of the Tribunal of Guarantees, F. Basterrechea, but the interview seems to have been directed more to the problem of the refugees in Bilbao than to the question of Guernica.[17]

How did the German press (and that of their Italian friends) respond to these attacks? The method used by the Germans was that employed by the Spanish Nationalists and by the French newspapers favorable to Franco. The first reports of the bombing were ignored, then without a preface the denials from Salamanca, with characteristic Nazi embroidery, were printed. The first news appeared on the morning of April 28. Most journals limited their accounts to the denial from Salamanca, but the *Berliner Tageblatt,* on its front page, headlined "AGITATION AGAINST GERMANY TO DISTRACT ATTENTION FROM ATROCITIES." "It has been alleged," wrote this newspaper,

> that the German air force cooperated in the attack on a day when flight was impossible. In view of the hundreds of French and Soviet airplanes which are helping the Reds, this manoeuver is too absurd to be effective. However, it is necessary to show it for what it is: a dull-witted effort to distract attention.[18]

On the following day, the *Deutsche Diplomatisch-Politische Korrespondenz,* described by the *New York Times* man in Berlin as the "semi-official organ of the Foreign Office," qualified as "pure lies" the reports that German planes had taken part in bombing Guernica and found a manner of replying by reminding its readers that the British had used air bombing in northwest India and Aden.[19] The French press was denounced along with the English on April 28,[20] but by April 30 it was admitted that the burden of blame lay more heavily on the English. "It must be recognized," wrote a Hamburg journal,

> that the French press has not fallen an uncritical victim of the Reuter-hoax. *Le Temps* refuses the campaign of lies against Germany. *La Liberté* confirms the guilt of the Bolskeviks, and *Le Jour* publishes as a conclusion of an investigation that anarchist Basque dynamiters blew Guernica up in the air. But *The Times* knows everything better. These facts cause one to think. They are looking for a campaign against Germany and the end justifies the means.[21]

There does not seem to have been, during the first days following the catastrophe, any general directive for the Italian press concerning what to print about Guernica. The correspondent of the *Gazzetta del Popolo,* reporting from London on May 28, seemed influenced by the English newspapers, to the extent of admitting and justifying the bombing:

> After the campaign of denigration and calumny against Italy [the battle of Guadalajara], it was to be expected that the anti-Fascist and ultra-democratic press of Great Britain would also begin an offensive against Germany. The occasion was furnished by the aerial bombing of the town of Guernica near Bilbao—an operation of an essentially military character, made necessary by the circumstances.[22]

To some extent the first dispatches about Guernica sent from other European capitals to Italy simply reflected the right-wing press opinion in the country of residence of the correspondent. The English right-wing Press admitted the bombing, hence so did the London reporter of the Italian newspaper. At the same time, an Italian journalist in Berlin denounced the press stories of Guernica as a propaganda maneuver, repeating the arguments of the German newspapers.[23] And an Italian correspondent in Paris reiterated the allegations of the French press of the right:

> Reacting to a new watchword which takes as pretext the destruction of Guernica, French political circles are once again mobilized for a campaign in favor of the Spanish revolution, attributing the act to the national airforce rather than to the incendiary torches of the fleeing Republicans.[24]

The general worldwide picture of what had happened at Guernica on April 26 seemed to bear a "Made in England" label. English news stories and editorial comment unfavorable to the Nationalists—and to the Germans—even in the conservative press, were plentiful. Public statements by public groups in England were numerous. On April 28 the Trades Union Congress General Council and the Labour Party National Executive declared:

> The dreadful sufferings of the Spanish people have reached a climax of horror and shame in the criminal bombing of Guernica by German airplanes under the command of the rebel generals.[25]

On the evening of April 30, Lord Cecil presided at a meeting of the League of Nations Union in London. The public, of some seven thousand persons, approved a resolution expressing horror at the bombing of Spanish towns and the slaughter of fleeing inhabitants.[26] On May 1 a letter published in the *Times*, with significant signatures, declared that "The description in your columns . . . of the total destruction by bombing of Guernica . . . must shock all humane persons irrespective of their political sympathies."[27]

Various prelates of the Church of England defended the Basque cause. The archbishop of York, Dr. Temple, stated:

> Surely the whole civilized world should unite to express its abhorrence of such methods of warfare. The moral judgment of mankind is in the long run, a potent force, but only exerts its influence when it is expressed. Let us, then, in the name of humanity itself, unite in condemnation of such methods as those employed in the destruction of Guernica.[28]

Peter Green, canon of Manchester, observed in a letter to the press that, "If a European war comes, as seems all too likely, the scenes in Guernica will be repeated in every big town in Europe," and added: "I may live to see all central Manchester in flames."[29] The bishop of Winchester, Dr. Cyril Garbett, qualified the bombing of the town as "a cruel deliberate, cold-blooded act against the laws of God and against every law of civilization." He continued:

> The crime was a cruel and cowardly act of terrorism, which the conscience of humanity should brand as a crime in such a way that no man will ever again order such a hideous and appalling deed to be committed.[30]

The ground swell of public opinion aroused in England as a result of the destruction of Guernica was unknown elsewhere. But the country where popular feeling most nearly approximated that of England was perhaps the United States. Eden told the British Cabinet on May 5 that American Ambassador Bingham had informed him that the news about Guernica had been received in America "with the utmost horror" and that it was considered "a practice for the bombing of London and Paris."[31] But America was far from Europe, and the United States belonged neither to the League of Nations nor to the Non-Intervention Committee, and this sentiment of "utmost horror" hardly weighed on the governmental and diplomatic steps taken following the tragedy.

American press opinion, except for that of the Catholic Church, was generally in favor of the Basque side of Guernica. The American ambassador, Claude Bowers, certainly the strongest pro-Republican sympathizer in Madrid's diplomatic-corps-in-exile in Hendaye, did not cable Washington of the bombing until April 30, at which time he informed the American secretary of state that Guernica had been destroyed by German bombers. Bowers was not a professional diplomat but a journalist and showed his confidence in the correspondent of the *Times*, "himself attacked with machine gun fire from German plane handled unexploded aluminum incendiary bombs on site of Guernica." Bowers considered "denials by insurgents and Germany following world reaction incredible."[32]

Despite American neutrality and American nonparticipation in the NIC, the question of Guernica was brought before both houses of the American Congress. Senator Borah of Idaho attacked Fascism on the floor of the Senate on May 6, and his speech included the most vigorous denunciation of the destroyers of Guernica delivered before a parliamentary body at any time.

> There is no tenet of democracy which Fascism does not challenge. . . . There is not a vital principle of free government with which this ruthless creed is not in conflict. It is built, and professes to be built, upon the ruins of democracy.

After stigmatizing the Italian attack on Ethiopia, he took up the war in Spain:

> Here Fascism presents to the world its masterpiece. It has hung upon the wall of civilization a painting that will never come down—never fade out of the memories of man. So long as men and women may be interested in searching out from the pages of history outstanding acts of cruelty and instances of needless destruction of human life they will linger longest and with the greatest horror over the savage story of the fascist war in Spain.

> Modern warfare, with its improved instruments of destruction of both property and life, is revolting at best. But it remained for the Fascist warfare to select the deadliest weapons which the ingenuity of man has contrived and to show to the world how thorough and effective these weapons are when used for the destruction of women and children. How effective are airplanes when throwing bombs and hand grenades into homes; how airplanes, swooping low

like winged monsters, can massacre thousands of innocent children without endangering in the slightest the lives of the brave assailants; and how at the same time they can set a non-combatant city on fire and leave the streets covered with the charred bodies of the slain, while the intrepid Fascist soldiers escape without a wound! Fascism boasts of courage, of the bravery of its soldiers; boasts how it makes men of its adherents, and tells other peoples that Fascism makes heroes of the young. And, as evidence of the fulfillment of its creed, it points to the subjugation of the wholly weak and disarmed Ethiopia and now doubtless will take pride in the successful slaughter of women and children throughout Spain. . . .

No language can describe the scene at Guernica, and Guernica was not a single instance; it was simply a culmination of a long line of unspeakable atrocities. It was not a military maneuver. . . . An unarmed, non-combatant city was singled out for the most revolting instance of mass murder in modern times. It was Fascist strategy.[33]

A few days after Senator Borah's anti-Fascist speech, Bishop Francis J. McConnell of the Methodist Episcopal Church, issued an "Appeal to the Conscience of the World," signed by hundreds of prominent Americans, including many senators and representatives, non-Catholic religious leaders, college presidents, and heads of labor unions. The appeal read in part:

The toll of slaughtered innocents exceeds 800 persons. This is the crime of Guernica. And this is the unspeakable crime of war on women and children, waged with a brutality and callousness unparalleled in modern times.[34]

The statement invoked as witnesses Canon Onaindia and "foreign correspondents, one of them a distinguished staff member of *The Times* of London."

On May 10, in the American House of Representatives, Jerry J. O'Connell, from Montana, brought up the subject of Guernica. He recalled that he and three other congressmen had a few days previously addressed a letter to Secretary of State Hull calling his attention "to the massacre of Guernica, reported by all the foreign correspondents of accredited newspapers to be the work of German planes, German bombs, and German pilots."[35] The congressman noted that

In his reply to our letter, the Secretary of State wrote that he agreed with Senator Pittman, who recently stated that "there is no evidence" that Germany and Italy are participating in the Spanish invasion.[36]

O'Connell then quoted from Steer's original dispatch reporting the presence of German planes in the Basque country as proof of Nazi aggression against Republican Spain.[37] It seems improbable that Hull himself believed what he wrote, for diplomatic reasons, to O'Connell. In his memoirs, written some years later, he spoke of "the savage bombing of the Basque city of Guernica by the Franco forces employing German and Italian planes."[38]

But if American popular indignation over Guernica was lost in the distance, and French sentiment was dulled by the ambiguous way in which the French press treated the subject, and by the Catholic convictions of the population, the situation was otherwise in England, where public opinion, aroused by the press, eventually brought the Conservative government under assault on two fronts: first, it came under fire from the Opposition in Parliament, and second, it came into conflict diplomatically with the German government. The fact that the British press had been largely responsible for the diffusion of the first Guernica dispatches had placed England in the role of accuser, while Germany was seen in the role of the accused.

The Guernica incident had thus developed, on the international scene, not so much as a contention between the Spanish Republican government in Valencia (the Basque government in Bilbao) and the Technical Junta of the Spanish Rebels in Burgos, but as a dispute between London's reluctant Tory government, obliged to consider public opinion, and the arrogant Nazis of Berlin, who did not even admit the presence of their air force in Spain, let alone that air force's responsibility for the bombing of Guernica. The English and German governments had two points of contact for the discussion of Guernica: one through normal diplomatic, ambassadorial channels, and the other through the Non-Intervention Committee, which held its sessions in London. Both of these were to be used by Whitehall, in an effort to calm down public feeling.

Popular feeling in England about the disaster of Guernica was quite naturally translated into parliamentary debate. In these skirmishes the Tory government cautiously sought, by all available means, to avoid any overt admission that Germany was guilty of the action. Twenty-four hours after the first news about Guernica was published in London, Sir Archibald Sinclair, a Liberal leader in the House of Commons, posed a question to Foreign Minister Anthony Eden:

> Is it not the case that, as regards the bombardment of Guernica, the civilians were deliberately pursued by aeroplanes with machine-guns and that, therefore, it was not a case in which civilians were killed in the course of an ordinary bombardment, but was a deliberate effort to use air power as an instrument of massacre and terrorism, and will not the right hon. Gentleman take some means of making an effective protest expressing the condemnation of British public opinion?

Eden's reply was properly diplomatic and noncommittal, and when another speaker stated, "In view of the fact that these massacres were committed by German machines apparently driven by German pilots . . ." the foreign minister declared: "The hon. Member is speaking without confirmation."[39]

The Guernica incident as such did not come before the House of Commons again until May 3, although on April 30, the Labourite Hugh Dalton questioned Mr. Eden concerning another episode of the propaganda war in the Basque country, a reported threat by Mola, which had appeared in the press on April 29. It read:

We shall raze Bilbao to the ground and its bare desolate site will remove the British desire to support Basque Bolsheviks against our will. We must destroy the capital of a perverted people, who dares defy the irresistible cause of the national idea.[40]

Eden replied that he had asked for a report on this statement from the British ambassador to Spain; he had not yet received an answer.[41] In effect, that very day Sir Henry was replying to the minister's request. He noted that the statement in question did not appear in the Spanish Nationalist press, but that he had seen it "in *Dépêche,* left-wing Toulouse paper and mention of it in other French papers."[42] He inquired about it from two Nationalist sources: Marquis Merry del Val and the military governor of Irún, Major Julián Troncoso.[43] The first assured the ambassador that "the general had only threatened to destroy military objectives."[44] If the marquis was referring to Mola's threat as stated in the *Daily Herald,* and it could not have been otherwise if Sir Henry correctly asked the question, then the marquis' answer constituted a confirmation of the declaration. If the statement had been made, as seems probable, it was not made for the Spanish Nationalist press or for the inhabitants of the Rebel zone: it was made for the already heavily bombed people of Bilbao. It was a part of the war of nerves and terror launched by Mola at the beginning of the Basque campaign.

The military governor of Irún, Major Julián Troncoso, replied to Sir Henry late on April 30

in a long and wordy letter denying that General Mola could have broadcast any speech on April 27th (as it was reported that he had) since broadcasting station is in Salamanca while he has not left the front for the last few days.

The letter from the military governor of Irún then stated "that General Franco cannot bother to deny the thousands of tendentious reports published by the foreign press." But he authorized the ambassador to say that, as for the threat "to raze Bilbao to the ground," it was "a matter for the military authorities." As for the second part

which refers to Englishmen it is sufficient to read the Nationalist press and the favorable foreign press to see that whatever may happen the Nationalists will respect every foreigner.

Sir Henry's report closed with this observation: "Military Governor's letter nowhere directly denies that General Mola spoke the words in question."[45]

Parliamentary questions concerning Guernica, addressed to Eden, were to be answered on May 3, and to prepare them, Sir Henry Chilton was queried for further information. The lead paragraph read: "Public opinion in this country has been deeply stirred by destruction of Guernica. . . ." Chilton was also informed that suggestions were "being made that some kind of impartial committee should be set up to investigate facts. . . ."[46]

More than a dozen questions were asked of Mr. Eden in the House of Commons on May 3 concerning the bombing of Guernica and the fighting in the Basque country. The Germans were openly accused of being responsible by members of the Opposition. The foreign minister replied that he had asked the British ambassador to Spain, who was in Hendaye and not in Spain itself, and the British consul in Bilbao "to forward as soon as possible any information which might assist in establishing the facts regarding the destruction of Guernica." Since "replies are still being received," the minister's information was incomplete, and he was not "in a position to make a considered statement" on the subject. But Eden did accept clearly the fact that Guernica had been bombed, and this had its importance:

> His Majesty's Government have, however, already expressed their views on the general question of the bombardment of civilian populations, of which the destruction of Guernica furnishes so deplorable an example.[47]

The London correspondent of the *New York Times* cabled to his newspaper:

> The Foreign Secretary and his fellow ministers are being careful not to accuse Germany of the Guernica bombing until they have irrefutable evidence, although evidence has been received in official quarters to show that the bombing was the work of German planes flown either by German pilots or by other airmen in General Mola's service.[48]

Eden's prudence hardly satisfied the German ambassador, who cabled to Berlin that the British foreign minister had "answered evasively" to the charges brought against Germany. He also informed his ministry:

> From various quarters the Embassy is receiving communications making German flyers responsible for the bombardment of Guernica, in spite of our denials. In private conversations Franco's denial is still given prominence and is construed to mean that Franco indirectly admits the attack was made by German flyers.[49]

"Franco's denial" to which von Ribbentrop made reference was more the result of an interpretation by the British press than of any specific Rebel statement. The widely read *Manchester Guardian* on April 29 published a dispatch, probably rewritten by the editors, relative to the destruction of Guernica. The theme was given in the headline: "WERE THE GERMANS ALONE RESPONSIBLE?" The text read in part:

> The rebel G.H.Q. at Salamanca officially denied all knowledge of the air raid. It did not deny that it had taken place, but declared that the rebel airforce had no part in it. . . . General Franco's repudiation of the attack on Guernica would appear to throw the direct responsibility for it on the German staff in North Spain.[50]

This interpretation by the *Manchester Guardian* did not take into account the fact that the Nationalist communiqués never admitted the existence of a German air force in Spain. The Nationalist statement, therefore, in Nationalist thinking and communiqué writing, did cover the German planes and pilots in Spain. At the same time, every newspaperman in London knew that there were in fact squadrons of German planes, manned by German pilots, in Spain; it was difficult at times not to write with this unspoken secret in mind. It is instructive that von Ribbentrop, perhaps influenced by the atmosphere around him, also tended to give credence to this interpretation of the Salamanca communique. Von Ribbentrop suggested that the charges uttered in the Commons on May 3 could be invoked to persuade Franco to issue "an energetic and very sharp denial, removing all ambiguity." [51]

This same day, the Havas-Botto dispatch on Guernica was published in France. This pro-Nationalist report was exactly what the Germans needed at this moment, and on the following day this information of French origin was printed on the front page of the tightly controlled and censored Nazi press of Berlin and the provinces, as proof of the lies published in the English press about Guernica. [52] The *Berliner Lokal-Anzeiger* clarioned on its front page: "STRUCTURE OF LIES DEMOLISHED. LIES OF TIMES UNMASKED BY HAVAS." By some queer reasoning, perhaps by simple Teutonic thoroughness, this newspaper, like many others that day in Germany, thought it well to reprint large extracts of Steer's first dispatch on Guernica before demolishing it with the Havas-Botto report. [53] The *Kölnische Volkszeitung und Handelsblatt* said the "Bolshevik horror stories" were being used to push the English people into rearmament, with no regard for "German honor." It then cited on its roll of honor *Le Jour* and the Havas-Botto dispatch, the headlines used by *Le Figaro* over the same dispatch, and Massot's similar report in *Le Journal*, before reprinting in its entirety Steer's original article. [54] Thus the beginning of the Guernica controversy—Steer's telegram—was finally widely printed in Germany, thanks to the unwitting intervention of Georges Botto and the Havas Agency.

On April 30 a new British ambassador had arrived in Berlin. This was Sir Neville Henderson, of whom his foreign minister was later to write that

> it was an international misfortune that we should have been represented in Berlin at this time by a man who, far from warning the Nazis, was constantly making excuses for them, often in their company. [55]

Four days later, when the Havas-Botto dispatch was on the front pages of the German press, Sir Neville conveyed his own misgivings about the *Times'* manner of handling the Guernica story, by sending the following cablegram to London:

> In view of the importance attached here to Guernica I should be grateful to be informed as soon as possible whether the "Times" report is correct or incorrect. If it proves incorrect I recommend that the fact should be frankly admitted by a Government spokesman in the House of Commons or elsewhere. The "Times" enjoys a high reputation in Germany for honesty and accuracy. Should it be established that they have been misled by their

correspondent they would be well advised in their own interests to make a handsome retraction. Both His Majesty's Government and the "Times" have much more to gain from such an attitude than they can possibly lose.[56]

On this same day the German Foreign Ministry sent a telegram to the embassy in Salamanca, repeating the previous day's telegram from von Ribbentrop with these instructions: "Please induce Franco to issue an immediate and energetic denial." The telegram ended with this endorsement of the Havas-Botto article: "Our press has rejected the false British reports, by using material meanwhile received which proves destruction of the city by the Bolshevists.[57]

A suggestion that England take "immediate steps to address a collective protest with other Powers to General Franco and Herr Hitler against the bombardment of the civilian population of open towns which is now being conducted in Spain" had been raised on April 28 by the Labour Party leader Clement Attlee, in a "Private Notice" to Eden. The foreign minister assured Attlee that the government

> deeply deplore the bombardment of the civilian population in the Spanish Civil War wherever it may occur and whoever may be responsible. . . . They will continue to examine the question whether further steps are possible to prevent the recurrence of such deplorable events.[58]

In France, the Socialists in the Popular Front government, and especially Prime Minister Léon Blum, were under fire from their coreligionists in and outside France. The indecisive attitude of the French government toward the cause of the Spanish Republic, and its silence concerning the destruction of Guernica, seemed inexplicable to Socialists in other lands. On the eve of May Day, the veteran Belgian Socialist, head of the Second Internationale, Émile Vandervelde, published an open letter to Blum, to emphasize the difference between the reaction in England, with a Conservative government, and that in France, with a Popular Front government, concerning "the blows of the atrocious happenings in the Basque country and the destruction of Guernica." "It is easy to understand," Vandervelde observed, "the movement of indignation in Great Britain and one can wonder if it is only in that country that there will be a reaction."[59]

On the same day, April 30, Yvon Delbos brought up a subject that was to permit both France and England to have the appearance of doing something about Guernica without really taking the risk involved in a positive endeavor: this was the sponsorship of an inquiry into the causes of the destruction of Guernica. Delbos addressed the Commission on Foreign Affairs of the French Senate, and the following communiqué was later issued:

> The Minister of Foreign Affairs reminded the Commission that it was the initiative of the French Government, joined to the British action, which obtained successively the Non-Intervention Committee and the Control Committee. A decision has now been taken to carry out an inquiry concern-

ing the conditions of the destruction of Guernica. The French Government, in agreement with the British Government, is preoccupied with the fate of women and civilians in all the Basque region, and of their eventual evacuation.[60]

There were various interpretations of what had happened at the meeting of the commission, and even of what had been written in the official statement. Some correspondents gave the impression that Delbos had talked with the press after the meeting. Ralph Heinzen, head of the UP bureau in Paris, wrote that Delbos

emphasized that the French enquiry would have a purely informational character, but indicated that if it were shown that the town was destroyed by German aviators with German planes, and that the bombs dropped were German bombs, as the Basques claim, it is possible that the efforts to obtain acceptance by the governments for the withdrawal of the volunteers now serving in both fighting armies be renewed.[61]

The punishment envisaged by Delbos could hardly be said to fit the crime.

The Communist deputy Gabriel Péri was not content:

I am surprised that, in speaking of the Spanish problem, the French minister did not seize on the occasion to stigmatize, as should have been done, the destruction of Guernica. . . . The violation of non-intervention is evident! The bombing was ordered by the German general headquarters! The airplanes which bombed and destroyed the town by dropping a thousand incendiary bombs were German airplanes![62]

Did Péri speak out in this fashion in the commission? One right-wing newspaper apparently thought so, and wrote that when Péri reproached Delbos for not protesting against the bombing of Guernica, the minister asked him: "Have you proof that the Valencia government is telling the truth?"[63] Such stories seemed to abound, and another journal of the right reported that a group of "deputies of the extreme-Left" visited Delbos to upbraid him for not protesting the destruction of Guernica, and the minister replied: "Gentlemen, if I have any advice to offer you, it is to speak no more of this lamentable affair. It could cause some disagreeable surprises."[64] One American news agency interpreted the note published after the commission's meeting (or perhaps interpreted a conversation with someone present at the meeting) to mean that "Great Britain and France have decided to conduct an investigation into the devastating bombing and machine-gunning of Guernica."[65] There was apparently no basis whatsoever for that assumption.

When Delbos appeared before the Senate commission, he certainly possessed full knowledge of one version of the destruction of Guernica. The French consul in Bilbao, Castéran, had notified Madrid on April 27 that Guernica had suffered an air attack and gave the opinion that its purpose was to cut communications of all the roads of the northern war front.[66] It is highly probable that this report was made, as was that of his British colleague Stevenson, after a visit to the burning town. Castéran was convinced of the culpability of the Germans in the attack, according to a statement made in 1969 by the man who was then the young French vice-consul in Bilbao, Antoine Molinié. Molinié himself visited Guernica, and actually held in his hands an incendiary bomb of the type described by the English journalists Steer, Holme, Monks, and the Belgian Corman.[67] These views were certainly made known to Delbos, and probably before he made his statement of April 30 to the Senate commission. In fact, an American journalist wrote from Paris that the Quai d'Orsay received on April 30 "an official report [which] indicates that the majority of the houses [in Guernica] have holes in the roofs made by air bombs, and that the city has the sorrowful aspect of desolation."[68]

However, no such clear opinion about Guernica shows up in the communications of French Ambassador Herbette, who was stationed in Hendaye. He found the British reaction to Guernica disproportionate to that caused by other incidents of the civil war, and attributed it to British commercial interests and to the strategic position of the Basque coast in case of a naval war.[69] The subject of an inquiry on Guernica came up in a conversation between Herbette and English Ambassador Chilton on May 1. Herbette said that he would advance no opinion about Guernica until an inquiry by specialists had taken place on the spot. Chilton replied that General Franco had extended him an invitation to visit the ruined town.[70]

Delbos's mention of an investigation into the causes of the destruction of Guernica might well have been inspired by the statement sent on April 29 by Aguirre to various governments—including the English and the French—denouncing the Rebel charge that "the destruction of Guernica and other towns was carried out by extremists in Basque territory" and asking for an international inquiry into the causes of the tragedy.[71] It is evident from existing documents that on April 30 no steps had been taken by either the British or the French to collaborate on an investigation into the causes of the disaster of Guernica. It was only on May 1 that Foreign Minister Delbos cabled to Charles Corbin, French ambassador in London and his government's representative to the Non-Intervention Committee. The message touched on the humanitarian aspects of the Basque problem:

> Because of the character assumed by the fighting in the Basque provinces, where the Insurgent aviation seeks to destroy completely open towns and civilian populations, the French government feels it its duty to take all the necessary steps to put an end to such excesses.

Delbos charged Corbin

> to ask the Secretary of State [Eden] immediately to consent to associate the British government with an urgent intervention of the French Government to refer the question to the Non-Intervention Committee.[72]

There is not a word here about any "investigation."

Corbin then saw the British officials and Soviet Ambassador Ivan Maisky. The British head of the Non-Intervention Committee, Lord Plymouth, intended to place as first item on the agenda of the May 4 meeting of the Chairman's Sub-Committee of the NIC an appeal to both of the warring parties in Spain to renounce the bombing of open towns. He pointed out to Corbin that the corollary to this appeal would be the establishment of a list of open towns, and Maisky noted that such a list would be extremely difficult to draw up. Strangely enough, Maisky gave Corbin the impression that he thought the Germans and Italians could be persuaded to put pressure on Salamanca to accept the proposed appeal, an illusion that, if true, was not to last very long. A phrase from Corbin's telegram of May 3 to Delbos shows how superficial most of the diplomatic reactions to the destruction of Guernica were in reality:

> It is moreover recognized that the decision requested from the Committee by the British government was above all a manner for giving satisfaction to a public outraged by the bombing of Guernica.[73]

The first effort of the British government to enlist international support for an action against what had happened in Guernica and its recurrence was thus made before the Non-Intervention Committee, with the encouragement of the French government and the foreknowledge of the Soviet government.

When the nine members of the Chairman's Sub-Committee of the NIC, the heads of the diplomatic missions in London of Belgium, Czechoslovakia, France, Germany, Italy, Portugal, Sweden, and the Soviet Union, plus the parliamentary under-Secretary at the Foreign Office, Lord Plymouth, chairman of the NIC, and the sub-committee's secretary Mr. Francis Hemming met at eleven o'clock on the morning of May 4, they found as the first item on the agenda, the following: "Possibility of addressing an appeal to the two parties in Spain regarding the bombing of open towns."[74] It is not made clear just when this topic was put on the agenda. As seen above, however, the subject was known to the French ambassador and to the Russian ambassador the previous day (May 3), and before 13h37, the time at which Corbin informed his minister in Paris.[75]

It is apparent from a speech of Guido Crolla, who was replacing Count Grandi, the Italian ambassador in London, and from a statement by German Ambassador von Ribbentrop that the British government had approached the governments concerned about the same matter through diplomatic channels. Nevertheless, the Italian and German representatives were obviously miffed by what they considered their tardy notification. Von Ribbentrop made a point of noting that he "saw this item on the Agenda this morning."[76] Offense was also taken in Lisbon by Oliveira Salazar, on learning that Portugal had not been informed of the British proposal before the sub-committee meeting.[77] When Monteiro saw Eden on May 7, he raised the point, and the foreign minister proffered excuses, saying that the Italians were informed of the project simply because he happened to see Grandi and had told him of the project "incidentally."[78] There was a bit of playacting in all this, for not only had the English government confided the project to most of the interested parties a day or two before the meeting but on the morning of May 3 Eden told

American Ambassador Bingham of his intention, "in the utmost of confidence." He also informed Bingham

> that he had felt out the Ambassadors and while the German ambassador
> showed the greatest reluctance to go into this question, he felt that no one of
> them could afford to refuse at least to discuss it.[79]

It was natural that Lord Plymouth open the meeting with an explanation of why he had so urgently added this matter to the order of the day: it was because "the United Kingdom are greatly exercised about this general question." He pointed out that the question was posed "in a tentative form," that his government sought "the advice and the help and the cooperation" of the other members of the sub-committee, not "with any desire to examine the past," but simply "to safeguard and to protect the civil population in Spain near those areas in that country round which the civil war is at present raging." The French representative Charles Corbin replied by saying that he had received instructions "on that point" last Saturday— that is, May 1. On receiving these instructions, Corbin had addressed a letter to Lord Plymouth, and he now handed it over.

This letter did not exactly agree with what Delbos was supposed to have said before the Senate commission concerning the intentions of the French government, but it did give full support to the "Possibility of Addressing an Appeal to the Two Parties in Spain in regard to the Bombing of Open Towns," and it did, alone of all the expressions made before the sub-committee, accuse the Rebels of the bombings in the Basque country.[80] Further support for the British initiative came from Russian Ambassador Ivan Maisky, Czechoslovak Counselor of Embassy Vilém Černý, Belgian Ambassador Baron Cartier de Marchienne, and Swedish Minister Baron E. K. Palmstierna.[81]

Portuguese Ambassador A. R. de S. Monteiro declared: "I think the Portuguese government will give its support to all measures which could be taken to end all the horrors of the Spanish civil war."[82] This was the first suggestion that an action on a broader scale might be taken, and it was not made by accident. The German had talked with the Italian and Portuguese representatives before the meeting. In a report to his government on this encounter, he wrote: "I shall have further contact with the Italians and the Portuguese, with whom we have worked very well together today."[83]

Taking his cue, von Ribbentrop then made a fairly long declaration, the sub-stance of which was that the committee should avoid being "concerned with something which might lead from non-intervention to intervention." This maneuver was aimed not at challenging the appeal itself as proposed by the British but at challenging the competence of the committee to undertake such an appeal. Baron Palmstierna observed: "Is it not the practice in international affairs generally that when there is a question of really humanitarian things, then we do not care too much about the form?" And Corbin opposed the trend of the German's thought: "I do not think that this case should be considered as an interference in the Spanish interior affairs." The Italian delegate, Guido Crolla, upheld von Ribbentrop's argument, suggesting that perhaps it was better that appeals come from governments and not from the committee.[84] After further discussion on methods of approaching the problem, Francis Hemming, secretary to the committee, began to draft a statement. This first draft was dismissed by France and the Soviet Union, with the approval of the Swedish representative, on the grounds, as expressed by the French ambassador: "The general impression given is that the British initiative has been met only with doubts, which is not the case."[85]

When the text was read again at von Ribbentrop's demand, Maisky gave this opinion:

> I think what passed this morning is that practically all the representatives, except two, expressed full agreement with the British initiative, and this fact should be expressed in our communiqué. The doubts are confined only to two representatives.[86]

This reference to Germany and Italy was opposed by Hemming, in part on clerical technical grounds, and von Ribbentrop rebutted the Soviet spokesman:

> I would in no circumstances agree that this should be again a Propaganda Committee, in no circumstances whatsoever, therefore I do not quite understand the Soviet Ambassador saying that everyone was in full agreement but two representatives. . . . I do not think that is right at all. We all rest in full agreement today to do everything we can to make the Spanish warfare as humanitarian as possible. That was the full agreement . . . in view of certain propaganda which has been made again during the last few days [concerning Guernica], I should strongly urge that we make this communiqué, if we make one at all on this question, as general and as careful as possible.[87]

Hemming made another try:

> After a preliminary exchange of views, representatives agreed to consult their respective Governments as to the method by which such an appeal should be made.

But here the Swedish and Russian ambassadors protested that they needed no further instructions on such a matter.[88] At this point, von Ribbentrop again referred, indirectly, to Guernica: "I could not agree with the propaganda which has been made lately." He continued:

> I should not agree that it would be defined only as the bombing of open towns. . . . I think the bombing of towns which has been going on on both sides continuously and probably in a very severe form, does not cover at all the whole subject of these atrocities in Spain, therefore I think if an appeal is made this should be made to the humanizing of warfare altogether in Spain, because otherwise referring to certain very unfortunate propaganda which is

very strongly objected to in my country [Guernica], the question would look very one-sided, and we should not agree to that.[89]

The Portuguese representative then intervened to support the German position:

If it is a question of addressing an appeal to the two sides in Spain dealing with the conduct of military operations, it becomes in my opinion an interference in the war. Evidently this interference can find excuses in humanitarian reasons; but it will be difficult to explain why such an intervention was not made at the beginning of the civil war, for such cruel actions have not had their commencement today; they date from the first day of the civil war. . . . People would not understand why the Committee should intervene exactly on this question of the conduct of the war when the horrors seem to have strictly a military origin, whereas so many cruel acts have taken place in this unfortunate Spain on other occasions. . . . The best thing would be not to publish a communiqué on this matter; but if one is published, it should be drawn up in very general terms, for evidently we do not wish to do propaganda work.[90]

In reality, the Portuguese ambassador had at no time the intention of condemning the bombing of Guernica, as is shown by the dispatch he wrote to Lisbon immediately after the May 4 meeting. He explained his opposition to the proposed text: "The communiqué was edited clearly in propaganda terms, seeming to give the impression that the Committee was condemning the recent bombardments."[91]

The Italian delegate upheld the German and Portuguese positions, the latter maladroitly, for he observed that "the Portuguese ambassador has also pointed out that the initiative now under discussion refers to a particular time." Here again was an oblique reference to the destruction of Guernica; it revealed the Italian's thoughts, for the British proposal in no wise referred "to a particular time." Von Ribbentrop also backed the Portuguese ambassador. Corbin intervened to remark that

it would be highly regrettable that in a situation . . . where we see the development of the war bring to the non-combatant population sufferings unacceptable to the civilized world, a scruple of this kind could stop us, and prevent the Committee from showing its opinion,

and he pointed out that the appeal would be directed to both the warring parties in Spain. The Belgian ambassador began to side with those who sought to water down the communiqué, and Hemming suggested the following:

The Sub-Committee had under consideration the possibility of addressing an appeal to the two parties in Spain to undertake that the present conflict should in future be conducted with the utmost regard possible to humanitarian considerations.[92]

The Swedish delegate thought this "too platonic!" and the Czechoslovak thought it better to have none at all than such a weak statement. The Soviet statesman: "I do not think it is worth while." The Portuguese ambassador continued to plead for a general statement against all atrocities.[93] And the Swedish representative exploded:

> We are getting rather far away from what are facts, the actual facts: at a certain spot certain aeroplanes went on to shoot women and children, went down to shoot them dead on the road, and a whole town, although the military people had left it, was extinguished. I mean it is a fact upon which world conscience has been aroused. Possibly next week we might see another and larger town dealt with in the same way. Our human feelings are aroused when cruelty reaches a certain point, and then we speak up. The word "propaganda" has been used. If I may so, if I can make propaganda against that sort of violence, I will do it, whoever has committed the crime, and I think several of us feel the same in this respect. If we talk as was done at the League of Nations, whether it is a legitimate or humane warfare or not, we shall be going on for years, nobody will find a solution. To stop what has now been executed, that is all the British government hopes for, I understand.[94]

This was the only moment of eloquence in the discussion. It was the nearest the word "Guernica" came to being pronounced before the sub-committee at this meeting, but von Ribbentrop could not allow even this slight reference to pass without protest. He was "amazed" by the words of the Swedish ambassador.

> We have known, for instance, if I may remind you here, that within the borders of Red Spain the Intelligentsia of the Right, men, women and children have been murdered, there is no one left, not one in [of?] the whole Right of Spain, but the human feelings of this Committee have evidently not been aroused. Well I cannot follow this at all, I am sorry. . . . I must of course insist that if consideration is to be given to the present situation, when through some absolutely misleading propaganda a certain bombing has been brought and placed before the world in an absolutely biased and propaganda way, I must insist that at least the whole question of humanization of the Spanish war must be brought under consideration, and if we make a communiqué at all, which I still think is in principle quite wrong at this stage, if we make one at all this would have to be put in some way, the whole situation should be seen quite in the right way and not in any sort of biased way.[95]

Monteiro, the Portuguese ambassador, then intervened to express his accord with the Swedish representative, but this was but a feint, "I would simply add one thing." He went on, "my pity, my emotion in this affair of the Spanish civil war date from the first day of the civil war." He thus returned to the general problem of atrocities during the conflict and suggested that the question raised by the British government be laid aside and that the committee study "all the problems of atrocities and of the humanization of the civil war."[96]

Maisky then ironically congratulated von Ribbentrop "on the very striking propaganda speech he has just made." He pointed out that the British government had recently intervened to ask both sides not to use poison gas; this was an example of a successful appeal on a particular subject. "The bombing of open towns is another case of special cruelty, absolutely unnecessary even from the military point of view." The Russian ambassador at this point launched an attack on the position held by the German, Italian, and Portuguese representatives:

> I am somewhat suspicious of the real motives of those who, instead of trying to do something concrete to eliminate the worst features of this warfare, advocate the discussion of the general problem of the humanization of the war. Do they desire to bring the possibility of definite results beneath the endless verbiage of a general discussion on humanization? I think it is not in the interests of those particular countries to give color to such a suspicion, and therefore I think it is in their own interests to accept and to support the initiative taken by the British government.[97]

Crolla replied that the positions taken by the Swedish, Soviet, and French ambassadors

> to certain particular facts . . . do not correspond to that broader view which the Committee would have to take if they really want to interpret indignation as human beings at the atrocities which have taken place in Spain for eight or nine months already.

These "certain particular facts" concerned the destruction of Guernica, a name nobody had mentioned. Nor did the following speaker, Lord Plymouth, say the word out loud, when he explained that the item had been placed on the agenda

> purely and simply because the public conscience and feeling, I think, all over the world have been aroused by certain reports that have been published in various parts of the press in different forms,

adding that he made "no observation as to whether these reports were justified or not."[98]

Von Ribbentrop challenged Maisky's last statement, perhaps unwisely. He strongly objected to the Russian ambassador's saying that "the discussion gave rise to the suspicion that certain members of the Committee did not wish this bombing to cease, but would like to continue this bombing of open towns." He and his government deplored "the form in which the Spanish civil war has been carried on." He again recalled "that thousands, tens of thousands and more, probably hundreds of thousands, have been killed in cold blood," and added:

> I do not think that anyone can say that this was necessary from the military point of view. Unfortunately, it has been the terrible method of the civil war, and I strongly object if now today there has been bombing on both sides, if on the part of General Franco's army there has been bombing, that this should be used in any biased way against General Franco. The Soviet ambassador said that this was absolutely unnecessary from a military point of view.

At this moment, Maisky interjected, "Absolutely." Von Ribbentrop continued:

> Well, neither he nor we all are in the Spanish civil war, but we have all had the experience—at least I had—that in war-time certain measures occasionally happen which may be very deplorable . . . if some of the civil population should have been killed through bombing lately on General Franco's side, which we deplore as much as anybody, then to compare this with these tremendous atrocities of murdering tens of thousands of people on the side of the Reds, I think, really, and I must emphasize again, the conscience of the Committee should make it take this question as a whole and see how these things really lie. . . . I am convinced that my government is in no way whatsoever prepared to lend a hand to any such biased propaganda against General Franco.[99]

A compromise statement concerning the day's discussion was then decided upon and the matter of the appeal in regard to the bombing of open towns put off to the next meeting.

The diplomatic skirmishing around the destruction of Guernica without even mentioning the name of the town makes unpleasant reading today. But von Ribbentrop's position is not without interest. He might have insisted that he did not know whereof the Swedish ambassador spoke, that at the "certain spot" to which Palmstierna apparently referred no proof was given that a bombing had occurred, that at any rate no Germans were involved in the action and that, therefore, he was in favor of such a condemnation. This sortie was ironically suggested to him by Maisky.

Throughout this maze of symbolic talk, the German, Italian, and Portuguese representatives played out their roles as if the acceptance of the British proposition on the "Possibility of Addressing an Appeal to the Two Parties in Spain in regard to the Bombing of Open Towns" would have constituted an accusation of the Spanish Nationalists, perhaps even of the Germans. Not once did any of the three declaim to his fellow diplomats the thesis being pleaded in public, that Guernica had not been bombed. On the contrary, the reader who analyzes the minutes of the May 4 meeting of the Chairman's Sub-Committee of the Non-Intervention Committee cannot elude the feeling that the ten personages, including Secretary Hemming, are acting out a charade to see who can come closest to designating Guernica without expressly uttering the forbidden word.

Von Ribbentrop obviously appreciated the niceties of such a civilized game. After the meeting he informed his ministry that the Swedish delegate referred aggressively to the "Guernica incident," but without mentioning Germany. If Germany had been mentioned, von Ribbentrop said, he would have left the meeting.[100] The German ambassador's report to his government was, of course, written outside the playground, and von Ribbentrop was not then bound by any diplomatic rule. In fact Baron Palmstierna did not break the regulations at the meeting, for he did not actually pronounce the word "Guernica."

May 5 in London was marked by a number of press and diplomatic events concerning Guernica. Someone present at the May 4 meeting of the Chairman's Sub-Committee, most probably Maisky, talked with correspondents, and articles such as the following one from the highly conservative *Daily Telegraph* appeared in the press of London and other Western capitals:

... ATTEMPT TO STOP BOMBING IN SPAIN. PLAN OPPOSED BY GERMANY. "IT IS SOMETIMES NECESSARY." CHANGE OF ATTITUDE CAUSES SURPRISE. By our Diplomatic Correspondent.

Herr von Ribbentrop, German ambassador in London, caused a surprise at yesterday's Non-Intervention Committee meeting. He opposed a suggestion of the Earl of Plymouth, chairman, that the Non-Interventionist Governments should appeal to both sides of the Spanish Civil war to abstain from bombing open towns. This suggestion was the result of the wave of feeling aroused by the recent news from Guernica. It was supported by the representatives of France, Sweden, Belgium, Czechoslovakia, Russia, and others. Herr von Ribbentrop declared bluntly that he could not agree to this proposal being considered by the Committee. He said it would amount to interference in the domestic affairs of Spain.

It was explained that the British Government's sole aim was to humanize the war struggle. Herr von Ribbentrop indicated that he would not object to the Committee discussing humanization of the war on some wider basis, but he could not assent to the proposal about bombardment of open towns. He considered it outside the competence of the Committee and added that from his own experience in the Great War, actions such as bombing of open towns, while they were regrettable, were sometimes necessary. Lord Plymouth offered to present a memorandum explaining what the British Government had in mind. Herr von Ribbentrop resisted even this proposal.

M. Maisky, the Soviet Ambassador, said Herr von Ribbentrop's attitude must arouse suspicion. It looked as though Germany was anxious to prepare the ground for further bombing of open towns. It will be interesting to learn whether Herr von Ribbentrop's view, that such bombardments are sometimes necessary, represents a definite change in German policy.[101]

Stories of this nature, which appeared in many of the London newspapers, were essentially accurate. A dispatch published in New York was more detailed:

Leftist-Fascist enmity flared here late today [May 4] when Joachim von Ribbentrop, German ambassador to Great Britain and Nazi member of the Spanish Non-Intervention Committee, defended the destruction of Guernica.... Ribbentrop's assertion that the bombing of undefended towns "sometimes is necessary" to achieve military objectives brought immediate and bitter retort from Ivan Maisky, Soviet Ambassador and committee member. "This looks very suspiciously like an attempt to shield a possible repetition of Guernica," he shouted.[102]

Nothing essential in the news stories in either London or New York was contrary to fact. The word "Guernica" was not mentioned at the meeting itself, but von

Ribbentrop did say, when he and everyone else at the meeting was thinking of Guernica, "in war-time certain measures occasionally happen which may be very deplorable." If Maisky did not shout exactly word for word the sentence quoted by the reporter, he did utter certain phrases that the German ambassador paraphrased during the session itself, as follows: "He said the discussion gave rise to the suspicion that certain members of this Committee did not wish this bombing to cease, but would like to continue this bombing of open towns."

But even the leaks to the press can be said to have served the diplomats and their games. Did they not give to many newspapers readers the impression that the ambassadors of the powers represented on the President's Sub-Committee—above all, Lord Plymouth—were resolutely facing up to their responsibilities? The contrary was true.

It might be argued that von Ribbentrop had not refused to discuss "the proposal about bombardment of open towns." He had merely insisted on diluting the proposal to change its substance. This was a diplomatic nuance, on which Anthony Eden seized to explain the German position before the cabinet on May 5. The "Cabinet conclusions" summarizing Eden's words read:

> It was untrue, as stated in certain newspapers, that the German Ambassador had refused to discuss the matter. . . . He himself [Eden] had seen the Ambassadors of the principal Powers before the meeting of the Committee. They had all agreed that the question of the bombing of the civil population should be discussed, except the German Ambassador, who had asked for time to consider the matter, though he had not refused to discuss it. . . . At the meeting of the Committee on the previous day everyone had agreed that the matter should be discussed, except the German Ambassador, who had again not refused, but had suggested that the scope of the discussion should be widened to include other forms of ill-treatment of the civil population besides bombing.[103]

The news leak from the Chairman's Sub-Committee was not the only significant item in the London press that morning concerning Guernica. On that day, not only had the *Times* published Holburn's cablegram from Vitoria, with its confirmation of the bombing, but it also printed an editorial position on that bombing, in the form of a reply to the all-out attack of the German press—supported by the Havas-Botto dispatch—against the *Times* of the previous day. The editorial has already been cited in part. The rest follows:

THE TIMES BOMBS GUERNICA

It was under this title that the official German news agency gave the State-controlled Nazi press its incitement for a violent outburst against Great Britain and the British press and this journal in particular. Official Germany now alleges that *The Times,* selecting a town "of which not one Englishman in a hundred had ever heard of before," fabricated a circumstantial account of its bombardment from the air in circumstances of peculiar, cold-blooded brutality.

It was left to the ingenuity of the individual German newspapers to provide motives for such singular conduct on the part of *The Times*. This was a formidable task; and the allegation, fantastic in itself, was rendered doubly so by various divergent efforts to convince the German public of its truth. The whole episode illustrated most poignantly the difficulties which beset international relations in our time.

The bombing of Guernica, which could have been foreseen by no one in this country, was reported by our special correspondent on the spot and by his colleagues of other newspapers as part of their ordinary journalistic duties. Since it was carried out by planes of a German type, the publication of the news embarrassed Germany. But where is the wisdom, from Germany's point of view, in allowing her embarrassment to inspire a press campaign which is calculated to damage her relations with Great Britain and which, consisting as it does, in a series of chimerical accusations, intemperately made, can only discredit her powers of self-control and—incidentally—arouse suspicions of her complicity in the bombardment?

What is the destiny of a world in which no responsible organ of the press can tell the simple truth without incurring charges of Machiavellian villainy?[104]

The German press did not tell its readers of the *Times* editorial, nor did the *Times* tell its readers of the Havas dispatch or of the use the Nazis had made of it.[105]

The Basque proposal of April 29 to investigate the causes of the destruction of Guernica had provoked no serious reaction; Delbos's suggestion along the same lines on April 30 had had no follow-up; and certainly the project being debated before the Sub-Committee of the N.I.C. without even a mention of the word "Guernica," could hardly lead to such an inquiry. Julio Álvarez del Vayo had brought up the question again on May 3, when he was in Paris coming from Geneva and returning to Valencia. In reply to a question by an interviewer, he asked for "an international enquiry on the spot to determine who had destroyed Guernica."[106] Now, on May 5, Pablo de Azcárate, Spanish ambassador in London, handed to the Foreign Office a note that said in part:

The Republican government considers, in view of the gravity of the happenings and their importance in the international situation, that it is essential that the responsibility for such an act [the destruction of Guernica] be decided in a conclusive manner. To this end, the government of the Republic asks Great Britain to adopt whatever action it may consider necessary to institute an international investigation with the purpose of deciding on whom reposes the responsibility for the destruction of the town of Guernica. The government of the Republic is disposed, for its part, to do all that lies within its power to ensure that such an investigation be conducted with the greatest efficiency.[107]

It seems evident now that neither the Basques nor the Republican government could have held out high hopes for such an investigation. Guernica was already in Rebel hands. But the proposal, after lying dormant for a week or two, was to take on new life, not to help the Spanish Republicans or the Basques but to help the Conservative government in England in its battle with public opinion.

The Non-Intervention Committee met in full session on May 5, and Lord Plymouth opened the meeting with a short statement concerning "the leakage of information" that had followed the previous day's reunion of the Chairman's Sub-Committee. He said

> versions appeared in some newspapers which were not only tendentious, but entirely incorrect. I cannot use words strong enough to condemn those who are responsible for this information leaking out in this particular form. . . . I wish to say that I feel this matter cannot be allowed to rest where it is at present. I have informed our News Department, who, in their turn, are informing the Press, that the only authentic version of what occurred at our meeting yesterday was that which appeared in the official communiqué and that all other versions are incorrect.[108]

This prissily firm position, not entirely in line with the truth of events, could not have displeased von Ribbentrop. He was, however, at least publicly, enraged and called on Eden after the N.I.C. meeting. Eden wrote that same day that the ambassador "said that he had come to speak to me of a grave matter." It was on British initiative that the sub-committee meeting had taken place, and the official communiqué "accurately summarized what passed." "Yet," the German ambassador continued, according to Eden's summary,

> in certain British papers the next day there appeared wholly inaccurate accounts of what happened, which attributed to the Ambassador, as German representative, views which he had never expressed and did not hold. Herr von Ribbentrop said that he was perfectly well aware of the source of these reports. If M. Maisky had at the Committee itself referred to Germany in connexion with Guernica as the press leakage now did, the Ambassador would at once have left the Committee.

If such an incident were repeated, von Ribbentrop "would strongly urge his Government to withdraw from the Committee."

The ambassador then brought up "the subject of Guernica and of the reports of the bombing of that town which had appeared in the British press." He claimed that the British press articles "were not accurate," and he "produced several counter-reports, including a message from Havas." Concerning Guernica, the foreign minister told von Ribbentrop

> that our evidence conflicted and that I could not agree with his view and that quoted in the "Echo de Paris." It was therefore quite impossible for us to

agree [to?] any statement on this subject. . . . An agreed statement on the subject of Guernica was not . . . possible.

Since Eden received von Ribbentrop after the N.I.C. meeting—that is, late on the afternoon of May 5—it is probable that he was aware of the Spanish note of the same date, requesting British initiative in setting up an "international investigation" into the causes of the destruction of Guernica. At any rate, he was aware of the Basque message along the same lines of April 29, and in his talk with the German ambassador he discountenanced the latter by suggesting that "since there was a conflict of evidence [concerning Guernica], would it not be best in the circumstances to have an enquiry to establish the facts?" According to Eden, von Ribbentrop "neither accepted nor refused" this suggestion.[109]

The German envoy took two steps following the visit to Eden. Despite the apparent casualness of Eden's words about an "international investigation," the German did not ignore his suggestion, and immediately asked Berlin for "the earliest possible instructions" concerning such a proposition for an inquiry. He thought that Eden might pursue the idea through the N.I.C. and added as an interesting afterthought (interesting, for it shows that von Ribbentrop thought he could count on the Belgian vote in matters of "Red atrocities") these words: "Possibly a proposal would have to be made by Belgium to extend the investigation to Red atrocities, or specifically to concrete instances of recent occurrences, if possible." To this end, he requested that Berlin forward to him at once a dossier on "Red atrocities." He was at this time—May 6—aware that on the previous day Valencia had requested Great Britain to take the initiative in "an international investigation" and suspected that the Russians would bring the subject up in the N.I.C.[110]

Von Ribbentrop's second reaction to his talk with the British foreign minister resulted from Eden's telling him that in view of their disagreement on the subject of Guernica, "there was nothing to prevent him issuing a statement of his Government's point of view from the German Embassy if he wished to do so."[111] In the declaration that he then made to the press, the German envoy said he had called Eden's attention to

> the false and tendentious allegations made by part of the English Press and in the House of Commons, concerning the pretended destruction of the Spanish town of Guernica. The Ambassador cited the reports of other foreign newspapers, based on eyewitness accounts and which agree with the results of German investigations, which show that the destruction of Guernica was carried out by the Bolshevists. The Ambassador expressed his surprise at the false and tendentious reports which have had unfortunate repercussions and which should not be allowed publication.[112]

This is a curiously worded statement. What did he mean by "the pretended destruction of . . . Guernica"? Was the town, then, not destroyed? The "other foreign newspapers" to which he referred were undoubtedly *Le Jour, Le Figaro, Le Journal,* among others, but what were the "results of German investigations"? At any rate, von Ribbentrop was quite satisfied with his effort and informed Berlin that

> my statement regarding the Guernica incident [was] given satisfactory publicity by almost the entire press. Only the *Daily Herald* and the *News Chronicle* add remarks which weaken the effect.[113]

This declaration was widely distributed by DNB and was printed in the Spanish Nationalist press, as an "official communiqué" from London, made to look as if it had been issued not by the German embassy but by the British government.[114]

Faupel in Salamanca replied on May 5 to Berlin's telegram of the previous day. He noted that "the denial agreed upon with Franco regarding Guernica has not been issued," but insisted that the Salamanca press handouts concerning the bombing, dated April 29 and 30, "in the sharpest terms . . . reject as lies and slander the Basque Government's report regarding the alleged destruction of the city by German fliers." He added: "The interpretation that this denial indirectly admits a German plane attack is malicious and unsupported by the text of the denial."[115] Faupel was, it would seem, right about the contents of the Salamanca press handouts. What is unexplained by the documents available is the full story of the "denial agreed upon with Franco."[116]

Other questions concerning Guernica and the war in the Basque country were raised in the House of Commons on May 5. Arthur Henderson raised the question already mentioned, concerning Mola's threat to Bilbao, and Mr. Geoffrey Mander inquired of Eden if he

> will consider the advisability of participating in the investigation being undertaken by the French government representatives as to the responsibility for the destruction of Guernica, either jointly or independently or through the appropriate organ of the League of Nations.

There was not, as we now know, any French investigation under way. Eden, in his answer, referred to the proposed action by the N.I.C. concerning the bombing of open towns, a procedure with which the French were in agreement.[117]

It was only on the following day, on the eve of the Whitsuntide holiday, that a genuine debate on the question of Guernica took place. The Opposition members who spoke on May 6 denounced the attack on Guernica in vehement terms and implicated the Germans. This soothed consciences, but what positive action could be demanded of the government? Nothing more vigorous than the "international investigation" proposed the previous day by the Spanish Republic was even suggested, and even this weak motion was by then impossible.

"It was an act of frightfulness," declared Mr. Grenfell, speaking of the "incident of Guernica."

It is said that the Germans are very sensitive, that they protest against the allegations that these airplanes were German airplanes. The allegation goes further and says that they were German pilots who flew those airplanes. Bombs were dropped; that cannot be disputed. The nationality of the pilots is a question to be decided by further evidence. In face of these denials and repudiations, and the counter-allegation that it was a journalist who conceived this dastardly act and that no such thing happened—the denial has taken that form—and that there was no air raid on that day, although the damage was done and it stands to be witnessed by anybody who cares to go there, I would ask the Foreign Secretary whether there is any reason why this peculiar example of the frightfulness of modern military minds should not be impartially investigated.

Mr. Mander, invoking Steer's second dispatch on the bombing, which had been printed that morning, declared:

> There is no doubt, I should have thought, that there has been a systematic bombing of Guernica. . . . The conclusion that I, at any rate, reached is that systematic bombing has taken place by German airplanes. I see no evidence anywhere to suggest that this is a case of mass suicide by the Basque people.

He also called for an inquiry, by neutrals or by the League of Nations.[118]

The chief defender of the Nationalist position, Mr. Donner, said that the bombing of Guernica "is a most lamentable and horrible thing—if it is true—and I say 'if' because there is insufficient and unreliable evidence. . . ." He based his argument on the Havas-Botto dispatch, a copy of which, he said, had been handed to him by a member as he came into the House. He interpreted the Havas-Botto report to mean that Mola's officers "were able to show that the burning of the town had been a voluntary act." When he was interrupted at this point, he remarked: "Hon Members opposite may disagree with my opinions, but it is futile to say that these things are not stated here." Donner then claimed that Guernica was "a legitimate military objective" and charged that the Spanish Republicans had bombed Motril and two other towns in Nationalist hands the same day, or at least the same week, that Guernica was said to have been bombed.

This provoked Wilfred Roberts to retort: "Will the hon. Gentleman explain which argument he is using? Was Guernica burned by the Basques, or was it bombed because of the munition factories that were in it?" Unabashed, Donner replied:

> My case is perfectly consistent and logical. The difficulty is that we do not know the facts. We have no reliable information of what happened at Guernica, but if German airplanes and or airplanes belonging to General Franco did, in fact, bomb Guernica, we should not without an investigation immediately jump to the conclusion that it is an open town; and, in any case, we should not pass over in complete silence the things which happened the very same week and which deeds were committed by the forces of the Government of Señor Caballero.[119]

Labourite Philip Noel-Baker continued the offensive against the position of the Baldwin government. The attack on Guernica was "not like anything that has ever happened before" and "it is not enough to make an appeal to both sides in the Spanish war to 'humanize' their conduct." To counter the evidence of the Havas-Botto telegram, he invoked Steer's "classic report in the 'Times'" and continued:

> We say that this is by far the worst atrocity that has happened; that, as a precedent, it is extremely dangerous to us and to the world . . . that such methods will become to be regarded as an accepted practice, which all too probably would be the starting point for the next war, and that in the first week of hostilities, if another war should ever unhappily break out, we should see repeated on a grand scale what a few dozen German aircraft did at Guernica.

The Labourite insisted:

> We believe that the case in regard to Guernica has been absolutely proved. We have the evidence of countless eyewitnesses, and we have the rebel case itself. . . . We have the evidence of British eyewitnesses. . . . We believe the case has been proved, and if the Government have any doubt, let them accept the plea of the Basque authorities and the Spanish Government for an international inquiry on the spot.[120]

The foreign minister answered the speakers of the Opposition and of the government. Aside from the fact that he refused to name the Germans as the culprits, he gave, in general, satisfaction to the partisans of the Basque and Spanish Republican cause. He admitted the bombing and the machine-gunning and he gave his blessing to an international inquiry.

"It is perfectly true," stated Eden in his intervention, "that this affair has stirred considerable depths of feeling in this country." He pointed out that this was "not the only example of the bombing of the civil population in Spain," and then sought to situate the Guernica disaster more precisely:

> It does seem, from the information which has come to us so far, a particularly deplorable example of bombing and machine-gunning from the air. I should like not only this House—in this instance I am speaking to a rather wider audience—but other nations to understand that the feelings in this country on this matter are not due, as some of them appear to think, to a desire to put any other country in the dock, or to a desire to accuse any other country, but they are due to a belief, which is widely shared in this country, on the evidence at present available, that there has been an exceptionally severe air bombardment and machine-gunning.

The minister then emphasized the wider implications of Guernica:

> It is the knowledge that if that kind of thing is repeated and intensified on a large scale, it is going to mean a terrible future for Europe to face which has resulted in this expression of opinion. This opinion is not confined to this

country at all, as some foreign nations think—not at all—but extends not only to the Dominions but, as I know, to the United States of America and elsewhere.

Reflecting the legitimate apprehensions of the government, he continued:

What we do want is to make of this event, if the event is of the nature that we think it is, an occasion for seeking to put a stop to the repetition of happenings which must have such tragic consequences in the future if allowed to be repeated.

The only proposal that Eden could suggest to halt such attacks as that on Guernica was the adoption of the suggestions of Grenfell, Mander, and Noel-Baker: an international investigation. The government was interested in "trying to establish the facts" about Guernica. He declared himself little optimistic about the chances of such an inquiry.

I should like to see, perhaps, a number of nationals of small neutral states endeavor to carry out that task. We shall be doing that, not in an effort to pillory the past, but in an effort to better the future.[121]

The most significant part of Eden's speech was that in which he admitted the bombing and machine-gunning at Guernica. No other governmental figure of his stature in the West had at that time gone so far. On what evidence did he base this position? The debaters on one side cited Steer's dispatches to uphold their arguments; opposing orators used the Havas-Botto telegram to prove their contentions. The foreign minister certainly knew these sources, and, as we shall see, had his own reasons for doubting the Havas-Botto telegram touted by von Ribbentrop; but he also had news from other correspondents: consuls and ambassadors.

When one studies the writings on the Spanish Civil War, one is struck by the fact that most newspaper correspondents, privately paid for public reading, were instinctively favorable to the cause of the Spanish Republic; but most diplomatic correspondents, publicly paid for private reading, were instinctively favorable to the cause of the Nationalists. One exception to this rule was the British consul in Bilbao, Ralph Stevenson, a conservative certainly, but deeply attached emotionally to the problems of the Basques.[122] He visited Guernica within twenty-four hours of its destruction, and his report doubtless influenced Eden's statement of May 6:

On landing at Bermeo yesterday I was told about the destruction of Guernica. I went at once to have a look at the place and to my amazement found that the township normally of some five thousand inhabitants, since the September influx of refugees about ten thousand, was almost completely destroyed. Nine houses in ten are beyond reconstruction. Many were still burning and fresh fires were breaking out here and there, the result of incendiary bombs which owing to some fault had not exploded in impact the day before and were doing so, at the time, of my visit, under falling beams and masonry. The casualties cannot be ascertained and probably never will [be?] accurately. Some estimates put the figure at one thousand, others at over three thousand. An inhabitant who went through it all told me that at about 4 p.m. three machines appeared overhead and dropped H.E. and incendiary bombs. They disappeared and ten minutes later a fresh lot of five or six machines came and so on for several hours, until after seven. All told he estimates the number of planes at fifty. After two or three visits panic seized the population. Men, women and children poured out of Guernica and ran up the bare hillsides. There they were mercilessly machine gunned, though with little effect. They spent the night in the open gazing at their burning city. I saw many men and women erring through the streets searching in the wreckage of their houses for the bodies of their dear ones.[123]

We know that Eden put great faith in Stevenson's report. On the day after the parliamentary debate—May 7—Eden had a conversation with Portuguese Ambassador Monteiro, who informed Lisbon that Eden told him that Guernica had been destroyed by "German airplanes." This was a statement the foreign minister did not care to make publicly before the Commons. Eden showed the Stevenson report to the Portuguese emissary and assured him that the author was "a well-balanced person, impartial and without any inclination towards the Reds." The essential facts of the Stevenson report were incorporated in the ambassador's message to Lisbon. [124] Unfortunately, what the head of British diplomacy told the Portuguese diplomat was never revealed to the British Parliament, or to the British people, and remained in the closed circuit of diplomacy. One can speculate on Eden's reasons for showing the Stevenson message to Monteiro. Perhaps he thought that Monteiro would tell von Ribbentrop, who would then probably cease pestering Eden with protestations of German innocence. Or did he also think that Lisbon would immediately inform the Burgos Junta? Eden maintained, years later, the stand he had taken with Monteiro, and in his memoirs wrote:

On April 26th, Guernica was destroyed by bombardment from the air with heavy loss of life. This was the first blitz of the second world war, carried out, according to our reports, by German aircraft.[125]

The man to whom Stevenson's telegram was addressed, and who forwarded it to London, Sir Henry Chilton, British ambassador to Spain, had less sympathy for the Basques than did his consul in Bilbao, and more faith in the given word of the Nationalists. On Thursday, April 29, the day Guernica fell, Sir Henry telephoned to London the Nationalist press denials of having bombed the town, and repeated the assertion that bad weather had kept the planes from flying, adding that Nationalists "accuse Government of having burned town as well as Eibar." Sir Henry had also asked for information from the military governor of Irún, who, he told London,

assures me airplanes were unable to fly on Monday, Tuesday and Wednesday of this week owing to low clouds. Prisoners taken stated that Guernica was set on fire by retiring Government troops.[126]

The military governor, Troncoso, promised the ambassador to put his declaration in writing, which he did, after a fashion. On May 2, Sir Henry telephoned to London:

Military Governor has in writing flatly denied that Guernica was burned *(sic)* by Nationalists and gives me his word of honor that the town suffered the same fate as Irún, Eibar, etc. (i.e., that it was burned by defenders) which he says can now be verified by personal visit.

On this same day—May 2—Sir Henry talked with the correspondent of the *Daily Telegraph,* Pembroke Stephens, who had visited Guernica the day it fell and cabled a dispatch to his journal on that date. Stephens told the ambassador "in confidence that he has no doubt whatever that raid took place." His testimony, as related by the ambassador, continued:

He visited the town on April 29 and spoke privately with the remaining inhabitants who confirmed reports. He also saw many unmistakable bomb holes. He has no evidence that damage was done by Government forces.

He also told the ambassador:

German and Italian air tactics have for the first time in Spain been properly employed in the present offensive and have had an overwhelming success. Raids similar to this one have been made on many small villages during the past month.

Sir Henry's message ended with this warning: "Please take care that this information cannot be traced back to my informant as he has to return to Spain."[127]

The foreign minister of Great Britain on May 6 thus knew a great deal more than he revealed to the members of the House of Commons about the destruction of Guernica. His consul in Bilbao had confirmed the bombing after a personal visit to the ruins; the correspondent of a conservative newspaper, who had sent a noncommittal dispatch to his newspaper about the destruction of the town, had expressed his confidential belief that Guernica had been bombed, and not by the Spanish government forces. Anthony Eden also had good and sufficient reasons to doubt the truthfulness of the Havas-Botto telegram, as shall be developed below. This confidential knowledge doubtless led him to state before the Commons his conviction that Guernica had suffered "an exceptionally severe air bombardment and machine-gunning."

On May 7 the chairman's subcommittee met again, and Lord Plymouth opened the proceedings with a statement on Item 1 on the agenda: "Unauthorized Publication in the Press of Information regarding the Proceedings in the Sub-Committee (To be raised by the Chairman)." Plymouth's declaration was so worded as to give full satisfaction to the German ambassador.

He wanted to put the position as clearly and as emphatically as possible. What occurs at our meetings is by general consent strictly confidential. . . . If we are unable to trust ourselves and are made to feel that any single word or sentence we use is liable to be quoted in the Press, and furthermore completely distorted for propaganda purposes, our deliberations here will become quite impossible.

Lord Plymouth also at this time gave as the sought-for result of the committee's activities this revealing formula: ". . . the Spanish conflict will be prevented from spreading outside Spanish frontiers and its dangers and horrors reduced to the lowest limit."[128] The strict application of nonintervention might have contributed to these results, but the definition said nothing about nonintervention in Spanish affairs. In fact the diplomats seemed more interested in keeping secret their talks than in preventing a repetition of the Guernica disaster. Jan Masaryk suggested that each delegation control the correspondents of its nationality and that if any correspondent published unauthorized information concerning the committee, he be sent home at once. The Italian ambassador made a grandstand play, rebuking Masaryk by saying virtuously, "I could not do that," whereas he was of course one of those present who could do precisely that, and within a few days his government was going to order all Italian correspondents in England to come home.[129] Masaryk replied with this naïve remark: "I think it is a terrible thing that there should be eight of us around this table and we cannot keep a secret. I think it is the most shocking thing I have known for years."[130] The Czech obviously did not consider the Russian ambassador a gentleman.

When the subcommittee reached Item 3 on the agenda, "Suggested Appeal to the Two Parties in Spain regarding the Conduct of the Present Conflict,"[131] the title of the item itself was sufficient to indicate a certain wavering of the British delegate's resolution. The practical difficulty of "drawing up a schedule of open towns, or of establishing safety zones in certain areas" was of such proportions that Lord Plymouth did not find "it possible to put before the Committee any detailed proposals of this character at this moment." He did, however, introduce a new proposal "that both sides should agree to renounce entirely the use of bombing from the air in this civil conflict." This was not "an exclusive proposal which would rule out any other attempts to humanize the conflict in Spain."[132]

This new proposal was unenthusiastically received.[133] If one can trust what was said at the meeting, and this would be unwise, the French delegate had no previous inkling of the new British proposition.[134] Plymouth pressed with great insistence for an agreement that each member of the subcommittee would put the proposal to his government. This insistence, and Plymouth's further insistence that the press communiqué mention the new proposal, would justify the conclusion that the British government wanted something, however unreal, with which to convince public opinion that action was being taken to prevent a recurrence of the attack on Guernica.[135]

Count Grandi, who had not been present at the May 4 meeting, intervened to inform the subcommittee that "as regards the question of the bombardment of open towns in Spain . . . today the National Government in Spain issued in Salamanca an official communiqué which has just reached me." He read the communiqué, part of which declared:

> The National Government, who are fighting in defense of the ancient Spanish traditions and world civilization, declare that non-military open cities have never been and never will be bombarded by National planes.

Grandi defined the paper as

> a particular and precise declaration by the National Government in Spain, in which it is emphasized that at least one party in the Civil War in Spain declares that non-military open cities have never been and never will be bombarded by National planes.

Grandi's colleagues were loath to believe the statement as far-reaching in its implications as the Italian ambassador pretended. There was a phrase read by the Italian delegate which seemed to justify the razing of Guernica: "Towns wherein military units take shelter, situated in a zone 10 kilometers from the front, are also lawful military objectives, and their civilian inhabitants should be evacuated." This prompted the French ambassador to note that "if you read the communiqué as a whole you will see that there may be some doubt about the conception of what is an open city."[136]

Grandi was not swayed by this observation, and attempted to include a reference to his "document" in the official communiqué of the subcommittee,

> by which international public opinion could realize that the Committee has already scored a success. We know now, by an official statement published everywhere, that at least one of the two parties in conflict in Spain undertakes a public engagement that they will never bombard open cities. I thought perhaps it was useful from the point of view of our work and the success of our work to take note of this.[137]

The matter was dropped when Maisky retorted:

> If, however, the Italian ambassador will insist upon putting his statement into the communiqué, then I have no alternative but to make a counter-statement, and to insist on its inclusion in the communiqué.[138]

It might have been embarrassing for the Italian delegate had he succeeded in getting official recognition for his "document," and embarrassing for the other members had they accepted the "document," for it was in reality but the tail end of a polemical editorial broadcast by Radio Nacional of Salamanca early on the morning of May 6, and not at all "a particular and precise declaration by the National Government." The basis of the Salamanca editorial was the London dispatches founded on the news leak following the May 4 meeting of the chairman's subcommittee, for Salamanca, not knowing that von Ribbentrop contested these reports, accepted them at face value. The Nationalist spokesman presented the

German ambassador as affirming that "Lord Plymouth's proposition of an appeal to stop the bombing of open towns was a barefaced intervention in Spanish matters" and claimed that the German delegate "asserted that the bombing of open towns was justified if they were militarized."[139]

The "document" so irresponsibly read by Grandi was but a continuation of this harangue and could hardly have been considered as a binding engagement of the Salamanca government. But it does constitute a revealing commentary by the Nationalist propagandists on the problem of Guernica: it seemed perfectly believable to them that their champion on the Non-Intervention Committee, von Ribbentrop, consider the proposed British appeal as intervention in Spanish affairs (whereas the bombing by German planes was not) and that he attempt to justify the air attacks on open towns.

The subcommittee came back to the British proposal, and after a good deal of bickering on the words to use in the communiqué, it was finally agreed that it read as follows:

> Lord Plymouth then put forward a suggestion on behalf of the United Kingdom that the Non-Intervention Committee should address an appeal to both parties in Spain that they should agree to renounce entirely the use of bombing from the air in the present conflict.

Member governments were immediately to give their instructions thereon. The communiqué also referred to the suggestion

> made by the German representative and supported by the Italian and Portuguese representatives that any approach to the two parties in Spain should be on a wider basis and should aim at doing what was possible to bring to an end all the inhumanities which had marked the present conflict.[140]

The subcommittee then adjourned for seven days.

The London correspondent of the *New York Times* observed pertinently:

> There is little hope in the Committee or elsewhere that either side in Spain will heed such an appeal, if made. The British feel, nevertheless, that it was necessary to do something to satisfy public opinion, and if possible to "humanize" the war in Spain. Today's meeting was important chiefly in that it shows all European powers again are anxious to preserve the appearance of non-intervention regardless of what their "volunteers" may be doing in Spain at the present time.[141]

The meeting of the chairman's subcommittee, scheduled for May 14, did not take place, and the subcommittee did not meet again until May 18. At that reunion the first item on the agenda was: "Suggested Appeal to the Two Parties in Spain regarding the Conduct of the Present Conflict." This suggested appeal, it can be remembered, did not ask for the ending of the bombing of open towns, as had the original British proposal, but sought the complete cessation of all air bombing in the civil war. Lord Plymouth recalled the position of the British government as outlined at the session of May 7, and the Soviet and Czech representatives expressed their support of the British statement. [142] The German delegate, Dr. Woermann, who attended in von Ribbentrop's absence, after reiterating the German position that the appeal in question was not within the competence of the committee, sought again to enlarge the scope of the appeal "by dealing with the problem as a whole." He observed:

> Otherwise there remains the danger that this action, which was started in the interest of humanity, would be directed against one party and could be used for propaganda purposes against them.

The unnamed shadow of Guernica lingered over the committee room. The German reasoned:

> At the present state of affairs it would be contradictory to the principle of not intervening into the warfare of the fighting parties, if one suddenly demanded the prohibition of a means of warfare which up to now was legal.

He expressed a preference for the original British proposal of May 4, "prohibiting the bombing of open towns," adding that "it goes without saying that such an appeal would only form one part of the problem of humanization."[143]

Crolla, the Italian spokesman, agreed with the German. He made an oblique reference to the incident at Guernica:

> As regards the sufferings of the civil population and the destruction of private or national property or of art treasures, the Italian government find it utterly irrelevant whether they be caused by bombs dropped from the air, by land or sea artillery, by mines placed by retreating troops, or by fire deliberately started.

The Italian also returned to the "official communique issued at Salamanca on the 7th of May," which his superior, Grandi, had presented to the subcommittee on that date; the Italian embassy was apparently still unaware that the statement in question was not an "official communiqué."[144]

The Portuguese ambassador upheld the stands taken by the German and Italian speakers concerning the noncompetence of the committee to deal with the problem of bombing open towns. As for widening the appeal to include the ending of all air bombing, he did not believe "that it will be possible, at the present stage of armaments, to lay aside so important an instrument of war." He then, perhaps unconsciously, revealed his feeling that the Nationalists were stronger in the air than the Republicans by stating that "for one of the parties to relinquish this weapon could result in a serious diminution of its power of attack and might accordingly amount to the giving of strong assistance to the other side." He added: "It should be remembered that bombing from the air does not, in the present conflict, appear to constitute the salient feature of the atrocities committed." The

Swedish ambassador would "support all measures to bring about a more humane dealing in any warfare, including this." The Belgian had not received his instructions.[145] Corbin, speaking for France, demanded immediate action on an appeal. He recognized the insufficiency of international law concerning aerial bombing, but he proposed that a distinction be made between, on the one hand, wars between nations, and, on the other hand, civil wars.[146]

There then followed a debate on procedure. Woermann said that if the intention was to go beyond "an appeal in very general terms," the matter would have to be delayed. Maisky stated: "I am more inclined to accept the British proposal and to limit an appeal for the time being to the question of aerial bombardment alone." The German disputed this interpretation of the "British proposal." Plymouth sought to placate the representative of Berlin:

> We were in sympathy with the proposals made by the German representative at the first meeting to the end that this appeal should be widened in order to include various forms of other inhumanities which unfortunately had occurred during the course of the war.

He concluded by stating that

> the question we have to resolve is whether we can all of us agree to make an appeal on the broader question, namely the cessation of bombing altogether, or whether we can only confine ourselves to the question of bombing of open towns.

Palmstierna saw "with the utmost delight and pleasure the British Government supporting the view of forbidding bombing from the air altogether." It was finally decided that the committee secretary should draft "the form of an appeal which might be made to the two parties in Spain, and base it on the discussions we have had today."[147] This draft was to be circulated before the next meeting.

The Germans did not lose sight of the possibility of an investigation into the responsibilities for the Guernica tragedy. The embassy in London persisted in demanding from Berlin a complete dossier—not on material with which to prove Nazi innocence for Guernica but on material to prove "Red atrocities," with which to combat any proposal for an inquiry into Guernica. Woermann repeated von Ribbentrop's request in a letter to Prince Bismarck on May 7.[148] A week later Bismarck asked for other material on the subject from the German embassy in Salamanca, alleging that such information as DNB had been able to prepare from Radio Salamanca's broadcast left much to be desired.[149] On the following day— May 15—State Secretary Lammers telephoned to von Mackensen, then state secretary at the Foreign Ministry, to give him Hitler's views on any investigation of Guernica. According to von Mackensen's note, Hitler

> expects that the Foreign Ministry in its instructions to London will emphasize that the investigation of a single event of the war lies far beyond all

possibility and that such an investigation should be unconditionally rejected.

The diplomat replied to Lammers that

> our orders have followed the thinking of the Führer and we stand in
> agreement with the War Ministry on this point, that an investigation of the
> Guernica incident must in all circumstances be refused.[150]

The Germans were resolutely against the investigation. And the French? It is
now clear that whatever Delbos may have said to the senate commission or to the
newspapermen, he never had any serious intention of actively pursuing an inquiry
into Guernica. On May 12, Sir Robert Vansittart, permanent under-secretary of the
Foreign Office, saw Alexis Léger, secretary-general of the Quai d'Orsay, and then
reported to his government:

> I asked M. Léger . . . whether there was any reason for supposing that the
> French Government was proceeding to some sort of enquiry into the Guer-
> nica case. M. Delbos had rather left this impression on our minds. M. Léger
> (and later M. Delbos himself) told me. that this must be an entire misunder-
> standing on our part. They were undertaking nothing of the kind; nor had
> they any means of doing so. M. Leger went on to say that any enquiry, even
> if it were nominally possible, would in his opinion be a mistake. From the
> diplomatic point of view, he said, *(cela ne rime à rien)* and it would lead us
> nowhere.[151]

The slow progress being made in the N.I.C. was perhaps responsible for the fact
that the British government now sought another method for demonstrating to the
English people that it was determined to take action against a recurrence of the
Guernica tragedy. This method was to revive the proposal, first made by the
Basques on April 29, then mentioned by Delbos on April 30, recalled to public
attention by Álvarez del Vayo on May 3 in Paris, and again reactivated by the
Spanish ambassador in London on May 5 in a note to the British government, and a
day later proposed by Opposition deputies and by Eden himself in the Parliament:
an international investigation into what had been done in the Basque country. It
was also the proposal that the French had refused verbally six days earlier. The
technical basis for launching this new campaign was the Basque note received 20
days earlier.

On May 19 an identical cipher telegram was forwarded from Whitehall to the
British ambassadors in Paris, Berlin, Moscow, Rome, and Lisbon, recalling that the
Basque Autonomous Government had communicated to the Foreign Office on
April 29 an official note "regarding the destruction of Guernica and other Basque
cities by foreign aircraft in the service of General Franco," and that in that note the
Basque government had declared that

> they are ready to receive all commissions, persons and institutions who desire
> to investigate on their own account the deeds that have been done in Basque

territory and express their fervent desire that these investigations should be done as fully as possible.

Each ambassador was instructed to inform the government to which he was accredited "of this communication and invite their observations on the suggestion made therein." The message ended:

> You should add that if, in their view, such an international enquiry could be usefully made, it could, if thought desirable, be extended to cover other incidents of a similar nature. For ourselves we should be ready to cooperate in such an enquiry whatever its scope.[152]

The first reaction came from the Portuguese. A verbal refusal was indicated to British Ambassador Sir Charles Wingfield, in a conversation with the secretary-general of the Portuguese Ministry of Foreign Affairs, de Sampayo. During this talk, Wingfield told the Portuguese diplomat: "Public opinion in Great Britain also felt that it would be disastrous for civilization if we let pass without protest such outrages as the destruction of undefended towns from the air."[153] This not only revealed to de Sampayo his interlocutor's thoughts about what had happened at Guernica, but also showed how the pressure of "public opinion" was working in the ambassador's mind.

On the following day, the Portuguese government definitely turned down the British proposal in a written note, incorporating the arguments used by de Sampayo. A résumé of the Portuguese memorandum was cabled to London, and this produced an interesting comment by C. A. E. Shuckburgh:

> The suggested enquiry was, in our minds, to be directed more towards establishing or disproving *German* participation in the Guernica incident, than as an enquiry into the methods of the Insurgents. The subsequent appeal to the two parties has somewhat obscured this distinction.[154]

In the memorandum, Lisbon declared that the proposed inquiry at this moment would certainly be viewed by General Franco with suspicions of "partiality in favor of his adversary." The Portuguese also found it

> difficult to explain the special interest aroused by the case of Guernica to the extent of proposing an international enquiry into it. Furthermore as Guernica is now situated in a zone of very active war operations, and as no enquiry could be carried out without the consent of General Franco, who could not grant it for that reason, the request of the Basque Government can only be made with the sole object of obtaining such a refusal and using it for ends which do not interest us and to which we cannot contribute.[155]

As of that date—May 21—no other replies were forthcoming.

Then on May 24 the subcommittee of the N.I.C. met again, and the other British proposal inspired by public reaction against the attack on Guernica, the appeal concerning the bombing of open towns, was the first item on the agenda. Hemming's draft appeal had been circulated among the members before the séance, as had been agreed on at the last meeting. This draft differed considerably from the original British proposals. The preamble begged "the two parties in Spain at once to take every step necessary for the protection of non-combatants, whether men, women or children," and one paragraph certainly recalled Guernica:

> In particular the International Committee urge with the utmost vigor that both sides should abstain from the bombardment from the air, or by land or sea, of all open towns and villages and other objectives of a non-military character.

But other paragraphs deviated into the problem of the treatment of hostages and prisoners of war and of "the civilian adherents of the opposite side in the territory under their control." The preamble, at one point, seemed far away from the reality of the Spanish war, calling upon "the two parties in Spain . . . to treat those who are their foes in the field of battle in a chivalrous manner, in accordance with the dictates of humanity.[156]

Lord Plymouth assumed the sponsorship of the new draft. Woermann, representing Germany, objected to the fact that the paragraph concerning bombing and open towns was more strongly worded than the others. He also thought that the appeal should mention "the burning of churches and so on." The Italian delegate wanted the system of hostages condemned. Monteiro said that the question of bombing open towns was general to all wars; the Portuguese public was sensitive to those acts of cruelty peculiar to the Spanish Civil War, for example, the *"exportation d'enfants sans autorisation des parents."*[157]

Samuel B. Cahan, sitting in for Maisky, then declared the draft "unsatisfactory." He recalled that the original British proposition had dealt with the bombing of open towns and nothing else; this had been changed to an appeal "for the complete cessation of bombardment from the air." Today, in the draft appeal "we see a number of 'points' included which obscured the original purpose of the appeal and the object which the British Government had in mind when they made their suggestion." Whereas the Republican air force bombed only military objectives, "The Rebels, on the contrary, have made a special point of terrorizing the civil population by the bombing of open cities and towns." Cahan protested against the paragraph on the treatment of political opponents, for it might "be interpreted as an attempt to deprive the Spanish Government of the right to take all measures necessary for maintaining the political stability and security of the State." The only part of the draft appeal the Soviet delegate would accept was that dealing with "the bombing of open towns."[158]

The debate went on. A phrase was changed here, a word there. Woermann sought again to include a denunciation of the burning of churches, "one of the most distasteful things in the civil war." Monteiro returned to his theme:

> the horrors and cruelties of which tens of thousands of persons in Barcelona, in Madrid, in Málaga, have been the victims; the judgments, the execution of

prisoners and of great numbers of civilians, the judgments by the "people's courts," the executions without judgment of thousands and thousands of men and families.[159]

The Soviet delegate continued to protest that

the whole appeal in its present form represents a complete watering down of the original proposal of the British Government which had as its object a concrete, definite purpose which my Government . . . was prepared to support.

But Plymouth was no longer defending the original British proposals and gave his support to the new draft. Cahan replied:

If a compromise has for its object the attainment of a certain practical purpose, that is a compromise which everyone will agree to, but if it is a compromise calculated to meet the desires of those who want to avoid the attainment of a certain definite object, then it is something to which I for one am not prepared to agree.[160]

Cahan found himself alone, with all the other powers ready to accept the new draft.

When the time came to prepare the day's communiqué, the appeal was again brought up. The decision was taken to circulate the draft, as amended during the day's meeting, among the members of the whole N.I.C., in spite of the fact that it had not been accepted by the Soviet delegate.[161] The text, which had begun as an appeal to stop the bombing of open towns, then had been changed to an appeal to stop air bombardments altogether, was now a paper of three paragraphs organized as follows: the first paragraph asked for the "protection of non-combatants, whether men, women or children, from the horrors to which they are now subjected," and asked for "a stop to the summary putting to death of individuals and to mass executions for political reasons." The second paragraph dealt with the treatment of hostages and prisoners of war held by either party" and of "the civilian adherents of the opposite side in the territory under the control of the respective parties." The third paragraph read:

Lastly, the International Committee urge that both sides should abstain from the destruction of all open towns and villages and other objectives of a non-military character, whether by bombardment from the air, or by land or sea, or by fire, mining or by other means.[162]

Even the initial indirect reference to Guernica had been sidetracked.

Two days later the N.I.C. met in plenary session, and again the first item on the day's business was the "Suggested Appeal to the Two Parties in Spain regarding the Conduct of the Present Conflict." Lord Plymouth explained to the members the development of the appeal, giving the history of its different revisions. The Italian delegate expressed the "complete agreement" of his country with the new draft.

But Cahan, again taking Maisky's place, said he could not accept the new version, which he called "a complete departure from the original British suggestion," and then proceeded to inject political reality into the diplomatic debate. He declared that his government "has absolutely no reasons for thinking that the Spanish Government has neglected the principles of humanity in its struggle against the rebels and interventionists" and charged that "the rebels have made it their special object to terrorize and persecute the peaceful population and to destroy cities devoid of any military significance." He became more precise:

> The bombardment of Durango and other Basque cities, and the most outrageous bombardment of Guernica and of the most densely populated quarters of Madrid are but a few illustrations of the "humane" activities of the rebels.

He declared that "the new elements brought into the present draft in lieu of the original British suggestion are an unjustified and unwarranted reflection on the Spanish Government," and stated that the first and second paragraphs of the draft were "unsatisfactory" and "unacceptable." He would agree to the third paragraph concerning "the abandonment of the destruction of open towns and villages" but not to the others.[163]

In the ensuing argument between Lord Plymouth and Mr. Cahan, the Russian defended the original British position, and the Englishman upheld the changes made at the request of Germany and Italy. The German representative felt that he must answer "some allegations . . . made about Guernica and other towns." But in his discourse he never did "answer" these allegations, contenting himself with remarking that he was "quite prepared to give details about the real cruelties in Spain, the burning of towns and churches, the murder of population and so on."[164] The French delegate, Corbin, accepted the new text, with a slight sentimental and rhetorical addition,[165] but he also made a passing reference that doubtless concerned Guernica but did not name it.[166]

Finally, despite Cahan's protestations—he wanted to send the whole matter back to the subcommittee—it was decided to meet again on May 28 "for the purpose of adopting an appeal of the two parties in Spain."[167] A new text of the proposed appeal was prepared for the May 28 meeting, incorporating some minor changes of phraseology made on May 26.[168] However, on May 28, the Soviet delegate had received no instructions from Moscow, and the final decision was put off until June 1.[169] The principal matter before the N.I.C. on May 28 had been attacks by Republican planes on Italian ships, officially engaged in naval observation work for the N.I.C. but resting in the harbor of Palma on May 24.[170] Then, on May 29, two Republican planes dropped bombs on the German battleship *Deutschland* anchored off Ibiza. There were thirty-one dead.[171] The German and Italian governments ordered their representatives to boycott the meetings of the N.I.C. The subcommittee meeting of May 31 was not very long, with Germany and Italy absent.[172] The appeal was again at a standstill.

The Opposition again brought the proposed investigation about Guernica before the Parliament. Labourite Noel-Baker formed a Parliamentary Question for May 26, asking the secretary of state for foreign affairs

> whether he can make a statement as to the progress made by the Non-Intervention Committee concerning the request made by the Spanish Government for a commission of enquiry regarding the responsibilities for the bombardment of Guernica.

Viscount Cranborne replied for the government, patiently explaining that the request came from the Basque government and that it was directed to the British government and not to the N.I.C. His Majesty's government had sought the observations of the chief European powers and was "awaiting replies from the Governments who have been consulted."[173]

These "observations" were slow in coming from Rome, Paris, Moscow, and Berlin; hence on May 28 Sir George Mounsey, of the Foreign Office, telegraphed to the British ambassador in each of the four capitals: "Please endeavour to expedite a reply of Government to which you are accredited."[174] This produced an immediate *note verbale* from Rome on the following day. The Fascist government said no. It again referred to other atrocities of the war in Spain, "murder of hostages, mass shootings, massacre of women, members of religious orders and children, the burning of sanctuaries and churches, etc.," and could not understand why a "specific episode should be suddenly chosen and this alone made the subject of an international enquiry." But, the note read, the Italian government has "gladly associated themselves with the appeal to the two sides which the Non-Intervention Committee has elaborated for that purpose."[175] On May 31, the Soviet government notified His Majesty's embassy in Moscow that it was ready to take part in an international investigation concerning the destruction of Guernica. "But no one else is" was the terse observation of a Foreign Office functionary.[176] This left the score: For the investigation, one (or two, if England went along); against the investigation, two.

What to do? The Opposition continued to hector the government about Guernica. Labourite Emmanuel Shinwell posed a Parliamentary Question on June 2, asking Eden

> whether it has now been established that German airmen were responsible for the bombing of Guernica; whether the matter has received the consideration of the Non-Intervention Committee; and with what results.

For that same day, Captain Ramsay, a Franco sympathizer, demanded to know whether Eden "is now in a position to give the House the correct facts regarding the destruction of Guernica." Eden put off the answers by referring to a "possible enquiry" into the matter.[177] All the facts we now possess show that there was no chance whatsoever for a "possible enquiry" and that Eden surely knew it.

One high Foreign Office official, reading the Italian reply, which reached London only on May 31, observed: "This is what we really expected," and suggested that the matter be allowed to drop.[178] Walter Roberts was of the same mind but felt that "it will be easier for His Majesty's Government to drop the idea publicly if the proposed appeal has been sent off." Roberts felt that the provisional boycott of the N.I.C. meetings by the Germans and Italians was not an insuperable obstacle; they had already agreed to the text of the appeal. The obstruction came from the Soviets. Roberts suggested asking for the German and Italian accord, then calling for a meeting of the N.I.C.

> If the Soviet representative still refused his assent to the appeal, the Committee would be recommended to publish its appeal and say that, as the Soviet Government refused to associate themselves with it, the appeal could not be sent from the Committee.

Lord Cranborne agreed that "it would be far easier for His Majesty's Government to drop the Guernica enquiry if this appeal could be sent off." If the German and Italian governments were still

> ready to play . . . the Committee could be summoned, and if the Russians remained obdurate, they would have to be shown up. This . . . could easily be done by publishing the text of the appeal in the communiqué of the Committee, explaining why it could not be dispatched. It would thus reach the two parties to the dispute, if indirectly, and the faces of the Soviet would be blackened, as they richly deserve to be.

Mounsey agreed that "the Russians ought to be shown up," but such an act would jeopardize the committee's existence. Vansittart agreed with Cranborne.[179]

Eden, however, was not sure that the Russians would have their "faces blackened" and suggested another effort to persuade the Soviets to agree to the appeal in the form it now had. Walter Roberts drew up a letter for Eden to send to the British ambassador in Moscow, requesting him to

> approach M. Litvinov reminding him that I spoke to him about this question recently in Geneva and express hope that his instructions will be sent at once to Soviet representative here to accept revised draft which all other governments represented on Committee have already approved.

This was sent on June 7.[180]

The French government, on June 8, however, upset British plans by informing London that, "while recognizing the difficulties, in the present circumstances, of an international enquiry," it was "ready to back any initiative which the British Government might take in the matter and would cooperate in its execution."[181] Shuckburgh found the tardy French reply "rather tiresome" and opined that the inquiry "would do more harm than good." He observed:

> Not only has considerable time passed since the bombardment of Guernica— during which time no doubt the Insurgents have doctored the evidence

there—but subsequent events have driven the idea of an enquiry out of the minds of most people (except Mr. Arthur Henderson) and it would only cause new wrangling to raise it again.

Walter Roberts put his finger on the essential strategy of the Foreign Office: Eden had agreed

that as far as we are concerned the idea of an enquiry should be abandoned but that this decision should, if possible, not be announced until the "appeal" to the two parties had been sent.

Roberts thought the French could be told that since a unanimous opinion had not been found for the suggested investigation, "we propose to answer that as far as we are concerned the matter is dead and to concentrate public attention on the appeal."[182]

These schemes produced results. When the N.I.C. met again in plenary session on June 18, Maisky agreed to the appeal, with several minor changes. However, he fired off a *baroud d'honneur* before leaving the field. "I feel strongly," he declared,

that whereas the original British proposal concerning the abolition of aerial bombardment made it a comparatively simple matter to detect infringement of this principle, this present appeal is altogether too vague and rambling to ensure easy detection of abuses; and I regret that the clear-cut British proposal should have become submerged in this rather formless appeal.

He denounced "the barbarous tactics adopted by General Franco, and exemplified by such cases as the indiscriminate destruction of open towns from the air, and the machine-gunning of refugees in flight."[183]

This indirect reference to Guernica terminated all discussion of the ruined Basque town before the Non-Intervention Committee. On the following day Bilbao was occupied by the Rebel forces. The final text read:

Resolution regarding the conduct of the present conflict in Spain. Deeply impressed by the sufferings inflicted upon the people of Spain by the tragic events which have marked the present conflict, and actuated by the desire to bring relief to the families and homes of the Spanish people, the International Committee for the Application of the Agreement regarding Non-Intervention in Spain, on behalf of the Governments of:—Albania, Austria, Belgium, United Kingdom, Bulgaria, Czechoslovakia, Denmark, Estonia, Finland, France, Germany, Greece, Hungary, Irish Free State, Italy, Latvia, Lithuania, Luxemburg, Netherlands, Norway, Poland, Portugal, Roumania, Sweden, Turkey, U.S.S.R., Yugoslavia which are parties to the Non-Intervention Agreement, appeal to the two parties in Spain at once to take every step necessary for the protection of non-combatants, whether men, women or children, from the dangers to which they are subject, and to put a stop to the summary or mass executions of individuals for political reasons.

The International Committee urge that hostages and prisoners of war, held by either party, should be treated in accordance with humanitarian principles, that for the future the system of hostages should be abandoned and that all non-Spanish nationals, held as prisoners and who have taken no part in the present conflict, should be released. These principles should be applied equally to the civilian adherents of the opposite side in the territory under the control of the respective parties.

Lastly, the International Committee urge that both sides should abstain from the destruction of all open towns and villages and other objectives of a non-military character, whether by bombardment from the air, or by land or sea, or by fire, mining, or any other means.

The International Committee for Non-Intervention in Spain earnestly hope that the present appeal which they believe corresponds with the ideals and the honourable traditions which have ever animated the Spanish people in the course of its history will evoke a response from the two parties and will help to lessen the cruel sufferings inflicted upon the civil population during the present conflict.[184]

This final text of the appeal was far from a condemnation of the bombing of Guernica. The appeal urged that open towns not be bombed from the air, as Guernica had been, but it also urged that open towns not be destroyed by fire or mining, as Franco's friends were proclaiming far and wide had been done at Guernica.

The appeal was communicated by Eden to the two warring parties in Spain. No reaction from the Republican government has been found, but Salamanca replied with a *note verbale* dated July 20, 1937, given to Chilton in Hendaye. It reaffirmed the virtuous conduct of the Rebel forces.

From the beginning the National Army and Authorities have practiced such humanitarian measures as are referred to or suggested in the above-mentioned appeal, as well as many others, such as the recognition of the rights of prisoners to work with pay, in manifest contrast to the barbarous and savage methods used by the Reds.[185]

As far as the British government was concerned, the proposal to undertake a multinational inquiry into the causes of the destruction of Guernica was also buried in the files. It had never been popular among Foreign Office functionaries. Mounsey's first draft of the note to be sent to the five ambassadors about the "international investigation" had carried the observation that

while the Basque Government express their readiness to facilitate the work of anybody entrusted with such investigations, Guernica and other affected towns are now in the hands of General Franco's troops.

Vansittart wrote on May 11:

Guernica is now in Franco's hands, and the entire mise-en-scène will have been rigged before any commission could get there. We shall then have local evidence contrasted with the stories of refugees. If there are any survivors left behind they will of course be too frightened to give evidence for fear of what might befall them now that they are in Nationalist hands.[186]

This perceptive reflection was unfortunately restricted for thirty years to an inner circle of the Foreign Office. The Portuguese note of May 21 had included, among Salazar's reasons for refusing to participate in the enquiry, the valid argument that "Guernica was situated in a very active war zone at this moment" and that "nothing could be done without the consent of General Franco."[187]

When Delbos said on May 12 that the French had no "means" of carrying out an investigation into the catastrophe of Guernica, he was merely being realistic. The reasoning of Salazar was also beyond dispute. The determining factor was the capture of Guernica by Italian and Spanish troops on April 29. It was evident by the following day when Delbos appeared before the senate commission that no visit to Guernica could be made without Franco's consent. Franco did allow visitors in the following weeks and months, but, as already seen, they were carefully screened by the military authorities. In any event, neither the Germans nor the Spanish Rebels had any intention whatsoever of allowing an international study of what had happened at Guernica.[188]

Any investigation carried out in Bilbao was more or less reduced to duplicating the task already admirably done by the newspapermen covering the war. That was shown by the only effort ever made at that time to inquire into the facts of the destruction of Guernica. It was sponsored by the Labour party, and was realized by a group that included R. McKinnon Wood, an aviation expert who had been head of the aerodynamics department of the Royal Aircraft Establishment at Farnborough for twenty years, until 1934, by an English lawyer named Geoffrey Henry Cecil Bing, and a mine expert H. Pursey.[188a] Their researches made manifest the inherent difficulties of such an investigation. They could not get to Guernica, and from Bilbao they could merely confirm what the newspaper correspondents had been saying. A part of their time was spent in trying to prove what everybody in Bilbao knew from daily experience: that recently arrived German planes with German pilots were bombing the Basque country.

Wood made a report to the press in Bilbao on May 25, in which he said that he had seen the Heinkel 111 and the Heinkel 51 in action over Bilbao.

> A priest from Guernica with whom I spoke was most positive in his identification of the Heinkel 111 as one of the types of planes taking part in the bombing, because it was a new type unlike the German Junkers 52 which had hitherto been the bombing plane used.

Wood thought it likely that the Heinkel 111s were being flown from Germany to Italy, then on to Spain. He was also convinced that such planes had not been seen on the Spanish front before March 20. Wood was trying to show that the Germans were deliberately violating the nonintervention agreement, apparently believing that such proof would cause a reaction in the Western democracies. He had also interviewed the German pilot Wandel.

> I think there can unfortunately be no doubt that the German flyers have orders to wage indiscriminate warfare. Wandel said that his orders were to machine-gun from the air anything moving.

Wood gave his professional opinion about the incendiary bombs being used by the Germans in the Basque country. They were, he said,

> of an old pattern, with which—in my opinion—accurate bombing from a height is impossible. They would not be satisfactory for use against a defended military objective. . . . It would seem that these bombs were intended for indiscriminate bombing.

He concluded with an opinion more concerned with the war in the Basque country in general than with the destruction of Guernica:

> In my opinion the air operations in the Basque country are being conducted by German airmen and Germany has sent both pilots and planes after the imposition of the ban on volunteers and the control.[189]

Lawyer Bing gathered three affidavits from witnesses to the bombing of Guernica. These were made before a notary, countersigned by the local man in the British consulate, A. Ojanguren, on May 28. Ojanguren had himself visited Guernica with the British consul Stevenson on the morning of April 27. But the affidavits were made in Bilbao, not in Guernica, and two of the three witnesses had already given their testimony, for one was Father Eusebio de Arronategui of Guernica, and another was José de Labauria Porturas, mayor of Guernica. Nevertheless, their statements here are more detailed. All identified the aircraft seen over Guernica as being German models, corresponding to photographs in *Jane's All the World's Aircraft*. Father Arronategui was bombed and machine-gunned while hiding under a bridge on the outskirts of the town. When the bombing ceased, he entered the town. "Many houses were already burning in the upper part." By nine-thirty the firemen were there, but there was little or no water available, for the mains were damaged.

José de Labauria said that on the date of the bombing the normal population of 6,000 people in Guernica had been swollen to 8,800 by the arrival of refugees. The market day, with a scheduled championship game of *pelota vasca*, had brought in another estimated 2,000. During a part of the bombing he was in the *abri* constructed in the city hall. When the bombing was over, the town was in ruins and on fire. He saw the bombers at different times and identified them as Heinkel 111s. He saw five or six bodies near the railroad station; their wounds indicated that they had been machine-gunned. At the asylum he found the bodies of some twenty-five elderly women, killed by a bomb. "In a refuge on which a bomb had fallen, I could discern the corpses of women, children and men, around forty in all." Also:

When I left the city hall, houses were burning in different parts of the town and I observed that the fire seemed to come from the upper stories. The fire spread rapidly and the bombs which had not already exploded did so from the heat of the flames.

There were three barracks and a revolver factory in Guernica, all outside the central part of the town, but they were untouched during the raid. He added that twenty-three persons, finding themselves on the river's edge, jumped into the water when aircraft approached, and sixteen of them were killed by machine-gun fire.[190]

The Opposition in England did not seem to consider the Guernica matter closed with the N.I.C. appeal, and as the Foreign Office had foreseen, on June 21 Arthur Henderson did again question the government about the replies received to the proposal for an investigation into the bombing of Guernica. Henderson, however, was not alone, and other questions concerning Guernica were posed by Eleanor Rathbone and by Seymour Cocks. Rathbone demanded to know if any progress had been made with the proposition for an investigation. Eden answered with the chronology of the messages and replies, regretting

that all the governments concerned do not concur in their views as to the value of such an enquiry even if it were extended as His Majesty's Government were willing to do to other incidents of a similar nature.

When Wedgwood Benn asked, "Has the Foreign Office taken note of the studied discourtesy with which the German Government replies to nothing?" another member demanded: "Is it not rather optimistic to expect the German Government to accept an enquiry into the destruction of Guernica by German airplanes?" Eden shortened his reply to: "I must point out that some other governments have taken a long time to reply."[191]

Seymour Cocks inquired concerning the replies the secretary of state for foreign affairs "has received to the request he made to British consular and diplomatic representatives for information regarding the bombing of Guernica." Eden had a month previously promised to inform the Parliament of progress concerning such information. D. Howard of the Foreign Office observed, in preparing Eden's reply, "This is rather awkward to answer." He noted the dispatches from Chilton and Stevenson: "Sir Henry had asked that his information not be rendered public, but Mr. Stevenson's is fairly definite proof of German participation in the raid."[192] Eden stated in the Commons:

I have received certain information on this subject and, as the House is aware, His Majesty's Government proposed an inquiry into the matter on an international basis. I am not in possession of any considered reports.

Cocks pressed him, asking to know the information received "from the consular authorities and the ambassador." Eden did not alter his position: "I said that I was not in possession of any considered reports, and I explained that such information as I have will be placed at the disposal of the inquiry." When Cocks persisted, "Cannot the right hon. Gentleman place it at the disposal of the House?" the minister affirmed: "I have no considered reports to place at the disposal of the House." To this, Lieutenant-Commander Fletcher retorted pointedly, "There is not the slightest prospect of this inquiry being held."[193]

Seymour Cocks returned to the charge again with two Parliamentary Questions for July 12, demanding to know

> whether any reply has yet been received from the German Government to the suggestion made by His Majesty's Government on 18th May that there should be an international inquiry into the destruction of Guernica;

and whether or not the idea of an inquiry had been abandoned; and, if so, whether or not Eden would "give the House the information on the subject received from British consular and diplomatic authorities which he had intended to place at the disposal of the inquiry?" Eden's reply was short:

> ... it has not proved possible to pursue the question of an international inquiry. No British official was present at Guernica at the time of its destruction. His Majesty's Ambassador at Hendaye has, therefore, received no first-hand evidence from any official under his jurisdiction on which he could base a considered report on the circumstances in which the destruction of Guernica took place.[194]

The most charitable comment that can be made is that Eden evaded a direct answer to the Parliamentary Questions concerning Guernica. When he replied to Henderson, Rathbone, and Cocks on June 21, he did have "considered reports" showing that Guernica had been destroyed by German bombs and German airplanes and German pilots. He knew on June 21 that no inquiry was foreseen, and by July 12 he could no longer make any pretense that an international investigation was possible. In his own mind he was evidently certain of what had happened. Not only did he have the dispatches of Chilton and Stevenson already signaled, but also the testimony of a secretary of the German embassy in Salamanca, who was in Saint-Jean-de-Luz on May 9 and "volunteered" to a member of the British embassy's staff "that he had visited Guernica and had seen plenty of bomb holes there." The report to London went on:

> In response to a decoy expression of "personal" opinion he "personally" agreed that it had been bombed by Whites as well as burned by Reds and said that this was the impression of most people at Salamanca.[195]

Eden had received further confirmation of the German bombing on May 13, in another message from Chilton, informing London that

> Herr von Goss, press attaché at the German Embassy in Spain, volunteered recently to Count Horace de Pourtalès of the International Red Cross, that "of course we" [i.e., the Germans] "bombed Guernica to smithereens."

This action was, according to the version given by von Goss, " 'A military necessity' and probably cost no more than a hundred lives, eighty of which he said were lost in one shelter which was unluckily set on fire by a bomb." Chilton concluded with this thought:

> In the face of such frankness on the part of a German whose word may surely be taken as final, it is harder than ever to understand what good the military authorities at Salamanca expected to do with their verbose and evasive denials.

This document placed Sir Henry definitely among those in the Foreign Office convinced that Guernica had been destroyed in a bombing attack carried out by the Germans. Shuckburgh, in an added note, wrote: "This is indeed a confession; Guernica has taught us what to expect from the Germans, and it has also shown how inefficient is the propaganda department of the Franco Government." This document was signed, with no contrary remarks, by the News Department, the Central Desk, Lord Plymouth, Sir George Mounsey, D. Howard, E. E. C. (?).[196] Many were the persons in the British Foreign Office who had reason to think the Germans had bombed Guernica.

Not all the news arriving at the Foreign Office told the same story, as we have seen from the visit of Cecil Gerahty. Gabrielle Herbert, an enthusiastic Catholic partisan of the Rebel cause, who had been with the hospital installation in Vitoria sponsored by the Catholic archbishop of Westminster,[197] called at Whitehall on June 3. She had come armed with a letter from General Franco, whose cause she pleaded, and was received by Lord Cranborne, undersecretary for foreign affairs. Herbert had visited Guernica shortly after its capture by the Nationalists, and she had also talked with eyewitnesses of the beginning of the fires. She had been

> appalled by the destruction [of Guernica], quite different from Irún or any of the other towns which had been bombarded during the war. There was literally not one stone upon another. The main street looked like a road with the materials for repair piled on either side—great heaps of rubble and nothing more.

Lord Cranborne asked her whether, "in her view, the town had been destroyed by bombing or by burning." She replied that "she had no doubt it had been burned. She had looked for evidence of bombs and could only distinguish 9 or 10 bomb holes in all." The troubling feature of the exchange of views between the ardent partisan of the Franco cause and the titled diplomat is that neither seems to have read or understood the basic text of the course: the newspaper dispatches sent from Bilbao. Nothing in their conversation reveals the slightest idea that incendiary bombs were used in the air raid.

Herbert had talked, however, with two young men "who had been in the front line of the insurgent army at the time of the destruction of the town." These two men were "quite illiterate" and, Herbert reasoned, "could not have got their facts from any newspaper or propaganda pamphlets." Their testimony was:

The town had been bombed, but not severely, and little real destruction had been done. It was not until the next day that the town was destroyed. It went up before their very eyes, as they described it, in a sheet of flame.

These eyewitnesses "were convinced that it had been either burned or blown up with dynamite."[198]

This declaration was dutifully taken down and commented on by Foreign Office officials, but the comments rarely constituted a criticism of the "facts" presented. Why did Herbert say that the destruction at Guernica was "quite different from Irún or any of the other towns which had been bombarded during the war"? What did this fact mean to her? Most other defenders of the Nationalist cause found a striking similarity between the ruins of Guernica and those of Irún, a similarity arising, they said, from the fact that both towns had been deliberately burned.

It was also significant that Herbert found many more bomb holes than had any correspondent who sent his report out through the censorship. More incredible still was the testimony of the two "quite illiterate" young soldiers. First, it could be noted that "quite illiterate" young soldiers can be propagandized, and we know from Carney's dispatch of April 28, already quoted, that loudspeakers were used to inform the soldiers of the Nationalist version of how Guernica was destroyed. We also know, from reading the testimony of other persons who visited Guernica and talked with inhabitants, that the peasants of the region usually knew what to tell inquisitive foreigners so as not to get into trouble. More to the point, it was physically impossible for two Nationalists soldiers, even "in the front line of the insurgent army," to know what was going on in Guernica on April 26, or to have seen on the following day or the day following that one the town go "up before their very eyes . . . in a sheet of flame." They were, from all the evidence from Nationalist sources, simply too far away. Finally, what is shown by Herbert's story is the extremely vague and incomplete conception she herself held of what had happened at Guernica and the total lack of any judgment on her part concerning what constituted believable evidence to uphold the faction she supported so passionately.

Perhaps Herbert realized that the Foreign Office might prefer the testimony of someone other than two "quite illiterate" young soldiers, and she produced a newspaper man, "*The Times* correspondent with General Franco's forces." "He had told her," the Foreign Office report said,

> . . . that his paper might not like it very much but if he were asked quite definitely what his view was, he would be obliged to say that the town had been destroyed by burning and not by bombing.

With whom had Gabrielle Herbert spoken? With James Holburn or H. A. R. Philby? She gave no name. Philby took over from Holburn on May 24. If it were Philby, such a statement would have been worthless, for part of his cover for his espionage activities on behalf of the Soviet Union was to express pro-Nationalist sentiments. Holburn comments: "I have no recollection whatever of the conversation [with

Miss Herbert] although as Miss Herbert discussed it with Lord Cranborne, it must surely have taken place." He added: "I was more likely to have said that the town was destroyed by burning caused by bombing, the Nationalists having admitted the bombing."[199]

In either case, Holburn or Philby, the correspondent was probably careful of what he said to Herbert, for they both doubtless knew, as Lord Cranborne noted in his writing, that "It must be remembered that Miss Herbert is a strong supporter of General Franco." Lord Cranborne told her after she had recounted her version of the Guernica incident that the Foreign Office "had very different accounts from other sources, but she could not be shaken."[200]

But although Foreign Office records today show that at least an inner circle of high functionaries were convinced by what they thought irrefutable evidence that Guernica had been bombed and destroyed by German aviators in German airplanes, on behalf of the Spanish Nationalists, they also show that this inner circle were reluctant to reveal this knowledge, even to others in the Foreign Service. As we have seen, Eden showed Stevenson's dispatch from Bilbao to the Portuguese ambassador. When Ambassador Henderson queried London about Guernica, suggesting a disavowal of the *Times,* he was told, nine days later:

> Reports received from H. M. Consul at Bilbao tend to confirm the gist of the "Times" report on bombing of Guernica. We are, therefore, by no means in a position to issue any denial of its truth. Pending receipt of further information no action on the lines suggested by you is possible.[201]

But D. G. Osborne, of the British Legation to the Holy See, was not allowed this frank a statement, perhaps because he displayed too open a partisanship for the Nationalists. He wrote to Whitehall on May 11 that he was disposed to share an opinion expressed to him by an English Jesuit friend, "that although Guernica was in the first instance bombed by Nationalist aeroplanes, the work of destruction was probably completed by incendiaries on the other side."[202] On June 4, Osborne wrote again, this time to Philip Nichols, of the Foreign Office, to ask him what was the official sentiment about what had happened at Guernica. He repeated his own "conviction" that "there was some bombing and that the work of destruction was then completed by the extremist element of the retreating army—for purposes of useful propaganda." He continued:

> If so, they were very successful, for most of the English Press, the B.B.C., the Deans and the whole liberal-intellectual element, all of which swallows anything that comes out of Valencia and disregards anything that comes from Salamanca, accepted the story of total destruction by bombing.

Osborne had seen his Belgian colleague that day and had heard two "interesting points." The Belgian

> said that no bombing planes could work so accurately as to destroy houses on both sides of the streets without doing serious damage to the surface of the

streets themselves, as was the case in Guernica; nor would they have been able to spare the two most revered Basque shrines, one a building—I think, the old parliament building or town hall or something of the sort and the other an ancient and respected tree (I suppose this is possible, but I may have misunderstood or misheard him).203

The Belgian diplomat was evidently employing the arguments of Douglas Jerrold, which had been published in Belgium in June. In London, Shuckburgh thought Osborne's letter "a little difficult to answer," and finally Walter Roberts signed a reply, which left the British envoy to the Vatican about where he was when he wrote his letter. The Foreign Office had

> received a great deal of conflicting evidence from both sides on this subject and it is impossible *in the absence of evidence from British official eyewitnesses* to give a definite opinion whether bombing from the air or incendiarism from within the city were mainly responsible for its destruction. It seems fairly evident from what we have heard that there was a very heavy bombardment of the town from the air with considerable damage to buildings and loss of life, and there is no doubt, judging by the reports of reliable people who were on the spot shortly after the event, that the bombardment had thrown the whole population of the town into a state of great terror. This terror could not have been simulated. On the other hand the possibility of incendiarism and destruction of buildings on a large scale by "Red" elements cannot be ruled out.204 (Italics added.)

Guernica slowly disappeared from the news columns, and if the tragedy was mentioned now and again in articles and books, it did not arouse English public indignation to the point of bothering the government. The initiative taken by the English government, first to appeal to both parties to stop the bombing of open towns, and then to investigate the responsibilities for the disaster, were never more than maneuvers to calm public opinion by make-believe that something was going to be done. This artful proceeding worked, in that it gained time for the government.

There is one other English diplomatic document to add to the dossier. In February 1938, the chargé d'affaires of Great Britain in Hendaye, G. H. Thompson, visited Bilbao and stopped at Guernica en route. He duly reported to Sir Robert Hodgson, the British agent in Salamanca, concerning his impressions. He wrote that Eibar, Durango, and Guernica "are now sad monuments to the ruthless efficiency of the German and Italian air forces on the Nationalist side." Guernica, he observed,

> ...hardly has a whole building left, and it is clear from the pitted and pockmarked condition of the walls still standing that it was heavily dosed with high explosive [bombs] and that incendiary bombs completed the destruction.

This was a revealing observation, for journalists who had entered Guernica immediately after its capture, nine months earlier—notably Botto and Massot—had been unable to see the "pitted and pockmarked condition of the walls still standing." Thompson also incidentially volunteered a curious piece of news:

> I know, as a matter of fact, that H.M.G. have full details of what occurred [in Guernica] from German sources; and if I seem to labor the point it is because I feel myself that the proofs so frequently furnished by this war of the extent to which the Germans and Italians believe in "frightfulness" afford perhaps the most menacing lesson the English people can learn from it.[205]

Further research has not unearthed the "full details of what occurred from German sources," although this statement may refer to the two dispatches sent to London by Chilton, concerning the testimony of a German secretary of embassy, and a German press attaché, already mentioned. Thompson's gloomy views of Nationalist Spain [206] had little apparent effect on the recipient of the message, for Hodgson remained a fervent supporter of the Franco cause.[207]

Thompson later confirmed his impressions in a book published in 1959, in which he recalled his visit to

> the ruins of Guernica which ... presented a melancholy tribute to the Luftwaffe, whose first experiment it had been with tactics to become only too familiar to the inhabitants of Britain less than three years later. ... Although at the time George Steer wrote the story movingly for *The Times,* there were all too many in Britain, especially on the right amid the Tory back benches, who chose to believe the Nationalist's allegations that the town had been destroyed not by German bombs, but by the retreating "Reds."[208]

In all this hypocritical world of Western diplomacy, there was but one ambassador who openly proclaimed his sympathies with the Spanish Republic. This was Claude Bowers, Roosevelt's ambassador to Spain. His profession was journalism and writing, not diplomacy. It was an open secret in New York in 1940 that Bowers was writing up his memoirs of the civil war and that they could not be published for as long as he remained in the American foreign service. There were even rumors that he was kept on as ambassador in Chile, not because of State Department fondness for him but to keep his book off the market. *My Mission to Spain* did not appear until 1954. Bowers reports that he was in Saint-Jean-de-Luz when he heard of Guernica. "I was horrified, most of all by the heartless complacency with which the bestial crime was accepted by many," he wrote, doubtless referring to other members of the diplomatic corps. Father Eusebio de Arronategui, the Basque priest who spoke on the Bilbao radio about Guernica, later told Bowers the details of the raid. Bowers naturally received the confidences of his newspaper friends. David Darrah, of the *Chicago Daily Tribune,* told Bowers of his inspection of the ruins, with an Insurgent officer. Darrah pretended not to understand Spanish, and when an old man told them that "the planes came in enormous numbers and kept on dropping bombs until everything was ruined," the officer translated as follows: "He says that just before the Army of Liberation entered the town, the anarchists set fire to everything." Virginia Cowles also told her Guernica experience to Bowers.[209]

Two other personages of political and diplomatic importance, both Spaniards, gave pronouncements on the destruction of Guernica. Their statements can be introduced here, for, though far from being diplomatic secrets, both weighed, or sought to weigh, on the higher spheres of English and American public opinion. Francisco Franco himself, on numerous occasions—three in July 1937—charged the "Reds" with responsibility for the catastrophe. He told a special correspondent of the United Press: "The Reds destroyed Guernica premeditatedly and for purposes of propaganda."[210] On July 14 a reporter for the *Liverpool Daily Post* observed to Franco: "There has been a great deal of discussion abroad concerning what took place at Guernica," and Franco was asked, "Can you give an official and exact version of what happened there?" Franco replied: "The Reds burned it as they burned Oviedo in 1934 and 1936, and as they burned Irún, Durango, Amorebieta, Munguía and many other towns during this campaign."[211] A few days later, in talking about Guernica, he manifested a sense of humor, albeit a rather macabre example of it. He handed some photographs to the marqués de Luca de Tena, owner of ABC, saying they were of Guernica in ruins. "Horrible, yes," he remarked.

> At times, the needs of warfare or of repression can lead to such horrors. This consideration is one of the reasons which have moved me to use these photographs which were sent to me some days ago. But, look closely: they are not of Guernica.

Everyone probably laughed. The Spanish journalist was vague as to what the photographs really were.[212] The following year Franco alluded to Guernica in his allocution to the Spanish people on July 18, 1938, the second anniversary of the outbreak of the civil war in the Peninsula. He challenged the patriotism of his adversaries and likened the "Crusade" he claimed to be leading to a "war of independence." He declaimed: "The incendiaries of Eibar, the destroyers of Guernica, the anarchists of Cangas de Onís and those of many other small towns of our Cantabrian lands, cannot invoke the name of the Fatherland."[213] Even after the end of the war, Franco continued to blame the "Reds" for the damage done to the town. He told his audience in Cádiz on October 14, 1948, that Guernica had been

> burned and destroyed by the Reds themselves, who, in their destructive fury, sought to blame the National squadrons. From this act of arson there rises the new Guernica, the most beautiful town in Spain.[214]

The other Spanish personage who gave his viewpoint on the destruction of Guernica was the prince of Asturias, Don Juan de Borbón. In a "foreword" to the English translation of the Carlist political work *The New State*, by Víctor Pradera,[215] he raised the question of atrocities in the Spanish Civil War. "May I," he wrote, "in this connection, deal with the traditional British view that, so far as atrocities are converned, it is 'six of one and half a dozen of the other.' " And he affirmed:

> Surely there is a universe of difference between accidentally killing civilians while attacking military objectives, and deliberately murdering men, women and children in cold blood.

It is not clear to which incidents he was referring with the words "accidentally killing civilians while attacking military objectives." Did he not mean the destruction of Guernica? Perhaps. He then stated: "The Badajoz and Guernica myths have been analyzed and refuted in Mr. Robert Sencourt's admirable book, *Spain's Ordeal*. I need deal no further with those points."[216]

Part Two

•

THE CONTROVERSY
FROM
1939 TO 1975

During World War II little attention was paid to Guernica by either historians or statesmen, except in Spain itself. It was in December 1939 that the height of Francoist cynicism concerning Guernica appeared, when the Spanish ambassador to the Vatican, Yanguas Messías, in the course of a year's end ceremony, presented to Pope Pius XII a crucifix in carved wood from one of the destroyed churches of Guernica. The Pope accepted the gift.[1] Equally cynical were the "adoption" of the town by Franco and its high priority in reconstruction accorded by the Nationalist government.[2]

Historians, inside and outside Spain, treated the subject of Guernica in many different ways from 1940 to 1975. I will attempt to follow the course of this development chronologically, interweaving the versions printed outside Spain with those printed inside, for despite the vigilant censorship in Spain, what was published outside Spain did eventually affect that published inside. In 1940 the Nationalist supporters were still proclaiming the theses on Guernica of "Sencourt," Thorning, Lunn, and Jerrold to be Holy Writ, but such was the stubborn nature of facts and logic that thirty years later, although Franco was still alive and the regime had not changed, these theses were being held up to public ridicule by a functionary of the Spanish state.

Three books published in 1940 in Spain treat the subject of Guernica in what was still a typical pro-Nationalist manner. Hitler and Mussolini were still in power, and the Axis seemed to be winning the new world war. Manuel Aznar, a journalist close to Franco, writing a semiofficial military history of the Spanish Civil War, reported that late on April 28, "the vanguards reach the first houses of Guernica, which is in flames, having been set on fire by Asturian dynamiters."[3] Luis María de Lojendio, member of a well-known Basque family, in another military history of the war, mentioned "the remains of Guernica, destroyed by the fire and dynamite of the Marxists demoralized in their flight."[4] Lojendio, however, was in an excellent position to know what had taken place at Guernica, for he prepared military communiqués for the foreign press during the war. He is now the Mitered Abbot of Franco's giant mausoleum, the Valley of the Fallen, near Madrid. Two other Spanish rightists, Alfonso Gutiérrez de la Higuera y Velázquez, a lieutenant colonel in the cavalry, and Luis Molins Correa, in another military study of the war, wrote that on April 29, Guernica

> was vigorously defended by eight Nationalist Basque battalions, two Asturian and three from Santander. The Red-separatists, forced to abandon the town with heavy losses, try to reduce it to ashes, as was done at Eibar, succeeding in great part.[5]

All four writers attempted to link the destruction of the town with the withdrawal of the Basque army.

A more cautious treatment of Guernica can be found in the eight-volume *Historia de la cruzada española,* a semiofficial work edited by Joaquin Arrarás, Franco's wartime biographer. In the pages dealing with the 1937 campaign in the Basque country, published in 1943, neither the bombing nor the burning of the town is mentioned in the text. However, the book does contain views of the ruins of Guernica, entitled simply, "An imposing view of the destroyed town," or "Ruins of Guernica."[6] It is difficult to believe that these Spanish Nationalist writers, either from their military positions or from their journalistic occupations, did not know what had really happened at Guernica.

During the years of World War II the theme of Guernica was dealt with in quite dissimilar ways in Nazi Germany and in Fascist Italy. The Germans rarely mentioned Guernica. Only one reference to the town has been found in any of the many books written and published by veterans of the Condor Legion and distributed widely throughout Germany during the war years.[7] However, the Luftwaffe did begin an account of the war in the Basque country and in an unpublished rough draft one can now read as follows:

> On April 26 an air attack was ordered on a bridge and crossroads to the East of Guernica; it was carried out by nine airplanes flying at 2300 meters in a single flight. Nine bombs of 250 kilograms and one hundred and fourteen of 50 kilograms, 7950 kilograms in all, were dropped. Observation found that no hits were made on the bridge. Visibility was quite insufficient, for the town was enveloped in fire and smoke. This bombing was seized upon by all the hostile world press, especially to attribute the blame for the destruction of

Guernica to German formations. It was utilized excessively to influence public opinion. But following their orders, all the flyers had spared the town. It was rather the system of the Red, through arson and explosion, to change the town into a pile of ruins. This also explains why the units engaged were strongly hindered in their visibility by the already burning town.[8]

In a revised version, the above paragraph was edited out, and a new reference to Guernica inserted:

Concerning the alleged destructive bombing of Guernica by National aircraft, especially by German formations, the frightfulness and horror of which the world press convincingly described with words of the greatest loathing, this subject will be treated in a special annex. It turns out that, following orders all the aviators spared the town, which according to plans was transformed by the Reds through arson and explosives into a heap of ruins.[9]

Manfred Merkes, who has done a great deal of work on the German documents, opined:

Both versions of the work are unfinished, since they go only up to the occupation of Guernica by the National troops. The "special annex" was possibly never written.[10]

The Italians were less disciplined or less sensitive about Guernica. Two writers, Ambrogio Bollati and Giulio del Bono, in 1937, stated that the twelve battalions in the town—eight Basques, two Asturian miners, and two Santander militia—preferred to retreat rather than to fight,

. . . but first they set fire to, and destroyed systematically, the city, which the Nationalists occupied without fighting. The antifascist French and British press tried in vain to attribute the destruction of the town to the Nationalists—and precisely to German airplanes; loyal foreign journalists, who received from General Franco the authorization to visit the town, testified that the destruction was due exclusively to the savage fury of the Reds.[11]

This verdict was repeated in 1939 by General Faldella, in his technical military book on the Civil War. Guernica was defended by twelve battalions, "who opposed no resistance, but destroyed and set fire to the town."[12]

A curious paragraph mentioning Guernica appeared in 1939 in the work by "General Belforte." He said that Italian bomber squadrons from Soria, accompanied by fighters from Logroño, had attacked, among eleven objectives in the Basque country, "the Guernica bridge." No date is given, but the following paragraph begins with a reference to the occupation of Elorrio on April 23. No reference is made to the destruction of Guernica.[13] Guido Mattioli, in the first edition of *L'aviazione legionaria in Spagna,* made no mention of Guernica.[14] But in a revised, amplified edition of that work in 1940, he copied almost word for word Belforte's paragraph, including the reference to "the Guernica bridge."[15] We can conclude, then, that the single source for the story is Belforte. Later, in 1942, another Italian, Tullio Rispoli, who had fought in Spain, asserted in a book on the Italian legionaries that Guernica was destroyed "by an air attack and by Red mines."[16]

Immediately after the end of World War II, with the Nazi bombings of Rotterdam and Coventry fresh in the public mind, the Basque government in exile in Paris sought to bring accusations against the Germans for the destruction of Guernica before the War Crimes Tribunal in Nuremburg. But the court refused to consider events that took place before World War II.[17] It has, however, been frequently reported that evidence concerning German guilt for the destruction of Guernica was presented to the War Crimes Tribunal. These reports are probably based on information that appeared in the Paris press in September 1945, saying that two Americans—Joseph Maier, identified as "Chief of the Briefing Analysis Section," and Sander, identified as "Chief of the Analysis Interrogation Section"—interviewed Göring in his prison cell concerning the bombing of Guernica. The former air marshal was said to have replied, after searching his memory, that the Basque town had been used as a "testing ground." He added: "A lamentable event. But we could not do otherwise. At that time, such experiments could not be carried out elsewhere."[18] Some such interview may well have taken place. Maier and Sander did exist, but their present whereabouts are unknown.[19]

One of the first post-World War II books dealing in any way with Guernica was from the pen of a Hollander favorable to Franco, Dr. E. Brongersma.[20] He presented the two versions of the destruction, crediting the *Times* with first giving a full account blaming the Condor Legion, and then with balancing that account by another from its correspondent on the battlefront to the effect that "the retreating Left Army had blown up the roads with land mines." Brongersma's conclusion is based, rather peculiarly, on arguments advanced by the Portuguese government against the British proposal for an international investigation.[21]

On July 3, 1940, Gonzalo de Cárdenas Rodríguez gave a talk in Madrid on the reconstruction of Guernica. He was the architect charged with the rebuilding of the zones devastated by the civil war. He said little about how Guernica was destroyed, noting only that among the "towns adopted by El Caudillo" there was Guernica "in whose name the enemies of God and Spain had raised the banner of rebellion."[22] He did, however, give some statistics on the destruction suffered by the town: of the 401 houses totally destroyed in the province of Biscay, not counting those in the capital city of Bilbao, 271 houses—that is, 65 percent—were in Guernica.[23]

In an official 1947 publication, perhaps published in conjunction with the exposition at which Gonzalo de Cárdenas Rodríguez spoke, we find another description of the disaster, which struck

the poor town whose destruction began the preparation of a vast cycle of calumny against the National Uprising—lies which deceived no one, but which in their day served to add spice to a poisoned propaganda.

The town, the writer said, had been "set on fire by this paroxysm of an army in flight and made mad by its cowardice."[24]

Charles Foltz, Jr., an AP war correspondent with the Franco forces, published his testimony on Guernica in 1948. He explained that although he had not seen the bombing, he "walked through the still smoldering ruins shortly thereafter." The army press officer who accompanied him told him that "the Basques had wantonly burned their 'holy city' as they retreated." Foltz went back to Vitoria, and that night after his dinner in a cafe, he listened "to young German airmen boasting of how they had levelled the town on Sperrle's orders."[25]

Another military witness, especially well placed to testify, for he had headed the first Nationalist troops entering Guernica, was General Martínez Esparza, who wrote of the destruction of the town in a Spanish technical military journal in 1949. "There was an arms factory there which produced trench-mortars and pistols as well as other weapons," he stated.

> Our planes bombed this factory, and they also bombed the railway station to prevent the arms being exported. But in Guernica I saw two completely different kinds of ruins. On one side, the bombed arms factory, the railway station and their surroundings; on the other, ruins of a more recent character, the result of arson and dynamite.[26]

This exposition, although being perhaps the first published in Spain to admit *a* bombing of Guernica, is in large part false. The arms factory was never bombed, and nothing done during the air attack prevented the trains from running. And why bomb an arms factory on April 26, when it might possibly fall intact into your hands on April 29? Martínez Esparza had a keen eye indeed if, on entering Guernica on April 29, he saw "the bombed arms factory" that was not bombed, and could distinguish between the results of the bombing of April 26 and the "ruins of a more recent character, the result of arson and dynamite."

The unconditional stand on Guernica adopted by historians inside Spain was difficult to maintain elsewhere, but a strenuous effort was made to that end by the American Catholic ultraconservative writer, Richard Pattee. He devoted four pages of his 1951 book, *This Is Spain,* to Guernica. Pattee's inspiration came chiefly from Sencourt.

> Just as Badajoz had loosed a wave of propaganda, so the bombing of Guernica takes its place as one of the celebrated episodes around which much fanciful legendry has accumulated.

Steer was "a free-lance correspondent who frequently sent in material to the London *Times,*" and his story "was played up for its propaganda value." After repeating Sencourt's unlearned remarks about "President Euzkadi" and the three priests in Guernica named Arronategui, he stated:

> The fact is that there were no competent foreign witnesses, and the stories as they have been woven are the result in every case of accounts and versions given after the event.

Pattee's curious logic—which confuses prediction of the event and the event itself—can be summed up in this fashion:

> The people in Guernica cannot be believed for they are Spaniards; nor can any other [foreign] witnesses be believed, for they were not there at the moment of the bombing.

It is also of interest to note that the Catholic Pattee cited neither the name nor the testimony of Father Onaindia.

Pattee did, however, admit that the first Nationalist version of Guernica was in error and that "Later it was admitted that Guernica had been bombed. That there were probably excesses in the attack admits of very little doubt."[27] He then quoted Holburn's dispatch in the *Times* of May 5, presenting it erroneously as a "consensus" arrived at after the "Guernica question was examined with considerable care."

Pattee also cited the French press of May 3, reciting the Havas-Botto report erroneously as the testimony of "a group of foreign correspondents." He also cited the opinions of Arnold Wilson, Page Croft, Yeats-Brown, and Wing-Commander James, whose "report"—he apparently thought they had all four issued a document in common—"showed that the number of bombs actually dropped was extremely small, perhaps a dozen and all were light weight." (On the preceding page he had said, "there were probably excesses in the attack." With a dozen "light weight" bombs?) After calling on Cardozo as an expert witness, the American Catholic historian concluded:

> It may be stated on the basis of all the evidence we have that there was an air raid; that German planes may very likely have done this bombing, but that the destruction of the city and its civilian population by air raids does not stand up to close scrutiny. The evidence points to destruction on the ground by the retiring Republicans.[28]

Juan Antonio Ansaldo, an important personage in Nationalist aviation circles, an early collaborator with the Spanish Phalanx, a monarchist who had turned against the regime after serving Franco as air attaché in Paris, Vichy, and London, in 1951 wrote of his impressions on visiting Guernica, shortly after it fell into Nationalist hands. He spent a day there, eating his noon meal with the artillery chiefs of the section and with Jorge Vigón. He wrote:

> I must honestly recognize that I did not feel extraordinarily impressed by the destruction and fires that I observed, in a quick visit through the ruins. . . . These seemed to me very similar to others contemplated before and in

particular to those of the frontier city of Irún, which according to Nationalist propaganda were caused by Asturian dynamiters in their well-known tactic of "the scorched earth."

This opinion was counterbalanced by the repetition of the newspaper article on the interview of Maier and Sander with Göring at Nuremberg. It cannot be ignored that Ansaldo's middle-of-the-road version of Guernica was published in Buenos Aires by the official publishers of the Basque government in exile.[29]

In 1953 there appeared the first post-World War II testimony concerning Guernica from an officer of the Condor Legion. This witness, Adolf Galland, who finished the war as a Nazi air force major general, was not in Spain at the time of Guernica. He landed in El Ferrol on May 8, 1937, two weeks after the event, and therefore knew only what he had been told by others. The Condor Legion was sent to destroy a bridge over which the Republicans were transporting troops. Visibility was bad, the crew inexperienced, the bombsights primitive. The bridge was unharmed, but the town nearby was badly hit. The operation was considered "a failure," the more so in that the orders of the German pilots were

> to destroy the enemy at any cost, but to spare as much as possible the civil population. The contrary had been achieved with the attack on the highway bridge near Guernica. For this reason at the time of my arrival in Spain spirits in the Legion were very low. No one spoke willingly of Guernica.

After denouncing the propaganda campaign of the Spanish Republicans on the subject of Guernica, Galland declared:

> And in fact Guernica, which was neither an open city nor a military objective, but an unfortunate mistake, such as later in the Second World War was countless times repeated by both sides, was to become the very essence of German wickedness and barbarity.

The man who was one of Nazi Germany's aces during World War II then invoked a series of later air bombings, the successors of Guernica, as possible explanations, if not justifications, of the bombing of the Basque town. "Even today", he wrote,

> after Rotterdam and Warsaw, after Hamburg, Kassel, Rothenburg and Berlin, even after the horrors of Dresden, Guernica still looms spiritually in the background of the hatred of Germany by its enemies.[30]

This theme, that after all Guernica was followed by still more horrible bombings, was to be picked up by other commentators.

Galland's account can be immediately recognized as a rewriting of the paragraph concerning Guernica in the document prepared by the German air force right after the end of the Spanish Civil War, "Die Kämpfe im Norden." Perhaps Galland was able to refer to a copy of the document while he was preparing his book. Or perhaps he had collaborated on the writing of the original. There was one signficant difference between the two texts. Galland did not suggest arson or dynamite as the cause of the destruction. In any event, this account of the bombing is hardly convincing in its details. The significance lies in the fact that the German pilot admitted the bombing, admitted that the town was badly hit and that the civil population had suffered. But we now know, from evidence from both sides of the controversy, that the town was not bombed accidentally as Galland pretended, but was struck by repeated waves of planes for three and a half hours, that the fleeing people were pursued by the airplanes in which gunners tried to kill those in flight on the ground. Nor do we find in any of the accounts of survivors or witnesses any evidence whatsoever to sustain the statement that there was poor visibility that day. In the official report on Guernica there are declarations of twenty-two witnesses, but not one indicates any sign of mist or fog.[31]

Two years later Galland's book was published in Spain, with the references to Guernica but slightly changed. Where Galland had written, "Guernica was neither an open city, nor a military objective, but an unfortunate mistake," the Spanish censor wrote: "In reality, Guernica was not an open city, nor was it destroyed."[32] Censors make poor editors. The Spanish version also eliminated the detailed references to what Galland called "the propaganda capital" found in the bombing by the "Reds." But the essential remained: Guernica had been bombed and badly damaged by the Germans, and the civilian population had suffered, and all this, though but a German confession, was printed in Spain.

Indalecio Prieto, a man of Bilbao, though not of Basque stock, in 1955 profited from the appearance of Galland's book to speak of the problem of Guernica. At this time the friends of Franco were waging a campaign in Mexico to persuade the government to recognize the Franco regime. As part of this campaign, the Mexican Catholic historian José Vasconcelos accused the Spanish left of destroying Guernica. "The truth," he wrote,

> is that a Nationalist bomb fell accidentally on the town, causing some damage, but also causing the departure of the Republican garrison and it was the Leftists who profited from this absence to set fire to the town and caused the destruction.

To challenge Vasconcelos, Prieto quoted from the interrogation of Göring by Maier and Sander, "high functionaries of the British investigation services," and from Father Onaindia. Prieto brushed off the evident inaccuracies of Galland's details and accepted what was positive and beyond discussion in Galland: the Germans had destroyed Guernica. Prieto also alleged that the Germans had for some time been seeking a target whereby they could "test the effects of a massive bombing." The Germans first wanted to try out an attack on a barrio of Madrid, but Franco said no, there were too many diplomatic establishments there, and the Fifth Column too numerous. "Why, then," asked Prieto, "did Franco choose Guernica for martyrdom? Because of what Guernica meant historically and politically."[33]

Sir Robert Hodgson, England's first envoy to Franco Spain, named commercial agent in November 1937,[34] wrote his Spanish memoirs and views on Spain in 1953 and, ignoring the report of his junior colleague in Hendaye, Geoffrey Thompson, left open the question of what had happened at Guernica. "Whether or not Guernica . . . was in fact destroyed by German planes and its inhabitants machine-gunned from them, remains a mystery." But after quoting a few sentences from Steer's dispatch, he found himself forced to admit that whether it was true or not, "it had every appearance of veracity" and was "a most powerful weapon in the hands of critics of the Nationalist regime and its German backing and was effectively used by them." Hodgson thought that "the belief that Germans were responsible for the barbarity did great harm to 'The Cause' both in Spain and in 'right' circles abroad."[35]

Sir Robert's book was translated into Spanish and published in Barcelona in 1954. The translation was generally more favorable to the Nationalist theses than was the original, but it curiously added a phrase not found in Hodgson's text to the effect that the version attributing the destruction of the town and the bombing of its inhabitants to German airplanes was "more or less established." A paragraph from Steer's dispatch, quoted by Hodgson, was also permitted publication.[36]

In 1955 Noel Monks wrote the memoirs of his journalism career, and in the pages on the Spanish Civil War, confirmed completely his dispatches on the bombing. He had passed through Guernica early on the afternoon of April 26 and was about eighteen miles east of the town when his driver

> pointed wildly ahead. . . . Over the tops of some hills appeared a flock of planes. A dozen or so bombers were flying high. . . . The bombers flew on towards Guernica.

Monks's car was strafed by Heinkel 52 fighters, while "over to the left, in the direction of Guernica, we could hear the crump of bombs." That evening in Bilbao, a government official came into the dining room, shouting out the news of the burning of Guernica. Monks was driven to Guernica.

> One middle-aged man spoke English. He told me: "At four, before the market closed, many airplanes came. They dropped bombs. Some came low and shot bullets into the streets."

Monks wrote that all the people he and Steer and Holme talked with told of the bombing. He, himself a Catholic, concluded with: "Rome put the official seal on Franco's denial, and to this day only 'bad' Catholics believe that the Germans destroyed Guernica."[37]

From 1956 to 1958, four more books with references to Guernica, by military authors, appeared in Spain. One, a biography of El Caudillo, was written by Franco's cousin Lt. Gen. Franco Salgado, in collaboration with the journalist Luis de Calinsoga. These writers charged that Guernica had been destroyed "by the

Reds, who before abandoning the town used this stratagem in order to attribute the damage to National bombings."[38]

A Catholic sympathizer with Franco, the British journalist S. F. A. Coles commented on Guernica in a biography of Franco, published in England and the United States in 1956. Coles wrote that he had inquired about Guernica of "the most knowledgeable person I knew in Spain, of whom none could say that he was a Right-wing partisan for he reported the Civil War from the other side," and was told:

> Guernica was a legitimate military target. It was a cross-roads. . . . There was a big munitions dump there, and I believe, a munition factory. These were the military objectives, and so far as I know only the houses in the immediate vicinity were affected by the actual raids. Who destroyed the rest of the town was anybody's guess.

Coles thought it significant that the Tree of Guernica was untouched in the catastrophe. After giving the most underhanded blow of all to Steer, by observing that he "lost his life on service in the Far East during the World War through a car accident after a celebration," he concluded his study of the Guernica problem with this sentence:

> Moreover it has been clearly proved that an American correspondent named Reynolds, who sent sensational reports about the "wanton destruction" of Guernica from the air, was, in fact, nowhere near the place at the time.[39]

The "American correspondent named Reynolds" was a product of Coles's mixed-up method of writing history. He doubtless meant Reynolds Packard, and it was Badajoz, and not Guernica, where he "was, in fact, nowhere near the place at the time."[40] But if Coles disqualified the imaginary Reynolds because he was not near Guernica when it was destroyed, why did he not go back to what Steer, Monks, Holme, Onaindia, and others who were at "the place" or "near the place" when it happened? Instead, he asked questions of men who had neither been there nor made any special study of the question. Coles is representative of a certain type of newspaperman, who unhesitatingly accepts anything he receives through the ear and never verifies anything by research. It is small wonder then that he affirms as "clearly proved" a fact false from beginning to end.

A year later, in 1957, Spanish General Díaz de Villegas, stated: "As in Irún, the Reds burned Guernica before leaving it, in order to blame the destruction on the Nationals. Guernica . . . is the great lie of Red propaganda."[41] That same year, General Jorge Vigón, Ansaldo's luncheon companion in 1937, declared in an ambiguous sentence that the Rebel troops found the town of Guernica "in a state of destruction, the responsibility for which must be laid to the criminal folly of those who pretended to be its defenders."[42] Still another Spanish military figure, Colonel José Gomá, relating the air history of the civil war, declared in 1958: "The Marxists, in their retreat, had blown up Guernica."[43]

Another person who had fought with the Nationalists, in the Foreign Legion, the Englishman Peter Kemp, published his memoirs in 1957. He gave a highly confused version of what had taken place at Guernica, relying a great deal on his friend Cardozo. "Certainly Guernica was bombed by the Nationalists," he wrote, "but it was not an open town at the time it was bombed." Kemp, following Cardozo, did not believe that Guernica was set on fire by incendiary bombs from Franco's planes, but that "the Republicans themselves had set fire to the town before leaving."[44] His views on Guernica and Republican propaganda will be studied later. Kemp's book was translated into Spanish and published in Barcelona in 1959.[45] Sir Geoffrey Thompson's book, with its important remarks on Guernica, which also appeared in 1959, has been commented on earlier.

The French historian Claude Martin, in his life of Franco published in 1959, refused to give an opinion about Guernica, and contented himself with observing that the town had been "destroyed by Italio-German flyers according to anti-Franco propaganda and burned by the Asturian '*dinamiteros*' on retreat, according to Nationalist sources."[46] When this book was published in Spain in 1965, a bizarre footnote was added. This consisted in a quotation concerning Guernica from Galland's book, translated from the original German, and therefore more complete than the Spanish version published ten years earlier. This new translation was not only more complete; it added details that the original German had only hinted at, and stated that the raid on Guernica caused "numerous victims." This phrase does not appear in the original German. Thus, the Spanish censor had passed not only a mention of the air raid but also a mention of "numerous victims."[47]

Publication in England in 1961 of Hugh Thomas's detailed work on Spanish Civil War gave added impetus to further studies. His account of Guernica is not without errors of detail, but his conclusion is interesting:

> The Germans deliberately bombed the town in an attempt to destroy it, observe in a clinical way the effects of such a devastating attack, and thus carry out the instructions of Mola of March 31.[48]

Thomas noted in a footnote: "The Basque [government] account is confirmed by conversations the present author carried out in Guernica in the summer of 1959."[49] Thomas's book was never published in Spain, but a Spanish-language edition was printed in Paris.[50]

A significant change in the manner of dealing with Guernica could be found in a 1961 edition of Manuel Aznar's *Historia militar de la guerra de España*. This journalist turned diplomat altered his 1940 attribution of the destruction of the town to "Asturian dynamiters" into an ambiguous but revealing statement:

> By the evening of April 28, the advance troops have reached the first houses of Guernica, which is burning, having been set on fire by aerial bombardment and by the action of dynamiting militiamen.[51]

The airplanes that carried out the "aerial bombardment" were not, it is true, identified by Aznar, but the average Spanish reader probably had no difficulty in identifying them.

Two Spanish generals also made interesting contributions in 1961 to the history of Guernica—General Rafael García-Valiño, who played an active role in the conquest of the Basque country, and General Alfredo Kindelán, head of the Rebel air force. Both participated in a discussion on the civil war at the University of Saragossa, later published in book form. García-Valiño spoke on "The Campaign in the North,"[52] and Kindelán, on "The Air Force in Our War."[53] Neither of the generals mentioned Guernica, which was perhaps an eloquent way of speaking of the destruction of the town.

It was in this same year, 1961, that the German scholar Manfred Merkes delved for the first time into the German archives of the Spanish Civil War period. He limited his remarks on Guernica to a footnote reference. "The Spanish Nationals do not deny that a few bombs were dropped, but declare that arson by the Reds was the principal cause of the destruction of the town." He quoted from Beumelberg, noted that Galland admitted a bomb attack on Guernica, and that the published German documents shed little light on the Guernica problem. His strangest observation was that Sencourt gave "an interesting analysis on the reports on Guernica."[54]

In 1962 four books were published with accounts of Guernica, each one by a writer of a different nationality. The German Hellmuth Günther Dahms, who throughout his book sought to play down German responsibilities in the Spanish Civil War, willingly conceded that "devastating bomb attacks of the Condor Legion (Sperrle) hit Guernica, Durango and Amorebieta, where the civil population suffered heavily."[55] In a footnote he accepted Thomas's figure of 1,654 for the dead, but added the charge that "dinamiteros" had destroyed a large part of the town.[56]

The American journalist Robert Payne presented his version of the Spanish Civil War in the form of a chronological anthology. For Guernica, he used extracts from Onaindía's statements and from the unpublished memoirs of Aristarco Yoldi, a sergeant in the Basque army, who entered Guernica at two o'clock on the morning of April 27.

> We came up in lorries, but when we came to Guernica we knew we would have to abandon them. We could not take the lorries through the flames. We jumped out and made our way as well as we could, dodging the flames. . . . The whole town was burning. . . . Men and women were still digging out the bodies. . . . Except for the roaring of the flames, there was no sound.[57]

Another of the 1962 books that commented on Guernica was *Spanish Fury,* by James Cleugh, an Englishman. Cleugh seems too confused in his own mind about Guernica to convey to his readers a clear picture of what had happened there. He admitted, "Today it is clear that Guernica was heavily bombed." On the one hand, "The Nationalists undoubtedly meant . . . to break civilian as well as purely military morale by a ruthless exhibition of force." On the other hand, "The Government leaders . . . equally undoubtedly, exaggerated the scale and deliberate brutality of the attack as well as unduly minimizing its necessity as an act of war." How could the government leaders have "exaggerated the scale and deliberate brutality" of what Cleugh himself calls "a ruthless exhibition of force" intended "to break civilian as well as purely military morale"? Cleugh does not mention the incendiary bombs, which were the technical explanation of what had happened; nor does he speak of the victims. Like many other pro-Franco writers, Cleugh is more impressed by the immorality of the Republican exploitation of the Nationalist atrocity than by the immorality of the atrocity itself.

It is curious that Cleugh, for all his sympathy for the Spanish Rebels, does not mention the Germans in connection with Guernica. He says that the Republican government blamed the fire on an "overwhelming and indiscriminate air attack by Mola's pilots." He also altered Virginia Cowles's story of the statement of the "tall staff officer" in Santander who angrily affirmed the bombing of Guernica, attributing that statement to a "young Spanish pilot" who had participated in the raid.[58] In 1963 Cleugh's work was translated into Spanish and published in Barcelona. The paragraphs on Guernica were kept intact, errors and all. This is probably the first book published in Franco Spain which says that Spanish Nationalist pilots took part in the bombing of Guernica.[59]

Also in 1962, the Barcelona professor and historian, Carlos Seco Serrano, in his illustrated history of the war, mentioned "the burning and destruction of the town," but he did not say who burned or who destroyed it. Picasso's painting *Guernica* was reproduced in this book, as was a photograph of the ruined town.[60] In a second edition in 1968, the text concerning Guernica was repeated, the photograph of the ruins was exchanged for another one, but Picasso's painting disappeared.[61]

In 1963, with the publication of a history of the Spanish Civil War by Georges-Roux, a new formula for dealing with the problem of Guernica made its appearance among the Nationalist sympathizers. This French writer of the extreme right did not hesitate to tell his readers of the bombing, of the incendiary bombs, of the fifteen hundred dead and more than eight hundred wounded. However, he found a way out for Franco and the Nationalists.

In this incomprehensible horror, the Spaniards [Nationalists] bear no responsibility. They make no effort to hide their reprobation. The manoeuver was carried out by a German squadron operating with no order from the High Command. The Hitlerians had simply had the idea of "carrying out an experiment to see the effects on civilian morale of the destruction of a defenseless town."[62]

There is not a word about Basque arsonists or Asturian dynamiters. The Spanish translation, published in Madrid in 1963, is faithful to the original, even to the point of placing the bombing on a Sunday instead of on a Monday.[63]

Hugh Thomas in 1965 revised his book, changing but one detail in his account of Guernica. Whereas he had originally given in his text, the total of the dead in the bombing as 1,654 and 889 wounded, he now changed the reference to a footnote, in which the dead were reduced to around a hundred.[64] Unfortunately, Thomas gives no authority for either figure.

Also in 1965, the author of what is perhaps the best general account of the Spanish Civil War, Gabriel Jackson, blamed the Germans for the destruction of Guernica, in what he called "one of history's most famous calculated experiments in terror." Jackson gave considerable weight to the statements of Onaindia, but he was wrong in saying that "the essential points of those statements were confirmed by the testimony of several German officers during the Nuremberg trials in 1946."[65]

During these years of the seventh decade of the century, a new generation was coming of age in Spain, and many of the younger writers and historians, even those favorable to a continuation of *Franquismo*, feeling few emotional ties with the propaganda of the civil war years, recognized the need for finding more valid explanations than those of their elders for such disputed topics as the destruction of Guernica. The Spanish government was also becoming aware of the necessity for cleaning up some of the dirtier chapters of the Nationalist version of the civil war. It has been written that a Spanish minister brought up this question at a cabinet meeting early in 1965, and it was decided that in order to combat certain hostile interpretations of the war and the origins of the regime, a "Section of Studies on the War of Spain" be established in the Ministry of Information and Tourism, then headed by Manuel Fraga Iribarne. The direction of this work was, in May 1965, entrusted to Ricardo de la Cierva, grandson of the monarchist minister Juan de la Cierva, known as the "Cacique de Murcia."[66] La Cierva brought to the task a great deal of energy and ambition, and a recognition not only that the old myths emotionally defended by the wartime generation of Nationalists were no longer valid but also that their maintenance often made the friends of the regime appear ridiculous and mendacious.

Eventually this Neo-Franquista school, in interpreting the events of the Spanish Civil War, was forced to confront the subject of Guernica. The leaders of this school of thought realized that the destruction of Guernica and the Nationalist accusations against the Basques for that destruction constituted a barrier to any understanding between Madrid and Bilbao, and that the strong sentiments aroused in the Basque country by the attack on Guernica were not dying down with the passage of time, but were possibly growing stronger. They further realized that the official maintenance of an unpopular position known to be based on falsehood was politically weakening to any regime. But they also knew that it was far from easy to manipulate an about-face on a subject as emotionally charged as that of Guernica, especially after thirty years of lying about it. It was therefore going to be necessary to do a great deal of backing and filling before deciding on the propaganda line.

The year 1966, looked at from the vantage point of 1975, may well seem the year when the Spanish censorship concerning the subject of Guernica broke down completely. Three books published in Spain at that time dealt with the story of Guernica, each one in a different manner. The book whose passage through censorship is the most difficult to understand is that of Carlos Rojas, a Spaniard teaching in a North American university. The ninth chapter of his *Diálogos para otra España* concerned *Guernica,* Picasso's painting, and the destruction of the town. The incident is presented to the Spanish reader as described by Steer, Holme, and other journalists. Thomas (first edition) is cited for the number of victims, and Cleugh as the indecisive defender of the Nationalist position. Two pages are given over to this exposition of the facts, twenty more to an aesthetic discussion of the painting.[67] The indulgence of the censorship may well have been due to the fact that Rojas's book was concerned with the philosophical problems of the two Spains, and not with the history of the Spanish Civil War. The tenth and last chapter of the book dealt with, in several instances, a possible dialogue between Castile and Catalonia. But, on the contrary, such problems as the two Spains or a possible dialogue between the Basque Country and Madrid are not at all evoked in the printed text of the penultimate chapter, that on Guernica. This chapter on Guernica, at least to this reader, seems alien to the rest of the book. Is it because the censorship eliminated the references to Guernica as a symbol that must be destroyed or conquered before the dialogue can be renewed between Bilbao and Madrid?

Another 1966 book that underlines the disarray (inefficiency?) of the censorship is the Spanish translation of Dahms's work. Whereas the German original of Dahms stated: "Devastating bomb attacks of the Condor Legion (Sperrle) hit Guernica, Durango and Amorebieta, where the civil population suffered heavily," the text in Spanish read:

> The devastating bombardments carried out by the National combat group (González Gallarza) and the Condor Legion (Sperrle) affected Guernica, Durango and Amorebieta, where the civilian population suffered heavily.

Here for the second time (the first being Cleugh's translated work), the reader in Franco Spain could learn that Guernica was bombed by *Nationalist* planes. In a footnote, the German author repeated Thomas's figures for the 1,654 dead. Dahms also attributed to Willi Münzenberg an active role in the propaganda battle around Guernica; this assertion, if offered with any proof whatsoever, would be of interest. Dahms also gave an unusual artistic judgment, writing that Picasso's painting, "The Death of Guernica" [sic], achieved "great fame" because of its title. This footnote was also, in all probability, the origin of a theme concerning Guernica which would be developed in the next few years by the Neo-Franquista school: the damage done to Durango was "relatively greater" than that done to Guernica, but Guernica was the subject of more propaganda. "This circumstance is another proof that in the news and commentaries about Guernica, propaganda weighed more heavily than strict objectivity."[68]

Dahms, then, having admitted the bombing and the heavy loss in lives, proceeded to argue that the bombing could hardly have done much damage. "A town like Guernica could not have been razed with the aerial means then available." Only three squadrons were in flying condition, and they could not have been used "massively." The planes could not have dropped bombs of more than 250 kilograms.

> A careful evaluation of the aerial photographs shows that in Guernica the exterior walls of the houses generally remained standing; therefore, the damage could not be attributed to the explosive effects of the bombs and must be charged to the fires.

These were the old arguments of Jerrold and his friends. A report, said to have been made by one Wronsky, now in the East Berlin files, which stated that 120 German planes attacked Guernica, was called "absurd" for the Condor Legion had at its disposition only forty-seven Junkers 52s and nine Heinkel 111s.[69] The objective sought by Dahms in this footnote is not clear. In his text he had written that Guernica was bombed by both the Spanish Nationalists and the German Condor Legion, killing many people. He then by a series of bizarre arguments sought to show that the damage done to Guernica could not have been wrought by the air force available to the Germans. (He could have added the Spanish air force, which he himself implicated in the raid, but in all truth, there is no evidence that it participated in the raid. Why then did the Spanish censorship pass the incriminating sentence?) But Dahms suggested no other responsibility for the razing of Guernica, not even the traditionally guilty Asturian *dinamiteros*. Many times in the long history of the Guernica controversy, arguments were advanced to prove that the damage done to Guernica simply could not have been done in an air raid, and this in spite of the wealth of incontrovertible evidence that it was precisely in an air raid that the town was destroyed. Dahms's arguments are of course basically faulty because he chooses to ignore the undeniable fact of the incendiary bombs. The explanation for such a blind attitude in 1966 lies perhaps in the maladroit corrections of the censor.

A third opinion on Guernica appeared in Spain in 1966, written by the novelist Tomás Salvador:

> Since the destruction of Guernica has been the cause of intensive propaganda, we shall say that the National airforce did carry out an intensive bombing of the town, and that the destruction was later finished by the dynamite of the Gudaris.[70]

What did Salvador mean by "the National airforce"? Did he limit the responsibility to the Spanish airmen, or did he include the Germans? A similar account was published in France in 1966 by a strongly pro-Nationalist sympathizer, Robert Cassagnau, who as a young journalist had spent the early weeks of the civil war in the Basque country. He wrote that the town was bombed by the Condor Legion on

April 26, but that later when it was about to fall into the hands of the Rebels, the "anarchocommunists" blew up and set fire to what remained.[71]

There was growing social agitation in the Basque country throughout 1966, and many young priests were implicated in "subversive actions." In June, the young Basque priest Victor Manuel Arbeloa published an article in *Signo,* an organ of the Catholic Action Youth Movement, in which he asserted: "I am not a partisan of those who, during the Civil War, killed bishops, priests, and readers of *Signo.* I do not back any murderer—neither those who bombed Guernica, murdered in Badajoz, or shot people on the roadsides of Navarre." [72] Arbeloa was arrested and charged with "calumny of the National Movement, incarnated by the F. E. T. y de las J. O. N. S."[73] When he appeared before the court in Madrid on March 13, 1967, he explained that he had been challenged to state openly whether or not he was on the side of those who had killed thousands of priests and bishops during the civil war and that he had simply replied that he was against all killers.[74] The prosecuting attorney asked that Arbeloa be condemned to four years and two months imprisonment. The defense attorney pleaded that there could not be calumny, for the facts listed by Father Arbeloa were true. "The accused wrote with the intention of discrediting the National Movement," cried the prosecutor. "How could I scorn that for which my father died?" replied the priest, recalling that his father, a volunteer in Franco's ranks, had died on the very day Guernica was bombed. Arbeloa's defender ended his plea by saying: "You can condemn the accused, but the verdict you will pronounce cannot rectify history."[75] There was considerable surprise when Arbeloa was freed on the following day. [76] This judicial decision— whether influenced by the government or freely arrived at by the court—marked an important step forward in the clarification within Spain itself of the facts concerning Guernica.

The court decision about Arbeloa prompted the French *hispaniste* Elena de la Souchère to arrive at a too optimistic conclusion in *Le Figaro Littéraire:* "The truth about the martyrdom of the Basque city Guernica is no longer illegal in Madrid."[77] This article was chiefly composed of quotations from the by now standard gallery of witnesses: Steer, Onaindia, Cowles, Galland, and Ansaldo, but a new and important witness also came forward. This was Angel Ojanguren y Celaya, the Basque employee of the British consulate in Bilbao, who accompanied Consul Ralph Stevenson on his visit to the smoking ruins on the morning of April 27. Ojanguren wrote:

> We walked through the town in all directions and questioned everyone we saw wandering through the rubble and ashes. All the witnesses gave the same reply: "Guernica was bombarded with high explosive and incendiary bombs for longer than three straight hours."

Ojanguren said that several British officers from the ships anchored in the estuary of the Mundaca, notably A. H. Still, captain of the cargo vessel *Hamsterley,* also visited the burning town. If any of them later made a statement, no record of it has been found.[78]

Another factor that weighed in the judgments of the "revisionist" school was the inability of the Franco government to prevent the people of Guernica from talking about what had taken place in their town. During the thirty years since the bombing, they were talking not only among themselves but to other people in Spain, and with the development of tourism, they talked with tourists and they also talked with writers and correspondents. It is probable that discontent with the regime and social agitation helped loosen tongues. We have seen that Hugh Thomas in his 1961 book wrote that the people in Guernica with whom he talked confirmed the bombing.

The American journalist William P. Lineberry visited the town in 1967 and found people willing not only to talk but to be quoted. "For many years it was a jailable offense in Spain to allege that anyone other than 'Red separationists' was responsible for the town's destruction," he wrote.

> Now this fiction is finally being put to rest. There is still plenty of controversy over what actually happened, but local authorities (obviously committed to "the regime," as Franco's government calls itself) are currently willing to concede that the Germans—and the Germans alone—were responsible.

The then mayor of the town and his predecessor both endorsed this point of view. Francisco Bilbao, vice-secretary of the provincial government of Vizcaya, was willing to admit that Franco did not really control the activities of the Condor Legion. He thought that the Germans in bombing Guernica were experimenting, "testing out new techniques of aerial warfare in preparation for the major conflict they knew was coming."[79] It is highly improbably that these three functionaries allowed their names to be used by the journalist without having previously cleared their statements with a higher authority.

At almost the same time, an Italian journalist Nello Ajello visited the town and listened to accounts of the air attack told by survivors. It is significant that Ajello does not name his witnesses, identifying them with only initials and trades. The planes are identified as being German, but no opinion is given as to any Spanish Nationalist participation or responsibility.[80] An instructive contrast can be established between these two sets of interviews. The functionaries were more willing to be identified as witnesses by name than were the humble people of the town. Was it, then, by 1967, more or less "official" policy in Spain to say that Guernica was bombed, on condition that the full responsiblity for the deed was thrown on the Germans?

In 1967 three books were published—one by an Australian, Brian Crozier; the other by George Hills, an Englishman born in Mexico; the third by Luis Bolín, the chief press officer in Salamanca in 1937—each of which in its peculiar way contributed to the development of the story of the destruction of Guernica. Bolín, as we have already seen, was responsible for the first crude communiqué sent from Franco's headquarters after the bombing, and it is therefore not surprising that, at the end of his career thirty years later, he should defend the discredited theses of his wartime years. Nor is it surprising that his long study should be a mass of contradictions.

Bolín's thinking about Guernica was blocked around the spring of 1937. He declared in 1967 that

> the story of the wholesale destruction of Guernica by Nationalist bombs during the Spanish Civil War is a myth. . . . Most of Guernica was deliberately dynamited or set on fire by the Reds. The report that the town and its inhabitants had been destroyed by German bombs was invented for propaganda purposes. It is one of the myths which our enemies conjured up to deceive public opinion in other countries during the Spanish Civil War.

He saw propaganda everywhere, and his ill-prepared explanation of what had happened at Guernica was doubtless embarrassing to the men of the Neo-Franquista school.

> But the Republicans in Bilbao needed a sensational story to offset their reverses. They dispatched Asturian miners to dynamite Guernica and set fire to its buildings and swore that they had been blown to smithereens by German bombs. Partly bombed previously for sound reasons—around Guernica there were military objectives of the first order—evidence of havoc was not wanting. Foreign correspondents, rushed to the spot from Bilbao shortly before our troops occupied the place and at a loss to distinguish the damage caused around the town by bombs from that wrought inside it by dynamite and arson, concluded that the whole of Guernica had been destroyed from the air and hastened to denounce the outrage.[81]

The reader will immediately recognize that Bolín was forced to use two misstatements of fact—that Guernica was bombed before April 26, and that only a short time elapsed between the visit of the correspondents (on April 26) and the capture of the town by the Nationalists (on April 29)—in order to build his fundamental misstatement of fact that Guernica was destroyed not by the bombing but by dynamiting and arson. Since the structure of his thesis depended on dates, he simply eliminated them from his relation.

Bolín made no reference to his own role in the original development of the Guernica story, but he depended greatly on the work of his friend Jerrold, "a writer gifted with the technique of sifting evidence," and he quoted at length Jerrold's "scholarly analysis" as reproduced by Arnold Lunn. He also cited several paragraphs on Guernica from Peter Kemp's book, "one of the best books written on the Spanish Civil War."[82]

Bolín presented documentary evidence. He cited, with extraordinary negligence, *Guernica: The Official Report,* but he did not identify the document with any name. In summing up the *Report,* he gave as part of the conclusions: "(3) planes bombed Guernica intermittently causing less than one hundred casualties."[83] (He had stumped his toe on his own evidence. The *Report* did say that there were less than one hundred casualties, but it did not attribute these casualties to the action of the planes. The *Report* certified also that the arms factory was undamaged,[84] but Bolín, trying to prove that Guernica was a military objective, brought forward as a witness General Martínez Esparza and his 1949 statement that "our planes" bombed the arms factory.[85]

Bolín's one new and original contribution to the story consisted of several Spanish army dispatches. What did they say? One, dated April 28, the day before the capture of the town, read:

> Our men were eager to enter the town. They already knew that the enemy had evacuated Guernica after criminally destroying it and was blaming our planes for its destruction, but Guernica itself is free of bomb-craters.

Another, also of April 28, read:

> Basque fugitives who had reached our lines were terrified by the tragedies enacted in towns such as Guernica, deliberately burnt and destroyed by the Reds while we were not more than ten miles away. There is much indignation among our troops against the Basque-Soviet leaders who blame Nationalist aviators for these barbarous acts. Our planes during the last few days were unable to fly owing to persistent fog and drizzle.

A third report, dated April 29, related: "The town of Guernica is destroyed and deserted. All that remains of it at the time of writing is on fire." In commenting on these dispatches, Bolín, the former chief press officer, assured his readers: "None of the dispatches quoted above was written for the public; their contents merely reflected what was seen and heard on the ground."[86]

But what was "seen and heard on the ground"? The Franco sympathizer and correspondent with the Nationalists for the *New York Times,* William P. Carney, cabled his newspaper on April 29:

> "Aguirre lies," says a note read today from the Salamanca radio station and heard plainly by loudspeakers set up here as well as all over the Basque region. "Guernica was destroyed by the gasoline and hand bombs of criminal incendiaries serving Aguirre. Nationalist aviation [Insurgent] did not fly at all Monday afternoon and all day Tuesday because of bad weather on the entire Basque front. Prisoners we took yesterday and the day before will testify that they saw Guernica set afire upon being evacuated."[87]

It seems highly probable that the field commanders were merely sending back to general headquarters the propaganda they were themselves receiving from general headquarters. In the second of the reports cited, that of the Army of the North, the author says that fugitives from Guernica were in his hands, he also says that "our planes" were unable to fly because of bad weather. But certainly the fugitives, if they told about the destruction of Guernica, gave the date of that disaster (April 26), and certainly the author of the report had sufficient memory to know that forty-eight hours earlier (April 26) the weather was not bad enough to prevent flying. If the author of the first report cited, that of the VI Army Corps, *knew* that there were no bomb craters in Guernica, it could only have been because he had learned of the photographs taken that very afternoon and handed into general headquarters at three-thirty.[88] Why should he include in his reports to general headquarters information that came to him from general headquarters? One can also doubt the value of such photographs, for the report of the army corps commander said that "A thick mist from the mountains blotted out visibility and prevented us from reaching Guernica."[89] These army reports were not so secret and confidential as Bolín pretends. The air of artifice hangs about all of them, and one, the second quoted, that of the Army of the North, was published in the Nationalist press on April 29.[90]

Bolín also quoted from the published German documents concerning Guernica. He cited the telegram from Berlin of May 4, 1937, which in turn cited that of von Ribbentrop, demanding "an immediate and energetic denial" from Franco.[91] The reply from Salamanca to Berlin commenced: "The denial agreed upon with Franco regarding Guernica has not been issued."[92] But Bolín in his text deliberately and unscrupulously eliminated this sentence and told his readers: "The denial had already been published"[93] This is an unpardonable falsification of documents. In fact, a further denial (of sorts) was sent from Salamanca on May 7, as we shall see below. But if Bolín knew of this message, he preferred to keep silent about it.

Since there was in these German documents no confession of the bombing of Guernica, Bolín drew the conclusion that the bombing did not take place.

> They were secret and were not meant for publication; there is no apparent reason why these official documents should have disguised the truth or altered it in any way.[94]

Bolín does not even consider the obvious fact that all the German documents were not printed, and that a number referring almost certainly to Guernica have never been recovered. This analysis of Bolín's documents shows how fragile they are as evidence, but they did impress some persons. Professor Stanley G. Payne, an American, in a review of Bolín's book, observed that the former chief press officer went

> to great effort to demolish what he terms "The Guernica myth," producing original documents to bolster the contention that most of the destruction in Guernica was deliberately carried out by the defenders to facilitate anti-Nationalist propaganda.

Payne conceded that "the evidence presented fails to obliterate the more commonly accepted version," but insisted that "it does introduce an element of doubt concerning the Republican account."[95]

Bolín, still trying to justify the false communiques of thirty years earlier, reprinted in 1967 the assault on Steer's integrity made by the *Tablet* in 1942 in reviewing Steer's book *Sealed and Delivered* and, in his turn, concluded: "In boasting of lies which he circulated in the world war, Mr. Steer is self-convicted as the author of mendacious propaganda." [96] Bolín did not see the quicksand on which he was treading. Steer was a war correspondent in 1937; during World War II, he became an officer charged with propaganda in Ethiopía against the Italians. In the course of his official duties, he later wrote, he spread certain falsehoods. On the other hand, Bolín was also a journalist, in England, in 1936; during the Spanish Civil War, he became an officer charged with the press relations of Franco's headquarters. In the course of his official duties, he spread certain falsehoods, notably about Guernica. Steer quickly admitted the falsity of his propaganda work. But Bolín has never admitted the falsity of what he said about Guernica in 1937, and thirty years later was still defending the undefendable. So undefendable was this position in 1967 that had Bolín looked   around him, he would have seen that in Spain itself he was quite along on the ramparts.

But outside Spain, as we have seen, Stanley Payne was impressed with Bolín's documentation. Another believer was found in the British journalist Brian Crozier, who published a biography of Franco late in 1967. Though it was late in the day for such a maneuver, Crozier attempted to exonerate the Germans completely. "So deeprooted is the belief that the destruction was the work of German bombers of the autonomous Condor division," he wrote,

> that it is not easy even to admit the possibility that this might not be the archetypal example, which I, for one, had always assumed it to be—being encouraged in this belief by the considerable success of Picasso's painting *Guernica.* [97]

This sentence probably contains the key to Crozier's mental processes. There is nothing in Picasso's painting to suggest the guilt of the Condor Legion, or of any other air force; there are no airplanes, no bombs, no pilots, no Condor Legion insignia. It was, moreover, not the painting itself but merely the "success".of the painting which encouraged the young Crozier to "assume" German guilt. It is small wonder, then, that he adopted another "assumption" about Guernica, the innocence of the Germans, on evidence equally bizarre.

Crozier was impressed by the "powerful evidence" collected by Bolín, which suggested "that the major part of the destruction was caused by retreating Republicans, who dynamited most of the buildings." Since Bolín's evidence was principally "Nationalist field reports that were not intended for publication," Crozier thought that "due weight must be given to it." He continued: "Whatever the proportionate degree of responsibility, it is clear that neither Franco nor Mola was consulted or informed about any German decision to bomb the town." [98] Crozier considered that it was "by no means certain that the Germans bombed Guernica at all," and found German innocence "the likeliest inference to be drawn from an exchange of telegrams found in the captured German archives."[99] He admitted that "Nationalist planes did, however, bomb the railway station and an arms factory— both legitimate military targets," and concluded, "Ironically, the balance of proba- bility seems to me to indicate that the Nazis—who have had so much to answer for—were wrongly blamed for the destruction of Guernica."[100]

When a critic wrote that Crozier "blunderingly denies that the Germans bombed Guernica,"[101] he answered:

Actually, I postulated the likelihood that they did not. Since publication, important new evidence in support of this tentative conclusion has come into my hands, and I hope to publish it soon. "Blunderingly" may then seem an odd as well as an offensive word.[102]

Crozier kept playing with the Guernica story, and when the *Times,* on June 26, 1969, recalled the destruction of the town, alleging two thousand dead, Crozier wrote a letter to the editor, denouncing the "hoary myth." The accusation against Franco and the Nazis was, he wrote,

incompatible with the evidence of the German Foreign Ministry archives and with other evidence now available, some of which I analyzed in my book on Franco. There was, in fact, a minor Nationalist raid, in which the targets were a railway station and an arms factory. Some German bombs may also have fallen on the town. But the massive destruction was caused by systematic dynamiting of one quarter—and one quarter only—by the retreating Repub- licans. Ironically, Picasso's masterpiece probably celebrated a non-event.[103]

Late in 1969, Crozier's book was published in France, and the same critic who had denounced his version of the destruction of Guernica when the book was published in England, brought the matter up again, and challenged Crozier to produce his "important new evidence."[104] Crozier, in reply, produced his proofs. His evidence came from an interview with Sir Archibald James, now a air vice- marshal, who as a Conservative Member of Parliament had visited Guernica in October 1937, as he had informed his parliamentary colleagues at the time and, shortly thereafter, the readers of the *Daily Telegraph.* Crozier had recorded on magnetic tape Sir Archibald's words, in part as follows:

I spent several hours in a close examination of the situation. What I verified is that three-fourths of the town had been systematically burned to the ground, in so far as it is possible to burn these solid Spanish buildings. The fires were absolutely uniform. One of the rare inhabitants who had remained told me that airplanes had flown over the town and dropped bombs. I, therefore, sought bomb craters. My examination of the three-fourths of the destroyed town revealed no damage attributable to bombs. On the other hand, I walked around in the town two or three times and I discovered about half-a-dozen bomb craters about a hundred meters from the perimeter, all caused by bombs which, in the First World War, would have been twenty-pounders. The meaning of the ruins was this: the northwest quadrangle, where the city hall, the sacred oak and the cathedral [*sic*] were located, was absolutely intact. Not a sign of damage of any kind. In the three other quadrangles . . . the destruction was complete and caused by fire.

Crozier summed up Sir Archibald's thoughts:

The damage seen could not, for evident reasons, be attributed to an air attack. For anyone who remembers the technological level of the air-planes of 1936-1939, it is in fact inconceivable that an aerial bombing, with either explosive or incendiary bombs, could have left a quarter of the town intact.

And Crozier added: "This testimony seems to be absolutely conclusive in itself."

Crozier insisted that in fact James's testimony but confirmed the evidence of the German archives. To pretend that the fact that certain documents might be missing from the German archives hindered their interpretation was, he said, but "soph-istry." Since the German diplomatic messages were secret, if von Ribbentrop thought the Nazis guilty, would he not have revealed his thoughts in the telegrams? To strengthen his position, Crozier revealed that he "has been able to examine the original texts which Luis Bolín had cited in his Memoirs," the Nationalist military field reports.

On reading these dispatches, as well as the German documents, I posed the hypothesis of the non-responsibility of the Nazis in the destruction of Guernica. The testimony of Sir Archibald James, posterior to the publication of my book, confirms this hypothesis.

Crozier reaffirmed his

primitive detestation of the Hitlerian regime and of the atrocities for which it was responsible. But one must admit that, among these atrocities, it seems out of place to include Guernica.[105]

From Crozier's different statements, it is clear that almost immediately after the publication of his book in England, he entered into communication with James. Either James did not tell him about his previous declarations of 1937 or 1938, or Crozier, for some unknown reason, chose to ignore them. If we can judge from the care with which he took down the air vice-marshal's precious words on magnetic tape, it would seem that Crozier thought he had stumbled on a rare document indeed. When a year and a half later, he wrote to the *Times*, he was evidently basing his letter on this "other evidence now available," but he did it in a careless manner. In the *Times* letter he insisted that only a quarter of the town had been system-atically destroyed, but James had told him that three-fourths of Guernica had been destroyed and only a quarter spared. In this same letter, Crozier affirmed that the destruction had been caused by dynamite, but James's testimony, as given by Crozier, spoke of fire, never of dynamite. When James spoke with Crozier, he was thirty years older than when he made his earlier declarations. To the historian, the earlier versions seem more reliable, especially for such details as those given by "one of the rare inhabitants," who said, "that airplanes had flown over the town and dropped some bombs." In his 1938 statement he had identified this person as "a middle-aged priest," who told him "that many airplanes came over, and many bombs were dropped, that the roads were machine-gunned." He also said that about a hundred were killed in the bombing. Such testimony did not enter into Crozier's thesis.

Thus ended one of the last efforts by anyone to deny German culpability in the destruction of Guernica. It is difficult to fit Crozier into any school of thought on Guernica. He was a cold-war journalist, and probably hated the Spanish Republicans[106] more than he loved Franco. On the question of Guernica, his inconsistencies are more weighted in favor of the Nazis than of the Nationalists. His book is one of few that affirm that "Nationalist planes" bombed Guernica.[107] It is true that he says that they bombed only "legitimate military targets," but why did he accuse the Nationalists of this military raid, for which he offers no proof whatsoever? Was he simply carried away by his passion to prove that no German plane ever bombed anything in Guernica?

Crozier was unlucky in that his book appeared right at the moment when the West German university world was on the point of admitting that the Germans had bombed Guernica, and when the Neo-Franquistas in Madrid were getting ready to proclaim a new truth about Guernica—all of which would leave Crozier holding the bag. The one point he was to have in common with the Neo-Franquista version was his unsupported statement, "It is clear that neither Franco nor Mola was consulted nor informed about any German decision to bomb the town." The rest of his argument was being disavowed in Madrid at the very moment in 1970 when his Spanish translation was being published, with no charitable soul on hand to correct his fantasies about Guernica.[108]

As mentioned earlier, another biography of Franco appeared in England in 1967. In this book George Hills, a journalist, developed in depth the idea suggested a few years earlier by Georges-Roux: total blame for the Germans, total absolution for the Spanish Nationalists. Hills spoke fluent Spanish, and while his fellow countryman Crozier was falling under the influence of Luis Bolín and the traditional interpretation of Guernica, Hills was finding newer sources of information, and his book can aptly be considered the first of the Neo-Franquista school on Guernica.

Hills attributed the destruction of the town to the Germans, with no mention of arson. He observed that the German bombers used in the Guernica attacks had previously been used for hitting tactical targets, "as required by Mola," but that "as many missiles had gone wild as had found their mark." The bombsights were unsophisticated (as Galland had said), and the crews without experience. "In these circumstances, the Germans, without consulting *any Spaniard,* chose . . . Guernica for the world's first experiment in saturation bombing."[109] Hills's short account of the bombing was "based on my cross-questioning of Basque and other eye-witnesses in the 1950s." This was essentially Steer's story, and Hills accepted the accuracy of the *Times* man's report.[110] Hills also accepted the figures of 1,650 dead and more than 800 wounded.[111]

But if Hills's description of the bombing itself was a summary of what the readers of the *Times* had known on the morning of April 28, 1937, his details of the subsequent relations between the German military in Spain and the Spanish Nationalists were new, based on "information willingly supplied by eye-witnesses [plural] to the scenes [plural] at General Franco's G.H.Q."[112] Hills was told:

> The first news we had of it [the destruction of Guernica] was from abroad. At first we didn't believe the news and thought it another piece of red propaganda. The Germans denied it, confusing the issue by telling Franco that none of their aircraft had taken off on the 27th, the date on which Franco's General Staff first thought the destruction of Guernica had taken place. When better informed, Franco ordered Colonel Funck [military attaché at the German embassy] to report to him. Pale with anger, he said to Funck: "I will not have war made on my own people."[113]

This account is of interest for the chronology—or rather the lack of precise chronology—established for what happened in Salamanca from the morning of April 27 on, concerning Guernica. We are told that the news came from abroad. This was probably true. But by what means? At what time? And what was the news? The bombing? Or the extent of the destruction? Hills does not tell us. But Vicente Talón wrote three years later that the news was received in the form of a Reuters telegram.[114] It was highly probable that Salamanca had some means of intercepting Reuters news service sent from London. We know that Holme, the Reuters man in Bilbao, sent off his telegram from Bilbao early on the morning of April 27, for it appeared in the London afternoon press of that same day.

But there is another element by which the chronological developments of the events of April 27 can be controlled, and which the Neo-Franquista historians have ignored: the Bilbao radio transmitter. In the Basque periodical published in Paris shortly after the bombing, one can find at least three reports concerning Guernica taken from the Bilbao broadcasts on April 27, all between ten and twelve o'clock that morning.[115] One cannot read these paragraphs without understanding that the bombing referred to had taken place on the previous day—that is, on April 26. Among the broadcasts reproduced by the Basque periodical is the Aguirre statement broadcast at noon on April 27. This was known to the Nationalists for the Salamanca riposte on the night of April 27, "Lies, Lies, Lies," was a refutation of Aguirre's allocution and did not mention the Reuters dispatch. A hasty reading of the Nationalist press is sufficient to show that the Republican transmitters were closely monitored by the Rebels, and there can be hardly any question that normal procedures were followed on April 27 and that the news programs of the Bilbao transmitter were known immediately in Salamanca. The news of the bombing of Guernica was therefore most probably known in Salamanca by ten o'clock on the morning of April 27, if we consider only the Bilbao radio, and still earlier if the Reuters dispatch anteceded this transmission.

If we depart with the premise that we are dealing with rational human adults in the Salamanca press office, and with people accustomed to receiving, judging, and interpreting news dispatches, it is impossible for us to believe that on receiving the news of the destruction of Guernica, not later than ten o'clock on the morning of April 27, these experienced press people could for a moment have thought that the information concerned an action that was to take place on the afternoon (or that had already taken place on the morning) of that same day.

Another chronological flaw in Hills's account appears in his description of the only one of the "scenes at General Franco's G. H. Q." which he offers to us—that between Franco and Funck. When did this take place? Hills does not give a date to the encounter, but immediately after it he writes, "Guernica was occupied by Mola's troops two days later."[116] This would place Franco's audience for Funck on April 27. There was a crowded calendar for that day, if we believe Hills. We are told that the Germans informed Franco that their planes had not flown on April 27, and that Franco's General Staff at first thought that the alleged bombing had taken place on that date. Such a reply from the Germans, in the past tense, could only have taken place after the end of the day's operations on April 27, but how could Franco's staff, which knew of the bombing immediately after ten o'clock that morning, accept for a moment such obviously falsified information?

Still more to the point, how could the Germans have given such information to Franco when their official communiqué of April 27, far from saying that their airplanes did not fly that day, told of several flights?[117] If, as Hills says, Franco's staff did accept the false information, when then was Franco "better informed," and at what time did he call in Funck on April 27? Hills is evidently as confused in his own chronology as he alleges Franco's men were. At any rate, in view of the contradictions in Hills's account, we cannot accept the version that the people around Franco were "confused" about the date of the bombing.

Nor is it only the date that is troubling about the scenes between Funck and Franco. In a note Hills reported that his "enquiries" produced evidence that "Franco did not order the bombardment ('How could he? We had plenty of friends, even in Basque towns.')."[118] Hills is a naïve person. Twenty-seven days before the bombing of Guernica, Durango was bombed. This was the kickoff for the campaign in the north. Durango was a Basque town, and presumably Franco had as many friends there, proportionally, as he had in Guernica. Yet 227 people were killed in the bombing or died subsequently as a result of wounds.[119] The bombings continued in the Basque country until the end of the campaign, none so deadly as that of Guernica, but still people, perhaps friends of Franco, were killed here and there. In fact, the Nationalist air raids continued until the end of the war, with especially devastating attacks on Barcelona, Nules, and Granollers. Had Franco no friends in these towns? How could Hills believe, and reproduce, the scene with Franco stomping his foot and crying, "I will not have war made on my own people"? Whom did he think he was making war on? This is on page 277 of Hills's book. Had he written 276 pages without realizing that Franco was making war on his own people?

When Hills's book was reviewed in England, a critic noted that "Hills admits the bombing of Guernica but denies Franco's responsibility for it," and that Hills also "presents a Franco furious with the Italians for bombing Barcelona" later in the war, and then he asked Hills: "Was the Caudillo powerless to keep the Fuhrer and the Duce from bombing Spain at their leisure?"[120] Hills replied: "The answer would appear to be yes."[121] If Hills thought that Franco was powerless to stop the German bombing, then he should have considered the "scene" between Franco and Funck at best as a bit of playacting.

Hills seemingly thought Franco *sans pouvoir et sans reproche,* going so far in his efforts to whitewash El Caudillo in the Guernica affair as to write that the press office statement of April 29 was "apparently issued without Franco's authority."[122] It is not clear just what Hills may mean by "the Press Office statement of April 29," but a United Press correspondent wrote and had passed through the Nationalist censorship the statement that the declaration of April 27, two days earlier, was by Franco himself.[123] Obviously, by April 29, even if Franco's powers were reduced to that of reading the Nationalist newspapers, he knew of the April 27 statement.

Hills might have made a stronger case had he identified his "eye-witnesses" (the word is in the plural) who testified "willingly." It is even more curious that the Neo-Franquista historians who followed Hills made not the slightest effort to corroborate this testimony, or to identify the "eye-witnesses," although it would still be fairly easy to make a list of those who might have been present at the "scenes" (this word is also in the plural). However, in a note Hills does tell us that one of the "eye-witnesses," was a "Spanish general," who when shown Galland's account of the bombing, called it "utterly absurd," adding that "there was no question of a mistake: Funck admitted that it was done as ordered by Keitel and that it was a try-out."[124]

To strengthen his case for the absolution of Franco and Mola, Hills quoted one of his "eye-witnesses" to the "scenes" at Franco's headquarters as saying that as a result of the Guernica incident, "at G. H. Q. relations between us and the Germans were at breaking point for a long time." If this was true, it is surprising that no hint of it can be found in the German documents available. Hills followed the statement of his witnesses by observing: "The Condor Legion's commander was eventually recalled,"[125] and in a note had one of his informants testify that "Sperrle's recall was maybe connected with Guernica, among other things: but it took time to be rid of him." Hills also wrote: "Sperrle and Faupel subsequently quarrelled."[126] This quarrel, however, antedated the bombing of the Basque town.[127] The argument connected with Sperrle's departure from Spain and its relation with Guernica became a cardinal point of the Neo-Franquista thesis on Guernica and will be considered later.

The theme of Guernica was also dealt with in the German-language Spanish Civil War anthology of Hans-Christian Kirsch, who illustrated the subject with citations from Onaindia and Aristarco Yoldi, as given by Robert Payne; Cowles, unidentified by name, as taken from Thomas's German edition; General Duval; and Galland, as quoted by Thomas.[128]

The year 1967 also saw another interesting step in the evolution of the Guernica story: the first effort of the official civil war propagandist of the regime, Ricardo de la Cierva. He was the chief editor of a serial history of the war, *Crónica de la guerra de España*,[129] begun in 1966 and which by October 1967 had arrived at weekly chapter 62, "Arde Guernica." This work, printed in Buenos Aires and distributed in all the newspaper kiosks of Spain, gave the ordinary Spanish reader for the first time a wide sampling of the different opinions in print about what had happened in Guernica. Among the historians and witnesses quoted on Guernica—some for the first time in Franco Spain—were: Hugh Thomas; the mayor of Guernica at the time of the bombing, Labauria; George L. Steer; Lojendio, Martínez Esparza, Ansaldo, and Bolín, among the Nationalists; then the Germans Galland and Dahms.[130] After the editor had presented accounts, he himself gave a vague and irresolute conclusion:

> Germany in 1937 could not carry out "tests" of urban destruction for the simple reason that the Luftwaffe was not conceived as a strategic arm until much later in the Second World War.... To speak of designs of urban destruction in connection with Guernica is to ignore the trajectory of modern aviation.... Guernica was simply an episode more, although an extremely sad one—but not so sad as that of neighboring Durango, less bruited about by propaganda —in the interminable chain of small and great tragedies which formed the Spanish Civil War.[131]

This verdict was an anticlimax, but the economic facts of life were that the publication had to please readers in both Spain and South America and not offend the Spanish censor. Who had, then, destroyed Guernica? The editor does not tell us. But he had warned us on the first page of the fascicule that his intention was "to leave, at the end, the path open to the reader's own conclusions."[132] This must have come as a shock to many readers, and it showed that the Neo-Franquistas were having difficulty in deciding exactly what position to take on this highly controversial event.

The confused and changing attitude existing in Spain in 1967 toward the question of Guernica can be further illustrated by three more examples. One is the treatment given to the subject in the translation of Edward Knoblaugh's 1937 book, now published in Madrid. Knoblaugh's paragraph on Guernica was unchanged in the text, including his statement that "the principal damage was caused by Anarchist incendiaries and Asturian dynamiters before they evacuated Guernica."[133] However, the editor felt impelled to give an explanation in a note. "The episode of Guernica," he wrote, "has been weakened by all sorts of propaganda." He then said that Bolín, in his recent book, "gives an interesting and documented version," and went on to contradict Bolín: "Of course, no one can deny the bombing of the Condor Legion, although it is also true that it did not have the character of a 'strategical' bombing, but simply that of a 'tactical' bombing." The editor then chided historians for overlooking the testimony of Galland and, apparently unaware that the book had been published in Spain (in censored form), quoted from it in a new translation.[134]

The bombing of Guernica was admitted in the 1967 work of the aging monarchist poetaster José María Pemán, who wrote the captions for a volume containing a thousand photographs of the civil war. Picasso's *Guernica* illustrated the title page and was reproduced inside the book. A significant remark for the Neo-Franquista school on Guernica was found in the caption of the photograph of a ruined house in the bombed town, with an exposed staircase, leading nowhere:

> Where does this wounded staircase lead to? To peace? to love? to hatred? This staircase must be continued, in a future of fraternity, formed with equal parts of much forgetfulness and sober remembrance.

Guernica a symbol of fraternity? Another scene of the ruined town was commented on thusly:

> ...Guernica bombed. One of the most profound sorrows of the war. And a sad fruit of violence. Fortunately, the Guernica later rebuilt has been reborn from its ashes.[135]

The other example can be seen in a letter published in the Barcelona magazine *Qué pasa?* late in 1967. This letter, pro-Nationalist and highly anti-Basque autonomy in tone, admitted the bombing of Guernica by the Condor Legion, denounced the Basque and Republican propaganda on the subject, and ended:

> It is the fault of National propaganda that the case of Guernica took on the propaganda dimensions that it did. Instead of facing up to the facts with courage and explaining that what had happened was a lamentable episode, such as happens in all wars, National propaganda kept saying: "Guernica was burned by the Reds." This was an error.[136]

Bolín was not named, but he was obviously the object of the attack.

The indecisive method utilized for explaining the catastrophe of Guernica by the editor of *Crónica de la guerra de España*, the balancing of contradictory testimonies and opinions, was followed in 1968 by Bernardo Gil Mugarza, editor of an expensive book of civil war photographs. *España en llamas, 1936* gave its readers five photographs of the ruined town, with texts from Galland, Father Onaindia, José de Labauria, Cleugh, and Peter Kemp. It also offered a reproduction of the document of the Basque clergy, addressed to the Pope from Bilbao, on May 11, 1937—as had the Argentine publication of the previous year—with a commentary by Hugh Thomas and extracts from an unpublished manuscript on Guernica by a journalist Vincente Tálon. This was Tálon's first appearance on the Guernica scene. His contribution did not touch on the responsibility for the destruction, which was, however, attributed to a "bombing," but dealt rather with the number of deaths caused by that bombing. He concluded that they were fewer than two hundred.

Gil Mugarza's book represented an advance over all else that had been said about Guernica in Nationalist Spain because of the editorial summary on the subject. First of all, the editor said that Guernica was destroyed in a bombing attack carried out by German bombers.

> Some writers have affirmed that the town was destroyed by Republican dynamite. Others have admitted that it was destroyed by the National bombing and by a fire started hours later by the Republicans. In reality, there exist no proofs that Guernica suffered any damage after the bombing of April 26.

This is certainly one of the first times, if not the first time, that such a clear statement about Guernica was printed in Franco Spain. The declaration was, however, hedged with reservations. Guernica, the summary said, was a legitimate military target. The death roll was less than two hundred, by Tálon's figures. The attack was not a saturation bombing, for the Germans at that time had neither the aircraft nor the techniques for such an operation. It was the Anglo-Americans later in World War II who invented that horror. These qualifications by the editor do not alter the essential part of the summary.

The positive elements of the editorial analysis indicated above were weakened by a halfhearted defense of the original Nationalist communiqués on Guernica.

> The National version of the first hours—Guernica was set on fire by Red dynamiters—was based on other facts, which were certain. Irún was burned by the CNT and Amorebieta by Asturian militiamen.[137]

That any story, true or false, could be based "on other facts" than its own is difficult to understand. But what were the "other facts?" Irún was burned before being left in the hands of the enemy; Guernica was set on fire sixty-seven hours before it was abandoned. And it is even more difficult to understand how the destruction of Amorebieta, by incendiarists or by air bombing, could have weighed on the decisions taken at Franco's headquarters on the morning of April 27, for Amorebieta did not fall into Franco's hands until twenty days later, on May 17.[138]

To this dishonest argument, Gil Mugarza added another one, at the same time introducing a new character in the Guernica story, a Socialist officer of the Republican army, Victor de Frutos, who, in a book published in the Argentine, told of plans to set fire to the old town of Bilbao, upon evacuation, thus "delaying the passage of the enemy forces and of his tanks."

This plan was not carried out, for the reasons given by Victor de Frutos:

> The old city was not transformed into flames because as we crossed the streets with incendiary bombs already prepared, cans of gasoline and matches, we could perceive the women who had remained in their homes and were watching us from the windows, clutching their little ones in their arms. The spectacle, which we did not expect, immobilized us. For this reason the old

town remained intact and thus it was found by the forces of Italians and Requetes when they occupied it.139

For thirty years the Franquistas had used the precedent of Irún, set on fire upon evacuation, as "proof" that Guernica had been destroyed by arsonists; the Neo-Franquistas had now found other proof in the fact that elements of the Republican army had planned to set the old part of Bilbao on fire upon evacuation but had not done so. From the first day of their reaction to the news about Guernica, the Insurgents had reasoned in this oblique, illogical manner. Now that they were seeking a new formula to explain what had happened at Guernica, they were reasoning in the same oblique, illogical fashion. Moreover, the Bilbao action, according to Frutos, was planned to delay the passage of the enemy and his tanks. This was a valid wartime reason. But the reason would not have been valid for such a Republican action in Guernica on April 26, for it would have affected not only the Franco forces but also the Republicans still to the east of Guernica. But, however feeble their reasoning, the Neo-Franquistas were to maintain their interpretation of the story of Victor de Frutos as an integral part of their version of Guernica.

Gil Mugarza expressed still another idea that was to become a fundamental part of the new history of Guernica. "Practically, the bombing of Guernica had a world-wide impact more because of the famous painting of Picasso than for the destructive effects of the bombs."140 The simple chonology of the development of this "world-wide impact" will suffice to show the absurdity of the idea, but we shall see how the conception of the magical power of Picasso's picture was to influence the activity of the Neo-Franquista school. Penrose tells us, in his study of Picasso, that the news from Guernica on April 29, 1937,

> roused Picasso from melancholy to anger. Acting as a catalyst to the anxiety and indignation mingled within him, it gave him the theme he had been seeking.

Then: "Before two months from the day Picasso made his first sketch had elapsed, the great canvas *Guernica* was ready to take its place in the Spanish pavilion at the Paris Exhibition."141

The worldwide reaction to the destruction of Guernica was immediate. Picasso shared this reaction and expressed his powerful feelings in painting. His large canvas certainly kept the thought of Guernica alive, and will continue to do so for the rest of history, but the "world-wide impact" was caused by the news, and the way in which the news was given, and not by the painting, which came later. In spite of these qualifications, Gil Mugarza's book did mark a significant advance in presenting to the Spanish people—or at least to that small segment of the Spanish people who could pay the equivalent of more than thirty dollars for a coffee-table book, or to that small portion of that small segment that would take the trouble to read the text in a book of photographs—a more realistic picture of what had happened at Guernica.

Spanish censorship in 1968 had allowed a frank avowal to pass in the Gil Mugarza book that Guernica was destroyed by German bombers. Such was the unpredictability of that censorship that in the same year it permitted the publication of a book by the official Servicio Histórico Militar, under the sponsorship of the Central General Staff of the Army, in which it was stated that on April 29, "the conquerors occupied the calcinated ruins of the historic town of Guernica, burned by the Reds in their retreat."[142]

By 1968 the sociopolitical situation in the Basque country was quite different from what it had been thirty-one years earlier, when Guernica was bombed. In 1937 the dominant political force was the Partido Nactionalista Vasco, which was conservative in its economic views, closely allied to a conservative clergy, and on the Republican side of the war more for the sentimental appeal of regional autonomy than for the basic economic interests of its members. All this had changed. The exile of the PNV leaders, the unpopularity of the highly centralized Falange and of the monarchist alternatives, had left a political vacuum, filled in large part by 1962 by a new movement called ETA (*Euzkadi ta Askatasuna*—the Basque homeland and its freedom), which announced as its objectives, "independence and reunification of the Basque territory, the transformation of the economic, social and cultural structures and the creation of a socialist regime."[143] Thus, for the first time in Euzkadi, Basque nationalism was allied with the workers' revolt in a political movement. This frankly revolutionary movement was supported by the younger elements of the Basque clergy, and passively, it would seem, by much of the population.

During the first months of 1968 frequent bombing attacks on public buildings, barracks, and newspapers considered "anti-Basque" took place in the Basque country.[144]   On June 7 a member of the executive committee of E. T. A., Javier Echebarrieta, was killed by police a few hours after a skirmish in which a civil guard had met his death. Echebarrieta was said to have been shot down in cold blood.[145] Echebarrieta's companion, Sarasketa, was captured and sentenced by a military court to fifty-eight years in prison. A higher military tribunal judged the verdict too lenient and condemned the man to death on June 27. The government later changed this to life imprisonment after an urgent meeting of the Council of Ministers.[146]

It was in this charged atmosphere that on August 2, Melitón Manzanas, chief of the political police in the province of Gúipuzcoa was shot down in Irún, on the doorstep of his home.[147] Madrid immediately decreed the state of alert, a modified form of martial law, for the entire province, and revived the decree for repressing "banditism and terrorism" which had become inoperative since 1963. A vast police operation was launched throughout the Basque provinces, and hundreds were arrested, among them lawyers, journalists, and priests.[148]

Detention of a priest, without the consent of his superior, was a violation of the Concordat linking the Catholic Church and the Spanish state. The lack of combativeness on the part of the bishop of Bilbao was interpreted as collaboration with Madrid and the Bilbao seminary was occupied by rebellious priests demanding that the Church "take position against the repression of which the Basque people are victims."[149] This immediate problem was resolved by the death of the bishop and the naming by the Vatican of the bishop of Santander, José Mariá Cirarda, a Basque and a reputed liberal, as apostolic administrator of the Bilbao diocese.[150]

On December 13 a military court sitting in San Sebastián sentenced three militant Basques, each to forty-eight years of imprisonment, for setting fire to a vacant house.[151] These condemnations were less than the death sentences requested by the prosecutor, but nevertheless, wrote the correspondent of the *New York Times*, they "shocked large elements of the community."[152] Churches in San Sebastián were occupied by women and priests to protest the verdicts, and were vacated only when the bishop promised to investigate ever-increasing charges of police brutality.[153]

This agitation was by no means limited to the Basque country. Mgr. Cirarda, as bishop of Santander, protested against the numerous detentions of workers in Santander and the rumors of torture by saying: "Any action which physically or morally violates the human person is infamous."[154] A strike in Asturias,[155] Carlist troubles in Pamplona,[156] churches occupied by protesting women in Madrid,[157] and student riots in Barcelona[158] —such was the news from Spain. A letter was addressed to Minister of the Interior Camilo Alonso Vega, who had commanded troops on the Basque front during the civil war, protesting against police brutality; it was signed by 1,300 figures from the literary, political, and religious worlds.[159] On January 16, the assembly of the Madrid bar—with 600 lawyers present—adopted by acclamation a petition to be sent to the government asking for the abolition of the Court of Public Order and the laws whereby political offenses were judged by military courts, and demanding better treatment for political prisoners.[160] The Barcelona bar association followed suit, and also requested from the minister of justice a report on the conditions of three lawyers in *residence surveillée* at San Sebastián.[161] Thousands of Madrid students manifested in the streets on January 22, following the death "by suicide" of a student held in police custody.[162]

On January 23, 1969, the government replied to these waves of unrest by decreeing a three-month nationwide state of exception. This was the first time such an action had been taken since Franco came to power.[163] This act was followed by numerous strikes in the Basque country. For the greater part of the month of February, more than 25,000 workers were on strike in Bilbao and more than 200 were arrested.[164]

The state of exception was raised prematurely on March 23, so that, in the view of observers, the country would not be under martial law when the thirtieth anniversary of Franco's victory was to be celebrated on April 1. The correspondent of *Le Monde* found the results of fifty-nine days of martial law very small indeed, writing that the state of exception "had not succeeded in stopping the strikes in

Biscay and Guipuzcoa provinces and had only 'tempered' 'the rebellious efforts' of the university students."[165]

The hunt for ETA members had not stayed. On March 6 a Basque named Francisco Javier Larena Martínez was arrested; on March 8, two more Basques were detained, and one of them, Gorostidi Artoli, with Larena Martínez, was later charged with complicity in the death of Manzanas, and judged by the military court in the 1970 Burgos trial.[166] On April 6 two Basques were reported killed near Pamplona, when their automobile blew up; police said they were transporting explosives. Five days later, five Basques were arrested in Pamplona, accused of organizing a series of bomb attacks.[167] These arrests brought to twenty-four the number of people jailed and charged with ETA membership since March 25, when the decree of martial law was lifted.[168]

On April 9 four Basques suspected of ETA activities were surrounded in their house in Bilbao by police; three surrendered, but one, Echevarria Iztueta, escaped and was later accused of having killed a taxi driver whose body was found in the nearby town of Orozco.[169] The three men detained were also later to appear in the Burgos trial.[170] Two days after the capture of the three Basques in Bilbao, another group of four Basques was arrested in Santander Province.[171] They also appeared as defendants at the Burgos trial, one of them being accused of complicity in the murder of Manzanas.[172]

On April 17, two priests were arrested in Bilbao. They were thought to have had relations with Echave, the priest arrested on April 11. A farmer and his wife were arrested at Orozco, suspected of having given aid to Echevarria Iztueta. Several priests, believed to have given aid to Echevarria, were in flight.[173] On April 22 five persons, including a woman, were condemned in Madrid, before the Tribunal of Public Order, to terms running from eighteen months to twelve years for allegedly belonging to ETA.[174] Foreign press agencies announced that in recent days a hundred persons had been arrested in the Basque provinces, accused of complicity in acts of "terrorism."[175]

The vicar-general of the Bilbao diocese, the bishop's first aid, was arrested on April 24, charged with aiding ETA members, but he was released two days later.[176] On April 26 the special correspondent of *Le Monde* cabled that eight Basque priests had been arrested during the preceding week.[177] Another Basque priest was arrested on April 28, for "complicity with ETA members."[178]

Le Monde announced on May 13 the establishment of two new military courts in Bilbao, bringing to four the number of such tribunals in the Basque country for judging ETA members and sympathizers.[179] Two days later a fifty-year-old Basque was killed in a church in Álava Province by police looking for ETA suspects. They thought his tolling of the bell was a subversive signal.[180] On May 30 five priests entered the Bilbao bishopric to begin a hunger strike. Before beginning the fast, the priests had, according to the police, distributed public appeals, one to the minister of justice, asking that the law on "banditism and terrorism" and the special military courts be suppressed; another to the International Red Cross, demanding an investigation into the tortures inflicted on the Basques; and a third to Mgr. Cirarda, asking that "once and for all the oppression and violence suffered by our people be ended and that he denounce to the Christian people the tortures employed by the police."[181] Four days later, on June 3, police entered the bishopric, without permission of the bishop, and arrested the hunger strikers.[182] On June 11 the five priests were brought before the military court in Burgos *in camera.* Two were given twelve years in prison, the other three, ten years each.[183]

Of the 133 political detainees condemned to prison terms in April and May, 33 or one-fourth of the total, were Basques. The harshest terms were for a young woman, who received twelve years, and a man, ten years, for ETA activities.[184] Five young Basques arrested on April 24 in Bilbao were tried before a military court in Burgos and sentenced on July 15 to from two to seven years in prison.[185] In May, June, and July, 213 persons were condemned to prison terms for political reasons in Spain. Of these, fifty-two were Basques, among them five priests.[186] On July 4 police stopped a Basque priest in his automobile and arrested him for transporting illegal propaganda. He was tried before the military court in Burgos, on August 20 and condemned to eight years imprisonment.[187] On August 6 the Burgos military court sentenced one priest to ten years, another to six years; a layman to eight years, and another to four years; all were Basques accused of distributing ETA tracts, which constituted "military rebellion" and "offenses to the army." [188] Again, on August 23, four Basques were condemned to prison terms of from six to sixteen years, for ETA activities.[189] On August 26, a letter addressed to Franco, bearing the signatures of more than 3,000 persons of Guipúzcòa Province, was made public; it demanded that Basque nationalists be judged by civil courts and not by special tribunals of exception, that the law on "banditism and terrorism," by which political offenses were judged by military courts, be abolished, and, finally, that all the priests and laymen condemned by military courts be amnestied.[190]

Harsh sentences continued to be meted out to the Basques. On October 5 four Basques were given twenty years each for placing a bomb in a newspaper office;[191] on October 11 two Basques were condemned to one year of prison each for "illicit propaganda"—that is, for having raised Basque flags near Bilbao, on the Republican anniversary of April 14, a year and a half earlier[192]; on October 16 two Basques received sentences of six years each in prison, for "illicit associations."[193] On October 24 the special military court in Burgos sentenced two Basques to fifteen years each in prison. They were accused of "military rebellion"—that is, of belonging to ETA and of having distributed propaganda tracts.[194]

The military court sitting in Burgos sentenced four Basque priests to terms ranging from two to ten years in prison for giving aid to Echevarria Eztueta, the presumed killer of the taxi driver on April 9. Mgr. Cirarda then addressed a note to the head of the Burgos military district, asking that such trials not be conducted *in camera,* as foreseen by the Concordat, but in the full light of day.[195] On the twenty-seventh of the same month, a young Basque, Antonio Arrizabalaga, charged with giving the order to put a bomb (which did not go off) in a police car, was condemned to death. His two accomplices had already received twenty-five years in prison.[196] On November 26 José Mariá Dorronsoro Ceberio was given a seventeen-year sentence for belonging to ETA.[197] On December 12 a Basque seminarist was condemned to four years, for "illicit associations" and "illegal propaganda."[198] According to one source, in the last six months of 1969, 147 Basques were brought before Spanish courts charged with political offenses.[199] At the end of 1969, twenty-one Basque priests were jailed in a special cell block reserved for members of the clergy in the prison of Zamora.[200]

> The lifting of the State of Exception signified for the Basque country an aggravation of the situation, the authorities having decided to intensify their operations against the separatists

observed a commentator in *Le Monde,* on October 29.

> Hundreds of persons have been held for questioning, kept incommunicado for several days. . . . Since the month of April, ninety Basques have been condemned, and of these, twenty at least, according to the press agencies, to terms running from six to sixteen years. Last June 19, the World Confederation of Labor protested against tortures in the Basque country. . . . The Basque clergy is particularly the target of the repressive measures. More than twenty-five priests, accused of "complicity with members of ETA," have been jailed since the month of April. According to *Pueblo* daily of the official syndicates, "a large part of the Basque clergy has participated and participates more or less directly in the activities of the clandestine organizations." . . . The action of the Basque priests who denounce the repression and demand the reestablishment of individual liberties is more and more frequently, if not approved, at least protected by the local hierarchy.[201]

The repression of the years 1968 and 1969 had put many Basques behind prison bars, but it had not brought peace to the Basque provinces. Everyone knew that the sixteen defendants accused of "military rebellion" and who were to appear before the military court in Burgos in 1970, in what history would know as the Burgos trial, were in the hands of the police and that the trial was being thoroughly prepared. It was against this background of social and political agitation, on the one hand and, on the other, governmental repression, police brutality and tortures, military courts, and laws of exception, that there developed another chapter in the Guernica controversy. The growing sentiment in Neo-Franquista circles, that a new Nationalist version of what had happened at Guernica was called for, now encountered unexpected political support: a new account of the destruction of Guernica, if artfully conceived, could perhaps help to bring calm to the troubled Basque country.

The demand for a revised version of Guernica was facilitated by another event: on September 3, 1969, Luis Bolín died,[202] and with him disappeared one of the last of the fanatical defenders, at least in Spain itself, of the original Franquista account of the Guernica incident. Shortly before Bolín's death, his position had been reaffirmed by Marqués Pablo de Merry del Val, like Bolín a former press officer, but in 1969 Spanish ambassador to Washington. "It is extremely doubtful that the city itself [Guernica] was ever bombed at all, as personally I am convinced that only the entrenchments, railway yards and road convoys were actually attacked," wrote Merry del Val. "The city itself was destroyed by the retreating anarchist forces, among which there were an untold number of 'dinamiteros'."[203]

There is still another event of 1969 which could have weighed in favor of a decision by the Neo-Franquista school to proceed to a revision of the Guernica story. This is the acknowledgment of the bombing by a West German historian, who had found his proof in the German archives. But there is no evidence that this work was even known to the Spanish revisionists. In 1969 Manfred Merkes, who had slighted the subject of Guernica in his earlier work, developed the theme in a revised edition. This is significant for our story; no one else has looked into the German documents concerning the Spanish Civil War as closely as has Merkes. In an annex he published all the references to Guernica that he could find. He first cited Beumelberg, who had worked in the Air Ministry, and whose remarks we have already seen.[204] Then he quoted from the first draft and then from the revised version of "Die Kämpfe im Norden," which have also been given at the beginning of this chapter.[205] In addition to these documents, Merkes has found four comments on Guernica, all written by German military figures who had been in Spain during the civil war.

Colonel Jaenecke, of Special Staff W, who was in Spain at the time of the attack on Guernica, later wrote an account of his four-week visit. In this he insisted on the fact that arson had been carried out in Eibar, and then wrote:

> On the other hand, Guernica has been destroyed by the Italians and on the last days by certain German bombs on bridges and crossroads, and since in the town, a great deal of wood was employed in house construction, contrary to the custom in the rest of Spain, the town went up in flames. The inhabitants took flight and could not extinguish the fires. . . . In itself Guernica was a complete success for the Luftwaffe. The only path of retreat on the whole Red coast was blocked by fire and two meters of rubble in the streets.

Merkes noted that the blocking of the retreat road was to be but partially effective.[206]

The chief of staff of the Condor Legion at the time of the bombing, von Richthofen, in a later report, wrote that a breakthrough to the south of Bilbao had presented the perspective of cutting off large masses of enemy troops east of Bilbao, by effecting rapid advances to the north. The retreat of the enemy troops was to be delayed by continuous attacks on crossroads and bridges. "It was possible to disrupt the Red movements on a wide scale, through combined attacks, of which that on Guernica was the most successful." However, since the Nationalist troops advanced hesitantly, the enemy was able to withdraw from the encirclement and bring his forces safely to the west of Guernica. This report was countersigned by Sperrle on July 11, 1938.[207]

Colonel Wilhelm Meise, who visited Spain for a week, from January 20 to 28, 1938, wrote on March 21 of that year, a report in which the following is found:

> It seems that specified targets are not being hit by the flyers. During the retreat in Asturias [*sic*] the aviators were to have destroyed a bridge near Goernica [*sic*], to delay the Red retreat. The bridge shows no sign of being hit and is undamaged. On the other hand, Goernica [*sic*] lies in ruins and wreckage.[208]

After the war, Colonel (ret.) Hans Henning Freiherr von Beust, who had served in the Condor Legion, gave a version that differed somewhat from that of "Die Kämpfe im Norden." He wrote that three squadrons of six airplanes each, flying at 3,500 meters from the north, with each squadron a kilometer apart, to attack a small bridge, lost their way over Guernica, and therefore most of the bombs fell short—that is, on the town itself. Merkes points out that von Beust gives the same objectives as did Jaenecke, and as Galland also later gave.[209]

Merkes's last citation is from Ansaldo's book, and concerns the supposed testimony of Göring while in prison in Nuremberg. The German historian notes that he has been unable to verify the statement.[210]

Merkes's summary of these papers was:

> Few statements on the subject have been found among the German documents. They confirm a German attack, but they contradict themselves in statements concerning the carrying out of the attack, although the purpose of the attack is clear.[211]

What can we conclude from this testimony found in the German archives? We can say that there does not exist in the German archives any definitive German report on Guernica, but that, nevertheless, in 1969, it could be proved by various documents in the German archives that Guernica had indeed been bombed by the German air force.

In 1969 there began a series of events, all related to Guernica, and each related to the others, and the whole to a propaganda campaign intentionally constructed to help pacify the Basque provinces. Since 1937, a barrier existed between Bilbao and the Franco regime, Guernica. Since the end of the war when the Nationalist leaders thought of Guernica, their thoughts increasingly turned not only to the tragedy itself but to the mysterious, symbolic representation of that tragedy: the painting of Pablo Picasso. Had not Crozier written that the "success" of the painting had been one of the causes for his belief that the Germans had bombed the town? And Gil Mugarza had declared that the painting, more than the bombing itself, had influenced public opinion. The painting had in recent years in Spain become the symbol of the civil war itself, reproduced in Seco Serrano's book, on the dust jacket for Carlos Rojas's book, in *Crónica de la guerra de España,* and on the book cover, on the endpapers, and in the text of Pemán's *Comentarios a mil imágenes de la guerra civil española.* The Spanish censorship, at any rate, had forgiven Picasso. And if this magic talisman were captured from the enemy, might not its strange power be made to work in favor of Madrid, rather than against Madrid? Was this the way official thinking was working in Madrid in 1969?

On October 23, 1969, Florentino Pérez Embid, director general of fine arts, and a prominent member of the Opus Dei movement, made a public gesture stating that *Guernica,* "this masterpiece of Picasso, should occupy the place that belongs to it," in the Museum of Contemporary Art, then under construction in Madrid.[212] This news was published all over the world. The idea had little success, and was publicly repulsed a few days later by Picasso's French lawyer, who made it known that the artist's long-time intention was that the picture, now at the New York Museum of Modern Art, "should be handed over to the government of the Spanish Republic the day the Republic is restored in Spain."[213]

Picasso's refusal to enter into the game plan of Madrid did not end the discussion about Guernica within Spain itself, where the debate was to intensify. On October 29, 1969, a reshuffling of the Spanish government increased the strength of Opus Dei, the friends of Pérez Embid. Fraga Iribarne left the Ministry of Information and Tourism, yielding his place to Alfredo Sánchez Bella, who with his two brothers formed a family group within the family of the holy Mafia.[214] It seems probable that at this time a more aggressive presentation of the revised version of the destruction of Guernica was decided upon. The first measure taken by the new government constituted a gesture of appeasement toward the Basque provinces: Arrizabalaga's sentence was commuted from death to thirty years in prison.[215]

On January 30, 1970, Spain's leading Falangist daily, *Arriba,* published a long interview with Ricardo de la Cierva, whose precise function within the Ministry of Information was to guide Spanish thinking on Spanish Civil War historiography. This was La Cierva's second effort to coordinate the facts on Guernica—his first being the rather noncommittal one found in the Codex-Argentina text—and he was to make at least seven more, each one contradicting parts of the others. In the *Arriba* article the subject of Guernica received heavy emphasis and new and sensational facts were revealed. The improvisation of these sensational facts would point to a hurried preparation.

La Cierva declared Picasso's painting *"fenomenal,"* and then presented for the first time before the Spanish people in a newspaper of mass circulation the information that Guernica had been bombed by the Germans. To this information, well known outside Spain (and inside Spain as well, it appears, for the news did not seem to upset many people), he added these details: Guernica was bombed by the Germans,

> but not by the Condor Legion, which was controlled by the National command, but by a special testing group which came directly from Germany,

destroyed Guernica and went back to Germany, without our knowing anything about it. . . . Since the National command had not given the orders for
the bombing, it said that the reports were lies, but in view of the international
uproar, it finally said that Guernica was blown up by Asturian dynamiters.
This is false.[216]

La Cierva exculpated the "Asturian dynamiters" of any blame, but he introduced new Spanish culprits: "Separatist Basque action groups, some of them
known by persons who were living in Guernica," had "contributed to the destruction." Such groups, he went on, "were under the orders of President José Antonio
de Aguirre himself, until shortly before the fall of Bilbao." La Cierva's intention
would seem to be to throw all the Spanish part of the blame for Guernica onto
Aguirre and the "separatists," the spiritual fathers of ETA. This could hardly bring
calm to the Basque country, especially since his assertion was unsupported by any
proof.[217] La Cierva also showed his interlocutor

a report, done two weeks after the destruction, with photographs and a map
with indications of all the bombs which fell there, with written testimonies of
persons who were there and are still living.

This report, he said, had not been published, because "it was contrary to the
propaganda theses held in those days." He also announced that Vicente Talón "is
going to publish a book that will be definitive and in which positions will be fixed
concerning Guernica."[218]

All this represented an uncommon amount of activity around a subject that had
been interdicted to all serious research in Spain for more than thirty-two years. This
statement on Guernica, by the official spokesman of the regime on civil war
matters, set the pattern for the Neo-Franquista version of Guernica. Placed against a
background of Picasso's "phenomenal" painting, three main elements could be
discerned. (1) Guernica had indeed been bombed, but the raid was an exclusively
German affair; (2) Franco had known nothing about the attack and was "disturbed" when he heard about it; (3) the number of the dead was small, "not even a
dozen." The word "disturbed" was to be strengthened in the future, and its
weakness may well have been the responsibility of the interviewer. The number of
the victims was also to climb rapidly in future texts. It can be seen that the
Neo-Franquista version was that given by Hills, except that Hills sinned by accepting a high figure for the victims.

La Cierva's revelation of the flight of the "special testing group" of German
airplanes that came from Germany, dropped their loads, and returned without even
saying hello to Franco was false at first glance for two reasons: First, according to
all accounts, three models of aircraft were used in the Guernica attack: the Junkers
52 bomber, the Heinkel 111 bomber, and the Heinkel 51 fighter. It is difficult to
find exact figures for the range of these airplanes, but no figures available come
anywhere near suggesting that any one of the three planes that took part in the raid
could have flown from Germany with a bomb load to Guernica and then back to its

German base. The distance from the German frontier to Guernica was approximately 750 miles, which would demand a flying range of 1,500 miles. These planes could not have made the flight.[219] Second, since the flying time from Germany to Guernica was around four hours for the bombers, and since all the reports confirm that there was an almost incessant flow of planes over Guernica, and the raid lasted almost four hours, no plane could have made the flight more than once. This operation would have demanded an enormous air fleet, which could hardly have crossed France unperceived. Evidently, La Cierva had not read very much in the basic texts of the Guernica controversy.

The precipitation with which La Cierva launched into the problem of Guernica can perhaps be explained by recalling another of his objectives: to have the history of the Spanish Civil War written by Spaniards inside Spain, or if written by foreigners, then by foreigners sympathetic to the regime. This objective had often been proclaimed. For example, in 1969, he wrote:

> The deposits of primary sources are here. . . . Up to now they have written history for us from the outside, without sources. This characteristic of the third stage, which is now beginning, is, as Stanley Payne has just said, "so much the better if the Spaniards have decided to write the history of Spain."[220]

During the *Arriba* interview, La Cierva held in his hands a copy of a Paris literary magazine that announced the preparation of a new work on Guernica. He referred to it three times during the interview, and on one occasion said: "What one cannot do is speak without any groundwork whatsoever. For example, that on Guernica, by Southworth."[221] It is quite probable that La Cierva himself, in addition to the Neo-Franquista historical reason for refurbishing the Guernica story, and the political reason of the situation in the Basque provinces, had this additional reason for his ill-prepared entry into the Guernica controversy: the desire to outdistance a competing version of Guernica, which he had all reason to believe would be less than favorable to the Nationalist regime.

Someone doubtless called La Cierva's attention to these grave flaws in his new theory, and when a commentary on his *Arriba* interview was published in *El Pensamiento Navarro*, he seized on the occasion to make an inelegant rectification. He wrote a long letter to the newspaper, published on the borders of the Basque country, and it was printed on the front page under the title: "THE TRUTH ABOUT THE BOMBING OF GUERNICA." He extricated himself in this way:

> Guernica was destroyed by a bombing attack of the German airforce, almost certainly of the Condor Legion, with a base on the Vitoria aerodrome. The thesis of the special group—*which I owe to another researcher*—is not probable. The German airforce of 1937 lacked, even for a testing project, such special groups.[222] [Italics added.]

La Cierva went on to justify the bombing by declaring Guernica "a military objective of the first order (communications, two armament factories)." And:

The principal and determining cause of the destruction of Guernica was the German bombing (in which not a single Spanish plane nor a single Spanish pilot participated, and for which orders were lacking as to the destruction of the town).

On April 27, 1937, in the Nationalist reply to the reports of the bombing of Guernica, the text said quite the contrary.[223] La Cierva added that "the cooperation, negative and positive, of the destruction commandos of the Army of Euzkadi, whose chief was President Jose Antonio de Aguirre . . . seems very probable." The "cooperation, negative and positive" was apparently an indistinct way of suggesting that the "destruction commandos" (1) *did not* help put out the fires, and (2) *did* help to set the fires. La Cierva's final point:

> The surprise of Mola and the indignation of General Franco on learning the complete facts were the motive for the unintelligent reaction of the propaganda services of the [Nationalist] zone (and perhaps the immediate destitution of the head of the Condor Legion; verify the dates).[224]

La Cierva's new thesis was, unfortunately for the Neo-Franquista school, as studded with contradictions as his previous one. He was prepared to admit that the Germans had bombed Guernica, but he ceded ground unwillingly on other positions. He advanced fragile arguments, built on rumor, hearsay, jumped-at conclusions, to exonerate the Spanish Nationalists from any responsibility in the tragedy of Guernica. La Cierva had pontifically assured his readers in *Arriba* that the Condor Legion "was controlled by the National command." Now, forced to withdraw from the battle his imaginary "special group," and to assign the bombing of Guernica to the Condor Legion, he conveniently forgot that it was "controlled by the National command" and declared Mola "surprised" and Franco "indignant" when they knew "the complete facts." He also declaimed that this knowledge of "the complete facts" by the two generals provoked "the unintelligent reaction" that we have seen in the early Nationalist communiqués on Guernica. If this means anything, it means that Franco and Mola were aware of the real situation on the evening of April 27 when the first "unintelligent reaction" was issued. It also means that they bear the responsibility for this "unintelligent reaction."

La Cierva also contradicted his *Arriba* interview, where he said that Euzkadi "destruction commandos" had "contributed" to the annihilation of the town. Two weeks later, he had withdrawn into a more prudent position, saying that their "cooperation, negative or positive . . . seems very probable." He also adopted Hills's suggestion of a link between Sperrle's recall and Franco's alleged rage over Guernica, inflating the German's departure from Spain four to six months after the Guernica incident into an "immediate dismissal." Did Sperrle go home in disgrace? Did his career suffer from his recall? Nothing offered by La Cierva proves it. La Cierva writes, "Verify the dates." They point to nothing "immediate,"[225] as will be subsequently shown.

It is useful to follow La Cierva's veiled attacks on Bolín, whom he does not yet name, but the "unintelligent reaction" was Bolin's; he was the author of what La

Cierva called "dull and awkward" propaganda.[226] One should also note here another argument to be used again and again by La Cierva, which appeared at this time. La Cierva observed that the Casa de Juntas and the Trees of Guernica suffered no damage, "in spite of their prominent position on the scene of the bombing and the silencing of all antiaerial defense after the first passage of the Condor Legion." This, he asserted, proved "the absolute lack of any symbolic intention in the bombing."[227] It also proved, then, the deliberate intention to destroy the rest of the town completely.

This letter from La Cierva, like his previous interview in *Arriba,* also suggested new revelations about Guernica. In emphasizing the military importance of the town, he observed: "I possess all the documentation on the exact emplacement of the bombs dropped on Guernica, which in their overwhelming majority fell near the military objectives." He admitted, however, that "enough of them fell on the city." Here it is obvious that La Cierva is referring only to high explosive bombs. How could he or anyone else know where the incendiary bombs had fallen? But he does not even mention the incendiaries, or the fire. He also referred again to important documentation uncovered by Air Force Colonel Ramón Salas Larrazábal concerning the Euzkadi "destruction commandos." "There exist specific documents which refer to the action of these special groups in Guernica itself." And he raised the possibility that the Carlist historian Jaime del Burgo might also make a contribution to the history of Guernica.

One of the reasons for La Cierva's feverish and ill-prepared activity around the question of Guernica was made evident in the Pamplona newspaper. First, he assured his readers that his new version of what had happened at Guernica (newer by two weeks) "with some finishing touches" could be upheld "documentally," as the "definitive" story. Then came this highly political phrase:

> And under the painting of Pablo Picasso—why not?—may this work of mine become another stepping stone to the end that the sacred name of Guernica— sacred for the Basque country and for Spain—be finally a symbol of reconciliation and of liberty for ALL OF US and not a symbol of resentment and of fear, as unfortunately is at times the case.[228]

Del Burgo, after this prompting, came forward with his version of the destruction of Guernica. He found two contradictory facts: "the center of Guernica, where there were many Carlists before the Uprising," was destroyed, a fact that pointed to a Republican reprisal; on the other hand, it could not be denied "that the city was bombed by a German squadron at the service of the Nationals." He reported a rumor that the Germans had bombed the town in reprisal "for the murder of one of their pilots, fallen days before in the enemy zone and who was practically quartered by undisciplined troops." I have found no confirmation of this murder.

Del Burgo observed:

> One cannot dismiss the possibility that dynamite was used after eight o'clock

that night, when explosions were continually being heard from the nearby places of Ajanguiz and Busturia. And National troops were still far away.

He further said that a sapper officer from Pamplona, while clearing up the rubble shortly after the bombing, showed him what was "beyond any doubt the traces of charges of dynamite placed after the bombing." He also stated that when he asked members of old Carlist families, who had lost everything in the destruction of the inner town, who was responsible, he invariably heard the answer: "The Reds. The Asturian dynamiters." Del Burgo frankly attributed such answers to "the passion that then dominated both sides of the struggle."

He criticized La Cierva's justification of the bombing. He thought the argument that Guernica was "the key point of the retreat of the Republican army in the last days of April 1937, with two munition factories," of doubtful strength. He pointed out that the greater part of the retreat passed south of Guernica, and he observed, "The munitions factories did not suffer too much." But, on the other hand, he judged La Cierva's reference to the Basque "destruction groups" to be well founded. "It seems beyond doubt that they acted in Guernica, as they had done in Mundaca."[229] A part of this testimony, but not all, was published in del Burgo's book, *Conspiración y guerra civil*, in July 1970. The book had been given to the printer twenty-seven months before, in March 1968.[230]

La Cierva advanced his views on Guernica again, in April 1970, in reply to a letter to the editor of *Historia y Vida*. He was again forced to retract a position taken a few weeks earlier. He now stated that the number of dead in the raid, "which had been greatly exaggerated," was around a hundred—that is, nine to ten times the figure he had announced in January. "The essential and determining cause of the destruction was the bombing of the Condor Legion, undertaken in a tactical operation," he again said. "Pilots and planes were exclusively German." Paying no heed to del Burgo's suggestions, he still another time declared that Guernica was "a clear military objective (essential communications for the retreat of the Basque army, two important arms factories)." He also repeated:

> In view of the documentation which I possess, I believe probable the negative and positive participation, in part of the destruction, of the special commandos for urban demolition and communications, which, beyond any doubt, existed in the Basque Army Corps commanded at that time by President don Antonio de Aguirre y Lecube himself.

He also insisted again that the lack of damage to either the Casa de Juntas or the sacred oaks was proof that the raid was not a symbolic attack on the traditions of the Basque country. Significantly, he returned to the *Guernica* of Picasso:

> The desires of the Spanish government to recuperate the painting *Guernica* of don Pablo Picasso show that in Spain a partisan political value is no longer attributed to this masterpiece.

And once again La Cierva announced the forthcoming publication of Talon's work, "a book of which I know certain elements and which, to my way of thinking, can be the definitive work on the subject."[231]

Ricardo de la Cierva profited from the fact that Víctor de Frutos was an Argentine to bring up the new version of Guernica in the second edition of his book *Leyenda y tragedia de las brigadas internacionales*, which was published in the spring of 1970. La Cierva thought Fruto's "essential testimony" opportune,

> . . .precisely because in these months we find ourselves on the eve of new and certainly definitive clarifications on another of the themes of the Spanish war most martyrized by propaganda: Guernica.

He again announced the book of the "young and brilliant journalist" Vicente Talón, in which "all the available sources are investigated, without respecting the mythologies of any kind." Guernica was also, he wrote, to be studied in a forthcoming monograph by Martínez Bande. But he wanted to underline the testimony of Víctor de Frutos,

> . . . which indirectly, yes, but with enormous efficacy, illuminates one of the aspects of the Guernica problem most unanimously denied by the propaganda of one of the tendencies: the possibility that, at least in part, and in collaboration with the bombing of the Condor Legion (another fact which cannot be denied today), Guernica was destroyed by special squadrons of the Army in retreat. This could have happened in Guernica, because as Víctor de Frutos is going to tell us, it was he himself who prevented these special squadrons from burning down, not Guernica, but the old town of Bilbao itself.

He then quoted from what he called the "sensational revelation" of Víctor de Frutos, of the plans to burn down the old town of Bilbao, plans that were not carried out. He concluded:

> In the light of this irrefutable testimony, the controversy over Guernica loses much of its importance. Víctor de Frutos is not a correspondent; he is not the author of a *novela-reportaje;* he is the chief of a fighting unit, who commands the sector, who reveals that fire was included in the habitual plans of the retreat in the North. In Guernica there were no women in the windows [this fact dissuaded the potential incendiaries of Bilbao from carrying out their mission] ; everybody was in the refuges, because of the aerial alarm given just before. Let the controversy on Guernica continue, although the work of Talón is about to dissolve it for all time; what is already history is that, by virtue of the most authorized and direct of witnesses, who is writing completely faithful to the cause for which he fought, it is already proved that there was a direct order so that, in case of the retreat of the Republican troops, the old town of Bilbao should be burned down. It is not necessary to weigh further the consequences which this revelation and this new focus can have on the history of the war in the North.[232]

The irrelevancy of Frutos's testimony about Bilbao, in a discussion of Guernica, has been argued in the analysis of Gil Mugarza's book. Those lines apply equally to La Cierva's evidence. Like Gil Mugarza, he fails to give Víctor de Frutos's reason for setting fire to the old part of Bilbao: "to delay the passage of the forces and the tanks of the enemy."[233] However, La Cierva does state that the plan of arson was to be applied "in case of retreat of the Republican troops." This removes from his "sensational revelation" all resemblance to the case of Guernica, where the Republican troops had not yet fallen back when the town was burned. The reference to Frutos's book was hardly "sensational," and it certainly was not a "revelation," for Gil Mugarza had used it two years previously.

To the five La Cierva versions of the Guernica incident, which we have now analyzed, must be added at least four others. According to Talón, La Cierva dealt with the subject of Guernica "in one of the documental chapters of his doctoral thesis, *Información, propaganda y poder,* presented at the University of Madrid in the Spring of 1970."[234] All efforts to consult this work have been fruitless.[235] A seventh version of Guernica by La Cierva appeared late in 1970, as a chapter of his two-volume work, *Historia ilustrada de la guerra civil española.* This included the promised documentation, hinted at throughout the spring of 1970. In the meantime, Talón's book had appeared around the middle of 1970. La Cierva's eighth account of Guernica was a criticism of Talón's book. Still another exposé on Guernica by La Cierva was published in *La Actualidad Española,* on May 18, 1972. And finally, in the twenty-sixth chapter of another weekly series, *Francisco Franco; Un siglo de España,* in 1973. These works will be studied in the chronological order of their composition (not of their publication). Since La Cierva's chapter in his *Historia ilustrada* was written before Talón's publication,[236] and since Talón's printing did not affect La Cierva's text, we shall first of all discuss La Cierva's different works, with the exception of his criticism of Talón, then take up Talon's book, and finally La Cierva's return to the matter in 1972, with two or three other commentaries on Guernica published in Spain and elsewhere since 1970.

Perhaps the lack of results from the Pérez Embid–La Cierva "Operation Guernica" had dampened the enthusiasm of the official historian. Nothing tangible had been gained by historical concessions to the Basques, not even Picasso's painting. At any rate, the élan and aggressiveness of the sole possessor of the Truth on Guernica seem to have escaped Ricardo de la Cierva in his seventh account of the tragedy, that found in the second volume of his *Historia ilustrada de la guerra civil española.*[237] This account began with a clear affirmation: "An incontrovertible fact: Guernica had been completely destroyed."[238] The questions were then: How was it done? Who had done it? Why was it done?

La Cierva analyzed the opposing arguments and reached this conclusion:

> It is very interesting to note that whereas propagandistic writers insist on one of the exclusory versions—incendiarism from the ground, or bombing—the witnesses who were inside Guernica and the military observers who entered shortly thereafter in the town still in flames, coincide in the thesis of the two more or less simultaneous causes.[239]

To understand this conclusion, we must evaluate the evidence and the arguments of La Cierva. His obvious purpose is to show that the propaganda of both sides was false, for both, he lamented, and had a hand in the destruction. Truth lay between the two. In the past La Cierva had attacked Bolín by heavy indirection; now he assaulted the man by name, and this was probably the first time that had been done in Spain. La Cierva denounced him for "the stupid and antihistoric posture of the National propaganda of that time." "The historian [La Cierva] does not understand," he went on, "how the services of Bolín could persist in applying the tactics of the ostrich to a fact for which hundreds of witnesses can be found." On the other hand, he decided, "The Republican posture is not more solid with regard to argumentation."[240]

In his indictment of Bolín and the Nationalist propaganda of 1937 and subsequent years, he cited from Bolín's memoirs[241] and from the Rebel handout that appeared in the Nationalist press of April 29.[242] His case against the Republicans was more detailed. He began with an undeveloped mention of Steer's dispatch and book, then he centered his evidence on the 1955 article of Indalecio Prieto, "the person who has best brought together the sources on which the position of Euzkadi is based." La Cierva presented Prieto's evidence as coming from Onaindia, on whom he made no comment; from "the declaration of Göring at the Nuremberg trial [*sic*]—which he called a 'vulgar invention,' " a judgment that history would in all probability not confirm.

In summing up Prieto's arguments, La Cierva wrote that all of the Socialist's exposition "is based on gratuitous, unfounded appreciations, for which he does not bring forth a single convincing proof."[243] This was a reference to Prieto's statement that Göring wanted to test the effects of a massive bombing on Madrid. Franco said no, and Guernica was chosen because of what the town meant, "historically and politically." Prieto had a primary interest in the war in the Basque country—his political power base was in Bilbao; he was also a newspaperman with a curiosity difficult to satisfy. It is significant, therefore, that whereas he had a clear idea of how Guernica was destroyed and who had destroyed it, he was reduced to undocumented theorizing as to why it was done. Only the Germans and the Spanish Nationalists really *knew* why the raid was carried out. All else was for the moment speculation. What is instructive here, however, is that Ricardo de la Cierva, with all the Spanish archives open to his wish, does not want to tell us any more about the motives of the bombing than did Indalecio Prieto, an exile in Mexico, fifteen years before.

Along with his presentation of the evidence brought forward in 1955 by Prieto, La Cierva underlined what he called the propaganda effort of the Bilbao government, signaling out for a preponderant place, "the famous letter of the mayor," which, he thought, "sounds too much of tearful propaganda composed in a sensationalist office and destined for exportation."[244] La Cierva makes a number of mistakes here. Labauria's letter, which La Cierva had first published in the *Crónica de la guerra española,* was not a cardinal piece of Republican propaganda,

nor was it the tearjerker that La Cierva pretends. He does not even identify the
letter correctly, although it was hardly a secret that it was addressed to Isabelle
Blume, a Belgian deputy, active in helping Basque refugees and who had obviously
asked for the letter, doubtless as propaganda for her refugees.[245] La Cierva also
found it sinister that the letter was dated "May 17, a suspicious two days before the
fall of Bilbao to the Nationals."[246] La Cierva is too suspicious. Bilbao fell not two
days after May 17, the date of the Labauria letter, but thirty-three-days later—to be
exact, on June 19. What is more useful in situating the place of Labauria's letter in
the propaganda structure of the Basques and the Republicans is the fact that it was
published in the chief organ of Basque propaganda in Paris only on June 10,
1937—that is twenty-four days after it was addressed to Isabelle Blume.[247]

La Cierva also included in his catalog of the Basque government propaganda the
May 11 letter signed by Basque priests, with the signature of Vicar-General
Galbarriatu in first place. He noted that it was probably signed by Galbarriatu
under pressure in Bilbao, and that later Galbarriatu recanted, probably under
Nationalist pressure. [248] The more vital question is: Was the information contained
in the letter to the Vatican concerning the bombings in Guernica, Durango, and
other Basque towns true or false? It was true. Then, when did the vicar-general do
his duty? When he signed the letter? Or when he recanted? The historian of the
Franco regime would have better completed his story had he added that Galbarriatu, in his recantation, did not go so far as to deny the bombing of Guernica, and
that even recanting, he was unable to escape confinement in Santo Domingo de la
Calzada, where he died a few months later.[249]

La Cierva gave a longer treatment to the relation of Galland, "the first of
the partially serious testimonies," from which he deduced an "incontrovertible"
fact: "The German airforce had bombed Guernica." To answer the question:
Why was it done? La Cierva added up the military factors that justified the
bombing:

1. The bridge, "Vital for the retreat" of Republican forces;

2. "An important factory for light and heavy armament";

3. The fact that "the bombing took place three days before the occupation
   of the town, while the enemy was in full retreat"; and

4. The fact that the bombing was "on important objectives from the military
   point of view."

As a commentary on the four military justifications of the bombing given by La
Cierva, we can observe that:

1. The bridge was not touched;

2. The two (and not one, as La Cierva writes) armament factories were
   unharmed;

3. There were no retreating troops in Guernica on April 26; and

4. Since no participant in the bombing raid has come forward to say what the objectives were and since La Cierva produced no document to name these objectives, we can presume that he is, in reality, ignorant of their exact nature. Whatever the reason for bombing Guernica, if it were to destroy precise military objectives, it was a complete failure.[250]

La Cierva repeated his themes of the nonsymbolic intention of the German bombing and of the high quality of Picasso's *Guernica,* but the emphasis of his pages on Guernica in *Historia ilustrada* was on implicating the Basques in part for the destruction of the town. He curiously dropped completely his argument that few were killed in the disaster. He also gave comparatively little space to pleading the nonresponsibility of the Nationalists in the attack. But he did return to the question of Sperrle's departure being caused by Franco's displeasure about Guernica, first raised by Hills, and then developed by La Cierva himself. La Cierva now noted that Sperrle's command was taken over "by von Richthofen something more than a month after Guernica" and explained that "Sperrle was not pardoned for having bombed Guernica without Franco's consent."[251]

La Cierva is either himself very much mixed up, or he is deliberately trying to mix us up. In his letter to *El Pensamiento Navarro,* he declaimed, in writing of Sperrle's leaving Spain: "Verify the dates." *"Algo más de un mes"* must surely mean more than thirty days and fewer than sixty. So let us "verify the dates" of Sperrle's departure from Spain, and also the reasons for that departure.

In fact, Sperrle had enemies in Spain, and they can be classified as follows: first, the Spaniards, who resented his hypercritical attitude toward their conduct of the war; and, second, Ambassador Faupel, and doubtless Johannes Bernhardt, because of Sperrle's critical position toward the trading company, Hisma, which Bernhardt controlled. According to Merkes, Sperrle had been highly critical of the Spanish way of waging the war almost from the day of his arrival in Spain. "Sperrle was very dissatisfied with the military situation," Merkes writes. "He saw the faults of the Spaniards but was unable to correct them."[252] Major Arranz, Rebel Air Chief Kindelán's first general staff officer, went to see Faupel on June 23 to speak "frankly" about Sperrle.

> He told me that General Sander [Sperrle] frequently made very pessimistic statements concerning the progress of the war, and derogatory remarks concerning Spanish conditions without considering that Spanish officers who spoke German, or at least understood it, were frequently present. . . .

wrote the ambassador to Berlin in a confidential note, some two weeks after the visit. Nor was this all.

> Thus Sander had also expressed himself in a very derogatory manner about Hisma. He, Arranz, knew the importance of Hisma for German-Spanish economic relations very well; he knew that Hisma was not a profit-making

enterprise and that such attacks on Hisma were calculated to damage German-Spanish cooperation, especially in the economic field.[253]

Faupel was in Berlin on July 19, and told von Mackensen, state secretary in the Foreign Ministry, in detail of "the untenable situation which had arisen between him and General Sander [Sperrle]." This was not a new situation, for according to von Mackensen, Faupel said he had submitted the matter to the Führer "several months ago" without success.

> In the meantime the situation had become worse from week to week, although he, Faupel, had been keeping entirely out of military questions for about 2½ months, which until then he had not been able to do, considering the personality of General Franco and his habit of speaking with him about military questions too.[254]

Von Mackensen did not spell out the details of "the untenable situation," but they were given by Faupel in his message of July 7 to Berlin: "During the last six months I have had to observe again and again that General Sander has a definitely hostile attitude toward Hisma."[255]

Von Mackensen also noted on July 19 that the War Ministry was thinking of replacing Sperrle "mainly because of Admiral Canaris' report on his latest impressions in Spain."[256] Merkes thinks that this report was made as a result of Canaris's visit to Spain in April. Franco gave high praise to Sperrle, but, Merkes adds, Canaris knew the Spaniards and concluded that Sperrle "was not equal to the political importance of his mission."[257]

Hills, who had first brought up the subject, had sought by suggestion, for proof was lacking, to tie in Sperrle's departure with the Guernica incident. He suggested that Arranz came to Faupel with "gossip" about Sperrle and Hisma, intending to provoke trouble between the ambassador and the aviator. This may well be true, but Hills cannot justify telling of it in a note dealing with Guernica, and adding: "Sperrle and Faupel subsequently quarrelled." [258] This simply does not seem to be true, for the dissension between the two men was anterior, and not subsequent, to the bombing of Guernica.[259] Franco evidently did want to get rid of Sperrle, and of Faupel also, but for reasons unrelated to Guernica.

Shortly after Faupel's call on von Mackensen, a decision was taken in Berlin to bring both men back to Germany. Keitel called on von Mackensen on August 19, and, according to the diplomat, "assumed that the Führer and Chancellor had ordered the recall of Ambassador Faupel as well as of General Sperrle."[260] Faupel made his farewell visit to Franco on August 20; on August 27, Eberhard von Stohrer was named ambassador but took over his duties only on September 19.[261] Sperrle took a bit longer to leave Spain. He went home on leave during the summer, and it was undoubtedly this absence, during which he was replaced provisionally by Chief of Staff von Richthofen, that La Cierva tried to convince us that Sperrle had been sent home in disgrace by Franco in fury, "something more than a month after Guernica." In fact, von Richthofen did not become commander of the Condor

Legion until November 1, 1938.[262] Sperrle returned to Spain on August 11, 1937.[263] Shortly thereafter, during the fighting around Belchite, he had another disagreement with the Spanish command.[264] Merkes wrote:

> In order to avoid attention, Sperrle was to return [to Germany] only after the conclusion of the current operations. On October 4, Hitler signed the order for his replacement by General Volkmann. On October 21 Gijón fell and on October 31 Sperrle's command ended.[265]

"Verify the dates," Ricardo de la Cierva had imperiously written. The date of Sperrle's departure has been verified, and it was not "something more than a month after Guernica," but, to be precise, six months and four days after the event. On this matter, as on others, the representative of the Neo-Franquista school had offered no documentary support for his bold affirmations.

La Cierva rejected Galland's explanation that the bombing of Guernica was "a mistake" and considered this excuse as "totally artificial." He had another explanation. At the same time that he enumerated the military reasons given above for bombing the town, he insisted:

> They do not explain the evident contrast between the incomplete destruction of these objectives and the almost complete destruction of the small town, a fact which can also be proved in spite of the incredible negative of Galland.[266]

Before going into La Cierva's explanation of why the small town was completely destroyed, we shall take a paragraph to digress on "the incredible negative of Galland." La Cierva had quoted at length from Galland's account, including the phrase that Guernica "was not an open city, nor was it destroyed." As La Cierva observed, this was an "incredible negative." But Galland never wrote that phrase. He had written that Guernica was "neither an open city, nor a military objective, but an unfortunate mistake." The phrase cited by La Cierva was written by the Spanish translator, or perhaps by the censor, trying to show that even though Galland admitted the bombing, he did not admit the destruction by the bombing. It is "incredible" that La Cierva, in daily contact with the censorship, did not automatically consult Galland's original German text. Hundreds of books on the Spanish Civil War have been translated into Spanish and published in Spain, and almost without exception each one—even those most favorable to Franco—has had to suffer the whims of the censorship of the moment. What a heavy legacy for those Spaniards who want to write on the civil war and who have at their disposition only these falsified translations. And how just that La Cierva, functionary of the Ministry of the Censorship, should fall into the trap!

What was La Cierva's explanation for the "almost complete destruction of the small town"? A part of his explanation lay in his great discovery, the documentary proof of which he had talked and written for almost a year. It was

> an important report, *unpublished as of this date,* in which are included innumerable affidavits signed by people of Guernica and detailed plans, visual

inspections, and an impressive collection of photographs. The investigating group, presided over by the Highway Engineer Estanislao Herrán, performed with this Report an inappreciable service to History, although during all these years *it was not thought convenient to publish it. It lay stored away in one of the civil archives* of the Spanish administration, where it was found by the author of this book [Ricardo de la Cierva] . [Italics added.]

La Cierva published in his book

some of the documents and photographs gathered by the special commission. In view of the objectivity of these reports, in which the fact of the bombing was recognized, a thesis contrary to that sustained by the official propaganda, *it was decided that the report would not be published and for this reason it has not been known until today.* [Italics added.]

On the basis of this report, Ricardo de la Cierva concluded: "The destruction of the city should be attributed to the simultaneous action of the bombing and of the arson commandos of the Republican army in flight."[267]

The "document" produced by Ricardo de la Cierva is beyond any doubt a significant element for the dossier on the destruction of Guernica, but it can be interpreted in various ways. The Nationalist authorities in 1937 interpreted it as being incompatible with their propaganda and suppressed it in Spain, but the English supporters of this same propaganda thought it of aid and comfort to their cause and *published* it, in 1938, more than thirty years before Ricardo de la Cierva "discovered" it in a musty archive. For this "unpublished" paper is neither more nor less than the original of *Guernica: The Official Report,* published by Douglas Jerrold (Eyre & Spottiswoode) in London, with the foreword by Sir Arnold Wilson. This was certainly not done without the accord of the Nationalist authorities.

A great mystery surrounds the methods of work of the official civil war historian in Franco Spain. In 1966, Ricardo de la Cierva was chief editor of the serial publication *Crónica de la guerra española.* The number of this series, dealing with Guernica, contained a special bibliography of five titles. One of these five was *Guernica: The Official Report.*[268] According to a bibliography edited by a team headed by Ricardo de la Cierva, in 1968, a copy of the London edition of this report is in the library of the service directed by La Cierva.[269] *Guernica: The Official Report* is mentioned, or alluded to, by many writers on the Spanish Civil War. The duchess of Atholl in 1938 devoted five pages of her book to a competent dissection of the Insurgent-sponsored report.[270] La Cierva criticized the duchess's book with disdainful phrases; hence, we must presume that he read it.[271] Did the references to the report mean nothing to him? Luis Bolín made references to the contents of the report, made by "Two magistrates and two qualified engineers, after hearing the depositions of twenty-five witnesses."[272] Did not La Cierva read this book? Why did he, in preparing his campaign on Guernica, not have the curiosity to open the book in his library entitled: *Guernica: The Official Report?*

In an earlier chapter of this book, a detailed analysis of the contents of *Guernica: The Official Report* has been given. It is not at all what La Cierva said it was, an honest report suppressed in Spain because it denied the official arguments. The "Report of the Commission" and the "Report of Investigation" are dishonest reports, twisting and perverting the honest part of the book, the "sworn declarations" of the witnesses. It is probably because these two "reports" cannot be reconciled with the sworn statements that no part of the investigation was ever published in Spain. It is true that when the report was finished in September 1937 (and not as La Cierva said, in *Arriba,* two weeks after the bombing), the Nationalist government had already admitted *a* bombing, but this admission was published outside Spain.

The two "reports" beginning the book could have been published in Spain, but the affidavits accompanying them could have been published only with a great deal of editing. La Cierva saw this difficulty with his "document"; he made a highly personal résumé of the conclusions of the commission, and then published extracts from but one of the "sworn declarations." This affidavit spoke of the suspicious breaking out of new fires after April 26, a fact that might have puzzled some of La Cierva's readers, because he does not explain to them how unfired incendiary bombs were triggered by falling masonry and other movements. This affidavit is one of the few that do not mention incendiary bombs, and the gravest fault committed by La Cierva at this point is that he studiously avoids mentioning the incendiary bombs, the element in the bombing raid which explained the destruction of the town.

In addition to the Herrán report *(Guernica: The Official Report)*, La Cierva advanced, in support of his positions on Guernica, a word-for-word reproduction of his already stated commentaries on the book of Víctor de Frutos.[273]

La Cierva's reasoning here seems to be that since elements in the Basque army seriously considered setting fire to a part of Bilbao, on the moment of evacuation, but did not do so, it is certain that they did set fire to Guernica, three days before evacuation. La Cierva adopted the thesis advanced by the commissioners in *Guernica: The Official Report,* that the town was set on fire by Basque elements during the air raid, while everybody except the incendiaries was in the shelters. There is nothing in *Guernica: The Official Report,* except in the undocumented conclusions of the commissioners, to support such a position. And this position is demolished by the affidavits of the witnesses, which La Cierva has surely read but which he does not fully reveal to his readers.

The Spanish reader who had followed the various interpretations of the evidence concerning Guernica advanced by Ricardo de la Cierva in 1970 was doubtless disappointed at the end. Little or nothing had been changed in the official account of Guernica as given in 1937. True, now one said that the Germans had bombed Guernica, but La Cierva was not the first to say so in Nationalist Spain. He had begun insisting that not a dozen were killed in Guernica, then backtracked, and at the end was forced to let the matter drop. He had insisted on the complete nonparticipation of the Spanish Nationalist command, Franco, Mola, and on down, in the foreknowledge of the raid, but in his final analysis he proferred no proof. His contribution to the historical knowledge concerning Guernica, was the Herrán report—published thirty-two years before in England, and hardly in the realm of "classified documents." He did not publish this "document" so that the Spanish people might judge it for themselves. Instead he made a false resume of a few paragraphs, and in his references to the report, noted that it was "in the archives of the author,"[274] a curious repository for the property of the state.

From 1937 to 1967, the Spanish regime, at least in any even semiauthorized statement, defended the thesis that Guernica had been destroyed in large part, if not entirely, by arsonists working from the ground—that is, by Basques and Republicans—and that little damage had been done from the air. The decision was taken to adopt a more credible explanation. The functionary entrusted with writing this new version was Ricardo de la Cierva. Being a paid employee of the government, he could not have been engaged in such work without official authorization or—more—official instructions to do so. In such a situation, what would he naturally have done? He would have gone to the Spanish archives and found the relevant papers and published them. Or he would have consulted the remaining military leaders of the time of war, beginning with Franco, and heard their stories. It is instructive that this was not done.

La Cierva has in recent years vaunted the research facilities of the Spanish archives for Spanish Civil War studies. In a journalistic survey of Spanish Civil War historiography, he denigrated the work of Hugh Thomas, giving as its chief defect, "that it is a book based on books. It does not go back to the primary sources. It does not deal with documents and knows nothing about the press." La Cierva went on to say that in his section of the Ministry of Information there was "the most complete library in the world on the civil war," and boasted that whereas he did not have all the documents in existence on the Spanish Civil War, "I believe that we do have them located and we know where they are."[275]

Let us look at the problem from another angle. The Technical Junta of the Spanish Nationalists in April-May 1937 was not a primitive, tribal establishment. Franco's headquarters was an organized affair. Records were kept, papers were written, documents were preserved. It is therefore impossible to believe that, from the morning of April 27 on, when the first news, not necessarily about the bombing, but perhaps about the reactions to the bombing, came into Nationalist headquarters, and for days and weeks following, there was no recorded references to Guernica somewhere in a dossier. Can we really believe that there was absolutely no written communication between the Franco Spaniards and Sperrle, between the Franco Spaniards and Faupel, between Salamanca and Berlin, relative to Guernica? Such a premise must be dismissed. On the other hand, there is every reason to think that somewhere in the Spanish archives the facts about Guernica could have been found. If such papers were not available to every curious eye, they were certainly at the disposition of La Cierva, a functionary entrusted with the elaboration of a government policy.

Leaving to one side the first tentative of La Cierva, the *Crónica* publication, we have seen during 1970 at least four articles or interviews giving his opinions on Guernica. What do we find there? An almost total lack of documentation. He confines himself almost exclusively to guesses and suppositions. His first exposition (*Arriba*) is based on a far-out extravagance, unsupported by a single one of his widely publicized documents, and he is forced to retract it within a few days. He did bring forward references to "documents on the organization of commandos for the destruction of towns and cities, belonging to the Basque Separatist army," but he never showed any relationship between these in fact never-revealed documents and the destruction of Guernica. It was here also that for the first time he disclosed that he held a significant "report" on Guernica, done two weeks after the incident, which had never been published, but he gave no details.

In his second effort (*El Pensamiento Navarro*), he alleged: "There exist specific documents which refer to the action of these special groups in Guernica itself." He again referred to the "documentation on the exact position of the bombs dropped," and expressed the hope to "find new documentation and new aids." In his third analysis (*Historia y Vida*), he again referred to the "direct and indirect documentation" which made probable "the negative and positive participation" of the Basques in the destruction.

It is only in the second volume of his *Historia ilustrada*, however, that he reveals his great discovery, his "documentary" evidence. And what is it? It is a document, and an authentic one, but it had also been published as a book in England in 1938. His other principal "evidence" comes from the book of Victor de Frutos, and has no relationship with Guernica, except in the frustrated thinking of the man who had a few months earlier destroyed Guernica in a bombing carried out by "special groups" come expressly from Germany for the purpose. Is it not the height of irony that, after making so frequently his spurious distinction between "his" documents in the Spanish archives (the primary sources) and the books (secondary sources) of the "others," he is himself reduced to published sources?

The documentation of secondary sources offered by La Cierva, however, touched on but a part of the Neo-Franquista version of Guernica: How was the town destroyed? By whom? In the details as he revealed them, there was nothing concerning either the number of the victims or the responsibility of the Nationalists. For either of these points, essential to his main thesis, he advanced not one iota of documentation. That the Spanish archives might be skimpy in material about the number of the dead and dying is understandable. The Spanish Nationalists never tried to find out the facts. But it is not possible that these archives contained nothing about the responsibilities of Franco, Mola, and the Spanish Nationalists in general about what had happened in Guernica. If La Cierva did not publish them, it is not because they did not exist but because they did not coordinate with the thesis he was instructed to defend.

Therefore we can summarize the results of the 1969-1970 Pérez Embid-La Cierva campaign to soften up the Basques as follows: Failure to obtain Picasso's painting. Success in proving that the Germans had bombed Guernica. Failure to prove any participation of the Basque "destruction commandos" or other Republican groups in the destruction of the town. Failure to prove the limited number of the victims, which he had first circumscribed to a dozen, then to a hundred, and which in his final paper La Cierva had dropped altogether. Above all, the failure to exculpate Franco, Mola, and the Nationalist authorities from any part in the disaster. On this vital point, he offers not a smidgin of proof but his bare affirmation, and this, as we have seen all too frequently on the preceding pages, is a highly variable measure and one that we can hardly take seriously.

There is another ironic facet to La Cierva's analyses: his bitter assault on Luis Bolín. Bolín was certainly panicky in reacting as he did to the first news from Guernica, but that reaction must be studied in the context of the historical moment and Bolín's person. La Cierva makes no effort to do this. It is, however, the key to the Guernica "controversy," as opposed to the Guernica "incident," and will be discussed below. Unfortunately for Bolín, the situation demanding—as he thought—the first lie, was to continue until his own death. Or perhaps at the end he really believed it. But if in 1970 the Franco regime, after thirty-three years of lying about Guernica, wanted to modify the position taken by Bolín in 1937, the one thing to avoid was to present another unconvincing version, another set of obvious lies. Yet La Cierva, in the course of a year and a great number of moves forward and jumps back, presented a series of unfortunate, inconsistent, temporary expedients. He produced many explanations; he never produced *the* explanation. This is the fact that makes the posture of Ricardo de la Cierva so difficult to understand: thirty-three years after Bolín, he gave a performance that, in view of the changed circumstances, was far more mediocre than that of his predecessor.

In the meantime, another event had taken place which rendered obsolete the efforts of La Cierva to explain the tragedy of Guernica. This was the publication of Talón's *Arde Guernica,* so frequently and favorably announced by Ricardo de la Cierva himself. It was published around the middle of 1970,[276] several months before La Cierva's *Historia ilustrada,* but this latter work, a luxuriously illustrated two-volume work, was doubtless already written, perhaps on the printing presses, before Talón's book was placed on sale. We can consider, then, that Talón's publication had no effect whatsoever on any of La Cierva's texts on Guernica published in 1970 (except for his review of Talón's book). We can even wonder why La Cierva apparently did not see all of Talón's manuscript before completing his own chapter on Guernica.

Ricardo de la Cierva, in one of his preceding articles, stated:

History must be written scientifically; it must be history and not a *reportaje* more or less documented. This has been an error of the régime. The history of the civil war was entrusted to outstanding journalists who wrote journalism, but not history.[277]

This ponderous judgment by La Cierva, who repeatedly describes himself as a "historian," is ludicrous in the case of Guernica, for it is the journalist Talón whose work approximates the status of historical research, and La Cierva, the self-proclaimed "historian," who writes journalistic propaganda, or *"reportajes* more or less documented."

Talón's basic purpose is to prove that Guernica was destroyed in a bombing raid on April 26, 1937, that the aircraft employed were German, manned by German pilots of the Condor Legion, and that no other agency—Asturian dynamiters or Basque demolition squads—was involved. He succeeds in this effort, and in such a way that his book falls outside the guidelines set up by the Neo-Franquista school. His book is in fact a rebuttal of the chief argument advanced by La Cierva in his final 1970 exposition on the problem of Guernica. When Talón refused to accept the participation of the Basque "demolition squads"—a theory based on La Cierva's "discovery" of the Herrán report—he demolished the thesis of the historian. Talón considered the Herrán report "highly dubious,"[278] a report that "offers not the slightest guarantee."[279] He called it "a succession of commonplaces of strong propagandistic motivation, which do not correspond to the facts." Talón also gave the evident reason why the report was not published in Spain in 1937:

> ... at the end of the original text quoted there is a long series of sworn statements which clarify much better what had happened and which go so far as to contradict what is expressed in the report itself.[280]

Talón gave other reasons for rejecting the arguments of the Herrán Commission:

> (1) Because after the raid and because of its destructive dimensions, there remained very little to destroy. (2) Because it is inconceivable that anyone should blow up and set on fire those parts of the town without military interest, while abandoning without the slightest damage the arms factories, the barracks and the Rentería bridge.[281]

He applied the same logic to an examination of the story published in *Unidad,* a Falangist newspaper—the same story as one of Massot's articles—in which the destruction of Guernica was said to have been carried out by militiamen who doused the buildings with gasoline and then flew over them and dropped incendiary bombs from a single airplane. It was, wrote Talón, easier to accept such a story than to explain how

> dynamiters, who destroyed entire blocks of houses which were to be of no use to the enemy, left to that enemy, intact, factories and barracks, as well as the strategic and vital bridge of Rentería.[282]

The refusal of the journalist Talón to accept the evidence sponsored by the historian La Cierva is all the more commendable in that Talón was warned of possible dangers in not being reasonable on this point. "Don't be too clear," he was told. "Leave things half-way. Say that Guernica was destroyed, half by the aviators, half by the dynamiters. In this way you will bother fewer people." The journalist added: "This piece of advice is among those I threw into the wastepaper basket."[283]

Another aspect of the Neo-Franquista argument—that of the excessively low number of victims in the Guernica disaster—was refuted by Talón, who arrived at the figure of around two hundred[284] —that is, eighteen times the first number advanced by Ricardo de la Cierva in January 1970. The figure given by Talón is the same as that he stated two years earlier in the Gil Mugarza book; the text is almost word for word. It was doubtless Talón's figure of around two hundred that persuaded La Cierva to abandon the subject of the Guernica dead completely in his *Historia ilustrada*, but it does not explain why the historian used the figure of less than a dozen in January 1970, when Talón had already published his higher figure in 1968. The question of the dead and dying in Guernica will be discussed in a later chapter.

Talón's book is uneven in documentation and in argumentation. Having effectively shown that Guernica was destroyed by explosive and incendiary bombs dropped from aircraft of the Condor Legion, that there was no serious evidence to indicate the participation of any other agency in the disaster, that Ricardo de la Cierva's "discovery," the Herrán Report, was erroneously interpreted by its discoverer, that the number of victims was far higher than the Neo-Franquista school wanted to admit, Talón then lets the quality of his research and his analysis decline. This is, above all, to be remarked in his discussion of the role of the Spanish Nationalists in the destruction of the town. (Were these conscious concessions? They may well have been. Certainly, had he taken a contrary position, or merely balanced the evidence available, his work would never have been published in Spain in 1970.)

Talón began working on his project in 1961, but as a working journalist—often outside Spain—he was obliged to use his odd moments to finish his manuscript. For several years, in his leisure time, he talked with the people of Guernica.[285] The fact that his wife was Basque undoubtedly facilitated his task.[286] He thus became quickly impressed with the fact that almost all that had been printed in Spain about Guernica was false. His persistance on a project that he must often have thought impossible to realize, unless he expatriated himself, is commendable. The publication of his work was impossible during the lifetime of Luis Bolín (unless the regime changed), and in view of the normal motions of the Spanish censorship, it is probable that unless the mechanism had been unloosened by the propaganda campaign in 1969 centered on the deposit of Picasso's painting in Spain, Talón's book would not have been published in Spain when it was.

Unlike the work of La Cierva, Talón's book takes into dominant consideration the action of the incendiary bombs on the town. Guernica was an ideal site for a town burning, he writes. "Narrow streets, which being oriented in the same direction as the wind, were veritable chimneys." Although the principal water deposit was untouched by the bombs, the distribution system was blown to pieces. He also tells what happened concerning the firemen. The city architect, after the end of the bombing, drove to Múgica, from where he telephoned to Bilbao for firemen. These came two hours later. They fought against impossible odds. At three in the morning, worn out and knowing their efforts useless, fearing capture by the Nationalists advancing on a broken front, the firemen returned to Bilbao. Talón explained again the phenomenon that seemingly had mystified the authors of *Guernica: The Official Report,* and also La Cierva, the recurring fires and explosions. "Such explosions," he wrote,

> came from the triggering of the incendiary bombs dropped during the aerial attack and which, in a high proportion, did not go off at the time, but exploded much later, from sympathy with the fires.[287]

The weakest part of Talón's work is that in which he sought to explain the actions of the Salamanca authorities, and to exculpate the Nationalist military from all responsibility for the tragedy. According to his account, the "National Government" learned of the bombing of Guernica through a telegram from the Reuters Agency. This is an important fact for our dossier, but unfortunately no source is given for the statement. Nor does Talón say how the telegram was received, or the day of reception (certainly April 27), or the hour of the day. We have already written that it was probable that Salamanca had a service for intercepting Reuters and other radio-telegraphic services, and that therefore the telegram was received around noon. (It was to be printed in the London afternoon newspapers.)

Talón then wrote:

> Hardly had the Reuter's telegram been received, when the Salamanca government requested clarification from the Condor command, for already corroborating information began to arrive through various channels. But the Germans said they knew nothing about the affair, "and as proof" of it offered the communiques on the activity corresponding to "the last few days," and in which no bombing of that nature was mentioned.

Which Condor Legion communiques were these? Talón mentions and quotes in full two, one of April 26 and one of April 27, the latter of which is described as "the first divulged by the Germans because they believed—or said they believed—that the accusations concerning the bombing referred to that day."[288]

There was, moreover, in the communiqué of April 26 a curious sentence that might have aroused the curiosity of the Salamanca military. Elsewhere, Talón points this out.[289] The sentence is:

All the air forces of the Condor Legion carried out various attacks against the enemy, who was retiring along the highways north of Mount Oiz, and on the bridges and roads west [*sic*] of Guernica.[290]

"All the air forces" of the Germans meant a great deal of air activity in the region of Guernica on April 26. Another disturbing detail, unmentioned by Talón: The daily reports of the Condor Legion were automatically sent to General Kindelán, at the Jefature del Aire.[291] Why all this comedy of *asking* the Germans for the reports?

Trusting in the German reports, Radio Salamanca then proceeded to broadcast the harangue entitled: "Lies, Lies, Lies." This long diatribe ended: "Our airforce, because of the bad weather, could not fly today and consequently could hardly have bombed Guernica."[292] We must repeat here: It is not conceivable that the Salamanca press people, receiving the Reuters telegram on April 27, should have imagined that it referred to that very day. There is no evidence whatsoever to show that the Salamanca press office made at this point but a simple human mistake. There was at least one brazen lie in the April 27 statement, appropriately called, "Lies, Lies, Lies." This was the final sentence claiming that the bad weather had kept the planes from flying. The German communique, if it guided the Spanish propaganda office, as Talon suggests, told them of at least three sorties that day. It is therefore impossible to accept Talón's position that "at the beginning of the affair the National Command believed that it was during the day [April 27] that the supposed bombing took place."[293]

Talón also sought to exculpate Franco and Mola from any responsibility for the attack on Guernica. This is done, not with documents but with anecdotes. Concerning Franco and Guernica, Talón repeats Hills's version, based on anonymous sources, which he did not seek to verify,[294] and then he gives another hearsay incident in which Franco exclaimed at a hunting party: "Guernica! Even now I cannot explain how that could have happened."[295] For Mola's innocence, Talón quoted Del Burgo, and then related still another anecdote, as follows: On April 29, a surgeon escaped from Guernica presented himself to Mola, who inquired concerning the destruction of the town. When the doctor replied, "Well, you know, general, the airplanes," Mola was furious and cried: "A lie! We have aerial photographs which show that it was burned down." The man from Guernica was jailed.[296] Talón accepted this story. But a few pages before, he had quoted from a Nationalist communiqué of April 28, which read in part:

> An airplane . . . in spite of the bad weather was able to reach Guernica, verifying the destruction of the town by the fires set before the abandonment of the town and obtaining photographs which were handed in to the General Staff at fifteen hours thirty.

These were certainly the photographs of which Mola spoke. Concerning them, Talón commented, "A pilot, flying a simple reconnaissance mission over Guernica in bad weather, could hardly verify that the town had been destroyed by those who occupied it."297 If this argument is accepted, and it seems valid, then it must be applied to Mola himself, and his performance before the Guernica surgeon becomes pure comedy. Moreover, the anecdote demands not only that we believe that Mola was in the dark as to what had actually taken place in Guernica at the time of the raid but that he was still in blissful ignorance on April 29. But Hills told us that, according to his unnamed eyewitnesses in Franco's headquarters, Franco, before April 29, was in possession of "more exact information" about Guernica. Did not Franco and Mola communicate about Guernica?

In any event, Mola used the photographs as if he thought they were gospel truth. This is seen in another document published by Talón, the letter that Cardinal Gomá sent to the Vatican concerning Guernica, which read as follows:

> Here the general [Franco? Mola?] defends himself against the imputation that the National army destroyed the town of Guernica. The authors of the systematic destruction are the Reds, instructed by the Russians, whose chiefs direct the defense of Bilbao. It is the *Russian system,* followed since Napoleon: leave but ruins to the enemy. Mola offers me photographs of Guernica which show that the town was destroyed by fire when the National army was still six kilometers away. They did the same in Eibar, where the Reds passed tarred cables from one house to the other to facilitate the burning.298

This missive, read carefully word for word, seems ambiguous, but this is probably the fault of the clerical prose, and we can conclude that Gomá wanted to inform the Vatican that the Reds had destroyed Guernica. This letter was dated May 8. If we admit (for this paragraph alone), in following Talón's recital, that Mola on April 29 really believed that Guernica had not been bombed, the same Talón tells us that very shortly thereafter he found out the truth. Then the general sent the photographs to Gomá under a false description, and by May 8 had made no effort to send a rectification. But did Gomá himself really believe such fabrications? Where was the clerical grapevine? Was the primate so far removed from the inner circles of the Nationalist military that he had no means of finding out the truth and on May 8 really thought Guernica had not been destroyed by bombing? It is difficult to believe. It should have been easier to fool the cardinal with the photographs than to fool the general. Insofar as is known, these photographs were never published, nor have they been studied since 1937. The basic fact is that everybody in the Neo-Franquista school who writes of the Nationalist reaction during the days following April 26 leaves the exact chronology blurred.

Nor were Franco and Mola the only Nationalist generals presented by the Neo-Franquista school as curious to find out what had really happened at Guernica. In still another piece of hearsay evidence, we are told that General Cabanellas came to Guernica on April 30 to inquire about the destruction. He had difficulty in drawing out information from the people he questioned, but was finally told, "We did it, general." Cabanellas then ordered that all the information known be gathered and sent to Burgos in a sealed envelope.299 This anecdote is intended to prove Nationalist lack of knowledge of the affair on April 30. What had aroused the suspicions of Cabanellas? What had provoked his visit? Such an anecdote might be proof of something if the contents of the envelope sent to Burgos were revealed.

Talón writes:

> Guernica was destroyed by German airplanes which received orders directly from Berlin and which on carrying out their aggression, gravely violated the sworn loyalty to the government of Salamanca.[300]

This may be so, but for the moment it is but an unverified supposition. Talón offers not a scrap of paper to prove it or even to suggest it. Nobody, neither La Cierva, Martínez Bande, Jesús Salas Larrazábal, nor any of the other lights of the Neo-Franquista school has produced any documentary evidence of Spanish Nationalist discontent with the Germans over the raid on Guernica.

There is indeed evidence to the contrary. It is documentary evidence. It was found by Vicente Talón in the Spanish archives and published in his book. It is the only known scrap of paper referring to the destruction of Guernica passed between the Spanish Nationalists and the German Nazis. It is an urgent, reserved, telegram sent to the head of the Condor Legion by the Third Section of the General Headquarters Staff at Salamanca, dated May 7, 1937. It reads as follows:

> I request Sander [General Sperrle] to inform Berlin that Guernica, a town of fewer than five thousand inhabitants, was six kilometers from the fighting line, is a highly important communications crossroad, has a factory for munitions, bombs and pistols; on the 26th it was a place for passage of units in flight and for the stationing of reserves. Front-line units requested directly to Aviation for the bombing of crossroads; this was carried out by the German and Italian [here Talon added a "sic"] airforce, and because of the lack of visibility, because of the smoke and clouds of dust, bombs from the planes hit the town.

> Therefore, it is not possible to agree to the investigation; the Reds took advantage of the bombing to set fire to the town. The investigation constitutes a manoeuver of propaganda and an attack on the prestige of National Spain and nations friendly to it. The Red airforce constantly bombs important capitals far from the front, such as Saragossa, Valladolid, Córdoba, Melilla and other cities, leaving more than 300 dead and 600 wounded.

> In no manner is it advisable to agree to [the investigation of] the matter of Guernica, which has no real importance. Civilians assassinated by the Reds with the blessing of their government number more than 300,000, all known by diplomatic representatives of England, France and Russia.[301]

Talón, who found this telegram in the Spanish Military Historical Service, thought the "investigation" mentioned was that of possible "journalists and technicians" who might visit the ruins and write of their findings. He interpreted it as a temporary position of the Nationalists to forbid such visits. However, the date indicates that the telegram in fact referred to the "international investigation," demanded by the Spanish Republican government of the British Foreign Office on

May 5, a fact known to the Germans and a suggestion for which had been made by Eden to von Ribbentrop in their May 5 interview. The German ambassador had informed Berlin at six o'clock on the afternoon of May 6.[302] The message quoted by Talón is possibly a reply demanded of the Spanish Nationalists by the panic-stricken Condor Legion, on learning, from Berlin, of the projected international investigation.

If the document is viewed in this light, it becomes a highly important piece in the Guernica dossier. It is undoubtedly authentic. It is therefore undeniable that in the only communication on Guernica between the Spanish Nationalists and the Germans of which we know today, there is not one single word of reproach against the Germans. Far from censuring the Condor Legion for having bombed the town, the Spanish command told Berlin that the raid was carried out at Spanish Nationalist request, justified the attack for military reasons, and excused the bombs that hit the town as being due to an accident combining bad visibility, smoke, and clouds of dust. As for the destruction of the town, Salamanca assured Berlin that it was due to the incendiary activities of the "Reds." Unless the Neo-Franquista historians can come up with a clear explanation of this telegram, all their theories about Franco's displeasure and Mola's rage with the Germans for the bombing of Guernica will have to remain where they have always been, in the undocumented realm of the anecdotist. The reader should note that the reference is to "rage" and "displeasure" over the incident, the bombing, and not to "rage" and "displeasure" over the controversy, the fallout of the bombing.

But the information sent by Salamanca via the Condor Legion to Berlin was false. Salamanca knew that it was false. The Condor Legion knew that it was false. Did Berlin know that it was false? Why send such information in an urgent, secret telegram? Why did the Salamanca air command connive with the Condor Legion to lie to Berlin? Somehow the statement of Salamanca bears the bizarre odor of a concocted message sent for the good of the cause. But it was in reply to a real situation, the threatened international investigation; it was not meant simply for the files. And if it were for the good of the cause, what was the cause? Were the Spanish Nationalists really covering up for the Condor Legion, before Berlin? Were the Spanish Air Command and the Condor Legion in league? For whom? Against whom?

At any rate, some people were deceived by the telegram or could later pretend to have been. For certain words and phrases in the Salamanca telegram have doubtless sounded to the reader as something already heard. The paragraph on Guernica published in *Die Kämpfe im Norden* and Galland's résumé of the same incident have too many similarities for us not to think that the historians of the Condor Legion and Galland were totally or in part inspired by the false information furnished to Berlin by the Spanish Nationalist Air Force.

Talón's major mistake was his failure to document convincingly his arguments concerning the true role of the Nationalist military in the destruction of Guernica. He also committed a series of minor mistakes in attributing censure and blame to

Aguirre and other Basque leaders, and to George Steer, for what were at most errors of judgment and possible oversights. He accused Aguirre of "Caeserism and phrase making" for beginning his statement on Guernica, "Before God and before History, which are to judge us, I affirm. . . ."[303] Talón at such moments loses all sense of proportion. It was the bombing of Guernica that was immoral and not the reaction of Aguirre. Talón criticized the May 11 letter addressed to the Vatican and signed in Bilbao by members of the Basque clergy, for the document's part in the "propagandistic battle." "This letter was not wholly exact," he wrote.[304] But in what way were the facts given about the bombings of Durango, Guernica, Arbacegui, and Guerricaiz in the letter inexact? Talón avoids telling us.

Talón indulges in unfounded accusations and snide remarks about George Steer, incomprehensible on the part of a man who himself knows the difficulties of a journalist. Steer writes too vividly; he has a "burning imagination."[305] Steer suggests that the Casa de Juntas was the only building left standing in Guernica on the night of April 26 when there were really others.[306] It is a cheap commentary for Talón to write that Steer's death in a road accident while serving with the British army in Burma was "a banal automobile accident."[307] Talón observed that Steer repeated in his book the same facts as in his dispatch on Guernica, facts that Talón considered to be in error: "the distance of Guernica from the front, the bucolic aspect of the town that April Monday, the priests consoling the multitude, etc."[308] Where the Spanish journalist goes too far out of bounds is in calling George Steer a liar. "The correspondent of *The Times* lied, in fact, on speaking of the raid," wrote Talón, "but said the truth about the fundamental things. That he should lie about this point was not surprising, for he was accustomed to doing so." Also: "Steer had as strong a taste for lying as for giving false ideas to the reader by means of negligently edited prose." This latter charge concerned Steer's statement that his friend Rezola had "disappeared" after the fall of Santander. This statement, said Talón, gave the impression that Rezola was "put up against the wall and shot, whereas in reality he died of illness in France."[309]

The word "liar" is one that should be used sparingly. Here Talón follows the great Franquista tradition. If one reads Franquista propaganda of the civil war years (and since),[310] the word turns up with surprising frequency, especially in the violent pamphleteering of priests and people who publicly wear a badge proclaiming themselves to be "Catholics." The Republicans were always charged with "lying." But if in the light of today's known facts, we look at what these abusive hands and voices themselves wrote and said, we find a great number of shall we call them misstatements? Misstatements, moreover, which they have never corrected, let it be said in passing. Talón could have read Steer's original English concerning Rezola, and quite frankly, he could with difficulty have concluded that Steer wrote that the Basque had been shot. Where Steer wrote: "And now he [Rezola] was seen no more; and the Basques, his people, were traded into captivity,"[311] the Spanish translator wrote: "*Ahora no se le volvería a ver mas. Y los vascos, su pueblo eran reducidos a prisión.*"[312] Talon should dig a bit deeper before calling "liar."

I am going to be more charitable with Talon than he was with Steer. Rezola was taken prisoner in Santoña, condemned to death, taken to the prison of Larriñaga, near Bilbao, then later to the penal of Burgos, with six hundred other Basques, all under the death penalty. After three years, his sentence was commuted, and after six years of imprisonment, he was liberated. He went to Madrid, where he was again arrested. Taken to San Sebastián, he escaped and reached France. He died in France on December 26, 1971.[313] Steer was right when he wrote in 1938 that Rezola "was seen no more." Talón was wrong when he wrote in 1970 that Rezola was dead, for he was at that time alive and well and in France. I do not say that Talón "has as strong a taste for lying as for giving false ideas to the reader by means of negligently edited prose," but I do say that he should dig a bit deeper before calling "liar."

Talón, referring to what he calls Steer's "political-historical-literary pirouettes," accepts uncritically the *Tablet's* harsh indictment of Steer for the revelations about his propaganda activities in Ethiopia in the book *Sealed and Delivered,* as repeated by Bolín.[314] It is not inappropriate here to recall Claud Cockburn's exposure of his own part in the preparation of a completely false news story about an anti-Franco uprising in Tetuán, during the Spanish Civil War. When Cockburn, unable to keep the secret, told about it later, he was prissily called to order by Richard Crossman, a Labour politician. "I was fascinated," wrote Cockburn,

> to find out that what fretted Mr. Crossman was not that the thing had been done, but that I seemed to be quite happy, retrospectively, to have had a hand in it.[315]

Cockburn was happy to have done it, but was also happy to tell about it, as was Steer. The cause of one or the other did not depend on the validity of that particular propaganda. The reverse would seem to be true of those on the Franco side in England, such as the editors of the *Tablet,* who wrote untruths about Guernica and have not yet informed their faithful readers of the misinformation they gave them during the war.

Talón admits that errors might slip into a journalist's daily copy, but

> in a book, the information is decanted. Everything has been measured, judged, screened. The author has, therefore, little margin for excuse. And Steer, in his book, reveals himself to us a passionate journalist, lacking in seriousness; one can conclude that his work, as a whole, is worth little.[316]

This statement about Steer is the height of absurdity. Steer's dispatch about Guernica is, if not the most significant newspaper report of the Spanish Civil War, easily one of the first five in significance. His book, *The Tree of Gernika,* is by far the best on the war in the Basque country. No book published in Nationalist Spain on the civil war can touch it with a five-foot innuendo. And if we were to judge Talón's book, by Talón's standards? When Talon tells his readers that the Herrán report was "kept secret until today,"[317] although he lists the 1938 published

English version in his bibliography,[318] there is no reason to call him a liar. He is simply mistaken, led astray by Ricardo de la Cierva and a lack of knowledge of the English language. When he asserts that the *Times* man on Franco's side on May 2, 1937 was Philby,[319] although in reality it was Holburn, Talon is not telling a lie. He is merely suffering from too much confidence in the writings of Luis Bolín. When Talon writes that "monsignor Mac Connel [sic], archbishop of New York," denounced the bombing of Guernica,[320] thus giving his readers a clear, though false, impression that at least one Catholic archbishop somewhere in the world took publicly such a position—What would the Catholic Church not give today if such an archbishop had then existed?—when in reality McConnell was neither "monsignor" nor "archbishop" but a bishop of the Methodist Episcopal Church, it is not necessary to shout that Talón is a liar. He is merely committing an error.

Once Talón had established his thesis that Guernica was bombed by the Germans, and that no other human agency was involved, that the death list was around two hundred, he let his work drift, with no sense of direction. The questions before the court are: How was Guernica destroyed? By whom? Why? Why did the controversy over Guernica develop as it did? Instead of digging in to find these answers, he calls Steer a liar. But if Talón wishes to play the amusing game of starting a list of people who lied about Guernica, he will not lack help. The first name on the list, hierarchically, is that of Francisco Franco y Bahamonde. If we accept, for this paragraph, Talón's facts about Franco and Guernica, El Caudillo knew the facts within two or three days of the bombing. But on numerous occasions after those dates, Franco, knowing the truth, lied to newspapermen and to the Spanish people about the incident, and not only during the war itself but as late as 1948. Was Cardinal Gomá lying when he wrote to the Vatican on May 8 about Guernica? If he was in ignorance at that date, and it is hardly probable, it cannot be admitted that he remained long in that state. Did he ever send a rectification to the Vatican? There is still another proved liar on Guernica: Luis Bolín, who invented the original lie on the subject. Bolín to the end of his days repeated the lies about Guernica. It is strange that Talón, in his fanatical passion to nail down the liars about Guernica, never came across the names of these three.

George Steer was a great newspaperman. True, he had attacks of enthusiasm and the disastrous vice of espousing lost causes—the Negus against the Fascists, and the Basques against the Franquistas. There were journalists who experienced sympathies as strong for the cause of Franco. Let Talón test Steer's work against theirs, against that of the Cardozos, the Bottos, the Héricourts, and the others. It is not always easy to judge a book like Talón's, published under the rules of a floating censorship. The judgment may be unfair and unjust. We know that Holburn, in his desire to get through the Nationalist censorship the news that Guernica had really been bombed, gave other details that he knew not to be always exact. But Holburn was writing in time of war, and Talón is writing a researched work of history, published in Spain, as they say, after thirty years of peace (and censorship). We can but conclude that after the manuscript had been currycombed by the Section of Bibliographical Orientation in the Ministry of Information, Talón accepted the result.

Talón's book received a strange welcome in a land unaccustomed to hearing a challenge to the Franco myths of the civil war. The publisher, apparently disinterested in selling the book, furnished no review copies to the press.[321] Ricardo de la Cierva reviewed it in *El Alcázar,* almost as soon as it was published. This review, although published before his *Historia ilustrada de la guerra civil española,* was evidently written after that book, and constitutes the eighth known version of Guernica by the offical historian of the regime. The review began by tying Talón's book to the Guernica propaganda campaign of Pérez Embid and Ricardo de la Cierva. The immediate and unfortunately negative results of Pérez Embid's declarations were of little significance for La Cierva.

> These declarations are a highly important step in the understanding preliminary to the definite reconciliation of the Spanish people on the subject of their recent and tragic history. When this perspective appears . . . the words of the Director of Fine Arts will acquire all their authentic dimension and will become in the memory of all the first of the final points of the Guernica story.

Pérez Embid, a caption under Picasso's painting (which illustrated the article) tells us, considered

> that "Guernica" (given by Picasso to the Spanish people) is part of the cultural patrimony of this people and should be on exhibition in Spain as proof of the definitive end of the contrasts and differences aroused by the last civil conflict.

The second of La Cierva's "final points" about Guernica concerns what happened at the Basque town.

> Guernica was destroyed on April 26, 1937 by various flights of the Condor Legion, which in agreement with general and specific German standards during three hours smashed the lovely symbolic city (the heart of the symbol, thanks be to God, remained untouched) with explosive and incendiary bombs.

But he added: "The supreme national command and the command of the Army of the North were not informed before the operation and manifested their indignation when they learned of the facts." At this moment La Cierva reneged on a point on which he had taken a firm position several times earlier in the year, concerning the "special commando squads" of the Basque army and their participation in the destruction of the town. "The soldiers of the defending army . . . although their intervention and their destructive proposals in other towns are documentally proved, did not intervene directly in Guernica." This statement is all the more surprising, for La Cierva's contrary stand was then at the printer's and would appear in a few months.

The third of La Cierva's "final points" concerns the "myth" of Guernica, the origins of which he attributes to the activities of Picasso, Onaindia, Steer, and Labauria. La Cierva considers that Talón makes plainly manifest their errors.[322]

La Cierva's criticism served as a guideline to the rest of the critics, who were surprisingly few. *Pueblo* reviewed the book by quoting extensively from La Cierva and then still more extensively from Talón.[323] *El Correo Español—El Pueblo Vasco,* of San Sebastián, solved the problem by reprinting La Cierva's article.[324] On August 30 the Madrid newspaper *Nuevo Diario* damned Talón's book with faint praise, concluding that its

> fundamental contribution lies—and I do not know to what extent it can be considered news—in establishing, once for all time, the certainty that Guernica was destroyed in an action carried out by German bombers. The thesis that the town was dynamited by its own inhabitants remains definitely eliminated in this book by an abundance of proofs.[325]

José Berruezo, writing in *Diario Vasco,* gave a Basque point of view, at the same time more generous to Talón, and historically more incisive.

> For those of us who lived through the civil war and especially for those of us who endured that war with our own flesh, for the people who suffered its consequences beyond the chronological limits of the drama, this book of Vicente Talón reveals nothing we did not know the day after the German bombs fell on Guernica. But if for those of us who knew the technique of war propaganda, genocide could not be masked behind official explanations nor behind orchestrated instructions which attributed to "Basque dynamiters" the destruction of the Biscay town, for the ordinary people whose good faith or whose passion was exploited in creating a certain state of public feeling, this book, which comes into their hands after thirty-three years, will be highly revealing.[326]

This forthright statement could hardly have pleased many people in Spain unprepared for the change in the propaganda line signified by Talón's book.

Spain's most influential newspaper, *ABC* of Madrid, waited until September 17 to write about the book. This review denounced Republican propaganda about Guernica, said that World War II bombings were worse than those at Guernica, and exculpated the Nationalist chiefs.

> Still less is the act attributable to any responsible Nationalists, who had no part whatsoever in the destruction . . . The testimony of Mola, Cabanellas and Juan Bautista Sánchez, all taken at first hand, leaves no doubt as to this.[327]

This testimony, as given in Talón's book, is, as already shown, not at all "first hand."

The propaganda campaign, "Operation Guernica," begun by Pérez Embid, and continued by Ricardo de la Cierva, can be considered to have come to an end with a dramatic scene in the *frontón* of San Sebastián on September 18, 1970. To understand this epilogue to "Operation Guernica," we have but to observe that the propaganda campaign of Pérez Embid and La Cierva was unaccompanied by any slowdown in the repression. Let us take a quick look at what had been happening in the Basque country during the first nine months of 1970. On January 24, 1970, in a military court of San Sebastián, a Basque was sentenced to six years for aiding a man sought by the police. The same court condemned two priests and another Basque to jail sentences for causing "public disorder."[328] The French press reported that in the last month of 1969 and the first month of 1970, the Madrid Tribunal of Public Order condemned ninety-five persons to prison; of these, twenty-four were Basques.[329] On the second day of February, six young Basques accused of belonging to ETA appeared before the Madrid Tribunal of Public Order. One of them, Francisco Javier Larena Martínez, was expelled from the courtroom when he refused to answer questions of a court, which, he said, "I consider incompetent, for it represents a State illegally constituted and against which I have always fought." Larena Martínez was already faced with a possible death sentence in the Burgos trials, which were being prepared.[330] On February 17, seventeen Basques were sentenced in Madrid to terms ranging from four months to twelve years in prison.[331] A number of arrests were made between April 2 and 4 of persons accused of distributing tracts for the day of the Basque Fatherland (Aberri-Eguna).[332] Twenty-two Basques were detained at Guernica on April 26, when several hundred people sought to mass in protest on the anniversary of the bombing.[333] Early in May, nine Basque Socialists were condemned by the Tribunal of Public Order to from one year and three months to four years and eight months, for allegedly trying to reorganize the Spanish Socialist party in the Basque country.[334] On May 12, two young Basques were sentenced to twelve years for "military rebellion," and another to five years, by the military court in Burgos.[335]

Nine more Basque priests were incarcerated in the Zamora prison on June 3. This brought to thirty the number of priests in that special cellblock.[336] The nine priests had been sentenced to imprisonment for reading and commenting on in their churches a document prepared by five other priests already in Zamora prison, charging police torture of Basque Nationalists. The five priests were those who had been arrested in the bishop's palace in Bilbao on June 3, 1969. The acting administrator of the diocese protested vigorously against the imprisonment of the nine priests, in a pastoral letter that claimed that their trial without the permission of their superiors was a violation of the Concordat, and which defended the acts of which the priests were accused.[337] According to the *Washington Post* correspondent, the declaration of the bishop was not printed in any Basque newspaper, because Franco's first assistant, Admiral Luis Carrero Blanco sent a written note to the press forbidding publication.[338] On June 24 eight of the nine priests were freed.[339] On July 7 the military court sitting at Burgos condemned two Basque country priests each to three years in prison. Two Basque students were given harsh terms, one thirty years, the other twenty years, for "terrorism and banditry."[340] A report prepared late in July 1970 by Spanish lawyers indicated that 187 Basque Nationalists were then in prison. Five were serving life sentences, after having been condemned to death and then reprieved. Ninety other Basques, including seven priests, were awaiting trial.[341]

In San Sebastián, on September 18, 1970, while General Franco was presiding over the world championship jai alai games, Eusebio Elosegi, a Basque Nationalist, jumped from the seven-meter-high walls of the *frontón,* his clothing in flames, crying *"Gora Euzkadi Askatasuna"* ("Long live free Euzkadi"). He fell in flames in front of General Franco. Elosegi was carried away badly burned, while Franco continued impassively to watch the game.[342]

Elosegi was a man marked by the fires that had ravaged Guernica thirty-three years earlier. He had been in command of the only military unit in the town on the afternoon of the air attack. It was Elosegi who fired the light machine gun, the only antiaircraft protection the town had, against the first of the German planes.[343] On May 14 Elosegi was in charge of the battery that shot down a German Heinkel fighter plane, piloted by Hans Joachim Wandel, in whose diary was found the word "Garnica." Elosegi saved Wandel from the fury of the Basque soldiers.[344] He was in Bilbao when the last Basque soldiers left to take the road to the west and the remaining prisoners, among them Wandel, were liberated.[345] Elosegi was taken prisoner, lodged in the Penal del Dueso, and when the officer preparing his trial learned that he had been in command of the troops in Guernica on April 26, he shouted:

> This is the man who destroyed Guernica, the sadistic officer who set fire to the sacred town of the Basques, the chief of the gang of dynamiters who sacked the town after destroying it, the man responsible for thousands of dead in an innocent and undefended town.[346]

The desperate gesture of Elosegi on September 18 was intended not to do physical harm to Franco but to bring before the eyes of the aging dictator the reality of the flames of Guernica. On August 28, before his immolation, Elosegi wrote: "I have already said that I do not intend to eliminate Franco. I want only for him to feel on his own flesh the fire that destroyed Guernica." Three days later, he wrote at the end of his diary:

> Forgive me; if I endeavor to light again the flame which destroyed Guernica, it is because Guernica represents for the Basques something more than a pile of stones. Its destruction signifies persecution and oppression. And the man who personalizes all this is there before my eyes.[347]

It is not too much to say that the flames from Elosegi's clothing also lighted the failure of the propaganda campaign to desymbolize the destruction of Guernica. A few days later, news of the imminent opening of the great trial in Burgos of sixteen miltant members of ETA, six of whom risked a death sentence, began to appear in the world press.[348]

The purpose of the 1969-1970 Guernica campaign, culminating with the publication of Talón's book, was to desymbolize Guernica, to end the controversy, at least within Spain itself. Was this end accomplished? The evidence shows that it was not. The admission in Spain itself that Guernica had been bombed by the German air force flying for the Nationalists was not sensational news to the Spanish people, according to at least two of the rare commentaries on *Arde Guernica* which appeared in Spain. The public confession of the bombing might well have been sensational news, but this was an aspect that few people in Spain itself cared to take up publicly. Nor was the fact of the bombing a novelty outside Spain; even in West Germany, the fact of the bombing had been acknowledged in scholarly circles before it was admitted in Spain. There was, nevertheless, reluctance to accept Talón's work as the final word, reluctance among pro-Spanish Nationalists inside Spain and outside Spain to abandon the 1937 (Bolín) version of the destruction as part of their cultural heritage; and reluctance by the Spanish Republican sympathizers to accept Talón's corollary thesis: the complete innocence of the Nationalist military, and the small number of victims.

We shall now look into the Guernica controversy subsequent to the Neo-Franquista campaign of 1969-1970. In Spain the work of Talón was at first unquestioned. An artillery colonel, José Manuel Martínez Bande, writing in 1971 of the war in the Basque country, continued unreservedly to follow Talón's arguments. Guernica was destroyed in a bombing carried out by the Condor Legion. The dead numbered around two hundred. The Spanish Nationalist authorities had no previous warning of the raid, and were lied to by the Germans. The Nationalist denial of responsibility for the raid was therefore justified.[349] In a footnote, Martínez Bande wrote, "For the study we are doing we consider the book of Vicente Talón, *Arde Guernica,* fundamental. From it we have taken most of the facts concerning the bombing of this locality [Guernica]."[350] Martínez Bande declared that the Rentería bridge near Guernica has been bombed by the Italians on March 31, but this was not confirmed by the reference he gives.[351] Surprisingly, he made no mention of the famous "unpublished documents" of Ricardo de la Cierva, nor did he speak of the May 7 telegram, from the Spanish command in Salamanca addressed to Sperrle, reproduced by Talón.

Another who wrote approvingly of Talón in 1971 was José Luis Vila-San-Juan, in a curious book entitled: *¿Asi fue? Enigmas de la guerra civil española.* Vila-San-Juan asked: "Who destroyed Guernica?" and after quoting Steer, Onaindia, Aguirre, and Labauria for the Basque side, and the Nationalist communiqué of April 29 for the other side, concluded that the town was a military objective, that it was bombed by the Germans without the foreknowledge of Franco, that it was not destroyed by dynamiting, and that it was set on fire by incendiary bombs.[352] On one of these points Vila-San-Juan took contradictory positions—Nationalist military foreknowledge of, and responsibility for, the air raid.

> It is known, positively, that Franco became extremely angry on learning of the operation [attack on Guernica] and its results. General Hugo Sperrle . . .

received a superlative Philippic.

But on another page of this book, we can read:

> It is possible that the German command had secret orders for a "total war try-out" of *planchado*. But it could hardly have been able *to organize* the operation (planning, observation studies, loading, control, initiation and results) without the go-ahead, or, at the least, the tolerance of the National command. The Vitoria airdrome was not a reserved ground of the Luftwaffe.[353]

When Vila-San-Juan states, "It is known, positively, that Franco became extremely angry on learning" about Guernica and its results, he is quite possibly relying on Hills's testimony, but neither Hills nor anyone else has proved this *positively*. Hills assigned to von Funck the unhappy role of the man lashed by Franco's tongue. Vila-San-Juan stated that it was Sperrle, and Sperrle would be the more logical object for Franco's ire, but Vila-San-Juan offered no more proof than did Hills. He quoted extensively and favorably from Talón and accepted without question Talón's figure of "some two hundred victims." [354] However, he did not mention, or draw any conclusions from, the May 7 telegram, cited by Talón. But this telegram, or Talón's interpretation of it, may well have inspired Vila-San-Juan's affirmation that, following its capture on April 29, Guernica "was completely closed, for almost two weeks, not only to foreign journalists, but to all except strictly official visitors."[355] This is of course completely false; probably more than twenty foreign journalists visited the town in the week following April 29. Vila-San-Juan also quoted with approbation from La Cierva.[356] He made no reference to the Herrán report, "discovered" by La Cierva, but in his own conclusions tacitly denied those of the Herrán report, sponsored by La Cierva.

The sharp turn on the question of Guernica taken in 1969-1970 by the Neo-Franquista historians was followed by other inexplicable changes of direction in 1972. On May 18, 1972, Martínez Bande, in Number 45 of a series on the Spanish Civil War, issued by the Madrid weekly *La Actualidad Española,* published an article in which the problem of Guernica was discussed, and also gave an interview on the subject. In that same magazine, Ricardo de la Cierva wrote about Guernica. Martínez Bande did not mention Talón or his book; La Cierva not only did not speak of Talón but he contradicted Talón's book by what he wrote. The accompanying bibliography, on "The Biscay Offensive and Guernica" and "The Capture of Bilbao," contained forty titles. [357] Talón's book was not among them. The Talón experience was momentarily over, insofar as the Neo-Franquistas were concerned, and it was an open secret in Madrid that the censorship had definitely refused the manuscript for a new and revised edition of *Arde Guernica.*

Martinez Bande's contribution to *La Actualidad Española* was a résumé of what he had written the year before in his book *Vizcaya,* but in his interview he showed a certain disposition toward recidivism in propaganda:

One cannot talk now about Asturian dynamiters although I believe that there probably were some in Guernica, although charged with other missions than that of completely destroying the city. Some blast holes must have been prepared, which added to the confusion . . . Yes, I believe that at least it is not nonsense to speak of dynamiters in Guernica, but, naturally, giving a distinct turn to the question. I have not been able to speak with anybody belonging to the sapper company which entered Guernica and who could perhaps clear up this question. . . . But, if the dynamiters did not destroy Guernica, they were certainly on the point of blowing up nothing less than "the seven streets" and the adjacent quarters of Bilbao.[358]

This is hardly a clarification of the problem of what actually did happen at Guernica. As to the quality of what Martínez Bande "believes," it is not improper to recall at this point that in 1965 he "believed" in the authenticity of the spurious "Communist documents"[359] touted by del Moral, Jerrold, Lunn, and other "believers" in the now discredited Nationalist versions of Guernica.

In 1970 Ricardo de la Cierva published a number of differing and contradictory versions of what had happened at Guernica. He also proclaimed to all who would listen that Talón's book on the subject would be the definitive work. It is a tribute to his imagination, if not to his scholarly rectitude, to note that in 1972 he published a still different account of Guernica and ignored completely the work of Talón. In the interview in *La Actualidad Española,* he said:

The Condor Legion bombed Guernica the second time. . . . Three hours before the German "raid" the Italians were on the scene. . . . It is evident that the first bombing was that of the Italians. The texts concerning this are clear: *L'Aviazione legionaria in Spagna* of Guido Marcoli [*sic*] ; the four volumes of General Francesco Belforte, et cetera.

These Italian texts, however, as has already been shown, make absolutely no reference to April 26. The real basis for La Cierva's new position appears to be a Nationalist war communiqué of April 26 which La Cierva asserts Ramón Salas Larrazábal has found in the Salamanca archives. This communiqué, according to La Cierva, states that three hours before the German raid—that is, around one-thirty in the afternoon—three Italian planes bombed the Rentería bridge, near Guernica. If this fact is true, it is indeed curious that none of the numerous witnesses in Guernica on April 26 spoke of it. La Cierva made no more definite reference to the document. If the document exists, it would place in doubt—from Nationalist sources—the pretended ignorance of Franco, Mola, and others on April 26 concerning the bombing. La Cierva seemed blithely unaware of this evident conclusion. "Neither Franco nor Mola had been informed," he declared once again. "Franco's reaction is clear. The great German general Sperrle was dismissed. Richthofen took his place." And once again, La Cierva offered no proof for his assertion nor for his next declaration: "Sperrle was an intimate friend of Göring and paid dearly for his exploit."[360]

In 1970 La Cierva prophesied that Talon's book would be one of the dozen works on the Spanish Civil War destined for immortality.[361] Yet Talón treated with utmost disdain La Cierva's great discovery, the Herrán report. Two years pass. The Perez Embid—La Cierva propaganda campaign on Guernica is over, an admitted failure. In 1972 La Cierva writes about Guernica as if Talón's book had never existed, affirming that the Herrán report was "a highly valuable work [which] has remained secret until now." La Cierva again demonstrated the peculiar ideas of the Neo-Franquistas about civil war propaganda:

> The Republican side immediately took advantage of the German raid on Guernica for its propaganda. Picasso painted his picture and thus began the Guernica case . . . Although Guernica received a hard bombing, other towns, such as Durango, suffered more from the war. In Durango, the bombing was more intense, but was not used for propaganda.[362]

Not only are La Cierva's ideas on propaganda completely cockeyed, but his chronology and his estimates on war damage are inexact. The controversy over Guernica was well under way in May, and Picasso's painting did not go on exhibition until June. Nor did Durango suffer more from the war than did Guernica.[363] Even if it had, it was bombed and shelled over a period of weeks, and its destruction did not strike the world's imagination as a terrible portent, as did Guernica, bombed and burned in one cruel attack. Durango was used in Republican propaganda,[364] but it was, understandably, overshadowed by the disaster at Guernica.

It is worth noticing that in 1972 La Cierva is more tender with Bolín than he was in 1970. Bolín's great mistake, wrote La Cierva, was his refusal to recognize his initial error, taken when both Franco and Mola did not know the facts. La Cierva is also capable of amusing us. He finds food for reflection in the "curious case" of having Steer at Guernica for the *Times* at the same moment that Philby, the Soviet spy, was representing the *Times* on the Rebel side.[365] The "curious" feature of the story is that La Cierva, with all the vaunted Spanish Nationalist archives at his disposal, does not know that Philby did not work for the *Times* in Spain until several weeks after the bombing of Guernica.

Among those unconvinced by the arguments of Talón and the Neo-Franquista historians was Joseba Elosegi, who had left behind him the day he climbed to the walls of the San Sebastián *frontón* a manuscript that was later published in France. The first pages of his book are in the form of a diary, beginning August 1, 1970, and ending on the last day of that month, eighteen days before Elosegi immolated himself in front of Franco. In the entry for August 5, he tells of reading Talón's work and, in a harsh judgment, puts his finger rightly on the weak part of the journalist's argument. He wrote that Talón's "lack of objectivity, of courage and of honesty lies precisely here: in seeking to absolve the *Franquista* leaders and Franco himself from blame." After dismissing the work of the "illustrious historian"

Ricardo do la Cierva, who "writes history for the mentally lazy" and for the "mentally backward," Elosegi explains why in his opinion Talón failed in his work:

> Well do I know that this gentleman can do no other than try to pass athwart the intricate and slippery field of censorship, but let him not presume either of valor or of honesty. I do not give him this first quality, because he who possesses it does not fear to say the truth when he wants to write history. And he is not honest, because he attempts to cover up for the guilty. I do not hold him for a fool and I am certain that he knows as well as I who are the promoters and accomplices of that barbarous act.[366]

In other details Elosegi's text implicitly contradicts that of Talón. He says that the weekly Monday fair did take place on the day of the bombing. After the bombing he saw the dead animals in the Plaza del Ferial.[367] Elosegi apparently does not accept Talón's figure of some two hundred dead, for in one place he speaks of "thousands of innocent victims," but this may be but a figure of speech.[368] The argument, advanced by La Cierva and others, that the town had been bombed in order to cut off the retreat of the Republican forces to the east is dismissed with the observation that "the later evacuation of troops and material from an important sector of the front was carried out through Guernica without great hindrance." [369] But Elosegi's book is more than the refutation of certain points of Talón's book. It also constitutes one of the best eyewitness accounts of the tragedy that we today possess.[370]

Elosegi did not die from wounds received as he fell in flames from the wall of the frontón. He spent 111 days in a hospital and then on February 17, 1972, he was tried before the Tribunal of Public Order in Madrid for illegal propaganda, for starting a fire, and for causing harm to others. He was condemned to seven years in prison and a fine.[371]

La Cierva, as the director of the historical conscience of the Franco regime, had sought to fabricate a new "definitive" version of the Guernica history, credible for the 1970s. But the affair was perhaps badly coordinated, and not everybody in positions of authority in Spain helped in the effort. (Even La Cierva himself had apparent second thoughts on the subject.) One result was that Talón's book, as noted above, received a minimum of critical appraisal in Spain. One could conjecture that the functionaries who finally permitted its publication had almost immediately regretted the rashness of their act. No translations of the book appeared. The fact that Talón's book was completely unknown outside Spain, in spite of its sensational contents, was made evident by the printing in New York in January 1973, in a national magazine, of an article embodying the arguments of Luis Bolín, thoroughly discredited in Spain itself. The article was written by a professor of English at Dartmouth College, D. Jeffrey Hart, a leading exponent of American right-wing thought; it was published in the *National Review,* the leading organ of ultra-conservative ideas in the United States.

Hart, in his article, entitled "The Great Guernica Fraud," repeats all the evidence and reasoning of Bolín, including the field dispatches that had impressed Professor

Stanley Payne and Brian Crozier.[372] Among the contributions of this professor of English to the Guernica controversy, the following should be noted:

Hart remarks that "the Left" says Guernica was bombed and that "the Nationalists" say it was deliberately destroyed by its defenders, and then asks, "How is the historian [Hart] to judge?" His answer: "Evidently, by the character of the damage." How does he go about discovering "the actual character of the damage"? By quoting Jerrold (unidentified), as quoted by Lunn (unidentified), as quoted by Bolín. Hart also proves that the bombing never took place by repeating the claim that the Nationalists simply did not have enough bombs to destroy Guernica. (Hart seems blissfully unaware of the incendiary bomb.) The professor of English thus proves again in 1973, by the technical arguments first advanced in 1937, that the bombing of Guernica never happened, and this despite a wealth of documentary evidence available to prove the contrary.[373]

Hart writes that Thomas's "evidence paragraph," which he describes as "very flimsy," will not stand up against the proofs advanced by Bolín. He considers the visit of the foreign correspondents to Guernica on the night of April 26-27, cited by Thomas, as highly suspect, and the bomb fragments they picked up, marked with German factory signs, as absolute proof of a propaganda plot. The May 11, 1937, letter to the Vatican, signed by a number of Basque priests, "including the Vicar General of the diocese," also smells of fabricated propaganda to Hart. His suspicions become certainties when he quotes Bolín to the effect that "the priest in question was *not* the Vicar General of Valladolid." Here Hart the "historian," following a tradition among pro-Nationalist writers, has mixed up his personages and his localities, confusing Galbarriatu, vicar-general of Vitoria, with Onaindia, canon of Valladolid.[374]

Hart asks: "Yet, if, as Bolín says, the German terror-bombing of Guernica is a myth, how is it that the myth prevailed over the truth?" In answering that question, fraught with ethical overtones, Hart is forced to this lamentation: "Invention is *free,* while history is limited by facts." Aguirre, he concludes, was probably incapable of concocting the "lie" about Guernica. Who did it? "We cannot perhaps know the truth," concedes Hart, "but I think we can make a pretty good guess." His "pretty good guess" is based on Bolín's report of Kemp's report (Kemp is unidentified) of Botteau's (Botto's) report of an alleged Havas report that a large sum of money was spent in Paris on Guernica propaganda. Hart also discovers that "Paris, indeed, seems to have been the center from which the whole effort was coordinated." Who was in Paris? And who had money? Willi Münzenberg, the Comintern agent, that's who. Ergo:

> It may be that Picasso was not the only great artist, or even the greatest one, connected with the mythologization of Guernica. He painted the picture, but Münzenberg invented the episode out of the whole cloth.[375]

Professor Hart is too modest. Münzenberg was perhaps in his day an artist of talent in inventing an "episode out of the whole cloth," but Hart has shown us real genius in inventing an "episode" involving Münzenberg with no cloth whatsoever.

The reaffirmation of the Bolín theses on Guernica, by an American professor in 1973, illustrates more than the stubborn survival of an historical myth; it illustrates the need of conservative right-wing elements in general in the perpetuation of the Nationalist myths of the Spanish Civil War. It is, after all, their great victory of the century. The Bolín version of Guernica was revised by the Neo-Franquistas, following a certain interpretation of an evolution in the local, specific situation of the Spanish right. But right-wing thought in general throughout the world was not necessarily served by an admission of Nazi guilt in the destruction of Guernica. Indeed, Hart refurbished the threadbare arguments of Bolín to serve a certain purpose of the Right. This purpose is given in an editorial heading to his article:

> 1972: U.S. Bombs the North Vietnamese Dikes. 1951: Germ Warfare in Korea. 1937: Nazi Planes Obliterate Guernica. What have all these stories in common: 1) They never happened, and 2) they helped the Communists.[376]

The proliferation of Hart's article would seem to indicate that it filled a need. It was reprinted in another American conservative publication,[377] and on March 18, extracts appeared in the *Washington Post.* Two weeks later, the same newspaper published an eyewitness account of the bombing by Pedro de Beitia, a Basque functionary during the war. This article, in addition to Beitia's own recollections of the bombing, presents an attestation from an unnamed American news agency correspondent, "who for several reasons cannot be identified," but whose name should be easily guessed by readers of this text. He says that on April 28, "Bolín ordered him, under penalty of losing his press credentials and being ousted from Spain, to report that Basques and 'Asturian dynamiters' had deliberately blown up Guernica's buildings, that there were no bomb craters in the city's streets and the like." When the journalist wrote the dispatch Bolín insisted on, "he attributed his information directly to Franco spokesmen, which led Bolín to tear up his copy in a frenzy, wave his pistol at him and order him to write another." The following is also of interest:

> Several [correspondents], in the months immediately following Guernica, had occasion in Salamanca or elsewhere to talk to officers of the German Luftwaffe's Condor Legion who made no secret of their connection with the Guernica bombing. The Germans claimed it had been requested by the Franco forces, who worried that the Basques intended to make a stand in the town.[378]

Within a few days of its appearance in New York, the *National Review* article was translated and reproduced in its entirety in the conservative German daily *Die Welt,* taking up almost a full page of the newspaper. It was illustrated with a reproduction of Picasso's painting and a photograph of Willi Münzenberg, whose responsibility for the bombing of Guernica seemed no longer in doubt. A suggestive heading asked if Hart's article was "the end of the legend."[379]

An immediate rebuttal to *Die Welt* came from the Madrid correspondent of the *Frankfurter Allgemeine,* and was headed "NO DOUBT ABOUT GUERNICA. FALSE 'REVELATIONS' " The writer cited in support of his arguments that Hart's evidence was fallacious, the position of La Cierva, described as "the unofficial historian of the Spanish Civil War in Franco Spain and a functionary of the Information Ministry," the declaration of Göring at Nuremberg, the books of Galland and of Vila-San-Juan.[380]

A more informative reply to the page in *Die Welt* was given by Karl-Heinz Janssen in the Hamburg weekly, *Die Zeit.* Janssen chided the editor of *Die Welt* for not telling his readers who Bolín was and that his book had been published five years earlier. More important, Janssen offered several significant bits of information:

When Hitler refused the British proposal for an international investigation into Guernica, he did so because Keitel had warned him of the great danger of finding traces of German bombs in the ruins.

A soldier, assigned to the information service of the Luftwaffe, had reported that immediately after the bombing, Minister of War von Blomberg asked Sperrle who was responsible for the destruction. The head of the Condor Legion replied: "Not the Germans!"

Sperrle's reply was confirmed by a report that Air General Karl Drum (ret.). when questioned by American military historians after World War II, replied that the Italians were guilty of bombing Guernica. He attributed the destruction to the Italian system of releasing all the bombs of a squadron at the same time, following a signal from the leader, and to the fact that the fire spread rapidly because all the inhabitants had fled to the neighboring villages. However, Janssen observes, this version hardly relieved the Germans of their responsibility, since all the air forces in the north depended on the Condor command.[381]

Germany was not the only country in which conservative elements eagerly adopted Hart's revelations. The Roman daily *Il Tempo,* on February 5, 1973, published a long résumé of Hart's resume of Bolín on Guernica; it was signed by Dante Pariset, who had been a wartime correspondent in Spain.[382] This article was headlined: "SENSATIONAL REVELATIONS WHICH ARE BREAKING UP A MYTH." Pariset gave full credit to Hart, but made frequent references to Bolín as the source of Hart's inspiration.[383] Three days later, a former colleague of Bolín's on the prewar *ABC,* Eugenio Montes, now Rome correspondent of the Madrid monarchist daily, sent a dispatch based on Pariset's article. It was printed under these headlines: "GUERNICA WAS NOT DESTROYED BY AIRCRAFT. AN ARTICLE IN 'TEMPO' SAYS THAT IT WAS SET ON FIRE AND DYNAMITED FROM INSIDE THE TOWN." Montes mentioned Hart but once, and the readers of the article are given the clear impression that most of the ideas on Guernica are those of Pariset himself. The name of Bolín does not appear in Montes's dispatch. Thus Luis Bolín's ideas on Guernica, officially repudiated in Franco Spain by the Neo-Franquista historians, were smuggled back across the frontier in Italo-American dress. It is of more than passing interest that Montes and *ABC* preferred to hide the Spanish origin of these ideas and chose to pass them off as the result of new American and Italian research.[384]

Montes's dispatch provoked a reply from Augusto Unceta, a former Nationalist mayor of Guernica, who was also one of Talón's principal witnesses to the bombing. "It is inconceivable that in this day and age," wrote Unceta, "and after the studies published by don Ricardo de la Cierva, Colonel Martínez Bande, don Vicente Talón and others, such nonsense should be published on the subject." This letter had its curious sentences. It did not give the nationality of the airplanes that Unceta accused of destroying the town and of machine-gunning the population. Unceta also sought to diminish the violence of the air raid, insisting that in all probability the total number of the victims did not reach two hundred, "fewer than those killed in the bombing of Durango, by *the national air force*" (italics added). This letter was written, according to the text, in the month of March, and was published in *ABC* on March 17—that is, thirty-seven days after the appearance of the report from Rome.[385]

There is an unsettling aspect to the 1973 journey of the 1967 writings of Luis Bolín (the 1937 writings of Douglas Jerrold), from Spain to North America, then to Germany and Italy, and later, in a fradulent cover, back to their place of origin, Spain. In 1970, Talón had published his account of Guernica, and before and later, the fact of the bombing was frankly admitted in Spain. It was not shouted from the housetops, but it was said openly and published. This information apparently never crossed the frontier. In the first months of 1973, nobody supporting the Hart (Bolín) arguments, and nobody attacking the Hart (Bolín) arguments, had apparently ever heard of Talón, nobody in New York or Washington, or Hamburg or Frankfurt, or Vienna or Rome. Is it so difficult for information to travel? Apparently not, for Hart's message got about very quickly. True, Hart is a professor in a reputable American university, and Talón is but a Spanish journalist. But this is hardly the explanation, for in 1969, a distinguished German professor, Manfred Merkes—unlike Hart, an authority on the Spanish Civil War—published a book in which the destruction of Guernica by German aircraft was proved by documents. Nobody in New York or Washington, or Hamburg or Frankfurt, or Vienna or Rome had apparently ever heard of it. Throughout the 1973 revival of Bolín, Talón was never correctly cited, and Merkes was completely forgotten; yet either was enough to drown Hart in ridicule.

Pariset's article served as a welcome escape hatch for Ricardo de la Cierva, in his tenth explanation of what had happened at Guernica on April 26, 1937. This version appeared in the twenty-sixth number of the weekly serial on the life of El Caudillo, *Francisco Franco: Un siglo de España*, written by La Cierva. Although La Cierva had three years before considered that Talón's book marked the end of the contention, he now admitted, "Many years after the bombing of Guernica, the polemic concerning the causes of the destruction of the town continues." He pointed out, "In Italy it has just been said that there was no such bombing," and he added, with the seriousness of a man who weighs the pros and cons, "It is difficult to deny this evidence." (This evidence, as La Cierva surely knew, came not from Italy but from North America, and the American Hart had got it from Luis Bolín; it was, then, evidence that La Cierva had himself denied in 1970. But we were now in 1973.) La Cierva seized on the occasion to continue his retreat to the 1937 Nationalist arguments on Guernica.

> One must admit that the aerial action of the Condor Legion may have coincided with some partial destructions due to the intervention of Basque *dinamiteros* who, as is known, took action at other points.[386]

In another paragraph he wrote. . . .

> the collaboration of the "scorched earth" squadrons [in the destruction of Guernica] —evident at other moments of the war in the North—continues to be very probable historically, confirmed by the Herrán report . . . and the indispensable testimony of Jaime del Burgo.

He showed further Basque responsibility in the disaster because "it seems evident that the Basques did nothing to prevent [*evitar*] the fire."[387]

La Cierva again repeated the basic arguments of Neo-Franquismo on Guernica. The Germans bombed the town, with not a single Spanish pilot participating in the raid. The "sacred sites" were unharmed; hence, the bombing of Guernica, "clearly tactical in purpose, lacked completely any symbolic intention."[388] He again discovered Talón, whom he had forgotten in 1972. Again we are told: "The definitive historical *reportaje* of Vicente Talón has ended, for all time, with the myth forged by Steer . . . and Picasso." He quotes approvingly Talón's undocumented statement that Guernica was destroyed "by German airplanes which received orders directly from Berlin." Talón, we are told, has shown that there was no public market in Guernica on April 26, 1937, and "has reduced to the figure of a little more than a hundred the habitually exaggerated list of the thousands of dead."[389]

La Cierva quoted Professor Trythall [390] and George Hills to prove the innocence of Franco. Bolín is not named at all in this final effort by La Cierva, but he is in a sense whitewashed, and the Germans are blamed not only for the bombing but for Bolín's propaganda blunders as well.

> The propaganda inspired by headquarters accumulated error after error; in great part because of German pressures, this propaganda reached the point of denying the evidence of the military objective, which can be verified by anyone who looks at a map of the zone. Salamanca fell into the German trap and thought initially that the denial of the bombing of the 27th applied also to the real date, the 26th.[391]

Independently of the impetus given to the Guernica controversy by Hart's article, the dispute was again revived by Brian Crozier, who used an obituary on Picasso in the *Economist* to trot out again his already much-used defense of the

Nazis. Once again he presented Bolín's evidence: the published German documents and the Spanish field dispatches. As to the latter, he proudly stated: "I have read them myself." He also quoted Wing-Commander James again, as if the testimony of that officer had never been challenged. But he did add something new: "I visited Guernica recently to see for myself and satisfied myself that the destruction could not be imputed to the Nazis." Just what Crozier did on that visit, or what he could have done on such a visit, to arrive at the conclusion he reached, he did not tell.[392] Crozier's letter to the *Economist* provoked a letter from Madrid informing the readers of that magazine of Talón's book, including the Spanish journalist's arguments for the sole responsibility of the Nazis and the complete innocence of the Spanish Nationalists.[393] This had no effect on Crozier, who replied that the position of the Spanish regime on Guernica did not interest him. "My only interest is in what really happened," he wrote, adding that "in view of the fact that a quarter of the city was spared, including the cathedral [sic], the Casa de Juntas and the oak tree, there is no rational explanation, other than deliberate destruction at ground level."[394]

There was also an inevitable reaction to Hart's article, in the editorial offices of the *National Review*. One reader wrote to protest that Hart had not sufficiently identified Bolín and had not told of his role in the civil war.[395] Then, eight months after the publication of Hart's first article, the magazine printed four comments on Hart's conclusions and a rebuttal from Hart. Two of the writers contested Hart's judgments, two defended them. The initial article, by Williamson Murray, a graduate student in history at Yale, accused Hart of writing "half truths, misstatements and just plain lies." Murray presented as evidence two German documents that he had found in Washington in less than two days of research. One was by a German naval officer, *Fregattenkapitän* Heye, who wrote a report during a visit to Insurgent Spain in the summer of 1938 and offhandedly admitted the bombing of Guernica. The other document was a study prepared for the United States Air Force by German Lieutenant General Herman Plocher, entitled "The German Air Force in the Spanish Civil War." Plocher's explanation corresponds roughly to what Jaenecke had written (as cited by Merkes) and what Drum had said (as cited by Janssen, in *Die Zeit*). The second item in the new series of the *National Review* was by a teacher, Lawrence Nevins, who revealed Talón's book to the American public by quoting from it the anecdotes concerning Mola and Cabanellas. He supported the conclusions of the Spanish journalist, exculpating the Spanish Nationalist command of any blame, and even approved of Talón's attacks on Steer. But essentially, his presentation of *Arde Guernica* constituted a sabotage of the book and made Talón an easy opponent for Hart. Nevins's basic misunderstanding of the Guernica incident and of the Guernica controversy can be seen in his suggestion that if Picasso had not called his painting *Guernica*, the attack on the town would long ago have been forgotten.

The third offering in the *National Review* was none other than Crozier's letter to the *Economist* of a few months earlier. The fourth contribution was by a New York lawyer named Zayas, who gave an amalgam of information on the subject, some of it original. He postulated two "revisionist" theories:

> 1) the Germans did not bomb Guernica at all and the town was systematically destroyed by the *Rojos;* 2) either the Germans or Italians (or both) bombed military objectives in the town and subsequently the *Rojos* completed the destruction for propaganda purposes.

He then presented his evidence for these theories. He quoted the first draft of the 1940 "Die Kämpfe im Norden," alleged that Sperrle in 1937 had denied the bombing, and cited General Drum's testimony. He cited Thomas and Ansaldo on Göring's testimony, without, however, understanding that the former head of the Luftwaffe was interrogated in a prison cell and not before the War Crimes Tribunal. More important, Zayas personally interviewed Galland and another German Luftwaffe general who had flown for the Condor Legion.

> They informed me that a limited attack was carried out against military objectives, but that owing to weather conditions, poor visibility, and primitive aiming equipment, certain non-military objectives had been hit. However, under no circumstances had the attack been a terror bombardment on the civilian population.

Zayas had also visited Guernica, where his questioning of the inhabitants produced contradictory statements. But he considered it important that he was told that "the explosions continued after the air bombardment had ceased and many buildings were deliberately and systematically dynamited or set on fire with petrol, including the Church of San Juan." The lawyer then cited Bolín to show that Guernica was a military objective, and indicated that he viewed Bolín's quotations from Spanish Nationalist military dispatches as vital evidence. He also quoted the fourteen conclusions of the Commissioners in *Guernica: The Official Report.* Zayas's conclusions upheld Hart's basic position:

> There is persuasive evidence supporting the thesis that the *Rojos* did in fact destroy the town of Guernica. . . . The evidence for a deliberate destruction of the town by Basque *dinamiteros* (or more probably by Asturian miners) is persuasive.

Zayas was, perhaps, too easily persuaded by doubtful evidence.

Hart was then given the final rejoinder and commented on the four comments on his article. He airily dismissed Murray's two German documents, much in the 1937 manner of Douglas Jerrold. Heye, he said, was not an eyewitness, and his remarks may well have been based on hearsay. As for the Plocher document, it "tends to support my view, not Mr. Murray's." Hart rejected Nevin's presentation of Talón as merely anecdotal. This was true, but why did not the scholar Hart have the curiosity to peruse Talón's book at first hand? Here was Hart's conclusion:

> The Germans and Italians did bomb the military targets. Some bombs may have fallen on the town. However, on balance, the evidence seems to me to

indicate that the defenders destroyed the town, as, everyone agrees, they had destroyed many others. At that point, the propagandists fabricated the Guernica Myth.[396]

One other by-product of Hart's article was an article in *Saturday Review/World* by Roger M. Williams, reporting from Guernica, where the people he talked with confirmed the fact of the bombing. Williams had also talked with Hart, who, despite his polemical position, claimed his interest in Guernica was "intellectual" rather than political. Of more interest is the fact that he talked with Vicente Talon, who confirmed to him that there would be no second printing of *Arde Guernica,* and not for commercial reasons. "It was clearly not good for my health to have more than one edition," Talón told the American journalist.[397]

Despite Talón's worries about his health if a second edition of his book was published in Spain, a few weeks after he made the statement, in December 1973 a second edition of his work did appear in Madrid.[398] This second edition has more pages than the first, but this is in part achieved by larger type, in part by the incorporation of footnotes of the first edition into the text of the second, and only in part by new material. Why did the Spanish censorship reverse its policy and permit the new edition? Did Hart's article provoke a reaction in official Spain? It is difficult to see how Hart could have irritated the Spanish regime. Moreover, Talón's few references to the American professor of English do not indicate that he takes Hart seriously.

One significant change between the two editions is Talón's attitude toward La Cierva. In the introduction to the first edition, there was a list of persons to whom Talón expressed gratitude for their help. The first name on that list was R. de la Cierva, who, Talón wrote in 1970, "as a writer, investigator and teacher, is developing such a worthwhile labor to clarify, establish and divulge the themes of the Spanish war."[399] This paragraph of thanks has disappeared from the new edition. In another reference to La Cierva in the first edition, Talón described him as a "historian."[400] The mention is repeated in the second edition, but La Cierva is no longer considered to be a "historian."[401] Another reference to La Cierva as "historian" in a footnote in the first edition[402] has been eliminated from the second edition, footnote and all.[403] But there is still a more direct attack on La Cierva. In the first printing, Talón had cited from the articles of La Cierva and Del Burgo published early in 1970 in *El Pensamiento Navarro,* and had concluded:

> I believe absolutely in the sincerity of Senor Del Burgo and in that of Señor de la Cierva, considering myself, moreover, among those who await, with authentic eagerness, the publication of these "specific documents."[404]

In the new edition, Talón repeated the above sentence, adding to it as the end, "although three long years have already passed since these [the specific documents] were announced and we have not yet seen anything."[405] There is evidently bad blood between Talón and La Cierva.

Perhaps the immediate reason for this new printing of *Arde Guernica* resides in the final pages of the book, wherein Talón exposes certain correspondence from members of the Institute for Research in Military History, of the West German Republic. From these German documents can be gleaned the impression that while the German military historians are prepared to admit that German planes did bomb Guernica, they are not prepared to assume Condor Legion responsibility for ordering the attack. To this newly developing position, Talón makes this comment:

> It seems to be evident, from these texts, that the intention of the German Institute is clearly exculpatory. It is even possible that they may publish the testimony of a former German interpreter of the [Spanish] General Staff according to whom the order for the bombing came, directly, from the Spanish command. Personally, I shall consider it highly unfortunate if matters crystalize in this manner. And it will be curious to see how the Germans, who, forgetting the thousand and one horrors of which they were victims [*sic*], have declared themselves the authors of all sorts of excesses . . . now deny that which is proved beyond any doubt.[406]

One other example of Neo-Franquista argumentation concerning Guernica was produced in 1973. The reader will recall that a year earlier, Ricardo de la Cierva had mentioned a document, concerning an Italian air raid of April 26 on the Rentéria bridge near Guernica, found by Ramón Salas Larrazábal. Salas revealed the details of this document in his four-volume work on the Spanish Republican army published in 1973. He said that there exists in the Spanish archives an Italian communiqué, handed in to the Spanish air force headquarters on April 26, 1973, reporting an attack on the Guernica bridge, at five hours twenty, by three Savoia 79s, each of which dropped twelve bombs of fifty kilograms (1,800 kilograms).[407]

Since it was still dark at five hours twenty in the morning, Salas deduces that the raid took place at five hours twenty (Nationalist time) on the afternoon of April 26—that is, at four hours twenty (Republican time). This hour coincides more or less with most of the other testimony concerning the beginning of the air raids on Guernica. But Salas then reasons that since night fell at seven hours thirty-six (Nationalist time), and the bombing had to take place in daytime, the raids in reality lasted but little more than two hours. Salas then arrives at the kernel of his arguments: no airplane could have dropped its bombs on Guernica, returned to Vitoria, reloaded, and bombed Guernica a second time in the time limits imposed.[408] Therefore the number of bombers over Guernica on April 26 could not have been more than twenty-nine, the number available for bombing on April 12, two weeks before the attack on Guernica, according to an official document.[409]

There is too much testimony from eyewitnesses of the bombing, fixing the duration of the attacks at three hours or more, for us to accept, without further proof, the arguments of Ramón Salas. In *Guernica: The Official Report*, twelve witnesses reported the time the bombing stopped: the earliest was seven-thirty (eight-thirty Nationalist time); twelve witnesses (not all the same persons) gave a time for the duration; it varied from a minimum of three hours to a maximum of five hours. Steer, after talking with a number of people who had endured the bombing, said that it lasted three hours and fifteen minutes, that it began at four-thirty, and that it ended at seven forty-five, "at the approach of dusk."[410] Canon Onaindia said that the bombing began shortly after four-fifteen and ended at fifteen minutes to eight, "of that radiant April evening."[411]

It is not possible to believe that all these witnesses, beginning with the testimony taken on the night of April 26, and then throughout the years, should have made the same miscalculation of time. What we have here is but another example, so frequently found in the course of the Guernica controversy, of expert analysis produced to prove that what had happened could not have taken place.

Ramón Salas agreed with Talón on the fact that "the bombing and the fires were the work of the air force."[412] He also concurred with the journalist's opinion concerning Nationalist involvement, though with a nuance:

> The fact seems then fully demonstrated that the attack was due to German initiative, without knowledge or consent of the Nationalist command, a fact which does not exempt the latter of moral responsibility.[413]

As a matter of fact, Ramón Salas did not demonstrate this "fully" or otherwise. Salas further followed the Neo-Franquista arguments in accepting Talón's statement that the Guernica market was not held on April 26, and then using that statement as a pretext for diminishing by half Talón's estimate of the dead.[414] Salas's propositions, which are not without their cleverness, are, like all the others of the Neo-Franquista historians on Guernica which we have studied, intended to reduce the front-page criminal act to a *fait divers* buried inside the newspaper.

Were Italian planes really involved in the bombing of Guernica? There is other proof to support Salas's statement. In the spring of 1975 an Italian journalist quoted extensively from a document that he had found in the government archives in Rome. This document reported the flight by three Savoia-Marchetti 79s on April 26; each dropped twelve fifty-kilogram bombs on the "bridge built on the Oca river in the Rentería quarter of Guernica and on nearby military objectives," at four-thirty in the afternoon. These were apparently the first planes that attacked the town. The Italians, according to this source, were unaware of the projected bombing by the Condor Legion. We can therefore assume that the confusion about the bombing of Guernica which has persisted throughout so many years existed in the Nationalist military commands on April 26. But can the Italian communique be trusted? Certainly not when it reads, "The bombs were dropped from a considerable distance, but the objectives were hit."[415]

What is the Neo-Franquista position on Guernica in 1975? It has retreated considerably from the summit of Talón's book in the summer of 1970, and from the unconditional acceptance of that work, itself highly blemished with concessions to the Franco regime. Now the Neo-Franquistas take what they need from Talón, such as the total accusation of the Germans and the denial of a public market on the day of the bombing, and they tend to discard the rest. Ricardo de la Cierva ignores Talón's dismissal of the Herrán report, and Ramón Salas reduces Talón's figure of around two hundred dead to less than a hundred. La Cierva openly places in doubt Taión's denial of the responsibility of any other agency than the German bombers in the destruction, although he accepted it without reservations in 1970. Talón was used by the planners of "Operation Guernica" in 1970, then he was shoved off to one side. The official spokesman on Guernica is not Vicente Talón but Ricardo de la Cierva. A certain nostalgia for the uncompromising days of Luis Bolín is clearly in the air, as evidenced by La Cierva's respectful treatment of Montes's ludicrous rehash of Bolín sent back from Rome in a new wrapping. Under the guidance of Ricardo de la Cierva, the Neo-Franquista historians are slowly retreating to a position where, if not all the blame for the destruction of Guernica can again be charged to the Basques, at least a good part of it can be.[416]

BOOK III

•

CONCLUSIONS

Introduction

We have now studied the newspaper reports of the Guernica incident, and we have also studied the various positions concerning the controversy about the incident, which followed the newspaper dispatches. The essential problems of Guernica—How was it destroyed? By whom was it destroyed? And why was it destroyed?—have in the course of these studies been joined by other problems, some of which abandon the restricted search for the truth about an event of the Spanish Civil War, and lead us into fields where historical research must be applied to the fragile nature of the newspaper telegram, into the political manipulation of news, and into propaganda analysis. These intrusive problems, these seemingly lesser problems (but are they?), must also be given an attempt at solution.

Two of these newer problems arise directly from the first part of this chronicle, which dealt with the telegrams of the newspaper correspondents: How can we explain the contradictions between the news forwarded by the reporters who visited Guernica on the night of April 26-27 and later during the few days the town remained in Republican hands, and the news sent out by the other newsmen who came to Guernica after it had fallen to the Rebels? How can we explain the curiously unprofessional attitude of the Havas Agency toward the news about Guernica?

There is also a problem, which might have been dealt with in a discussion of the destruction itself, but which I have preferred to treat independently: How many casualties were caused by the destruction? And yet another problem has arisen during the long, detailed research into the controversy: Why did this polemical discussion begin? And why has it persisted to our day? These problems will now be approached, and in this order:

1. The problem of Steer, Holburn, Botto and the Havas Agency.
2. The dead and the dying.
3. How was Guernica Destroyed? By Whom? Why?
4. The reasons for the Existence and Persistence of the Guernica Controversy.

1

The Problem of
Steer, Holburn, Botto,
and the Havas Agency

After the English publication of *Guernica: The Official Report,* to the careful reader there remained little of substance to the "technical" arguments advanced early in the controversy by del Moral, Croft, Jerrold, Lunn, and others, pleading the Nationalist cause. Perhaps for this reason, Sencourt concentrated his ire on the person of Steer, and kept his praise for "the regular correspondent" of the *Times,* the mysterious "investigator," and the man from the Havas Agency and his unidentified aides, "a number of foreign journalists." In the development of the controversy, although it was plain to the persons who read the testimony of the witnesses convoked by the Burgos commission that Guernica was set on fire by incendiary bombs, there did remain to explain some fragments of the charges against Steer,[1] the dispatch of the *Times* man from Vitoria (Holburn), in part favorable to certain Nationalist positions, and the telegram distributed by the Havas agency, extremely favorable to the Nationalist position.

It is now time to look into these three cases, and we shall start with that of George Lowther Steer. Steer was a highly respected newspaperman. His book *The Tree of Guernica* is superbly readable and historically authoritative.[2] None of his detractors produced a work to rival it, certainly not Robert Sencourt, whose book *Spain's Ordeal* is worthless today, save as a source for study of Nationalist propaganda in England and the United States.[3] The telegram from the *Times* to Steer, which Father Thorning "revealed" with such great éclat, in no way reflected on Steer's work. The editor of the *Times Archives* states:

We have no trace in our Archives of the out-message to Steer which [the telegram produced by Thorning] you quote. But there is nothing extra-ordinary about it. Ralph Deakin, who was Foreign News Editor at the time, sent out many such telegrams in his long career in that post. His aim was the normal journalistic one of telling the correspondents that other papers had reacted differently and inviting him, if he thought fit, to send a further message backing up the earlier one or amending it in the light of further information if that should seem to him necessary. It has long been the tradition of *The Times* to appoint its correspondents with great care and then to trust them.

He then added, to place the telegram in its correct, and not in Father Thorning's, perspective,

We have no reason to doubt the accuracy of the telegram, which typically shows the care taken by our Foreign Department to keep the news record true and accurate.[4]

But, as has already been shown, there was never any reason to doubt the *Times'* trust in Steer. Positive proof of the newspaper's complete confidence in its corre-spondent was available to any impartial critic who wanted it, on May 5, 1937, in the editorial printed that day in the *Times*. This editorial, which neither Jerrold, Thorning, "Sencourt," Code, nor Williams—the chief defamers of Steer's good name—had the intellectual honesty to mention, not only upheld Steer's original report but warned the reader of the "political and military censorship" under which the *Times* man with the Nationalists (Holburn) was working. Still more, on the following day, the *Times* published Steer's "further judicious statement," which it had requested in the telegram later revealed by Father Thorning. The headline over this dispatch read: "BOMBING OF GUERNICA. FRESH EVIDENCE." It is not conceivable that the newspaper would have published the article, in this fashion, if it had not had absolute faith in the integrity of the man who sent it. In this cablegram Steer confirmed his first dispatch:

I personally talked with over 20 refugees from Guernica in the outskirts of the town on the night of its destruction. Except for minor details about the number of airplanes which destroyed Guernica, their stories agreed on every point. Between 4:30 and 7:45 that evening Guernica was destroyed by aircraft which most of them could distinguish as belonging to the insurgents, while priests were able to describe the well-known Junkers type which was responsible for the heaviest bombing. . . . The fact remains that General Franco's airplanes burnt Guernica and the Basques will never forget.[5]

It can be seen, then, that on May 6, two days after the *Times* sent to Steer in Bilbao the telegram that later fell into Thorning's hands, the newspaper, far from demonstrating any doubts about Steer's first telegram, published another one confirming the first one.[6] There was therefore no basis whatsoever for anyone's suggesting that George Steer was not a highly respected member of his profession. It is impossible today to understand how Douglas Jerrold, Father Thorning, Robert Sencourt, Father Code, and Major Williams could have read the dispatch from Vitoria in the *Times* of May 5, 1937, and not have read the editorial on Guernica published in the same edition or Steer's correspondence of the following day, and that having read them, they were unable to correlate each with the others, and then to interpret the message, that Thorning so proudly proclaimed to be a "Hitherto Unpublished Telegram," in the light of the evidence published in the *Times* itself.

The treatment of the Guernica incident in the *Times,* especially the moral support given to Steer's cablegrams, is all the more remarkable, because it ran counter to the political line consciously followed by that conservative newspaper. The *Times* in April 1937, more than a year before the Munich pact, was deliberately trying to discover a way by which England and Nazi Germany might reach a *modus vivendi,* appeasement before the Great Day of Appeasement. On May 23, less than a month after the bombing of Guernica, the editor of the *Times,* Geoffrey Dawson, sent, in a letter to the paper's Geneva correspondent, what K. W. Watkins called "the most pathetic paragraphs that can ever have come from the editorial chair of *The Times* in its long and great history."[7]

"But it would really interest me to know precisely what it is in *The Times* that has produced this antagonism in Germany," wrote Dawson.

I did my utmost, night after night, to keep out of the paper anything that might have hurt their susceptibilities. I can really think of nothing that has been printed now for many months past which they could possibly take exception to as unfair comment. No doubt they were annoyed by Steer's first story of the bombing of Guernica, but its essential accuracy has never been disputed, and there has not been any attempt here to rub it in.[8]

But while we admit that the *Times* showed courage and honesty in sustaining Steer and his coverage of the Guernica bombing in 1937, we must also show that a few months later the *Times* was to display a most shabby attitude toward the correspondent. He apparently did no reporting for the *Times* after the end of the Basque campaign. He certainly then spent some months writing *The Tree of Gernika,* and during a part of 1938 and 1939 he wrote a series of articles on German and Italian colonial claims in Africa for the *Daily Telegraph,* and produced two more books, *Judgment on German Africa* and *A Date in the Desert.*[9] Phillip Knightley tells us that "then, in 1939, Steer began a libel suit against a critic who said he had left *The Times* after a dispute over the accuracy of the Guernica story," and "the newspaper gave him little help."[10]

From Knightley's evidence, this would seem to be an understatement. The *Times* wrote on April 6, 1939, to Steer's solicitors that he had worked in Spain for the newspaper only in August and September 1936. Then, in a letter dated May 1, 1939, the *Times* grudgingly admitted that Steer had done further work for it in Spain, but phrased the admission condescendingly in a statement that Steer "also acted on his own initiative as an occasional correspondent from April to June, 1937." This satisfied neither Steer nor his solicitors, and the *Times* finally produced the following formula on July 11, 1939:

> We write to inform you that the report of our former occasional correspondent, Mr. G. L. Steer, on the bombing of Guernica had no connection whatever with the cessation of his service with the *Times*. He gave up the temporary work he was doing in Spain for the *Times* entirely on his own initiative and for private reasons.[11]

These references to "occasional correspondent" sound very much like Sencourt's description of Steer. The only book published in England at that time which could have provoked Steer to engage proceedings as described by Knightley was Sencourt's *Spain's Ordeal*. This book was dedicated, "To Ernest Grimaud de Caux to whom I owe a debt . . . in admiration of his courage, his judgment and his style, and in gratitude for his warmth and openness of heart."

De Caux was one of the senior correspondents of the *Times*. He had been in Madrid before the civil war, where his dispatches were remarked for their pro-monarchist opinions and conservative views. He stayed on in Madrid when the civil war broke out, and the Republicans tolerated his hardly favorable reports. He was actively opposed to the Republic,[12] and highly considered in the Rebel zone. Bolín, during a visit to the *Times* in London in June 1937 praised De Caux's messages from the besieged capital, and even suggested that De Caux come to visit Franco and the Nationalists.[13] In view of Sencourt's friendship with De Caux, it is highly probable that the latter was aware of the former's attempts to discredit Steer, and it is equally probable that Sencourt was thus in part responsible for the reluctance of the *Times* to be even halfway decent to Steer. Apparently the suit was never heard, perhaps because of the outbreak of World War II.

The *Times* gave Lieutenant Colonel G. L. Steer a handsome obituary when he died, including the mention that he "became a special correspondent for the *Times* in Spain, where the Civil War raged."[14] An even more honorable mention was granted Steer in the official history of the *Times* in 1952:

> George Lowther Steer was already, before his thirtieth birthday, one of the paper's most successful war correspondents. A South African by birth, and a scholar at Winchester, and New College, he entered the paper's service in 1935 to report the Abyssinian campaign from the victim's side, and was moved to Spain soon after the Italians expelled him from Addis Ababa in May 1936. His *Tree of Gernika* described his experience with the Basques with a vigor its readers will not easily forget. He was killed in active service in the South-East Asia Command in 1944, at the age of 35.[15]

The greatest success as a war correspondent of George Steer, one of the *Times'* "most successful war correspondents," was won in the Basque campaign; his work there had been but a few years earlier scorned by the *Times* as that of an "occasional correspondent."

We can now dismiss as totally unfounded the charges brought unjustly and vindictively against George Lowther Steer. But there remains the dispatch of his colleague with the Insurgent forces, James Holburn.[16] If Steer was an honest reporter and of sound mind, how can the critic reconcile his cablegram with that of Holburn? This is not so troublesome a problem as it might seem, once we look at Holburn's telegram, not with the prejudiced vision of a Jerrold, a Lunn, or a Sencourt, but with the text before us and the knowledge of how it was written, of how it was "filtered" through the censorship from Vitoria to London.

This task is facilitated by the fact that Holburn is still living, retired from the *Times*. He was across the frontier, in the French Basque country, when the first news of the destruction of Guernica was printed. He did not visit Guernica with Botto, Massot, and the others on May 1, but came in a day later, unescorted, as he remembers it.[17]

Holburn wrote in 1969, after having read his Guernica article for the first time since he wrote it in Vitoria, as follows:

> The main point of the dispatch was to report, from the Franco side, that Guernica had been bombed "intermittently for three hours" as the Franco authorities admitted to me. But to be able to send that out I had to put their case that the destruction was not due to the bombing but, as they claimed, to arson by the retreating Basques. The use of phrases as "public opinion here" and "it is felt here" was my way of not identifying myself with their story.
>
> Reading the dispatch reminded me that I met a man, in Guernica or Vitoria, who purported to be chairman of a commission of civil engineers appointed by Franco to inquire into the causes of the burning of Guernica. The comparisons with Durango, Eibar, Elgueta and Irún must have been made to me by him, for I never saw Durango, Eibar or Elgueta. His must be the opinion that "it will be difficult to establish exactly how the fire started."[18]

Holburn was also asked for an explanation of the sentence, frequently quoted and probably the part most favorable to the Nationalist position in his telegram, which read as follows:

> In view of these circumstances it is difficult to believe that Guernica was the target of a bombardment of exceptional intensity or was selected by the Nationalists for an experiment with incendiary bombs, as is alleged by the Basques.

He replied that

> it was no doubt intended to be sugar on the pill, the pill being the admission of the bombing. But if I wrote it precisely as it was published, the phrase had been better not written. Cablese always magnifies the margin for error in the mechanical and editorial handling of dispatches but I do not recall whether I used cablese much from Spain or not.

Holburn, as he affirms today, had but one intention in writing his telegram on Guernica: to get out to London, through the Rebel censorship, the admission of the bombing.[19] His message was understood in London, as evidenced by the editorial position taken by the *Times* on the very day his article was printed, an editorial, moreover, which made a specific reference to Holburn's article. This editorial position—that Guernica had indeed been bombed—also, as already underlined, mentioned the hardships of men like Holburn who were working in the Insurgent zone. This constituted a warning to the reader to go slow in interpreting Holburn's dispatch—a warning that Jerrold, Thorning, Sencourt, and others ignored. The obstacles placed in the path of the working newsman in the Franco zone were well known to the *Times* people, in Paris as in London, as evidenced in one of the letters Scott wrote to Bailby.

The publication of Holburn's dispatch in the *Times*, and the interpretation made editorially by the newspaper of that dispatch, resulted in Holburn falling into Aguilera's bad graces.

> As to why I was in trouble with the Nationalists over the dispatch, the answer is that it conveyed abroad an impression the opposite of that which they had hoped it would convey. I recall one of my colleagues telling, or warning, me that the Nationalists regarded me as a correspondent who was out to put something over on them whenever opportunity offered. The Guernica dispatch was the climactic offense.[20]

A few weeks after he had sent his Guernica telegram,[21] Holburn left Spain and returned to work for the *Times* in Berlin.[22] The distinction made by Sencourt between Steer, "a free-lance journalist," and Holburn, "the regular correspondent of *The Times*," thus had no stable basis in fact. Holburn was in Spain on a temporary assignment, and Steer was on the same footing. No war correspondent is ever on a permanent appointment. However, Steer went to Spain for the *Times* before Holburn did, and stayed on after Holburn had left. Holburn was certainly a more permanent employee of the newspaper than was Steer, but this arrangement seemed to suit Steer. When he left the *Times*, after the collapse of the northern front, it was in order to write *The Tree of Gernika*.

Holburn's place in Spain was filled by a young and promising correspondent, H. A. R. ("Kim") Philby, whose pro-Nazi connections doubtless facilitated his acceptance by Bolín, who little imagined that he was welcoming a Soviet spy.[23] Bolín, in fact, later credited Philby with Holburn's report on Guernica.[24] Today, Holburn, on rereading his Guernica telegram that was, unbeknownst to him, the center of so much violent controversy, has the tendency to disparage its composition. "I feel that in writing this dispatch my intentions were better than my performance."[25] In all honesty, there is no reason to accept this judgment. Viewed in the context of the time and conditions of its writing, compared with what others wrote on the same subject for the same censorship, it is competent journalism. Holburn got the essential facts of his story out to London, and that is what he was supposed to do. It was not the fault of the journalist if Jerrold misinterpreted his telegram, if Sencourt misquoted it, and if all the English and American friends of Franco ignored the *Times* editorial it had in part inspired.

With George Steer absolved of the charges brought against him, and James Holburn's telegram placed in historical perspective, there remains only the problem of Georges Botto, author of the pro-Nationalist dispatch sent from Vitoria and distributed by the Havas Agency in Paris on May 3. Botto is no longer here to testify; he died in 1952 and is buried in Auteuil cemetery in Paris.[26] However, the documents of the Havas Agency tell us the principal parts of his story. If the reader will recall the earlier chapter on the hazards of reporting in the insurgent zone, he will remember that when Botto came to Spain in February 1937, his predecessor, Malet-Dauban, was in durance vile and possibly condemned to death. With d'Hospital on leave in France, Botto was the only Havas man in Vitoria. When he came into Guernica on the afternoon of April 29, with Captain Aguilera and the other correspondents, he found his compatriot and colleague Georges Berniard, who had just escaped being shot as a spy and who now risked being shot for having worked on the Basque side of the war, after having previously worked with the Nationalists. Berniard was still a prisoner in Botto's apartment when, on Saturday, May 1, Botto went with Aguilera and the other reporters to write about the ruins of Guernica. Botto then sent out a story tailored to Aguilera's wishes. No other reporter—with the possible exeception of Max Massot and Pierre Héricourt—wrote so much of the presence of gasoline, of the absence of bomb holes, in Guernica. This telegram was, as already noted, picked up and printed widely in Germany, used by certain elements of the French press to attack Steer and the *Times,* used by Nazi sympathizers in London to disprove the statements of the Basque government.

This situation was irritating or, better said, embarrassing, to the English government. The story of the bombing of Guernica was generally considered, and rightly so, sponsored by the English press. The Havas Agency was generally considered, and rightly so, an agent of the French government. Sir Eric Phipps, who had, a few days earlier, been accredited as British ambassador to France, made inquiries concerning the Havas dispatch at the Quai d'Orsay. He was told,

> . . . in confidence, that there is reason to believe that the Havas representative in question did not write the story at first hand, but had it imposed upon him by the Nationalists.

Phipps's informants added, "that no use can be made of this information for fear that the man in question will be shot."[27]

French Foreign Minister Yvon Delbos, on May 4, told Sir Eric "confidentially that the Havas telegram arrived with the following addition: 'It is begged that the greatest possible publicity may be given to the above'." This formula, Sir Eric told his superiors in London,

> strange to say, is apparently the formula generally used to indicate that the news given is incorrect or only given under pressure, which was the case in present instance. A high official in the Havas Agency, however, decided to take the message *au pied de la lettre* and the widest publicity was given.

The ambassador added:

> This is, of course, unfortunate, as the German press published it and have
> made capital out of the fact that the "perfidious" British press suppressed a
> true account of the investigation into the "so-called" bombardment of
> Guernica.[28]

From this evidence, one can conclude that by May 5, both the French and
British Foreign Offices knew that the Botto message was untrue. Eden undoubtedly
had this information when he talked with von Ribbentrop on that day, and this
knowledge permitted him to oppose the German's version of events in Guernica,
based on the Havas message.

In the "Guernica" file of the Havas documents in the National Archives in Paris,
there are a great many papers, letters, and notes, but there is nothing precisely
concerning the validity of the Botto telegram, or of any interest of the Quai
d'Orsay in the matter. However, we have seen that on May 4, officials of the French
Foreign Ministry, and even the French foreign minister, were perfectly acquainted
with the nature of the Botto dispatch. There is another curious detail. All the
original news telegrams received from correspondents by the Havas Agency during
the Spanish Civil War have been destroyed, with one sole exception, and this
exception is Botto's telegram concerning Guernica. It was dated "Saturday May 1
19 hours" and ended with the words: "NOTER DIFFUSER LARGEMENT CETTE
DEPECHE."[29] These words are easily the journalistic cablese equivalent of the
diplomatic English of Sir Eric Phipps, "It is begged that the greatest possible
publicity may be given to the above."

It was customary for correspondents of the Agence Havas working in the
Nationalist zone of Spain (and perhaps in the other) to take the precaution of having a
code ready so as to be able to let Paris know when they found themselves under
pressure to send incorrect or doubtful information. There is evidence in the Havas files
to show that Havas had given Botto such a code, but nowhere is the exact wording
spelled out. However, d'Hospital's code was clearly given. On August 15, 1936, when
d'Hospital was preparing to enter Insurgent Spain, he cabled his Paris office: "KEEP
IN MIND ALL DISPATCHES WILL BE CENSORED STOP WATCH SIGNATURE
WITH FIRST NAME MEANS OBLIGATORY OR DOUBTFUL NEWS."[30]

When the truthfulness of the news contained in an article sent from Majorca by
d'Hospital in October 1937 was contested, a Havas note read as follows:

> When Mr. d'Hospital cannot guarantee the affirmations in his dispatches, he
> ends them by a mention signifying this fact to the editors and permits them
> to use these dispatches with circumspection. No mention of this kind figured
> at the end of the telegram in question from Palma.[31]

When, months later, Botto sent a cablegram with information thought to be
doubtful in Paris, Havas reproached the reporter for not using the proper code to
warn his editors.[32]

It can therefore be asserted that the Botto dispatch, distributed by Havas, confirming the destruction of Guernica by arson and clearing the Nationalists and Germans of any guilt in the disaster—quoted by Jerrold, by Lunn, by Thorning, by Sencourt, and by others, hailed in Nazi Germany as proof of Steer's lying, used by von Ribbentrop in his conversation with Eden, quoted by Franco's friends in the House of Commons, cited by Leon Bailby in his quarrel with Scott—was purely and simply a fradulent message, known to be false by the man who wrote it, known to be false by the news agency that distributed it, known to be false by the French Foreign Ministry and then by the British Foreign Office.

The initial fault can be attributed to Georges Botto. There is no proof that he was under irresistible pressure on May 1 to send out false information. Berniard had the impression that Botto was on friendly terms with the Insurgent military. He recalls that Botto discussed military strategy with the Spanish officers.[33] Botto had, after all, fought in World War I and had been decorated with the Croix de Guerre and the Legion of Honor. He held the rank of reserve captain in the French army.[34] But at times the Spanish military were suspicious of French reporters with military knowledge. Was Botto frightened by the fate of Malet-Dauban? By the possible fate of Berniard? Be that as it may, Berniard was told of his freedom only at midnight on Saturday, May 1; Botto had handed in his telegram five hours earlier.

Botto risked nothing in sending out his false message, for he had forewarned Paris that the information was suspect and the telegram written under constraint. Botto also certainly knew that the Havas Agency needed him on the job. He had probably been instructed, as was d'Hospital, to do his work of reporting and to avoid any action that might bring about an expulsion.[35] As the only Havas man in the Nationalist zone, he was vulnerable to Insurgent pressure. In the struggle over the Latin American news market, Havas had to keep someone in the Rebel area or lose customers and prestige. Botto knew of his vulnerability, as did Aguilera and Bolín. Whether any of these elements in play affected Botto's decision to send the telegram is not known, at this writing. But if Botto did not compose under irresistible pressure, if he did not write the message to help bring about the freeing of Berniard, then he did write it for personal reasons. These, both political and financial, can be found.

Botto's political beliefs led him naturally to a sympathy with the Spanish Rebels.[36] In his reports to Paris, even when uncensored, he always called the Republicans, "the Reds."[37] This partisanship for the Nationalists became more open after the episode of the Guernica telegram. Botto had entered the Havas Agency in December 1932,[38] one editor among many; before going to Spain, he had never been a "Special Correspondent," with the perquisites and renown (and dangers) that that title could bring. In Paris he was paid 1,850 francs a month.[39] His salary was raised to 4,000 francs when he went to Spain, with all expenses paid.[40] A management report on him later noted:

He is a fellow who, before leaving for Spain, led a poor existence and, probably, had a good many debts. Since he has been a Special Correspondent, he has seen the situation change completely.[41]

He was, in the words of one of his colleagues, "un arriviste."[42] Berniard has been impressed with Botto's "sumptuous" apartment.[43] Barré, returning from his unfortunate month in Rebel Spain, mentioned to someone in Havas's Paris headquarters Botto's "propensity to good living and to seeing big, both as to the present and as to the future."[44]

Curiously enough, the Havas files contain not a word to show that Havas and Botto ever mentioned to each other the false news they gave to the world.[45] Botto was certainly not censured by the Nationalist press officers for sending his telegram, but neither can one find any signs of special favors granted in payment. Did the false news about Guernica have any value? The record shows only two persons who thought so, that most naïve of adventurers in the Spanish Civil War, Peter Kemp and Georges Botto. Kemp—then a working journalist—wrote in 1957:

> The Republicans were countering the Nationalist offensive against Bilbao with a propaganda offensive of their own; at this time it was concentrated on the famous Guernica incident. It was very cleverly handled, and a great deal of money was spent on it abroad—Botteau [sic] was told by his head office that the Republicans spent about six hundred thousand pounds in Paris on propaganda about Guernica alone. The story circulated—and widely believed—was that Guernica, an open town, was destroyed by incendiary bombs dropped by Nationalist aircraft.[46]

Peter Kemp's book shows that he readily believed anything that agreed with his class prejudices,[47] but a journalist should reflect before repeating an absurdity and giving the impression that he believed it. That Botto told the story to Kemp is probable, that anyone from Havas told the story to Botto is highly improbable, and that the story contained any truth is impossible. Six hundred thousand pounds is a lot of money for propaganda today, and it was a lot more in 1937. Moreover, any Havas editor capable of reading the daily press in France would have known that the news about Guernica, far from being exaggerated through huge subsidies from the Republican propaganda funds, was not even being treated as a normal news story. Botto must have told this rumor about the Guernica propaganda budget to Kemp during the time the young Englishman shared an apartment in Vitoria with the Havas man and Cardozo. Kemp left this apartment not later than June 19, 1937.[48] This date fixes the time during which the "six hundred thousand pounds" were spent in France, as well as the time for Botto's hearing (or inventing) the gossip and passing it along.

Nowhere in the Havas papers for this period is there a sign of any such communication about Guernica propaganda; more pertinent, nothing in the Havas files indicates that Havas in Paris was in the habit of sending such gossip to any of its men in the field of Spain, let alone to a man who had just cabled 308 words of false information on the same subject—Guernica—to his employers. Nor is there at any time in the Havas files any suggestion that Havas was in the habit of sending men from Paris to confer with its correspondents from the Rebel zone at the frontier.

But if it is highly improbable that anyone from Havas reported to Botto the tale of the six hundred thousand pounds, and impossible that the tale be true, it is quite possible and quite probable that Georges Botto told it to his credulous young friend Peter Kemp. This is the interesting part of the story. Georges Botto, the person who suggests to Peter Kemp that there was money to be made in spreading "propaganda" about Guernica is precisely that Georges Botto, the person who cabled the lying information about Guernica to the Havas Agency. If anyone was paying for a "propaganda offensive" about Guernica, it could well have been those who profited most from the false news telegraphed by Botto—that is, the Spanish Nationalists and the Nazis. Only one person in our cast of characters was living beyond his means (as will be seen): again, Georges Botto.

The Havas Agency seemed rather pleased with their "Envoyé Spécial" who had cabled the false information. On the first of June he was given a 25 percent increase in salary, and the notifying letter read in part,

> We do not doubt that this action taken will please you and that you will see therein evidence of satisfaction on our part for the manner in which you have carried out, under particularly difficult conditions, the mission which we have entrusted to you. Nor do we doubt that you will see therein a valuable encouragement to continue on this path.[49]

Botto replied:

> All my efforts go towards informing you in the most exact and the most rapid manner possible, and at the same time to make for the Agency the place which it should occupy: the first.

Botto did not have the insolence to underline the word "exact." In this note Botto also wrote the following to Paris:

> I think I am on the right track. It has been hard going upstream, but I think the worst is over and that soon we shall be able to gather the fruits of our labor. I have already some small results which permit me to hope for better ones in the future.[50]

Botto was referring to exclusive stories, special interviews, favored treatment on his messages, and so forth. But on July 1, d'Hospital came back to Spain. Both correspondents held equal rank, both were "Special Correspondents," but doubtless d'Hospital, because of his greater experience, was the more highly regarded by Paris.[51]

Generally, Havas did not sign correspondents' names to their dispatches, and it is difficult to follow Botto and d'Hospital in their coverage of the military fronts.[52]

Botto apparently followed the end of the campaign in the north, for on October 21, he finished a dispatch with the following sentence:

> The Special Correspondent of the Havas Agency has presented to Colonel García Valiño the congratulations of the foreign press for the brilliant conduct of his brigade during all of the Northern offensive.

This sentence seemed in bad taste to Paris, and it was cut out of the text as distributed. Later, a note of the Havas management observed: "It is evidently not the work of our representative to congratulate a Spanish officer, and still less to inform us of his act."[53] This telegram seems to have marked the beginning of Botto's decline.

On November 17, a telegram from Botto, too patently pro-Nationalist, produced comments such as these in Paris: "This paper of Botto's is really absurd," and "This is certainly a miserable report."[54] A few days later he sent a message from Hendaye, announcing an offer of mediation on the part of the English, an offer that involved the restoration of the monarchy in Spain. Botto insisted that this telegram, which he pompously claimed as an exclusive for the Havas Agency, be datelined not from Spain but from France.[55] This precaution was evidently taken so that inside the Insurgent zone Botto would not be thought the author of the news. His telegram indicated no source for the information, and it immediately aroused the mistrust of Botto's superiors in Paris. An inquiry in London confirmed the suspicions aroused, and the story was not distributed.[56]

Two days after the first telegram from Hendaye, Botto sent another, saying that

> it was learned from an authorized source that after a profound study of the British proposition on mediation of the Spanish conflict, the *Generalísimo* has not been able to take it into consideration.

Botto appended to this telegram a note informing Paris that "all this series of telegrams has been given me by the diplomatic cabinet of the *Generalísimo,* which has been extremely surprised not to find in the newspapers the first dispatch announcing the English démarche."[57]

Havas had reason to believe that the first telegram on this subject was false, that the English mediation offer was inexistent. A second telegram announcing Franco's reaction to an inexistent offer smacked of insolence. Havas threw this message into the wastebasket along with the first one, and then published, instead, a report from Paul-Louis Bret, its correspondent in London, denying as unfounded rumors the news contained in both of Botto's dispatches.[58] The Havas management was probably further irritated when Botto's first message was printed in *Le Jour* under the signature of Henry de Vilmorin, whom the Belgian reporter Hoornaert had already described to Havas as being "the most favored" of French correspondents in the Nationalist zone.[59]

Sending this telegram was an error on the part of Botto, for, unlike the Guernica message that was equally false, it carried no warning to Havas. "It would have been of the most elementary honesty on the part of Mr. Botto to inform us of the origin of his information," wrote one of the Havas managers. He summed up:

> One concludes from this that Mr. Botto accepts to tell us everything he is asked to tell us; that he fails to surround himself with precautions of elementary prudence; and that henceforth the editorial board will accept his communications with extreme mistrust.[60]

Unfortunately for Botto, the matter did not stop with his troubles in Paris. His two telegrams with false information may have pleased certain monarchist elements in the diplomatic cabinet at San Sebastián, but not other and more influential persons at Salamanca and Burgos. How these persons became aware of the intrigue is not revealed by the Havas papers, but on December 1, d'Hospital telephoned from Hendaye to inform Paris that a commission was in San Sebastián to inquire into the false news sent by Botto concerning the English offer of mediation. Botto was unable to produce any documentation to support his telegram, but a certain Baráibar of the Diplomatic Cabinet more or less recognized that he had given the information to Botto. Baráibar was released on parole. There were rumors of Botto's arrest, and when he tried to cross the frontier to Hendaye on November 29, the Spanish police refused him passage. However, everything now seemed arranged, said d'Hospital.[61]

But as Botto's affairs cleared up in Spain, they worsened in Paris. A Havas "Note for the Management," dated December 4, 1937, read in part:

> There seems to be no doubt that Mr. Botto is suffering from a form of megalomania. . . . With this state of mind, it is not surprising that Botto should act in a complaisant manner towards the Nationalist authorities and consent to send us at times rather amazing communications. If he behaved with more subtlety, he could be amiable with them and at the same time warn us by the proper "notes de service"; in doing so, he would, moreover, be doing only his duty. Instead of this, he has the effrontery to present false information to us as a Havas exclusive, the publication of which would have caused considerable bother. . . . The fault committed by Botto in sending us, under the circumstances indicated, the false information on English mediation, would justify the recall of our collaborator.[62]

Botto was not, however, immediately recalled. Instead, for the moment, Havas changed the hierarchy of its representatives in the Franco zone. D'Hospital was named head of all Havas activities, and Botto his "informateur"; any political news that Botto wrote had first to be approved by d'Hospital before going to Paris.[63] This arrangement did not last long. On February 3, 1938, the distinguished savant in science and amateur in politics, Georges Claude, published an article on Spain in *L'Action Française,* in which the managers of Havas could read:

> I am happy, not only to confirm by what I have seen and heard, all that has been published by our courageous correspondents, Real del Sarte, Héricourt,

Le Boucher, Dourec—with whom I want to associate Claude Farrère and Botto—but to say how great is the authority which *L'Action Française* enjoys in Nationalist circles.[64]

The classification of their correspondent, supposedly politically neutral and rigidly professional in his outlook, with those of *L'Action Française* was more than the directors of Havas could tolerate. For this gaffe on the part of Claude, Botto was recalled to Paris with a telegram dated February 4. This message is not in the Havas files, but Botto immediately called Paris from the French frontier, protesting to Meynot that he had not asked to leave Spain and that his health was excellent. Meynot explained to Botto that the references to his demand to leave Spain and to his health were but pretexts to save him embarrassment. "It is, then, a disfavor," observed Botto.[65]

However, Meynot told Botto, he could remain in Spain until a replacement was found. In spite of the salary paid, Havas found it difficult to find a competent man to go to Nationalist Spain; the work was dangerous, and the Insurgent authorities were slow to accept candidates. Nor was Botto in a hurry to leave, exchanging the affluence he knew in Spain for the drudgery of Paris. Finally the name of André Vincent was accepted by the Rebel press office,[66] and Botto was told to come back to Paris.[67] Botto then had someone telegraph to Paris to say that he was engaged in a series of farewell visits to Spanish officials in Saragossa, Burgos, and Seville.[68] Havas telegraphed to d'Hospital, requesting Botto's immediate return: "We unreservedly blame his attitude in absolute contradiction with orders given him."[69] Botto finally crossed the frontier, after visiting Saragossa and Burgos,[70] and took some weeks of vacation then due him. His mother died on April 30, 1938, and at the funeral service in Auteuil he caught cold.[71]

Havas was then informed that Botto was ill and could not come to work.[72] On May 20, an emissary from Havas found the correspondent in bed.[73] A month later the visit was repeated, but this time Botto was absent, having gone, the visitor was told, to see the doctor.[74] Botto had not come back to work by July 6. A Havas management memorandum of that date read:

> A curious detail concerning a collaborator who in Paris was always short of money: M. Botto has received only an advance of his salary for April (payable at the scale of Special Correspondent) and has not received any of his salary for May and June (payable at the Paris scale). . . . In any case, if M. Botto comes back to the editorial services, I should have a strongly unfavorable bias against him.[75]

On July 20, Botto's doctor gave him fifteen additional days of rest.[76] The Havas Agency then sent a doctor to visit Botto, who was absent on July 21,[77] absent on July 25.[78] On July 27, the Havas doctor finally found Botto and declared him fit to resume work in August.[79]

But already in July the dossier of complaints against Botto was growing fatter, including not only disloyal actions against his colleagues of the agency but also political denunciations of Frenchmen to the Insurgent authorities. Leon Guillet, member of the Institute, director of L'Ecole Centrale, wrote to protest that one of his former students, a French industrialist in Saragossa, had been "denounced by a correspondent of the Havas Agency, as being a Republican sympathizer, which is certainly false."[80] Botto had also, Havas was told, taken pains to give a bad reputation, politically speaking, to a French vice-consul.[81] D'Hospital, "invoking the testimony of colleagues, had already told of certain manuevers of M. Botto directed against him,"[82] and Botto's successor, André Vincent, had informed Havas "that his arrival in Spain had been prepared in a rather singular manner by his predecessor."[83]

An official of the Havas Agency, M. Fis, by chance found himself in Hendaye. Learning that he was from Havas, the hotel keepers began to talk about Botto. Although Fis had not come to Hendaye to make this inquiry, he felt obliged to inform Paris. A report dated August 3 told all about the correspondent who "led such an easy and outrageously expensive life in the region that everyone talks about him." "People tell me," the author of the report went on,

> of their astonishment that an agency such as ours would have tolerated for so long a person who spent money so obviously out of all proportion with his possible salary, money which could only have come, to say the least, from falsifying expense vouchers.

The report said Botto "played *le grand seigneur*" and mentioned "the crazy expenditures of our former correspondent."[84]

Botto's chauffeur, who claimed his last weeks were unpaid, charged his former employer with disloyalty to his Havas colleague.

> It even happened, several times, that Botto, having learned that d'Hospital was preparing to go to France, told his chauffeur to increase his speed. "That way we shall get first to the military post," he explained, "and I'll arrange for them to refuse a pass to d'Hospital." The chauffeur did not tell me by what shameful means Botto achieved his ends. One fears to guess.[85]

This report was handed to the head office of Havas on August 4. That very same day Botto telephoned in to say that he would report for work on the afternoon of August 5, at four in the afternoon. The following paper in the files is Botto's letter of resignation, dated August 6.[86]

Thirteen days later, Botto wrote to thank the Havas management for sums given to his family. He spoke of his "resignation" in quotation marks, protested his loyalty to the agency, and announced his immediate departure for Spain.[87] This marks the end of Botto's dossier in the Havas files, except for visits of bailiffs and tax men, one on the subject of a fine amounting to almost five times Botto's yearly salary in Paris.[88]

Couderc, of *L'Action Française,* who later served as press attaché of Pierre Héricourt, then Petain's consul-general in Barcelona during the years of Vichy,[89] and who knew Botto well, finds it strange that the former Havas man said he was returning to Spain in August 1938, for Couderc never saw him there, and Couderc was everywhere in Rebel Spain at the time. "He was a collaborationist with the Germans," goes on Couderc,

> which was rather strange, for he was certainly not pro-Boche when I knew him in Spain. He got used to spending money and couldn't stop. He was administrator of Radio Paris, the German transmitter in Paris, and I think he left Paris with the Germans. I never saw him after 1940.[90]

A further reference to Georges Botto can be found in the memoirs of Jean Hérold-Paquis, the ill-famed speaker of the Radio-Journal of Paris. The reference is to August 16, 1944; the French collaborators with the Nazis are leaving Paris, and with them the personnel of the Radio-Journal, including Botto. An employee of Radio Paris

> had during the day, bought two automobiles, through the intervention of M. Botto, this curious factotum, former editor at the Agence Havas, become by some unknown miracle, administrative director of the *Radio-Journal,* former tenant of a real town house, Square of the Bois de Boulogne, a fact which marked a change for him and his tribe, from the mediocre apartment which he formerly occupied in the 15th *arrondisement.* . . . Not one of the automobiles bought by Botto and paid for—cash-and-carry—would run. There were shouts of sabotage! I would have preferred that one speak of imbecility! Unless Botto . . . But everyone will tell you that he was a very honest man. They will tell it to you very quickly, true enough![91]

We have perhaps lingered too long over the sad, degrading story of Georges Botto. But he was one of the chief witnesses in the controversy over Guernica, as was George Steer, as was James Holburn. Jerrold, Lunn, Father Thorning, Sencourt, Father Code, Major Williams—all attacked the testimony and character of George Steer, and, in the course of this study, the evidence available, concerning both Steer's testimony and his character, have been examined. The study would be incomplete if the evidence concerning the testimony and the character of the other two journalists involved was not also examined. This has been done with Holburn, and now it has been done with Botto.

The evidence brought forward against Steer was never more than supposition and innuendo. The analysis of the telegram found in the Bilbao post office by the Nationalists, as advanced by Father Thorning, Father Code, and Major Williams was amateurish, and finds no support in the archives of the *Times.* The evidence against Botto is of another *cru.* The document in the British Foreign Office concerning Botto's telegram is confirmed by the original telegram itself, the only such original news telegram of the Spanish Civil War preserved in the Havas files. The Havas files are not lacking in evidence of doubtful morality against Botto, quite different from the unfounded accusations irresponsibly voiced against Steer.

The situation of Botto is then clear: Botto did send a false telegram about Guernica; he sent other telegrams containing false information; he lost the confidence of the editors of the Havas Agency; he left his employment under a cloud of suspicion. Botto was a French collaborator with the Nazis. Steer was killed in military service against the Japanese. It is perhaps but poetic justice that the charges read by the English and American Catholics against George Steer, the defender of the Basques, should in the final accounting be found to be a true bill against Georges Botto, the defamer of the Basques, and himself the chief witness of these same English and American Catholics.

But it is manifestly unjust to declare Georges Botto the dishonest employee of honest employers. Insofar as the Guernica telegram goes, Botto did not cheat his employers; he cheated the Basques, the Spanish Republic, and the newspaper-reading public, but in this particular swindle, Botto had at least one accomplice, probably two. Back of Botto stood the Havas Agency, which sent out the Guernica cablegram and in so doing, cheated its clients, the newspaper-reading public, the Basques, and the Spanish Republic (and the *Times*, Steer, and so forth).

The telegram about Guernica, signed by Botto and received by Havas, can be accepted as Botto's original. It was not exactly what was later printed in the French press. It read:

> . . . agy 512 vitoria 308 [words] 1 [May] 2145 [hours] biscay front satur-
> day nineteen hours stop headquarters officers mola today conducted foreign
> journalists guernica to permit them visit thoroughly ruins town guernica
> paragraph one recalls reds spread whole world story that nationalists had
> themselves destroyed town by series methodical air bombings with heavy
> bombs paragraph havasman who went over town all directions stop pene-
> trated smallest nook stop questioned complete freedom few civilians who had
> courage await arrival franco troops [Havasman] saw for himself bistop that
> all sections walls still standing bear no traces even slight bomb splinters on
> other hand all windows are girdled traces flames stop wooden beams burning
> still today dash three days after occupation dash rubble shows collapse
> buildings stop [Havasman] can still follow ravages fire which probably began
> south town and which fanned by sea breeze spread northwards stop [Havas-
> man] remarks also that places where fire did not take hold especially houses
> reinforced concrete were drenched gasoline and [Havasman] sees interiors
> still intact traces flames which must have been started by kerosene because
> smoke deposited very greasy soot paragraph elsewhere bombs may possibly
> have left traces explosion stop no bombholes found despite meticulous
> searching stop only some outskirts town especially near roads serving Guer-
> nica paragraph beyond doubt nationalists unparticipated this devastation stop
> civilians state clearly reds began evil work monday evening 26 and their
> declarations are easily verified because [Havasman] can follow advance
> scourge stop moreover reds exploded town itself four mines craters of which
> still unfilled greatly bothering traffic stop significant that this only town
> where communists used this method paragraph no doubt for persons on spot
> that responsibility this disaster attributable to quote marxists unquote botto
> suggest wide publicity be given this dispatch botto.[92]

This telegram, timed at seven o'clock on the evening of Saturday, May 1, by Botto, was timed at nine o'clock that same evening by the telegraph services in Vitoria and delivered in Paris by Eastern Telegraph, on the following day, Sunday, May 2, on seven pages of telegraph paper. The first page bears the notation "4.50" and this probably means "four hours and fifty minutes" on the morning of that day. This telegram was edited in the Havas offices. At that time the editor in chief at Havas was Louis Perrin; his assistant was Léon Chadé. Perrin is dead, but Chadé is now managing director of *L'Est Republicain,* an important French provincial daily published at Nancy. Chadé remembers Botto and his "profascist opinions." Botto, he writes, "espoused the Franco cause unreservedly." Chadé does not remember the Botto dispatch on Guernica, but he thinks that such a cablegram, received on a Sunday, may well have passed through his hands. "I was doubtless on duty at the agency, the day the cablegram was received, because on Sundays I replaced, as assistant chief editor, the editor in chief," he writes. "It is therefore highly probable that this dispatch went through my hands, unless it was published, before my arrival around nine o'clock, by the night service."[93] But there are good reasons for doubting that this particular telegram was edited by Chadé, aside from the fact that it probably arrived at the Havas offices at 4.50 in the morning, and Chadé came in around nine.

The journalist who edited Botto's telegram did his rewriting, as was customary, on the face of the telegram itself, changing phrases, eliminating sentences, adding articles, punctuation, and capital letters to the abbreviated telegraphic style. His work gave us the following text:

> Biscay Front, from the Special Correspondent of the Havas Agency. Officers of General Mola's general staff yesterday conducted foreign journalists to Guernica where they were permitted to make a thorough visit of the ruins of the town.
>
> One recalls that news from a government source has said that the town had been burned by the Nationalists in a series of methodical air bombings by means of heavy bombs.
>
> The foreign journalists were able to go through the town in all directions and questioned with complete freedom the few civilians who had awaited the arrival of General Franco's troops. They have been able to see for themselves that all the sections of walls still standing bear no trace of bomb splinters and that on the other hand all the windows are girdled by traces of flames. The beams are still continuing to burn, three days after the occupation. Nationalist officers drew the attention of the journalists to the fact that nowhere did one find signs of bomb splinters and that the absence of any traces of projectiles, as well as verifications made elsewhere, showed the evident arson in the town. One could even follow the havoc wrought by the fire which must have begun in the south of the town and which, fanned by the sea breeze, spread to the north. The attention of the journalists was also drawn to the fact that the places where the fire did not take hold, especially the houses of reinforced concrete, were drenched with gasoline, and they could see in the

interiors still intact traces of flames which must have been started by kerosene because the smoke deposited a very greasy soot.[94]

At this point in the telegram, the first editor stopped his work. But the text just given did not constitute the final dispatch distributed by the Havas Agency. There was another editing (or editings). Why did the first editor stop his work? Who did the final editing? These are questions difficult to answer today.

We have, then, three versions of Botto's dispatch: the telegram sent through the Vitoria censorship and received by Havas in Paris, a first attempt at editing in the Havas offices, and the final, published version. There are singular differences among the three. Let us, first of all, compare the Botto telegram with the first and incomplete editing. Botto's telegram was an extreme statement of the Nationalist position. He found no traces of bombs or of bomb splinters. He did find evidence of the use of both gasoline and kerosene in starting the fires, which he unequivocally attributed to "Marxists," "Communists," and "Reds." He denied any Nationalist responsibility whatsoever for the disaster. (In a way, Botto was betrayed by the Nationalist censorship, for within twenty-four hours Holburn sent through that censorship a cablegram admitting that Guernica was bombed "intermittently over a period of three hours.")

But Botto told his editors that they could not place any trust in the content of his message. Nevertheless, the journalist who began the editing in the Havas offices and the journalist (or journalists) who wrote the final version, not only made no effort to weaken the extreme pro-Nationalist statement sent by Botto but in some places these strong statements were made stronger. Botto, nowhere in his original message pretended to be the spokesman of all the foreign journalists who visited Guernica on that day, but the first editor who worked on his telegram changed the text so that Botto's convictions and conclusions became those of all the foreign journalists who visited Guernica on May 1. Where Botto had telegraphed the word "Havasman," the editor substituted "the foreign journalists," and in two other places in his editing he added the phrase "the foreign journalists" where Botto referred only to himself, and in one other place he substituted a plural verb (referring to "the foreign journalists") for the singular verb used by Botto to refer to himself.

There is no journalistic justification for this change, and this is especially true of a cablegram containing false information. We have seen that the change resulted in the generalized belief among Franco's partisans in England—and in France—(or so they said) that Botto spoke for all the foreign journalists in Vitoria.[95] It is true that the effect was softened by the subterfuge of adding such phrases as "Nationalist officers drew the attention of the journalists to the fact . . ." and "The attention of the journalists was also drawn to the fact that . . ." but these subtleties were usually lost on the newspaper-reading public and completely lost on Franco's partisans.

Where Botto had cabled: "[Havasman] does not see anywhere fragments projected by explosions stop arson is evident . . ." the editor wrote that nowhere did one find signs of bomb splinters and that the absence of any traces of projectiles, as well as verifications made elsewhere, showed the evident arson in the town.

The editor not only arranged Botto's prose to fortify the pro-Nationalist content, but he also added the phrase "as well as verifications made elsewhere." Botto did not speak of these "verifications," and they existed only in the editor's imagination. There is no defense for this act. It was also this editor who crossed out the only part of Botto's message that might have enfeebled his pro-Nationalist stance: "Elsewhere bombs may possibly have left traces explosion."

We can now study the further changes made in the Botto telegram by the final editor or editors, changes that resulted in the text distributed by Havas to the press. No effort whatsoever was made by the new editor to weaken the pro-Nationalist content of this message, which was, however, known to be of highly doubtful quality. The alterations made by the first editor were accepted. The sentence in Botto's cablegram that, curiously, repeated through the Vitoria censorship the accusation of the Basques ("one recalls reds spread whole world story that nationalists had themselves destroyed town by series methodical air bombings with heavy bombs") was transformed into:

[The officers of General Mola's staff yesterday conducted the foreign journalists to Guernica] to let them see for themselves, with their own eyes, that contrary to the news from a government source, the destruction of the town was not the work of the Nationalists.

This is, from the Franco point of view, a more positively favorable statement than Botto's original.

This editor also continued the practice of changing Botto's statements into the collective experiences of "the journalists." He revised the following phrase of Botto's cablegram: "Moreover, . . . reds exploded town itself four mines craters of which still unfilled greatly bothering traffic." This became: "Moreover, the journalists were shown, in the town itself, four craters resulting from mines. . . ." He removed from the representative of the Havas Agency the full responsibility for stating that the craters were caused by mines and not by bombs; and attributed the responsibility to Botto's colleagues (and to the Nationalist officers), leaving but a small part of the opinion to Botto himself. It should be observed also that the editors left in the text the flagrant contradictions in Botto's telegram: he saw no bomb holes, then he did see some on the outskirts; he had seen four craters in the middle of the town, but these he attributed to mines.

Some of Botto's affirmations that aggressively adopted the Insurgent version of Guernica were, however, eliminated in the corrected text by the last editor. "Beyond doubt nationalists unparticipated this devastation" was dropped, as was "No doubt for persons on spot that responsibility this disaster attributable to quote marxists unquote."

But the cuts made in the final part of the message were perhaps done in the interest of brevity. One can say, in summing up, that the editing done by Havas on the basis of Botto's doubtful telegram reinforced, rather than weakened, its pro-Nationalist content. The editors sought also to eliminate personal references to Botto and to his opinions by attributing them generally to groups of journalists who, as such and with such opinions, simply did not exist.

If Chadé had helped in this veritable conspiracy and if he had edited a telegram so widely discussed, it seems likely that he would remember it today. Everything we know about the Botto message indicates that it was not handled by Havas as a run-of-the-mill news item. The French foreign minister told the British ambassador: "A high official in the Havas Agency . . . decided to take the message *'au pied de la lettre'* and the widest publicity was given." We can presume that high officials of the agency did not see and take decisions on ordinary news telegrams. The statement of Delbos as reported by Phipps suggests a decision taken after weighing all the elements involved. And this decision was known the following day to certain officials of the Quai d'Orsay, even to the foreign minister. The telegram itself was kept, the only news telegram of its time still in the Havas files. The wording of the telegram was the subject of discussions in Paris newspaper circles and, as we have seen, Pierre-Louis Falaize, writing in *L'Aube* of May 19, 1937, knew the terminal, and significant, words of Botto, although he did not realize their true meaning.

But it was not only Botto's telegram about Guernica that was treated in this abnormal manner by the Havas Agency. Every piece of news concerning Guernica was manipulated by Havas in the same fashion. From the first moment that news about the destruction of the Basque town was received in Paris (the message from Fontecha), Havas managed this information in an unusual manner for a news agency. Fontecha's message was botched; no amplification of this botched job was ever sent out; most of the news of the English reaction to the bombing came from special correspondents of Paris newspapers and not from the Havas Agency; Onaindia's interview was poorly distributed (if distributed at all), and, still later, Holburn's cablegram to the *Times* was incorrectly interpreted in the version sent out by Havas. In fact, at only one moment, during the week when Guernica dominated the headlines, did Havas show normal journalistic zeal and energy: this was in distributing the knowingly false information contained in Botto's telegram. The existence of a Guernica problem in the Havas offices of 1937 can be verified today by the thick dossier of Guernica material that Havas prepared at the time.[96]

To what can be attributed the manner in which Havas manipulated the news about Guernica? Why was the decision taken to distribute Botto's telegram, despite the knowledge that its contents were doubtful? Did the agency fear reprisals from the Spanish Nationalists? It is pertinent to recall here the need of the Havas Agency to have, at all costs, a representative in the Insurgent area. This man was supposed to send a thousand words, or two thousand words, a day, to be published not in the French press but in the Latin American press. If Havas had no man in Franco Spain, it would have but a one-sided (Republican) coverage of the war. Under these conditions, it might well have lost customers in South America, but Havas did not maintain this service because the Latin American revenues were important but because the French Foreign Office thought it worthwhile and necessary.

It has been written above that there was in all probability a third accomplice in the publication of the false Botto telegram on Guernica. This was the Quai d'Orsay. Relations between the French Ministry of Foreign Affairs and the Havas Agency were extremely close, so close that the first paid the debts of the second. The Havas Agency was composed of two activities: an advertising service that made money, and a news service which did not make money.[97] The balance sheet results were the addition of the profits of one service and the losses of the other.[98] Poincaré had opened a monthly credit in 1924 "for the reimbursement of part of the transmission costs to Latin America."[99] In 1931, Briand as foreign minister signed an accord with Havas general manager, Charles Houssaye,[100] which provided for the payment by the Quai d'Orsay of up to 800,000 francs a month for "the expenses incurred by the Agency in strengthening its posts and foreign services in Europe, America and Asia." The accord stated that these sums were paid not for political reasons but "for the diffusion of French thought."[101] In July 1938 another agreement was signed under which "the deficit of the 'Information Branch' of Havas would be paid by the Foreign Ministry during a period of ten years."[102]

In view of this collaboration between the agency and the ministry, or as we might say, in view of the control of the "Information Branch" of the agency by the ministry, the almost total absence of references to this relationship in the Havas files is surprising. However, there are one or two small bits of paper, which might have been overlooked in any determined attempt to rid the files of such evidence. And one of these small bits of paper concerns Guernica. After the publication of the Botto telegram, Havas cabled its representative in Bilbao, Fontecha, asking him to send "urgently other very precise testimonies on destruction of Guernica."[103] Fontecha responded with an account of the talks of the mayor of Guernica and of Father Arronategui on the Bilbao radio.[104] This cablegram arrived in Paris in Spanish and was immediately sent to the South American desk for transmission. But when translated into French, an editor thought it too propagandistically favorable to the Basques, rewrote the story, and handed it to the management.

> This modified text was submitted by M. Bassée to the Quai. The Quai after some slight changes and after having suppressed the final sentence, which I had left in, attributing the responsibility of the destruction to the Germans, had the text published.[105]

This incident shows that within forty-eight hours of the publication of the Botto telegram, other information concerning Guernica was being controlled not only by the Havas management but also by the Quai d'Orsay. The Quai d'Orsay was more severe in its censorship than was the agency, and this censorship was being exercised in a manner that weakened the Basque charges against the Germans. The Havas Agency, which had distributed a false dispatch accusing the Basques of destroying Guernica, then distributed another dispatch only after eliminating the Basque accusations of the Germans. A remark is justified at this point. The Fontecha telegram was edited twice, once by a Havas editor, once by an editor in the Quai d'Orsay. The Botto telegram was also edited twice. Were they the same hands that put the finishing touches to both messages? A factor other than the Spanish Civil War was also involved in the editing of these cablegrams: Havas' service to Latin America. Jacques Dumaine, a former chief of protocol of the French Foreign Ministry, described the situation as follows: "The *Service de l'Information et de la Presse* of the Quai d'Orsay organizes and directs, in agreement with the Havas agency, French news sent to foreign countries, and especially to America."[106]

Only one other example of French Foreign Ministry censorship of Havas telegrams during the Spanish Civil War can be found in the files today. On August 11, 1937, Botto sent a message to Paris to the effect that von Goss, identified as the director of the German news agency, DNB, who was residing in Saint-Jean-de-Luz, had been expelled by the French authorities. Someone has written on this teletyped dispatch the following notation: "The Quai is absolutely opposed to our talking of this affair."[107]

In view of all this evidence it is difficult to think that the "high official" of Havas decided to distribute the Botto telegram without previous consultation with, and the accord of, the French Foreign Ministry. Officials of the Foreign Ministry, even the foreign minister, were well aware of the situation on May 3, as is shown by the message sent by the British ambassador to London. Significantly, this diplomatic message makes no effort to explain why the Botto telegram, known to be false, was distributed. The diplomatic message explained merely why, after distribution, its lack of veracity could not be announced. But this explanation is not convincing. If on May 3, the Havas Agency and the Quai d'Orsay feared that Georges Botto would be shot in case the truth were told about his telegram, the correspondent could have been recalled to the French side of the frontier (where, moreover, he frequently went) and held there while the truth was revealed publicly. This procedure was not even envisaged. Such an action would have been a blow to Havas, certainly; perhaps all the other French correspondents would have been expelled from Insurgent territory. The nonexistent relations between Paris and Salamanca might have worsened; relations between Paris and Berlin might have greatly deteriorated. But the truth would have prevailed, this truth that news agencies like so much to speak of.

There is, then, strong evidence for assuming that not only the Havas-Botto telegram but all the Havas coverage of the Guernica incident was censored, by both the Havas high command and the Quai d'Orsay. This censorship worked to the disadvantage of the Spanish Republicans and the Basque government, and to the advantage of the Franco forces and their German Nazi allies. Why was this done?

The nominal head of the Foreign Ministry was Yvon Delbos, a Radical Socialist with a reputation for being against any help to the Spanish Republic.[108] He was also the author of a book frequently cited in anti-Communist campaigns during the Spanish Civil War.[109] More important, the secretary-general of the Foreign Ministry, Alexis Léger, was firmly opposed to intervention in the war—that is, to aid for the Republicans.[110]

It is not difficult to imagine that in the higher spheres of the Ministry, as in the same spheres of other foreign ministries of Western Europe, enthusiasm for Franco was rampant. It seems plausible that the first news of the destruction of Guernica received by Havas was held back by the agency and by the Quai d'Orsay; when the news from London showed the strong reaction in the British press on the afternoon of April 27, an almost incomprehensible dispatch was finally issued for the morning papers of April 28. Havas was of course beaten by the competition, but according to one observer, Jacques Dumaine, this was a frequent happening when politically sensitive reports were held up, awaiting the "confirmation" of the Quai d'Orsay.[111] The same policy was doubtless followed on all the other news about Guernica. The probable purpose was to prevent popular feeling in France from reacting violently and demanding aid for the Spanish Republic. We have seen how the full publication of the news of Guernica provoked a public reaction in England, which for more than two months embarrassed the government with acerbic debate and demands for more information. By depriving the French people of the first alarming news, the French government (the Foreign Ministry and the Havas Agency) defused the possible repercussions the full truth of the destruction of Guernica might have had on French public opinion.

One of the most competent commentators on the French press of the 1930s has written that throughout the Spanish Civil War, Havas manipulated the news. Thanks to its control of the sources of news and of the budgets for publicity—including those of the government—the management of Havas could suppress news or invent news at its will.

> Usually an unofficial denial, a hint of dreadful consequences to come, were quite enough to bring those who had dared open their mouths back into line,

wrote Pertinax. And in a phrase that will recall to readers Jean Richard's article in *L'Aube* telling of his interview with Father Onaindia, Pertinax continued:

> But what did it matter, after all, if a few isolated journalists did speak out? The tens of thousands of readers whom they kept posted were insignificant in comparison to the millions led astray. Fully seventy out of one hundred Frenchmen never knew that the Italian planes sent to the assistance of the Spanish generals crashed near Oran at the end of July 1936; that the acts of piracy in the Mediterranean, denounced by the Nyon Conferences (September 1937), were chargeable to Italians; that German aviators bombed Guernica.[112]

2

The Dead and the Dying

One of the more puzzling features of the Guernica controversy was the reluctance of the defenders of the Nationalist position to make any reference to the victims of the disaster. Yet the victims constitute the essential element of the incident. Had the explosive and incendiary bombs touched only the wood and stone construction of the Basque town, which contained no extraordinary monuments (aside from the Casa de Juntas and the oak trees, which were untouched), it would have been an unpardonable aggression. Guernica held a sentimental place in Basque hearts, but such an aggression would, after all, have been of minor international consequence if people had not died in the raid. The wiping out of a town in an aerial attack, as happened in Guernica, for the first time in history, was in itself a sensational event. But doubtless what touched the imagination of so many people in the world, not yet wearied of the murderous accounts of Coventry, Dresden, Hiroshima, and Hanoi, was the fact that people were killed and wounded in Guernica.

How many were the killed and the wounded? This question cannot be answered with precision today, and it was probably never possible to give an accurate answer. Twenty-seven days before the bombing, at seven-twenty on the morning of March 31, the Basque town of Durango was attacked by four bombers and nine fighters. Durango was some distance from the fighting line and remained in Basque hands for twenty-nine days after the bombing; the attack was but the opening shot in the northern campaign, and the Basques still had the morale to take the time and care to document the casualties. This documentation is not without significance for our story, as shall be seen. But the attack on Guernica was of another dimension. The town was wiped out. There was not enough time to search the ruins for bodies. The town fell to the enemy less than seventy-two hours after the bombing. Thus the Basque government lost all control over the counting of the dead eventually found in the debris or in the surrounding fields.

For there were victims, and this fact was known from the moment the first news was received. Yet we find in almost all of the pro-Franco disquisitions on Guernica a complete silence concerning any possible casualties. A Spaniard in the Rebel zone, whose only source of information was the press of that area; a French conservative, whose view of the war was limited to that given by a newspaper such as *Le Figaro*; an Englishman, whose knowledge of the Guernica incident was obtained from the writings of Jerrold, Lunn, and the like—all these people might well have demanded the reason for the uproar about Guernica. The sources of their information never talked of the dead and the dying.

Preliminary to our effort to try to find out how many victims perished in Guernica, we shall try to estimate how many people were in the town on April 26, 1937, and the extent of the damage done to the town. Nobody really knows the population of Guernica on the day of the bombing. There were figures for the *normal* population of the town, but the situation in Guernica was not normal on April 26, 1937. People had left the town because of the war. How many? Nobody knows. Refugees had come into Guernica, fleeing before the Nationalist troops. Again, nobody knows how many these were. A third element enters into our calculation. April 26 was a Monday, and Monday was market day. How many people attended the market that Monday? There was some disagreement on all these points.

Steer said that the population of Guernica on April 26, 1937, was seven thousand plus three thousand refugees.[1] He also noted that Monday was the market day for the region, that at four-thirty "the market was full and peasants were still coming in."[2] Holme's Reuters dispatch likewise fixed the population at 10,000 and stated that "the raid occurred on market day when the town was full of peasants."[3] Noel Monks also gave Guernica a population of 10,000 in his first report from Bilbao,[4] and later 6,000 when he was back in England.[5] Still later, in his book, Monks wrote that he had passed through Guernica at three-thirty on the afternoon of April 26. "Guernica was busy. It was market day."[6] Ralph Stevenson, the British consul, told his government that the number of people in Guernica was "since the September influx of refugees about ten thousand."[7] In one interview, Father Onaindia estimated the normal population of Guernica at 7,000 and the refugees and market visitors at 5,000, for a total of 12,000 people on April 26.[8] He wrote that on arriving in Guernica, some minutes before the air raid, the town "offered us the spectacle of its streets animated by the weekly market," and he repeated the existence of the market in his memoirs.[9] The anonymous witness of Víctor Montserrat stated:

It was a Monday, the town was very lively because of the market attended by the inhabitants of the neighboring villages. Hundreds of honest peasants accompanied by their wives and children.[10]

The four Basque nurses who spoke in Paris on the night of May 22 gave the town a population of 12,000, of whom 6,000 were refugees and market visitors.[11]

Few writers who favored the Nationalist position gave any population figures for Guernica. Sencourt wrote that Guernica was "a town normally of some five thousand inhabitants," and he did not suggest the presence of either refugees or visitors.[12] *Guernica: The Official Report* gave the normal population of the town as "approximately 6,000 inhabitants,"[13] and said there were neither visitors nor market that day ("neither the cattle nor the attendants at the fair were anywhere to be seen") and that many inhabitants had fled that very day before the attack,[14] thus suggesting that the population on April 26 was smaller than normal. But on this detail as on many others, the report of the commissioners was contradicted by the testimony of a witness, this time a municipal employee, who told of finding in a shelter

. . . .forty-five dead persons, of whom the corpses had not all been identified, but that they appeared to be those of villagers who had attended the market which had taken place that day in Guernica.[15]

The Valladolid University report said the normal population of Guernica was 5,561 persons.[16] The Italian journalist Segàla cabled his newspaper that there were 7,000 persons in Guernica; they were forced to flee by the "Reds," who then dynamited the town.[17] Sandro Sandri adopted the same way out: the Asturian dynamiters forced the people to leave before blowing up their homes.[18] The English Catholic editor Douglas Woodruff, probably inspired by *Guernica: The Official Report*, wrote in 1938 that "the death roll in the event was under a hundred" because "the inhabitants had already, as a matter of common prudence, withdrawn in great numbers from what was obviously going to be a scene of military operations."[19] Many years later, Luis Bolín, rather foolishly in the light of what was known, declared that Guernica was "a small town of some 3,000 inhabitants."[20]

When postwar writers gave a figure for Guernica's population—for example, Thomas,[21] Georges-Roux,[22] and Hills,[23] —it was 7,000. Talón does indirectly give a population figure, but his special contribution to this phase of the controversy lies in his insistence on the fact that there were few visitors in Guernica, for a government official, fearing danger, had canceled the market and the jai alai game and placed pickets on the roads to stop the incoming peasants.[24] Talón himself places in doubt this testimony, for in a footnote he names eighteen localities around Guernica in which he found "traces of the people who disappeared during the bombing" of the town.[25]

If eighteen of the surrounding hamlets contributed to the day's death roll, there must have been a throng of visitors.

Elosegi declared that there were many countrymen in to the cattle fair that day.[26] Martínez Bande gave 5,000 as the town's population and considered that the number of people who had fled because of the war was more or less equaled by those who had come in for the same reasons. He also accepted Talón's statement that the market had been called off that day.[27]

But whether there were 6,000 people in Guernica on April 26, or a few more or a few less, what is certain is that the town was largely in ruins by nightfall. There is no doubt about the material damage done to Guernica. *Guernica: The Official Report* stated:

> Guernica possessed some 300 houses; of these, 71 per cent have been completely destroyed, and 7 per cent have been badly battered about. The remaining 22 percent are damaged, but not to the same extent.[28]

This would mean that about 213 houses were "completely destroyed" and 21 "badly battered about." An official Spanish publication of 1940 increased the figure of "houses destroyed" to 271. This figure was said to represent almost three-quarters of the number of houses destroyed in all of Vizcaya during the war, not counting the capital, Bilbao. The value of the damage done in Guernica was calculated at twelve million pesetas of the time—that is, almost one-third of all the damage suffered in the province, still excepting the capital city.[29]

We now know that on April 26, 1937, Guernica was a town whose population varied from 3,000 to 12,000 according to the political point of view, and that the town, if we look at only the official Spanish Nationalist statistics, was left in a state of total desolation. Of these, let us say 6,000 persons, who were in the town that was completely destroyed, how many were killed? The figures here vary. Partisans of the Basques were inclined to give a high figure; the Spanish Rebels to diminish the number of the dead to almost zero. Steer wrote:

> It is impossible to state yet the number of victims. . . . In the hospital of Josefinas, which was one of the first places bombed, all the 42 wounded militiamen it sheltered were killed outright. In a street leading downhill from the Casa de Juntas I saw a place where 50 people, nearly all women and children, are said to have been trapped in an air raid refuge under a mass of burning wreckage. Many were killed in the fields, and altogether the deaths may run into hundreds. An elderly priest was killed by a bomb.

When Steer came back on the afternoon of April 27, "About 30 dead were laid out in a ruined hospital."[30] In another article, Steer wrote of a "ruined hospital" where there were 40 dead,

> of whom I saw 14 laid out. They were mostly women, freshly dead and known by name to the Guernicans who were with me. They had not been killed by petrol but by bomb wounds, except two by bullets. On the same day Bilbao published a list of over 50 people from Guernica who were being treated for bomb wounds in Bilbao."[31]

Later in his book Steer gave no figures for the dead and wounded, not because there were none but because of the impossibility of calculating in the midst of chaos.

> Some of the witnesses were quite dumb. They were digging them out of ruined houses—families at a time, dead and blue-black with bruising. Others were brought in from just outside Gernika with machine-gun bullets in their bodies; one, a lovely girl. The militia cried as they laid her out on the ground in the broken hospital; they could give no reason for their tears—they just cried.[32]

There was no attempt here to exaggerate the number of the victims.

The Reuters dispatch, by Holme, published in the conservative *Morning Post,* read in part as follows:

> It is not yet known how many hundred civilians—men, women and children— lost their lives from shells or fire during the three and a half hours' bombardment.

It added these details:

> The Church of St. John was destroyed as was the Convent of Santa Clara, which was being used as a hospital. Many of its helpless inmates perished. Another small hospital, with 42 beds, was completely wiped out together with its 42 wounded occupants. Yet a third hospital was wrecked. . . . In one bomb shelter over 50 women and children were trapped and burned alive.[33]

Noel Monks cabled London on April 27 that "hundreds of bodies had been found in the debris."[34] In a second cable he noted:

> The full death roll in Guernica may never be known, for although bodies are being unearthed hourly from wrecked homes and buildings, it is believed that many will never be recovered.[35]

When Monks went home a week later, he asserted: "I saw bodies in the fields spotted with machine-gun bullets. . . . I saw 600 bodies."[36] Monks was less specific in his later book. He told of seeing, that night of April 26, "Basque soldiers collecting charred bodies that the flames had passed over." He wrote that "the smell of burning human flesh was nauseating." Again, "A sight that haunted me for weeks was the charred bodies of several women and children huddled together in what had been the cellar of a house."[37] Watson, of the *Star,* speaking over Radio Bilbao, said he saw "the mutilated bodies of some 500 civilians."[38]

Mathieu Corman, in his first dispatch to *Ce Soir,* gave the figure of 800 killed,[39] and in his second report stated that the number of the dead was larger still.[40] Corman also wrote in his book of the dead of Guernica.

> Here and there, a vague form in the red night, a body, human or animal. The smoke carries at times the smell of grilled meat. Nightmare. The bodies show

extravagant wounds. Here, a head opened like a cocoanut, the brains spilled out. There, an arm, a leg pulled off, the bone sticking out from the flesh. And over there, a body slashed as if a sadistic murderer had written out his fury with his knife, in the stomach and the flanks. Some of the dead are marked only with bullet wounds. I shall never forget—I shall never forget anything— that young girl, lovely still in death, half undressed by the deflagration, whose pelvis was but bloody pap.[41]

In a dispatch to the *News Chronicle,* Fifi Roberts, in Bilbao with her father's cargo vessel, wrote, "Among the victims were 42 wounded men and ten nurses burned alive."[42]

Each of these correspondents wrote according to his qualities as an observer, and according to the style of his newspaper. Several articles described the same victims, for example, the 42 wounded killed in the hospital. But it is impossible to read these accounts without realizing that many people were killed in Guernica on the afternoon of April 26. Even the mutilated Havas dispatch spoke of "victims," noting that their number was "unknown."[43] The press agencies reporting from outside the territory controlled by Bilbao also told of the numerous dead. The United Press from Hendaye said 800 persons had perished in the holocaust.[44] The Hearst Universal Service, in that curious dispatch supposedly sent from Vitoria, reported that "an estimated 900 men, women and children" had been killed in Guernica.[45]

Ralph Stevenson, the British consul in Bilbao, after his visit to the burning ruins on the morning of April 27, wrote:

The casualties cannot be ascertained and probably never will be, accurately. Some estimates put the figures at one thousand, others at over three thousand.[46]

Angel de Ojanguren y Celaya, who accompanied Stevenson, stated:

Scattered over the ground we saw several bodies but it will be very difficult to ascertain the exact number of the victims, for most of them perished in their own homes and their corpses disappeared calcined by the terrible fire.[47]

The figure advanced by the Basque government in Bilbao, and by the Basque delegation in Valencia, in the first days following the disaster, was 800 dead.[48] On May 4, Jesús María de Leizaola, minister of justice and education in the Basque government, in a radio address, alluded to two persons who had died in Bilbao hospitals following wounds received at Guernica and gave the figure of "590 others who died here in Bilbao as a result of such wounds after Guernica."[49] During that same radio program a parish priest from Guernica, Eusebio de Arronategui, said that he had seen "thousands of his fellow townsmen suffocated, wounded and dead pay tribute to brutality." The mayor of Guernica, José de Labauria, that same evening, spoke of "thousands upon thousands of innocent victims."[50] Basque

President José Antonio de Aguirre later wrote of Guernica as being "an immense bonfire, in which were burning hundreds of innocent victims," and declared that "almost two thousand" perished in the tragedy.[51] According to a Nationalist historian, Aguirre wrote to Prieto that there were 1,654 dead and 889 wounded in the Guernica bombing.[52] Father Onaindia in one interview was quoted as saying the dead were more than a thousand[53] and in another as expressing his belief that the number of the "victims" was "not inferior to 2,000."[54]

Four Basque nurses who were in Guernica on April 26 told a Paris audience a few weeks later that 2,000 persons had been killed in the air raid, giving these details:

> We remember a woman, the widow of Gazteiz, about 55 years old. She fled in terror in the street with her two daughters, 25 and 27. A bomb dropped from a plane left the two girls in pieces; the widow herself, wounded and out of her mind, reached the hospital, covered with blood and calling for her daughters. We cared for a child of three, Ángel Luis Badiola, badly wounded by shrapnel . . . the child died three days later in Bilbao. A woman, Pilar Ajuria, was badly hurt, driven half crazy; her husband was killed at her feet by a bomb as they were leaving their house. We also gave first aid to a civil guard and his wife, both wounded by shrapnel; the guard died a few days later in Bilbao. . . . We also know that there were persons of all ages and conditions buried in the ruins and torn to pieces in the streets and in the fields.[55]

The letter addressed to the Pope on May 11 by a delegation of Basque clergy spoke of "hundreds of casualties" in the destruction of Guernica.[56] The figure of 1,600 dead has been attributed to the mayor of Guernica,[57] and one writer contends that the figures of 1,645 (1,654?) dead and 889 wounded were given "in pamphlets printed abroad for the Republican government."[58] The numbers which were, apparently, first given by Aguirre, 1,654 dead and 889 wounded were used by the duchess of Atholl in 1938; she attributed them to "the latest official statement."[59] Pedro de Basaldúa, close collaborator of Aguirre, later wrote of more than 3,000 dead in Guernica.[60]

The newspaper reports from Bilbao and elsewhere and the charges of the Basque government concerning Guernica constituted a double accusation against the Nationalist forces and their Nazi allies. This indictment charged the Rebels and their foreign aviators with the destruction of the town, and it also charged them with the slaughter of many of the inhabitants of the town. The defenders of the Nationalists replied at length to the first part of the indictment, but rarely to the second. The arguments of the friends of the Nationalists accused the Basques, the Reds, the Anarchists, the Asturians, and others of dynamiting and setting fire to Guernica, but almost never did the pro-Nationalist writers accuse their enemies of killing anybody in the process of this destruction. They ignored this part of the indictment, and it can appear to the reader of their tracts that they were unable to bring themselves to speak of the dead in Guernica. For, in replying to the charges, just as they cried, "No, we did not destroy Guernica; you did it!" they should, in all normal circumstances, have at the same time cried, "No, we did not kill these people; you killed them!" But, except in a rare case or two, the defenders of the Franco position never charged the Basques or other Republican forces with killing anyone in Guernica. There was thus throughout the controversy a fundamental difference of expressed opinion concerning the very nature of the crime committed at Guernica.

Douglas Jerrold did not tell his readers that anyone was killed in Guernica. On one page, he wrote that the Republican army, by setting fire to the town, "endangers the lives of its subjects." On the same page, he perceived a contradiction in what he called Steer's "first excited account," because the correspondent wrote that the town was completely destroyed "but that the deaths were, fortunately small." But, the Catholic editor continued, the deaths "could hardly have been small if the town had been slowly, systematically, pounded to pieces. They might have been if it was being fired and mined."[61] Steer never wrote that "the deaths were, fortunately small." He wrote:

> It is impossible to state yet the number of victims. In the Bilbao press this morning they were reported as "fortunately small," but it is feared that this was an understatement in order not to alarm the large refugee population of Bilbao.

This deliberate attempt by Jerrold to use Steer as the authority for stating that few perished in the bombing is significant. From the first moments, the Nationalists and their spokesmen either ignored the victims of the disaster completely or sought to lower their total number. There was logic in Jerrold's reasoning, but the logic was equally valid for assuming, in case the town had been "slowly, systematically pounded to pieces," that there were many dead. Steer certainly suggested this probability. If Jerrold had read him carefully and quoted him correctly, he could have seen that the journalist thought "the deaths may run into hundreds." He cabled that the "42 wounded militiamen it [the Josefinas Hospital] sheltered were killed outright." He reported that "50 people, nearly all women and children, are said to have been trapped in an air raid refuge under a mass of burning wreckage," that "many were killed in the fields," that "an elderly priest named Arronategui was killed by a bomb," and that when he returned on the afternoon of April 27, "about 30 dead were laid out in a ruined hospital."

Arnold Lunn followed Jerrold's policy and said nothing of the victims in Guernica, although he did have a chapter of his book entitled, "The Inconvenient Dead."[62] These were the dead on his side, killed by "the Reds." Sencourt, in quoting Steer and the other correspondents at length in order to refute them, had to take notice of the charges that the dead "may amount to several hundreds," but he quickly added that "this hypothesis was never confirmed."[63] Nor did the marqués del Moral indicate that there were any victims in the diaster. He invented a new formula that got rid of the problem of the dead: "Most of the population had been evacuated by the Reds to Bilbao."[64] The audience that heard Father Thorning defend the Nationalist cause before the American Catholic Historical Association did not learn from the speaker that there were any victims at Guernica.[65] The American Jesuit Wilfrid Parsons denounced with ill-placed humor "the lurid story that Hitler's planes had bombed it [Guernica] flat and killed nobody knew how many women and children (never any men)."[66] Father Code did bring the supposed victims to the attention of his readers by denying "the mass murder of its [Guernica's] citizens by the forces of Franco."[67] Cardozo had the poor taste to attempt irony to belittle the charges of deaths in the bombing:

> Suppose this little Basque town . . . had really been bombed, and that really hundreds of its inhabitants had been killed. . . . So the hundreds of people shot down by the machine-gunning planes or killed by the bombing had all disappeared.[68]

Croft discounted the large number of dead reported in the news dispatches from Bilbao and noted that "the total number of bodies observed did not exceed fourteen." He wrote: "The suggestion that there was a massacre of vast numbers of civilians from machine gun fire must also be discounted." [69] On this point it can be observed that according to *Guernica: The Official Report*, Florencio Madariaga Arabia, twelve years old, died on May 9 of machine-gun wounds received during the bombing.[70]

It was in *Guernica: The Official Report*, published by Jerrold's firm, that for the first time pro-Nationalist elements in England admitted that there were victims in the Guernica disaster. This report, which rarely mentioned the dead was extremely taciturn concerning details about the victims, and concluded simply that "The number of victims in Guernica on the 26th April did not reach one hundred."[71] This figure, adopted by the investigating committee, was probably based on the statement of the stationmaster, who testified

> that the deaths which occurred in Guernica due to the destruction of that town did not amount to one hundred, a point on which he is able to give evidence, because he helped to extract from the ruins of the shelter in Santa María Street and of the Calzada Asylum the bodies of those who perished therein.[72]

It must be noted here that the extraction mentioned took place after April 29—that is, after the capture of the town by the Rebels.[73] Elsewhere the report says that forty-five persons perished in the Santa María shelter alone,[74] and in still another place lists fifty corpses "found in the various shelters in Guernica," from May 4 to June 17. The compiler of this list noted that "many of those who succumbed in the hospital [Asilo Calzada?] are missing" from the Civil Register.[75] A municipal employee

> states that in a certain unnamed shelter were found forty-five dead persons, of whom the corpses had not all been identified. . . . He also states that twenty-five inmates of an asylum perished and that these were identified.[76]

This municipal employee and the above-mentioned stationmaster were the only ones among the twenty-two witnesses who even referred to the victims, although it was evident that it was the victims who gave the basic significance to the destruction of the town and prompted the inquiry. One can conclude from the lack of testimony on this particular that few questions were asked on the subject. The report had no great effect on believers in the Nationalist cause. Foss and Gerahty cited the report, but summed up the conclusions in such a fashion as to leave the reader in doubt whether the "casualties" of less than a hundred were caused by bombers or by arsonists.[77]

For some years after the end of World War II, non-Spanish writers, in dealing with the question of the dead in Guernica, continued to follow their political alignments; those who sympathized with the Nationalists ignored the dead; the pro-Republicans, on the contrary, insisted that there were victims in the tragedy. Richard L. Pattee adopted the same position as Sencourt and Cardozo, and concluded that "the destruction of the city and its civilian population by air raids does not stand up to close scrutiny."[78] Peter Kemp, who was enjoying the hospitality of Cardozo and Botto either at the time of the bombing or immediately thereafter, did not seem to understand that there were any dead people in Guernica.[79] Manfred Merkes was equally blind on the subject.[80] Hugh Thomas, in his first (1961) edition, used the figures of the duchess of Atholl for Guernica: 1,654 dead and 889 wounded.[81] But for some whimsical reason, when he revised his book in 1965, he reneged on these figures and wrote in a footnote that it was impossible to establish the number of persons killed: "Estimates vary from 1,600 to 100. The lower estimate is likely."[82] Galland admitted heavy casualties.[83] James Cleugh did not realize that anyone was killed when Guernica "was practically destroyed by fire."[84] Dahms, however, acknowledged that the civil population had suffered heavily when Guernica was bombed.[85]

The Neo-Franquista formula of admitting the bombing but attributing it exclusively to the Germans permitted more flexibility to the pro-Nationalist writers in mentioning the dead and the wounded. Thus, Georges-Roux wrote: "The dead bodies were scattered about the ruins or strewn around the streets. There were 1,500 dead, more than 800 wounded."[86] George Hills, defending Franco and blaming the Germans, used the numbers advanced by Hugh Thomas in his first version: "1,650 dead or dying and over 850 wounded."[87] His fellow countryman Crozier, writing in the same year as Hills, 1967, reverted to the old formula, and did not mention the dead in his wholesale denial of the bombing.[88]

Nationalist authors of memoirs or history touching on the war in the Basque country, writing since the end of the civil war, have taken little notice of the dead in Guernica. Aznar said not a word,[89] nor did Lojendio.[90] The semi-official *Historia de la cruzada española*, which appeared in 1943, did not speak of the dead and wounded at Guernica, but then it did not even mention the destruction of the town in the text.[91] Galinsoga,[92] Díaz de Villegas,[93] Jorge Vigón,[94] José Gomá[95]—all failed to tell of the dead. General García-Valiño passed over the Guernica incident; including the victims, in silence. [96] General Kindelán, writing of the aviation during the civil war, forgot to mention the most noted exploit of the aviators on the Rebel side, including the victims. [97] The historian Seco Serrano said not a word about the victims of Guernica in either his first [98] or second (revised) [99] editions. Pemán, in his commentary on the ruins of Guernica, stayed mute concerning the dead. [100]

It was generally only in the translations that the Spanish reader could learn that there were victims in Guernica; in Galland, [101] in Georges-Roux, [102] in Dahms, [103] in Hills. [104] Galland of course called the bombing a technical error; Dahms excused it as a military necessity; Georges-Roux and Hills blamed the Germans and absolved Franco. Peter Kemp[105] and Cleugh,[106] in their Spanish versions, as in their original English, forgot to tell about the dead. Luis Bolín, in whose account one paragraph contradicted the other, managed to deny the destruction of the town by bombing on one page, while admitting on another page that a bombing had caused almost one hundred casualties. [107]

However, in 1966, Carlos Rojas, significantly a Spaniard living in the United States, published in Spain an account of the destruction of Guernica, based on Thomas, with the number of victims given as 1,654 dead and 889 wounded. [108] This paragraph probably drew little attention, for the book deals with philosophy, political theory, and art, rather than history. Two years later another tentative step forward in establishing the facts about Guernica inside Spain came with the publication in Barcelona of an extract from Talón's then unpublished work. Talón wrote that nobody in Guernica "placed at more than two hundred the number of dead." This figure was based essentially on the testimony of Pedro Calzada, who said that he had carried most of the dead to the burial ground. Talon said that the figures given by Pedro Calzada would be verified by almost anybody in the village today. "Moreover, these figures can be verified by looking at the death registers in Guernica and at those of the surrounding villages," Talón wrote. "The victims of the bombing are recorded one by one with a surprising scrupulousness."[109] Talón's statement probably had little impact in Spain, for it was published in a book priced beyond the means of most Spaniards.

It was only with the advent of the 1969-70 propaganda campaign, built around a new version of Guernica, that the subject of the dead in the air raid became a topic in the daily press. The Neo-Franquista school had as one of its objectives to diminish the number of the Guernica dead, thus reducing the tragedy to the status of a *fait divers*. Ricardo de la Cierva began the attack as maladroitly as possible, referring in his *Arriba* interview to "The myth of Guernica, where not even a dozen perished."[110] It is extremely difficult to understand how La Cierva, charged with the mission of preparing a new and rational explanation of the tragedy, based on an admission of the bombing for which he gave exclusive blame to the Germans, could have started with such an evidently false figure. La Cierva had two conclusive reasons for knowing better than to pretend that "not even a dozen" had perished in Guernica. First of all, in his interview he spoke of Talón's "definitive" work soon to appear, and even if he had not read that manuscript, he certainly knew the extract already published in 1968 in Gil Mugarza's book, giving the figure of "not more than two hundred." Second, he began in this interview his references to the Herrán report, in which the number of the dead was placed at around a hundred.[111] La Cierva was guilty either of inexcusable negligence or of deliberately falsifying his figures of "not even a dozen."

But this figure was too low to be maintained for long. In his letter to *El Pensamiento Navarro* La Cierva did not mention the victims, nor did Jaime del Burgo bring up that question in his reply to La Cierva. But already in April, La Cierva was writing:

> I have the personal impression that the figure [of the dead] is much nearer the lower limit generally admitted (some hundred) than the thousands bruited about in propaganda.[112]

But in his *Historia ilustrada,* La Cierva inexplicably avoided giving any figure for the dead and wounded. Only in his citation from Galland did he by indirection admit that there were victims.[113] This is all the more curious in that he here unveiled his "unpublished" document, the Herrán report, in which the figure of fewer than one hundred was given in the conclusions of the Commissioners.[114] It was only in his review of Talón's book, written later than his *Historia ilustrada,* though published earlier, that La Cierva arrived at the figure of "around two hundred" for the victims of "the bombing and the fires,"[115] that is a figure more than eighteen times the preliminary figure he had put forward a few months earlier.

Talón devoted many pages to the question of the dead from the bombing.[116] He reproduced what he had already published in the Gil Mugarza book, with certain curious changes, and many more details. He had two principal sources of information: (1) Persons who were in Guernica during the bombing or shortly thereafter; and (2) The death registers of the cemeteries of Guernica and eighteen surrounding villages. His conclusion was, as in 1968, that the total number of the dead did not surpass 200.[117] He was so sure of this figure that he wrote that he could easily compile an almost complete nominal list of those who died in the raid.[118] It is to be observed that he did not present this list, and it is to be regretted.

But Talón's figures of not more than 200 dead in Guernica were not to be upheld for long by the Neo-Franquista historians. Vila-San-Juan quoted Talón's estimates in 1971,[119] and Martínez Bande quoted them in 1970[120] and in 1972.[121] But La Cierva, writing about Guernica in 1972,[122] said nothing about the dead. A year later, he told his readers that Talón, in his book, had reduced the number of the dead in Guernica "to a little more than a hundred."[123] It is difficult to see how any honest mental process now known could change the figure of "not more than two hundred" into a "little more than a hundred."

La Cierva repeated this sleight of mind in a newspaper interview later in 1973, saying that Guernica was "a tragedy in which perished one hundred or two hundred persons—depending on the version."[124] That same year another Neo-Franquista, Ramón Salas Larrazabal, after studying Talón's account, decided that it would be difficult to arrive at even a hundred, in adding up the list of the Guernica dead.[125]

We can only conclude that the Neo-Franquista historians, with Ricardo de la Cierva at their head, are now seeking once again to diminish the number of the dead at Guernica, and we should not be surprised to find that number once again fixed at "less than a dozen," the number at which Ricardo de la Cierva began his "research."

It is obvious to the reader that the Basque government people in Bilbao who gave out casualty figures for Guernica could not know exactly how many had perished in the shelters and ruins. The town—or the ruins of the town—was in the hands of the enemy, and there had not been time enough to search through the still-smoldering debris for the dead before the town was abandoned. Moreover, when Leizaola gave a figure on May 4, it pretended to cover only the Guernica dead in Bilbao hospitals; Leizaola did not pretend to know how many corpses were still in the ruins of the town. It is equally clear from reading the extremely few pro-Nationalists who advanced a studied figure for the Guernica dead that they were considering only those who were found dead in Guernica when the Nationalists entered or thereafter, and that they were largely ignoring the Guernica dead in Bilbao and elsewhere (save in the surrounding hamlets).

We thus have two sets of figures for the dead in Guernica. The Basque figures are those given by Leizaola, in his radio allocution of May 4: 592 dead in Bilbao hospitals, and a later figure, attributed to Republican sources, of 1,654 killed and 889 wounded in the raid. For the Nationalists, we have the figures of *Guernica: The Official Report,* fewer than 100, and the figure of Talón, not more than 200.

We can take a closer look at the figures in the Nationalist report. According to witnesses before the commission, 45 persons died in the Santa María shelter[126] and 28 in the Hospital Calzada Asylum.[127] A list of 50 victims is given at the end of the book. Of these 50, only 30—that is, 60 percent—are identified by name. Thirty-eight of these dead were taken from Guernica shelters; the others died between May 8 and June 17, from different causes.[128] Among these 38 bodies found in the Guernica shelters, 11 came from the Hospital Calzada Asylum and 23 from the Santa María shelter. Then, if we add to the list of 50 dead, 17 (28 less 11) from the Calzada Asylum, and 22 (45 less 23) from the Santa María shelter, we get the figure of 89. This figure does not include the dead buried before April 29 near Guernica, or carried to Bilbao for burial, or anybody badly enough wounded to have been transported to Bilbao, where he perhaps later died, or anyone burned to death in the fires, the debris of which was cleaned up years later. This report is obviously deficient.

Vicente Talón put a ceiling of 200 on the number of the Guernica dead. This estimate was first published in 1968—that is, 31 years after the 1937 official report. Talón's principal witness was one Pedro Calzada, who said that he and his oxen carried many of the dead to the cemetery. Talón's 1968 citation from Calzada read as follows:

> That painful task was prolonged for *many* days, even continuing when the town was in National hands. I transported *almost all* of the dead. They were

seventy-five or thereabouts. Others, *not many more,* were carried on stretchers, on window shutters, on ladders, on anything that could be found. (Italics added)129

The 1970 version is slightly different:

> That task which was carried out as a sad monopoly, or, for the least, with hardly any competition, was prolonged for *several* days, even continuing when the town was in National hands. "I transported *many* of the dead. Some seventy-five or thereabouts. Others, *the same number or perhaps fewer,* were carried on stretchers, on window shutters, on hand ladders, on everything that could be found. (Italics added)130

In the 1970 book by Talón we are told that Calzada "took charge of the bodies which appeared in the Santa María refuge, the Calzada Asylum and the debris of the houses."131 *Guernica: The Official Report* tells us that there were 45 bodies found in the Santa María refuge and 28 in the Calzada Asylum, which add up to 73 in all. Calzada told Talón that he had transported around 75 bodies. He also told Talón that his

> painful task prolonged for many days [later, "several days"], even continuing when the town was in National hands.

This phrasing suggests that the greater part of Calzada's work was done before the Nationalist occupation. But the 73 bodies that Calzada carried from the Santa María shelter and the Calzada Asylum were transported after the occupation. Who were, then, the bodies that Calzada conveyed before April 29?

We must also note that Talón's direct quotation from Calzada, in the 1968 version, suggested that his number of dead known about by the ox driver was more than 150 but, in the 1970 version, was less than 150. This change may have been made by the author for reasons of style, or by the censor for other reasons. Talón also tells us that Calzada transported the bodies from "the debris of the houses." But he explains that in these houses

> there were few human remains for, because of the characteristics of the houses and of the town, the attack permitted the people to escape or to put themselves under cover. Only some old or infirm persons continued in their homes during the lapse of time between the appearance of the first airplane . . . and the arrival of the following waves.132

First, there must inevitably have been a certain number of old and infirm, and if they stayed in their homes, they were certainly burned to death. How many bodies were found in the debris when, months and years later, it was cleaned up? Talón does not tell us. Second, if Talón's argument is understood, he means to say that everybody except "some old or infirm persons," on hearing the first airplane, left their houses or took to shelters, because on hearing the first plane, they knew that it would be followed by others. How can we be certain? On this point, an eyewitness of the bombing, Elosegi, wrote that after the first bomber had dropped its load and gone away, "We believed that the danger had passed and that the enemy was satisfied with the punishment inflicted."[133] It is also a well-known fact that many people, neither old nor infirm, feel as safe in their houses during a bombing as in a shelter, and are even opposed to going to shelters. People would hardly stay in their homes if it were known that the town was going to be fire-bombed, but Talón can hardly pretend that the people of Guernica knew this. Nor can he pretend to know today how many people remained in their homes and were killed either by explosive bombs or by fire.

Guernica suffered more from the fire than from the explosive bombs or from the machine-gunning. But the dead enumerated in *Guernica: The Official Report* did not die from the fire.[134] The dead whose tale is told by Calzada and Talón did not die from the fire. Yet there were certainly some dead from the flames, and from the known intensity of the fires, they could have been many indeed. The eyewitness, María Goitia, told the Havas man in Bilbao:

People were dying under the debris of the crumbling houses. . . . When the explosions stopped, one could hear hair-raising screams.[135]

Steer had written:

So, as the houses were broken to pieces over the people, sheathed fire descended from heaven to burn them up.[136]

How many were caught and consumed in the flames nobody knows and nobody will ever know.

According to the German military writer Colonel (Ret.) Rudolf von Xylander, who wrote many articles on the Spanish Civil War for a leading German military weekly, the "Nationals" achieved great success with thermite bombs in the Basque campaign; they were used to start brushfires and produced a heat of 3,000 degrees centigrade.[137] These were the same bombs that, according to many witnesses, were used in Guernica, not to start a brushfire but to set aflame the partly wooden houses of the town.[138] One can well imagine that anyone trapped in these flames of 3,000 degrees centrigrade—wounded, aged, infirm, or in good physical condition—had little chance of survival or even of leaving behind him a trace of his physical existence. This was suggested by Ojanguren y Celaya, in his account of the visit to Guernica on the morning of April 27, as already noted.

We have observed that the four men who wrote the "Report of the Commission" in *Guernica: The Official Report* did not take into consideration the Guernica dead who might have died in Bilbao. It would appear that Talón has made the same mistake. He writes:

Some of the trails concerning the deceased must be documented, however, in the archives of the Basurto hospital, of Bilbao, where the most seriously wounded were taken after the raid.[139]

He then cites the names of three persons who died there, but two of these names were those given in Leizaola's radio talk of May 4, in which he stated that there were 590 others who had died in Bilbao hospitals from wounds received in Guernica. Talón's ambiguous statement does not indicate that he sought information in the Bilbao hospital archives. It is of interest that Martínez Bande seized upon this obscure assertion of Talón to inform his own readers that Talón's figure of "not more than 200" included references concerning the dead found in Bilbao.[140]

Earlier in this chapter, mention was made of the bombing of Durango on March 31 and of the figures released by the Basque government concerning the dead and wounded on that occasion. Talon tells us that 127 persons died in Durango.[141] This is an error difficult to understand, for at least 258 persons died as a result of that bombing. The figure advanced by Talón represents in fact less than 45 percent of the deaths caused by the Durango bombing, according to statistics established by the Basque government. It seems difficult to challenge these statistics, for of the 258 persons, 207 are identified by name, 7 by military numbers, and only 44 are unidentified. This percentage—15 percent—of unidentified is far less than that given in *Guernica: The Official Report*, where 40 percent were unidentified. With these figures were given the names of 110 wounded who had entered the Basurto Hospital on March 31 and had not died, and of 35 others who entered hospitals in other towns on that date. That is, according to official statistics difficult to contest, there were 258 dead and 145 wounded in the Durango bombing, some 45 days after the event.[142]

Of the 403 casualties in Durango, the dead represented 64 percent. Talón tells us that the figures of 1,654 dead and 889 wounded, given by Republican authorities according to the duchess of Atholl, then repeated by Thomas before his recantation, is open to suspicion because "in a tragedy of this nature the number of the wounded is usually higher than that of the dead."[143] (Talón should reflect on the number of the wounded given five minutes after an accident, and the number of these wounded who are among the dead a few weeks later.) Here is a statistic that merits meditation: if the total number of casualties in Guernica is taken at 1,654 dead plus 889 wounded, the number of the dead represents 65 percent of the whole, one percentage point off from the figures given for the Durango casualties, figures that Talón could challenge only with great difficulties, and which he, in his book, for some unknown reason, lowered by 55 percent—by more than half.

We have observed that Calzada's statement indicated that he had probably transported more bodies before the Nationalist occupation than later. He also said that he had carried "seventy-five or thereabouts." And it was shown that the dead from the two shelters from which he said he brought bodies after the occupation by themselves alone amounted to 73. He also brought bodies from "the debris of the houses." Then either he did not transport any bodies before the Nationalist occupation or else he did, and if he did, then his total was far more than "seventy-five or thereabouts."

In this same statement quoted by Talón, Calzada described a scene where "Others . . . were carried on stretchers, on window shutters, on ladders, on everything that could be found." This scene has nothing to do with the laborious extraction of bodies from the Santa María shelter after the capture of the town; it describes the terrible night of April 26 and the hopeless day of April 27. What happened to the bodies transported on window shutters? What happened to the bodies carried by Calzada before the Nationalist entry?

The scene described by Calzada is not alone of its genre. All the correspondents who wrote about Guernica, all the eyewitness stories about Guernica, all told of the same scenes. Steer wrote that 42 wounded militiamen had been killed outright in the Josefinas Hospital. This was repeated by Holme and also by Fifi Roberts, who added that 10 nurses had also perished there. On April 27, Steer saw 14 of the 40 dead in a hospital, laid out. It is a known fact that a priest named Arronatagui was killed in the bombing. There was also "the lovely girl" Steer saw dead from machine-gun bullets. Monks saw "bodies in the fields spotted with machine-gun bullets and "the charred bodies of several women and children huddled together in what had been the cellar of a house." When Monks went back to Guernica on April 27, he later wrote that he saw 600 bodies.[144] He was writing for a sensational newspaper, and perhaps he exaggerated a bit. But that does not mean that he did not see hundreds of bodies. Bodies were still being extracted from the ruins when Monks was in Guernica on April 27. When Yoldi came into Guernica late that night after the bombing, "Men and women were still digging out the bodies."[145] Elosegi saw his liaison man disappear in the ruins, and he never saw him again. He dug a three-year-old child out of the ruins and handed it dead and bleeding to the mother.[146] After the bombing, he wrote, there were unfortunates caught in the fallen masonry condemned to death by fire. Others were caught by falling walls as, mindlessly, they sought lost members of their families.[147]

Talón cannot dismiss all this testimony simply by calling Steer a liar. What happened to these hundreds of wounded and dead? After the bombing of Durango, 84 bodies were buried in two common graves, 42 in each one; only 33 were buried individually in graves. All of this was done in Durango.[148] But the complete destruction of Guernica precluded any such local solution. Certainly the wounded were taken to Bilbao, and in all probability the dead also. Talón himself wrote that "many wounded from Guernica and its zone were taken to Bilbao on the night of the 26th."[149] Yoldi wrote that on his arrival in Guernica, "Army ambulances were coming up from Bilbao."[150] Elosegi noted that at some time that night, "Help has come from Bilbao. Firemen and sanitary personnel. Also a strong force of motorized police. They can organize the evacuation of the wounded in better order."[151] As we have seen earlier in this chapter, the Basque nurses testifying in Paris mentioned two wounded persons, one by name, who were evacuated to Bilbao and later died there.

After the attack on Durango, 276 wounded were carried to hospitals in Bilbao and other towns; of these 47 percent, or 131, died. Is it not conceivable that after the raid on Guernica many more wounded were transported to Bilbao in the following forty-eight hours? A UP report said that on the night of April 26, "a constant cortège of ambulances was transporting the wounded from the devastated zone to Bilbao."[152] Talón paid little heed to the wounded sent to Bilbao after the air raid. He paid little heed to the old, infirm, dead, and wounded who were burned in the ruins of Guernica. It is thus that he was able to limit his dead to not more than 200.[153] It is not possible that the bombing of Durango, which nobody can pretend was as brutal as that of Guernica, which was carried out by far fewer planes in far fewer flights, which lasted not one-sixth as long, and which did not include the dropping of incendiary bombs, was still more murderous.

This is not to pretend that the figures of 1,654 dead and 889 wounded are correct. Martínez Bande says that Aguirre used them in a letter to Prieto, dated June 11, 1937, and suggests that the desperate plight of the Basques encouraged them to exaggerate these tragic figures.[154] Nobody knows how many people were killed in the bombing of Guernica. It is evident that the Basques were unable to establish any definitive figures before the town fell to its captors three days after the bombing and cut them off from one of the principal sources of statistics, the dead still in the smoldering ruins of Guernica. We do have, however, the statement of Leizaola that on May 4, 592 people from Guernica had died in Bilbao hospitals. We know also that it is probable that the population of Guernica on April 26, 1937, was swollen beyond its normal size and that, despite Talon's witnesses, there were numerous visitors to the weekly market. The fact that 40 percent of the dead enumerated in *Guernica: The Official Report* are unidentified by name could lend credence to the suggestion that there were numerous people from outside the town in Guernica that day. It is regrettable that the conquerors of Guernica never made a serious effort to ascertain how many perished on April 26. However, from what we do know, can one say that the number of 592 Guernica dead in the hospitals of Bilbao on May 4 was improbable? Can we say that the number of 1,654 dead from the bombing was improbable? From what I have learned in the course of preparing this study, I am of the opinion that these estimations of the Basques are far nearer the truth than the "fewer than a dozen" of the Neo-Franquista historian Ricardo de la Cierva, then the "fewer than a hundred" of the 1937 Nationalist Commission, than the not more than 200 of Talón. It was a grave psychological error for the Nationalists to accuse the Basques of destroying Guernica. It is an equally grave psychological error for the Neo-Franquista historians to haggle about the number of the dead.

The success of the Neo-Franquista version of Guernica depended, not on proving that the town had after all been bombed to destruction—the bombing was admitted in West Germany before the opening of the 1970 propaganda campaign—but on proving that the Nationalist command had nothing to do with the bombing, and that the death list was after all quite short (so why all the fuss?). The latter point has not been proved. In the next chapter we shall look at the first point.

3

How Was
Guernica Destroyed?
By Whom? Why?

The destruction of Guernica—the event itself—has presented us with three questions for which answers must be attempted:

1. How was Guernica destroyed?

2. By whom was Guernica destroyed?

3. Why was Guernica destroyed?

Of the three questions asked concerning the destruction of the town, the reader will have seen that there exists today a general agreement on but one of them, the first: How was Guernica destroyed? A Nationalist military figure has recently described the action:

On June 26 [sic] the sky over Guernica was cloudless. Towards four-fifteen an airplane appeared and dropped several bombs. Ten or fifteen minutes later, the first wave arrived, followed by others, until quite long after seven o'clock.
    The airplanes took off from the Vitoria airdrome, flew beyond the littoral and then, making a half turn, followed the Oca valley, attacking Guernica from North to South. There were apparently three types of planes: Heinkel 111 and Junkers 52, for bombing, and Heinkel 51, for pursuit and machine-gunning. They must have formed two groups, which took turns, and as for the number in each group there exists a general discrepancy. We can suppose that some 15 to 20 airplanes, bombers and fighters, took part in each wave.

These were enough. Their tactic consisted in dropping first of all ordinary heavy explosive bombs, then clusters of small incendiary bombs and, simultaneously, in machine-gunning the persons in the open, not only those in the town but also those in the surrounding country and even in the neighboring parishes. The old town, where wood was a fundamental element in construction, practically disappeared, but left many high outer walls standing. . . . After the bombing, explosions continued during several days even after the town was occupied by National troops and several buildings, previously untouched, were set on fire.[1]

If we correct the date, putting April 26 in the place of June 26, mention the probability that the first planes in the attack were Italian, and add the important fact that the wind was favorable for propagating the flames, we have a record of the bombing of Guernica which few today would contest, unless it be Brian Crozier or Professor Jeffrey Hart.

The second question concerning the Guernica incident—Who was responsible for the destruction of the town?—is the subject of disagreement. As we have seen, for more than thirty years the pro-Nationalists accused Republican elements of razing the town with fire and dynamite. In very recent years the destruction by bombing has been admitted by the Nationalists, but always with the proviso that the bombing was exclusively the work of the Germans, and that the Nationalists were in no wise implicated, not by action, not by knowledge, not by consent. Unfortunately for those who uphold this thesis, Vicente Talón in his book, perhaps unwittingly, produced a Nationalist document that stated that the attack on Guernica was asked for by Rebel ground troops, ordered by the Spanish Air Command, and carried out by German and Italian planes. If this document can be believed, the Spanish Rebel command knew of the attack before, during, and immediately afterward. This telegram of May 7, 1937, sent by Franco's headquarters to the Condor Legion for the information of Berlin in effect covered up for the Condor Legion vis-à-vis its superiors.

We shall repeat here the essential lines of that telegram:

> I request Sander [Sperrle] to inform Berlin that Guernica, a town of fewer than five thousand inhabitants, was six kilometers from the fighting line, is a highly important communications crossroad, has a factory for munitions, bombs and pistols; on the 26th it was a place for passage of units in flight and for the stationing of reserves. Front-line units requested directly to Aviation the bombing of cross-roads; this was carried out by the German and Italian airforce, and because of the lack of visibility, because of the smoke and clouds of dust, bombs from the planes hit the town . . . the Reds took advantage of the bombing to set fire to the town.

The request "directly to Aviation" meant that the "front-line units" had asked for the bombing to the *Jefature del Aire* of General Kindelán, and that he in turn requested the Germans and Italians (?) to carry out the attack. On this point, it is interesting to note that the Neo-Franquista expert on the aviation aspects of the civil war, Jesús Salas Larrazábal, also wrote that the Condor Legion had been *ordered* to carry out the attack.[2]

An essential element of the Neo-Franquista version of Guernica is not only that Franco and Mola were unaware of the plans for the bombing but that when Franco learned of the true facts, he was extremely angry. Thus far no defender of the Nationalist position has produced any evidence for this. George Hills tells of conversations with persons who supposedly were present when Franco delivered his vigorous protests. We do not know who Hills's witnesses were, though they were to all appearances military persons. If they could talk with Hills, they could speak to others. But nobody of the Neo-Franquista school, not La Cierva, not Talón, not Martínez Bande, nobody at all has sought to nail down this evidence with more details.

The scenes portrayed for Hills of Franco in rage are in contradiction with the dispatch of the telegram of May 7. The telegram is a document; Hills's interlocutors are anonymous persons. Hills suggested that Franco's anger led to the eventual recall of Sperrle. La Cierva assured us that this was a fact. Then why did Franco's headquarters send a telegram to Sperrle on May 7, asking him to lie to Berlin in the name of the Rebel command, a lie whereby Franco assumed the responsibility for the attack on Guernica? Here was for Franco a hell-sent opportunity to get rid of Sperrle.

This telegram tells us still more. It tells us that Berlin did not really know what had happened at Guernica. Salamanca is in effect telling the Condor Legion to lie to its Berlin headquarters, for even if we accept the Nationalist versions of what happened at Franco's headquarters in the days following the tragedy of Guernica, by May 7 Salamanca, as well as the Condor Legion, knew that the statement that "the Reds took advantage of the bombing to set fire to the town" was completely devoid of all fact. Yet if Berlin had known the truth, the whole truth, it is inconceivable that Salamanca would have told the Condor Legion to tell its superiors in Germany a version of the destruction of Guernica which both the Nazi aviators and the Spanish generals knew to be false. The only conclusion that we can draw from this set of facts is that the attack on Guernica was decided by the Spanish High Command—perhaps in collaboration with the Condor Legion—and carried out by the latter, with no forewarning known to Berlin.

This hypothesis is not difficult to accept if we look at the situation as it was on April 25, rather than as it was on April 27 or April 28. The town of Durango had been bombed on the morning of March 31, and 258 persons at least had been killed. Churches were bombed, and nuns were dead. This attack was never mentioned in the Nationalist communiqués or in the Spanish Nationalist press of the time. Some writers today, seeking to downgrade Guernica, even pretend that Durango suffered more destruction than Guernica.[3] Then, why should the people who decided to bomb Durango on March 31, have hesitated to bomb Guernica twenty-six days later? Steer wrote:

> Their [German] activity on this day [March 31] corresponded exactly to
> their activity on April 26th following, when Guernica took the place of
> Durango in their destructive scheme. But they were not yet using incendiary
> bombs behind the line.[4]

Incendiary bombs had been used earlier in Madrid with mediocre results.[5] Perhaps
the wooden houses of Guernica would burn better.

It is essential to recall here that when the Spanish generals and the Condor
Legion decided to bomb Guernica, they did not know exactly what would happen.
Incendiary bombs had been dropped on Eibar the day before but Eibar was not a
virgin field, and had been the target for explosive bombs for some days. In Guernica
everything worked perfectly for the attackers, even the wind was blowing as they
would have wished, to spread the flames from house to house. The bombing of
Guernica was, as a German colonel cited by Merkes observed, "a complete success
for the Luftwaffe," and the then chief of staff of the Condor Legion, von
Richthofen, with the approval of Sperrle himself, later described that attack as "the
most successful" of those April days. There were no difficulties until the news
arrived. The reaction in England threw Bolín into a panic, and what had been a
military success turned into a diplomatic and propaganda disaster. Everything had
been foreseen, except the presence of the three British journalists in Bilbao, and the
providential arrival of Father Onaindia in Guernica just before the bombs began to
fall.

It is not impossible that there were angry scenes of recrimination between the
Germans and Franco. Franco might well have reproached the Germans for not
telling him that the destruction of Guernica would provoke a world-wide reaction.
And the Germans may well have replied that they had not, any more than Franco
or Mola, known that the flames would spread so rapidly, that the attack would be a
success. For after all, if the journalists had not been in Bilbao, if Father Onaindia
had not come to Guernica just when he did, the Guernica story the world knows
would never have existed. There would have been delayed news stories; the press
services from the frontier would have sent their telegrams, but the story would
never have had the same impact. The bombing of Guernica was a lot like the tree
that falls in the forest. If nobody hears it fall, does it make any noise? There were
people who heard Guernica fall, and if there were disputes between the Spanish
Nationalists and the Germans in Spain after the bombing, they were more probably
caused by the resulting scandal in the world press than because of the military
action itself.

The two responsible for the bombing, the Spanish Nationalist command and the
Condor Legion officers, in order to cover their act, lied to everybody, including the
air officials in Berlin. We can be certain that cablegrams were exchanged between
Berlin and the Condor Legion when Berlin learned of the reaction to the bombing.
We lack copies of these cablegrams, as well as many other messages concerning
Guernica, but obviously Berlin inquired about the true situation and obviously a

reply was given. We can deduce that the Condor Legion chiefs answered Berlin with the same version as that found in the May 7 telegram of Salamanca, for it is inconceivable that the Spaniards would have asked that the Condor Legion lie to Berlin, if they had not known that their telegram was a confirmation of the news already sent to Berlin by the Condor Legion. The actual message from the Condor Legion to Berlin on May 7 has not been found, but presumably it relayed the information found in the Salamanca telegram of that same date.

The hypothesis that Salamanca and the Condor Legion presented a common front before the whole world, including Berlin, to hide their act finds support in the testimony of Adolf Galland, who wrote that "no one spoke willingly about Guernica" and whose account was that bad weather and primitive bombsights changed a routine bridge bombing into an attack on a town. We know that Galland's relation was inexact, but perhaps it was the version he learned from the uncommunicative men he met who had participated in the attack and who thereafter formed a fraternity of silence. Galland's version of Guernica bears a close resemblance to the information that Salamanca asked the Condor Legion chief, Sperrle, to transmit to Berlin.

The six documents found in the German archives and cited by Merkes likewise reflect in general terms the contents of the Salamanca telegram and of Galland's testimony: crossroads and bridges are named as the targets, and the actual bombing of the town, if mentioned, as an accident. Is there not reason to believe that there existed a general agreement among the Condor officers and pilots to hush up the whole matter, even to their superiors in Berlin, even to comrades in the Luftwaffe such as Galland, who entered the scene after the "accident" and to whom "no one spoke willingly about Guernica"? We must also remember the story that Sperrle denied to von Blomberg that there was any German responsibility for the destruction of Guernica. This falsification of the facts was aided and abetted by the Spanish Nationalists, accomplices of the Nazi flyers, and what one finds in the incomplete German archives of today is the reflection of the information sent by the Condor Legion, at Salamanca's request, to Berlin, and of the rehearsed stories told to curious German military visitors by Germans and Spaniards in Spain.

There are other consequences to our acceptance of this interpretation of the known facts. Must we conclude that in all probability von Ribbentrop was not too well informed about what had happened at Guernica, when on May 4 he discussed the question with Eden, that the English foreign minister knew the facts better than the German ambassador? It was at this time that Norman Davis, a Roosevelt emissary, told Lloyd George's confidant Thomas Jones that "he had met Ribbentrop who complained of the attitude of the British press towards Germany over the bombing of Guernica, and of the American press."[6] Did Göring, when questioned by the two Americans in prison during the Nuremberg trials, reply as vaguely and imprecisely as he did for the simple reason that the version of Guernica he was given by the Condor Legion was also vague and imprecise?

We have now concluded that Guernica was destroyed in an air raid carried out by the Condor Legion and requested by the Spanish Nationalist command. There remains to be answered the third question: Why was Guernica destroyed?

President Aguirre declared on the day after the attack that

> the German airmen in the service of the Spanish Rebels . . . have sought to wound us in the most sensitive of our patriotic sentiments, once more making it entirely clear what Euzkadi may expect of those who do not hesitate to destroy us down to the very sanctuary which records the centuries of our liberty and our democracy.

Steer cabled in his first report: "The object of the bombardment was seemingly the demoralization of the civil population and the destruction of the cradle of the Basque race." Some years later, Aguirre wrote that Guernica was "the stage chosen by Franco and Germany to carry out . . . the first attempt at total war."[7]

The Nationalists and their supporters were to suffer a certain embarrassment over the years in trying to rationalize their version of Guernica, to explain *why* the "Reds" destroyed Guernica. The earliest efforts followed the formula expressed by General Queipo de Llano on the evening of April 29:

> I believe that the Asturians and Basques destroyed Guernica and accused us of the deed, in order to arouse the indignation of their militia and encourage them to fight us.[8]

These primitive explanations of the Nationalists became more sophisticated after May 4, when, at least in the English and American press, it was admitted that Guernica had been bombed "intermittently." Douglas Jerrold offered the classic example of this elucidation: Guernica was bombed by the Germans, but the bombing did little damage. The bombing was amply justified for military reasons (Guernica's strategic situation, the small-arms factories, presence of troops). But the bombing did not destroy the town. It was burned. Why did the Basques burn their town? According to Jerrold: "In order to provide the material for propaganda in neutral countries." He elaborated on this idea as follows:

> Finally, the question can be cynically determined by reference to that old question "cui bono?" When the alleged destruction of Guernica took place it was in process of being evacuated; an advance had taken place on all fronts and nothing could have saved the town. General Franco had nothing whatever to gain by destroying it. The Basque government, if they could get their story accepted, had everything to gain. The "incident" would stiffen the resistance of the Catholic Basques. It would influence neutral opinion; strengthen the attitude of the British government in regard to the blockade of Bilbao and possibly even lead to its abandonment.[9]

Jerrold's arguments were accepted by Arnold Lunn.[10] The Nationalist commissioners wrote that "the corpses of the dead would serve admirably for the purpose of propaganda against the Army of Liberation."[11] Sencourt wrote that the German bombing, perhaps "unnecessarily ruthless," was

> exploited by those purely destructive conspirators who had already set fire to Irún and Eibar . . . basely to exploit as propaganda against the Nationalists the criminal destruction for which again they were responsible themselves."[12]

The Catholic author Richard Pattee reasoned similarly:

> The evidence points to destruction on the ground by the retiring Republicans who sensed—and in this they were right—that they had in this spot a made to order propaganda appeal to the world, ready to swallow almost any tale that came out of Spain, provided it reflected no credit on the Nationalists.[13]

Bolín as late as 1967 repeated the standard story:

> But the Republicans in Bilbao needed a sensational story to offset their reverses. They dispatched Asturian miners to dynamite Guernica and set fire to its buildings and swore that they had been blown to smithereens by German bombs.[14]

A more rational reason for the Basques or other Republican forces to have destroyed Guernica was the "scorched earth" operation blamed on "retreating troops." This argument was officially advanced by the Salamanca authorities to the outside world, as is shown by a bit of local news in *La Nación,* informing the Argentine people that the representative of the Rebels, Juan Pablo de Lojendio, had received instructions to deny the differing versions being bruited around concerning the destruction of Guernica, a town that, the bulletin stated, "was set on fire by the Red elements who occupied it, before fleeing."[15] Here are some other examples: this argument was used by Father Thorning, who accused "Spanish anarchists in their retreat";[16] by Father Code, who blamed "the retreating Leftist army";[17] by Knoblaugh, who attributed the damage to "Anarchist incendiaries and Asturian dynamiters before they evacuated Guernica";[18] by Cardozo, who imputed the burning to "communists and anarchists enraged at having to abandon [Guernica] to a hated foe";[19] by Foss and Gerahty, who said "the town had been destroyed by fire by the retreating forces of the Madrid government";[20] by Yeats-Brown, who thought the anarchists fired the town before leaving it;[21] by Arnold Wilson, who accused "the retreating forces";[22] by del Moral, who wrote that the destruction was done by "retiring Bilbao Reds";[23] by Wing Commander James, who charged the crime to "retiring defenders";[24] by Vice Admiral Joubert, who declared that "the Reds systematically destroyed the town before their departure";[25] by the count of Saint-Aulaire, who declared that "the Reds had burned it [Guernica], as was their habit, before evacuating it";[26] by Arthur Loveday, who declared that Guernica had "met the same fate as Irún, destruction at the hands of the retreating militia";[27] by Brasillach and Bardèche, who stated that Guernica "was, above all, burned upon evacuation, exactly as Irún";[28] by General Duval, who admitted that perhaps "a part of the damage could not be imputed to the rage of the defenders forced to retire";[29] by Pattee, who charged "retiring Republicans" with the crime;[30] by Crozier, who accused the "retreating Republicans";[31] by Major Al Williams, who repeated an opinion he attributed to "various reputable Englishmen" that ". . . the principal damage to the city was not done by air bombs, but by the dynamite and incendiarism of the Reds and anarchists who were driven from this town by Franco's air and land forces";[32] by Juan Estelrich, who wrote that the destruction "was caused by the Reds before retreating";[33] by Antonio José Gutiérrez, who said that the destruction was done by the Reds "when they fled";[34] and by L. F. Auphan, who wrote that "government troops set fire to the town from which they were being driven by Franco's troops."[35]

We have now seen several explanations for the destruction from those who accused the Republicans of the deed. There were other students of the civil war, and not all were sympathetic to the cause of the Republic, who blamed the Germans and/or the Nationalists. What reasons did they give? Hugh Thomas admitted that

> Guernica might have been regarded as a military target . . . but it is difficult not to conclude that the Germans deliberately bombed the town in an attempt to destroy it, observe in a clinical way the effects of such a devastating attack.[36]

Georges-Roux wrote that the Germans wanted "to carry out an experiment on the effects of destruction on civilian morale in an undefended town."[37] George Hills considered Guernica to be "an experiment in saturation bombing."[38] James Cleugh thought the Nationalists undoubtedly sought to break civilian as well as military morale.[39] Gabriel Jackson considered the bombing an "experiment in terror."[40]

The Neo-Franquista campaign of 1969-70 found new answers (for Spain) to the first two of the questions we have asked concerning the destruction of Guernica. The Neo-Franquistas said that Guernica had been bombed and that the Germans had done it. (La Cierva introduced the activity of arsonists and dynamiters to account for part of the damage done, but he was not always followed by the other Neo-Franquistas.) Why did the Germans bomb Guernica? The answer to this part of the examination was not always forthcoming. La Cierva gave no explanation as to why his imaginary "special testing group which came directly from Germany" had bombed Guernica, although one could imagine it was to test the effects of the bombing. This theory suggested a special test bombing but not enough to destroy the town completely, for La Cierva insisted that "Action groups of Basque separatists" contributed to the destruction.[41] In his letter to a Navarese newspaper, La Cierva again blamed the Germans and suggested a specific reason for their action in the claim that Guernica was a "military objective of the first order." He also took pains to claim that there was an "absolute lack of symbolical intention in the bombing," shown by the fact that neither the Casa de Juntas nor the oak trees suffered any damage, "despite their prominence on the scene of the bombing." This time La Cierva insisted that it was "very probable" that "destruction commandos" of the Basque army helped in the destruction.[42] In *Historia y Vida,* La Cierva said the German air attack was of the "tactical type," that there was no symbolical intention in the bombing, and that it was "probable" that "special commandos for urban demolition and communications" of the Basque army participated in the destruction.[43] We then arrive at La Cierva's fundamental work on Guernica, his *Historia ilustrada.* He explained the German air attack as being against "military objectives." He then noted "the evident contrast between the incomplete destruction of these objectives and the almost complete destruction of the small town." This "evident contrast" was explained by the work of the "arson commandos of the Republican army in retreat."[44] La Cierva divided the blame between the Germans and the Basques. The Germans had carried out an ordinary bombing on military objectives; the Basques had carried out an ordinary (for them) devastation project as they retreated. That is, as defined by its chief practitioner, the Neo-Franquista school was more or less back where the class had opened in 1937 under Douglas Jerrold. But La Cierva had little choice, for he had no ready explanation for the fact that the Germans had bombed the town as brutally as they had in fact done. And if La Cierva believed that the Germans had bombed merely the military objectives and were not responsible for the complete destruction of the town, why does he take such pains with false evidence to prove that the Nationalists did not consent to the bombing?

Jaime del Burgo sought to explain the bombing by the Germans as a reprisal for the killing by the Basques of a German pilot who fell behind their lines. But he, like La Cierva, also blamed the Basque "destruction groups," who, he wrote, "appeared beyond any doubt to have taken action in Guernica."[45] Vicente Talón, who, in contrast to La Cierva and Del Burgo, allotted all the blame for the destruction on the bombing, rationalized the air attack as "a necessity for finding a testing ground for the Luftwaffe."[46] Martínez Bande, who accepted Talón's ideas, said the raid was carried out as it was because Sperrle wanted to win the war in a hurry, and the only way to do this without an increase in troops and supplies was "to impose a destructive tactic which would terrify the civilian population in the rear-guard and, by rebound, the troops at the front."[47] Ramón Salas wrote that the object of the raid was to prevent the retreat of the enemy and that the raid was a "tactical action."[48]

We must also take into consideration the reasons for the bombing offered in the six opinions found by Merkes in the German documents. Two attributed the burning to arsonists operating at the same time the Condor Legion was correctly attacking military objectives in the vicinity. Three others thought of the destruction as accidental. We now come to the most important, that of von Richthofen, who was chief of staff of the Condor Legion at the time of the bombing, and whose opinion was confirmed by Sperrle. He said that in order to cut off large forces of the enemy in retreat, a number of attacks were carried out on "cross-roads and bridges" and that of these, "that on Guernica was the most successful." He did not make any references to the destruction of the town.[49]

Finally, there is the Salamanca telegram of May 7, which said that the attack on "the crossroads" was a normal military effort, and the bombs dropped on the town were an accident. The destruction of the town was largely caused by arsonists.

The early pro-Nationalist arguments as to why Guernica was destroyed were singularly inept. The original Rebel thesis that Aguirre destroyed Guernica to encourage his troops to fight was irrational and quickly abandoned. The immediate replacement—the destruction as a propaganda ploy—which came from Jerrold (Bolín?) was equally illogical but is worth a bit of inspection. The argument was frivolous but it was seriously motivated by the acute inferiority feeling of the Catholic defenders of the Nationalists in England on the subject of propaganda.

A more rational hypothesis was that which blamed the destruction on "retreating troops." The major difficulty here was that Guernica was destroyed on April 26 and did not fall to the enemy until April 29. Had the Basques burned Guernica on April 26, they would have risked cutting off their own troops. This pro-Nationalist argument is in fact demolished by the pro-Nationalist counter argument, advanced by Galland, von Richthofen, and others, to prove that the real intention of the bombers was to destroy the Rentería bridge and other means of communications, to cut off the Basque retreat. Many of the advocates of this theory, to add weight to their arguments, were forced to ignore chronology and to try to combine the date of the destruction with that of the Republican retreat.

There was more of a ring of credibility to the words of those who held that the Germans had indeed bombed Guernica, to test their airplanes, to experiment with their bombs, to try out civilian morale when faced with these weapons. This hypothesis inevitably designates an operation guided from Berlin. Pertinax had blamed Göring immediately after the bombing, and thirty years later Hills had blamed Keitel. Talón recognized this relationship, and when he explained the bombing by the need "to find a testing ground for the Luftwaffe," he said it was done following "direct orders from Berlin." The chief obstacle to the acceptance of this theory is that there exists no known documentary proof whatsoever. Moreover, if Guernica had been bombed for any reason on orders from Berlin, there would not have been subsequently any need for Salamanca to explain the operation to Berlin, let alone to lie to Berlin, as was done in the collusive telegram of May 7.

Talón had no believable explanation, supported by documents, of the bombing; Ricardo de la Cierva's contradictory theses are unsatisfactory, and he himself, in his review of *Arde Guernica*, turns his back on his own arguments, adopting those of Talón. He later reneged on his support for Talón, further destroying his credibility. The Neo-Franquista effort to explain the destruction has but one well-argued text, that of Martínez Bande. He tells us that Sperrle feared the war was going too slowly and that he bombed Guernica in the manner it was bombed in order to spread terror and help end Basque resistance. This is, curiously enough, what George Steer cabled his newspaper on April 27, 1937.

The Neo-Franquistas are in agreement on this sentence: Guernica was destroyed by a bombing that was carried out by the Condor Legion, without the knowledge or consent of Franco. But they are not in agreement on the reason for the bombing. Yet the credibility of the sentence on which they are in accord depends on finding a believable motive.

The question is: was the bombing of Guernica a tactical operation or a strategical one? We have three Neo-Franquista theses, each one in contradiction with the other two. La Cierva pretends that the bombing was a simple, tactical operation. Talón and Martínez Bande have different arguments, but each implies a strategical bombing, be it, as Talón insists, to try out the material, or as Martínez Bande writes, to break down Basque morale and bring the northern campaign to an end. But La Cierva perceived the weakness of his argument; the destruction inflicted on Guernica surpassed that of a tactical bombing. Therefore he resurrected the old tale of Basque dynamiters and incendiaries. Neither La Cierva nor Talón nor Martínez Bande has produced a scrap of documentation to support their versions of why Guernica was bombed as it was. The only Spanish document that gives a reason for the bombing, the May 7 telegram, we know from other sources to be false in its *explanation* of the bombing. But this document does tell us one important thing: on May 7 the Spanish command was willing to assume vis-à-vis Berlin full responsibility for having requested the bombing. We know that the Spanish command and the German command in Spain were in agreement on the bombing. If we look again at Martinez Bande's conclusion—that Guernica was bombed by the Condor Legion in order to break Basque morale and hasten the end of the northern campaign—why should we not conclude that the Spanish command was in agreement with Sperrle?

We have written above that the military authorities who ordered the attack and those who carried it out did not know what the military results would be, and especially did not know what the propaganda and diplomatic results would be. Professor Trythall, a recent biographer of Franco, has written that "the Nationalists were clearly unprepared for the international cry of horror that was raised." This does not signify that their intention was not to burn Guernica down to the ground. Guernica was burned as part of a plan, not by accident. (The accidental part came from the presence in Bilbao of Steer and the other correspondents and from the passing through Guernica of Father Onaindia.) The incendiary bombs were not loaded onto the airplanes by error. If this was done to break Basque morale and speed the war to an end, is it not possible that the Nationalist request to the Condor Legion was a request to fire bomb Guernica to break Basque morale rather than a routine request to destroy a bridge or cut a road? "The bombardment certainly exceeded what was militarily justifiable except inasmuch as civilian morale is a factor in war," wrote Trythall.[50]

Let us, first of all, look at the evidence adduced against this supposition. It is weak indeed and consists mainly of Martínez Bande's qualification to his proposition concerning Sperrle's terrorist bombing of Guernica. "This policy," he wrote, "clashed with the other determining factor of the conduct of General Franco in the direction of the operations: the feeling that the war was taking place on Spanish soil and against Spaniards."[51] Martínez Bande's analysis is contradicted by the entire record of the conduct of the war by the Spanish Rebels before April 26. This record shows not only no reluctance to killing Spaniards on Spanish soil but also an unmistakable enthusiasm for carrying out the act and for surrounding it with an aura of terror. The threat of killing, the act of killing, and the subsequent publicity given to the killing—these were normal happenings in Andalusia from the first days of the campaign of the Army of Africa, which employed against the Spanish people the ruthless techniques learned from skirmishing in the Rif.

Queipo de Llano employed against the peasants and villagers of Andalusia both the word and the deed of terror. The Radio General would threaten a village on the radio, and the following night recount in sanguinary detail how the menace had been carried out.[52] The Moorish troops were allowed (encouraged?) to rape and pillage.[53] Prisoners were killed and mutilated. Back in his African apprenticeship, Franco once congratulated a bugler for killing and cutting off the ears of an unarmed Moor he had taken prisoner.[54] If the massacre of Badajoz caused, to the great surprise of the Franco military, unfavorable publicity in England, such stories, on the contrary, when bruited about Spain helped to break down the resistance of the untrained men of the Republic. Great was the fear of falling into Moorish hands. Steer told of the fear of capture in the Basque campaign:

> When the bombardment was over, and the mere noise of it in their shaken smoky dug-outs was enough to disorganize the Basques, they came out to find that they were being shot from behind. The terrible cry of panic arose that had broken the line before Ochandiano—*estamos copados!* In the Spanish Civil War, where the rebels made a practice of killing all prisoners taken arms in hand, and all officers whatever their *tenue,* the militia—when ill-led—did not think it worth their while to fight a battle in a salient. "We are cut off!" they shouted, and away they ran down the back of Tellamendi between the flanking machine-guns. By midday the red and yellow flag floated from the summit of Tellamendi, and the militia were scattering southward in the fresh brushwood below.[55]

The technique repeatedly used by Queipo de Llano in Seville a few months earlier, the threat and the ruthless execution of the threat, was copied by Mola for use in Biscay. Instead of talking over the radio, Mola dropped leaflets. His airplanes blanketed the Basque towns with his menace to "raze all Vizcaya to the ground" if the Basques did not surrender. As a sample, on March 31, he bombed Durango. This was twenty-six days before Guernica was bombed. Two hundred and fifty-eight persons were killed, all Spaniards on Spanish soil, and the bombings continued throughout those twenty-six days, except during bad weather. Martínez Bande's argument is especially weak in that he acknowledges the dead in Durango to be at least 248 (quoting Steer, whom he does not contradict) and fixed the dead in Guernica at not more than 200 (quoting Talón).[56] If the bombing of Durango was more murderous than that of Guernica, how had the tenderheartedness of Franco failed to intervene before the bombing of Guernica, after the destruction of Durango? In reality, the barbarous attack on Durango was an essential part of the battle plan, including the menace of Mola, the existence of which Martínez Bande acknowledges.[57] It is not with such arguments that one can draw a portrait of Franco the Sentimental. Martínez Bande's supporting footnote is a quotation from Salvador de Madariaga, who wrote that the bombing of Guernica must have caused Franco "deep disgust,"[58] but Martínez Bande forgets that Madariaga on most disputed points of civil war history takes the side of Franco.[59]

We have noted how Queipo de Llano used a system of threats over the radio, followed by pitiless executions, which were in turn followed by a recital over the radio—a cycle of terror, inspiring terror. Mola threatened to raze Vizcaya, and the Condor Legion bombed Durango, to show how it could be done. Then the Condor Legion bombed Guernica, and this act was immediately followed by a rumored statement of Mola, supposedly made over the radio. This has already been quoted, but we shall repeat it here:

> We shall raze Bilbao to the ground and its bare, desolate site will remove the British desire to support the Basque Bolsheviks, against our will. We must destroy the capital of a perverted people, who dares defy the irresistible cause of the national idea.[60]

Papers in the English archives tend to support the authenticity of this statement.[61]

It is difficult to see how anyone could dispute the authorship, but England's leading Catholic weekly immediately misinterpreted the message. It rejected the idea of the *Times,* that "the motive [of the bombing] was unquestionably to terrorize the population of Bilbao by showing what it might expect." This "plausible" explanation, "corroborated to some extent by the strong language attributed to General Mola about razing Bilbao to the ground," was contradicted by the denial of the Nationalists, which true or false, "shows no sort of desire to turn to account the threat of destruction from the air." "If terrorism is the motive, these denials are senseless," the *Tablet* wrote.

> The enemies of Nationalist Spain in Great Britain immediately jumped to the conclusion that here was the savagery they are always expecting. But even they will find it hard to explain why, if the Nationalists are as bloodthirsty as they allege them to be, they should so weaken the effects of their deeds by denying them.[62]

The *Tablet* was reading Mola's menace by the light of London, whereas it should be read by the light of Bilbao. Nationalist denials of the bombing and of Mola's menace might have an effect on English Catholic editors but they had no effect on the inhabitants of Bilbao, where it was well known how Guernica had been destroyed and where Mola's preferred menace sounded possible and probable. Steer found it difficult to think Mola had uttered the words. "I do not yet believe that he did," he later wrote.

> But they had their currency in our city [Bilbao] , and it moved from hand to hand as quickly as any fearful inflation. Bilbao was trembling; only the men at the top kept their nerve.[63]

If the effect of the words attributed to Mola was further to terrorize the people of Bilbao, why should one not think that they were uttered with that purpose in mind, just as in July and August of 1936, Queipo de Llano had played word games over the radio with the hapless peasantry of Andalusia?

We have now seen that, contrary to Martínez Bande's affirmations, there is nothing in the record to show any reluctance on the part of Franco or of any of the other Rebel leaders to support a murderous operation such as that which destroyed Guernica. We can therefore accept Martínez Bande's reason for the bombing, cutting from it, however, his disclaimer of any responsibility by the Spanish command. Guernica was destroyed by the Condor Legion, with Spanish assent in order to break Basque resistance. How could the barbarous attack on Guernica help bring the Basques to their knees? The objective of the Nationalist offensive launched on March 31 was to capture Bilbao. Bilbao. What did Bilbao mean to the Spanish military mind in 1937? Bilbao was "the city of sieges"; it had been four times beleaguered in the past century, during the two Carlist wars, and had never fallen to the Carlists.[64] The Spanish military mind in the first months of 1937 was also preoccupied by the disturbing fact that Madrid had been practically under siege since early November of the year past, for more than five months, and showed no signs of yielding. Are we not justified in believing that the possibility of a new siege of Bilbao weighed on the calculations of the Nationalist planners, and that they, as well as their Nazi helpers, were prepared to take the measures necessary to prevent the realization of that possibility?[65]

We know that the idea of a new siege of Bilbao was in the journalistic air and in the propagandistic air. Douglas Jerrold echoed this sentiment, and saw in such an action the most despicable of human behaviors. "What is even more criminal," he wrote, "they [the Republicans] deliberately plan a house-to-house defense of Madrid and Bilbao."[66] This apprehension, linked with the siege of Madrid, is the more significant in that Bolín was in England when Jerrold wrote his words, and it is inconceivable that they had not seen each other. A commentator for *La Nación,* Constantino de Esla, also coupled the beleaguerment of Madrid with the possible siege of Bilbao. The Basque capital, like that of Spain,

> had two doors open to receive enough air to avoid asphyxiation, the sea and the zone to the West. . . . Bilbao is a city with experiences of sieges and would accept another one to add to its History. . . . Mola is ready to follow the footsteps of Zumalacárregui, hoping to find a happier ending to the adventure.[67]

"BILBAO HAS NEVER FALLEN," proclaimed a headline in a London newspaper, and part of the text read:

> Sixty-seven years ago this week was raised the siege of Bilbao in the Second Carlist War. The siege lasted 125 days; there was hardly a house left standing; the citizens suffered terrible privations. But Bilbao held out. General Mola, preparing to besiege Bilbao once more, knows that he has a traditionally hard nut to crack.[68]

The *New York American,* aggressively for Franco, headlined a story from the Basque front, a few days after the bombing, "CITY DIGGING IN FOR SIEGE."[69] The *New York Times,* in an AP dispatch from Bilbao dated 29 April, wrote that the army defending Bilbao fell back on the town's defenses "and dug in for a long insurgent siege."[70] An article from the French-Spanish frontier, published in the *Times* just after the bombing read in part:

> Should they maintain the present rate of progress the Nationalists expect that within a few days Bilbao, already known as "the city of sieges," will once more be beleaguered.[71]

Can we not assume that the razing of Guernica was a murderous warning to the Basques that if they tried to defend Bilbao, that town would also be burned to the ground? "Attack and counter-attack do not exhaust war's strategems," observed an editorial writer in the *Glasgow Herald.*

> There is the psychological weapon. What, it can be argued, is more likely to terrorize Bilbao into surrender than a not too distant demonstration of frightfulness?[72]

Guernica was but 30 kilometers from Bilbao.

The theory of a terror bombing of Guernica was advanced in 1938 by Arnold Toynbee, who countered Wing Commander James's assertion in the *Daily Telegraph* that the Spanish Rebels had no motive for destroying the town by observing that "they may well have considered that such an example of 'frightfulness' would increase the Basques' feeling of helplessness under the Nationalists airplanes and show them how useless it was to resist."[73]

Unlike Madrid, Bilbao was not defended. The city, with the iron mines, fell undamaged into the hands of the Spanish Nationalists, and of the Nazis. The intention had been to defend the city with an "iron belt" of fortifications, but the engineer, one captain Goicoechea, who planned the defense system and helped build the finished part of it, deserted to the Insurgents, with the plans in his pockets.[74] The town could have been defended house-to-house; the iron mines could have been sabotaged. Shortly after the capture of Bilbao, the mines were producing for the Germans. When the English diplomat Geoffrey Thompson came through Bilbao in February 1938, he saw a German ship loading iron ore.[75] Another British observer, the Catholic editor Douglas Woodruff, wrote a few months later:

What made Bilbao so great a prize was, in part, the iron ore mines, and in part the elaborate smelting and factory equipment. It was a prize which the Carlists in the first and second Carlist wars never succeeded in taking.[76]

Had the Basques defended Bilbao, as a few years later Leningrad was defended, had they fought house-to-house as the Russians did at Stalingrad, they might have won the moral disapprobation of Douglas Jerrold, but they might also have won a few precious months for the Spanish Republicans. The fact that they did not defend their city might well have been in part because of the morale-breaking example of Guernica.

Of the three questions propounded concerning the destruction of Guernica, two have been answered, with documentary proof. The third has been answered with a hypothesis. I do not know why Guernica was destroyed as it was. As all readers of crime fiction know, in cases of murder the most difficult point to resolve is: Why? We have identified the murderer with the bomb in his flying machine. We have identified his accomplices. But we shall never know with certainty why Guernica was destroyed in the brutal manner that it was, until someone who was in on the planning comes forward to inform us. There are, in all probability, people still living in Spain and in Germany[77] who know the precise motive for the terror bombing. Perhaps one of them will now speak up.

4

The Reasons for the Existence and the Persistence of the Controversy

We have now finished with the three questions concerning the incident—the destruction of Guernica. There remains to answer the question about the controversy. Why was there a dispute over the facts of the destruction, over whether there had even been a bombing, and if there had been a bombing, over its effects?

The controversy resulted from the Nationalist counterstatement on April 27 and the following days refuting the press reports--especially those appearing in England that day—and answering Aguirre's statement. Knowledge of why this denial of the reports from Bilbao was made will help us to understand not only the origins of the controversy but also why it has continued up to this very day.

Why did the Nationalists deny the bombing? There have been any number of more deadly bombings carried out since April 26, 1937, but none has had its causes, or its very reality as a bombing, seriously contested.[1] During the years when this denial was considered gospel truth in Spain, and a man risked death if he controverted it,[2] no explanation of why it was promulgated was thought necessary. Even during the past two or three years, since the 1937 Nationalist explanation was officially discarded (in part), no serious attempt has been made to tell the Spanish people why Franco's headquarters lied about the matter.

Two positions have been adopted. One is simply to call the person judged responsible for the Nationalist communiqués, Luis Bolín, dimwitted. Ricardo de la Cierva called Nationalist propaganda of 1937 concerning Guernica "incredibly dull and awkward,"[3] and said "it had a stupid and antihistoric posture."[4] On another page he referred to the "immobile and recalcitrant posture of National propaganda . . . faithful to the dictates of Luis Bolín."[5] Jaime del Burgo wrote that Nationalist propaganda was "lying, manifestly untrue and false."[6] Talón and Martínez Bande, on the other hand, thought the Nationalist position to be the result of misinformation. Talón mentioned the "errors" of Nationalist propaganda but was willing to consider them honest mistakes.[7] Martínez Bande followed this lead: the Nationalist denial was understandable, for the Salamanca headquarters was really ignorant of the facts.[8] Neither of these theses can be maintained. We must find an explanation other than Bolín's stupidity or his ignorance. After all, he was not directing operations, and his communique was accepted by both the Nationalist military and the Condor Legion. He upheld it to the end of his life. The Neo-Franquista school, even today, has not told us the truth about the destruction of Guernica. The reason must, then, be one that touches profoundly the bases of the regime.

The person accused by La Cierva, undoubtedly with good reason, of responsibility for the initial communiqués on Guernica was Luis Bolín Bidwell. Part of the explanation for his action lies in his background and personality. His mother was half English (Bidwell), and he had spent a great part of his life in England. His maternal uncle was Roman Catholic bishop of London. He had been London correspondent for the monarchist Madrid daily *ABC* during the years of the Republic. He had been active, as we have already seen, in the fight against the Republic during the years 1931-1936, but always from an English base, with such men as Jerrold and del Moral. He reacted to the problems of the Spanish Civil war, not so much like a Spaniard or like a typical Englishman but like a militant English Catholic, like a Jerrold or a Lunn. This militant English Catholic minority had taken up arms for Franco, some of them, like Bolín, before the fighting broke out.

Bolín, serving as a press officer with Franco, was unduly sensitive to English feelings about the war, as was shown in January and February 1937, when he overreacted to a letter published in the *Manchester Guardian* concerning the Badajoz massacre five months earlier. He bullied the UP and Havas agencies into signing papers that he could interpret as denying the massacre.[9] He had hardly weathered this crisis when he saw the first of the Guernica cablegrams, with their accounts of British indignation against the Rebels. Bolín panicked and did exactly what he had done about the Badajoz massacre. He denied everything, even that Nationalist airplanes had taken to the air on April 26.

Another question arises: Why did Bolín (and Franco's headquarters) not simply admit the bombing, claim that it was a military necessity, and that war was hell? This was the argument of the officer who spoke with Virginia Cowles in Santander. The reason is that the Catholic propaganda forces in the "neutral" countries, especially in England, France, and the United States, were proclaiming not the hellishness of the Spanish Civil War as practiced by the Franco forces but the sanctity of it. The Spanish Civil War, they had been saying for months, was a Holy

War, a Christian Crusade for Saving the Roman Catholic Church and Western Civilization from the Oriental Menace of Communism.

There was no way out for Bolín. If he admitted the destructive and murderous bombing, he would have had to name the persons responsible. If he threw all the blame on the Germans, as his successors were to do in 1970, he would have to admit the presence of a large German air force in Spain. This would not only spoil the romantic tale of the crusaders but would play havoc with the Non-Intervention Committee and tear holes in the diplomatic facade of April 1937. If Bolín said the bombing had been done by the Spaniards, he would at the same time have demolished the arguments for the Holy War. He fell back on the solution that the Franco propaganda activists had employed since the outbreak of the fighting: he denied everything, telling a great many lies in the process.

Bolín may well have panicked as he did because he was nervous also about his personal situation. He was quite probably being unfavorably criticized at Franco's headquarters. His arrogant, bullying manner had made him enemies, among his Spanish colleagues as well as among the foreign pressmen. The frequent lamentations by friends of Franco about press hostility to the Spanish Rebels could easily be, and doubtless were, turned at times into accusations against Luis Bolín. Even Lunn, while boasting of his friendship with Bolín, mentioned disapprovingly "the restrictions of which the journalists complained."[10] McCullagh, on one of the many pages in which he expressed his dislike of "Bustamente," gave this aside:

> Were this only my opinion, I should hestiate to express it, but it is at present the opinion of all the English-speaking correspondents in Nationalist Spain, and of all the Spanish officials I have met outside Spain.

Guernica was apparently the high point of Bolín's career as a domineering press officer. On May 2, the Nationalists began to change the script for the destruction of Guernica. This represented a disavowal of Bolín. According to his memories, he spent three weeks in England in June 1937. Some news of the approaching publication of McCullagh's book, with its pages on "Bustamente" may have reached Bolín. He asked to see McCullagh, then sixty-eight years old and whom Bolín had treated with insufferable rudeness on several occasions but a few weeks earlier, when he was riding high in Salamanca. McCullagh refused to see him.[11]

Bolín's memoirs do not tell us what he did during the last half of 1937. No evidence has been found to show that he worked again as a press officer. A list of the press officers who served with the Nationalist forces, prepared by one who himself labored in that capacity during most of the Civil War, indicates that Bolín left the service in April 1937.[12] He was probably made the scapegoat of all the public relations gaffes committed by the Nationalists up to that time, including Guernica.

No journalist mentioned an encounter with Bolín, or with Aguilera, after April 1937, for good or for bad. Captain Eddy Bauer, who spent a few weeks in

Nationalist Spain in July and August 1937 as a correspondent, gave thanks in his preface to "M. Paul Merry del Val, chief of the *Prensa y Propaganda* service at Burgos, and Lt. Colonel Lámbarri, who commands the column of war correspondents."[13] The climate at press headquarters had changed since the days of "Bustamente," when a journalist waited hours, if not days, to be received. "Towards eleven in the morning," wrote Bauer, "we arrived at the office of *Prensa y Propaganda,* where we were handed, in exchange for our safe-conduct pass, an orange card which authorizes us to circulate in the front zone, accompanied by a Press Officer."[14] Merry del Val, described as "the providence of the journalists," invited Bauer to visit Oviedo in a car placed at his disposition;[15] he asked to visit a prison camp and "the authorization was accorded without difficulty";[16] when he arrived at San Sebastián, he was warmly greeted by Lámbarri.[17] True, he was a friend of the Rebels, but then so was McCullagh.

When Virginia Cowles was in Salamanca in August 1937, Merry del Val was "head of the Foreign Press."[18] A few months earlier he was considered a mere press officer.[19] On June 12, 1937, Georges Botto of the Havas Agency, described Merry del Val as "Chief of the Press Bureau at General Headquarters in Salamanca."[20] Bolín had disappeared, but nobody mentioned his disappearance, or thought of linking it with his activity during the Guernica crisis.

Bolín is vague as to his work during the last six months of 1937, but he wrote that on the last day of that year he suggested to Franco that he go to Teruel, then under Republican attack, to talk to the journalists. His suggestion was not accepted.[21] On February 16, 1938, Bolín was named head of the Spanish State Tourist Department.[22] This was hardly a top-ranking post for a country with a lot of war and few tourists or potential tourists. It was certainly lower in the hierarchy than the post held by "Bustamente" when he was swaggering around Salamanca.

The frequently proferred explanation—that Bolín was honestly mistaken when he composed (or helped to compose) the first communiques concerning Guernica—does not stand up. Bolín was not that simpleminded, and until the end of his life he chose to hold onto the deceitful statements of the first days after the bombing, rather than to excuse them as the errors of a fool. It was absolutely impossible, in view of the international situation at that time, in view of the basic falsehoods of Nationalist propaganda, for Bolín to have told the truth about Guernica. He was a victim, probably a willing victim, of the "tangled web" of lies that he himself had helped to weave since July 1936 and even before. Moreover, if his intention was to win the war for the Nationalists, he did the right thing. By lying about Guernica, Bolín and all the other Nationalist propagandists helped maintain a certain pro-Franco discipline, at least among British and American Catholics and other conservatives. This would have been extremely difficult, if not impossible, had the truth been told.[23]

We have already mentioned the feeling of inferiority experienced by the English Catholics on the subject of Spanish Civil War propaganda. This feeling persists to this day among the Nationalists, as evidenced by the words of Vicente Palacio Atard in 1968, echoing the writings of Lunn and Jerrold published precisely at the time of the Guernica bombing.[24] Lunn, who boasted of his friendship with Bolín, and who, according to Palacio Atard, "aided the propaganda" of the Burgos government,[25] deplored the fact that on Spanish matters, "the champions of advanced views should be so much more articulate than the supporters of Christian culture."[26] Republican propagandists were sharp and had lots of money. "The Madrid government have discovered that it is impossible to over-estimate the gullibility of English progressives," Lunn told his readers in a pamphlet. "When, therefore, the Nationalists submit proofs in support of the facts which they allege, the Reds content themselves with broadcasting reckless assertions in support of fiction."[27] In a book, Lunn advanced the same arguments:

> Meanwhile England has been doped by propaganda as corrupt as it is brilliant, as cynical as it is successful. The resources behind this propaganda are unlimited, for Russia is the second greatest gold producing country in the world and the Valencia Government has control of the gold in the Madrid banks, while the committee of Englishmen who are trying to counteract Red propaganda have to argue for hours as to whether they can afford to print, or must be content to roneograph, a letter or pamphlet contradicting Red lies.[28]

Jerrold was almost psycopathic when he contrasted poverty-stricken Nationalist "truth" with rolling-in-money Republican "lies." "Propaganda is not merely a subsidiary weapon of the Valencia Government, but its only weapon," he told the readers of *The Nineteenth Century and After*, the very month Guernica was bombed.

> There is no Valencia Government. There is a Red Spanish Army; there is no Red Spain; there is only Red propaganda. And it is believed all over the world, and even in Spain . . . Red propaganda is not, like ours in the last war, a political exaggeration or a merely favorable presentation of facts, but the deliberate circulation of lies.[29]

Jerrold bemoaned the fact "that this fiction is still believed," and it was, he asserted, "the fault of the Salamanca Government who affect an indifference to world opinion. . . ."[30] His obsession with the successes of Republican propaganda and the failures of that of the Nationalists led Jerrold to this finding, revealing though exaggerated: "And so it is, in the Press—which is where this war is being fought."[31]

This fearful preoccupation of Bolín, Jerrold, Lunn, and others with the subject of Republican propaganda in general found its force concentrated on the subject of propaganda on Guernica in particular. It was but a step from writing (and believing) that it is "in the Press . . . where this war is being fought" to believing (or thinking that others could be made to believe) that towns were being blown up for a propaganda victory. The subsequent step was to believe that the destruction of

Guernica was shamelessly exploited by the Republicans for the vile purposes of propaganda. Immediately after the destruction of Guernica, Jerrold declaimed:

> It should by now be obvious to everybody that the chief weapon of the Red revolutionaries in Spain is propaganda, and that the chief purpose of this propaganda is to arouse public opinion in the neutral countries.

Guernica was, Jerrold stated, "the greatest, if only because it is the one victory, of the 'red' government."[32]

Vice Admiral Joubert explained the success of the Republican version of Guernica by the fact

> that the Red propaganda is admirably done and does not draw back from any lie, whereas Franco, who at first was totally lacking in propaganda, seems still to have too much confidence in the intrinsic force of truth.[33]

Father Thorning considered the news on Guernica to be "The crowning achievement of Red propaganda."[34] Cardozo wrote of "such claptrap lies as were furnished by the ever-fertile propaganda office of Bilbao,"[35] while Foss and Gerahty said that "the story of Guernica" had given to "the fiction factory" an "incredible success with its false news department."[36] Knoblaugh considered that "the bombing of the Basque town of Guernica was one of the most fortunate bits of material for the propaganda machine."[37] Pattee denounced "the fanciful legendry . . . accumulated around Guernica."[38]

Dahms, in his German edition, said that the bombing provoked an enormous campaign of propaganda,[39] and in his Spanish edition amplified this to state that the campaign begun in Bilbao "was supported by Münzenberg and in part of the Anglo-Saxon and French press."[40] But Cleugh blamed the Republican government, writing that "this disaster was immediately used advantageously by the Republican government at Valencia."[41] E. Allison Peers, the prolific writer on modern Spanish history, was uncertain as to what had "happened there [at Guernica], or was alleged to have happened," but he was certain that "in Great Britain" it was "skillfully exploited by propagandists."[42] Another who believed the Republicans had mounted a great propaganda offensive around Guernica, as we have seen, was gullible Peter Kemp. He reflected the general feeling of inferiority of the Nationalist partisans of Franco in England on the subject of propaganda:

> It seems to me that nothing illustrates better the superiority of Republican propaganda over Nationalist than the Republican story of Guernica [which] was given immediate and world-wide publicity and is still generally believed; whereas the Nationalist case scarcely received a hearing.[43]

Gil Mugarza declared that on Guernica had fallen "more tons of ink than of bombs."[44] Talón contrasted Republican propaganda cleverness on Guernica with Nationalist blundering. "While from the so-called antifascist front the theme of Guernica is exploited with extraordinary skill and intelligence, errors were accumu-

lating in the opposing trenches."[45] He confused the reality of the bombing with
the attendant publicity given to the event. "The destruction of Guernica," wrote
Talón, "has been more than anything else a master motive of political propaganda. . . . Above all, Guernica constitutes a unique model of well-produced political publicity."[46] Jeffrey Hart, as late as 1973, concluded that Willi Münzenberg
had "invented" the story of the bombing to launch "an international propaganda
campaign about Guernica."[47]

This widespread feeling among the Nationalists that Guernica was exploited by
the Republicans has little basis in fact. The impact of the destruction of Guernica
on world public opinion did not result from the few pamphlets published by the
Basques before Bilbao fell[48] or in England[49] or by Basque sympathizers in
France.[50] The Nationalists and their sympathizers show, at least publicly, a false
conception of how propaganda is done. Propaganda is a plan, an organized effort to
spread an idea. *Information to be effective as propaganda must be presented in such
a manner as to make converts among those persons who would normally be
counted among those opposed to that information.* This rule explains the effect of
the information concerning Guernica on public opinion in England, France, the
United States, and elsewhere. The news about Guernica was presented in England,
France, and the United States not in a propaganda pamphlet but in the *Times,* the
Daily Express, and, through Reuters service, in all the British press; in the *New
York Times* and, through the news agencies, in all the American press. The story of
Guernica reached the English and American public through the conservative press—
that is, *in such a manner as to make converts among those persons who would
normally be counted among those opposed to that information.*

Such was the manner in which the news about Guernica was presented in
England that, in spite of the efforts of the Quai d'Orsay and the Agence Havas to
suppress the information, it rebounded onto the front pages of many French
newspapers. But this rebound of the news from England does not fully explain the
influence that this information finally had in France. It was the interview in *L'Aube*
with Father Onaindia that broke the Quai d'Orsay-Agence Havas conspiracy, and
split French Catholic public opinion on the Spanish Civil War.

In England, conservative people found the atrocity story of Guernica on the
front pages of their daily newspapers, and many of them believed it, because it was
from the correspondent of the *Times,* from the correspondent of the *Daily Express,*
from the correspondent of the Reuters Agency. In France, many French Catholics
found the testimony of a priest on the front page of a small Catholic daily, and
they believed him. This Catholic priest, Father Onaindia, was invited to small
gatherings by people who had read the article; his sincerity convinced these people
and provoked a schism in the Catholic ranks of France on the question of Franco
and the Basque country. The information about Guernica in each case—in England
among conservative newspaper readers, in France among the select Catholic readers
of a small Parisian daily—was presented in such a manner as to make converts

among those persons who would normally be counted among those opposed to that information.

These two operations were carried out in the most normal fashion in the world. There was no mastermind behind them, no Willi Münzenberg. The journalists did their daily task of reporting the news; the correspondents in Bilbao cabled what they saw; the reporter in Paris interviewed an eyewitness. None of these persons, to the best of our knowledge, realized the power he was wielding. But to the English, American, and French Catholic defenders of the Nationalist cause, all this seemed part of a mysterious conspiracy of "propaganda," an art of which they knew so little as to imagine that towns like Guernica were blown up as part of the daily task of a propagandist.

The only element of high propaganda in the whole history of Guernica was the dispatch sent by Georges Botto and distributed by the Havas Agency, with the blessing of the Quai d'Orsay, and then utilized by the Nazis and other defenders of the Nationalist lie about Guernica, such as Jerrold, Thorning, Sencourt, Pattee, and many others. This was propaganda such as Willi Münzenberg never dreamed of. It was this same Georges Botto who had amused himself by telling Peter Kemp that his head office in Paris told him that "the Republicans spent about six hundred thousand pounds in Paris on propaganda about Guernica alone." This same Georges Botto was the only person who mentioned Guernica, propaganda, and money in the same sentence—he and Peter Kemp, who repeated Botto's story.

What on earth did Peter Kemp think had been done with the money? Did he imagine that Francisque Gay had been bribed? Did he have any idea of how many pamphlets could have been printed with that much money?

The rule of propaganda we have enunciated above applies equally to Botto's dispatch. It was believed, in many circles, because it was vouched for by the Havas Agency, just as Holme's report was guaranteed by Reuters. The Havas-Botto telegram was certainly utilized by the Nazis, because of the Havas reputation. The lesser successes of Franco propaganda about Guernica, with the reports of Massot and of the men of *L'Action Francaise,* were lesser successes because they were from partisan sources. The same is true of Corman's story, which, verified by all witnesses today, carried less weight in the France of 1937 because it appeared only in a left-wing journal. It convinced the readers of that newspaper, but they were already convinced. On the contrary, *L'Aube* carried the message of Guernica into the territory of the enemy, among readers who were not all convinced, and was highly effective. The relatively small propaganda effort about Guernica realized by the Basques and Republicans is explained by the very evident reason that their work was being done for them by others; in the "neutral" countries, by the great press, or by the liberal Catholics.

In spite of Catholic lamentations, Nationalist propaganda was not all that unsuccessful; nor were Nationalist propaganda resources so limited as the poor-mouthing of its advocates might lead us to think. The Catholic Church controlled numerous publishing houses in England, and one needs only to look at the list of pro-Franco material published during the civil war by these houses to realize their strength. There are probably still many people somewhere in the world who believe all of that 1937 Bolín-Jerrold fantasy on Guernica, thirty-seven years after it was first pronounced. This has been shown by the success of Jeffrey Hart's article. That is not bad for an easily demonstrable lie. So let us ask: Why was this irrational story, so evidently false today, accepted by rational human beings for years and years?

There are several reasons that rendered this propaganda credible to a mass of people. The first and foremost is that it was spoken and written by priests and prelates, published in the official Catholic press. To the average Catholic layman the priest possesses both knowledge and wisdom, and is incapable of lying. Who would question what he was told about Guernica by a Father Thorning, a Father Parsons, a Father Code? These same qualities were unconsciously attributed to those laymen, who presented themselves as Catholic spokesmen, such as Lunn, Jerrold, Joubert, Sencourt, and others. On the subject of Guernica, they were neither knowing nor wise, and since they glibly accused their adversaries of lying, one can at least pose the question: Were they simply ignorant, or were they lying? At the very least, they were guilty of speaking out on a subject on which they had not done the necessary groundwork to have the right to speak, and they abused the confidence placed in them by other believers in their faith.

The basis of the Catholic arguments—no damage by bombing but destruction by arson—has since then been denied in Franco Spain itself by the Neo-Franquista historians. Yet the special pleaders of the Rebel cause and their press, in England and elsewhere, insofar as is known, have never corrected the false information printed about, or apologized for the calumnies thrown at, the Basques. Father Thorning, in his address to the American Catholic Historical Association in 1937, wildly attacked the *New York Times* and demanded that it "make an 'amende honorable' for three savagely partisan editorials about the Guernica affair."[51] It is not the dean of the American press who should apologize but Father Thorning and his fellows.

At the same time one must admit that the 1970 about-face of the official Franquista historians on the subject of Guernica leaves Franco's German military allies and his vociferous Catholic propaganda allies of the civil war years in a somewhat embarrassing situation. Without the German air force and the Catholic propaganda, one can place in doubt the victory of the Nationalists. These wartime allies have been paid for their services in dubious coin. The Germans can shrug off the charges, leaving them at the door of the defunct Nazi regime. The position of the Catholic press is more delicate, for here more than elsewhere in the political world there is continuity—and there is also the eighth article of the Decalogue.

Another reason for the acceptance of Nationalist propaganda about Guernica can be found in the parade of "experts" who came forward to prove by military service, scientific expertise, and journalistic experience that Guernica was never bombed, and if bombs had been dropped on the town, they had done no harm. A part of Jerrold's success lay in his air of knowing what he was talking about when he said that the outer house walls still standing proved that Guernica had never been bombed, although in reality he was spouting nonsense. All those who pontificated on the matter—Cardozo, Russell Palmer, General Fuller, Major Yeats-Brown, Sir Arnold Wilson, General Maxwell-Scott, Major Al Williams, the marqués del Moral, Grey Grey, Wing Commander James, and the interminable list of Spanish Nationalist military figures, the man who is now the mitered abbot (no less) of the Holy Cross of the Valley of the Fallen and was then a military press officer, Luis María de Lojendio; another press officer, the marqués Pedro Merry del Val, now risen to ambassadorial rank; Cardinal Gomá y Tomás; and even General Francisco Franco y Bahamonde—all were experts, and all were wrong about Guernica. Some were honestly mistaken, blinded by partisan feeling; others were simply lying for the good of the cause. The reader can judge for himself.

Another factor that permitted those pleading for the pro-Franco version of Guernica to maintain their arguments without too much embarrassment was the silence of the two "neutral" governments that knew the fundamental facts about Guernica: France and England. France was the greatest sinner. If the Havas Agency suppressed the first news from Guernica, or gutted it of all meaning, and then a few days later distributed a mendacious report favorable to the Nationalist arguments, these acts were certainly done with the knowledge of the Quai d'Orsay. This took place under a popular front government, but minister of Foreign Affairs Yvon Delbos was a Radical Socialist, unfriendly to the Spanish Republic.

Delbos may have had little control over the permanent functionaries of his department, but the argument that he gave to the British ambassador, that the false Havas-Botto telegram could not be corrected, lest Botto be shot, was peurile. If Delbos had wanted to correct the lie, it would have been a simple matter, as has already been shown, to call Botto to Biarritz, and tell him to stay in France and bear witness before the whole world that the contents of his telegram were false. On the contrary, there is no evidence that the Havas official responsible for releasing the telegram was ever disciplined, or that Botto himself was ever later questioned about the matter. Anyway, it is highly probable that the Quai d'Orsay preferred to keep quiet, and for the same reasons that it had permitted the distribution of the Botto telegram and censored the first dispatch about Guernica: to keep French public opinion uninformed and to avoid any massive protests in the streets of Paris against the destruction of the Basque town. There are but two alternatives: either the French government was extremely fearful of public reaction if the truth about Guernica were frankly proclaimed, or the Quai d'Orsay and the Havas Agency were making public policy without informing the government.

In England, public opinion was better informed than in France, because the entire press had printed the news. But the English government kept to itself, to a restricted circle in the Foreign Office, the sources of the knowledge that enabled Eden to tell the Commons that Guernica had indeed been bombed. The British government permitted the Nazis to slander the *Times* and George Steer without ever taking any measures, even years later, to set things aright. Eden never told the House of Commons of what the consul in Bilbao, Ralph Stevenson, had informed the government. Nor were any of the other reports concerning Guernica made public until thirty years after being received. The British government proposed a resolution on Guernica to the Non-Intervention Committee; when the proposal met with opposition from Franco's friends Germany, Italy, and Portugal, the British allowed it to be watered down to meaninglessness.

The Spanish Civil War was fought so that the possessing class in Spain, those who owned the land, the factories, and the banks could keep their holdings. This economic and social reality was generally masked behind the argument of the Holy War. The position of the Basque country in the Civil War, Spain's most Catholic people on the side of the Republic, constituted a challenge to the great design that portrayed the Spanish Nationalists as crusaders. In the Basque country, these crusaders stood Catholic priests (Basques, but priests, nevertheless) up against the wall and shot them. Is it by chance that the best-known atrocity of the atrocious Spanish Civil War was the bombing of Guernica, the bombing of a Catholic town full of practicing Catholics by the Fascist mercenaries of the twentieth-century crusade? It is no wonder that the crusaders lied, lied, and lied again rather than admit this particular atrocity. Nor is it any wonder that the simple truth about Guernica cannot be published in Nationalist Spain today and that so much artifice has been employed recently in Spain to present a new model of Guernica, as conceived by the Neo-Franquista school.

The Neo-Franquista school sought by "Operation Guernica" to help pacify the Basque country and to end the Guernica controversy. Neither object has been attained. The Guernica controversy has not ended, because the regime that spread the false news about Guernica in 1937 cannot bring itself to confess the truth about Guernica in 1970 or in 1975. Yet the fact of Guernica remains an immovable obstacle opposed to any understanding between Madrid and Bilbao. Guernica might, under other political circumstances, be a symbol of reconciliation, on the condition that all the truth be proclaimed concerning the attack and the lies afterward told about it. The frustrated effort of the Neo-Franquista historians indicates the unwillingness of those implicated in the 1937 attack to accept the consequences of telling the truth. The Germans today can say that another regime, the Nazis, bombed Guernica. The Franco government, having never changed, cannot take this way out. The brutal economic and social reality of the Spanish Civil War, the not-yet-ended Spanish Civil War, is still masked behind the banner of the crusade.

The final paragraph of this history belongs to the irony of history. Many of those who lied so vehemently about Guernica, unjustly accusing the Basques of destroying their town, thought (or said they thought) they were saving the Roman Catholic Church in Spain. However much their work may have aided Franco and the economic interests that he was defending during the war, it can be doubted today that their work will be in the long run of any help to the Church. Today that Church seeks to disassociate itself from the Franco regime, and in the traditional Basque country the clergy are more and more *"contestataire."* A Spanish prelate said recently, "The majority of the Spanish clergy today considers the attitude of the Church during the Civil War as a sort of sin to be washed away." [52] Among these sins are the lies told about the bombing of Guernica.

NOTES

Notes

Foreword

1. Pierre Nora, *Faire de l'Histoire*, I. "La retour de l'événement" (Paris: Gallimard, 1974), pp. 210-217.

A Preliminary Note

1. "A de Lizarra" (José María de Irujo), *Los vascos y la república espanola*, p. 24.
2. Steer, *The Tree of Gernika*, p. 73.
3. The facts given in this short résumé of the political, economic, and military situation in the Basque country on 26 April 1937 have been taken from the following works: Arenillas, *Euzkadi, la cuestión nacional y la revolución socialista*, supplement to no. 68, La Batalla; Fernández Exteberría, *De Euzkadi nación a España ficción*; Garcia Venero, *Historia del nacionalismo vasco*, pp. 411-471; "Lizarza," *op. cit.*, pp. 19-96; Sierra Bustamente, *Euzkadi de Sabino Arana a José Antonio Aguirre*, pp. 161-181; Steer, *op. cit.*, pp. 11-104. I also recommend the recently published book, Ortzi, *Historia de Euzkadi. El nacionalismo vasco y ETA.*

BOOK I

Chapter 1
The News from Bilboa

1. " . . . at ten o'clock [P. M.] Antonio Irala [secretary-general of the presidency of the Basque government] rang up. 'Gernika is in flames,' he said." (Steer, *The Tree of Gernika*, p. 242). "Gernika" is the Basque spelling of the Castilian "Guernica." Steer, correspondent of the *Times*, had been told at seven o'clock that Guernica had been bombed, but the extent of the bombing and the resultant holocaust were not then imagined (ibid.). The Belgian correspondent Corman also confirmed that he had been informed of the destruction of Guernica by Irala, but he did not indicate the hour (Corman, *"Salud camarada!"* p. 290). Another correspondent, Noel Monks, writing years later, recalled that "a government official, tears streaming down his face, burst into the dismal dining room crying: 'Guernica is destroyed. The Germans bombed and bombed and bombed.' It was about 9:30 P.M." (Monks, *Eyewitness*, p. 96).

2. Steer mentioned as being present in Bilbao at the time of the Guernica disaster, aside from himself, Christopher [*sic*] Corman, Holme of the Reuter Agency, Monks of the *Daily Express* (hereafter, D. E), and an unnamed reporter from the *Star* (*op. cit.,* p. 247). Hugh Thomas places six foreign correspondents on the scene, adding to the above five, a man from the *Daily Telegraph* (*The Spanish Civil War* [1961], p. 419). In an editorial on 29 April 1937, the *New York Times* stated that it had received "cabled reports of three press associations, though less detailed" than that of Steer. These were doubtless from the three American agencies, whose representatives in Bilbao were probably Spanish journalists; these agencies also received news from correspondents stationed in France, on the Basque frontier.

3. On 26 May 1937 an Air Pyrénées commercial airplane was shot down by Nationalist planes while flying from Biarritz to Bilbao with five passengers, including one woman; the French pilot was wounded. (*Times,* 27 May 1937).

4. Steer—a South African by birth—had worked for the *Times* during the Italian-Ethiopian war, on the side of the Negus. Peter Kemp, a young Englishman who fought with the Spanish Rebels, wrote that Steer was with the Nationalists in Toledo in November 1936 and later expelled (*Mine Were of Trouble,* pp. 41, 52). However, this is not confirmed by Steer's book, in which it is evident that Steer was in the Basque country for at least the greater part of that time. Christopher Holme wrote in a letter dated 25 July 1968: "I, of course, unlike Steer, worked for some months also on the Nationalist side." The editor of *The Times Archives* wrote: "We regard with grave doubts suggestions that George Steer was once expelled from Nationalist Spain. There is nothing whatever in our papers to indicate this, and we feel sure that if he had been expelled *The Times* would have stated so in the news columns" (letter signed by W. R. A. Easthope, 5 May 1969). George Steer was killed while with the British army in Southeast Asia in 1945.

5. Monks was born in Australia; he had also covered the Italian-Ethiopian war with the Ethiopians, and had been expelled from the Nationalist side in Spain. He arrived in Bilbao three or four days before the destruction of Guernica (*op. cit.,* pp. 80-83, 90-91). Monks is now dead.

6. Holme also covered the war in Ethiopia, but with the Italians. He had also been with the Nationalists before going to the Basque front (Kemp., *op. cit.,* pp. 41, 52; Monks, *op. cit.,* p. 94). On 1 April 1937 Holme was at Hendaye and was refused permission to enter Rebel Spain (Archives Nationales, Paris (hereafter AN), 5 AR 272, letter in Havas files). Holme is now with the BBC.

7. Corman had been in Spain during the Asturian revolt in 1934 (Corman, *Brûleurs d'idoles* [Paris-Ostende, 1935]). He was on the Aragón and Madrid fronts in November 1936 (Corman, *"Salud camarada!"*) He wrote, in a letter dated 25 January 1969: "While passing through Paris, I had given a part of the manuscript [*"Salud camarada!"*] to a writer named Fels who was intending to publish some extracts in a magazine of which he was editor. This part was read by Jean-Richard Bloch (editor, at that time, of *Ce Soir*) who got in touch with me when I was going back to Spain. It was he who asked me to go to Bilbao. The manuscript being at the printer's, I completed the book with the texts which I sent from Spain."

8. These were: 1. Fifi Roberts, daughter of Captain W.H. Roberts of the *Seven Seas Spray,* who sent stories to the London *News Chronicle,* while her father's ship, the first food ship to run the blockade, was in Bilbao harbor; 2. Elizabeth Wilkinson, described as a "member of the British Women's Committee against War and Fascism," who happened to be in Bilbao on 26 April and cabled to the London *Daily Worker;* 3. an unidentified reporter for the *Star,* whose message about Guernica was one of the first printed and one of the most widely quoted; 4. Christopher Martin, identified as the London *Daily Telegraph*'s "Special Correspondent with the Basque Forces"; and 5. an unidentified "Special Correspondent," who sent a telegram to the Labour Party's *Daily Herald.* According to Vicente Talón, quoting *El Liberal,* Bilbao, 30 April 1937, a man named Watson was correspondent for both the *Star* and the *Daily Herald* (*Arde Guernica,* pp. 64, 66, 140). *Arde Guernica* was first published in 1970; a second edition appeared in 1973. All references are to the 1970 edition, unless otherwise indicated.

9. AN 5 AR 272, Fontecha file. The archives of the Agence Havas are perhaps the richest source of information on news agency journalism during the Spanish Civil War now available. Fernández-Fontecha arrived in Bilbao on 20 April 1937. He signed his cables "Fontecha" and his name is thus used throughout the text. Only one printed cable from Bilbao signed with his name has been found, in the *Toronto Daily Star,* 30 April 1937.

10. *Daily News,* New York, 26 April 1937, UP dispatch from Bilbao.

11. The first number of *Ce Soir* appeared on 2 March 1937. The two directors were Louis Aragon and Jean-Richard Bloch. Paul Nizan held a high position on the newspaper. Contributions were not limited to Communists, and, if we can judge Corman by his writings, his sympathies were with the Spanish anarchists. The newspaper was reportedly financed with Spanish Republican money (Prieto, *Cómo y por qué salí del Ministerio de Defensa Nacional,* p. 13).

12. Noel Monks, for example, was sent to Bilbao to cover not the fighting at the front but the British challenge to the Rebel blockade (*op. cit.,* p. 89).

13. "I drove back to Guernica . . . it was nearly two in the morning–to send my message" (Monks, *op. cit.,* p. 89). Corman and Holme sent their telegrams in time for the afternoon newspapers of 27 April but Steer, knowing that his paper could print nothing before the morning edition of 28 April, "drove back to Guernica and slept on my story" (*op. cit.,* p. 245).

14. The *Star,* 27 April 1937. The *Star* article was headlined: "HUNDREDS DEAD IN WORST AIR-RAID YET. WHOLE TOWN LAID IN RUINS. FLEEING PEOPLE MOWN DOWN BY AERIAL MACHINE GUNS. 1,000 BOMBS. 50 WOMEN AND CHILDREN PERISH IN A SHELTER." This correspondent said he was at Guernica at five o'clock in the afternoon. "When I left the district at 4 a. m. today, Guernica was still blazing and the sky was reddened for miles."

This afternoon daily is no longer published. Talón gave the name of Watson to the reporter for the *Star* (see n. 8). Steer, as noted above, said that there was a reporter of the *Star* covering the story of Guernica (*op. cit.,* p. 247). Also, there are details in the *Star*'s story which are not found in any printed version of Reuter's dispatch. Cf. the *Evening News, News Chronicle,* of 27 April; *Morning Post* of 28 April. One example: the *Star* tells of the destruction of the Josefinas Hospital; no other mention of this fact has been found in an afternoon newspaper of 27 April. Such details are not invented in London newsrooms. However, Christopher Holme does not today remember anyone from the *Star* (letter from Holme, dated 16 August 1968).

15. *New Chronicle,* 27 April 1937, p. 1. The heading: "FLYERS WERE GERMANS, BASQUES CHARGE." On April 28, this newspaper stated editorially: "The story of the bombing of Guernica exceeds in its sickening horror even the worst that the Italians perpetrated in Abyssinia. . . . Guernica is merely a foretaste of what will happen to other cities, larger and nearer home, unless the rule of law and decency can be exerted over the brutalities of militarism. Every bomb that falls on an open town, anywhere in the world, threatens our lives, and exposes the bankruptcy of statesmanship that can allow such actions to go unpunished." On 29 and 30 April, the *News Chronicle* carried short articles about Guernica sent by "Fifi" Roberts.

16. *Evening News,* 27 April 1937, p. 1. This was a sister paper of the *Daily Mail,* but despite the generally pro-Nationalist position of the Rothermere papers, the *Evening News* headlined the Guernica story: "THE MOST APPALLING AIR RAID EVER KNOWN. GERMAN WAR PLANES ATTACK IN RELAYS FOR HOURS. HUNDREDS KILLED." All these stories in the English press on the afternoon of 27 April were based on Reuters, except for that of the *Star,* but they were not necessarily the same word for word. Each newspaper arranged Reuters facts according to its own style.

17. *Evening Standard,* 27 April 1937, p. 13. This, like the *Daily Express,* was a Beaverbrook paper. Headlines: "TOWN WIPED OUT BY REBEL RAID."

18. *DE,* 28 April 1937, p. 1. Noel Monks' story began: "I have seen many ghastly sights in Spain in the last six months, but none more terrible than the annihilation of the ancient Basque capital of Guernica by Franco's bombing planes." This article was reprinted in the Basque propaganda pamphlet *Foreign Wings over the Basque Country* (hereafter, *FWOBC*) (London, 1937), pp. 37-38.

19. *Glasgow Herald,* 28 April 1937, p. 13. Headlines: "BASQUE TOWN NOW HEAP OF RUINS." This newspaper, like the *Times* and the *Manchester Guardian* did not print news on the front page.

20. *Manchester Guardian* (London edition), 28 April 1937, p. 11. This article is credited to "Press Association Foreign Special," but is mainly a rewrite of Reuters news.

21. *Daily Herald,* 28 April 1937, p. 1. The headlines read: "GERMAN AIRMEN ATROC-

ITY SHOCKS WORLD." The dispatch signed by Christopher Holme was on page two, under headlines saying: "GERMAN EAGLES ON GUERNICA BOMBS. DEFENSELESS TOWN NOW IN RUINS." On page one, the *Daily Herald* printed another, short dispatch, attributed to "A Special Correspondent," not otherwise identified. See n. 8.

22. *Daily Worker*, 28 April 1937, p. 1. This Communist Party newspaper also quoted from the *Star* of the previous afternoon. The headlines were: "THEY MURDERED HUNDREDS IN GUERNICA. FASCIST BOMBERS BLOT OUT UNPROTECTED BASQUE TOWN. PLANES RAINED BOMBS."

23. *Morning Post*, 28 April 1937. "BASQUE TOWN DESTROYED. MASS SLAUGHTER BY GERMAN PLANES. CIVILIANS SHOT IN FLIGHT," were the headlines in this conservative journal. H. A. Gwynne, editor of the *Morning Post* since 1910, was hysterically pro-Franco, and in June 1937 wrote: "Further, we may say that our experience of the Nationalist forces confirms our view that General Franco and his staff are Spanish officers and gentlemen, humane and civilized in their conduct and outlook" (*Controversy on Spain*, p. 19). A measure of the English reaction to the destruction of Guernica can be found in an editorial in the *Morning Post* on 29 April, in which the newspaper adopted a cautious and neutral attitude. Under the heading "HORROR AND MYSTERY," we read: "Public opinion in this country is naturally and properly shocked by the accounts which have been coming from Spain of the bombing of Guernica. . . . Who, then, did the deed which cannot be denied? Here we pass from horror to mystery. On this point the Basques themselves are the most material witnesses; and they flatly accuse the Germans. . . . This accusation does not prove the guilt of the accused; but it does justify the suspension of judgment, until inquiry has established the unquestioned facts." What is important here is that the *Morning Post* did not question the bombing of the town; it reserved judgment concerning who did the bombing.

24. *Daily Mail*, 28 April 1937, p. 1. The account in the *Daily Mail* was signed by Reuters and the British United Press. The international edition of the *Daily Mail*, published in Paris, also used Reuters dispatch on April 28, on page one, declaring that Guernica had been wiped out by German bombers.

25. *Daily Telegraph*, 28 April 1937, p. 1. The *Daily Telegraph* article was signed by "Christopher Martin, 'D. T.' Special Correspondent with the Basque Forces," and laconically reported that Guernica "had also been bombed out of existence."

26. *New York Times* (hereafter, *NYT*), 28 April 1937, p. 1. This article was signed "G. L. Steer" and thus, at least in the United States, there never was any mystery about who had written the article. However, the London article had not been signed, for in those days dispatches in the *Times* were not signed. There are slight editing differences between the London and New York English-language versions. The London version was reprinted in *FWOBC*, pp. 5-11. Steer's article was also printed in *La Nación* of Buenos Aires, p. 1, and in the *Nieuwe Rotterdamsche Courant*, p. 5, on the morning of 28 April.

27. *Times*, 28 April 1937, p. 17. This dispatch was printed, exceptionally, on the editorial page; a paragraph on a foreign news page called attention to it. This *mise en page* constituted, for the conservative *Times*, the equivalent of giant headlines:

28. *DE*, 29 April 1937; *FWOBC*, pp. 39-40.

29. *DE*, 11 May 1937; *FWOBC*, pp. 41-45, where the date of publication in the newspaper is erroneously given as 1 May. Monks was outraged to think that people in England could doubt that Guernica had been bombed by German planes and pilots. "I will swear to it that Franco's German aviators bombed Guernica, and that they killed 1,000 civilians," he wrote. "When Franco hastened to deny that German planes had wrecked the ancient Basque capital, he was trying to make liars of the three accredited war correspondents who were on the spot. Another London newspaper correspondent, Reuter's correspondent, and myself."

30. *Evening News*, 29 April 1937, p. 1.

31. "The denial by Salamanca of all knowledge of the destruction of Guernica has created no astonishment here, since the similar but less terrible bombing of Durango was denied by them in spite of the presence of British eye-witnesses. I have spoken with hundreds of homeless and distressed people, who all give precisely the same description of the events. I have seen and measured the enormous bomb holes at Guernica, which, since I passed through the town the day before, I can testify were not there then."

32. "Thus, although Durango is full of bomb holes, all the churches have holes in the roofs, every house in a wide circle round the churches is shattered from attic to floor, the dead number 200, including 14 nuns, who were machine-gunned from the air as they were running across the convent garden, and every wall is nicked with dozens of machine-gun bullets, it is blandly asserted that this was the work of a "Marxist" mob which does not exist in Vizcaya. When Eibar was burned, this was described by the insurgents as the work of Asturian miners, who were never quartered in the Eibar sector; and when Guernica was reduced to ashes they alleged that the fire was started by Anarchist Militia—aided, presumably, by the clergy, who led the hopeless work of rescue and with whom I talked."

33. *Times*, 6 May 1937, p. 15. *NYT*, 5 May 1937, p. 18. The time lag doubtless accounts for the earlier publication in the New York paper. Also *La Nación*, Buenos Aires, 6 May 1937, p. 2, *Nieuwe Rotterdamsche Courant*, 7 May 1937, p. 2, *FWOBC*, pp. 12-16.

34. *Times*, 28 April 1937, p. 17. *NYT*, 28 April 1937, p. 1. *Chicago Daily News*, 27 April 1937, p. 1, UP. President José Antonio de Aguirre did not go to Guernica on the night of April 26-27 (Aguirre, *De Guernica a Neuva York pasando por Berlín*, p. 28). The only member of the Basque government at Guernica that night was Minister of the Interior Telesforo de Monzón.

35. "Before the tribunals of God and of History, where we must all be judged, I declare that for three and a half hours German airplanes bombed with unparalleled ferocity the civil population of the heroic town of Guernica, reducing it to ashes, pursuing with machine-gun fire women and children, who perished in great numbers, and leaving the rest to flee in panic (*Times, NYT*, 30 April 1937).

36. See Book II, part 1, Chap. 2.

37. *Times*, 6 May 1937, p. 15; *FWOBC*, pp. 48-49; *NYT*, 6 May 1937; *New York Herald Tribune*, 6 May 1937, p. 12; Havas dispatch, 5 May 1937, AN 5 AR 272, "Affaire 'Destruction de Guernica' " file. The most complete text is found in *Euzko Deya* (hereafter, *ED*), Paris, 9, 13 May 1937, p. 1.

38. *Times*, 15 May 1937, dispatch from Bilbao; *FWOBC*, pp. 17-20; *NYT*, 15 May 1937. In reality the word written in Wandel's diary was "Garnica," and he tried to pretend that it was a girl's name. See Steer, *op. cit.,* pp. 281-283. Wandel had left Germany on 22 April by commercial plane for Rome, from where he flew to Seville the following day.

39. Steer, *op. cit.,* pp. 183-185. *La Intervención de Alemania en favor de Franco en las operaciones del territorio vasco*, pp. 31-35. Sixty-three persons were killed in the air raid on Bilbao in which Sabotka himself perished. He had left Berlin on 6 April and was in Seville two days later.

40. The automobile and its occupants were captured on 15 April near Ochandiano. Captain Garsten von Harling was killed, and the interpreter, Pablo Freese, a German with long years of residence in the Basque country, was wounded. Kienzle, twenty-four years old, had left Germany early in February on the merchant ship *Ilma* and entered Cádiz the 16th or 17th of that month. Schulze-Blanck, 22 years old, had left Hamburg on the ship *Monte Roxe*, landed in Lisbon, and entered Spain on 30 December (*La Intervención de Alemania en favor de Franco en las operaciones del territorio vasco*, pp. 27-30, also photographs of persons and documents; Steer, *op. cit.,* pp. 170-171). Corman saw Kienzle in prison (*"Salud camarada!"* pp. 310-324). See also, for the trial, the *Times*, 22 May 1937; unsigned article by Steer; another by Reuters; *FWOBC*, pp. 22-27; the *Times*, 24 May 1937; *NYT*, 22 May 1937.

41. *Chicago Daily Tribune*, 27 April 1937, p. 4. This dispatch was the first item in the Spanish civil war news of the day, and was clearly marked as having been received on Tuesday, 27 April, to distinguish it from most of the newspaper's contents, dated 26 April. This short, succinct report, also published in *La Nación* on the following day, read: "Hundreds of civilians were killed and this ancient city, once capital of the Basque country, was left a mass of blazing ruins today after a three and a half hour insurgent aerial bombardment."

42. *Boston Evening Transcript*, 27 April 1937, p. 1; *Toronto Daily Star*, 27 April 1937, p. 2. This afternoon paper did not give a source for its news, but the text corresponds to the AP text, identified elsewhere as such; however, some news from Reuters, labeled as such, is also incorporated in the article. See also: *La Presse*, Montreal, 27 April 1937, p. 2.

43. *Montreal Daily Star*, 27 April 1937, p. 1. This is an afternoon newspaper.

44. *Chicago Daily News*, 27 April 1937, p. 1. On the following day, Edgar Ansel Mowrer,

of the *Chicago Daily News* foreign service and one of the best-known foreign correspondents of that time, cabled other news about Guernica from Paris.

45. *New York American,* 28 April 1937, p. 1. The headline read: "RAINING FIRE AND EXPLOSIVES REBEL FLIERS KILL 900 NEAR BILBAO." This newspaper regained its normal pro-Rebel posture during the following days, in its reports on Guernica. See *New York American,* 29 April 1937, p. 2; 30 April 1937, p. 2.; 2 May 1937, p. 2; 4 May 1937, p. 10.

46. *New York Herald Tribune,* 28 April 1937, p. 1; New York *Daily News,* 28 April 1937, p. 20; *Washington Post,* 28 April 1937, p. 1; *La Prensa,* Buenos Aires, 28 April 1937. The phrases quoted are from the *Washington Post.* This article was undoubtedly written by A. Hérisson-Laroche, who covered this frontier listening-post for the United Press throughout the civil war. "My comments and information were phoned twice a day to Ralph Heinzen [head of Paris UP office].... Every day before writing my articles I had to listen to both radios and translate papers from both sides as well as to receive important people arriving from Burgos or from the Republican side" (letter from Hérisson-Laroche, 5 February 1969). The *Times* also had a man on the frontier, and on 29 April, p. 16, published a dispatch beginning: "Reports that a large part of the town of Guernica had been destroyed by fire are confirmed by travellers arriving on the frontier coming from Spain." Reuters also maintained a correspondent on the frontier. See the *Times,* 29 April 1937, p. 16.

47. *Daily News,* New York, 28 April 1937.

48. *La Prensa, Correio da Manhã,* 28 April 1937.

49. *NYT; Gazette,* Montreal, 28 April 1937.

50. *New York Herald Tribune,* 6 May 1937. This Father Arronategui was the brother of the priest of the same name reported killed in the air raid in Steer's original dispatch.

51. See David Wingeate Pike, *Conjecture, Propaganda and Deceit and the Spanish Civil War* (Stanford, 1968), pp. 111-121. This study of the French press during the Spanish Civil War has been extremely useful.

52. Jean Mottin, *Histoire politique de la presse, 1944-1949,* pp. 22-23.

53. *Ce Soir,* 28 April 1937, p. 1. This newspaper, like all the other afternoon dailies in Paris, carried the date of the following day.

54. This was Fontecha's address on 4 May, and presumably he was there on 26 April (AN, 5 AR 272, "Affaire 'Destruction de Guernica' " file). Lodging was difficult to come by in refugee-swollen Bilbao, and the hotel was doubtless requisitioned for journalists and other personalities.

55. *L'Humanité, L'Oeuvre, La Nación,* 28 April; *L'Ordre, Journal des Débats Politiques et Litteraires,* 29 April 1937.

56. See the "Contrôle" sheets, concerning a comparison study of the amount of copy from each of the competing news agencies printed by certain South American newspapers, established by the "Agence Havas (Services Etrangers)" in 1938 and 1939 (AN, 5 AR 272).

57. *La Nación,* 28 April 1937, p. 1. This newspaper not only used Havas, the AP, and the *Times* for news of the Spanish Civil War but also had its own special reporters in Spain on both sides and elsewhere in Europe to report on the war in Spain.

58. *Correio da Manhã,* 28 April 1937, p. 1. The name "Hérisson-Laroche" was frequently anglicized into "Harison-Laroche" or "Harrison-Laroche." This newspaper never published a Havas story from Bilbao about Guernica. On 29 April it featured the continuation of the Guernica story on its front page, beginning with a Havas report from London on the English reaction to the news of the bombing. On the following day, however, it published a Havas dispatch from the Nationalist zone denying reponsibility for the destruction of the Basque town.

59. *Aftonbladet,* 27 April 1937, p. 3. This tabloid-sized newspaper gave a full-page headline to the story.

60. *Nieuwe Rotterdamsche Courant,* 28 April 1937, p. 5.

61. The *Montreal Daily Star* used the AP dispatch from Hendaye on the afternoon of 27 April. The French-language Montreal daily *La Presse* also used the AP service for its account of the bombing of Guernica on 27 April. The *Toronto Daily Star* published information from the AP and Reuters about Guernica on 27 April, but not a line from Havas. All three newspapers normally used Havas items on the Spanish Civil War.

62. The *Journal de Genève* did not mention Guernica until 29 April.

63. *La Métropole* also waited until 29 April to mention Guernica, and never reported the initial story of the bombing. This newspaper was frankly pro-Nationalist.

64. *La Libre Belgique*, a liberal Catholic organ, also had nothing about Guernica until 29 April.

65. *L'Indépendance Belge* printed Havas dispatches, from Valencia, Salamanca, and London, to inform its readers belatedly of Guernica on 29 April.

66. See telegrams from Havas in Paris to their correspondent in the Nationalist zone, Jean d'Hospital, at Avila, dated 8 and 9 March 1937 and letter dated 12 March (AN, 5 AR 271, d'Hospital file).

67. *Toronto Daily Star,* 30 April 1937, p. 2, printed a Havas article signed "By Fernando Fontecha." It is a sequel to the Guernica story, and shows not only that Fontecha could write a professionally correct newspaper dispatch but also that he held firm ideas concerning what had happened in Guernica. "I witnessed late Thursday afternoon in this little suburb of Bilbao another such massacre of defenseless civilians by German-made insurgent airplanes and bombs as wiped the Basque "holy city" of Guernica off the map last Monday. The horrible slaughter began at 4:30 P. M.—the exact hour at which Gen. Francisco Franco's angels of death opened their merciless attack on Guernica four days ago. By the time the raiders had flown off over the horizon, the terrified population was convinced Franco's emissaries were determined to annihilate the entire Basque country, down to the last and tiniest hamlet. . . . Forest fires crackled and raged in numerous nearby pine groves. In the horror and confusion which followed it was impossible to obtain anything like an accurate count on casualties, which must have been high. I myself saw numerous unexploded incendiary bombs bearing the stamp of German manufacture—Rheinsdorf 1936. . . . According to all authoritative accounts of the Guernica massacre, this raid on Galdácano was in every way analagous. The airplanes flew in similar formations and adopted the same tactics. first driving the civilians into the open with bombs and then systematically mowing them down with well-placed machine-gun fire." The headline read, over two columns: "MASSACRE OF CIVILIANS IS CONTINUED IN SPAIN."

The text of the dispatch quoted above is sufficient to show where Fontecha's sympathies lay. It should also be noted that, in order to get to Bilbao, he had left Republican Spain and entered France. He could have asked to go to Nationalist Spain, or to stay in France, had his political desires been in those directions. He worked with the Free French radio in Dakar as a journalist during World War II and later (interview with Antonio Pérez-Torreblanca y Guardiola). I have found no recent trace of him.

68. The bombardment of Guernica, according to all other accounts, lasted from three hours to three hours and a half. The "8 hours" in the Havas cable could only have been an error of transmission from Bilbao or of editing in Paris. Since the Havas message was sent too late for publication on the afternoon of 27 April, the editors at Havas had two means of controlling the duration of the bombardment: by reference to Corman's article published in *Ce Soir;* and by reference to what the London papers were printing. Since some French newspapers waited until at least 29 April to publish the Havas dispatch, and then printed the error of "8 hours," it can be concluded that Havas made no effort to send out a correction.

69. *L'Humanité,* 28 April 1937, p. 1. On the following day, the Communist daily cited at length both Steer's telegram and the editorial from the *Times* of 28 April; Gabriel Péri continued with another editorial. The different manner in which each French newspaper treated the news about Guernica gives importance to French press circulation figures. Two sources have been used: Bodin and Touchard, *Front populaire 1936,* pp. 283-291 (hereafter, B.-T.); and Jean Mottin, *Histoire politique de la presse,* 1944-1949, pp. 23-24. According to these sources, the circulation of *L'Humanité* was 320,000.

70. Arthur Koestler wrote: "The Loyalist government had at last managed to set up an international news agency. . . . It was called "Spanish News Agency" in England and *Agence Espagne* in France. The European head office was in Paris, directed by Otto [Katz], the London office was run by Geoffrey Bing. The first two war correspondents to go to Spain for *Agence Espagne* were Willy Forrest. . . . and myself" (*The Invisible Writing,* p. 335).

71. *Le Populaire,* 28 April 1937. This newspaper was of course strongly in favor of the Spanish Republic. On 29 April, it published photographs of the ruined town on its first page,

with three headlines: "MASSACRE OF BASQUE PEOPLE. 'OUR WAR AGAINST FRANCO IS FINISHED. IT IS GERMANY WHO MAKES WAR ON US,' DECLARES BILBAO GOVERNMENT DELEGATION. SEPARATE PEACE OFFERS REFUSED BY EUZKADI, HITLER'S MEN SYSTEMATICALLY CARRY OUT THREATENED PLAN OF DESTRUCTION." Circulation: B.-T., 100,000; Mottin, 60,000.

72. *Le Petit Journal,* 28 April 1937, p. 3. This *modéré* newspaper, markedly pro-Basque in its treatment of the Guernica incident, did not print the Havas dispatch from Bilbao. On 29 April it reported declarations from the Spanish embassy and the Basque delegation, both in Paris. It also declared: "London aroused with indignation by bombardment of Guernica." Circulation: B.-T., Mottin, circa 160,000.

73. *L'Oeuvre,* 28 April 1937, p. 3. This newspaper, the voice of Radical-Socialism in Paris, specialized in foreign news; its foreign news specialist, Genevieve Tabouis, had an international reputation. Circulation: B.-T.; Mottin: 115,000.

74. *Le Matin,* 28 April 1937, p. 1. This newspaper carried the Guernica story objectively— that is, it reported the news available. See cable from London, reporting message from Holme, saying he had himself verified presence of Junkers 52s, Heinkel 51s and Heinkel 111s over Guernica (*Le Matin,* 30 April 1937, p. 3). Holme's original cable, *Evening News,* 29 April 1937. Circulation: B.-T., 275,000; Mottin, 300,000.

75. *Le Petit Parisien,* 28 April 1937, p. 1. The headlines over this comprehensive account read: "DESTRUCTION OF GUERNICA BY GERMAN AIRPLANES OF FRANCO'S ARMY. HOLY CITY OF BASQUES IN FLAMES. METHODICAL CARNAGE OF MORE THAN THREE HOURS ON MARKET AFTERNOON. HEAVY BOMBERS FIRST CRUSHED TOWN AND SURROUNDING FARMS UNDER AVALANCHE OF HEAVY PROJECTILES AND GRENADES. LOW FLYING FIGHTERS THEN MACHINE GUNNED PANIC STRICKEN PEOPLE FLEEING. EIGHT FEET DEEP SHELTERS PIERCED BY HEAVY BOMBS. HUNDREDS DEAD." This story was accompanied by a Havas dispatch from Vitoria, reporting a denial of the bombing by a Rebel transmitter called "Radio Requeté." On the following day, *Le Petit Parisien* reported the debate in the House of Commons over Guernica and a Radio Nacional denial from Salamanca. This newspaper was described in the pro-Republican *Journal des Nations,* of Geneva, 29 April 1937, p. 1, as "very favorable to Franco's cause." It had the largest morning circulation in Paris: B.-T., 1,312,129; Mottin, 1,370,000.

76. *L'Echo de Paris,* 28 April 1937, p. 3. The significance of the air raid escaped the attention of the newspaper's editors on 28 April, as did a similar incriminating dispatch, that of the editors of the *New York American,* on the same date. On the following days it regained its normal posture, as did the *New York American,* and, despite the fact that it had reported the raid on 28 April, subsequently spoke skeptically even of the town's destruction. (*L'Echo de Paris,* 28 April 1937, p. 3; 30 April 1937, p. 1). The *Journal des Nations,* 30 April 1937, p. 1, considered *L'Echo de Paris* one of the "unofficial organs of the Franco cause in France." René Rémond wrote of *L'Echo de Paris,* in *Les catholiques, le communisme et les crises,* p. 271: "In the years of the 1930s, the most faithful expression of the conservative Right: has an important Catholic audience." Circulation: B.-T.; Mottin (p. 24), less than 100,000.

77. *Le Journal,* 28 April 1937, p. 5. This consistently pro-Nationalist newspaper had, as Spanish Civil War news on its front page that day, a dispatch from Vitoria by its correspondent, Max Massot, telling of Republican barbarities and incendiarism in Eibar. On 29 April, it published a dispatch containing a denial of Nationalist responsibility for the disaster at Guernica. It never did print an account of the bombing. The circulation of *Le Journal* was 400,000 (B-T., Mottin), making it the second-ranking Paris morning newspaper.

78. *Paris-Soir,* 29 April 1937, p. 5. At this time, *Paris-Soir* had the largest circulation in France, according to B.-T. and Mottin, around 1,800,000.

79. *Ce Soir,* 29 April 1937, p. 1. Two days later, *Ce Soir* published an interview of Corman with a "reporter-photographer" of the newspaper who had been in Guernica.

80. *Le Temps,* 29 April 1937, p. 2. This conservative afternoon newspaper of *"grande information"* was reputed to be well acquainted with the viewpoint of the Quai d'Orsay. Its printing was around 100,000, which placed it rather low among Paris newspapers of its category (B.-T., and Mottin).

81. *L'Action Francaise* (hereafter *AF*), 29 April 1937, p. 2. Since December 1926 this

newspaper had been forbidden to Catholics, but it had nevertheless a large Catholic reading public. Circulation: B.-T., circa 100,000; Rémond, *op. cit.*, p. 269, and Mottin, 50,000.

82. *Le Jour,* 29 April 1937, p. 3.

83. *Le Figaro,* 29 April 1937, p. 3. On the following day, *Le Figaro* published a photograph of the ruins of Guernica with this caption: "The historic town of Guernica which has just been destroyed by an aerial bombardment." However, the caption on a photograph cannot always be taken to denote an editorial position; it was, more probably, the idea of the photographic agency. Also on 30 April, on page 1, "Guermantes" (Gérard Bauer), a regular *Figaro* contributor, published an evocation of Guernica, based more on touristic nostalgia than on a political position, and concluded indecisively: "However, the ruins and the dead are there, whether the fire fell from the skies or was set by men in flight." The news columns of *Le Figaro* had never mentioned any dead in Guernica; Guermantes must have been reading some other newspaper. This refusal to take a stand was further underlined in the newspaper on May 5, when Wladimir d'Ormesson wrote on the front page: "All these contradictory news are suspect. It is, however, probable that the two facts are exact and that Guernica was destroyed by an air raid and by fires set here and there." Circulation: B.-T., 90,000; Mottin, 50,000.

84. *Journal des Débats Politiques et Littéraires,* 29 April 1937, p. 1. Circulation: B.-T.; Mottin, 25,000.

85. *L'Excelsior,* 29 April 1937, p. 3. This dispatch came, surprisingly enough, from the American agency, UP. *L'Excelsior* was, according to my research, the only Paris newspaper that used a foreign news agency. From time to time it printed brief UP telegrams; if it received a full UP service on the Spanish Civil War, it did not make good use of it and, in fact, published little about the conflict, from either side, from any source. Circulation: B.-T., 90,000; Mottin, 130,000.

86. *La Croix,* 29 April 1937, p. 5. Circulation: B.-T., 150,000-170,000; Mottin, 100,000.

87. *L'Aube,* 29 April 1937, p. 1. Circulation: B.-T., circa 20,000.

88. *L'Ordre,* 29 April 1937, p. 3. B.-T. placed the circulation at less than 20,000.

89. *L'Ordre,* 30 April 1937, p. 3.

90. *Paris-Midi,* 29 April 1937, p. 3. Circulation: B.-T., 87,362; Mottin, 120,000.

91. *L'Intransigeant,* 30 April 1937, p. 3. Circulation: B.-T., 200,000; Mottin, 170,000.

92. *Le Petit Parisien,* p. 1; *L'Oeuvre,* p. 3; *Le Petit Journal,* p. 1, all 30 April 1937; *La Croix,* 1 May 1937, p. 2. A reprint of this Havas dispatch can be found in the pamphlet, *Guernica, la mainmise hitlerienne sur le pays basque,* p. 9. This report undoubtedly came from Fontecha and shows his pro-Republican leanings.

93. See *Journal des Nations,* Geneva, 1 May 1937, p. 1; *Glasgow Herald,* 30 April 1937, p. 13; *Le Petit Marocain,* Casablanca, 30 April 1937, p. 3. *Montreal Daily Star,* 29 April 1937, p. 23. This latter dispatch was credited to "C[anadian] P[ress] -Havas."

94. *L'Humanité,* 13 May 1937, p. 1. Their stories concorded with those of other survivors interviewed earlier in Guernica, Bilbao, and elsewhere.

95. *Le Petit Journal,* 8 May 1937, p. 5, article signed by Jacques Klein; *Le Matin,* 8 May 1937, p. 2. Havas cabled to South America a story about the arrival of *La Habana,* but if it included details about Guernica, these were not printed (*La Nación,* 9 April 1937, p. 1; *Correio da Manhã,* 9 April 1937, p. 1). The name of the Cuban newspaperman was given as Martín Arrisbaya in *Le Petit Journal* and as Martin Arrigola in *Le Matin,* but *La Nación,* citing *Le Matin,* printed it as Martin Arrigada. *L'Humanité,* on 9 May, p. 4, quoted from the article in *Le Petit Journal.* The reporter for *Le Matin* remarked on "The dozens of concordant testimonies concerning the events of 26 April."

96. *La Dépêche, Journal de la Démocratie,* 28 April 1937, pp. 1, 4. This newspaper belonged to the Sarraut family, important in the Radical-Socialist party. It had 23 editions according to B.-T.; Mottin gave the circulation as 270,000.

97. *Ibid.,* 29 April 1937, pp. 1-2.

98. *La France de Bordeaux et du Sud-Ouest,* 29 April 1937, p. 1. The adjective "radical-isante" is taken from Mottin. Circulation: B.-T.; Mottin, 235,000.

99. *La Petite Gironde,* 28 April 1937, 3. The paucity of news about Guernica in this newspaper did not indicate a lack of interest, for on the following day it sent a reporter-

photographer, Berniard, to Guernica to cover the story. See Book I, chap. 4. Circulation: B.-T., Mottin, 325,000.

100. *Chicago Daily News*, 29 April, p. 2.

101. *La France de Bordeaux et du Sud-Ouest*, 29 April 1937.

102. *L'Oeuvre*, 30 April 1937, p. 1.

103. A right-wing conclusion was that French public opinion was less moved by the Guernica affair than was that of some other countries. "This affair, which has not been cleared up, has nevertheless provoked a profound emotion abroad, especially in England" (*L'Illustration*, 8 May 1937, p. 48).

104. This study has found but one Paris newspaper that at this time attributed news dispatches to a foreign agency. See n. 85.

105. Havas held a monopoly on the news published in France in the spring of 1937. Some French newspapers had occasional bits of information from a financial news service, Fournier, and others from "Agence Radio," but such published items did not account for one percent of the general information distributed by news agencies in France. "Agence Radio" was, moreover, a Havas "satellite" (*Histoire générale de la presse française*, T. 3, p. 468).

106. Letter from Christopher Holme, 16 August 1968.

107. Public Record Office (hereafter PRO), FO371/21293, W 10657, folio 203. Gilbert, American consul at Geneva, cabled Washington on May 29: "Pierce [*sic*], representative of the London *Times*, who has just returned from Bilbao showed me an extensive collection of photographs of documents respecting German participation in the Bilbao campaign with particular reference to the bombardment of Guernica. Among these was a map annotated by directions in German for the aerial bombardment of Guernica and he asserted that the actual bombardment followed these directions" (*Foreign Relations of the United States, Diplomatic Papers* [1937], I, 306). Since we know that Steer was in Geneva on 29 May, it is certain that "Pierce" was in reality Steer. No other mention of such a map has been found.

108. Monks, *op. cit.*, pp. 97-98.

Chapter 2
Riposte from Salamanca

1. Galland, *Die Ersten und die Letzten*, pp. 42-45; Bolín, *Spain: The Vital Years* (hereafter, *STVY*), p. 274; Talón, *Arde Guernica*, p. 270; Martínez Bande, *Vizcaya*, p. 114. The only one to make the obvious reference to the murderous bombings of North Vietnam by the American air force is Talón (*op. cit.*, p. 55).

2. "Guernica was the first town ever bombed in order to intimidate a civilian population," wrote the English critic John Berger. "Thus, Picasso's personal protest at a comparatively small incident in his own country afterwards acquired world-wide significance. For many millions of people now, the name of Guernica accuses all war criminals" (*Success and Failure of Picasso*, p. 166). Picasso had been working on a project of this general nature for some time, as evidence by the two sheets of nine etchings each, entitled, "Dreams and Lies of Franco," dated 8 January 1937. A part of Picasso's short introduction reads: "Cries of children cries of women cries of birds cries of flowers cries of timbers and of stones cries of bricks cries of furniture of beds of chairs of curtains of pots of cats of papers." Hugh Thomas strangely refers to these etchings as "a series of comic strips" (*The Spanish Civil War*, p. 421). They were "cartoons," but this word does not always mean "comic strips." Picasso had been commissioned by the Republican government to do a painting for the Spanish pavilion at the Paris Exposition. The destruction of Guernica evidently crystallized his ideas, and he undoubtedly used conceptions he had already established before 26 April in the masterpiece now known as "Guernica." It was first shown at the Paris Exposition in 1937 and is now at the Museum of Modern Art, New York.

3. "La victoire de Guernica," first published in *Cours Naturel* in 1938.

4. *Die Kinder von Gernika*, first published in Amsterdam in German in 1939, and in that same year in English, *The Children of Guernica*. It was reprinted after the war with a preface by Thomas Mann. See *Les enfants de Guernica*, (Paris, 1954); *Die Kinder von Gernika* (Hamburg, 1955).

5. *L'Aube,* 2 June 1937, *"La signification de Guernica,"* by Luigi Sturzo. This may well have been published earlier in England, in English.

6. *Le Journal,* 28 April 1937. This dispatch is from Vitoria, but it is not signed.

7. Aguirre's charges were carried by the Bilbao radio station, and the Nationalists felt obliged to reply to them as part of Spain's internal propaganda war. What was said on the internal propaganda front was not always the same as that said outside the country.

8. *Heraldo de Aragón* (hereafter, *HA*), 28 April 1937.

9. *ABC,* Seville, 28 April 1937. Before the war this newspaper was published in both Madrid and Seville. During the civil war, the Madrid edition was a Republican newspaper of Azaña's Left Republican party, and the Seville edition was a Nationalist daily. In this work all references are to the Seville edition. There was never an official text for the radio talks of General Queipo de Llano. There may have been a semiprepared text, or series of notes for the speaker, but there was also apparently a great deal of improvisation. The text published by the Nationalist press was taken down by shorthand reporters listening to the radio, and the quality of their text doubtless depended on the quality of radio reception at any given moment. This fact explains the differences found in Queipo de Llano's text as reproduced in a Seville newspaper and in one from Saragossa. It is worth noting that the text of these speeches was frequently censored in the press of Seville itself. The "siri-miri" is not a wind, but a fine drizzle.

10. A correspondent of the United Press cabled from Salamanca on 28 April: "We have seen the sheets of paper of General Franco replying to Aguirre's charges." The date of the dispatch and the material quoted by the correspondent would indicate that the reference is to the article entitled, "Lies, lies, lies." See *La Nación,* 29 April, p. 1.

11. *The Tree of Gernika,* p. 246.

12. *ABC,* 16 April 1937. Arias Paz was described as a "highly cultivated major of the engineering corps, author of technical works."

13. San Román Colino, *Legislación del Gobierno nacional,* primer semestre (1937), pp. 93-95. Before the creation of the delegation, interior censorship had been in the hands of General Millán Astray, founder of the Spanish Foreign Legion. He had in turn succeeded the right-wing journalist Juan Pujol. See García Venero, *Falange en la guerra de España: la unificación y Hedilla,* pp. 273-274. Pujol was editor of Juan March's Madrid newspaper *Informaciones* before the civil war. Pujol was subsidized by the Nazi government (Viñas, *La Alemania nazi y el 18 de julio,* pp. 167-168). Pujol had been named head of the *Gabinete de Prensa* on 9 August 1936, with Joaquín Arrarás as his assistant (San Román Colino, *op. cit.,* segundo semestre [1936], p. 25). Gay, the first head of the delegation, was an extreme rightist, a Catholic anti-Semite (Gay, *Estampas rojas y caballeros blancos,* p. 37). His chief aide was Ramón Ruiz Alonso, ex-deputy from Granada for Gil Robles's CEDA, a man considered today to bear the chief responsibility for the death of García Lorca (Gibson, *The Death of Lorca*). Before the civil war, Gay had openly proclaimed his sympathies for Nazi Germany and Fascist Italy, but he was not a Falangist. See Gay, *La revolución nacional socialista* (Barcelona, 1934), and *Madre Roma* (Barcelona, 1935). He had also received subsidies from the Nazis before the civil war (Viñas, *op. cit.,* pp. 168-169). Like most of the Nationalists charged with press and propaganda work, Gay was strangely insensitive to world public opinion, as is shown when he wrote in 1937, with indifferent approval of the summary execution of women prisoners: "Father Laureano de las Muñecas offered spiritual aid to some militia prisoners at San Rafael. Among them were two young girls. One aged seventeen years accepted and confessed to the priest and died a Christian"(*op. cit.,* p. 153). On leaving the head office of the delegation, Gay was named chief of intellectual relations with the countries that had recognized the Nationalist regime—that is with Germany, Italy, and Guatemala.

14. *Crónica de la guerra española,* Núm. 62, Vol. IV, p. 45. This publication was brought out with the assistance of the Spanish Ministry of Information and Tourism. The chief of the Section of Studies on the Spanish War in the Ministry, Ricardo de la Cierva, served as an editor of the work. See R. de la Cierva, *Importancia histórica e historiográfica de la guerra española,* front cover fold.

15. *HA,* 27 April 1937, article by Fernando Ors.

16. *Op. cit.,* p. 233.

17. See this confirming dispatch in *Le Temps,* 27 April 1937, p. 8. "Vitoria, 26 April. Towards 17h30 Sunday, twenty trimotored bombers coming from the South, protected by 15 fighters, passed over Elgueta, and a few instants later, one could hear from the direction of

Eibar, a thundering noise which seemed never to end; and the airplanes spilled their bombs. A little later, one could see, from the heights of Enchorta, all the valley of Eibar filled with smoke caused by the bursting of the projectiles." This was also published in *La Nación*, 27 April 1937, p. 1, where it was identified as coming from the Havas Agency.

18. The strongly pro-Nationalist *L'Echo de Paris* reported on April 27: "Eibar is in flames. . . . Before abandoning the town, the Reds have destroyed the factories and workshops for arms and bicycles which formed the wealth of the Spanish Saint-Etienne." See also n. 36.

19. Wing-Commander A. W. H. James, a strong partisan of the Nationalist position on Guernica, wrote in the *Times*, 14 December 1937, "The destruction of many places upon evacuation, such as Guernica . . . may be excused as acts of war." He later wrote, in the *Daily Telegraph* of 19 February 1938, that the defenders "had every reason and military right to destroy it [Guernica] upon leaving."

20. *HA*, 28 April 1937.

21. As noted in the previous chapter, the Havas dispatch containing the denial from Salamanca was frequently found among the first dispatches concerning Guernica printed by many French newspapers. See *Le Temps, L'Action Francaise, Le Jour, Le Figaro*—all for 29 April 1937. This press handout was doubtless sent by the local Spanish employee of the Agence Havas as part of his routine chores, or was perhaps picked up by the Havas radio receiving station, rue de Richelieu, in Paris (An, 5 AR 272). This Havas dispatch was also printed in the following newspapers on 29 April 1937: *Tribune de Genève, Le Matin, La France de Bordeaux et du Sud-Ouest, Neue Zürcher Nachrichten, La Vigie Marocaine*. The Salamanca denial can also be found in the *Times*, dispatch from Franco-Spanish frontier; *NYT; New York American*, dispatch from Universal Service—all of 29 April 1937.

22. Not one of the "fugitives" mentioned at this time was ever produced later, even for the preparation of the official study, *Guernica, Being the Official Report of A Commission Appointed by the Spanish Nationalist Government to Investigate the Causes of the Destruction of Guernica on April 26-28, 1937* (hereafter, *Guernica: The Official Report*).

23. The distance of fifteen kilometers from the Nationalist lines to Guernica, on 26 April 1937, as the crow flies, is substantially correct. The Rebel army on this date was at Monte Oiz, which was approximately this distance from Guernica; elsewhere the Nationalists were farther away: Eibar, some twenty-five kilometers distant, fell on 26 April; Marquina, some fifteen kilometers from Guernica, fell on the twenty-seventh, and Durango, twenty kilometers from Guernica, fell on the twenty-eighth.

24. *ABC*, 29 April 1937. This statement, merely repeating the themes of the previous day, was infrequently printed outside Spain. Parts were published in *L'Echo de Paris* on 30 April, p. 1, as a dispatch from Salamanca dated the previous day. William P. Carney cabled on 29 April that he had heard the communiqué broadcast to the Nationalist troops by loudspeakers (*NYT*, 20 April 1937).

25. *ABC, HA*, 29 April 1937. This seems to be the first attempt by Nationalist spokesmen to use a technical interpretation of the ruins to prove that Guernica had not been destroyed by air bombs.

26. *ABC*, 29 April 1937; *HA*, 30 April 1937. The day before, according to a Reuters dispatch from Saint-Jean-de-Luz, dated 28 April, "Foreign journalists at Vitoria and San Sebastián have been invited . . . to visit the aerodrome and verify these facts by inspection of the essential records, pilots' log-books, petrol registers, etc." (*Manchester Guardian*, 29 April 1937). I have never found a report of any such visit.

27. *Times*, 29 April 1937, p. 16. *International Daily Mail*, Paris, 29 April 1937, p. 1.

28. "I picked up one incendiary shell which failed to explode. It was made of aluminum, weighed nearly two pounds, and was liberally stamped with German eagles" (*Manchester Guardian*, 28 April 1937). If Queipo de Llano were right about the venality of Christopher Holme, then Holme's press colleagues were equally guilty, for they all claimed to have seen the German bombs. "Of incendiary bombs, a journalist with me picked up three, all German, dated 1936," wrote Steer (*Times*, 6 May 1937). Steer repeated the statement in his book (*op. cit.*, p. 245, photograph, pp. 256-257). Steer also found bomb splinters. "They are the same metal as the bombs lately used by General Mola's German aircraft on the front," he wrote in the *Times* on 6 May. Steer found the same type of incendiary bomb, with the German eagle and the

RhS factory markings, in Galdácano on 29 April, after that village was bombed (*Times*, 30 April 1937). Corman had equally told, in his newspaper and later in his book, how his feet had struck an unexploded incendiary bomb. "It was marked with three German eagles and the following inscription:

$$114 \text{ K-Bi } \frac{H}{344} \qquad 36 \qquad 118 \frac{Rh.S.}{143} 1936"$$

(*Ce Soir*, 29 April 1937; *"Salud, camarada!"* p. 292). *Guernica: The Official Report* claimed, p. 15, that the incendiary bombs "were not stamped with the German eagle, nor with the word 'Rome' as alleged in Red propaganda." This reference is to the dispatch of Noel Monks in the *Daily Express* of 29, April 1937. "More than a dozen 'dud' incendiary bombs have been found. All are branded with the German double eagle. Two 'dud' torpedo bombs have also been found. They have 'Roma' branded across their base." Monks was the only one of the correspondents in Bilbao to identify any of the bombs found in Guernica as of Italian origin; he also claimed to have seen Italian planes near Guernica on the afternoon of April 26 (*ibid.*). Monks later wrote: "One of my colleagues found three 'dud' incendiary bombs. They were German bombs, branded with the German eagle" (*DE*, 10 May 1937). Stevenson, the British consul in Bilbao, sent two dismantled incendiary bombs from Guernica to the embassy in Hendaye (letter of Stevenson, 2 May 1937, PRO, FO371/21337, folio 140).

29. *HA*, 30 April 1937. This declaration was also reproduced in *ABC* of Seville of the same date. In the *Heraldo* quotation, the date of the siri-miri is 26 April; in *ABC*, 16 April, doubtless a misprint. No proof whatsoever had been brought forward concerning the presence of any Asturian troops in Guernica, although their mere presence would have proved nothing about the destruction of the town. Steer identified the troops in or near the town as "two Basque Nationalist battalions" (*op. cit.*, p. 236). See also Elosegi, who says his "company" was the only military unit in the town (*Quiero morir por algo*, p. 145).

30. *HA*, 30 April 1937.

31. *Times*, 4 May 1937. No source is given, but the report doubtless came from Reuters in Salamanca. The *Morning Post* printed the communiqué the same day, attributing it to Reuters. See also *NYT*, 4 May 1937; *New York American*, 4 May 1937, Universal Service report from Salamanca, dated May 3.

32. *ABC*, 4 May 1937; *HA*, 5 May 1937. The marqués del Moral wrote that this communiqué was "issued" by General Franco. See *Address Given by the Marquis del Moral to Members of the House of Commons on Wednesday, May 26th, 1937*, p. 9 (hereafter Moral: *Address*).

33. This propaganda policy of bringing the battle line closer to Guernica at the time of its destruction became standard from now on. William Foss and Cecil Gerahty in 1938 brought Nationalist troops to "within four miles of Guernica" on 26 April (*Spanish Arena*, p. 439). A year later Yeats-Brown declared Guernica to have been at the time of the bombing "a vital military objection five miles [eight kilometers] from their [the Nationalists'] front line" (*European Jungle*, p. 272). Luis Bolín in 1966 situated the Basque town as "part of the front line" at the time of its destruction (*STVY*, p. 274). Sinning on the other side, Hugh Thomas wrote that on 26 April 1937, Guernica "lay some thirty kilometers from the front" (*The Spanish Civil War* [1961], p. 419).

34. *Guernica: The Official Report*, p. 31.

35. *Ibid.*, pp. (x), 2.

36. See article by Fernando Ors, *HA*, 27 April 1937, p. 7. "The factories have disappeared. . . . In the more modest workshops one can still see parts of revolvers which could not be finished. But the great factories which employed hundreds of workmen are crackling in the flames before our eyes." See also n. 18.

37. *Daily Telegraph*, 27 April 1937. See also *La Prensa*, 27 April 1937, and Juan Pascual de Orkoya, *La verdad sobre la destrucción de Gernika*, pp. 29-30.

38. *Morning Post*, 28 April 1937. This article was unsigned, as was the custom on that newspaper.

39. *Il Telegrafo*, 27 April 1937.

40. *New York American,* 27 April 1937, p. 1; *Los Angeles Examiner,* 28 April 1937. The bombing of Arbacegui and Guerricaiz by Nationalist planes on 26 April was confirmed at the same time by the correspondents stationed in Bilbao. See following pages of text.

41. *L'Echo de Paris,* 27 April 1937.

42. *La Prensa,* 27 April 1937; Pascual de Orkoya, *op. cit.,* p. 30.

43. *Correio da Manhã,* 27 April 1937.

44. *La Prensa,* 27 April 1937. Heinzen was chief of the Paris office of UP. He usually cabled a roundup story of the situation in Spain, or a feature story on some element in the Spanish news, to customers in Latin America. These dispatches were rarely printed elsewhere.

45. *Il Messagero,* 28 April 1937, p. 1.

46. *HA,* 27 April 1937.

47. *ABC,* 27 April 1937.

48. *HA,* 27 April 1937.

49. *Ibid.,* 28 April 1937.

50. *Ibid.*

51. *Times,* 29 April 1937, p. 16.

52. *Ce Soir,* 28 April 1937. This was published on the afternoon of 27 April. Corman later wrote: "We return to Bilbao, Times, Reuter and I, to telegraph the story of the raid of which we were victims" (*op. cit.,* pp. 289-290).

53. *Manchester Guardian,* 27 April 1937.

54. *DE,* 29 April 1937. Monks was apparently not with the other three newspapermen but in another automobile.

55. *Ibid.,* 10 May 1937.

56. "Insurgent aircraft half destroyed the mountain villages of Arbacegui, Guerricaiz, Marquina and Bolívar, family seat of the great South American liberator" (*NYT,* 27 April 1937). This dispatch, not signed but a "Special cable to *The New York Times*" from Bilbao on 26 April, could have come only from Steer, who wrote some months later: "We had experienced quite enough that day [April 26], and we went on without stopping to Bilbao to write our stories" (*op. cit.,* p. 236). The *Times* used a more formal, impersonal style of journalism than did the newspapers of Corman and Monks. Monks later explained: "These were the days in foreign reporting when personal experiences were copy, for there hadn't been a war for eighteen years. . . . We used to call them 'I' stories, and when the Spanish war was ended in 1939 we were as heartily sick of writing them as the public must have been of reading them" (*Eyewitness,* pp. 95-96).

57. *Op. cit.,* pp. 234-236.

58. *Op. cit.,* pp. 285-289.

59. *Op. cit.,* pp. 94-96.

Chapter 3
Working Conditions of the Foreign Press

1. Bolín, *STVY,* p. 221. There were three cable heads in prewar Spain: Vigo, Máiaga, and Bilbao. When Bilbao fell on 19 June 1937, all three were in Nationalist hands. However, the Republicans controlled the telephone and could easily communicate with the outside world.

2. Letter from Richard G. Massock, AP correspondent, dated 27 October 1969. On 5 March 1937, a Havas correspondent, Jean d'Hospital, wrote to his Paris office: "Apart from the censorship at the office of origin, there are other censorships exercised along the road, up to Vigo" (AN, 5 AR 271, d'Hospital file).

3. Frances Davis, *My Shadow in the Sun,* pp. 85-93. Miss Davis's experiences concerned the early weeks of the war, when the Vigo cable head was not working (*ibid.,* p. 154). However, throughout the war in the Basque country, messages were carried across the Spanish-French frontier (AN, 5 AR 271, d'Hospital file). The Portuguese frontier was also used during the first weeks of the fighting. Harold G. Cardozo, of the *Daily Mail,* wrote: "The result was that a message censored, say at Talavera, might be censored again—with all the inherent delays—at Badajoz" (*The March of a Nation,* p. 222).

4. This title was given to Bolín in *Índice Histórico Español*, nos. 48-49 (Jan.-Aug. 1967), p. 56. Bolín does not assign himself a specific title in his book of wartime reminiscences *Spain: The Vital Years*. See Book III, chap. 4, n. 12.

5. Bolín's mother was half English; her brother was the Catholic bishop of London. His younger brother was the first husband of Constancia de la Mora. See her book *In Place of Splendor*, p. 89-178. Bolín had had some journalistic experience at the front during World War I (STVY, pp. 57, 219).

6. *The Spanish Republic* (London, 1933), *La República española* (Madrid, 1933). The authorship of this book has been disputed. Douglas Jerrold, then director of Eyre and Spottiswoode, wrote in 1937: "We scored a tactical victory with our book on The Spanish Republic, the fruit of an active collaboration between Luis Bolín, the Marques del Moral and myself, working on the foundations of a brilliant pamphlet by Calvo Sotelo" (*Georgian Adventure*, p. 361). Bolín, however, declared in 1967: "In 1933 I wrote a book called *The Spanish Republic*. . . . The book was signed 'Anonymous,' for to append my own name would have been risky" (*STVY*, p. 122). However, it is difficult to believe that the author or authors were unknown in Spain. The cataloging services of the British Museum credited the book to three persons: L. Bolín, Frederick Ramón de Bertodano y Wilson, marquis del Moral, and to D. Jerrold. In the Spanish version of *Spain: The Vital Years*, Bolín wrote: "Months later, without anyone's authorization, a Spanish version of my work appeared in Madrid and was widely sold throughout Spain" (*España: los años vitales*, p. 135). This statement does not appear in the English version of Bolín's book. Moreoever, it is untrue. The Spanish edition of the 1933 book bore a clear authorization from the English publishers of the work and was translated, prologued, and annotated by Joaquín del Moral y Pérez-Aloé.

7. See Bolín, *STVY*, pp. 11-54; also Jerrold, *Georgian Adventure*, pp. 370-375.

8. Bolín, *STVY*, pp. 167-172.

9. *Ibid.*, p. 187.

10. Koestler, *Spanish Testament* (1937), p. 27. "In Seville a Press Office was established, which I directed for a brief period" (Bolín, *STVY*, p. 187). This office was set up because some reporters were going down to Gibraltar or Tangier to file stories that the censorship would not allow to be sent from Seville. "Meanwhile, not all correspondents attached to us were submitting their writings to censorship, as is customary and usual in all wars. In certain cases we could not even find their contributions in the papers they allegedly represented, which were printing stories with the dateline 'Seville' signed with names we had never heard of. It took time to sift credentials, the genuineness of which could not be doubted, from others, undoubtedly false, but we got to know that some of these journalists, after spending a few days with us, were taking advantage of the freedom which they enjoyed to file their pieces under other names in Tangier or Gibraltar" (Bolín, *STVY*, p. 186). The Spanish version of Bolín's account here differs also from the English. For example, he says in Spanish that the Seville press office was established "on my proposal" (*España: los años vitales*, p. 197).

11. René Brut, of Pathé newsreels, and Jean d'Esme, of *L'Intransigeant*, were given a permit in Seville to go to the front on 15 August; two days later they arrived in Badajoz, which had fallen to the Nationalists on 14 August. Brut took many pictures of the scenes of execution and of the bodies of the dead; he paid someone one hundred pesetas to take the film across the frontier to Lisbon and forward it to Paris. He was ordered back to Seville on 18 August. On 30 August he left Seville, with a pass given by Bolín, visited Burgos, then came back to Cáceres, where Bolín ordered him to return to Seville. "I hung around Seville for a day or two . . . but since we were the object of continual bullying, due simply to the fact that we were Frenchmen, we decided to leave Seville." Brut asked for an exit permit. It was not granted; instead, on 5 September, he was taken into custody and accused of having sent out films unfavorable to the Rebel cause. Pathé had shown Brut's films in Paris, and Bolín had heard of them. After interrogation, Brut was allowed to go back to the hotel under surveillance. At Bolín's dictation, Brut sent a telegram to Pathé to ask that copies of his films be sent back to Seville. Bolín told Brut that if he was responsible for the films in Paris on the massacre at Badajoz, he could expect "the worst." "Thus, the specter of execution rose before me for the first time." On 8 September, Brut was arrested and put into a prison with 1400 other persons. "Each morning, I trembled at the thought of being designated for one of those trips which took the prisoners to a

destination from which nobody ever returned." After five days in jail, Brut was released. Pathé in Paris had intelligently revised the films before returning them to Seville for inspection. See interview with René Brut, written by Antoine Mazella, for *Le Petit Marocain,* 15 September 1936, pp. 1, 2.

12. Koestler, *Spanish Testament,* p. 27. When Koestler was arrested in Málaga six months later, he compiled a resumé of Bolín's career since he had seen him in Seville: "Captain Bolín had acquired a certain reputation amongst the international press correspondents in Spain. I do not know whether he was responsible for the execution of Guy de Traversé, correspondent of *L'Intransigeant* in rebel Majorca, but I know that it was he who arrested in Seville, amongst others, René Brut.... Brut was saved and so was S. of the 'Chicago Tribune,' whom Captain Bolín ordered to be shot.... And, last but not least, it was Captain Bolín who expelled a number of Conservative and Francophile [pro-Franco] British press correspondents from rebel territory" (*ibid.,* p. 220). "S." was Alex Small, who was arrested in Irún in November 1936. See *Foreign Journalists under Franco's Terror* (hereafter, *FJUFT*), p. 17. Koestler wrote that Bolín arrested Small, mistaking him for Edmond Taylor, of the same newspaper. Baron Guy de Traversay, as Bernanos named him, accompanied the ill-fated expedition of Captain Bayo which invaded Majorca on 16 August 1936 and was driven out seventeen days later. Traversay was shot by the Nationalists with the other prisoners taken, and all the bodies were burned on the beach. He had protested that he was a French journalist doing his work, but he had on him a paper of recommendation from the generalitat, and his case was decided in a matter of minutes (Bernanos, *Les grands cimetières sous la lune,* pp. 194-195).

13. Portela, *Nas trincheiras de Espanha,* p. 228. Portela, a Portuguese correspondent, found Bolín to be "strict, very English and curt with newspapermen."

14. *STVY,* pp. 195-196.

15. Arrarás, and Jordana, *El sitio del Alcázar,* pp. 294-295. Among the reporters mentioned by Arrarás in a newspaper article reproduced in the book were d'Hospital, of the Havas Agency, and Hans Rosel, of the *Berliner Tageblatt* and the *Frankfurter Zeitung.*

16. See Southworth, *Le mythe de la croisade de Franco,* pp. 52-68. Bolín wrote that he gave the news on which the AP story (*NYT,* 30 September 1936) and the Seville press stories (*ABC,* 30 September 1936) were based. Manuel Aznar, in an effort to explain the errors of the AP story, later wrote: "Under the circumstances of war no journalist had the time to check his story carefully" (*The Alcázar Will Not Surrender,* p. 53). The fact is that the foreign correspondents were kept out of Toledo during the first days of its capture and were forced to rely on the news such as given by Bolín, Arrarás, and other journalists serving the Rebel cause.

17. "Early in October ... my task was to organize War Correspondents and I endeavored to do this on a pattern similar to what I had seen at the British Front in Franch during the First World War. Spanish and foreign press representatives were supplied with passes at Salamanca. Our Press Officers in Ávila and Talavera de la Reina spoke a variety of languages, arranged visits to the Front, and escorted newsmen in cars specially assigned for the purpose" (*STVY,* p. 219). But in the Spanish version, Bolín gave another explanation of his organization policy, attributing it to "the norms I had received from my superiors" (*España, los años vitales,* p. 230). The differences between Bolín's English and Spanish versions can, ironically enough, be attributed to the Spanish censor.

18. This was the conclusion reached by Sir Percival Phillips, a veteran reporter, in Nationalist Spain for the Tory journal *Daily Telegraph,* as told by another reporter, Francis McCullagh: "Franco rewarded him [Bolín] by putting him in charge of the Press, though why he didn't find him some other post beats me, for he has made himself hated like poison by the English and American correspondents, and this reacts on the whole news service and propaganda of the Nationalists. Busty [Bolín] ... was never a real correspondent himself" (*In Franco's Spain,* pp. 106-107).

19. Denis Weaver, *Front Page Europe,* pp. 46-54; Frank C. Hanighen, editor, *Nothing but Danger,* "Through the Enemy's Lines," by Denis Weaver, pp. 99-115. A few hours after the capture of the journalists, and at almost the same place, an English bank manager, and Captain E. C. Lance, an honorary English military attaché, were also taken prisoner and brought before Bolín, Lance, although fervently pro-Nationalist, found Bolín to be "sneering, sarcastic, and contemptuous" and called him, "Quite the most unpleasant creature I've ever met" (C. F. Lucas Phillips, *The Spanish Pimpernel,* pp. 75-78).

20. *Manchester Guardian,* 19 January 1937. This letter was signed by Andrew Rothstein.

21. *New York Herald Tribune,* Paris edition, 16 August 1936, p. 1; also printed in *La Prensa* of Buenos Aires, 16 August 1936, p. 6. This latter dispatch was unsigned. Agency messages were sometimes signed by the name of the bureau head in the country of origin, whether he wrote the message or not. This explains the mistake made in Paris in attributing the telegram to Packard; the event did take place in what was technically Packard's territory.

22. Reynolds and Eleanor Packard, *Balcony Empire,* pp. 31-38. The Packards do not tell of this incident, nor do they volunteer an opinion about Bolín's work.

23. Geoffrey McNeill-Moss, *The Siege of Alcazar.* The original title in England was *The Epic of the Alcazar.* Copies of these telegrams were probably communicated to McNeill-Moss by Bolín.

24. See *La Prensa,* 17 August, p. 6; 18 August, p. 7; 19 August, p. 10; 20 August, p. 7; 22 August, p. 8—all 1936.

25. McNeill-Moss, *op. cit.,* p. 309. The *Manchester Guardian* of 28 January 1937, published a letter from Webb Miller, and on 16 February, Harry Flory, assistant European news manager of the UP, wrote to McNeill-Moss saying: "Mr. Packard never was in Badajoz and never wrote anything concerning the capture of Badajoz. At that time he was in Burgos, and the details referred to by you were erroneously published under his name. He did not write anything at the time remotely resembling the material which appeared by error under his name in the New York *Herald Tribune*" (McNeill-Moss, *op. cit.,* p. 305). Incredibly enough, this denial that Packard had sent the telegram was interpreted by McNeill-Moss and many others to indicate that the telegram was false. But the UP never said the contents of the telegram were not correct. See Southworth, *op. cit.,* pp. 179-186. Rothstein, the author of the original letter in the *Manchester Guardian,* was not fooled by the UP denial, and wrote, "At no time has the authenticity of the story itself been denied by the Agency which issued it—the United Press" (*Spectator,* 9 July 1937, p. 63).

26. AN, 5 AR 271, Dany file. Marcel Dany addressed a letter to Havas in Paris on 18 August 1936; it was received in Paris on 24 August, having been posted in France itself, to avoid the Portuguese censorship. It read: "Gentlemen, Following the instructions in your telegram of August 13, I went to Elvas [Portuguese town on Spanish frontier, near Badajoz] on the night of August 13-14. From there, I addressed to the editors in Paris three dispatches on the 14th, four on the 15th, and 4 on the 17th. Three dispatches of the 15th and three of the 17th were stopped by the Portuguese censorship, although they concerned only Spanish events which took place in Spain. These dispatches, in fact, constituted a reportage on the aspect of, and the situation in, the town of Badajoz. Warned by a man I trust in Elvas, whom I cannot otherwise name, that my telegrams 'would have some trouble,' I came back to Lisbon during the night of August 16-17, not wishing to continue spending money if I could not do my work as a journalist. In fact, in Elvas, a Portuguese frontier town, everything happened as if I were in Rebel Spain.

You may count on me to keep you informed of this strange affair, for this must be the first time that one can see a censorship exercised on behalf of a foreign group, in rebellion against a government officially recognized, concerning events which took place on foreign territory."

When d'Hospital cabled Havas in Paris on 25 January 1937 concerning Bolín's inquiry, Havas found in the files three telegrams from Dany for 14 August, three for 15 August, one for 16 August, and one for 17 August. A Havas interior note dated 26 January 1937 read: "The service on the capture of Badajoz was assured by M. Dany, whose reportage had a great success in the press." There was thus no denial of Dany's telegrams by Havas.

27. A glance at the Buenos Aires newspapers, such as *La Prensa* and *La Nacion,* with two more pages of news about the Spanish Civil War in each number, will suffice to indicate the great quantity of news about the conflict sent out to the Spanish- and Portuguese-language American subscribers of the news agencies. These newspapers frequently printed ten times or more as much news about the war as did an ordinary newspaper in Paris, London, or New York. *La Prensa* used the UP service, and *La Nación* took both Havas and the AP and also had rights to the *Times* foreign service. Neither Reuters nor the Hearst Universal Service was widely used in Latin America. Many news service articles were written especially for the Latin American market. Jean de Gandt, of the UP, for example, wrote his cables, sent to London, in Spanish.

28. Koestler, *Spanish Testament,* pp. 222-223. Bolín, *STVY,* pp. 248-249.

29. Cardozo, *op. cit.* Cardozo was fanatically pro-Nationalist. He was an honorary Carlist and wore the red beret, as did some other journalists (*ibid.*, pp. 299-301; see photographs pp. 190, 199). According to André Jacquelin, De Vilmorin, of *Le Jour;* Botto, of the Havas Agency; Héricourt and Couderc, of *L'Action Française,* also sported Carlist accoutrements (*Espagne et liberté,* p. 83). Cardozo wrote: "Not once have I heard any serious accusation of any form of atrocities having been committed by the soldiers of the Nationalist Army" (*op. cit.,* p. 74). This statement has been contradicted to me personally by d'Hospital who frequently shared an apartment with Cardozo. Of course one man may consider an "atrocity" what another thinks of as "military justice."

30. Cardozo, *op. cit.,* pp. 221-222.

31. *In Franco's Spain.* It was published by Burns Oates & Washbourne in 1937. This publishing house proclaimed itself officially "Publishers to the Holy See," a detail that makes McCullagh's remarks concerning Bolín significant. In the preface, dated June 1, 1937, the author wrote: "The articles on Spain in which have appeared over my name in the newspapers, have been described to me as unduly optimistic, as mere Nationalist propaganda, but my critics should remember that only optimistic articles are allowed to leave Salamanca, and that the articles which I consider to be my best were detained without my knowledge by the Censor" (*ibid.*, p. xxii).

32. *Ibid.,* pp. 104-105. "Bustamente" (Bolín) is treated at length on pp. 101-145, 214-217, 318-323.

33. *Ibid.,* pp. 106-112.

34. *Eyewitness,* p. 73.

35. *DE,* 5 April 1937, quoted in *FJUFT,* p. 23. Monks observed: "I am not sorry that I have been expelled, because the lot of a British journalist in Franco's Spain is made impossible by the obstructive methods of the Spanish censors—about the only 100 per cent Spanish unit in Spain today.... Hardly a day passes that British journalists are not subjected to insults by the press authorities."

36. F. Theo Rogers, *Spain: A Tragic Journey,* p. 135. Rogers stated his political position clearly: "I have come out unequivocally for the side of General Franco" (*ibid.,* p. 204).

37. Nigel Tangye, *Red, White and Spain,* p. 67.

38. Cecil Gerahty, *The Road to Madrid,* p. 139. Gerahty had been a *Daily Mail* correspondent.

39. Renzo Segàla, *Trincee di Spagna,* p. 102.

40. Cowles, *Looking for Trouble,* p. 84. See also Cardozo, *op. cit.,* pp. 288, 296-301. Lámbarri was apparently a more humane person than the other press officers. He evidently knew Franco, for he had attended military academy with him (Bauer, *Rouge et or,* p. 74).

41. Arnold Lunn, *Spanish Rehearsal,* p. 70.

42. Sefton Delmer, *Trail Sinister,* p. 277.

43. Lunn, *op. cit.,* p. 50; *Nothing but Danger,* "Assignment in Hell," by Edmond Taylor, p. 64.

44. John T. Whitaker, *We Cannot Escape History,* p. 108; *Nothing but Danger,* "Assignment in Hell," by Edmond Taylor, p. 64.

45. Whitaker, *op. cit.,* p. 109.

46. Kemp, *Mine Were of Trouble,* p. 50.

47. Letter from Cassell and Company, London, dated 27 March 1968.

48. Interview with Jean d'Hospital by the author, 14 September 1968.

49. Whitaker, *op. cit.,* pp. 108-110. Here are other observations by Aguilera as recorded by Whitaker: "You know what's wrong with Spain? ... Modern plumbing! In healthier times—I mean healthier times spiritually, you understand—plague and pestilence could be counted on to thin down the Spanish masses. Hold them down to manageable proportions, you understand. Now with modern sewage disposal and the like they multiply too fast. The masses are no better than animals, you understand, and you can't expect them not to become infected with the virus of bolshevism. After all, rats and lice carry the plague.... We'll make other changes too.... We'll be done with this nonsense of equality for women.... If a man's wife is unfaithful to him, why, he'll shoot her like a dog.... The people in Britain and America are going communist the way the French have gone. There's that man Baldwin in England. Doesn't even

know he is a red, but the reds control him. And, of course, that man Roosevelt is a howling red. But it goes back farther than that. It begins with the Encyclopedists in France—the American and the French revolutions. The Age of Reason indeed! The Rights of Man! The masses aren't fit to reason and to think. Rights? Does a pig have rights? . . . You people had better clean up your own houses. If you don't, we Spaniards are going to join the Germans and Italians in conquering you all. The Germans have already promised to help us regain our American colonies, which you and your shameful Protestant liberal imperialism stole from us" (*ibid.*).

50. *Nothing but Danger,* "Assignment in Hell," by Edmond Taylor, p. 64.

51. *Op. cit.,* pp. 89-92.

52. *Ibid.,* pp. 96-99.

53. *Op. cit.,* p. 42. Lunn felt that he had been "enlightened" by Aguilera's "general philosophy" (*ibid.,* p. 108).

54. Delmer, *op. cit.,* pp. 276-278. After the war, Aguilera told Delmer in London that he had been expelled at the demand of the Germans.

55. Cardozo, *op. cit.,* p. 301. Cardozo went into Bilbao with the first contingents, and his Carlist beret produced ovations from the crowds. "Major Lámbarri merely laughěd when I mentioned it to him, and said, 'Don't boast; I was kissed by much prettier girls than you.' Captain Aguilera, I am afraid, was not quite so pleased."

56. Gerahty, *op. cit.,* pp. 35-36. This was on September 6, 1936. Gerahty had met Aguilera some days previously in Burgos. Aguilera would thus seem to be one of the first press officers in service on the northern front.

57. H. R. Knickerbocker, *The Siege of Alcazar: A Warlog of the Spanish Revolution,* p. 138. A harsh judgment on this book was given by the English critic V. S. Pritchett: "He [Knickerbocker] is the gossipy war correspondent, Francophile for no particular reason, and he writes the sort of news which dies the moment it is printed and is ten times dead by the time it gets into a book" (*Spectator,* May 14, 1937, p. 910).

58. *Foreign Relations of the United States* (1937), I, 279. American ambassador, Claude Bowers, a former newspaperman, then living, as were many other diplomats accredited to the Republican government, in Saint-Jean-de-Luz, wrote of Knickerbocker's plight in a message to Washington. He also wrote: "I find some significance, too, in the fact that General Franco is becoming more and more intolerant toward war correspondents with his armies. He turned them all away when the attack on Málaga began. The men he then turned away had been with him for months and had written the most pronounced pro-Franco articles. No war correspondent with him could have been more satisfactory to him than Knickerbocker" (*ibid.*).

59. *New York American,* 29 April 1937. Knickerbocker later wrote: "The Gestapo had had me arrested and thrown into a death cell in San Sebastián for thirty-six hours, whence I escaped by the determined vocal efforts of my friend and fellow-correspondent, Randolph Churchill" (Knickerbocker, *Is Tomorrow Hitler's?* p. 25-26).

60. This dispatch, from the *Washington Times* of 10 May 1937, was reprinted in the appendix of the *Congressional Record* on 12 May 1937 in an "extension of remarks" by Representative Jerry J. O'Connell of Montana. O'Connell was a tireless defender of the Spanish Republic and in the same "extension of remarks" had quoted extensively from the articles by Steer. Other extracts from Knickerbocker's article, quoting Captain Sánchez [Aguilera]: " 'It is a race war, not merely a class war. You don't understand because you don't realize that there are two races in Spain—a slave race and a ruler race. Those reds, from President Azaña to the anarchists, are all slaves. It is our duty to put them back into their places—yes, put chains on them again if you like. . . .' Sánchez was melancholy for days after the American election returned a Roosevelt landslide. He said: 'All you Democrats are just handmaidens of bolshevism. Hitler is the only one who knows a "red" when he sees one.' His favorite exclamation was 'take 'em out and shoot 'em.' On labor his view is that all trade-unions must be abolished and membership be made punishable by death. . . . His idea for peasants is a benevolent serfdom. On education he declared: 'We must destroy this spawn of "red" schools which the so-called republic installed to teach the slaves to revolt. It is sufficient for the masses to know just enough reading to understand orders. We must restore the authority of the Church. Slaves need it to teach them to behave.' Sánchez himself is not religious, but supports the Church as a useful instrument of social discipline. 'It is damnable that women should vote. Nobody should

vote—least of all women.' On Jews the major affirmed: 'They are an international pest.' On liberty: 'It is a delusion employed by the "reds" to fool the so-called democrats. In our state, people are going to have the liberty to keep their mouths shut.' "

61. Charles Foltz, Jr., *The Masquerade in Spain*, p. 116. " 'Sewers' growled the Count. 'Sewers caused all our troubles. The masses in this country are not like your Americans, nor even like the British. They are slave stock. They are good for nothing but slaves and only when they are used as slaves are they happy. But we, the decent people, made the mistake of giving them modern housing in the cities where we have our factories. We put sewers in these cities, sewers which extend right down to the workers' quarters.' " Foltz considered Aguilera "in earnest, dead earnest" and as being representative of Spain's landowners.

62. *Morning Post*, 12 September 1936, quoted in *FJUFT*, pp. 27-28. Rice was also accused of mentioning "insurgent frightfulness" in writing about the campaign for Irún. This latter dispatch had been dated from France, "where, presumably, I might write freely. It seems that I was mistaken in this presumption." The *Morning Post* wrote editorially on 12 September 1937, that Rice's expulsion "proclaims *urbi et orbi* than any news emanating from Right [Nationalist] sources belongs rather to the realm of propaganda than to that of fact" (*ibid.*, pp. 28-30).

63. Davis, *op. cit.*, p. 136.

64. *Op. cit.*, p. 64.

65. Davis, *op. cit.*, pp. 131-154.

66. D'Hospital was sent to "the region of St.-Jean-Pied-de-Port/Pamplona" on 31 July 1936. He was expelled and informed that in order to return he had need of "an attestation from the Havas Agency accrediting him as a special correspondent to the "Provisional Government of Burgos" and "two letters of recommendation, above all one from M. Quiñones de León [former Spanish ambassador to France under the monarchy], addressed to generals Mola and Cabanellas." D'Hospital got his *laissez-passer* on 13 August 1936, after someone from Havas had seen Quiñones de León; he was in Burgos on the following day. D'Hospital covered the war from 13 August 1936 until the end, except for brief trips across the Spanish-French frontier and an extended leave in 1937, including part of April and all of May and June. He had intended to write of his experiences during the civil war, but all of the papers he had left in a hotel in Saint-Jean-de-Luz were lost during World War II. This is highly unfortunate. The research for this work has discovered many books of reminiscences of the Spanish Civil War by American and British correspondents, quite a few by Portuguese and Italian—even Swiss—correspondents, but few by French correspondents: Andre Jacquelin, *Espagñe et liberté, 1939-1945*, (*L'Indépendant*, Perpignan); Jean Riotte, *Arriba España!... Espagñe, eveille-toi!*, 1936 (*La Liberte du Sud-ouest*, Bordeaux); Yves Dautun, *Valence sous la botte rouge*, 1938 (*Le Petit Parisien*); Robert Cassagnau, *A l'Est de Saint Sebàstien*, 1966 (*Jeunesse 36*, Bordeaux?), *Souvenirs san fin* (III) by Andre Salmon, 1961 (*Le Petit Parisien*). Others such as *Front de la liberte*, 1938, by Simone Téry; *Pourquoi Franco vaincra*, 1937, *Pourquoi mentir? l'aide franco-sovietique a l'Espagne rouge*, 1937, *Les soviets et la France: fournisseurs de la revolution espagnole*, 1398, *Pourquoi Franco a vaincu*, 1939, all by Pierre Hericourt; *Vers l'Espagne de Franco*, 1943, by Charles Maurras; all these books by French journalists who were in Spain during the civil war are more collections of newspaper articles than accounts of personal experiences. Such books were perhaps not very popular in France but the French reporters like d'Hospital went from the Spanish Civil War into World War II, the defeat of France, the Occupation and the Resistance with scarcely a minute out for writing a book. Those who had the time to write were not always published. Jacquelin's book, published in 1939, was refused by the French censorship and was not put on sale until 1945 (*Espagne et Liberté*, p. 7). For a short account of the Spanish Civil War writings of the Italian and Portuguese correspondents, see Southworth, *op. cit.*, pp. 52, 77-78.

67. Albert Grand arrived in Seville on 28 August 1936 (AN, 5 AR 272 Grand file.). See also previous quotations from Arthur Koestler.

68. Interview with Jean d'Hospital, 14 September 1968.

69. AN, 5 AR 271, d'Hospital file. News of this nature was rarely published by the agencies. The Nationalists had a standing policy of leaving bodies around for a few days in order to discipline those left alive. This particular stretch of road lined with corpses was well known

to the correspondents, although not everybody counted as high as Grand. Webb Miller of the UP and some others reporters were driving back one evening to Talavera de la Reina. He wrote: "Bodies of men and animals which had been lying in the fields beside the road and partly across the road for several days were still there. . . . Several times our cars had to turn to avoid hitting them. Around Santa Olalla the bodies (we heard there were about three hundred in this area) had lain nearly two weeks. The stench was revolting; the faces had turned quite black" (*We Cover the World,* "The Little World War in Spain," by Webb Miller, p. 423). See also *Nothing but Danger,* "Assignment in Hell," by Edmond Taylor, pp. 71-72, and Gerahty, *op. cit.,* p. 75.

70. AN, 5 AR 272, Alderete file. Alderete may well have been on a list of undesirables because of his relations with the Spanish royal family. See Alderete, . . . *Y estos Borbones nos quieren gobernar.*

71. D'Hospital cabled to Paris: "I DO NOT KNOW REPROACHES MADE TO GRAND OFFICER HAS SIMPLY TOLD ME THEY ARE EXTREMELY GRAVE AND COULD BRING HEAVY SANCTIONS" (AN, 5 AR 271 d'Hospital file). According to Frances Davis, d'Hospital attributed Grand's expulsion to the fact that he had previously been on the Republican side, had not told the Rebels, and they had found out. Miss Davis wrote that d'Hospital said: " 'He is lucky to be alive. He would not be the first one who had been shot. By accident . . .' " (*op. cit.,* p. 178).

72. Telegram from Mme. Grand to Havas, Paris, 19 November 1936 (AN, 5 AR 271, d'Hospital file).

73. Gés' name was proposed on 27 November 1936, turned down on 8 December (AN, 5 AR 271, d'Hospital file).

74. Malet-Dauban arrived in Spain on 21 December 1936 (AN, 5 AR 271, d'Hospital file).

75. L'Humanité, 18 February 1937, wrote that Malet-Dauban was "formerly the secretary of [Eduardo] Aunós" [Minister of Alfonso XIII under the dictatorship of Primo de Rivera; later Franco's Minister of Justice]. Malet-Dauban "formerly wrote articles for Catholic newspapers of Spain and South America" (AN, 5 AR 272, note dated 16 December 1936, Malet-Dauban file).

76. AN, 5 AR 271, d'Hospital file.

77. According to the Havas files, Paris first heard of Malet-Dauban's arrest on 27 January 1937, when M. Perret of *Le Journal* informed Paris that the hotel rooms of d'Hospital and Malet-Dauban in Ávila had been searched and that compromising notes had been found in the room of Malet-Dauban. He was being kept in solitary confinement and, thought M. Perret, would probably be expelled. Perret said that Malet-Dauban "has served the Nationalist cause but it is now fairly certain that they will never thank him for it" (AN, 5 AR 272, Malet-Dauban file).

78. D'Hospital informed Havas in Paris on 30 January 1937 that he had written to Franco about Malet-Dauban and that he had been told that his colleague was suspected of espionage (AN, 5 AR 271, d'Hospital file).

79. Hubert de Lagarde, of *L'Action Française,* just returned from the Rebel zone, telephoned to Havas in Paris on 3 February to say that the press corps was worried over the fate of Malet-Dauban. D'Hospital could not leave Spain and de Lagarde had been told in Salamanca that the frontier was closed, but on arriving at Irún he had no difficulty in crossing into France. At Saint-Jean-de-Luz he met Armand Magescas, a Frenchman active in Spanish right-wing, monarchist politics. See E. Vegas Latapié, *El pensamiento político de Calvo Sotelo,* pp. 104-105. According to de Lagarde, "M. Magescas had learned that M. Malet-Dauban had been condemned to death and quite possibly has already been executed" (AN, 5 AR 271, Malet-Dauban file). The Havas note was signed by Chadé.

80. On 10 February, another right-wing French journalist, Alline, also of *Le Journal,* arrived from Salamanca with news of Malet-Dauban. Bolín had also told him that the frontier was closed, but he crossed with no difficulty. Perrin, an editor of the Havas Agency, wrote a note as follows after his talk with Alline: "He has the impression that they are simply trying to keep the French journalists from talking of the Malet-Dauban affair. D'Hospital is very tired and depressed by this matter. He would like to come to France as soon as possible. Malet-Dauban is still in solitary and will probably be tried just any day now. . . . D'Hospital is convinced of the innocence of his colleague and believes that he is in reality less the victim of

the Spaniards than of the Germans. Certain drawings are said to have been found on him. . . . In d'Hospital's opinion, Malet-Dauban will either be acquitted—an unlikely hypothesis—or condemned to death and executed. An intervention is urgent" (AN, 5 AR 271, d'Hospital file). D'Hospital was always ready to help his colleagues in trouble. André Jacquelin was arrested in Salamanca on 28 October 1937, after certain papers unfavorable to the Rebel cause had been found in his hotel room. He later attributed his liberation to the aid of d'Hospital, Packard, Leon Bancal, of *Le Petit Marseillais,* and of two German newspapermen. Bancal was able to secure Italian Fascist intervention (Jacquelin, *Espagne et liberté,* pp. 80-81, 87, 155).

81. Throughout the war, Havas was limited to two men in the Rebel zone. Whenever one of the two Havas men was either in jail, ill, or recently expelled, there was but one man on the job. On 12 August 1936 d'Hospital protested to Paris that he was alone to cover the whole of the Nationalist territory, whereas the UP and the Hearst Universal Service had two men each. Again, on 23 December 1936, d'Hospital informed Paris that two of the American services, AP and UP, had each three men in the Rebel zone (AN, 5 AR 271 d'Hospital file). Georges Botto of Havas cabled Paris from Hendaye on 19 June 1937 to say that on the Biscay front, UP had four correspondents and a European director; AP, three men; DNB and Stefani, four reporters each (AN, 5 AR 272, Botto file).

82. Botto was a reserve captain in the French army, decorated with the Légion d'Honneur and the Croix de Guerre (AN, 5 AR 271, d'Hospital file; 5 AR 272, Botto file).

83. Telegram from d'Hospital to Paris (AN, 5 AR 271, d'Hospital file).

84. *Ibid.* D'Hospital's irritation was evident. "After the Grand incident, the Alderete incident, the Malet-Dauban incident—too many incidents."

85. See article by William P. Carney, in *NYT,* 7 December 1936; Knoblaugh, *Correspondent in Spain,* pp. 185-198; Dautun, *Valence sous la botte rouge.* See Book I, chap. 4, n. 10.

86. Maximiano García Venero, *Falange en la guerra de España: la unificación y Hedilla,* p. 227. García Venero also quoted from a decree, supposedly proposed by General González Carrasco (and not since denied), published by Manuel D. Benavides in Appendix 5 of his book *Guerra y revolución en Cataluña.* Article 5 of the decree read: "All publications of any category are subjected to military censorship, all daily newspapers are for the moment suspended. News will be given by an official newspaper and radio stations" (*ibid.*).

87. McCullagh, *op. cit.,* p. 111.

88. *Ibid.,* pp. 107-108.

89. Cardozo, *op. cit.,* pp. 221-222. "Propaganda" here meant information of any sort.

90. AN, 5 AR 271, d'Hospital file.

91. *Ibid.* André de Hoornaert was also a lawyer accredited to the Brussels bar. De Hoornaert's statement was written down by a Havas representative who talked with him at a railroad station. Here is his description of the treatment reserved for the Havas correspondents: "The treatment is as follows: Constant and close surveillance; limited field of movement; rare and laconic official information; pitiless censorship directed by an incompetent person, a former orange vendor from Barcelona; open and ignorant hostility shown even in the vexations imposed upon our representatives within the press office itself: no table, insufficient light, although the censor himself has at his disposition a powerful lamp which he carefully shuts off when he is absent, so that others may not make use of it."

92. *Ibid.* The doctor's certificate is dated 1 March 1937. He and Cardozo had already had an automobile accident the previous October.

93. *Ibid.* Paris asked d'Hospital for a thousand words a day. D'Hospital replied that four UP men were not sending that much copy.

94. *Ibid.*

95. AN, 5 AR 272, Holstein file.

96. AN, 5 AR 271, d'Hospital file.

97. The negotiations that led to this exchange are not revealed in the Havas files, which have been almost completely denuded of all papers involving the Ministry of Foreign Affairs. The news was given in a Reuters dispatch from Bilbao on 28 May 1937. That same day the *presidencia* of the Basque government informed Havas of the exchange. The Basques freed two German aviators, Kienzle and Schulze-Blanck, a Swiss named Maurer, and a German resident of Bilbao condemned to prison for life; the Rebels freed three aviators, of whom one was a

Russian, and the French journalist. A. Meynot, of the Havas Agency, wrote to Franco on 5 June to thank him for "the gracious measure" he had taken in favor of Malet-Dauban, but Franco had already been paid for his grace, and it was the Basques who had paid him. Havas also sent a letter of thanks to Troncoso in Irún. Malet-Dauban, however, in a telegram sent to Havas on 31 May expressed his gratitude to d'Hospital, "who has not hesitated an instant in his fraternal defense of my life, exposing his own and certainly saved my life" (AN, 5 AR 272, Malet-Dauban file).

98. AN, 5 AR 272, Botto file.

99. AN, 5 AR 272, Barré file. In recommending Barré, Havas had pointed out to the Nationalist authorities that he had covered the war in Ethiopia on the Italian side and that he had frequently accompanied Mussolini on his trips.

100. Southworth, *op. cit.,* pp. 180-185.

101. Whitaker, *op. cit.,* p. 109.

102. Tangye, *op. cit.,* p. 11.

103. *Ibid.,* p. 67.

104. *Op. cit.,* pp. 109-110.

105. *Op. cit.,* pp. 320-321.

106. Southworth, *op. cit.,* pp. 180-181.

107. McCullagh, *op. cit.,* pp. 320-321.

108. *Op. cit.,* pp. 79-84.

109. *Ibid.,* p. 82.

110. Koestler, *Spanish Testament,* p. 38.

111. This word appears frequently as a euphemism for "German pilots" in the writings of certain persons who have all just come from Salamanca; it is logical to presume that their use of this word in this special sense was part of the special instructions they received while in Salamanca. It should also be noted that of the persons given below as examples, but one or two were working journalists. A study might show that when the professional correspondent failed to write what Bolín wanted, another species of writer was sought out, one more pliable and more easily influenced.

112. *Spanish Rehearsal,* p. 147.

113. "There are no German fighting troops and never have been. There are a few Germans, in the technical services, behind the lines—mainly, I believe, in the depot services and in the repair shops." (*Nineteenth Century and After* [April 1937], "Spain: Impressions and Reflections," by Douglas Jerrold, p. 481; Reprint, same title, p. 12; *American Review* [April 1937], "The Issues in Spain," by Douglas Jerrold, p. 16; Douglas Jerrold, *The Issues in Spain,* unpaged.)

114. "The Marquis said he saw no German troops at all. He saw a number of technicians connected with aircraft and anti-aircraft work, etc. He believed that there were a certain number of German airmen flying, but in comparison with the total number it was a very small number indeed" (Moral, *Address,* p. 19).

115. "The only German organizations which could be called self-contained units are the staffs of mechanics and technical supervisors" (*The Aeroplane,* 5 May 1937, p. 528). (See Book II, part 1, chap. 1, n. 157.)

116. "There were few Germans in Nationalist Spain, and they mainly technicians, but they were held in high repute" (Sir Arnold Wilson, *Nineteenth Century and After* [October 1937], p. 503).

117. "With regard to the number of Germans who were alleged to be fighting for Franco, the General pointed out that many of these Germans were on technical jobs, behind the lines" (General Sir Walter Maxwell-Scott, *Spain* [London, 31 May 1937], p. 6).

118. Tangye, supposedly an aviation expert, wrote that the *Legión Cóndor,* Hitler's air arm in Spain, was "an organization which is formed by German volunteers for mechanical units" (*op. cit.,* p. 151).

119. When Alline talked with Perrin of the Havas Agency in Paris on 10 February 1937, he told him that "he had not seen any German soldiers, only some technicians" (AN, 5 AR 271, d'Hospital file).

120. Sir Percival Phillips told McCullagh, "Busty [Bolín] won't let us mention Italians or

Germans in our dispatches, but they're here all the same" (*op. cit.*, p. 122).

121. *Ibid.*, p. 322. Complaints by Catholic journalists like McCullagh were heard by Catholic editors in London. The *Tablet* noted editorially a few weeks after the Guernica catastrophe that despite some improvements in "the facilities for journalists at Salamanca . . . it is still insufficiently recognized how very important it is to make the work of journalists as easy and agreeable as possible." The Catholic weekly, however, admitted that there were reasons for the precautions taken by the Rebel authorities at Salamanca. "The Spanish Nationalists say that they have to be very careful; that so many men calling themselves journalists are in fact secret agents; that French journalists of the Right may be primarily concerned with observing the German military equipment." But there were also reasons for discontent among the newspapermen. "There are still cases, of which we have heard details, in which telegrams sent from London papers to their correspondents in Nationalist Spain have not been delivered, but the journalist has been told roughly the substance of the messages and asked what answer he would like to make. Newspapers have their dignity. Very often an attitude is much more due in reality to irritation or offended dignity than to any political considerations" (*Tablet*, 12 June 1937, p. 833).

122. Noel Monks and Christopher Holme had been expelled from Franco Spain shortly before the Guernica bombing. See Book I, chap. 1.

Chapter 4
The News from Vitoria

1. A Havas dispatch published in *La Nación*, 1 May 1937, p. 1, said that the Brigade of Navarre entered Guernica at eleven-forty on the morning of 29 April. But the Italian correspondent Renzo Segàla, who entered Guernica with the first troops, wrote a year later in his book *Trincee di Spagna*, p. 173, that the first soldiers to enter Guernica were the *Frecce Neri*, with a company from the IV Brigade of Navarre. However, the Italian military chronicler Sandro Piazzoni, wrote that the Italians slowed their advance in order to permit the Navarese to be the first to enter Guernica, as had been promised by the Italian command to General Mola (*Las tropas Flechas Negras en la guerra de España (1937-1939)*, p. 56).

2. *La Petite Gironde* (hereafter, *PG*), 1 May 1937, p. 1. Berniard wrote that he was taken prisoner by the Rebels in Guernica at eleven-fifty, 29 April.

3. Sandri, in *La Stampa*, 30 April 1937; Segàla, in *Corriere della sera*, 1 May 1937, Franzetti, in *La Tribuna*, 1 May 1937; Saporiti (Stefani), in *L'Osservatore Romano*, 1 May 1937. Sandri was killed shortly after the Basque campaign, in China, when the gunboat *Panay* was bombed (Sorrentino, *Questa Spagna* [1939], p. 353). Segàla died on 22 August 1961, according to a letter from *Corriere della sera*, 27 February 1969. A letter from Pierre Saporiti, dated 20 April 1969, states that Franzetti is also dead. Saporiti now lives in the south of France. He worked with *Time* magazine after the end of World War II. Segàla does not mention his presence in Guernica, but a dispatch from Bayonne, published in the Toulouse newspaper *L'Express du Midi*, 30 April 1937, says that the Stefani correspondent was among those who recognized Berniard. Saporiti probably did not travel with the other three Italians. Segàla, Sandri, and Franzetti, each working for a newspaper in a different town, were not neccessarily competitors, but Saporiti, an agency man, was the competitor of all three.

4. Stephens was later killed in China, at the same time as Sandro Sandri.

5. *Kolnische Volkszeitung und Handelsblatt*, 30 April 1973, p. 3. See also a DNB report published in *L'Indépendance Belge*, 1 May 1937, p. 5 which began, "The Special Correspondent of the DNB accompanied the first Nationalist detachments which entered Gernica." See also DNB dispatch in *O Seculo*, 1 May 1937. The DNB reporter wrote: "The enthusiasm of the men and women, who had taken refuge in subterranean canals or in the hills, was enormous." The German reports on Guernica are uninformative. German journalism during the Spanish Civil War was dull and stolid. The Italian reporters were flamboyant, high spirited, and confident of marching toward a Fascist future. The German correspondents had few friends, and rarely identities. Frances Davis met a German reporter, but she never learned his

name. "He sits among us blond and glacial, never fraternizing, above the easy run of our talk and comradeship. He would prefer to have nothing to do with any of us. But the German papers are not as rich as the American papers. He finds himself dependent upon favors for bed-space in our rooms, for seat space in our cars" (*op. cit.,* p. 130). Few German correspondents are even named in the books of other pressmen writing about the civil war; they were doubtless there, but usually invisible. André Jacquelin, however, had two German journalist friends, Hermann Fiddickow of *Der Angriff,* and Bruno H. Fiefiger of the *Berliner Böersenzeitung (Espagne et liberte,* p. 153). Koestler had a run in in Seville in August 1936 with the son of August Strindberg, who was working for the Ullstein papers (*Spanish Testament,* p. 38). Only one German correspondent wrote of his civil war experiences, Karl-Georg von Stackelberg, author of *Legion Condor: Deutsche Freiwillige in Spanien.* It is a colorless, impersonal account.

6. Massot died in Lyons during the German occupation (interview, Southworth with "Jean Dourec," 19 March 1969).

7. No trace of Mévil since the Spanish Civil War has been found.

8. Méjat lives in Paris but refuses to talk about Guernica. On 12 July 1973, he appeared on a French television program and talked at length about the war in Spain. He told a totally false story about the Toledo Alcázar and the death of one of the sons of Moscardó (an event of which he had no personal knowledge) and, concerning Guernica (an event of which he did have personal knowledge), he limited his remarks to a general statement of the troubles of his friend Berniard.

9. "Jean Dourec's" real name was Jean Couderc. During the war in Spain he also used the names of "Jean Marot" in *Le Journal* and "Jean Chateau" in *Paris-Soir.* He held the rank of honorary lieutenant in the Requetés. Berniard does not mention his being in Guernica on 29 April, but Dourec insists that he was with the other French correspondents when they entered Guernica and found Berniard a prisoner. This is confirmed in his article in *L'Action Francaise,* 5 May 1937. Dourec lives in Paris today. He claims to have enjoyed considerable influence with the Nationalists during the civil war (interview, Southworth with Dourec, Paris, 18 March 1969). André Jacquelin wrote in 1939: "Is there not a correspondent of a royalist daily published near the Rond-Point of the Champs-Elysées who belongs to the Deuxième Bureau of Franco? Was he not charged to enquire into the political opinions of his French colleagues, in Franco Spain? Moreover, was he not the sole journalist authorized to cross the frontier at the International bridge from Irún to Hendaye, when this bridge was closed by the Franco authorities as was frequently the case?" This paragraph was followed by this phrase: "This question is addressed especially to MM. Coudère *[sic]* et Héricourt, of *L'Action Francaise*" (*op. cit.,* p. 83).

10. *AF,* 11 May 1937, p. 1. However, if Héricourt sent a message concerning Guernica on 1 May, the newspaper did not print it.

11. "All along the road an uninterrupted line of Basque peasants, who were leaving their homes, carrying in the most varied types of transport, their most precious belongings. On the other hand, there were few soldiers" (Berniard, *La Petite Gironde,* 1 May 1937, p. 1). This scene, sent through the Franco censorship, would seem to belie the assertion frequently made from Salamanca that the Basque soldiers were forcing the peasants to flee before the Insurgent armies. This dispatch was sent from Vitoria by Havas—that is, by Botto. Pike has misinterpreted the date of Berniard's entry into Guernica (*op. cit.,* p. 112).

12. *PG,* 1 May 1937, p. 1, article by Berniard.

13. *Ibid.,* 6, 7, 8 May 1937.

14. *Trincee di Spagna* (1st ed., Milan, May 1938; 2d ed. June 1938). This book is dedicated to Sandro Sandri.

15. The words and actions of the lieutenant constituted contradictory behavior for someone who was supposed to believe that whatever harm might have befallen the shrine was the fault of the Basques and not of the Nationalists. This act, however, does constitute a clear denial of the later charge that the Basques had used the shrine as a stable. The capture of Berniard and Urquiaga was mentioned in July 1949 by one of the first Rebel officers to enter Guernica, Major Martínez Esparza, but he had forgotten their names (*Ejército,* quoted in *Cronica de la guerra española,* no. 62, IV, p. 41, and in Talón, *Arde Guernica,* p. 100).

16. *PG,* 7 May 1937, p. 1.

17. *Ibid.*, 1 May 1937, p. 1.

18. Segàla, *op. cit.*, pp. 175-176.

19. *PG*, 1 May 1937, p. 1. These three names were given by Sandro Piazzoni, who added that they were accompanied by an Inspector of "Fascios" in foreign countries. Piazzoni wrote that Guernica "was still smoking from the last fires set by the fugitive Reds" (*op. cit.*, p. 56).

20. *PG*, 8 May 1937, p. 2.

21. *Ibid.*, 1 May 1937, p. 1. Aguilera and Berniard knew each other from Berniard's past experiences on the Rebel front. The editors of *La Petite Gironde* wrote on 4 May 1937, p. 3: "We have learned in fact that there exists a decree of General Franco, condemning to death any journalist having worked at his profession on the Nationalist side and subsequently found to be with the Republicans." Bolín confirmed the custom and justified it, when writing of Koestler's arrest in Málaga. "Koestler's position was more serious. He had gone over to the enemy after being for some time on our side. I recalled what a Scottish captain, one of my officers on the British front, had told me during the First World War when I expressed the wish to have a look at the Germans. 'Don't do it,' he said. 'If you went to Germany and we caught you afterwards, we would not hesitate to shoot you' " (*STVY*, p. 249). Talón also confirmed the existence of this severe penalty, while giving the name of "George Bernard" to the journalist-prisoner (*op. cit.*, p. 99).

22. *PG*, 1 May 1937, p. 1. The Basque government telegram arrived after Berniard's telegram from Vitoria.

23. Interview Dussauge-Berniard. Berniard says that when the director of his newspaper received the telephone call from the American correspondent, he asked his *chroniquer taurin* to intervene with a Frenchman in Berlin who was influential in Nazi circles. This Frenchman got in touch with General von Brauchitsch, who telephoned to Mola.

24. AN, 5 AR 272, Berniard file, Havas note dated 30 April 1937.

25. In his book, Segàla does not write that Franzetti was with him in Guernica, but on p. 177 he says that Berniard was met by "three Italian journalists," and a photograph, taken in Guernica on 29 April, reproduced opposite p. 112, shows Berniard with Sandri, Segàla, Franzetti, and a Spanish lieutenant (Pedro Sanz?).

26. *Daily Telegraph,* 30 April 1937.

27. *L'Express du Midi,* 30 April 1937, dispatch from Bayonne.

28. *Le Journal,* 30 April 1937; AN, 5 AR 272, Berniard file.

29. The *Frecce Neri* were "formed of Italian volunteers [*sic*] and very young Spanish soldiers brought in from the Falangist organizations" (Segàla, *op. cit.*, p. 169).

30. Packard, *op. cit.*, p. 38.

31. During the battle of Guadalajara, Havas in Paris cabled twice to d'Hospital in Ávila to inform him that the newspapers in Italy were receiving a better coverage of the military activities from their men in Spain than was Havas in Paris from its representatives (AN, 5 AR 271, d'Hospital file, telegrams 8, 9 March 1937).

32. Sorrentino, *op. cit.*, p. 300. "The Spaniards had a difficult time dislocating Bill Carney, of *The New York Times* and Pembroke Stephens. . . . They were among the first to have seen the journalistic advantages of reporting the war with the help of Italian press officers as compared to working only through the Spanish Press Bureau and, as a result, had established connections which were difficult for the Spaniards to break" (Packard, *op. cit.*, p. 39).

"Reynolds avails himself of this [Italian] service. Returning to Vitoria . . . he was severely reprimanded by Major Lámbarri . . . for having anything to do with the Italians. Lámbarri said that any future excursions made by non-Italian correspondents to the front in the company of Fascist officials would be punished by immediate expulsion" (*ibid.* p. 38).

33. Letter from Saporiti, 20 April 1969. The Packards had little love for Saporiti, and wrote: "One of the chief Fascist press officers was Piero Saporiti, who, when the war ended, came to the United States as correspondent for Virginio Gayda's *Giornale d'Italia* and proceeded to send the most virulent attacks upon President Roosevelt and the United States' attitude toward World War II" (*op. cit.*, p. 39).

34. See n. 54. The Italians wrote that Berniard was loquacious about famine conditions in Bilbao.

35. *Le Journal,* 30 April 1937, dispatch datelined San Sebastián.

36. AN, 5 AR 272, Berniard file.

37. *Ibid.* This note is addressed to M. Perrin and signed by H. Hubert. It is dated 30 April 1937. Havas sent the news about Berniard to Portugal (*Diario de Noticias, O Commercio do Porto,* 1 May 1937).

38. *PG,* 1 May 1937.

39. *Ibid.,* 8 May 1937, pp. 1-2. The Rebel military were free in their threats to kill journalists. Just before Noel Monks was expelled, he was summoned to Salamanca and shown a photograph published in his newspaper which displeased the censor. " 'I have a good mind to take you out and shoot you. How dare you publish that?' the censor said." A day or two later, when he was arrested in Seville, because of an article in his newspaper, he was told: "We know you did not write it, but your paper printed it, and I think you will be shot" (*DE* 5 April 1937, quoted in *FJUFT,* pp. 24-25).

40. Interview Dussauge-Berniard.

41. *PG,* 8 May 1937.

42. Interview Dussauge-Berniard.

43. *PG,* 8 May 1937, p. 2.

44. Interview with Jean Dourec in Paris, 18 March 1969. Ungría was certainly an officer in Franco's confidence. He was one of the two officers who treated with Republican emissaries for the surrender of Madrid at the Burgos airport on March 23, 1939 (Casado, *The Last Days of Madrid,* p. 225).

45. *PG,* 8 May 1937, p. 1.

46. *Ibid.,* 4 May 1937, p. 1.

47. AN, 5 AR, 272, Berniard file.

48. Interview Dussauge-Berniard.

49. *PG,* 1 May, p. 1; 7 May, p. 1, 1937.

50. Steer wrote that Esteban Urquiaga, Berniard's guide, was "a poet who was chief of the propaganda Department of the Basque Nationalist Party. The young propaganda man was shot (this was the kind of boy in whom the Rebels really enjoyed cutting off the springs of poetry" (*The Tree of Gernika,* p. 256). Talón wrote of Urquiaga that "in view of the post he occupied and the circumstances of the moment, his capture meant a death sentence" (*Arde Guernica,* pp. 98-100).

51. Berniard, in *PG,* 8 May 1937, p. 2.

52. Interview Dussauge-Berniard.

53. *PG,* 8 May 1937, p. 2.

54. "Hardly had the reporter returned to France when he took off his mask and wrote two articles in his newspaper in which he told of his adventures in false and tendentious terms, maintaining among other lies that Guernica had been destroyed by the Nationalists and saying nothing of meeting with three Italian journalists and the generous, providential intervention of Sandro Sandri" (*op. cit.,* p. 177). This is perhaps unjust, because if Berniard did not mention the names or the nationality of his benefactors in his first dispatch of 29 April, or even tell of the incident in his articles written in France, it was probably because Captain Aguilera let him know that the Nationalists did not want it known that Italian troops and journalists were among the first into Guernica.

55. *AF,* 5 May 1937, p. 2.

56. *HA,* 8 May 1937.

57. AN, 5 AR 272, Berniard file, telegram datelined "Guernica, Thursday 20 hours."

58. *Correio da Manhã,* 30 April 1937, p. 1. "The city was completely burned before its evacuation by the troops of the Government." The original was less ambiguous: Guernica "fut totalement incendiée par rouges avant leur départ" (AN, 5 AR 272, "Affaire 'Destruction de Guernica' " file).

59. *La Nación,* 1 May 1937. This article, datelined, "Guernica, 30 April (H[avas]-Esp[ecial]" has not been found in a newspaper in France. The capture of Berniard is also recounted in this dispatch, but no indication is given of the peril in which the correspondent found himself. Evidently, Havas took the decision not to mention Berniard in the news distributed in France but to release such news elsewhere. *Le Petit Marocain,* a morning daily published in Casablanca, printed the Havas account of Berniard's difficulties on 1 May 1937, p. 3, but did not give the source. A Havas article identified as such, concerning the capture of

Guernica, containing some of the material published in Buenos Aires but also additional paragraphs, was published in the Casablanca afternoon daily, *La Vigie Marocaine,* on 30 April 1937, p. 3. This latter article did not mention Berniard; it told of the desolation in Guernica, but did not charge anyone with the responsibility. *Le Petit Marocain,* on 30 April 1937, p. 3, published a short article, as follows: "The Nationalist troops, on entering Guernica, have been able to verify that the town was systematically destroyed, not by bombs, as Red propaganda falsely pretends, but by fire. As in Eibar, only the bourgeois quarter was set on fire. The rest of the town is intact and all the houses used as depots for war material were unharmed." No source is given. It may have been compiled by someone who listened to Radio Sevilla.

60. *Le Journal,* 30 April 1937, p. 5. It can be noted that no date was given for the air attack (or attacks) on Guernica, that the air raiders are carefully acquitted of any blame for the fires, which are attributed to "the forces of the government," who started the flames "before withdrawing."

61. *Le Journal,* 3 May 1937, p. 5. According to André Hoornaert, Massot was very favorably viewed by the Rebel authorities (AN, 5 AR 271, d'Hospital file).

62. *Corriere della Sera,* 1 May 1937. This charge of "crime" for burning Eibar rather than leave its industrial installations in the hands of the enemy is ridiculous. Nor has it been advanced with any proof at all. More people were killed in Eibar by bombs and shells from Nationalist planes and artillery than from any last-minute fires started in a ruined and abandoned town.

63. Segàla, *op. cit.,* pp. 172-174. All the journalists who entered Guernica at this time knew that the Italians were in the forefront of the occupying troops, but this information could not be passed through the Spanish censorship. The Italians made their own rules. Franzetti, in *La Tribuna,* 1 May 1937, p. 2, wrote openly of the *Frecce Neri* entering Guernica. Sandri and Segàla were more discreet: the former, in *La Stampa,* 30 April 1937, p. 1, mentioned the "mixed brigades"; the latter, in *Corriere della Sera,* 1 May 1937, p. 1, referred to the "National troops."

64. *La Stampa,* 30 April 1937, p. 1. The word "scempio" used by Sandri would seem to refer to human suffering, and thus constitutes one of the rare references in these Italian reports to the dead and wounded in Guernica. Yet Sandri said the town had been evacuated before destruction.

65. *La Tribuna,* 1 May 1937.

66. *Corriere della Sera,* 1 May 1937, p. 5.

67. *HA,* 28 April 1937, in Nationalist communiqué.

68. *Daily Telegraph,* 30 April 1937.

69. *La Prensa,* 2 May 1937. Both *La Nación* and *La Prensa,* conservative newspapers, throughout the civil war referred to the Franco forces as "revolutionaries." This article, datelined "Guernica 1 May Special" and with "United" at the end, bears no signature. Jean de Gandt, who was a UP man in Rebel Spain at the time, says he did not write the article, nor does he know who did.

70. *NYT,* 2 May 1937, p. 1; *New York American,* 2 May 1937. This dispatch is not signed, but Massock says that he was the man there (letter from Massock, 27 October 1969, Coral Gables, Florida, where he now lives). Concerning his dispatch, Massock later wrote in a letter dated 30 January 1970: "The brief item you quote seems much shorter than my file must have been. I remember mentioning that there were no obvious bomb craters, but that there was much rubble in the streets. . . . I doubt if AP New York or the *Times,* for that matter, would have shortened the story much, unless the details had been duplicated from other sources. My file could very well have been cut in transmission. Communications were so atrocious on the Franco side that we never knew if our dispatches were arriving within twenty-four hours of the filing time or later. . . . A censor at the relay office and/or one at Vigo could have passed judgment on the messages and deleted parts before they were cabled from Vigo to London, without our knowing of it." Since the same text was published in two New York newspapers, we can conclude that the published text was that distributed by AP; hence, if Massock sent a longer article (which seems probable), it was cut either during its Spanish transmission or in the AP office in New York (hardly probable for a story of this importance). Concerning the destruction itself, Massock wrote in the same letter: "It was a burned out, silent town. Nobody

was there to tell what had happened. There was not an animal, any bird. A city still in death, motionless. I saw no reason to doubt the stories refugees had told in Bilbao. There was nobody in Guernica to confirm or deny anybody's story. The dead, presuming many of the populace had been killed, had been buried, I suppose, There was not even left the nose-pinching stench of death with which we all were so familiar. The prisoners, presuming some stragglers had been taken, had been taken elsewhere. . . . The buildings had not been toppled, just burned out. I suppose fire bombs work that way."

71. AN, 5 AR 272, "Affaire 'Destruction de Guernica' " file. The original cablegram is in the Havas papers in the National Archives in Paris. The telegram was signed Botto, but the printed dispatches are unsigned.

72. This reference to "three days" is in the original telegram and is therefore an error on the part of Botto.

73. See *Le Temps*, 2-3 May 1937, p. 8; *Le Figaro*, 3 May 1937, p. 5.

74. *La Métropole*, Brussels, 3 May 1937, p. 3, short article based on Botto but with no source given; 4 May 1937, p. 2, longer dispatch, attributed to Havas.

75. *Journal de Genève*, 4 May 1937, p. 14; *Tribune de Genève*, 4 May 1937, p. 8; *Journal des Nations*, Geneva, 3 May 1937, p. 3.

76. *Glasgow Herald*, 3 May 1937. This is a shortened version, but attributed to Havas.

77. *Le Petit Marocain*, 3 May 1937. No source is given.

78. *La Nación*, 3 May 1937.

79. *Diario de Noticias; O Seculo; A Voz*, Lisbon, 3 May 1937.

80. *Le Figaro*, 3 May 1937, p. 5. The Havas-Botto dispatch was published in *Le Jour*, 3 May 1937, p. 1, 3, with these headlines, "GUERNICA WAS DESTROYED BY FIRE AND NOT BY BOMBS." *Le Matin*, 3 May 1937, p. 3; *Journal des Débats*, 3 May 1937, p. 4; *L'Echo de Paris*, 3 May 1937, p. 3; *AF*, 4 May 1937, p. 2. However, other French newspapers, for political or other reasons, did not publish the Botto telegram, for example, *Paris-Midi*, *L'Instransigeant*, *Le Petit Journal*, *L'Humanité*, *Le Populaire*, *L'Oeuvre*, *La France de Bordeaux*. *L'Express du Midi*, of Toulouse, 3 May 1937, p. 1, a strongly pro-Nationalist newspaper, presented the Botto dispatch as coming from "a correspondent, who does not hesitate, on occasion, to show his pro-Republican sympathies." This would be difficult to prove.

81. AN, 5 AR 272, "Affaire 'Destruction de Guernica' " file.

82. The English press commented on the German charges against the English newspapers, but no bulletin has been found in which the role of the Havas dispatch was noted. The French press was largely silent, because Havas issued no news about how the Nazi press used the Botto report. The special correspondent of *Paris-Midi* in Berlin, Robert Lorette, telephoned on the morning of May 4: "The most curious feature is that Berlin political circles as well as the press are basing their position on the clarification published by certain French newspapers, as well as on a dispatch from the correspondent of the Havas Agency with the Nationalists, to qualify as a lie the 'vile accusations' brought by the English against Germany" (*Paris-Midi*, 4 May 1937, p. 1; AN, 5 AR 272, "Affaire 'Destruction de Guernica' " file).

83. *ABC*, Seville, 4 May 1937, p. 9. *HA*, 5 May 1937, p. 5, has a longer Havas account, with no DNB credit.

84. *HA*, 6 May 1937, p. 6. This was presumably spoken on the night of May 5. This part of the general's talk was condensed in *ABC*, Seville, 6 May 1937, p. 10, in a line or two. The use of the Havas-Botto report can be clearly seen in reference to the burning beams "three days after the town was abandoned by the Marxists."

85. *Le Petit Marseillais*, 3 May 1937, Mévil "was not a regular editorial employee of *Le Petit Marseillais*, but he was a regular contributor. . . . It is exact that he was responsible for some reportages from Spain" (letter from Marcel de Renzis, news editor of *Le Provençal*, of Marseilles, 13 February 1969). A book by Mévil, *Sang d'Espagne*, with a preface by Louis Bertrand, of the French Academy, was published in Grenoble in 1942. Bertrand wrote: "I hope above all that the reader will retain the same lesson, the same horror of the abject myth of the Revolution, and that he will feel the same gratitude towards Spanish heroism. Without the valor of Spanish youth, we should have seen in France the ignoble regime which almost killed Spain" (*Sang d'Espagne*, p. 8). Mévil published in 1957 a short novel entitled *Un amour défendu*. This tells of a French engineer who is working for the Spanish government; he escapes with a lady of

noble birth to the Nationalist side. He returns to France, and she dies gloriously as a nurse in a hospital. Newspapers sometimes credited to their own reporters dispatches that in reality came from Havas. On 3 April 1938 d'Hospital cabled to Havas in Paris to protest the publication by *Le Jour-Echo de Paris*—these two newspapers had shortly before been merged—of one of his dispatches, which the newspaper had attributed to "One of Our Special Correspondents" (AN, 5 AR 271. D'Hospital file).

86. *Le Journal*, 3 May 1937.

87. *Kölnische Zeitung*, 4 May 1937.

88. *HA*, 5 May 1937.

89. *Ibid.*, 6 May 1937.

90. *Le Journal*, 8 May 1937.

91. *HA*, 2 May 1937. Despite this previous publication in the Saragossa newspaper, the forgetful editors of the *Heraldo de Aragón* reprinted Massot's latest article as if were news for their readers, on 12 May 1937. Someone later nominated Massot for the Albert Londres prize in journalism for his reporting on Guernica. It is not made clear which of his contradictory dispatches was thought worthy of the award (*ED*, 13 June 1937).

92. Letter, Holburn to Southworth, 24 September 1969.

93. It is asserted in one place that Philby, who was later known to have been a Soviet spy throughout his time in Spain, took Holburn's place on 24 May 1937 (Page, Leitch, and Knightley, *The Philby Conspiracy*, p. 73). Holburn, however writes that from his cancelled passports, "[I] can say pretty definitely that I crossed the frontier from Spain, on my last exit, on June 21, 1937. . . . If I didn't leave Spain until June 21, Philby cannot have taken over from me on May 24" (letter from Holburn, 24 September 1969). Philby's outspoken pro-Nazi sympathies—his espionage cover—doubtless won him an immediate acceptance by Bolín (*The Philby Conspiracy*, p. 71). The authors of *The Philby Conspiracy* consider that Philby's reports had "a Nationalist slant," and Bolín told them that Philby was a "decent chap who inspired confidence in his reports because he was so objective." "Again and again Spanish officers concerned with the foreign press echo the judgment of Merry del Val and Bolín: "Philby was a gentleman. Philby was objective" (*ibid.*, pp. 74-75). However, Bolín's memory was not always trustworthy. In his 1967 memoirs, he credited the Holburn dispatch of 5 May 1937 to Philby (*STVY*, p. 279). Bolín's error was dutifully followed by Talón (*Arde Guernica*, p. 259, n. 29), and R. de la Cierva (*La actualidad española*, 18 May 1972, "La guerra de España," 45, pp. 774).

94. *Times*, 5 May 1937, p. 16; *NYT*, 5 May 1937, p. 1; *La Nación*, 5 May 1937, p. 2. The headlines are unjustified, for essentially Holburn confirmed the bombing, and his was not a "rival view." *NYT* featured the dispatch as follows: "INQUIRY DOUBTFUL OF GUERNICA FIRE. NO EVIDENCE IS FOUND THAT BASQUE TOWN WAS SET AFLAME BY BOMBS FROM PLANES." Here also the headline writer failed to understand the dispatch.

95. See editorial in the *Times*, 5 May 1937, reproduced in *NYT*, 5 May 1937, and in this text. An intelligent summary of Holburn's dispatch in a Melbourne newspaper ended with a summary of the editorial (*Sun News-Pictorial*, 6 May 1937, p. 2) that was too often overlooked.

96. The Salamanca press office may well have given the reporters an outline of the general Nationalist position. Some correspondents vaguely recall such a paper today, but nobody has kept a copy of it, if it did exist. At any rate, Steer was wrong about the engineers' report; this did not appear until some months later.

97. Steer, *op. cit.*, pp. 248-249.

98. Interview Southworth-Holburn.

99. Letter from Holburn, 24 January 1969.

100. The *Times* no longer has the original cablegram from Holburn. The version published in New York agrees with that published in London. The *Times* is today unable to indicate other possible subscribers to their 1937 foreign service. Letters to Canada, Australia, New Zealand, South Africa, and elsewhere have given no positive result. If the Buenos Aires translation is correct, then London cabled Holburn's original message to the Argentine, rewrote it for London, and cabled the rewritten version to New York. But this is not the only part of the Buenos Aires translation which differs from that printed in London and New York. The following sentences were published in Buenos Aires, but not in any English-language version now known: "An employee of the city hall of Lequeitio, a town which has also suffered from

fire, has stated that he saw no flames when he came out of the refuge [in Guernica] where he was hidden during the aerial attacks. [In view of these circumstances . . . airplanes were responsible.] We can give an assurance that, contrary to what has been published, the bombers did not touch the farm houses—*caseríos*—on the hills surrounding Guernica, for we have seen many of these white-walled and red-roofed constructions and they are all intact. It is very difficult to prove how the fire began, but it is believed that the Asturian miners who formed the military guard are guilty. The existence of these companies is beyond doubt, for the Insurgents have captured the flag of one of them." These sentences, which were either cut from Holburn's original when published in London or were added in Buenos Aires—a farfetched suggestion—are significant in that there are two more confirmations of the bombing. No explanation for the fires that Steer saw on the mountains around Guernica on the night of 26-27 April, and thought to be *caseríos* in flames, has been found.

101. *NYT*, 5 May 1937, p. 18. Carney's cablegram might have been longer than the printed version and cut down because the paper also had Holburn's article. Efforts to find the original cablegram have been unsuccessful. Carney had been correspondent for *NYT* in Madrid before the civil war broke out. He had difficulties with the Republican authorities and left Madrid, probably early in December 1936. His long article in *NYT* on 7 December 1936 revealed his strong bias on behalf on the Nationalists, and shortly thereafter he was assigned to Salamanca, where he remained until the end of the war. This article was reprinted as a Catholic pamphlet (*Catholic Mind*, Vol. XXXV, no. 1 [8 January 1937]), with subheadings: "No democratic government in Spain," "Russia's part in Spain's civil war," "Murder and anti-religion in Spain." The article was criticized by Republican sympathizers for having revealed to the Nationalists the emplacements of the antiaircraft defenses of Madrid (Seldes, *The Catholic Crisis*, pp. 195-200; *Lords of the Press*, pp. 365-369). Carney was a harsh critic of the Republican censorship. "The censorship established in Madrid, both for the Spanish press and for foreign correspondents, was on lines much more in keeping with Soviet ideas than with the customs of a democratic regime. All telephoned and telegraphed dispatches had to be passed personally by a censor, and objections that the censors raised were constantly of such a nature as to exact strict adherence to government policy and the removal of all critical statements with regard to the situation in Madrid" (*Catholic Mind*, 8 January 1937). Other viewpoints on Republican censorship can be found in C. de la Mora's *In Place of Splendor* and in Arturo Barea's *The Clash*. Conditions of work in Salamanca were apparently more to Carney's liking, for he never protested, to public knowledge. His dispatches were consistently, at times absurdly, in favor of the Insurgents. The day that Guernica was destroyed, 26 April, he cabled to *NYT*, that the Basques had a hundred airplanes at their disposal (*NYT*, 27 April 1937, p. 1). Since the Basques did not have even 10 percent of this number of planes at their disposal, Carney certainly did not know, either from observation or from very reliable information, the facts that he cabled. Phillip Knightley tells of how Carney falsified the news about the Rebel recapture of Teruel early in 1938 (*The First Casualty*, p. 199). He was acclaimed a journalistic hero by American Catholics and, after the war, was decorated by the Knights of Columbus, an American Catholic fraternal association. He did not write of his Spanish experiences after the war. He never received another important foreign assignment from the *New York Times*, and he left the newspaper during World War II to enter United States government service. His present whereabouts are unknown. Holburn does not remember Carney, but is positive that he did not visit Guernica with him, although their dispatches are dated the same day. Carney, as previously noted, traveled with the Italians. Segàla tells that the first entry into Bilbao was made by nine journalists: eight Italians and Carney. He does not mention any press officers (*Trincee di Spagna*, p. 208). Cardozo claimed the same honor for himself and his group of correspondents, probably Massot and Botto, accompanied by Major Lámbarri and Captain Aguilera (Cardozo, *The March of a Nation*, pp. 286, 296-297). Massock sometimes traveled with Cardozo's group, but he did not go into Bilbao with them, for he had already been transferred to Moscow late in May (letter from Massock, 30 January 1970).

102. *NYT*, 7 December 1937; *Catholic Mind*, 8 January 1937, p. 7.

103. *AF*, 5 May 1937. Dourec said he entered Guernica with the troops, but he qualified this somewhat by saying that he was enabled to write his article "thanks to the support of the Spanish authorities and the aid of some of our French confrères." He wrote his article, he said,

to contradict the Bilbao radio, the French left press, and the French state radio stations.

104. *Ibid.,* 11, 19 May 1937.

105. *Op. cit.,* pp. 279-284. "I admit that I was not present at Guernica when the so-called bombardment took place. . . . I have visited Guernica not once but a dozen times" (*ibid.,* p. 280).

106. *The Masquerade in Spain,* pp. 54-55. It is not clear when Foltz went into Guernica. He was with the Insurgents; therefore his visit had to be on or after 29 April. He wrote: "I walked through still smoldering ruins shortly thereafter [the bombing] " (*ibid.,* p. 54).

107. *Sunday Times,* 17 October 1937; Cowles, *op. cit.,* pp. 70-71, 75.

108. There were other reports, equally contradictory, which perhaps did not pass through the censorship. *Le Jour,* on 30 April 1937, published an article by Henri de Vilmorin, without indicating from where it was telegraphed, which stated that "the Reds" had burned the tree of Guernica and that "following a battle between Basques on the one hand, on the other communists and Asturian anarchists, the latter groups destroyed Guernica by placing dynamite cartridges in each room of the buildings which they then sprayed with gasoline and set on fire." André Hoornaert, correspondent with *La Libre Belgique,* told M. Lepeltier of Agence Havas in Paris on 18 March 1937 that "the most favored of French journalists [by the Nationalists] is beyond a doubt M. de Vilmorin, representative of *Le Jour.* All doors are open to him and he is free to go where he will and to write as he pleases. Besides he is a lieutenant in the Requetés and wears their uniform" (AN, 5 AR 271, d'Hospital file).

BOOK II, PART ONE
THE CONTROVERSY DURING THE SPANISH CIVIL WAR

Chapter 1
The Public Controversy in England
and the United States

1. E. Allison Peers, *Spain in Eclipse* (1943), p. 3. Peers was professor of Spanish in the University of Liverpool and editor of the *Bulletin of Spanish Studies.* His influence among teachers and students of Spanish in England and the United States was enormous. Not only was the *Bulletin,* which he edited, strongly indoctrinated in favor of the Nationalists but Peers himself wrote at least six books, in one way or another favorable to the Franco cause. It was not until 1943, when Franco's partisanship for the Axis cause could not be ignored, that he confessed that, though during the war itself he had had "every hope, once it was over [Spain] would enter upon 'a new and brilliant day,' " he was now forced to admit that "that hope, down to the present, remains unfulfilled" (*Spain in Eclipse,* p. v). Peers was an Anglican, not a Catholic. Some measure of the feeling in England concerning Guernica can be seen in the fact that the *Bulletin,* normally pro-Nationalist, presented the pro-Republican version, in the section entitled "A Diary of the Civil War," that "Guernica has been practically destroyed by the most ruthless air-raid of the war" (*Bulletin of Spanish Studies,* July 1937).

2. *The Tree of Gernika,* p. 246.

3. At about the time Guernica was bombed, Antonio Ramos Oliveira wrote that "there exists in London various centers of rebel propaganda, directed by the Marquis del Moral, Señor Merry del Val, and the Marquis de Portago" (*Controversy on Spain,* p. 11).

4. When the monarchy fell, Jerrold wrote, "on the initiative of Sir Charles Petrie . . . we had formed our small committee to study and get full reports on Spanish affairs. The energizing factor on this committee was the Marquis del Moral, whose remarkable and buoyant personality and overflowing hospitality kept our small group in being and in remarkable amity over a number of years" (*Georgian Adventure,* p. 362).

5. Statement by the undersecretary of state for the Home Office, Mr. Geoffrey Lloyd, in

the House of Commons on 3 May 1937 (*The Parliamentary Debates* (henceforth, *PD*), *House of Commons Debates,* 3 May 1937, Col. 774).

6. PRO, FO 371/20538, W 10767, folios 254-266. Photocopies were included. Del Moral placed a high value on his "documents," and wrote Seymour: "The man who sent it has risked his life in doing so. Unfortunately, I only received it three days ago." Since, as shown in Southworth, *Le mythe de la croisade de Franco,* p. 174, two of the "documents" of del Moral had been published in a Madrid newspaper on 30 May, 1936, it is doubtful that anyone risked his life to get them to the marquis after that date.

7. A note addressed to C. J. Norton (named private secretary to the permanent undersecretary of state in 1930) on 8 September read as follows: "Mr. [H. J.] Seymour was unable to deal with this before he left. We understand Mr. [R. G.] Leigh to have told him the document was a forgery. Is this so?" Norton wrote below the single word, "Yes." Walter Roberts, acting counselor to the Foreign Office, on 14 September suggested that del Moral be told this. Norton replied on 16 September: "I should much prefer not to put anything in writing to the M. del Moral. I assume that he is on the side of the military party. He does not ask for an answer. If he returns to the charge we could tell him orally that we don't believe them to be genuine" (PRO FO 361/20538, W 10767, folios 255-256). This information was apparently given to the marquis. Details concerning Foreign Office personnel in this work are taken from the *Foreign Office List and Diplomatic and Consular Year Book for 1937.*

8. Loveday published the "documents" first in his book *World War in Spain,* pp. 176-183, then in a second book, *Spain 1923-1948, Civil War and World War,* pp. 251-257. In the second book, he wrote (p. 48), referring to the "secret document," that "a copy was received in England by the writer of this history in June, 1936 . . . and handed to the British Foreign Office, who curiously enough rejected it." The only reference to the "documents" which I have found in the Foreign Office files is that of del Moral. This would seem to indicate that the Loveday documents were those handed in to the Foreign Office by del Moral.

9. The "documents" were real, in the sense that even a forgery exists. They were concocted before the civil war, by some right-wing or Fascist agency, to convince the Spanish people that the left was planning a Red uprising and to prepare them for the Franco counterrevolution. These documents were used to justify the military revolt in Spain itself and in other countries after it had taken place. Now that the documents have been shown to be fraudulent, pro-Nationalist writers such as Ricardo de la Cierva dismiss them as being "absolutely trivial." See R. de la Cierva, *Historia de la guerra civil española,* T. I, pp. 708-709. This is not so. The documents are important evidence. But they should be taken out of the dossier formerly used to convict the Spanish left and placed where they belong, in the dossier of evidence against the Spanish right. It should be noted that according to La Cierva, the documents were originally fabricated by the right-wing journalist Tomás Borrás (*ibid.,* p. 709).

10. Southworth, *Le mythe de la croisade de Franco,* pp. 163-176.

11. *Das Rotbuch über Spanien,* pp. 71-73.

12. The "historical Note" is not signed. However, it does make a reference to the documents, the first public reference known in England, and we know that del Moral knew about the documents. He also doubtless knew that the Foreign Office thought them forgeries. Eyre and Spottiswoode, the publishers of *A Preliminary Official Report on the Atrocities,* state in a letter that their files were destroyed in a bombardment during World War II, and they do not today know who wrote the "Historical Note." At any rate, it was written by the man who received the journalist Nigel Tangye at Spanish Nationalist headquarters in London in December 1936. This person was "a man with the finest features I have ever seen . . . he was tall and slim, and his face revealed the breeding and culture that somehow one expects from the Spanish aristocracy. His hair, worn rather long, was white, and in his eyes was a look of inestimable sadness" (Tangye, *Red, White and Spain,* pp. 14-15). He told Tangye, who was going to Nationalist Spain: "But before you go, read the book on the Spanish atrocities. In it I have written a brief history of the events that led up to the revolution" (*ibid.*). This was an obvious reference to *A Preliminary Official Report on the Atrocities.* Tangye had an undoubted flair for recognizing Spanish aristocratic features, even when the person possessing them was born in Australia and had an English mother. This description could fit del Moral, according to a letter from Sir Arthur Bryant, dated 23 July 1969. Sir Arthur wrote the preface to the succeeding

volume, *The Second and Third Reports on the Communist Atrocities,* but he does not know who wrote the "Historical Note." The fact that it was unsigned would indicate del Moral, for he stayed carefully in the background. His success in staying out of the public eye despite his intense activity in aid of the Spanish Rebels can be gauged by the fact that his name does not appear in either K. W. Watkins's *Britain Divided,* subtitled *The Effect of the Spanish Civil War on British Political Opinion,* or Wm. Laird Klein-Ahlbrandt's *The Policy of Simmering,* subtitled *A Study of British Policy during the Spanish Civil War 1936-1939.*

13. *Daily Worker,* London, 29 April 1937, p. 1. Del Moral's letter was written on 23 April. It dealt with the House debates on the blockade of Bilbao. The Marquis felt that the tactics used by the government in the House were giving the impression "that the Government are pursuing an unpopular policy for which only Party discipline secures the necessary support." He felt that if the debate were broadened, the cause of nonintervention would appear more widely supported. "Now if I am right," he said, "this is a matter of critical importance not only for Franco's cause, but for Great Britain also." Del Moral asked Lord Howard, one of the country's leading Catholics: "Can you help by supporting our case for ever more neutrality?" He continued: "Unless our friends rally to the counter-attack, I am sure we shall have to face a crisis. There is plenty of material for a counter-attack and I shall be only too happy to supply you with shot and shell." Thus, four days before the news of Guernica burst upon the English political scene, the friends of Franco felt themselves in a difficult position over the Rebel offensive against Bilbao. The publication of the letter brought del Moral's activities before the House of Commons on two occasions in the succeeding days (*PD, House of Commons,* 3 and 6 May 1937, Cols. 774-775, 1271).

14. Sir Henry Page Croft had entered Parliament in 1910 and had done his military service during World War I. He was named Baron Croft of Bournemouth in 1940 and served as undersecretary of state for war from 1940 to 1945.

15. Croft—along with del Moral and Jerrold—was active in the propaganda group called "The Friends of National Spain," organized at about the time of the Guernica incident. "It was under these circumstances, having knowledge of the real facts, that I, along with a few Conservative friends, decided to inform the country on the Spanish issue. . . . I first intervened in June 1937." See Croft, *My Life of Strife,* p. 266. It is to be noted that in this autobiography, published after World War II, there is no mention of Guernica. Croft's views on Spain indicate that he may have served as model for the caricaturist Low's character Colonel Blimp. It was Croft who, speaking at a meeting in Queen's Hall, London, on the same platform with Douglas Jerrold and Arnold Lunn, on 23 March 1938, made the famous statement: "I recognize General Franco to be a gallant Christian gentleman" (*ibid,* p. 275; *Spain,* 5 April 1938, pp. 4-7). Croft repeated the phrase some years later: "His [Franco's] clemency in the hour of victory, and the whole conduct of the operations in Spain proclaimed him, as no Spaniard whether friend or foe in the years of tragedy will deny—a Christian gentleman" (*My Life of Strife,* p. 276). This was written after the end of World War II when the truth about the hundreds of thousands executed after the Nationalist victory was known. He also wrote: "Although I hold no brief for Franco, I can say that rarely in any war did any general show such wisdom, chivalry, and mercy. As the Conqueror of Red Spain . . . never did he allow indiscriminate bombardment either from the air or land artillery on non-military objectives" (*ibid.,* p. 275).

16. "Directly it was observed that the great Guernica story was creating such a sensation and being used with such skillful propaganda zeal by British left-wingers, friends of the writer proceeded to Spain" (Croft, *Spain: The Truth at Last,* p. 15). We can presume that one of the "friends" was the Marquis del Moral. Who were the others? Or was the plural used to hide the truth? However, the marquis stated on 26 May that "the question of Guernica had nothing whatever to do with 'his visit to Spain' " (Moral: *Address,* p. 4). This publication was marked "Strictly Private and not for Publication." The marquis insisted on this point in another place a while later, writing that he "visited Spain, recently, for quite another purpose." See "The Legend of Guernica" by the Marquis del Moral, in *Spain at War, 18th July, 1936-18th July, 1937,* p. 7. This article was mainly a condensation of what he had said on 26 May. He was probably protesting too much. On that same day, 26 May, he told the Portuguese ambassador to London, Armindo Monteiro, that "he went to Salamanca in the name of a great number of English friends of Franco." In del Moral's account of his conversation with Franco, as

communicated to his government by the Portuguese envoy, the problem of Guernica occupied the first place (*Dez anos de política externa (1936-1947)*, IV, 333).

17. Moral, *Address*, p. 4.

18. Croft, *Spain: The Truth at Last*, p. 15.

19. Moral, *Address*, p. 15.

20. *Ibid.*, p. 4; *Spain at War, 18th July, 1936-18th July, 1937*, p. 7. Jerrold told of this as follows: "A friend of mine, with long experience of war and military intelligence work, visited General Franco last week, and the last words General Franco said to him were: 'You *must* go and see Eibar, Guernica and Durango. You will see the difference between Durango, where the destruction was the work of aerial bombs, and Eibar and Guernica, where it was the work of dynamiters and incendiaries.' My friend did as he was requested" *Tablet*, 5 June 1937, p. 802).

21. See Bolín, *STVY*. "When I heard what the foreign press was publishing about Guernica," wrote Bolín, "I went to see General Franco." The visit took place on a Sunday, probably the first Sunday after the Guernica catastrophe—that is, on 2 May. The subject of conversation turned to relations between Salamanca and London. "I ventured the view that it was time we had somebody in London, qualified to speak for us in the right quarters" (*ibid.*, p. 281). Bolín shortly thereafter went to England, where he "spent three busy and pleasant weeks that late spring and summer" (*ibid.*). It is not known precisely what kept Bolín "busy" in England. "The Friends of National Spain" were organized about this time. The Spanish Press Services, Ltd., were established, and the first number of Franco's propaganda organ *Spain* was dated 11 September 1937. The duke of Alba came to England during the summer of 1937, as Franco's semiofficial representative. And Bolín was in England when Jerrold was busily defending the Nationalist theses on Guernica.

22. *Dez anos de política externa*, IV, 333-334.

23. Moral, *Address*, p. 3. Among the public were the duchess of Atholl, Admiral Sir Murray Sueter, General Clifton Brown, Captain Ramsay, Sir John Wothers, Sir Ernest Lamb, Mssrs. Donner, Pilkington, Turton, Wedgwood Benn. The majority favored the Nationalist cause. The only person present who showed Republican sympathies in her questioning was the duchess of Atholl (*ibid.*, pp. 17-22). Sir Henry presented his speaker as "a British subject, who had fought in three wars for the British Empire" (*ibid.*, p. 3). He did not tell his hearers that the marquis was a Spanish citizen. In the House of Commons debate on 3 May, in which the marquis' activities were under attack, Mr. Thurtle asked: "Is the Under-Secretary aware that one word from a marquis counts for more than a thousand from an ordinary man with members of the Tory party?" (*PD, House of Commons*, 3 May 1937, Col. 775).

24. Moral, *Address*, p. 6. "Not one of the houses of Elgueta destroyed by airplane bombing or shelling was set on fire. Also: "Durango was destroyed by the Nationalist forces chiefly by bombs from airplanes and some shelling" (*ibid.*, pp. 6, 7). Del Moral's phrase would indicate his belief that the Rebel bombing and shelling had destroyed nothing in Eibar.

25. *Ibid.*, p. 9.

26. *Ibid.*, p. 8.

27. *Ibid*, pp. 10, 11.

28. *Ibid.* Nobody else ever mentioned these entrenchments, and one can suppose that they did not really exist. During the questioning, Mr. Patrick Donner, a parliamentary defender of the Nationalists, evoked a story he said he had had from a French source. "The Basque troops dug lines of trenches immediately outside Guernica and so close to the town that when these trenches and fortifications of Guernica were bombed, and rightly bombed as military objectives, it was necessary for airplanes to fly over the town and since they were flying low it was perfectly easy for the inhabitants to believe that the noise they heard and the explosions came from within the town and not from the trenches. Would it not be extremely difficult for the inhabitants to distinguish between dynamite in the town and the bombing of the trenches outside?" The *Address* goes on: "The Marquis agreed. .He said he had said little about the trenches in connection with Guernica because he had not had the time in daylight to go and see these" (*ibid.*, p. 19). But Donner and del Moral had also walked into a trap (which remained unsprung). How could the inhabitants have confused the two operations (dynamiting in the town and bombing of the trenches) unless they took place at the same time, the same day? Then was the marquis admitting that the outskirts of Guernica were bombed on 26 April?

29. Steer never said that he had found an incendiary bomb; he saw those found by others. All four of the professional foreign correspondents who went to Guernica either found incendiary bombs or saw those found by others. See Book I, chap. 2, n. 28.

30. Moral, *Address*, pp. 8-9.

31. *Ibid.*, p. 21.

32. *Ibid.*, p. 10. Del Moral also said that the Nationalist communiqué published in the *Times* on 5 May constituted "a complete denial of the false accusations made by *The Times* Bilbao correspondent and the Bilbao Government" (*ibid.*, p. 9). However, that communiqué, even as quoted by the marquis, confirmed the bombing of the town; it neither affirmed nor denied that the bombing was carried out on April 26. Vagueness on such an important point could only be intentional.

33. *Ibid.*, pp. 16-17.

34. *Spain at War, 18th July, 1936-18th July, 1937*, p. 7. In his *Address* to the Members of Parliament, del Moral stated that other correspondents than that of the *Times* "at Vitoria asserted most positively to me that it [the destruction of Guernica] was never done by General Franco's forces" (Moral: *Address*, p. 10). It is regrettable that these other correspondents were not identified.

35. Moral, *Address*. Captain Ramsay, an active supporter of the Franco cause, helped extricate del Moral from this difficulty. "Captain Ramsey thought that some of the questions were directed to the fact that two arguments appeared to be slightly contradictory, which he was sure was not intended. The first was that General Franco would have been justified in having bombed Guernica and the second was that he had not in fact done so. He thought several questions had suggested that the Marquis started by saying that General Franco did not destroy Guernica, but that, on the other hand, had he done so, there was no doubt he would have been entirely justified; that it was necessary to include Guernica in the scheme of operations, but that he had not carried these operations to the extent of destroying it in the manner in which it had been" (*ibid.*, p. 21). A strange war was the Spanish war: Franco had good reasons for destroying Guernica, but the Basques had done it for him. Del Moral also involved himself in contradictions concerning the bombing and shelling "during several days preceding the 26th April," when he added that "the few bombholes visible were mostly to be seen at the outskirts of the town." He thus removed the bombing activity from the town itself. However, elsewhere he said he had found a bombhole "outside a shop (adjoining a garage or machine shop which had been completely gutted)" and "another in a neighboring street." He also said, "A bomb fell on a large church." He added, "In both cases the neighboring walls showed the scarring and pitting of the walls by bomb splinters" (*ibid.*, p. 8). This testimony constituted a refutation of that of the Havas man Botto, who had written "that nowhere does one find signs of shrapnel" and "in spite of meticulous searching, the journalists have found no bomb holes; some have been located on the outskirts."

36. *Ibid.*, p. 8.

37. *Ibid.*, p. 10.

38. Moral, *Address*, p. 19.

39. *Spain: The Truth at Last*, pp. 15-16. This pamphlet was published at Bournemouth, in Croft's electoral district, doubtless as an explanation of his policy to the voters. The pamphlet is not dated; it was probably published shortly after the fall of Bilbao on 18 June 1937.

40. *Ibid.*, p. 13. Sir Henry put into doubt the truthfulness of Steer's story of being fired upon by German planes on the afternoon of 26 April (*ibid.*), and in effect called him a liar for his report in general. "But how the Press, responsible Socialist Members of Parliament, and let it be regretfully admitted, even some [Anglican] Bishops, could have accepted this flimsy story of a journalist as proved without waiting for confirmation, it is difficult to understand" (*ibid.*, p. 15).

41. *Ibid.*, p. 14-15.

42. *Spain: The Truth at Last*, pp. 12-13. Del Moral had pooh-poohed the idea that Guernica was destroyed on a market day, remarking that "he saw a statement in *The Times* as to its being market day but there had been so many misstatements that he did not pay much attention to it" (Moral, *Address*, p. 17).

43. *Spain: The Truth at Last*, p. 15. Del Moral had called the account of machine-gunning fleeing people "an absolute fabrication." See n. 36.

44. Jerrold was editor of the *National Review,* an ultraconservative monthly, and director of the publishing house of Eyre and Spottiswoode. This house had published the Bolín-del Moral-Jerrold book, *The Spanish` Republic* in 1933. During the Civil War, it published the English versions of the reports on alleged Republican atrocities in southern Spain *(A Preliminary Report . . . ; The Second and Third Reports on the Communist Atrocities . . . ;* and also *Guernica: The Official Report.* The atrocity reports were fraudulently presented to the English public as having been "Issued with the authority of the Committee of Investigation appointed by the National Government at Burgos." The Spanish-language original reveals no such committee. An important analysis of Jerrold's role in the proappeasement, pro-Fascist movements can be found in Margaret George, *The Warped Vision,* pp. 115-120.

45. See Jerrold, *Georgian Adventure,* pp. 369-374; Bolín, *STVY,* pp. 16-19. Jerrold also intervened to help find machine guns for the Spanish fascists of José Antonio Primo de Rivera *(Georgian Adventure,* pp. 367-369; *STVY,* p. 148).

46. PRO, FO 371/21287, W 5279, folios 204-206. Note from the English ambassador to Spain, Sir Henry Chilton, then in Hendaye, France, to Foreign Minister Anthony Eden, dated 11 March 1937. Yeats-Brown had called on Sir Henry on 10 March on his way back to Paris. Sir Henry was impressed, and told his minister, "I hope it may be possible for more gentlemen of that calibre to make visits to General Franco."

47. Major General J. F. C. Fuller, C.B., C.B.E., D.S.O., *The Conquest of Red Spain.* He attacked the press in his foreword. "This pamphlet has not been written for purposes of propaganda—a word I detest—but solely for enlightenment. For months I read of the Spanish Civil War in our Press, and, feeling certain that much was being suppressed, a few weeks ago I decided to visit Nationalist Spain. This I did, travelling nearly 2,000 miles along General Franco's front. Of my visit I can certainly say this: *That my experiences were a revelation of the power of the press to suppress the truth.*" This foreword was dated 1 June 1937. He mentioned the bombardment of Guernica, but had evidently returned to England before that event. Fuller was a well-known military historian, an enthusiastic supporter of fascist causes. See his *The First of the League Wars,* a defense of Italy in its attack on Abyssinia.

48. Article in the *Observer* 22 August 1937, p. 19.

49. *European Jungle* (London, 1939), published by Jerrold's house, Eyre and Spottiswoode.

50. "Spain: Impressions and Reflections," in *The Nineteenth Century and After,* April 1937, pp. 470-492: reprinted as a pamphlet in England; and later in Spain, *España: Reflejos e impresiones;* published in New York in the *American Review,* April 1937, and later as the first part of the pamphlet *The Issues in Spain.*

51. *Georgian Adventure.* The preface is dated June 1937. References to Jerrold's trip to Nationalist Spain in March, pp. 378-385.

52. "The Truth about Guernica," *Tablet,* 5 June 1937, pp. 801-803. This article was published in French in the Brussels publication *La Revue Catholique des Idées et des Faits,* 16 Juin 1937.

53. "Red Propaganda from Spain," in *American Review,* Summer 1937, pp. 129-151. This is simply an enlargement of the *Tablet* article; it is therefore hardly true that it was "especially written for the American public," as the editor of the *American Review,* Seward Collins, claimed (p. 129). This article was also reprinted in *The Issues in Spain.* Where this revised version of Jerrold's article differs from that in the *Tablet,* it will be indicated; otherwise only the *Tablet* article will be mentioned.

54. *Spectator,* 18 June 1937. The *Spectator* had from the first adopted the Basque version of the destruction of Guernica. "Never in modern history has Europe known anything comparable," read an editorial statement on 30 April 1937, p. 785. "The sickening butchery of Guernica has no parallel. It takes rank among crimes which their very hideousness prints indelibly on history." A week later it said: "That the town was relentlessly bombarded from the air is irrefutably established by the evidence of reputable British journalists, apart from any Spanish testimony." And it added logically: "That much of the damage was due to fire is likely enough, for all the earliest reports speak of incendiary bombs being used; the suggestion from Insurgent headquarters that the town was fired by the Basques themselves is unconvincing" (*ibid.,* 7 May 1937, p. 845).

55. *Ibid.*, 2 July 1937, p. 21.
56. *Ibid.*, 23 July 1937, p. 150.
57. *Ibid.*, 30 July 1937, p. 208.
58. *Tablet*, 5 June 1937, p. 801. Jerrold wrote aggressively about the Spanish Civil War, and his writings were filled with boundless vanity. He began the article that first appeared in *The Nineteenth Century and After*, April 1937, by informing his readers that to "understand the Spanish situation . . . it is necessary . . . to know a good deal of recent Spanish history, to have made some little study of the art of war, to have a journalist's training in the assimilation of facts, and above all to realize the part played by propaganda in a conflict of vital interest, on the one hand, to Spain, and, on the other, to the revolutionary forces who have made Spain their battleground." Of course Jerrold was convinced that Jerrold understood "the Spanish situation."
59. *Spectator*, 23 July 1937, p. 150.
60. This is a reference to the campaign begun in the German press on May 4 against the *Times* and the English press in general. See Book II, part 1, chap. 3.
61. *Times*, 5 May 1937, p. 17.
62. Steer also failed to cite the *Times* editorial in his reply to Jerrold, but perhaps he had not seen it, since he was outside the country when it appeared. It is more difficult to understand why the Basque propaganda pamphlet *FWOBC* failed to reproduce it.
63. *Tablet*, 5 June 1937, p. 801.
64. See *The Tree of Gernika*, p. 242; also Steer's own reply to Jerrold, *Spectator*, 30 July 1937, p. 208, cited below.
65. *Tablet*, 5 June 1937, p. 801. The reader will note that Croft in his attack on Steer was more aggressive on this point.
66. See Southworth, *op. cit.*, pp. 179-186, for a study of how Jerrold, Arnold Lunn, and the American priests Joseph F. Thorning and Joseph B. Code attacked Jay Allen and other journalists for their exposure of the Badajoz massacre.
67. *American Review*, Summer 1937, pp. 142-143.
68. *Spectator*, 2 July 1937, p. 21.
69. *Ibid.*, 23 July 1937, p. 150.
70. Steer repeated the fact of his second visit in the *Times*, 6 May 1937. Jerrold wrote to the *Spectator* on 2 July 1937, p. 21: "My article in *The Tablet*, of course, made full reference to both *The Times* correspondents."
71. *Tablet*, 5 June 1937, p. 801. Jerrold admitted that "there is no reason to doubt that they [the Germans] bombed Guernica on occasions" (*ibid.*). The use of "intermittently," a word straight out of Holburn's article, would seem to be an effort to align Holburn's dispatch with Jerrold's false interpretation of it.
72. *Ibid.*
73. *Spectator*, 23 July 1937, p. 150.
74. *Ibid.*
75. *Guernica: The Official Report*, p. 18, noted only that a pistol factory lay near the railroad tracks, and beside it a machine shop was producing munitions, and that neither was damaged during the bombing. According to Talón, at the time of the bombing, there were three arms factories in Guernica (*op. cit.*, p. 81).
76. *Times*, 4 May 1937.
77. *Guernica: The Official Report*, p. 18.
78. See Steer's article, *Times*, 28 April 1937, reproduced in Book I, chap. 1.
79. *The Tablet*, 5 June 1937, pp. 801-802.
80. Jerrold may have taken this idea from Croft, who wrote that "to have reduced Guernica to ashes in such incredibly short time would have necessitated the use of a vast number of incendiary bombs" (*Spain: The Truth at Last*, p. 15). It is a bit startling to find out that a few dynamiters and *petroleurs* could produce in a few hours the destruction that would have taken a month's ammunition from Franco's army.
81. *Spectator*, 2 July 1937, p. 21.
82. *Dez anos de política externa* IV, 333.
83. *Spectator*, 23 July 1937, p. 150.
84. This may well have been true (and perfectly justified) about Irún, but not true about

Eibar (though equally justified), as we have shown above. Jerrold proclaimed: "And again, Eibar was also, and admittedly, burnt. It was never suggested by Bilbao that it had been severely bombed till two days after the Guernica story had shocked the world" (*Tablet*, 5 June 1937, p. 801). On the contrary, the Salamanca censorship, as already shown, passed bulletins announcing that Eibar had been bombed the day before its capture.

85. *Spectator*, 23 July 1937, p. 150.

86. *Ibid*. The article mentioned by Jerrold was written by a journalist "who entered Guernica with General Franco's forces," but it was based more precisely on the visit the journalist (Botto) made forty-eight hours later. Jerrold credits to several journalists the work of one man, Botto, and the "unanimous conclusion" was one taken by Botto in conference with himself.

87. *Times*, 5 May 1937, p. 16. See Book I, chap. 4.

88. *Le Figaro*, 3 May 1937, p. 5. Max Massot wrote in the same vein in *Le Journal*, 3 May 1937, p. 5. See Book I, chap. 4.

89. It is quite possible that neither Botto nor Holburn saw any bomb-scarred walls in Guernica, but this fact can hardly prove that no explosive bombs fell on the town. Only a small proportion of the walls was still standing in the bombed-out part of Guernica when the correspondents visited the ruins. Not only were walls constantly falling but they were being pulled down, because of the danger that they represented.

90. *Durango, Bilbao, 1937; Guernica, Bilbao, 1937*. These publications were the work of Esteban Guerequiz (letter from Antonio Guerequiz, 31 August 1975).

91. *Times*, 28 April 1937. See Book I, chap. 1.

92. Gerahty went to Spain in late August 1936 and stayed until late November. He had been in Morocco during the Spanish campaigns against the Moors and knew many Spanish officers. He had curious recommendations when he first sought to enter Spain: he went to see the Spanish doctor who was chief of the Spanish Phalanx in Tangier, then entered Morocco with the Phalangist letters. Gerahty went back to Spain early in April. See *The Road to Madrid*.

93. PRO, FO 371/212, W 11635.

94. *Ibid*. Sir Richard Roy Maconachie of the BBC, a former envoy extraordinary and minister plenipotentiary to Kaboul, sent Gerahty to Maclean.

95. *The Road to Madrid* (London, 1937).

96. It is not clear whether Gerahty meant the changeover from Gay to Arias Paz or the takeover by the Phalangists after the Unification Decree of 19 April 1937. See Maximiano García Venero, *Falange en la guerra de España: la unificación y Hedilla*, p. 274. Or did he mean the Bolín incident? See Book III, chap. 4.

97. In 1937, "Donald Maclean was attached to the Spanish desk of the Western [European] and League of Nations Department of the Foreign Office" (Cookridge, *The Third Man*, p. 45).

98. *Op. cit.*, p. 242.

99. *Spectator*, 23 July 1937, p. 150. The reader will note the importance Jerrold gave to Gerahty's testimony, that of the only English eyewitness. His word obviously outweighed that of hundreds of Spaniards.

100. *Spectator*, 30 July 1937, p. 208. Steer wrote about Guernica not only in the dispatches that appeared in the *Times*, and in the letter in the *Spectator* but also in an article in the *London Mercury*, August 1937. His 1938 book, *The Tree of Gernika*, easily among the dozen best on the civil war, has had a surprisingly limited printing life. It has never been reprinted in England and was never published in the United States. A Spanish translation appeared in the Argentine in 1963, *El árbol de Gernika*.

101. *Ibid.*, p. 209.

102. This is probably a reference to Holburn's dispatch, which apparently irritated Steer considerably.

103. *Spectator*, 30 July 1937, p. 209.

104. *Ibid.*

105. *The Road to Madrid*, p. 242.

106. *Spectator*, 30 July 1937, p. 209. There is also a contradiction in Gerahty's statement to Maclean or in Maclean's transcription. Gerahty is reported to have said that he went to

Burgos on Wednesday, the day after "the bombing" and "saw the bombers still in the same position as he had seen them on the [day] previous to the raid. But the day previous to Gerahty's raid was Monday, and according to his book he was then in Vitoria.

107. Douglas Jerrold, *Britain and Europe, 1900-1940*, p. 142.

108. *Observer*, 5 September 1937, reproduced in Bryant, *Humanity in Politics*, pp. 344-345.

109. Arnold Lunn, *Spanish Rehearsal* (London), pp. 230-235. See also Lunn, *Spain and the Christian Front*, p. 20; *Revolutionary Socialism in Theory and Practice*, pp. 58-59.

110. Bolín, *STVY*, pp. 276-279.

111. Frances Davis, who was working for the *Daily Mail* and Cardozo during the early weeks of the civil war, wrote: "I don't like the stuff I send. The *Daily Mail* calls these [Nationalist] armies the "Patriot" armies. Captain Rosales likes this and points it out with pleasure every time he stamps a story with the "censored" stamp. And then John [Elliott of the *New York Herald Tribune*] gives him his story, and in John's stories they are the "Rebel" armies and in fury Rosales tells him that he will not stand for it" (*op. cit.*, p. 131). Also my conversation with d'Hospital.

112. Peter Kemp, who shared an apartment with Cardozo and Botto for a few weeks at this time, wrote: "He [Cardozo] was in Guernica immediately after its occupation by the Nationalists, and so was able to make a pretty thorough examination" (*op. cit.*, pp. 88-89). Cardozo does not insist in his book *The March of a Nation* that he was in Guernica "immediately" after its occupation.

113. Kemp, *Mine Were of Trouble*, p. 88.

114. *Op. cit.*, p. 281. Italian participation in the raid on Guernica seems more certain now than when the French version of this book appeared in 1975. See Book II, part 2.

115. *Ibid.*, p. 280. Peter Kemp reported thusly on his May 1937 conversations with Cardozo: "It was clear to him, he said, that the Republicans themselves had set fire to the town before leaving" (*op. cit.*, p. 89). This statement is contradictory to Cardozo's later text, published before Kemp's, that Guernica was burned on the day of its "so-called bombardment" (*op. cit.*, p. 280). The "so-called bombardment" took place on 26 April and the "leaving" of the Republicans did not take place until 29 April.

116. Cardozo criticized Steer ("One of the principal organs of opinion, through its correspondent in Bilbao"), for having declared that "the bombing planes had set fire to all the farms around and that they were blazing like torches." He went on: "I have visited Guernica not once but a dozen times, and by every road into the town, and not a single farm or homestead outside of Guernica has been touched by flame or smoke" (*ibid.*). Holburn also attacked this detail in his dispatch from Vitoria. But Monks had also written in his dispatch published on 28 April in the *Daily Express*, "There is hardly a farmhouse intact for five miles around the city." Holme also cabled: "It is now known that the Nationalist planes bombed and set fire to isolated farm houses for a distance of five miles around Guernica" (*Morning Post*, 28 April 1937). No explanation has been found of what Steer and the other reporters saw that night. Fires seen during the night sometimes seem more important than the results of these flames viewed days later. Cardozo also denounced "another report from Bilbao," which he called "lying nonsense," describing "how the crew of the German planes leant out of the planes, swooped down and threw their 'hand grenades' at the people" (*op. cit.*, p. 280). This description came from the Reuters dispatch. See *Evening News*, 27 April 1937, and the *Star*, 27 April 1937. There were no air defenses, and this scene may have been true or appeared true to a panic-stricken peasant. It is not essential to the story.

117. *Op. cit.*, pp. 280-281.

118. *Ibid.*, pp. 281-282. In the first sentence of this quotation, it is evident that Cardozo meant to say "Durango" and not "Guernica." It is strange that Cardozo should make the same error that was made in Holburn's story as printed in the *Times*. See Book I, chap. 4.

119. *Ibid.*, p. 280. Noel Monks wrote on May 11, on his return to England: "We correspondents at Bilbao were in Guernica before representatives of the government were there. We went alone" (*DE*, 11 May 1937).

120. *Op. cit.*, p. 293.

121. *Sunday Times,* 17 October 1937, reproduced in 1941, in Virginia Cowles, *Looking for Trouble,* p. 71. Cowles spelled Rosales in the Catalan fashion with two "ll's."

122. *Sunday Times,* 17 October 1937; *Looking for Trouble,* p. 75.

123. Steer, *op. cit.,* pp. 249-250. Steer did not know the identity of the writer, for the article in the *Sunday Times* was unsigned.

124. Hugh Thomas cites the *Sunday Times* (*op. cit.,* p. 421), not Cowles's book. Although the book is in his bibliography, he did not credit Cowles with the *Sunday Times* article. This article appeared in October 1937, and Thomas placed the incident during the same month. However, the text of both article and book makes evident the fact that the visit of Cowles to Guernica took place at the moment of the fall of Santander—that is, in August 1937. A recent anthology on Spanish Civil War writings, *Der spanische Bürgerkrieg in Augenzeugenberichten,* p. 271, edited by Hans-Christian Kirsch, cites a part of the *Sunday Times* article without mentioning Cowles. The incident is again placed in October 1937. Cowles had told the story to American Ambassador Bowers in Saint-Jean-de-Luz when she crossed the frontier (*My Mission in Spain,* p. 346).

125. Knoblaugh left Republican Spain around the middle of 1937 (*Correspondent in Spain,* pp. 222-233). His book was published in October 1937, by the Catholic house Sheed and Ward. The nature of Knoblaugh's writings on events of the civil war can be judged by his dismissal of the Badajoz bullring massacre as "a hoax" (*ibid.,* p. 172).

126. *Ibid.,* p. 176. Knoblaugh, like Gerahty, did not visit Guernica after it fell into Franco's hands. The word "Loyalist" was frequently used to designate the Republicans.

127. This speech was published in the *Standard and Times,* official weekly of the Roman Catholic archdiocese of Philadelphia, 31 December 1937, on the first page under a two-column title: "PRIEST TELLS HOW PRESS AND ITS CORRESPONDENTS SLEW TRUTH ABOUT SPAIN." With a few corrections, the speech was reprinted in brochure form in 1938, by the International Catholic Truth Society, with the title *Why the Press Failed on Spain!* Knoblaugh's book had just come out, and the Catholic press was singing its praises. Father Thorning used it generously. "Catholic editors and publishers merit the compliment which Edward H. [*sic*] Knoblaugh paid to the Nationalist High Command at Salamanca: that never once were Franco's press officers responsible for the announcement or publication of false information" (*op. cit.,* p. 20). What Knoblaugh really wrote was somewhat different, but equally absurd. "It is only fair to say that not once during all those months did the newspapermen or neutral military observers catch the Rebel official radio in a deliberate misrepresentation of the facts as we knew them" (*op. cit.,* pp. 144-145). Anyone who had followed the development of the news concerning Guernica, including Thorning and Knoblaugh, could have known not only that the first news of this event given out by the Franco press officers and broadcast by the official Nationalist radio was false but that it was very soon admitted to have been false. Knoblaugh's remarks concerning Guernica were reprinted in the *Catholic World,* January 1938, p. 480.

128. Subtitles in Thorning's pamphlet are such as "The Lies about Badajoz" (p. 4), and "The Lies about Guernica" (p. 9). At the same time that Thorning attacked the secular American newspapers and their correspondents, he praised the American Catholic press and its writers: "The news, as reported in the Catholic press, may not always have been sensational, but it was correct" (*Why the Press Failed on Spain!* p. 20).

129. Holburn's dispatch was also, as noted above, published in the *New York Times,* a fact that Thorning did not mention, perhaps because it showed the objectivity of that newspaper. Also, on the day when Holburn's report was published in the *New York Times,* a cablegram on the same subject was printed, in a secondary position, coming from the newspaper's own correspondent with the Rebel forces William P. Carney. Thorning and the American Catholic press at this time were carrying on a feud with the *New York Times,* praising Carney's reports and denigrating those of the newspaper's correspondent with the Republicans Herbert L Matthews. Thorning asked, in the course of his address: "Why should the feature spot be reserved for the dispatches of Herbert L. Matthews morning after morning? Why were the reports of William P. Carney kept for many months on the inside page or in a subordinate place?" (*Why the Press Failed on Spain!* p. 18). Thorning and other American Catholic writers used anti-Semitism by innuendo in their running fight with the press, charging that the publishers of the *New York Times* and of other newspapers "allowed their antipathy for (or

valid grievances against) Hitler and Mussolini to influence their judgment in the placing and spacing of news" (*ibid.*).

130. *Ibid.*, p. 10.

131. *Ibid.*, pp. 9-10.

132. *Ibid.*, p. 11. This telegram had obviously been found in the Bilbao telegraph office when the Nationalists took the town. Someone, perhaps Bolín, turned a copy over to Father Thorning. Major Yeats-Brown wrote in the *Observer*, 22 August 1937, p. 19: "I have seen in Salamanca, a large room full of documents seized when the Nationalists entered Bilbao. There is a telegram from Comrade Dimitrov. . . . There is a telegraph book showing the cables sent from Bilbao to all parts of the world. . . . To me, the most interesting find in this room was a correspondence between an English M.P. and a journalist in Bilbao who excelled himself in describing the Guernica affair [Steer?]." Father Thorning fancied himself as a correspondent and went to Spain as a reporter for the news service of the American hierarchy, the National Catholic Welfare Conference News Service. "A writer who has travelled as foreign correspondent . . . In the words of Archbishop Curley, 'he is one of the greatest authorities in the nation today on Spanish affairs' . . . In 1946 he was presented the Grand Cross of the Order of Isabella the Catholic, with the rank of 'comendador' by the Spanish government" (Matthew Hoehn, *Catholic Authors. Contemporary Biographical Sketches, 1930-1947*, pp. 732-733). Thorning was proud of his copy of the telegram to Steer, which he described as a "hitherto undisclosed telegram, of which I submit a photostatic copy" (*Why the Press Failed on Spain!* p. 10).

133. *Ibid.*, p. 10. Thorning doubtless got the idea of the nonexistent "committee of international correspondents" from Knoblaugh.

134. *Ibid.*

135. *Ibid.*, p. 12. Palmer was later to hold a high editorial position on *Reader's Digest*.

136. *Ibid.*, p. 10. Thorning failed to see, or did not want to see, that the dispute lay not in whether fires had caused the damage but in the nature of the incendiary agency: incendiary bombs dropped from Nationalist airplanes, dynamite, or gasoline used by incendiarists on the ground.

137. *Ibid.*, p. 14. Thorning asserted here that "The final editorial blast came on May 7, long after every responsible editor in New York and London had ample reason to doubt the misleading report of Mr. Steer." This statement is completely false. As for the more personal charges against Steer and his motives, it can be noted that, far from being influenced by the editorials in the *New York Times*, Steer probably never saw the editorials in question, and may not even have been aware that the New York paper published his story.

138. *Ibid.*, p. 11.

139. *Times*, 14 December 1937.

140. *Columbia*, July 1937, "Atrocities Made to Order," by Wilfrid Parsons, S. J., p. 21.

141. ·Father Parsons received his doctorate from the University of Louvain and, from 1925 to 1936, was editor of the principal Jesuit publication in the United States, the weekly *America*. In 1937 he was professor of political science at Georgetown University.

142. *Columbia*, July 1937, "Atrocities Made to Order," by Wilfrid Parsons, S.J., p. 21.

143. *The Conquest of Red Spain*, p. 11.

144. Yeats-Brown spoke of being in Salamanca on 2 August 1937 (*Observer*, 22 August 1937, p. 19). "I spent a long time in Guernica, piecing together that tragic story." He had called in at the Foreign Office early in March to give his impressions of Spain. One Foreign Office functionary observed: "It may be mentioned that Major Yeats-Brown is a Fascist" (PRO, FO 371/21287, W 5279, folio 204).

145. *Observer*, 22 August 1937, p. 19. Yeats-Brown excused the original Nationalist version of "bad weather" as a "mistake." See also *European Jungle*, p. 271.

146. *Observer*, 22 August 1937, p. 19. In *European Jungle*, Yeats-Brown changed "Reds" to "dinamiteros," p. 275.

147. *Observer*, 22 August 1937, p. 19; *European Jungle*, pp. 271-272. This military information has not been confirmed elsewhere.

148. *Observer*, 3 October 1937, p. 24. Wilson found the "inhabitants" talkative, but Yeats-Brown said the evidence "of civilians hiding in cellars is not very reliable," and that "all

the witnesses" he questioned "stated that the place caught fire, that the fire brigade arrived from Bilbao, and that it was sent away again by the Red authorities" (*Observer,* 22 August 1937, p. 19; *European Jungle,* p. 271). Wilson's article escaped the attention of his biographer John Marlowe, who wrote that during his September visit to Spain, "his hosts managed to keep him away from Guernica, where his military experience and his uncompromising honesty might have led him to prefer the finding of G. L. Steer, *The Times* correspondent to those of such committed Francophiles as Douglas Jerrold and Capt. Yeats-Brown" (*Late Victorian,* p. 358). Wilson's visit to Guernica seems perfectly clear in the book used by Marlowe (*Thoughts and Talks,* pp. 377-378), but it is certainly clearer in the *Observer* article.

149. According to James's speech in the Commons, he visited Guernica around October 7, 1937. It is interesting to see under what conditions James traveled in the Rebel zone, compared with the restrictive life of the average newspaper correspondent. "a car was put at my disposal, and I was allowed to take with me an Englishman speaking fluent Spanish, not a minion of the government at all, but a businessman—and I was told I could go anywhere I liked and no restrictions of any sort were put upon me" (*PD, House of Commons,* fifth series, vol. 327, 21 October 1937, col. 103).

150. In reality, James spent two hours in Guernica, as he told the House with complete frankness (*PD, House of Commons,* fifth series, vol. 327, 21 October 1937, col. 107). "Simultaneous incendiarism from inside" could probably be more easily caused by an airplane dropping incendiary bombs than by a group of arsonists on the ground.

151. Guernica was apparently shelled by the Basques after evacuation, on 30 April and 1 May. See Talón, *op. cit.,* pp. 104-106. But this fact was not emphasized by James, who seemingly was talking of shelling before the capture of the town. See text.

152. *Daily Telegraph,* 19 February 1938.

153. *Ibid.* James was called in as a witness by Father Thorning, although not by name. See above. But in this testimony, James completely contradicts the clerical orator.

154. Joseph B. Code. *The Spanish War and Lying Propaganda,* p. 29, quoting the NCWC News Service, 8 April 1938. Code had studied at Paris, Oxford, Heidelberg, and Louvain; at the latter university he was awarded a doctorate in historical sciences (Hoehn, *op. cit.,* pp. 147-148).

155. *Spain,* 31 May 1938. Meeting of Friends of National Spain, 12 May 1938, at Perth.

156. *Aeroplane,* 5 May 1937, "On Stories from Spain," by C. G. G., p. 528. C. G. Grey held a place of high esteem in aeronautical circles. He was one of the two editors of the annual *Jane's All the World's Aircraft,* from 1936 to 1939, the years of the Spanish Civil War. He had recommended Tangye to the marqués del Mérito, aide-de-camp to the Nationalist air commander General Kindelán (Tangye, *op. cit.,* pp. 12-13).

157. Grey repeated this formula, whereby all the German pilots in Nationalist Spain were reduced to an indistinct "technical" quality, exactly as did del Moral, Lunn, Tangye, and others. See Book 1, chap. 4, nn. 113-121. "Actually as a number of reliable visitors to Spain have borne witness, there are no regular German troops, or Air Force, in Spain and hardly any German fighting men except a few volunteers. The only German organizations which could be called self-contained units are the staffs of mechanics and technical supervisors who are running the Junkers and Heinkel machines for the Nationalist Government. They are there for two reasons, one is to see that the machines are properly 'serviced,' to use that abominable American expression, and the other is to observe how the German aeroplanes and motors and their armament behave in those conditions. That is to say they are playing precisely the part of that new sort of salesman in the motor business and others, who is called a Service Representative." It is difficult to imagine one of the two men responsible for the world's principal aeronautical reference book of these years so misinformed. Of course he may not have been so ignorant as he pretended, but that poses a moral problem. He did add as an afterthought: "Actually there are German volunteers flying in Spain. Some are there to try out the German machines in actual war, and others are there to get personal experience of war. Some also are there because any fight against Communism is a righteous war" (*Aeroplane,* 5 May 1937, pp. 528-529).

158. Williams, *Airpower,* p. 282. This 1940 book was a tract for American isolationism, a movement upheld by most of Franco's friends in the United States. Williams's views of the

Spanish Civil War were inspired by Yeats-Brown, Knoblaugh, and McNeill-Moss. He denied the Badajoz massacre and accepted the fraudulent Communist plot documents of del Moral, Jerrold, and others (*ibid.,* pp. 227, 230-231).

159. *Ibid.,* pp. 127-128.

160. This reference was misunderstood by Steer, who considered that the greater part of the dispatch of his colleague "was mostly a rewrite of a document published for the whole foreign and 'nationalist' press at Vitoria, and purporting to be a report of civilian engineers of the causes of the burning of Gernika" (*The Tree of Gernika,* p. 248). Holburn does not now remember too vividly the engineers in question. He later wrote, in a letter dated 24 January 1969, "Reading the dispatch [*Times,* 5 May 1937, p. 16] reminded me that I met a man, in Guernica or Vitoria, who purported to be chairman of a commission of civil engineers appointed by Franco to inquire into the causes of the burning of Guernica."

161. *Germany and the Spanish Civil War* (hereafter, *GSCW*), pp. 280, 290. *Documents on German Foreign Policy, 1918-1945,* Vol. III.

162. This description is taken from page one of the English-language translation of *Guernica: The Official Report.* A part of the commission's argument can be found in the title, which indicates that the destruction took place during three days, from the twenty-sixth to the twenty-eighth.

163. "The Commission of Investigation . . . met in the town of Guernica on the 9th of August 1937" (*ibid.,* p. 17).

164. This does not mean to suggest that information could not be secured at this late date. Information can be secured even today, from survivors and so forth. I wish merely to point out that the correspondents under attack were there a hundred days earlier. They were as trustworthy in their profession as, and certainly possessed more freedom of expression than, the investigators who came a hundred days later. It is difficult to understand today the reasons for the long delay in beginning the investigation, which was undertaken only after the capture of Bilbao. The duchess of Atholl commented: "In the meanwhile, there had been ample time to fill in bombholes and pull down roofs. The photographs published with the Report suggest that this had been done very systematically" (*Searchlight on Spain,* p. 195).

165. Bolín is in error when he gives the number of twenty-five witnesses. See *STVY,* p. 358. Some witnesses testified a second time.

166. The report is signed: "Burgos, September 1937" (*Guernica: The Official Report,* p. 16).

167. See Book II, part 2.

168. The duchess of Atholl gave a competent and incisive analysis of *Guernica: The Official Report* in *Searchlight on Spain,* pp. 194-198. Her book was first published in June 1938. *Guernica: The Official Report* was probably published during the first trimester of 1938. There is an unjustified tendency to denigrate the duchess' book today, especially by Ricardo de la Cierva. See his *Cien libros básicos sobre la guerra de España,* pp. 154-158. La Cierva should reread her pages (187-199) concerning Guernica and compare them with those written by Nationalist defenders, even thirty years later.

169. Sir Arnold was quoted in the *Manchester Guardian,* 11 June 1938, as saying, "I hope to God Franco wins and the sooner the better" (Cited in Watkins, *Britain Divided,* p. 118).

170. The manager of the Guernica Workshops declared to three German officers that "in his opinion . . . the incendiary bombs dropped over Guernica were dropped by the Reds." He claimed that fuses for incendiary bombs, fashioned after a German model, had been manufactured in Guernica, and he based that opinion "on the fact that certain stains which he actually saw on the Rentería bridge [near Guernica] had the same characteristics as those which resulted from the tests carried out with incendiary bombs by the Red Separatists in the *Talleres de Guernica*" (*Guernica: The Official Report,* p. 43). Vaguely confirmatory testimony was offered by a foreman in the same factory, (*ibid.,* p. 47).

171. *Ibid.,* p. 15.

172. *Ibid.,* p. iv. "Something might have been urged if, as alleged by the Red propaganda, the barracks of the militiamen, the munition factories, the Tree of Guernica and the Parliament House in Guernica had all been destroyed. On the contrary, all the above remained untouched" (*ibid.,* p. 13). When the Nationalists accused the Basques of burning Eibar, they charged that it was done to destroy arms factories.

173. The person who talked with Virginia Cowles said the airplanes were German and Italian. The priest interviewed by Wing Commander James did not identify the aircraft. See n. 148. None of the eyewitnesses of whom the Rebel spokesmen had boasted in the early communiqués was ever brought before the commission. "Moreover, we have witnesses to the burning of Guernica by the Reds, witnesses to their work with incendiary material and petrol" (dispatch from correspondent on Franco-Spanish frontier, quoting Nationalist communiqué, *Times,* 30 April 1937); also Steer, *op. cit.,* p. 249.

174. *Guernica: The Official Report,* p. 23.

175. *Ibid.,* p. 25.

176. *Ibid.,* p. 26.

177. *Ibid.,* p. 28.

178. *Ibid.,* p. 31.

179. *Ibid.,* p. 33.

180. *Ibid.,* p. 38.

181. *Ibid.,* p. 39.

182. *Ibid.,* p. 40.

183. *Ibid.,* p. 43.

184. *Ibid.,* p.,46.

185. *Ibid.,* p. 49.

186. *Ibid.,* pp. 34-35.

187. *Ibid.,* p. 4.

188. *Ibid.,* p. iv. It is worth underlining the fact that at this point Sir Arnold openly contradicted one of the chief conclusions of the work he was prefacing in a supposedly friendly manner.

189. *Ibid.,* p. 13.

190. *Ibid.,* p. 22.

191. *Ibid.,* p. 24.

192. *Ibid.,* p. 26.

193. *Ibid.,* p. 28.

194. *Ibid.,* p. 33.

195. *Ibid.,* p. 36.

196. *Ibid.,* p. 39.

197. *Ibid.,* pp. 43-44.

198. *Ibid.,* pp. 48-49.

199. *Ibid.,* p. 49.

200. *Ibid.,* p. 8.

201. *Ibid.,* p. 16.

202. *Ibid.,* p. 13.

203. *Ibid.,* p. 9.

204. *Ibid.,* p. 24.

205. *Ibid.,* p. 26.

206. *Ibid.,* p. 31.

207. *Ibid.,* p. 35.

208. *Ibid.,* p. 37. Another witness said that "When he left at about nine or ten at night only some twenty houses were burning in the sector which he saw" (*ibid.,* p. 46). We do not know of which sector of Guernica he was talking, but twenty houses were not a negligible number.

209. *Ibid.,* p. 49.

210. Cárdenas Rodríguez, *Texto taquigráfico de la conferencia pronunciada por el arquitecto de la dirección general de regiones devastadas . . . el día 3 de Julio de 1940,* p. 29.

211. *Guernica: The Official Report,* p. v. Sir Arnold's figure of a "quarter of the town" was in reality slightly higher than that of the witnesses.

212. *Ibid.,* p. iv.

213. *Ibid.,* p. 24. "That once in his house, he was able to see that the house immediately next to his, on the corner of Santa María Street, was burning, but not his house nor any other house in Santa María Street towards the North, which was the way the wind was blowing. That as soon as his own house caught fire, and in order to save the remaining houses in that street, he

asked the militiamen for dynamite to blow it up and so establish a fire-break. This they categorically refused, and so the fire continued burning all the following night and day without anyone doing anything to check it, and that the street was totally destroyed." Here, clearly, the flames were carried by the wind.

214. *Ibid.*, p. 25.

215. *Ibid.*, p. 27.

216. *Ibid.*, p. 28.

217. *Ibid.*, pp. 15-16.

218. *Ibid.*, p. 22.

219. *Ibid.*, p. 24.

220. *Ibid.*, p. 25.

221. *Ibid.*, p. 26.

222. *Ibid.*, p. 28.

223. *Ibid.*, p. 29.

224. *Ibid.*, p. 31.

225. *Ibid.*, p. 35.

226. *Ibid.*, p. 36.

227. *Ibid.*, p. 37.

228. *Ibid.*, p. 39.

229. *Ibid.*, p. 40.

230. *Ibid.*, p. 44.

231. *Ibid.*, p. 46. This witness, later in the same declaration, rectified the time for the ending of the bombing, fixing it at seven-thirty.

232. *Ibid.*, p. 48.

233. *Ibid.*, p. 49.

234. In the duchess of Atholl's examination of *Guernica: The Official Report,* she noted that none of the pressmen who visited Guernica that night or on the following day heard these explosions (*Searchlight on Spain,* p. 196). The "Report of Inspection," included in *Guernica: The Official Report,* stated, "Very few indeed were the houses destroyed by the action of explosives" (p. 20).

235. *Guernica.*

236. *Guernica: The Official Report,* p. 16.

237. There are no eyewitness accounts of any dynamiting by the Basque forces. There are, on the contrary, declarations that the Basque authorities refused to heed the pleas of home-owners to blow up certain houses to establish a firebreak. (*ibid.,* pp. 24, 25, 31, 41, 46). It is not difficult to imagine today what would have been said about "Basque dynamiters" if these requests had been acted on.

238. *Spectator,* 30 July 1937, p. 209. Letter by Steer.

239. *Guernica: The Official Report,* p. 16.

240. *Ibid.*, pp. 26, 27, 29, 30-31, 31, 32, 35, 36, 38, 41, 43, 45. These references are not always to different houses.

241. *Ibid.*, pp. 10-11.

242. PRO, FO 371/21291, W 8861, folio 236. The report is dated "Bilbao, 28 April 1937."

243. *Guernica: The Official Report,* p. 16. Steer's dispatch on this point is informative. "When I entered Guernica after midnight houses were crashing on either side, and it was utterly impossible even for firemen to enter the center of town" (*Times*, 28 April 1937, p. 17).

244. *Guernica: The Official Report,* p. v.

245. Steer, *op. cit.,* p. 237. See also *Guernica: The Official Report,* p. 46. "That during the bombing the Telephone Exchange was burned, and that he supposes that the service was interrupted."

246. *Guernica: The Official Report,* p. 50.

247. *Ibid.* A librarian said that "he heard . . . that the firemen from Bilbao refused duty" (*ibid.,* p. 35). A baker asserted that "the people did not make up their minds to put out the blaze" and "that the same thing happened with the firemen when they arrived from Bilbao" (*ibid.,* pp. 37-38). An industrial engineer said that police and firemen came from Bilbao, "but that none of them did anything towards extinguishing the fire" (*ibid.,* p. 46). This point of view was contradicted by Steer and by others.

248. Steer, *op. cit.*, p. 244. What was the water pressure in Guernica that night? A bank clerk declared that "one of the explosive bombs cut his water-supply and the main." (*Guernica: The Official Report*, p. 36). A businessman said that the firemen sprayed water on his house for fifteen minutes, then received orders to remove the pump. He tried to bribe them to continue, but they refused (*ibid.*, p. 50). They may well have been discouraged by the immensity of the task and their own lack of resources. This is the conclusion of Talón (*op. cit.*, pp. 43-45).

249. *Guernica: The Official Report*, p. vi.

250. This form of reasoning is deep-rooted in the Spanish Nationalist soul. The Palace of the Infantado in Guadalajara was bombed and set afire by Nationalist planes on 6 December 1936. Francisco Layna Serrano, writing in 1941 of this event, blamed the Republicans for not putting out the flames (*El Palacio del Infantado en Guadalajara*, p. 81).

251. *Guernica: The Official Report*, p. 15.

252. *Spectator*, 30 July 1937, p. 209.

253. *Guernica: The Official Report*, p. iv. Wilson himself was not in agreement with the commissioners concerning the bombing, but perhaps he did not realize this fact. Wilson's biographer Marlowe has overlooked Wilson's contribution to *Guernica: The Official Report*, just as he overlooked the *Observer* article with Wilson's visit to Guernica. It is indeed curious that there was nothing in Wilson's personal papers referring to his preface to the Rebel document.

254. *Ibid.*, p. vii.

255. Kemp, *Mine Were of Trouble*, p. 104. Kemp convalesced at Wilson's home after being wounded in Spain (*ibid.*, p. 202; Wilson, *More Thoughts and Talks*, pp. 182-183).

256. Code, *The Spanish War and Lying Propaganda*, p. 29.

257. Foss and Gerahty, *Spanish Arena*, pp. 438-440.

258. Universidad de Valladolid. *Informe sobre la situación de las provincias vascongadas bajo el dominio rojo-separatista*, p. 39.

259. *Ibid.*, pp. 202-203. The letter is signed by Juan Antonio Llorente and dated August 1937.

260. The "Report" is printed in Spanish, German, English, Italian, and French, which shows that it was intended to be used as propaganda outside Spain; the greater part of the book—the attestations or *actas*—is in Spanish only. There are also 104 plates in the books, four of which concern Guernica in ruins—ruins attributed to burning, never to bombing.

261. The reader will remember that the Burgos Commission considered the fact that the Casa de Juntas was undamaged as proof positive of incendiarism from the ground. For the Valladolid committee, it was positive proof of the compassion of the Nationalist air force. See n. 172. In reality, the Casa de Juntas was not in the center of the town, where the bombing was highly concentrated.

262. Universidad de Valladolid. *Informe sobre la situación de las provincias vascongadas bajo el dominio rojo-separatista*, p. 46. This quotation is taken from the "Report" as given in English.

263. This book is dedicated to Ernest Grimaud de Caux, who was, before and during at least a part of the Spanish Civil War, correspondent in Madrid of the *Times*. His sympathies were doubtless with the Nationalists. In the preface to *Spain's Ordeal*, Sencourt gives special thanks to Professor Allison Peers, to his book *The Spanish Tragedy*, and to the learned quarterly he edited, *Bulletin of Spanish Studies*. He also acknowledged a debt for information received from Sir Walter Maxwell-Scott (pp. vii-viii). A second edition of *Spain's Ordeal* came out in 1940, but I have been unable to consult it.

264. *Spain's Ordeal*, p. 243. "More disquieting still is the fact that when Franco issued his official report which quotes many witnesses, he was able to show that explosions were continued in the period after Mr. Steer's arrival in it [in the report? or in Guernica?], and such was Mr. Steer's demeanour that he was taken by the inhabitants to be the Dean of Canterbury." This is all that Sencourt has to say about *Guernica: The Official Report*. Nowhere does the text of the Burgos report state that Steer was mistaken for the Dean of Canterbury, although some of the inhabitants apparently mistook one of three unidentified Englishmen for the dean (see pp. 50-51). Dean of Canterbury Hewlett Johnson was a strong friend of the Basques and had visited Durango shortly after it was heavily bombed, earlier that same month. If the inhabitants of Guernica, weary and frightened, mistook Steer for the dean, it was probably because he

spoke English and seemed a friend. It is difficult to understand how such an incident, if true, could be held against Steer. Nor is it very clear what Sencourt is trying to prove when he finds "disquieting" the fact that certain witnesses said the explosions continued during the night. In Sencourt's opinion, who was dynamiting what, and why? He could hardly pretend that houses were being blown up. The Burgos commission wrote: "the destruction of Guernica was caused by fire" (p. 15). See n. 234.

265. *Spain's Ordeal*, p. 244.

266. *Ibid.*, p. 247.

267. Sencourt's footnote refers to "*The Times*, 4 May 1937, p. 15d," but he evidently meant the *Times* of the following day, when Holburn's report was published.

268. *Spain's Ordeal*, p. 245.

269. *Ibid.* Sencourt is mixed up in his citations from the press. He quoted in one place the "Havas Agency, repeated in *Le Temps*, 3 May," and in another, *L'Echo de Paris* of the same date, without realizing that both newspapers were using, in one way or another, the same telegram, written by Botto and distributed by Havas.

270. *Ibid.*, pp. 245-246. Sencourt did not seem to comprehend that the priest quoted by James was in reality confirming Steer's report in its important parts. But James did cast doubt on the reports of at least two of the reporters who were in Bilbao, by noting that they "were both young persons, without any such experience" as he himself had had in World War I. But no town was destroyed as was Guernica during the earlier conflict.

271. *Chicago Daily Tribune*, 30 August 1936, p. 1.

272. Marcel Acier, *In Spanish Trenches*, pp. 3-8; Alvah Bessie, *The Heart of Spain*, pp. 83-89; Robert Payne, *The Civil War in Spain*, pp. 96-101; *Somebody Had to Do Something. A Memorial to James Philips Lardner*, pp. 15-23; Hans-Christian Kirsch, *Der spanische Bürgerkrieg in Augenzeugenberichten*, pp. 128-132. This article is usually entitled, "Blood Flows in Badajoz."

273. For other information concerning the work of Mario Neves, see Southworth, *op. cit.*, pp. 182-185.

274. *Spain's Ordeal*, p. 241.

275. This possibility was suggested by Father Joseph B. Code in his pamphlet *The Spanish War and Lying Propaganda*, p. 29.

276. *Op. cit.*, pp. 242-243.

277. *Times*, 6 May 1937, p. 15.

278. *Op. cit.*, p. 243. Sencourt offered, in commenting on this, at worst, printing error, this admonition: "Mr. Steer should have been more careful to avoid giving the impression that he was confused." He also said that there were "discrepancies" between Steer's story and those of the *Star* man and Reuters. In reality, all the news stories sent from Bilbao were in basic agreement and never varied later. Sencourt attacked Steer on another point: "One's doubt is increased by an expression he [Steer] used in the second message which *The Times* printed on May 6: 'Sniff where I might, I could catch no odor of petrol.' . . . But why did Mr. Steer sniff for petrol at all, if he believed that all the roar of flames around him was the work of incendiary bombs?" (p. 242). Steer was doubtless "sniffing" that night because he was a conscientious reporter. One should, moreover, note that this statement by Steer is found in the telegram he sent in reply to London's request for confirmation.

279. *Ibid.*, p. 239.

280. *Ibid.*, p. 237.

281. *Ibid.*, p. 245.

282. *Ibid.*

283. *Ibid.*, p. 243.

284. There were of course exceptions for such special "correspondents" as Jerrold, Lunn, Thorning, Yeats-Brown, Fuller, Palmer, James, and so forth. But these people were usually invited, or came like Tangye, armed with recommendations from Franco's people in London or Washington, or were already known to Bolín.

285. *Ibid.*, pp. 246-247. Sencourt's undocumented assumption that everybody who talked with Steer was lying or crazy is unacceptable. Sencourt's scenario for the events of the night of 26 April demands a *mise en scène* far beyond the possibilities of the time and place; nor is there any evidence that Steer believed just anything he was told in Spain.

286. *Ibid.*, p. 245.

287. *Ibid.* Sencourt also quoted Cardozo to the effect "that the majority of the burned houses . . . showed not the slightest sign of damage by bombing" (*ibid.*, p. 243). But Cardozo had published his book in 1937; in 1938, before the publication of Sencourt's book, *Guernica: the Official Report,* a volume cited by Sencourt, had effectively shown, through numerous references to incendiary bombs on roofs and balconies, that the burned houses themselves were "signs of damage by bombing."

288. *Spanish Arena* was, aside from the normal book outlets, distributed in England by the Catholic Book Club and the Right Book Club. Here is a sample of the political thinking behind the book: "We have shown that Spain was the victim of a vast Communist plot, inspired and controlled by continental Freemasons, largely Jewish, and international agitators, working with certain Spaniards as their tools and assistants, to establish a world domination for the Comintern" (*Spanish Arena,* p. 429). It is legitimate to point out that this anti-Semitic, anti-Masonic and pro-Fascist book was recommended by some of the most prestigious names of England's aristocratic and political world, notably by Lord Halifax, then foreign secretary. Twenty-three members of Parliament were on the committee of the Right Book Club. No publication date is indicated in the book, but the text shows that it was printed shortly after May 1938.

289. The Italian edition, *Arena spagnola,* was published by Mondadori in 1938. Extracts had already appeared in *Corriere della Sera* in August and September of that same year (*Arena spagnola,* p. 18). These details indicate an extremely rapid translation and publication, and an accord predating publication by some weeks at least. The anti-Semitic contents of the book, though already heavy, did not entirely satisfy the Italian converts to the National-Socialist "science," and new anti-Semitic observations were added by the Italian translator. No date is given for the German publication. No other pro-Nationalist book, originally published in England during the civil war, was subsequently published during the war in both Italy and Germany.

290. *Spanish Arena,* pp. 438-440.

291. *The Spanish War and Lying Propaganda,* pp. 28-29. This pamphlet bore the "Nihil obstat" of the Archbishopric of New York.

292. *Ibid.*, p. 29. According to Father Code, this telegram as well as that sent to Steer by the *Times* on 4 May "had been made public by Dr. Thorning" on 23 December 1937 (*ibid.*, p. 29). He also stated that *The New York Times* refused "to place on record the photostatic copy of two telegrams which indicate that *The Times* of London had been the victim of one of its propagandizing reporters" (*ibid.*, p. 28). If the *New York Times* refused to publish the copies of the telegrams, it was doubtless because its editors, knowing more about journalism than Fathers Thorning and Code, evaluated the telegrams at their just value. Father Code also wrote that "these two papers had taken no steps to deny it [Steer's story] until December 26, 1937." Nothing in either the *Times* or the *New York Times* of that date (or of any other) substantiates the assertion of the Jesuit priest. This is probably a reference to Father Thorning's misinterpretation of an article by James. See above.

Chapter 2
The Public Controversy in France

1. Father Onaindia had dined with President Aguirre on the night of 25 April. "The news from the front was not good that day. Some key positions were being abandoned and the president suggested that I go to Marquina on the following day and bring back members of my family because of the danger they could run if they fell into the hands of the *Franquistas*" (Onaindia, *Hombre de paz en la guerra, Capítluos de mi vida,* I, 237). His traveling companion was Florencio Marquiegui, mayor of Deva, who was shortly thereafter captured by the Nationalists and shot. The danger to the Onaindia family was not imaginary. Alberto de Onaindia's brother, the Abbot Celestino de Onaindia, was shot by the Franco forces on the evening of 28 October 1936 in Ondarreta (*Le clergé basque,* pp. 102-103; *Montreal Daily Star,* 30 April 1937, p. 41, UP Interview with Alberto de Onaindia).

2. Onaindia, *op. cit.*, pp. 238-240. This account agrees with the known interviews Onaindia gave the press in France.

3. Father Onaindia had documentation that permitted him to requisition transport (conversation with Father Onaindia).

4. An air attack on the Bilbao airport prevented Father Onaindia from leaving for Paris on the afternoon of 27 April (Onaindia, op. cit., p. 244).

5. "A curious incident: the world press published my declarations and presented them, each according to his manner. Each one emphasized the aspect which he found interesting, without always limiting himself to objective truth. Naturally, all the production of journalistic fantasy was placed in my mouth. It was my first experience with international journalism. Then I understood how difficult it was to know truth exactly in its details and specific circumstances" (*ibid.*, pp. 246-247).

It is not very clear to which interviews Onaindia is referring. His own recent account does not differ greatly from those published in 1937. It is probable that he was upset more by sensational headlines than by the contents of the reportages. The UP account also contained Onaindia's accusation that he had seen "blood-crazed Moors move through a town at night, raping wives and daughters of the innocent." It seems improbable that Onaindia either *saw* this or said that he had seen it.

6. See *Daily Herald* (p. 2); *Daily News* (p. 6); *Chicago Daily News* (p. 1); *Montreal Daily Star* (p. 41); *La Prensa* (p. 8)—all of 30 April 1937.

7. PRO, FO 371/21292, W 9579, folio 187.

8. *La Prensa*, 1 May 1937, p. 1.

9. *L'Aube*, 30 April-1 May 1937, p. 1. A reprint can be found in *Esprit*, June 1937, pp. 445-456. For a study of the political role of *L'Aube*, see Francoise Mayeur, *L'Aube: Étude d'un journal d'opinion*. The Guernica incident, as dealt with in *L'Aube*, is examined on p. 135, but the Onaindia interview is not mentioned.

10. *L'Aube*, 6 May 1937, p. 1.

11. Conversations, Southworth with Onaindia. It would seem certain that in 1937 Father Onaindia was not too well acquainted with foreign news agencies. He stated: "I confirm what has been published by the Havas Agency. Any other commentaries or evaluations published by the press have been made under the personal responsibilities of the journalists who have signed them." But the UP article was expressly signed with Onaindia's name. Does it not seem probable that this would be the interview he was guaranteeing? Since neither the UP article nor, apparently, that of Havas was published in France, it is doubtful that Onaindia had seen either when he made his declaration.

12. *La Libre Belgique*, 1 May 1937, p. 3. This Belgain daily was described as a "conservative Catholic newspaper, which has always adopted an ultra-Francoist position" (*ED*, 6 June 1937, p. 4).

13. *L'Echo d'Alger*, 4 May 1937, p. 3. There are slight editorial differences between these two articles attributed to Havas, but they are the same basic dispatch. Both the Brussels and the Algiers printings were sent from Paris, but the Brussels story was dated 29 April and the Algiers story, 3 May. The latter date could easily have been altered by an editor in Algiers.

14. Havas might have felt that since *L'Aube* had printed an Onaindia interview, it was hardly news. But *L'Aube* was a small-circulation newspaper, and nothing shows that the Havas interview was not given before that of Jean Richard in *L'Aube*. No sign of this Havas dispatch has been found in *La Nación* of Buenos Aires, certainly one of Havas' most important foreign customers. However, on 2 May, the newspaper published a comment by its military commentator Colonel (R) Carlos A. Gómez, on "the declarations of a Basque Canon who went to Paris to complain of the bombing of Guernica, which act we believe to be a fable invented by the incendiaries themselves to inflame the Basque Nationalists" (*La Nación,* 2 May 1937, p. 2; also Carlos A. Gomez, *La guerra de España* (1936-1939), I, 251-252).

15. *L'Aube*, 19 May 1937, p. 1.

16. *Nieuwe Rotterdamsche Courant*, 30 April 1937, p. 5.

17. *La France de Bordeaux et du Sud-Ouest*, 1 May 1937, p. 3. The article came from Paris and was dated 29 April.

18. The similarities merely suggest that the person who wrote the interview was present at the same news conference as that attended by the Havas man.

19. *L'Humanite,* 5 May 1937, p. 3. This article was copyrighted by *L'Humanité* and the author. Such a procedure would not have been used if the newspaper had not thought the interview to be sensational news. Therefore, no signs of a Havas interview with Onaindia had been perceived by the editors. An interview had appeared in *L'Aube* five days previously, but the article had not given Onaindia's name. Moreover, few people who read *L'Aube* also read *L'Humanité,* and vice versa.

20. *Le drame d'un peuple incompris. La guerre au pays basque* (1937), pp. 70-75; (1938), pp. 78-83. "Víctor Montserrat" was the pseudonym of the abbot Jean Tarragó.

21. *Times, Glasgow Herald, Manchester Guardian,* all dated 3 May 1937. The introduction in the *Times* read: "The following details of his [Onaindia's] report were received yesterday by the London Delegation of the Basque Government." This information was forwarded to *La Prensa* by UP, despite the fact that the agency had already cabled the first interview with Father Onaindia (*La Prensa,* 3 May 1937, p. 7).

22. *Guernica.* This booklet is partly in English and partly in Basque; it was also published in French and Basque, and probably also in Spanish and Basque. This edition contains an English-language translation of Onaindia's statement; it is more complete than that issued by the Basque delegation in London, and is not the same translation.

23. The Bordeaux newspaper frequently published items on the Spanish Civil War, of pro-Republican tendency, which could only have come from l'Agence Espagne. See article on Father Arzuaga, 13 May 1937, p. 3, mentioned below. L'Agence Espagne was inaugurated in Paris in October 1936, according to D. W. Pike (*La Presse francaise a la veille de la seconde guerre mondiale,* p. 21).

24. *Guernica: The Official Report,* pp. 2-3.

25. *La Destruction de Guernica,* pp. 11-12. No source is given for this statement, although most of the other articles are credited to one publication or another.

26. Jerrold wrote: "Nor is the case for his [Onaindia's] veracity improved by the discovery that he is the author of another account of the bombardment appearing under another signature and confirming that which appeared under his own name" *Tablet,* 5 June 1937, p. 801). This reference is an ill-intentioned interpretation of an article in *Catholic Herald,* 14 May 1937, p. 1. See n. 63.

27. René Rémond, in the preface to Mayeur's study of *L'Aube* (p. ix). Mayeur noted in her introduction that the newspaper "never had as many as twenty-thousand subscribers before the war" (p. 1).

28. *L'Aube,* 30 April-1 May 1937, p. 1. The newspaper was never quoted approvingly in the rightist Catholic press, but was at times in the left press. See *La Dépêche,* Toulouse, 30 April 1937, where the catholic journal's remarks on Guernica are cited.

29. Conversations, Southworth with Onaindia. José Antonio de Aguirre told of this trip, without revealing the name of Onaindia, in a lecture given in Santiago, Chile, 3 September 1942. He referred to Onaindia simply as "an illustrious Basque Canon." Onaindia was sent to Rome to pose this problem to the Vatican: "if the Basques, in defending their rights, did well or not; if morally, they were on the right path." Mgr. Pizzardo replied, "after several days of study, during which the Basque case was submitted to an examination by theologians and moralists, as follows: 'Morally, there is nothing for which to reproach the Basques.'" But an unnamed Vatican functionary intervened with: "It is exact that morally there is nothing for which to reproach the Basques, but politically, they are mistaken, because you have chosen the path of those who are going to lose." Onaindia then replied: "Sir, let us hope that this war in which we are involved will end, and then that other war, of which ours is but the forewarning; and on the day that that other war ends, we shall then see who has taken the right path and who has taken the wrong path." (José Antonio de Aguirre y Lecube, *Cinco conferencias,* pp. 138-139). Canon Onaindia, doubtless through discretion, does not repeat the final part of this conversation in his later account of his trip to the Vatican (*op. cit.,* pp. 75-90).

30. Onaindia, *op. cit.,* p. 233, and conversations with Father Onaindia.

31. *Montreal Daily Star,* 30 April 1937, p. 41. See also *La Prensa,* 30 April 1937, p. 8, where the above statement is said to have been made in Paris. The interview in *La Prensa* was the most complete version of the UP dispatch. There Onaindia was said to have shown a letter he was going to send to Cardinal Gomá. Onaindia stated: "I believe it my duty to tell him of this abominable crime and to ask him to use his influence to obtain a promise from the Nationalist leaders to change these barbarous methods."

32. PRO, FO 371/21292 W 9579, folios 186-187. Mgr. Mugica wrote to Onaindia on 30 April 1937, and the letter showed his belief that Guernica had indeed been bombed (Onaindia, *op. cit.*, pp. 255-256). Cardinal Gomá replied to Onaindia on 5 May. The letter of a militarist, thought Onaindia, who answered with a ten-page letter on 17 May (Onaindia, *op. cit.*, pp. 253-255).

33. PRO, FO 371/21292 W 9579, folio 188.

34. *La Prensa*, 30 April 1937. No mention of this incident has been found in the French press.

35. *Ibid.*, 2 May 1937. The news was sent from Paris by UP. No similar story has been found in the French press. Once again, Havas failed to report an interesting development in the Guernica dossier.

36. PRO, FO 371/21292 W 9579, folios 187-188.

37. *La Prensa*, 2 May 1937.

38. *Ibid.*, 6 May 1937. No similar information has been seen in the French press.

39. PRO, FO 371/21292, folios 186-187.

40. *Ibid.*, folio 184. Copies of these documents were given to Osborne by the "English Jesuit," but not sent on to London. Osborne opined: "I imagine these documents to be genuine, but I cannot, of course, vouch for them."

41. *Ibid.*, folio 185.

42. *El clero vasco, fiel al Gobierno de la República, se dirige al Sumo Pontífice, para hacer constar que la vandálica destrucción de Durango y Guernica se debió exclusivamente a la acción de los aviones alemanes* (This pamphlet, published by Ediciones Españolas in Spanish, French, English, and Italian, 16 leaves, 15 x 10 cm., on thin paper, was probably destined for propaganda in the Rebel zone); *Times*, 11 June 1937; *FWOBC*, pp. 51-52; *El clero y los católicos vasco-separatistas y el movimiento nacional*, pp. 85-87 [this latter book is generally attributed to Constantino Bayle, S.J.] ; Rafael G.[arcía] García de Castro, *La tragedia espiritual de Vizcaya*, pp. 254-259. This latter book says that the manifesto was published in *Euzkadi*, semiofficial organ of the Bilbao government on 11 June—that is, one month after its date—and concluded that this delay covered a sinister maneuver (pp. 261-262). However, it is evident that the text was made public only after the delegation to Rome had returned. This was simple courtesy toward the Vatican. G. Garcia de Castro's book is interesting because of the fact that he was a priest in the Bilbao zone during the last few months of the war in the Basque country; although published in 1938 in Franco Spain, the book takes an obscure position concerning the destruction of Guernica.

For Father G. García de Castro, "the ruins of the Biscay towns [were] caused almost in their entirety by the hordes which fought at Aguirre's side" (*op. cit.*, p. 97). He praised rather than excoriated the work of the Nationalist air force. "The National airforce inaugurated its very brilliant campaign bombing the mountains surrounding Biscay; and that frightful noise which had begun on a Sunday of March, at four in the afternoon, would continue dinning in our ears almost without ceasing until the triumphant entry of Franco's hosts into Bilbao" (*op. cit.*, p. 293). Hugh Thomas mistakenly wrote: "Twenty Basque priests, of whom nine were eye-witnesses of the bombing, and including the Vicar-General of the diocese, wrote to the Pope" (*op. cit.*, (1961), pp. 419-420). Ten of the priests who signed the document were eyewitnesses to bombings in the Basque country, but only one was an eyewitness to the bombing of Guernica.

43. *ED*, 17 June 1937, p. 1.

44. Conversations, Southworth with Onaindia; Aguirre, *Cinco conferencias pronunciadas en un viaje por América*, pp. 141-144.

45. Conversations, Southworth with Onaindia. Thomas, *op. cit.*, n. p. 420; Onaindia, *op. cit.*, pp. 257, 263.

46. *Times*, 11 June 1937; *L'Aube*, 11 June 1937.

47. P. Altabella Gracia, *El catolicismo de los nacionalistas vascos*, pp. 38-41. The entire text of the statement is on pp. 37-43. Here the paper is dated simply, "Bilbao, June 1937." A great part of this text can be found in *El clero y los católicos vasco-separatistas y el movimiento nacional*, pp. 89-92. Constantino Bayle, S.J., in his pamphlet ¿*Qué pasa en España?* p. 72, says that Galbarriatu's document was published in *Gaceta del Norte*, Bilbao, on 11 July 1937.

Crónica de la guerra española, no. 62, p. 42, states that the document was addressed to Cardinal Gomá, but the authors of this work—among them, Ricardo de la Cierva—have probably confused this statement with the latter one of the Vitoria chapter. See below.

48. Elosegi, *Quiero morir por algo*, p. 183. Fourteen Basque priests were shot by the Nationalist authorities in the early months of the fighting (Antonio Montero Moreno, *Historia de la persecución religiosa en España, 1936-1939*, p. 77). Many more were imprisoned and exiled (*Le clergé basque*, pp. 47-49, 109-143). Especially, Onaindia, *op. cit.*, pp. 97-123.

49. Onaindia, *op. cit.*, p. 245.

50. PRO, FO 371/21334, W 10222. If this document is representative of English diplomatic and press reactions in Rome, these would seem to be strongly inclined toward the Fascist version of Spanish events. This document and its appended Foreign Office comments also show that not everyone at the *Times* or the Foreign Office was on Steer's side. One person noted that the diplomatic correspondent of the *Times* had told someone at the Foreign Office that the newspaper "suspected their messages from Bilbao of not being objective."Another remarked that Steer "is definitely sentimental and of Left tendencies," adding: "This should be remembered."

51. *NYT*, 5 May 1937.

52. *ED*, 27 June 1937, p. 3.

53. *AF*, 16 May 1937. This text of the declaration of the cathedral chapter of Valladolid was taken from *El Diario Vasco*, of San Sebastián, 7 May 1937.

54. *HA*, 7 May 1937. According to the quotations from the chapter declaration, cited in *L'Action Francaise* of 16 May 1937, p. 1., the declaration had been sent to the chief of state (Franco), Queipo de Llano, the English catholic publication *Catholic (Herald?)*, the FET of Valladolid, and some local newspapers. It was in neither *ABC* of Seville nor *Heraldo de Aragón*. The Spanish Nationalists made few references to Father Onaindia.

55. *Times*, 3 May 1937, p. 13. The error was apparently made by the office of the London delegation of the Basque government, which distributed the text attributed to Father Onaindia. But in the pamphlet in English, *Guernica*, which reproduces the same text, Father Onaindia is given his proper title of "Canon."

56. *Tablet*, 5 June 1937, p. 801.

57. *Spain and the Christian Front*, p. 20. Lunn also quoted Jerrold's observation about Father Onaindia in his own book *Spanish Rehearsal*, p. 231.

58. *Spain's Pilgrimage of Grace*, p. 11.

59. *Universe*, 7 May 1937, p. 1; *ED*, 23 May 1937, p. 4.

60. *ED*, 6 June 1937, p. 1. Dom Luigi Sturzo stressed the historical similarities between the sinking of the *Lusitania* by German submarines in 1915 and the destruction of Guernica (*ibid.*, 20 June 1937, p. 1). Republican Foreign Minister, Julio Alvarez del Vayo, also saw this parallel (*Journal des Nations*, 5 May 1937, p. 5). The comparison was troubling to the Fascist powers, who remembered that the *Lusitania* incident had been one of the emotional factors that led to United States intervention in World War I. *Gringoire* wrote, 14 May 1937, p. 1: "A hypocritical campaign, skillfully orchestrated, seeks to convince world public opinion that the holy city of the Basques, Guernica, was set afire by the Nationalists. An effort is being made to create a movement similar to that which, after the torpedoing of the *Lusitania*, determined the entry of the United States, at the side of France. A bagatelle, as is evident. It has now been proved that the Marxists and separatists dynamited the 'Mecca of the Basques' and set it on fire."

61. *ED*, 20 June 1937, p. 1.

62. *Catholic Herald*, 7 May 1937, pp. 1, 9. A subheading spoke of "Basque Priest's conflicting reports." Nothing in the text confirms this "conflict."

63. *Ibid.*, 14 May 1937, p. 1. A headline read: BASQUE PRIEST'S TWO STORIES," and the newspaper underlined the fact that the interview in *L'Aube* was milder than other interviews credited to Father Onaindia. This difference between *L'Aube* and the more sensational press of the news agencies is easy to understand. See nn. 5, 26. *L'Aube*, 12 May 1937, p. 1, mentioned with satisfaction the fact that the *Catholic Herald* had reproduced the interview of Jean Richard; *L'Aube* did not realize that the English Catholic editors were going to disavow the report of Father Onaindia. Onaindia had one other encounter with the *Catholic*

Herald, in October 1941, in wartime England, while he was delivering a lecture on the Basque country and the Spanish Civil War at a Dominican convent. When Onaindia had finished speaking, the editor of the *Catholic Herald,* Mr. F. A. Fulford, rose and denounced before the assemblage the "Red canon" and the Basque attitude during the civil war. Onaindia then, for the first time, exposed publicly his 1936 visit to the Vatican and his interviews with Papal authorities. An account of the declaration of Onaindia was published in the *Catholic Herald.* Cardinal Arthur Hinsley, archbishop of Westminster and primate of the Catholic church of England and Wales, then entered the fray. "This high prelate was madly *franquista.* . . . He made it known that from then on nothing favorable to the Basques or unfavorable to Franco should be published in the English Catholic press. . . . Days later Mr. Fulford came to see me. He was sad and depressed. He was the father of six or seven children, and he told me that because of the article published about my lecture he was forced to abandon the weekly and go to Freetown, British Guiana, where he would continue to work as a Catholic journalist" (Onaindia, *op. cit.,* pp. 89-90). An attack against Onaindia, who is, however, not mentioned by name, and which undoubtedly had its origin in the offices of one of the English Catholic weeklies, is reported with satisfaction by the English Catholic doctor and writer Halliday Sutherland (*Spanish Journey,* pp. 113-114).

64. *Catholic Times,* 30 April 1937, p. 12.

65. *Ibid.,* 7 May 1937. This publication was fascinated by the detail in the news stories that sheep had been machine-gunned by the airplanes. The readers were told that this was impossible, for there were no sheep left in the region to be killed. These editors were sadly misinformed of conditions in the Basque country. In an editorial (p. 12) the publication declared that the reports on the Guernica air raid constituted "the biggest hoax of the war."

66. Onaindia, *op. cit.,* pp. 23-38; *ED,* 27 June 1937, p. 3: *Montreal Daily Star,* 30 April 1937.

67. Mgr. Gandasegui died on 17 May 1937 (*ABC,* Seville, 18 May 1937, p. 11). for the bombing of Galdácano, see *Times,* 20 May 1937.

68. *La Liberté du Sud-Ouest,* 27 May 1937, p. 1. The article was written by Alfred Camdessus and given three columns on the first page.

69. *ED,* 27 June 1937, p. 3.

70. An overwhelming majority of the Spanish priesthood sided with the Rebels, but those in the Nationalist zone who did not were killed, imprisoned, or exiled. It is thus that several thousand priests were killed on the Republican side, but in the final accounting each side killed the priests who sympathized with the enemy, just as it killed other Spaniards. If there were more Nationalist priests killed than Republican priests, it was in part because there were more of them. Very few priests took an anti-Nationalist position, outside the Basque country, but when one did, if he could not be shot or imprisoned, he was treated as was Father Onaindia. He was thrown out of the Spanish Church. This was what happened to Father Leocadio Lobo, a Madrid priest, who was declared "no longer in good standing" when he took the side of the Republic. This did not prevent him from ending his years protected by the Archbishopric of New York, never noted for liberalism. See *AF,* 16 May 1937, p. 1, for a denunciation of Father Lobo. For details of the unjust treatment handed out by ecclesiastical authorities to the Republican sympathizer Franciscan Father Luis de Sarasola, see Onaindia, *op. cit.,* pp. 83-84. The editors of the wartime writings of Cardinal Gomá exulted in informing the reader that Father Arzuaga was expelled from the Jesuit order for opposing the pro-Nationalist position of the cardinal. See Goma, *Por Dios y por España,* p. 82

71. Onaindia, *op. cit.,* p. 251; *ED,* 23 May 1937, pp. 1-2.

72. PRO, FO 371/21292, W 9579, folios 184-185.

73. The French Jesuit monthly *Études,* 20 May 1937, p. 540, in a moderate note concerning what had happened at Guernica, observed: "The Bilbao government accused the German airforce in the Nationalist service of causing the destruction; head-quarters in Salamanca charged the destruction to Basque militia, who were said to have burned the town before evacuating it. This second version is clearly contradicted by the statements of Basques who were eyewitnesses, among them, two priests." The editors of *Etudes* were also impressed by Eden's Commons statement on May 7. See Book II, part 1, chap. 3.

74. *ED,* 7 February 1937, p. 1.

75. *Op. cit.*, p. 246.

76. Preface by Jacques Maritain to *Aux origines d'une tragédie*, by Alfredo Mendizábal, p. 55. This statement did not appear in *La Nouvelle Revue Francaise,* June 1937, where Maritain's article was first published, but was added later, with the date of August 1937, when Maritain was reading the proofs of the preface.

77. *L'Humanité,* 5 May 1937, p. 3. This meeting was held in the house of Joseph Ageorges, Paris correspondent of the Brussels Catholic daily *La Libre Belgique.* He wrote an article, probably before this reunion, in which he stated his personal conviction that Guernica had been bombed by the Germans. "The bombing of Guernica by German airplanes has produced a distressing impression in France. The number of newspapers which have expressed their indignation is considerable.[?] Just as one must stigmatize the abominable crimes committed by the Red side, so must one blame the excesses committed by the Nationals. . . . Does not the Catholic journalist have the right to beseech his Catholic brothers, wherever they may be, to act like Christians? It is for this reason that we persist in believing and in crying out loud that the German planes, in destroying a village without defense, a village which was moreover a respected spiritual center, have committed a crime against the Christian order and that can hardly be the cause which General Franco and his partisans mean to defend" (*La Libre Belgique,* 1 May 1937). Onaindia later wrote, concerning Liebermann's article, "The contents of the article were exact and corresponded to reality" (Onaindia, *Experiencias del exilio,* p. 297).

78. *L'Aube,* 6 May 1937, p. 1. *La Croix,* 8 May 1937, p. 2. This was the first mention of Father Onaindia in *La Croix.* Talón completely misunderstood the reason for Onaindia's statement on the article in *L'Humanité,* attributing it to what Talón considered to be errors of fact in the interview (*op. cit.,* pp. 160-161).

79. *AF,* 6 May 1937.

80. *Ibid.,* p. 1.

81. *Le Nouvelliste de Bretagne.* Maine-Normandie-Anjou. Quotidien regional catholique. 6 May 1937, p. 1.

82. *Ibid.,* 8 May 1937, p. 2. *La Liberté du Sud-Ouest,* 27 May 1937, p. 1, repeated Terriére's doubts as to the existence of Onaindia expressed on 6 May, but did not take notice of the correction of 8 May.

83. *La Croix,* 4 May 1937, p. 1.

84. *Le Figaro,* 5 May 1937, p. 1. The fence-straddling example of, first *La Croix,* then *Le Figaro,* may well have been the inspiration of *Le Nouvelliste de Bretagne* seen above.

85. *L'Aube,* 6 May 1937, p. 1.

86. *Ibid.,* 8 May; *La Croix,* 8 May; *Le Petit Parisien,* 10 May; *La Vie catholique,* 15 May, 1937.

87. Father Onaindia was not pleased with what *L'Osservatore Romano* was writing about the Basque country and in his letter to Msgr. Múgica said that it was impossible to get the truth into the Press of the right, observing that "even *L'Osservatore Romano* will say who knows what" and suggested that Msgr. Múgica should speak to the directors of the Vatican newspaper (PRO, FO 371/21292, W 9579, folio 189).

88. *L'Osservatore Romano,* 9 May 1937, p. 6. This Nationalist report of a recent bombing of Valladolid, causing 148 casualties, was a pure invention. See Book II, part 2, n. 137.

89. AF, 10 May 1937, p. 2.

90. The Committee for Civil and Religious Peace in Spain was presided over by Maritain, and the secretary general was Claude Bourdet. The committee had addressed a telegram to the cardinal, secretary of state of the Vatican (Pacelli), on the occasion of the destruction of Guernica, saying that the Committee,"PROFOUNDLY DISTURBED BOMBINGS DURANGO, GUERNICA, DANGER EXTERMINATION CATHOLIC BASQUE PEOPLE, BEGS HOLY FATHER RECALL CHRISTIAN PRINCIPLES AND PROTECT NONCOMBATANTS." See Sierra Bustamente, *Euzkadi,* p. 15; Gutiérrez, *Sentido y causas de la tragedia española,* p. 164.

91. *L'Osservatore Romano,* 19 May 1937, p. 1. There was no reference to Guernica, either in the extracts from Maritain's letter or in the newspaper's commentary on that letter, but the title on the article was the same as that used by the newspaper on 9 May, concerning the 8 May manifesto: "Per i noncombattenti."

92. *La Croix,* 19, 22 May 1937.

93. *Sept,* 14 May 1937, p. 6; Aline Coutrot, *Un courant de la pensée catholique. L'hebdomadaire "Sept" (Mars 1934-Aout 1937),* pp. 212-213.

94. *Sept,* 28 May 1937, p. 20. F. Mauriac, *Mémoires politiques,* p. 81; Coutrot, *op. cit.,* p. 213. Coutrot wrote: "These few lines express the point of view not only of F. Mauriac but of all those connected with the publication, a point of view which situated its reflection and its action concerning the Basques on the plane of charity." She also wrote: "This attitude of *Sept* concerning the Basques is not guided by political considerations, but by a sentiment of pity" (*op. cit.,* p. 212). *Sept* was suppressed in August 1937 by orders of the Holy See (Coutrot, *op. cit.,* p. 287-302). Father Bernadot, the leading personality behind the magazine, told Father Onaindia in 1953 that he was in part responsible for the disappearance of the most liberal of the official Catholic publications in France (Conversations, Southworth-Onaindia). Bernadot doubtless meant that the testimony of Onaindia had forced the liberal French Catholics still further into a position of opposition to the Vatican on the question of Spain.

95. *Je Suis Partout,* 23 July 1937, p. 4. *La verdad sobre la guerra española,* p. 105. *Je Suis Partout* had taken a pro-Nationalist position concerning Guernica from the beginning. René Richard wrote in the issue of 1 May: "The destruction of Guernica bears too clearly their [of the anarchists] brand for one to hesitate to attribute it to them, even in the absence of other proofs" (p. 9). A week later he wrote: "If the destruction of Guernica, mendaciously attributed to the Nationalist airforce, is a crime, those who have risen to protest this crime should direct their indignation against those proved guilty: the Red incendiaries" (*ibid.,* 8 May, p. 9). The article by Fathers Carro and Beltrán de Heredia was later incorporated, under the title, "Respuesta al manifiesto de un grupo de escritores franceses," in the booklet *La Verdad sobre la guerra española,* of Dr. Carro, pp. 95-112. See pp. 102-103 for lines quoted. A note in this Spanish edition read: "We first published this Reply to the Group of French Catholic Writers in Rome, and we reproduce it again because we believe it still in the news, in spite of the capture of Bilbao and its province. The novelist Mauriac and the philosopher Maritain, who signed the manifesto, have continued writing fantasies about the Spanish war. Once again it is seen that the confession of an error is an act of sincerity and humility that is not within the reach of all minds and of all hearts" (*ibid.,* p. 97). An Opus Dei intellectual, Vicente Marrero, commenting favorably on the work of Father Carro and Father Beltran de Heredia, described them "as excellent historians of universal fame" (*La guerra espanola y el trust de cerebros,* pp. 195-196).

96. *La verdad sobre la guerra española,* pp. 81-82.

97. Steer, *op. cit.,* p. 385.

98. *La verdad sobre la guerra española.* "Epístola fraternal al 'Comité francés [sic] por la paz civil y religiosa en España," by Dr. V. Carro, pp. 113-118.

99. *La Libre Belgique,* 20 August 1937, p. 1.

100. But one Spanish text of this document has been found, in G. García de Castro, *op. cit.,* pp. 261-265. Extracts are given in *El clero y los católicos vasco-separatistas y el movimiento nacional,* pp. 87-88n. This paper was never used by the Nationalists in their propaganda. It was given to the Brussels newspaper by count van der Burch, who possibly thought its affirmations more significant than they were.

101. *La Libre Belgique,* 20 August 1937, p. 1. This text gives the impression that the newspaper had photographs of anarchists with dynamite in their hands.

102. *Je Suis Partout,* 3 September 1937, p. 1.

103. Estelrich, *op. cit.,* p. 135. Though published anonymously in France, the book very shortly thereafter appeared in Argentina and Italy with the author's name. It was also published anonymously in Rumania and Czechoslovakia.

104. *La Nouvelle Revue Francaise* (hereafter *NRF*), 1 July 1937, "De la guerre sainte," pp. 21-37. Preface to Mendizábal, *Aux origines d'une tragedie,* pp. 7-56. Maritain's doubts concerning Franco's Holy War were expressed again in 1947 (*Raison et raisons,* pp. 272-273).

105. Preface to Mendizábal, *Aux origenes d'une tragédie.* This does not appear in Maritain's original essay in 1 July 1937.

106. *NRF,* 1 July 1937, p. 31. Mendizábal, *op. cit.,* p. 43.

107. *NRF,* 1 July 1937, p. 31, n. 2. Mendizábal, *op. cit.,* p. 43, n. 2.

108. Joubert, *La guerre d'Espagne et le catholicisme (Réponse a M. Jacques Maritain,*

pp. 20, 32-33. Les Amis de l'Espagne Nouvelle published a number of pro-Nationalist pamphlets. Joubert gave as the sources of his information on Guernica, *La persécution religieuse en Espagne*. This work, published anonymously, was now openly credited to Estelrich by Franco's friends in France. The Jesuit Father Ignacio G[onzález] Menéndez-Reigada was at this time confessor to General Franco (García Venero, *Falange en la guerra de España: la unificación y Hedilla*, p. 307). He had made this declaration about the "holy war" in an article entitled "La guerra nacional española ante la moral y el derecho," published in *La ciencia tomista*, Fasc. 1 and 2, in Salamanca early in 1937, and later widely distributed as a pamphlet under the same title as the original article. Maritain had seen the article in *La ciencia tomista*. When Father G. Menéndez-Reigada saw Maritain's article in *La Nouvelle Revue Française*, he answered with another article in *La ciencia tomista*, "Acerca de la 'guerra santa.' Contestación a M. J. Maritain," which was also reproduced in pamphlet form under that title.

109. *L'Espagne de Franco. Synthèse de trois conférences données du 17 Janvier au 10 Février 1938*, par H. Joubert, pp. 32-33. This pamphlet, like the preceding one by Joubert, was sponsored by Les Amis de l'Espagne Nouvelle. Later that year of 1938, Joubert spoke again on Spain and Guernica. The town had been bombed, but "The town was methodically destroyed by the Reds before their retreat. There is an essential difference between the sporadic effects of a bombing and the sytematic incendiarism of a town, house by house" (*La Tragédie espagnole. Conférence donnée au Théatre des Ambassadeurs, le mercredi 27 Avril 1938 par . . .*, p. 24). The chief speaker was Henry Lémery, senator and former Minister of Justice. Also speaking on this occasion were Generals Duval and Jouart, and in the printed text Joubert changed uniforms, becoming also a "general."

110. Maritain, *Questions de conscience* (Paris, 1938), p. 278. Spoken during his toast at the banquet of the Amis de *Temps Présent*, 17 February 1938.

111. *Questions de conscience*, p. 223. More than three hundred persons were killed in the bombing of Granollers, near Barcelona, behind the Republican front, on 2 June 1938.

112. *Sentido y causas de la tragedia española*, pp. 167-168; references to Maritain, pp. 101-191, 230-243. For Gutiérrez, Maritain was a "furious racist Jew" (p. 152), a "converted Jew" (p. 164). The truth is that Maritain was a Protestant converted to Catholicism. The tactic of demolishing the moral authority of Maritain by accusing him of having a Jewish origin was widely used in Spanish Nationalist circles, especially by Ramón Serrano Suñer in his discourse celebrating the first anniversary of the capture of Bilbào by the Spanish Rebels, on 19 June 1938. See Southworth, *op. cit.*, pp. 141-142. The persistence of the belief in Maritain's Jewish origin, and in the relevance of the belief as an explanation of his stand on the Spanish Civil War, can be seen in the fact that Talón repeats it in 1971 (*op. cit.*, p. 158).

113. Gutiérrez, *op. cit.*, pp. 165-166.

114. *Ibid.*, pp. 168-169.

115. Mgr. Franceschi disembarked in Gibraltar. He had been sent by the Argentine primate, Cardinal Copello, with ornaments for two hundred churches "destroyed by the Reds." See *ABC*, Seville, 23 April 1937; *HA*, 27 April 1937. He went on to Salamanca, where he delivered to the bishop of Salamanca twenty-seven cases of church ornaments (*HA*, 4 May 1937). A full six-column headline announced: "MONSIGNOR FRANCESCHI COMES TO SPAIN IN REPRESENTATION OF THE CATHOLICS OF THE ARGENTINE." See also *HA*, 2, 13 May 1937.

116. Franceschi, *En el humo del incendio*, pp. 159-161. This article, entitled "The Eclipse of Morality," was sent from Vitoria on 11 May 1937. The meeting where Lord Cecil and Pierre Cot spoke in London was held at the Albert Hall, under the auspices of the League of Nations Union (Toynbee, *Survey of International Affairs* (1937), II, 160). Franceschi's first article from Spain was from Málaga, dated 22 April 1937 (*En el humo del incendio*, p. 151).

117. Juan Pascal de Orkoya, *La verdad sobre la destrucción de Gernika. Réplica a Monseñor Gustavo J. Franceschi*, p. 31.

118. *En el humo del incendio*, p. 203, article dated 9 June 1937.

119. Gustavo J. Franceschi, *El movimiento español y el criterio católico*, p. 3. This pamphlet was later incorporated into *En el humo del incendio*, pp. 217-267, with certain changes.

120. *El movimiento español y el criterio católico*, p. 25; *En el humo del incendio*, pp. 258-259.

121. *El movimiento español y el criterio católico,* p. 28. This quotation does not appear in the essay of the same title, incorporated into *En el humo del incendio.* Franceschi was correcting the proofs of his pamphlet when the July 1937 number of *La Nouvelle Revue Française* reached Buenos Aires. He replied to Maritain in a long footnote, in which he again thought he had found the explanation of Maritain's attitude in the fact that he was a Frenchman. In his article, Maritain had written that "the war in Spain . . . gravely threatens our country in certain fundamental conditions of its foreign security" (*Aux origines d'une tragédie,* p. 50).

122. *Pope Pius XI and World Peace,* p. 265n. Clonmore told an anecdote to show the humanitarian effort of the Nationalist air force and, incidentally, how Guernica was destroyed. "A Basque lay-brother in Rome received a letter from his sister, a Basque working-woman, living in Ermua, a small town occupied by the Nationalists a few days before Guernica. After describing the indignities suffered by her family during the Red occupation she told how Ermua was being prepared by the Reds for mining when a Nationalist bombardment cut off the electricity supply. 'Otherwise,' she wrote, 'the Reds would have blown it all to pieces like they did to Eibar and Guernica.' " It is interesting to see that this testimony from two unnamed persons, neither of whom was in Guernica, outweighed all the other evidence for Lord Clonmore. Clonmore also cited Jerrold's article in the *Tablet* of 4 June 1937.

123. The Vatican had forbidden Catholics to read *L'Action Française* in 1926, and the interdiction was lifted only on 15 July 1939 (Weber, *L'Action Française,* pp. 262-282).

124. *AF,* 19 May 1937, p. 2. This dispatch was datelined Bermeo, 18 May, retransmitted from Bayonne by telegraph. Héricourt wrote four books on the Spanish Civil War; he did not mention Guernica in any of them.

125. *Ibid.,* 11 May 1937, p. 1.

126. *Ibid.,* 19 May 1937, p. 2.

127. *Ibid.,* 11 May 1937.

128. *Ibid.,* 19 May 1937.

129. *Ibid.,* 14 May 1937. This article contained one of the rare mentions of Steer's 6 May telegram in the right-wing French press. Jacques Delebecque was a Protestant (Weber, *op. cit.,* p. 424).

130. *L'Émancipation Nationale,* 15 May 1937, p. 3. Salmon's letter was addressed to two of Doriot's collaborators, Paul Guitard and Camille Fégy. Salmon did not mention this incident or even the destruction of Guernica in his memoirs. At the end of his two short chapters on the war in Spain, he noted that "la politique n'est pas mon fort" (*Souvenirs sans fin,* III, 50).

131. *AF,* 24 May 1937. In Maurras's article, the attack on *L'Aube* is presented as part of Salmon's letter, but this part did not appear in *L'Émancipation Nationale.*

132. *AF,* 29 July 1938. Reprinted in a pamphlet entitled *Diez días en el norte de España conquistado por Franco.* This brochure contained a translation of the five articles by Auphan, printed in the newspaper between 28 July and 2 August 1938.

133. This was printed in *La Croix,* 6-7 May 1937, and credited to Havas. Also *La Liberté du Sud-Ouest,* 6 May 1937; *La Dépêche Algérienne,* 6 May 1937.

134. This statement is based on negative evidence. These dispatches have not been found in print, and it is considered improbable that they were distributed and not printed. *Esprit* reprinted in the number of June 1937, pp. 449-473, a collection of the material published in France relating to the destruction of Guernica. Neither the editorial of the *Times* of 5 May nor Steer's article of 6 May appears there, although both were extremely favorable to the cause defended by *Esprit.* One can conclude that the editors were unaware of them. *L'Aube* mentioned the editorial in the *Times* of 5 May and Steer's article of the following day, and *L'Action Française* spoke of Steer's article of 6 May, but it is clear from the text that both were referring to something seen in the *Times* itself and not to reprints in the French press. See n. 129.

135. Bret does not mention Guernica or even the Spanish Civil War in his later book of memoirs, *Au feu des événements. Mémoires d'un journaliste.*

136. Onaindía, *op. cit.,* p. 248. Liénart was the most liberal prelate in France at that time. "Cardinal Liénart intervened on several decisive occasions to define the doctrine or recall the ethical position, to defend the syndicates unjustly criticized, to warn against the political

leagues [Croix de Feu, etc.], to censure the campaign of calumny which had pushed a political figure [Salengro] to suicide. He does this in all circumstances with courageous and intelligent firmness" (Rémond, *Les catholiques, le communism et les crises, 1929-1939*, p. 18). Not all the French-speaking prelates welcomed Canon Onaindia as did Liénart. Cardinal Van Roey, archbishop of Malines, primate of Belgium, made known that if Onaindia repeated in Belgium what he had said about Guernica in Paris he would deprive the Basque priest of all right to say mass in Belgium. "This illustrious Prince of the Church did not concern himself with finding out if what I had said about Guernica was true or not; he did not want a priest to speak out against the 'crusaders' " (Onaindia, *op. cit.*, p. 251).

137. *La Dépêche*, Lille, 9 May 1937, p. 1. The article was signed by Jean de la Deûle. This newspaper did not have a large printing, but it was important as representative of right-wing Catholic thought in Liénart's region.

138. *L'Aube*, 12 May 1937, pp. 1, 3. This article was not signed, but was perhaps written by Pierre-Louis Falaize.

139. *Le Jour*, 6 May 1937, p. 1. Bailby drew some conclusions for his readers. The first one was: "Once again they have lied to us."

140. *La Flèche*, 9 May 1937. *La Flèche* was the "organ of the Common Front." See Claude Estier, *La gauche hebdomadaire, 1914-1962*; also Michele Cotta, *Le Frontisme et "La Flèche" de 1934 a 1936*, mémoire de l'Institut d'Études Politiques, typescript (Paris, 1959); *Esprit* (June 1937), pp. 468-469.

141. Frances Davis wrote of Scott: "The French government has decorated him for correspondence in which he has aided France by brillantly interpreting her to England. . . . He has that stiff thing in his character we call integrity. He would never write except what he believed—and that with clarity, courage and conviction" (*op. cit.*, p. 227). Scott has been dead for some years.

142. These details come from Falaize's article in *L'Aube*, 19 May 1937.

143. This reference was to the article in *L'Action Française* of 16 May 1937, concerning the denunciation of Father Onaindia's activities by the metropolitan chapter of Valladolid.

144. *Le Jour*, 18 May 1937, p. 1.

145. *Le Populaire*, 18 May 1937, p. 2. The Socialist newspaper wrote that Scott's letter "caught *Le Jour* in *flagrante delicto* of lying."

146. This phrase is found in no signed article by Falaize. He can therefore be referring only to the unsigned article of 12 May 1937. See n. 138.

147. Bailby's reproduction, however, agrees word for word with the Havas dispatch published in *La Croix*, 6-7 May 1937.

148. *L'Aube*, 19 May 1937, p. 1. The headlines read: "GUERNICA AGAIN. M. LEON BAILBY EDITOR OF *LE JOUR* HAD GIVEN A FALSE QUOTATION FROM *THE TIMES*. CONVICTED OF LYING, HE RELAPSES INTO CRIME." The article also noted that "*L'Aube* was first of the press, thanks to Jean Richard, to place in the dossier a paper which is and will remain an important document of history." *L'Aube* did not mention that *Le Populaire* had already published Scott's letter, twenty-four hours earlier.

149. *L'Aube*, 25 May 1937, p. 1. Scott's letter was dated 19 May 1937. The headline in *L'Aube* read: "THE BOMBING OF GUERNICA. DEFINITIVE RECORD ESTABLISHING THE MENTAL DEFICIENCY OR THE BAD FAITH OF M. LÉON BAILBY OF *LE JOUR*."

150. *Gringoire*, 7 May 1937, p. 2.

151. *Ibid.*, 14 May 1937, p. 2.

152. *Esprit* (June 1937), pp. 449-473.

153. Steer's dispatches of 28 April, 6 and 15 May (but the first two dates are incorrectly given as of 29 April and 7 May); Monks' article of 11 May; Jean Richard's interview with Onaindia, from *L'Aube*; the testimony of the four Basque nurses; the statement of President Aguirre and the Catholic appeal of 8 May.

154. Massot's article of 3 May and the reference to the dispatch in *Le Jour* are from a press handout of a Francoist agency in Paris, called "Bulletin d'information espagnole." This section in *Esprit* also included a quotation from Radio Burgos dated 15 May to the effect that for the first time "Marxist" airplanes appeared on the Basque front, causing great damage to the Casa de Juntas in Guernica (this was printed because it demonstrated that according to Nationalist

sources there were no Basque airplanes to bomb Guernica in April; the Casa de Juntas was never touched by a bomb); article in *Le Temps*, 13 May 1937, concerning the Nazi campaign against the *Times;* Falaize's article in *L'Aube*, on 19 May, and *L'Aube's* reply to *La Dépêche* of Lille. All this constituted an invaluable dossier on what had been printed in France concerning the destruction of Guernica.

155. *Esprit* (June 1937), p. 473.

156. *La France de Bordeaux et du Sud-Ouest*, 13 May 1937. This dispatch was probably sent out by L'Agence Espagne. The complete text can be found in *Euzko Deya*, 16 May 1937, p. 1. Dom Sturzo gave full credence to the arguments of Arzuaga (ED, 6 June 1937, p. 1).

157. *La destrucción de Guernica*, p. 19, quoting *L'oeuvre* 13 May 1937. The preface of this pamphlet is by Jacques Madaule. A severe denunciation of Arzuaga, or Arsuaga, was given by G. García de Castro, *op. cit.*, pp. 241-250. He wrote: "The most shameful spectacle was given by Father Ramón Arsuaga, of the Society of Jesus" (p. 241).

158. *Candide*, 1 July 1937, p. 1.

159. *Occident*, 10 November 1937, p. 1. This exact statement does not appear in the pamphlet Farrère published about this trip. Therein he merely declared that "Marxists" had "dynamited Guernica." *Visite aux espagnols (Hiver 1937)*, p. 14. The end of this text is dated October 1937.

160. Marcel Sauvage, *La corrida*, pp. 158-159. Another French journalist, Georges Oudard, gave his opinion about Guernica. The Germans did not destroy the town, for "even a massive drop of incendiary bombs would not produce such a result," and moreover Guernica looked just like so many other towns "burned before their departure by the most vile elements of the government troops" (*Chemises noires, brunes, vertes en Espagne*, pp. 82-83).

161. *Ibid.*, pp. 161-162.

162. Géneral Duval, *Leçons de la guerre d'Espagne*, pp. 149-150. The preface was written by General Weygand, an open supporter of the Nationalist cause. Géneral Duval did not mention Guernica in his second book on the Spanish Civil War, *Les espagnols et la guerre d'Espagne*.

163. Eddy Bauer, *Rouge et or*, pp. 66-69; other testimony by Olazábal, *Guernica: The Official Report*, pp. 45-46.

164. Comte de Saint-Aulaire, *La renaissance de l'Espagne*, pp. 196-197.

165. *Ibid.*, p. 199.

166. *Ibid.*, p. 192.

167. *Je Suis Partout*, 7 January 1938, article by Saint-Aulaire, p. 1. *La Renaissance de l'Espagne*, p. 197.

168. Saint-Aulaire, *op. cit.*, p. 197n.

169. *Ibid.*, p. 198.

170. *Occident*, 25 March 1938, p. 2.

171. Bardèche et Brasillach, *Histoire de la guerre d'Espagne*, pp. 297-299.

172. Robert Brasillach, *Notre avant-guerre*, pp. 248-249. "We had not forgotten Spain. . . . We decided on a short trip of two weeks, at the beginning of July 1938. . . . We were three, Pierre Cousteau . . . Maurice Bardèche and myself. We thought about gathering material to write *Histoire de la guerre d'Espagne.*"

173. *Histoire de la guerre d'Espagne*, pp. 321-322.

174. Conversations, Southworth with Onaindia.

Chapter 3
The Secret Controversy Among the Diplomats

1. *Evening News*, London, 27 April 1937, p. 1. This was based on the Reuters message sent by Holme, which was also carried by the *Evening Standard* and the *News Chronicle*. The *Star* report also implicated the Germans.

2. *Boston Evening Transcript*, 27 April 1937, p. 1. This was an AP story. See also *Chicago Daily News*, 27 April 1937, p. 1, a UP story, equally implicating the Germans.

3. *Daily News*, N.Y., 28 April 1937, UP dispatch.

4. *Washington Post*, 28 April 1937, p. 1, UP.

5. *Petit Parisien*, 28 April 1937, p. 1. This was a "neutral" newspaper. The Germans were also implicated in accounts appearing in *Le Populaire*, *L'Humanité*, and *Ce Soir*, all newspapers of the left.

6. *Morning Post*, 29 April 1937, p. 1.

7. *Ibid.*, 30 April 1937.

8. *NYT*, 30 April 1937, p. 1.

9. *Chicago Daily News*, 29 April 1937.

10. *New York Herald Tribune*, 30 April 1937. Dorothy Thompson signed the appeal concerning Guernica issued on 8 May by Bishop McConnell of the Methodist Episcopal Church (see below). A few weeks later, Miss Thompson began having doubts, apparently because "the statement is categorically made by a large part of the Catholic press of this century that Guernica was burned by retreating communists." She noted that "Supposedly independent reporters asserted categorically that Guernica was bombed by German planes." When she cabled journalists abroad "whom we have known for years, in whose honesty and disinterestedness we have complete belief" and asked them for "entirely confidential information," all the replies "confirmed that the Germans did bomb Guernica." Miss Thompson concluded with ambiguity: "This column believes on the basis of every scrap of evidence that could be assembled that the Germans bombed Guernica and machine-gunned women and children, and that it was an international outrage. But it does not entirely trust, now, any sources of information" (*New York Herald Tribune*, 2 June 1937). Merwin K. Hart, an ardent supporter of the Franco cause, quoted extensively from Miss Thompson's two articles, and decided that "she was grossly misled" and that "practically all of the facts on which she relied were wholly untrue" (*America, Look at Spain!* pp. 90, 92). According to Hart, Miss Thompson later said: "I wrote a piece on the bombing of Guernica which, I believe, has been translated into most of the European languages and used as propaganda by the Loyalists" p. 90). The extensive research for this work has uncovered no translation of Miss Thompson's article.

11. PRO, FO 371/21333, W 8913, folios 11-13.

12. *Times*, 30 April 1937, p. 15. See also article by dean of Canterbury, in the *Manchester Guardian*, 5 May 1937: "President Aguirre voiced the feeling of the nation to a man in a telegram which reached me at midnight protesting in passionate terms and appealing before God and before history to the testimony of journalists and consular representatives who with terror contemplated how far the instincts of destruction of the mercenaries at the service of the Spanish fascists can go." This was probably the same message as that sent to Baldwin on 28 April.

13. State Department Files, 852.00/5280.

14. *Ibid.*, 852.00/5274. This same message was sent to Foreign Minister Eden (PRO, FO 371/21290, W 8414/41, folios 161-162).

15. State Department Files, 852.00/5274. See also *ED*, 6 May 1937, p. 4.

16. *Documents Diplomatiques Français, 1932-1939*, 2d Series, Tome V (hereafter, DDF), p. 656n.

17. *ED*, 6 May 1937, p. 4.

18. *La Prensa*, 29 April 1937. *Die Nachtausgabe* and the *Deutsche Allgemeine* were cited as limiting their news to the Salamanca denial. The *Berliner Tageblatt* was widely quoted. See the *Gazette*, Montreal, 29 April 1937, CP-Havas dispatch; *NYT*, 29 April 1937. This same argument was advanced the same day by the *Lokal-Anzeiger* of Berlin (*Le Temps*, 29 April 1937, the *Gazette*, Montreal, 29 April 1937).

19. *NYT*, 30 April 1937. This German dispatch was forwarded to London by the British embassy in Berlin (PRO, FO 371/21332, W 8469, folios 188-189).

20. The *Gazette*, Montreal, wrote that the *Völkischer Beobachter* charged that "lax, shameful, Jewish journalism of intellectuals sheltered on French soil was systematically poisoning the atmosphere to provoke a war" (29 April 1937, p. 14). *La Prensa*, in a UP dispatch from Berlin, wrote that the *Nachtausgabe* observed that "a certain part of the French and British press amused itself in recent days with the publication of fantastic accounts of the bombings of Guernica" (29 April 1937, p. 9).

21. *Hamburger Fremdenblatt,* 30 April 1937.

22. *Bulletin périodique de la presse italienne,* no. 306, p. 15. The author of this report summed up: "The bombing of Guernica was presented by the Italian press as an invention of the friends of the reds to ensure support abroad for a cause now in desperate straits, but the first dispatches recognized and justified the bombing." He gave as an example the London reporter for the *Gazzetta del Popolo. La Stampa* of 29 May printed this commentary from London: "The bombing of Guernica has furnished the occasion for the adversaries of the government to "bomb" it with questions and to seek once more to place it in difficulty because of its position of neutrality regarding Spain" (Bulletin, p. 16). This analysis was not too false.

23. *Ibid.,* quoting the *Corriere della sera.* This text is word for word the same as the text in the *Berliner Tageblatt,* previously cited.

24. *Ibid.,* quoting *Popolo d'Italia,* of 29 May. *Le Temps,* 2 May 1937, p. 2, said that the Italian press was repeating Salamanca's claims of no flights because of bad weather and the charges that the retreating "Marxists" had set fire to Guernica.

25. *Daily Herald,* 29 April 1937.

26. *Times,* 1 May 1937.

27. Among the signers were Katherine Atholl, Noel-Buxton, Arthur Salter, Ellen Wilkinson, Eleanor Rathbone, Irene Ward, Megan Lloyd George, John Withers, Harold Nicolson, Thelma Cazalet, Philip Noel-Baker, Anthony Crossley, Lytton, Patrick Hannon, David Grenfell.

28. *Manchester Guardian, La Prensa,* 30 April 1937.

29. *Manchester Guardian,* 30 April 1937, p. 24.

30. *Manchester Guardian,* London edition; *La Prensa,* UP dispatch, 3 May 1937.

31. PRO, FO 371/21291, W 9029, folio 39.

32. *Foreign Relations of the United States. Diplomatic Papers* (1937), I, 290-291. Cablegram, Bowers to secretary of state, from Saint-Jean-de-Luz, 30 April, 1937, 6 P.M.

33. *Congressional Record, Senate,* 6 May 1937, pp. 5521-5522. It is not to contest the sincerity of Senator Borah's speech to note that in his state of Idaho there were more Basque immigrants than in any other state of the union. These were sheepherders organized in the Basque Sheepherders Association. The recent governor of the state of Nevada, which borders on Idaho, Paul Laxalt, was a descendant of French Basque immigrants. Among Congressional critics of the bombing of Guernica were Senators Matthew Neely of West Virginia and Gerald P. Nye of South Dakota; Congressmen John T. Bernard and Henry Teigan of Minnesota, John H. Coffee of Washington, and Jerry J. O'Connell of Montana. See Taylor, *The United States and the Spanish Civil War,* pp. 124-125; Guttmann, *The Wound in the Heart,* pp. 107-108.

34. *NYT,* 10 May 1937, p. 5. A preliminary " 'Appeal to the Conscience of the World,' to protest against the killing of non-combatants, largely women and children, in the recent bombing of Guernica," sponsored by Bishop McConnell, Senator Capper; James Rowland Angell, retired president of Yale; Carrie Champan Catt, champion of women's rights; Harry Emerson Fosdick, Protestant leader; Leland Stowe, the journalist; and others, was issued on 4 May. See (*NYT* 5 May 1937, p. 18). The 10 May statement was signed by numerous university presidents; by William Green, president of the American Federation of Labor; by Alfred Landon, former Republican candidate for the presidency; by Newton D. Baker, former secretary of the Navy; by congressmen and senators. Among the senators who signed the appeal were Wagner of New York; Bone of Washington; Glass of Virginia; Nye of South Dakota; Thomas of Oklahoma, Borah of Idaho and Capper of Kansas. Senator Capper was reproached by American Catholics for having given his signature to the paper, and on 11 September 1937, he wrote to his friend Dr. Stephen S. Wise, rabbi of the Free Synagogue in New York City and a well-known leader of American liberal Jewish thought: "I signed it [the Guernica protest] . . . after consulting two or three of my friends in the Senate, in whom I had confidence, because I am in sympathy with the Loyalists in the fight against the fascist insurgent forces in Spain." But, the senator went on: "Since the statement was published I have received letters from prominent Catholics who make a very vigorous protest against this document 'Crime of Guernica' on the grounds that it does not state the truth." Capper was troubled by these Catholic letters and asked Dr. Wise if, "in the light of later information" he thought the statement "unfair." Wise replied in part as follows, ten days later: "I know that some of our good friends contest the claims of the English war correspondents with regard to Guernica. But

I believe the truth to be incontestable. It was for that reason I joined the committee, as you did." Both letters are in the Special Collections, Library, Brandeis University, Waltham, Massachusetts. *The Crime of Guernica* is the title of a pamphlet published in New York containing the text of the appeal concerning Guernica and the names of the signers.

35. *Congressional Record, Appendix.* 12 May 1937, p. 5817. The three other congressmen who signed O'Connell's letter were Coffee, Teigan, and Bernard. See *Foreign Relations of the United States* (1937), I, 294.

36. Key Pittman, of Nevada, was chairman of the Senate Committee on Foreign Relations. There were Basque sheepherders in Nevada, as in Idaho, but they did not affect Pittman's pro-Franco convictions.

37. *Foreign Relations of the United States* (1937), I, 294-295, reproduces Hull's reply to O'Connell, dated 7 May 1937, but not O'Connell's letter to the secretary of state.

38. Cordell Hull, *The Memoirs of Cordell Hull,* I, 511. For Hull's accounts of American diplomacy and the Spanish Civil War, see pp. 504-517.

39. *PD, House of Commons. Official Report, in the Second Session of the thirty-seventh Parliament of the United Kingdom of Great Britain and Northern Ireland.* Fifth Series, Seventh Volume of Session 1936-37, col. 318-319.

40. *Ibid.,* col. 685. When the statement attributed to Mola appeared in the press, Hugh Dalton immediately informed Eden of a "Private Notice Question" that he intended to ask on the following day (PRO, FO 371/21290, W 8634, folios 219-220). Mola's threat appeared in the *Daily Herald,* 29 April 1937, p. 1, British UP dispatch. This was the newspaper text quoted in the Foreign Office (PRO, FO 371/21290 W 8501, folio 182, and W 8634, folio 223). The *Morning Post,* 29 April 1937, printed a similar story, from its "Special Correspondent on the Franco-Catalan Frontier," as did *Le Populaire,* 29 April 1937, p. 1, dispatch from Bayonne.

41. *PD, House of Commons, op. cit.,* cols. 685-686. When Eden received Dalton's note of 29 April, a telegram was immediately forwarded to Chilton. Cranborne's note was phrased in a fashion favorable to the Nationalists. He told Chilton that the declaration attributed to Mola "seems to conflict with statements of General Franco with regard to the bombing of Guernica," and suggested to the ambassador that if Mola's declaration was not authentic, "General Mola would be well advised to make an immediate public démenti" (PRO, FO 371/21290, W 8501, folio 182).

42. PRO, FO 371/21290, W 8552, folio 186. The fact that the news had appeared in what Sir Henry called a "left-wing paper" seemingly diminished its veracity in the eyes of the diplomat. Jay Allen, probably the ablest correspondent who covered the war, wrote from the Basque frontier at this time: "The ambassadors of France and England, accredited to Republican Spain, of course carry on astonishingly. Neither Monsieur Jean Herbette, ambassador of the French Popular Front government to the Spanish Republic, nor Sir Henry Chilton, His Britannic Majesty's ambassador, hide their passionate enthusiasm for General Franco. They make admiring small talk with a Rebel 'government' in Burgos and Salamanca which Paris and London have not met socially. . . . Sir Henry at a dinner party declared that Franco is defending the interests of 'our class.' . . . A monocled secretary of the British Embassy follows the doings of the International Brigades with passionate interest. The day Ralph Fox, the British poet who followed Byron's precedent and went to fight for the underdogs, was killed in Madrid, the secretary announced joyfully: 'Fine! In this way all of us British, French, and Americans will get rid of our undesirables' " (*Chicago Daily News,* 11 May 1937, p. 2).

43. The military governor of Irún was probably the Nationalist official most readily available to the diplomatic corps in Hendaye. The Foreign Office telegram had suggested that he be queried on this matter. For Troncoso, see Jaime del Burgo, *Conspiración y guerra civil,* pp. 172, 664. The most brilliant exploit of Troncoso was undoubtedly the discovery of a "plot" by the painter Luis Quintanilla and the writer Max Aub (both were then attached to the Republican embassy in Paris, where Luis Araquistain was ambassador) to send into Nationalist Spain two men whose scarified bodies were carriers of deadly bacilli, thus causing epidemics. Millions of dollars were involved in this dastardly conspiracy, nipped in the bud by Troncoso only days before the destruction of Guernica. See texts and photographs in *Vértice,* June 1937. This heavy-handed fable is not mentioned by Jaime del Burgo or by Bertrán y Musitu, who worked closely with Troncoso. See Bertrán y Musitu, *Experiencias de los servicios de infor-*

mación del nordeste de España (S.I.F.N.E.) durante la guerra. For further and more unfortunate adventures of Troncoso, see Pike, *Les français et la guerre d'Espagne,* pp. 251-253.

44. PRO, FO 371/20290, W 8552, folio 86.

45. *Ibid.,* W 8569, folio 200. A surprisingly accurate report on Troncoso's reply to Chilton appeared in *La Croix,* 4 May 1937, p. 2, in a dispatch from London, with no agency source given. Mola's threat came up again more than once. Arthur Henderson asked, in a Parliamentary Question on 5 May (deferred from 3 May), whether the foreign minister intended to place the matter immediately before the League Council. There was considerable doubt in the Foreign Office that the threat had been uttered (PRO, FO 371/21291, W 8971, folios 21-23). Wilfrid Roberts wrote to Eden on May 19 that he had been informed by the Basque delegation "that they had received information from Bilbao that threats are being made by General Mola in pamphlets dropped from his aeroplanes that unless Bilbao is surrendered, the whole of Biscay will be treated in the same way as that in which Guernica and other villages have been dealt with" (PRO, FO 371/21293, folio 69). The Foreign Office was skeptical (folio 71).

46. PRO, FO 371/21290, W 8623, folios 212-214.

47. *PD, House of Commons, op. cit.,* Eden's statement, col. 769; debate, cols. 769-776.

48. *NYT,* 4 May 1937, p. 8.

49. Auswärtiges Amt, Pol. III, 2000 serial 3373 HE 01876. Telegram from London, dated 3 May 1937, 23 hours. Quoted in telegram sent to Salamanca from Berlin on following day (*GSCW,* p. 279). This is the first reference to Guernica in the published German documents and, insofar as I have been able to ascertain, the earliest German diplomatic or military reference concerning Guernica known today. It is of course impossible that Guernica was not mentioned before this date, and many times, in official German communications. These have, unfortunately, been lost, at least for the time being, or destroyed. The German embassy in Madrid might have kept copies of such telegrams, but if it did, they are not made available; perhaps they were destroyed in 1945. The few references to Guernica found in the published documents have led certain writers, notably Luis Bolín, to conclude that no others were ever written. Brian Crozier and Stanley G. Payne, by giving credibility to Bolín's arguments, seemingly adopt this illogical point of view (Crozier, *Franco,* p. 246; Payne, *NYT Book Review,* 1 October 1967).

50. *Manchester Guardian,* 29 April 1937. This reference is the one in the Foreign Office files. The Reuters dispatch also appeared in the *Times,* 29 April 1937, p. 16. See also *Continental Daily Mail* of same date, p. 1: "The anti-Reds do not deny that the raids occurred, but they say they had no part in it."

51. Auswärtiges Amt. Pol. III, 2200, Serial 3373H, E 01976.

52. The Havas-Botto dispatch was apparently picked up as early as the afternoon of 3 May, for on that date Sir Neville Henderson, British ambassador in Berlin, cabled London to inform Eden that a DNB message from Paris featured in the German press stated that "it has now been established that Guernica was destroyed by the Bolshevists." Henderson also mentioned *L'Echo de Paris.* He did not speak of any campaign against the *Times* (PRO, FO 371/21332, W 8736, folios 233-234).

53. *Berliner Lokal-Anzeiger,* 4 May 1937, pp. 1-2. In this newspaper, as in many others, the space given to Steer's translation was greater than that used for the Havas-Botto counter-proof.

54. *Kölnische Volkszeitung und Handelsblatt,* 4 May 1937.

55. The Rt. Hon. The Earl of Avon, *The Eden Memoirs: Facing the Dictators,* p. 504.

56. PRO, FO 371/21332, W 3853.

57. GSCW, p. 279.

58. *PD, House of Commons, op. cit.,* col. 318.

59. *La Nación,* 1 May 1937, quoting *Le Peuple* of 30 April, Havas dispatch from Brussels.

60. *Le Temps,* 1 May 1937. This published communiqué contains the only existing information concerning the meeting of the commission on Foreign Affairs of the French Senate, on 30 April 1937 (letter dated 18 June 1969, from the Secretary General of the Senate, signed by François Goguel). See also the *Times,* 1 May 1937, dispatch from Paris, dated 30 April: *Le Petit Parisien,* 2 May 1937.

61. *La Prensa,* 1 May 1937.

62. *L'Humanité,* 30 April 1937.

63. *L'Echo de Paris,* 30 April 1937.

64. *AF,* 10 May 1937, in "Revue de la Presse."

65. *Boston Evening Transcript,* 30 April 1937.

66. Letter from the head curator of the Diplomatic Archives of the French Republic, 31 July 1969. Madrid was Herbette's official station and was probably a euphemism for Hendaye, where Herbette really was.

67. Conversation with M. Antoine Molinié, 16 July 1969. "At the time of this tragedy, I had the conviction that Guernica had been bombed by German airplanes and that it had been destroyed by incendiary bombs."

68. *La Prensa,* 1 May 1937, p. 6. This would have been better expressed by saying that "the majority of the houses *still standing . . .*" (italics added).

69. Letter from the head curator of the Diplomatic Archives of the French Republic, 31 July 1969. The French Foreign Ministry does not normally release documents until fifty years after the event; it can, however, when it so desires, communicate a résumé of certain documents. It is worth observing that the ideas of the French ambassador were the same as those advanced in the Non-Intervention Committee (hereafter, NIC) by the representatives of Germany, Italy, and Portugal.

70. *Ibid.* Chilton and Herbette were both favorable to the Nationalist cause. Jay Allen wrote as follows: "The France of Mr. Blum wants one thing and the France of Mr. Herbette wants another" (*Chicago Daily News,* 11 May 1937, p. 2). In view of Chilton's accreditation to the Madrid government, his reaction to Franco's invitation was highly irregular.

71. *La Prensa,* 1 May 1937, p. 6, cablegram from Paris. See also PRO, FO 371/21333, W 8913, folio 12.

72. DDF, pp. 646-647.

73. *Ibid.,* p. 656.

74. International Committee for the Application of the Agreement regarding Non-Intervention in Spain. The Chairman's Sub-Committee (hereafter, Sub-Com). "Stenographic Notes of the Forty-Ninth Meeting of the Sub-Committee, held in the Foreign Office, S.W.1, on Tuesday, May 4, 1937, at 11 A.M." (PRO, FO 371/21388, W 9235/169/41, folio 3). The essential work of the NIC was carried on by the much smaller subcommittee.

75. DDF, p. 656. Telegram from Corbin to Delbos, sent from London, 3 May, at 13h37, received in Paris, same day, 15h30.

76. Sub-Com, 49th meeting, folio 5.

77. *Dez anos de política externa* (1936-1947), IV, 263. Telegram from Oliveira Salazar to Monteiro, dated 5 May 1937. Oliveira Salazar was Portuguese premier and also foreign minister.

78. *Ibid.,* p. 267. Telegram from Monteiro to Portuguese foreign minister, dated 7 May 1937.

79. *Foreign Relations of the United States. Diplomatic Papers, 1937.* I, 87. Memorandum of Ambassador Bingham, dated 3 May, concerning a conversation that had taken place the morning of that day.

80. Sub-Com, 49th meeting, folio 3. The letter was in French. The part that referred, indirectly, to Guernica, read: "Because of the character taken by the civil war in the Basque provinces where open towns and civilian population are running the risk of complete destruction under the bombings of the Insurgent airforce, the French government considers it its duty to undertake any effort susceptible of putting an end to such excesses." The French ambassador generally spoke in English, as did all the other representatives except, strangely enough, the Portuguese ambassador, who preferred French.

81. *Ibid.,* folio 4. Czechoslovak Minister Masaryk attended the latter part of the meeting. The Belgian ambassador said: "I feel sure my government would like to associate itself with any approach to the two parties in Spain in regard to the bombing of open towns."

82. *Ibid.,* in French in original.

83. Auswärtiges Amt., Pol. III, 2213, no 257, 4 May. Message from von Ribbentrop to German Foreign Office, E 255217.

84. Sub-Com, 49th meeting, folios 5-8.

85. *Ibid.,* folio 9. In part, the statement read: "In the course of a preliminary exchange of

views doubts were expressed whether it would be within the competence of the International Committee, as such, though not of the participating governments, to address an appeal of the kind comtemplated."

86. *Ibid.*, folio 10. Maisky apparently sought to separate the German and Italian representatives from their Portuguese colleague.

87. *Ibid.*

88. *Ibid.*, folio 11. Palmstierna included the Belgian in his summing up. "The Belgian ambassador has got his instructions, we do not need to consult on a self-evident case."

89. *Ibid.*

90. *Ibid.*, folios 11-12. In French in original.

91. *Dez anos de política externa (1936-1947)*, IV, 259-261. Telegram from Monteiro to Portuguese minister of foreign affairs, Lisbon, 4 May 1937.

92. Sub-Com. 49th meeting, folios 12-13. Corbin spoke in French.

93. *Ibid.*, folios 13-14.

94. *Ibid.*, folio 14.

95. *Ibid.*

96. *Ibid.*, folios 14-15.

97. *Ibid.*, folio 15. Maisky does not tell of this incident in his book concerning his work with the NIC, nor does he go beyond a general statement in mentioning Guernica. However, he does give detailed portraits of Plymouth, Corbin, Cartier, Palmstierna, Masaryk, Grandi, and von Ribbentrop. He had little respect for his committee colleagues and their actions on Spain, and spoke well only of Palmstierna and Hemming (*Cuadernos españoles*, pp. 66-83).

98. *Ibid.*

99. *Ibid.*, folio 16.

100. Germany, Auswärtiges Amt., Pol. III, 2213. E 255214, Serial 4906. Telegram from von Ribbentrop to Berlin, dated 4 May 1937. Woermann, von Ribbentrop's deputy, telephoned earlier to Berlin (*ibid.*, Pol. III, 2209 E 010879). See also Toynbee, *Survey of International Affairs, 1937*, II, 380-381.

101. *Daily Telegraph*, 5 May 1937. See also the *Daily Herald*, 5 May 1937, article signed by W. N. E. The *News Chronicle* article of the same date, also page one, was by Norman Cliff, the newspaper's foreign editor. "There were fireworks. It was Herr Ribbentrop, the German ambassador, who rose indignantly to protest against the very idea that anyone should dare to question the propriety of recent happenings at Guernica." The *Daily Express'* "Diplomatic Correspondent" wrote, also on 5 May that "Hitler's ambassador von Ribbentrop objected that the bombing of open towns was sometimes a painful necessity."

102. *NYT*, 5 May 1937, UP dispatch from London. The New York newspaper also published a similar telegram from its own London representative, reading in part: "Germany, through the mouth of her ambassador to London, today opposed any ban on the bombing of undefended towns in Spain. Such bombings are inevitable in war, Joachim von Ribbentrop told a Non-Intervention Sub-Committee and warned that it would be folly for any government or group of governments to try to prevent them. . . . Mr. von Ribbentrop told the Sub-Committee that noncombatants were bound to be killed in air raids and that there was no way to prevent such occurrences. The German Government could not possibly consider a proposal to prohibit the bombing of open towns, he said, for such a proposal would not be workable." The *New York Times* correspondent gave an indirect source: "Mr. von Ribbentrop's speech was not mentioned in the communique but it became known in the usual manner from various sources soon after the Sub-Committee adjourned and the delegates returned to their respective embassies."

103. PRO, FO 371/21291, W 9029, folio 39.

104. *Times, NYT*, 5 May 1937. All the German press of 4 May used the news about Guernica which had appeared in the French newspapers of the day before. The *Berliner Lokal-Anzeiger* proclaimed in headlines: "THE LIES OF THE TIMES UNMASKED BY HAVAS." The *Hamburger Fremdenblatt* entitled its article, "FAIRY TALES OF HORROR," and the *Kölnische Zeitung* wrote in large letters, "FALSE NEWS ABOUT GUERNICA," and "A LYING REPORT OF THE TIMES." The *Kölnische Volkszeitung* developed another argument in headlines: "THE LIES ABOUT GUERNICA AND THE ENGLISH LOAN FOR

RE-ARMAMENT," and "THE TIMES REFUTED." The relationship between the interest aroused in England by the destruction of Guernica, and English rearmament was established on an argument advanced by the *Neue Zürcher Zeitung*: the English press was trying to persuade the English public that its own towns were in danger of bombardment in order to encourage British rearmament. The *Neue Zürcher Zeitung* had already on 3 May commented on Botto's dispatch, published in *Le Temps* on 2-3 May. The Zurich daily pointed out that the absence of bomb holes and bomb splatter did not prove that the town had not been attacked by incendiary bombs, but it was strongly impressed by Botto's references to "gasoline" and to "kerosene," and it concluded that Guernica had been bombed by the Nationalist air force, and then burned by the Basques. It is significant that the newspaper interpreted the conclusions presented by the article in *Le Temps* as being the result of a visit by a group of foreign war correspondents (*"einen Besuch den Ausländischekriegskorrespondenten"*). See Book III, chap. 1, n. 95.

105. *Times*, 5 May 1937, dispatch from Berlin dated 4 May. "The abuse officially let loose in connection with the account given in *The Times* of the bombing of Guernica continued today. The articles in the provincial press, mostly under such headlines as 'How *The Times* Lied,' show the efficient manner in which the campaign was set on foot." Franklin Reid Gannon does not mention, any more than did the *Times* itself in 1937, the French source for "the abuse officially let loose" against the *Times* (*op. cit.*, pp. 113-114).

106. *NYT*, 4 May 1937, p. 8.

107. PRO, W 8896/1/41 See also *La Prensa*, 7 May 1937, p. 9.

108. PRO, HO 107/2052, W 9382/41. International Committee for the Application of the Agreement regarding Non-Intervention in Spain. "Stenographic notes of the Twentieth meeting of the Committee, held in the Locarno Room, Foreign Office, S.W.1, on Wednesday, May 5, at 11 A.M." folio 4.

109. PRO, FO 371/21333, W 9079, message from Eden to the British ambassador, Sir Neville Henderson, dated 7 May.

110. GSCW, pp. 283-284, urgent telegram from London, 6 May 1937, 4:24 P.M.

111. PRO, FO, 371/21333, W 9070, folio 49.

112. *Times*, 5 May 1937.

113. GSCW, p. 283, telegram from von Ribbentrop to Foreign Ministry in Berlin, 6 May 1937. W. N. E., writing in *Daily Herald* of 6 May 1937, p. 1, reported, "Herr von Ribbentrop, much disturbed by the publicity which his performance in Tuesday's Non-Intervention Committee received, yesterday made a vehement protest to Mr. Eden."

114. *ABC*, Seville, 6 May 1937, p. 9.

115. *GSCW*, p. 281.

116. Luis Bolín, writing many years later, insisted that the statement of 29 April was the "denial" in question (*Spain: The Vital Years*, p. 359). This was chronologically improbable.

117. PRO, FO 371/21333, W 8968, folios 36-37.

118. *PD, House of Commons, op. cit.*, cols. 1340-1346.

119. *Ibid.*, cols. 1356-1358.

120. *Ibid.*, cols. 1376-1378.

121. *Ibid.*, cols. 1382-1383. Lloyd George considered the speeches on both sides of the debate on Guernica and the war in the Basque country to have constituted "one of the most interesting debates I have heard in this House" (*ibid.*, col. 1374). Eden echoed his praises (*ibid.*, col. 1380). This was doubtless parliamentary courtesy. The London correspondent of the *New York Times* gave another opinion: "What characterizes all speeches on the subject, however, was the bitterness that seems to grip the House of Commons whenever the Spanish Civil War is discussed" (*NYT*, 7 May 1937).

122. Sir Henry Chilton considered Stevenson too pro-Basque (letter of Chilton to Sir George Mounsey in the Foreign Office, 26 May 1937, PRO, FO 371/21337, W 10419). Stevenson's sympathies seem remarkably like those of Steer, pro-Basque, but not pro-Spanish. See also, FO 371/21291, folio 260 (pp. 3-4), Stevenson's report of 13 April 1937.

123. PRO, FO 371/21291, W 8661, folio 236.

124. *Dez anos de política externa (1936-1947)*, IV, 267.

125. *The Eden Memoirs*, p. 443.

126. PRO, FO 371/21290, W 8403, folio 148.

127. *Ibid.*, W 8572, folio 204.

128. PRO, FO 371/21389, W 9614/169/41. NIC, "Stenographic Notes of the Fiftieth Meeting of the Sub-Committee, held in the Foreign Office, S.W.1, on Friday, at 4:30 P.M." folios 2-3.

129. *Ibid.*, folio 6. All Italian journalists left England on 8 May to protest "the anti-Italian attitude" of the British government. 9 May was the anniversary of the foundation of the Italian Empire. See newspapers of 9 May, 1937. The occasion was hailed in Franco Spain (HA, 9 May, 1937, p. 5). According to a Rome dispatch, only the *Daily Mail*, the *Evening News* and the *Observer* were allowed to enter Italy (*L'Aube*, 9-10 May, 1937, p. 1). The Dominican publication *Sept* (14 May 1937, p. 2) attributed the recall of the Italian pressmen to the position of the English press on Guernica.

130. Sub-Com, 50th meeting, folio 6. Masaryk adopted a far from generous attitude toward the Spanish Republic. Hugh Thomas, who was allowed to see the unpublished memoirs of Pablo de Azcárate, Republican ambassador sent to London shortly after the outbreak of the civil war, wrote: "Azcárate was received perfectly by all London's diplomatic corps, except for Jan Masaryk, the Czech Minister, who refused to deign to call on the "red Ambassador," and for Grandi, the Italian ambassador. Ribbentrop . . . was always very correct." Thomas added that Vansittart "welcomed [Azcárate] very coldly on his first visit to the Foreign Office" (*The Spanish Civil War*, p. 270n.).

131. Sub-Com., 50th meeting, folio 2.

132. *Ibid.*, folios 9-11.

133. *Ibid.*, folios 10-13. Jan Masaryk said: "I am going to ask my government's opinion, but I could not altogether say that they would support your statement in every detail" (*ibid.*, folio, 12).

134. *Ibid.*, folio 10.

135. *Ibid.*, folios 12-13. At one point Lord Plymouth said, regarding his proposal: "I want to impress upon the Sub-Committee the view of my Government that this matter is, naturally, one of urgency. If anything effective is to come out of our discussions, the sooner we act the better."

136. *Ibid.*, folios 11-12.

137. *Ibid.*, folio 24. This was, from any point of view, a blatant attempt to include Nationalist propaganda in the subcommittee statement. It was obvious from the text that Madrid, for example, was not considered a "non-military open town." It had been, said the Nationalist text, "criminally converted into a military objective by the Red forces entrenched behind its walls with the purpose of defending it." The statement also justified the bombing of Durango and, curiously enough in view of Nationalist propaganda elsewhere, the bombing of Eibar. It also accused "Red aviation" of "bombarding open towns devoid of any military character." Among these towns were Valladolid, where "dozens of children leaving school [were killed] and nearly a hundred [were wounded]." This raid, announced shortly after the publication of the news from Guernica, was apparently imaginary. According to *L'Aube*, 13 May 1937, p. 3, "Mgr. Henson, rector of the English College at Valladolid, has telegraphed our Catholic colleague in London, *The Universe*, that the news from Burgos announcing a new bombing of Valladolid by governmental aircraft, with one hundred and forty-eight victims, of whom eighty-three children in a playground and sixty-five persons in the Plaza de la Independencia, is pure invention."

138. Sub-Com, 50th meeting, folios 23-24.

139. *HA*, 6 May 1937. This dispatch was timed "three o'clock in the morning."

140. PRO, FO 371/21389, NIS (C) (36). "Conclusions of the Fiftieth Meeting of the Sub-Committee . . ." folio 161 (p. 3).

141. *NYT*, 7 May 1937, p. 6.

142. PRO, FO 371/21389, W 10507/169/41. "Stenographic Notes of the Fifty-First meeting of the Sub-Committee . . . May 18, 1937, at 4 P.M." folio 49, pp. 2-3.

143. *Ibid.*, p. 4. The German delegate had presented a "memorandum" concerning his country's position on the "humanization of the Civil War in Spain" on 13 May (PRO, CAB 62/44 [897]).

144. Sub-Com, 51st meeting, folio 50, p. 6. The Italian position concerning the British proposal was stated in a document dated 18 May 1937, and presented to the chairman of the NIC (PRO, CAB 62/44 [897]).

145. Sub-Com, 51st meeting, folio 50, p. 6. This time the Portuguese representative read a paper written in English, which he later distributed among the delegates. The Portuguese government stated its position on the "problem of humanizing the war" in a paper dated 18 May 1937 (PRO, CAB 62/44 [897]).

146. Sub-Com, 51st meeting, folio 50, pp. 8-9.

147. *Ibid.*, pp. 9-11.

148. Auswärtiges Amt, Pol. III 2370, E 010896. Von Bismarck was deputy director of the political department of the foreign ministry.

149. *Ibid.*, Pol. III 2618, E 010899.

150. *GSCW*, p. 290.

151. PRO, FO 371/21291, W 9534, folio 166. C. A. E. Shuckburgh, on 24 May, wrote on the cover of this document (folio 165): "We can clearly not expect any encouragement from the French Govt. for our suggested 'enquiry.' " This was of course after the British had put forward their proposal (see below).

152. PRO, FO 371/21333, W 8913, folio 15.

153. PRO, FO 371/21334, W 10204, folio 46.

154. *Ibid.*, W 9870, folio 271.

155. PRO, FO 371/21335, W 10842, folios 37-38. Also, *Dez anos de política externa*, IV, 309-310.

156. PRO, CAB 62/46. NIS (C) (36) 66.

157. PRO, FO 371/21389, W 10508/169/41, folios 4-6. Monteiro spoke in French.

158. *Ibid.*, folio 6.

159. *Ibid.*, folios 10-13. Monteiro spoke again in French.

160. *Ibid.*, folios 15-16.

161. *Ibid.*, folio 23. PRO, FO 371/21389, W 18388, folio 57, p. 2. "Conclusions of 52nd Meeting of Chairman's Sub-Committee."

162. PRO, CAB 62/51, N.I.S. (36) 527.

163. PRO, FO 371/21389, N.I.S. (36) 21st Meeting, folios 3-6.

164. *Ibid.*, folios 7-8.

165. *Ibid.*, folio 9. Corbin referred to "the ideal and to the profound sentiment of honor which have animated the Spanish people in the course of their history." The original is in French.

166. *Ibid.* Corbin criticized the text, referring especially to the absence of any mention of "certain particular incidents which have caused a profound emotion in public opinion." Corbin spoke in French.

167. *Ibid.*, folio 16.

168. PRO, CAB 62/51 904, N.I.S. (36) 553.

169. PRO, FO 371/21389, W 12939, folio 29.

170. *Ibid.*, NIC 22nd Meeting, 28 May 1937.

170. *Ibid.*, N.I.S. (36) 22nd Meeting. "Stenographic Notes of the Twenty-Second Meeting of the Committee . . . May 28, 1937, at 3 P.M." The Italian ships were not "on duty" in Palma; they were in a port controlled by the Rebels. Only the Soviet spokesman Cahan raised the question of what the Italian ships were doing in Palma at the moment of the bombing.

171. Thomas, *op. cit.*, pp. 440-441.

172. PRO, FO 849/27 N.I.S. (C) (36). Sub-Com 53rd Meeting, folios 170-171.

173. PRO, FO 371/21334, W 10270, folio 61.

174. PRO, FO 371/21333, W 8913/7/41, folio 16.

175. PRO, FO 371/21335, W 10815, folio 13.

176. *Ibid.*, W 10652, folios 194-195; W 10827, folio 122. The comment is by Shuckburgh, folio 194.

177. *Ibid.*, W 10786, folios 258-262.

178. PRO, FO 381/21334, W 10518, folio 122. This observation is also by Shuckburgh.

179. *Ibid.*, folios 123-125. Lord Cranborne's remark was dated 3 June.

180. *Ibid.*, folios 125-132.
181. PRO, FO 371/21336, W 11145, folio 162.
182. *Ibid.*, W 11093, folios 144-145.
183. PRO, FO 849/1/N.I.S. (36) 23rd Meeting. "Stenographic Notes of the Twenty-Third Meeting of the Committee . . . Friday, June 18, 1937, at 4:30 P.M." folio 6.
184. PRO, CAB 62-52 N.I.S. (36) 575, annex, folios 2-3.
185. PRO, CAB 62/55 N.I.S. (36) 638.
186. PRO, FO 371/2133, W 8913, folios 7, 8bis.
187. *Dez anos de política externa (1936-1947)*, IV, 309-310. The arguments presented in the written note are summed up in a telegram to Monteiro in London from Oliveira Salazar in Lisbon, dated 22 May 1937 (*ibid.*, pp. 316-317).
188. *GSCW*, p. 290.
188b. See Pursey's letter, *Times Literary Supplement*, 18 July 1975, p. 805.
189. The English text is taken from a paper found in the archives of Mr. Wood, and kindly furnished to me by his son, David McKinnon Wood. Wood arrived in Bilbao on 22 May and left on 28 May. A Spanish text is printed in *Euzko Deya*, 3 June 1937, p. 2, where Wood is called "Mackinson."
190. *Ibid.*, 7 June 1937, pp. 1-2. The third witness added little to the known evidence.
191. PRO, FO 371/21337, W 12044, folios 125, 130, 131.
192. *Ibid.*, W 12047, folio 137.
193. *Ibid.*, folio 131. Reproduction of House of Commons debates.
194. PRO, FO 371/21341, W 13503, folio 132.
195. PRO, FO 371/21291, W 9438, folio 139. Shuckburgh called this "an interesting confession."
196. PRO, FO 371/21392, W 9586, folios 197, 198. Von Goss, a long-time resident of Spain, had been named press attaché at the German embassy in Madrid in June 1935. He was, in reality, an agent of Canaris's Abwehr, the Nazi German Intelligence Service (Viñas, *La Alemania nazi y el 18 de julio*, p. 168).
197. During the month of May 1937, Peter Kemp was ill in Vitoria, and among those who came to see him was Gabrielle Herbert. Kemp also saw a great deal of "Botteau" (Botto) and Cardozo during those days. Herbert's story about Guernica concorded more or less, as did that of Kemp, with those of Botto and Cardozo. See Kemp, *Mine Were of Trouble*, p. 89.
198. PRO, FO 371/21295, W 12216, folio 59. Sir Robert Vansittart, in a commentary on Herbert's testimony concerning the two "quite illiterate" young soldiers, wrote: "You can get propaganda through the ear." Sir Robert favored a middle path. "The truth might well be (as usual) halfway between the 2 versions. . . . Perhaps the little town was *both* bombed and burned." This latter remark shows how meager was Sir Robert's knowledge of the incident; he seemed not to realize that the Basque version included bombing and, subsequently, burning from incendiary bombs.
199. Letter, Holburn to Southworth. Sir Robert Vansittart, in commenting on Herbert's statement, confused Steer, who was with the Basques, and "The Times' correspondent with General Franco's forces." He exclaimed: "But it was the *Times* correspondent himself who *wrote* such a circumstantial story in the opposite sense!" (PRO, FO 371/21295, W 12216, folio 59.) If the British diplomat believed that Steer was attached to the Nationalist forces and that his dispatch had passed through the Rebel censorship, his conception of journalism during the civil war was curious indeed.
200. PRO, FO 371/21295, W 12216, folio 59-60. Cranborne added: "I am quite certain that the view which she [Herbert] stated was based on a conviction arising from her own observation and not merely from what she had been told." Vansittart thought her "evidently the complete partisan."
201. PRO, FO 371/21332, W 8853/7/41, folios 260-262. This is a minute signed by D. F. Howard.
202. PRO, FO 371/21292, W 9579, folio 185.
203. PRO, FO 371/21236, W 11411, folios 235-236.
204. *Ibid.*, folio 234, 238.
205. PRO, FO 371/22621, W 1725, folio 242. Thompson's paper was dated 2 February

1938, and a copy was sent to Sir George Mounsey at the Foreign Office.

206. *Ibid.* "Bilbao itself struck me as a sad city. . . . I noticed a German ship loading ore. . . . Details of the numbers executed are, of course, virtually impossible to obtain, but they certainly run into several hundreds. . . . The situation in Santander is worse . . . the Cuban consul there . . . estimates the number shot in round figures as one thousand." Thompson recognized that some Republicans shot by the Nationalists were guilty of murders, but he added: "I am afraid that only a percentage of those shot since the Nationalist occupation fall within this category. . . . There are thousands in prison in Vizcaya and Asturias, and I don't suppose the world will ever know what happened after the capture of Gijón. In Bilbao I saw that the prison ship in the river was crowded. . . . In writing about Nationalist Spain I do not reflect any great optimism. The fact is there is little to be optimistic about—Spain to-day is a sad and suffering country and I personally experience a great feeling of relief when I get out of it."

207. See Hodgson, *Spain Resurgent* (London, 1953). Thompson later observed that Hodgson believed "that the Civil War in Spain was another Bolshevik revolution and that the three dictators Hitler, Mussolini, and Franco, were protecting Western Europe from the Bolsheviks. While the illusion was widely entertained by right-wing politicians at home, I personally never had any sympathy with those that suffered from it" (*Front-Line Diplomat*, p. 335).

208. Thompson, *op. cit.*, pp. 138-139.

209. *My Mission to Spain*, pp. 343-346.

210. *Palabras del Caudillo* (1938), p. 120. The question asked of Franco is not given. The technique of the Franco interview was given as follows by Reynolds and Eleanor Packard, who represented the UP in Nationalist Spain at this time: "Bolín told Reynolds to write out a list of questions. Reynolds . . . made out the list immediately, on Bolín's typewriter. Two days later, Bolín said half of the questions had been thrown out and that the remaining five had been answered by one of the staff officers. He hoped within the next forty-eight hours it would be possible for Franco to read the answers and approve them. The approval was duly given, and Reynolds received the answers which bore Franco's initials, F. F. B. Reynolds was then permitted, after being searched for weapons, to see the rebel chief in his private office for two minutes, but was not allowed to ask any questions" (Reynolds and Eleanor Packard, *Balcony Empire*, pp. 47-48). The interview thus described was previous to that given the UP in July 1937. Also, *El pequeño libro pardo del general*, p. 34. Ricardo de la Cierva, commenting on the contents of this book (*El Alcázar*, 4 December 1972, p. 5), alleged that the phrases attributed to Franco were generally taken out of context and said that in his forthcoming biography of Franco, he would use all these phrases, but in their proper context. In *Francisco Franco: un siglo de España*, however, not only does La Cierva make no explanation of Franco's statements on Guernica—he does not even mention them.

211. *Palabras del Caudillo* (1938), pp. 132-133; *El pequeño libro pardo del general*, p. 34.

212. *Palabras del Caudillo* (1938), p. 144; *ABC*, Seville, 18 July 1937; *El pequeno libro pardo del general*, pp. 34-35.

213. *HA*, 19 July 1938, p. 2.

214. Franco, *Textos de doctrina política*, p. 675.

215. *El estado nuevo* was first published in 1935, in Madrid, by Cultura Española, a publishing house belonging to the Accion Española group. A second edition was printed in Burgos in 1937, a third, in Madrid in 1941. All three bore the Nihil Obstat. The final phrase of the book reads: "we have discovered that the New State is no other than the Spanish State of the 'reyes católicos,'" to which a footnote adds: "Ferdinand and Isabella" (*The New State*, p. 320).

216. *The New State*, p. 7.

PART TWO: THE CONTROVERSY FROM 1939 to 1975

1. Bernanos, Georges, *Les enfants humiliés*, p. 198, citing a Vatican dispatch, printed in a Brazilian newspaper.

2. Decree 23 September, 1939, *Boletín Official,* 21 October 1939 (*BO* 26, no. 299, p. 5989, Ref. Leg. 1496).

3. *Historia militar de la guerra de España* (1940), p. 406. The unwary reader could believe from Aznar's text that the town was set on fire on 28 April.

4. *Operaciones militares de la guerra de España,* pp. 281-282. Lojendio was press attaché in the Diplomatic Cabinet of general headquarters in Salamanca, at the time of Guernica. Later he was press officer at Franco's Headquarters, from July 1937 on (*ibid.,* pp. 14-15).

5. *Historia de la revolución española. Tercera guerra de independencia,* p. 236. A photograph of the ruins of Guernica on page 237 bears the caption: "Parochial church and houses burned by the separatist militiamen on abandoning the town."

6. *Cruzada,* VII, 322-323.

7. Werner Beumelberg, in *Kampf um Spanien: Die Geschichte der Legion Condor,* p. 98, spoke of the entry of the Nationalists into Guernica, "which was completely destroyed by the Reds." The following sentence read: "The bombs of the attackers finished it off." This does not necessarily mean air bombs. Nothing about Guernica has been found in: Wulf Bley, *Das Buch der Spanienflieger;* Max Hoyos, *Pedros y Pablos;* Hellmuth Führing, *Wir funken fur Franco;* Fritz von Forell, *Mölders und seine Männer.* References to Guernica can, however, be found in a book published in Berlin in 1937, written by a Dutch woman journalist, Maria de Smeth. The ruins of Guernica reminded her of Irún, and she had no doubt that explosions carried out by the Reds had caused the damage (*Viva España! Arriba España!,* p. 221). This book was published by Nibelungen Verlag, the Anti-Komintern editorial house.

8. Bundesarchiv, Militärarchiv, Freiburg. Akte Br. II L 14/3 "Die Kämpfe im Norden," p. 47. See Merkes *Die deutsche Politik im spanischen Bürgerkrieg, 1936-1939,* p. 397.

9. Bundesarchiv, Militärarchiv, Freiburg, Akte II, L 14/2, p. 77.

10. Merkes, *op. cit.,* p. 397.

11. *La guerra di Spagna, sino alla liberazione di Gijon,* p. 228.

12. *Venti mesi di guerra in Spagna,* p. 310.

13. *La guerra civile in Spagna,* Vol. III, *La campagna dei volontari italiani, dalle Baleari a Teruel,* p. 148. Belforte's real name was J. Biondi Morra.

14. This book was published in the year XVI of the Fascist Era, and was probably written early in 1938.

15. *L'aviazione legionaria in Spagna* 1940–XVIII, pp. 89-90.

16. *La Spagna dei legionari,* p. 132.

17. *ED,* 30 April 1946, p. 6.

18. I have not found the original newspaper report on this interview, but the essential elements have been often repeated. See Ansaldo, *op. cit.,* p. 179n; Basaldua, *op. cit.,* p. 114. Unfortunately, there is a tendency to confuse the testimony at the trial itself and the preparatory, unofficial conversations between the accused and the investigators which took place in the cells. See G. M. Gilbert, *Nuremberg Diary.* Gilbert does not mention Guernica, or even the Spanish Civil War.

19. A letter from the General Services Administration, National Archives and Records Service, Washington, D.C., 19 February 1969, reads in part as follows: "Several of our staff members, now working with the captured German records of World War II, were connected with the Nuremberg trials in administrative positions. Through their referrals, we were able to find a man here in Washington who had been associated with Maier and Sander. He informed us, 'I knew them, I worked with them, but I have not seen either of them since 1949, and I have no idea how to get in touch with them.' Mr. Charles Thomas, of our staff, while in Graduate School, made a brief study of Guernica. It was his experience that it was difficult to find reliable sources about what had happened at Guernica."

20. *Voorproef in Spanje, 1919-1939,* p. 165.

21. *Ibid.* This book was probably prepared for publication in 1943, the date found at the end of the preface.

22. *Texto taquigráfico de la conferencia pronunciada por el arquitecto de la dirección general de regiones devastadas . . . el dia 3 de julio de 1940,* p. 3.

23. *Ibid.,* pp. 29-30.

24. *La reconstrucción de España,* n.p. There are six photographs of Guernica in ruins, two of the reconstructed town.

25. *The Masquerade in Spain*, pp. 54-55.
26. *Ejército*, July 1949, cited in Bolín, *STVY*, p. 359. Also cited in *Ejército*, October 1957, p. 42.
27. *This Is Spain*, pp. 227-229.
28. *Ibid.*, pp. 229-231. Pattee wrote that Guernica was occupied by the Nationalists on 28 April (*ibid.*, p. 227).
29. *¿ Para que . . .?*, pp. 178-179n. Jorge Vigón was the brother of Mola's chief of staff, and certainly knew all about the destruction of Guernica, although he seems to have said nothing to Ansaldo.
30. *Die Ersten und die Letzten*, pp. 42-43.
31. On the contrary, witnesses gave evidence concerning the high visibility over Guernica on 26 April. See *Guernica: The Official Report*, pp. 28, 34, 37.
32. *Memorias. "Los primeros y los últimos,"* pp. 53-54.
33. *Convulsiones de España*, I, 351-355. The original article was published 16 March 1955, but, unfortunately, the editor does not state where.
34. Hodgson's "neutrality of spirit" can be seen in the hardly credible fact that his military attaché, an Irish Catholic, was a nephew by marriage of Admiral Cervera, head of the Franco navy (Hodgson, *Spain Resurgent*, p. 80).
35. *Ibid.*, pp. 69-70. Hodgson is a careless historian. He wrote: "The German Embassy in Spain was ordered at once to induce Franco to issue an 'immediate and energetic denial' of British reports attributing the bombardment of Guernica to German airmen and on 29 April an article was issued by the Press Bureau declaring that the town was 'set afire and reduced to ruins by the "Red" hordes in the criminal service of Aguirre' " (*ibid.*, p. 70). The telegram to the German ambassador requesting "an immediate and energetic denial" was sent on 4 May; the 29 April article was, then, hardly related to the Berlin request. Hodgson also referred in his text to the conclusions of "a commission consisting of two magistrates and two engineers"—information presumably taken from *Guernica: The Official Report*, and declared that the commission, "after examining twenty-five witnesses expressed itself as satisfied that: (i) on 25 April Guernica was occupied by Basque troops; (ii) The market that day was sparsely attended because people had been warned of 'impending destruction'; (iii) The town was bombed intermittently by aeroplanes, the total casualties being less than 100; (iv) The Town was destroyed by fire by the 'Reds' within it" (*Spain Resurgent*, p. 70). It is not of course absolutely certain that Hodgson got his information from *Guernica: The Official Report*, for he does not mention the title either in his text or in his bibliography.
36. *Franco frente a Hitler*, pp. 84-85.
37. *Eyewitness*, pp. 94-99.
38. *Centinela de occidente*, p. 292.
39. *Franco of Spain*, p. 44. Coles is unlucky. He does not name his first informant (perhaps Henry Buckley), nor does he give Steer's name. The only person he names in connection with Guernica is "Reynolds," who had absolutely nothing to do with the Basque town.
40. See Book I, chap. 3. See also Southworth, *op. cit.*, pp. 180-181, 185, 215-216.
41. *Guerra de liberación (La fuerza de la razón)*, p. 201.
42. *General Mola (El conspirador)*, p. 316.
43. *La guerra en el aire*, p. 207.
44. *Mine Were of Trouble*, p. 89.
45. *Legionario en España*, pp. 114-115.
46. *Franco, soldat et chef d'état*, p. 231.
47. *Franco, soldado y estadista*, p. 268.
48. *The Spanish Civil War*, p. 421. "Guernica," pp. 419-421. "Conclusion," p. 421.
49. *Ibid.*, p. 420n.
50. *La guerra civil española*. "Guernica," pp. 351-353.
51. *Historia militar de la guerra de España*, II, 147. This edition was considered the third. The first edition was in one volume in 1940; the second in two volumes in 1940. The first volume of the third edition appeared in 1958; the third volume in 1963.
52. *La guerra de liberación nacional*, pp. 259-314. The only reference to Guernica concerns the fighting on the Amorebieta-Guernica highway on 9 May (p. 290).

53. *Ibid.,* pp. 353-386
54. *Die deutsche Politik gegenüber dem spanischen Bürgerkrieg,* p. 96.
55. *Der spanische Bürgerkrieg,* p. 176.
56. *Ibid.,* p. 319.
57. *The Civil War in Spain,* Onaindia's statement, pp. 222-224; it is attributed to "Guernika, by Father Alberto de Onaindia, Bilbao, 1937," on p. 366. This is not the text found in the English-language pamphlet, entitled *Guernica,* probably published in Bilbao. Yoldi's testimony, pp. 225-233; the entire manuscript of Yoldi has never been published.
58. *Spanish Fury,* pp. 162-163.
59. *Furia española,* pp. 130-131. A second edition was published in 1963. A paperback edition came out in 1967; the Guernica text is on pp. 129-130, the same text as in the other editions.
60. *Historia de España,* VI, *La época contemporánea,* pp. 168, 220, 222.
61. *Ibid.,* 1968, pp. 257-259.
62. Georges-Roux, *La guerre civile d'Espagne,* pp. 190-191. The opinion of Georges-Roux concerning the destruction of Guernica cannot be taken lightly, for he combines historical writing with faith-healing, and is believed by his followers to be Christ returned to the earth, or, at times, God present on the earth. As such he should know the truth about Guernica. It was perhaps Divine Intervention that persuaded the French Academy to award a prize to this book which has neither literary nor historical worth.
63. Georges-Roux, *La guerra civil de España,* p. 217.
64. *The Spanish Civil War,* p. 537.
65. *The Spanish Republic and the Civil War,* pp. 381-382. A Spanish-language edition was published in Mexico in 1967.
66. *Arriba,* 31 January 1970, interview by Pedro Pascual. Foreign Minister Castiella had read Jackson's book *The Spanish Republic and the Civil War* and brought it to the cabinet meeting. La Cierva denigrated Jackson's work in the interview, calling it "highly fragile" and saying that it "was quite discredited among North American scholars." It is not too difficult to recognize the probable sources of La Cierva's opinion. This interview has recently been reprinted in Pascual, *Proceso a una guerra,* pp. 17-40.
67. *Diálogos para otra España,* pp. 230-231. The chapter on Guernica runs from p. 230 to p. 253, including notes. The discussion on Picasso's painting runs from p. 232 to p. 251; the notes from 251 to 253. There is a reproduction of the painting among the illustrations. The jacket reproduces the painting.
68. *La guerra española de 1936,* p. 254. The footnote is also on p. 254.
69. *Ibid.,* pp. 254-255. Dahms wrote that this fact was verified in 1937 by such "international experts in questions of aerial warfare as Grey Grey, Caldwell, Bouché and Niessel." He gave as reference the *Aeroplane,* 5 May 1937, which offered Grey's opinions, but not the verifications announced by Dahms.
70. *La guerra de España en sus fotografías,* p. 196.
71. *A l'est de Saint-Sebastien,* pp. 256-257. Cassagnau cited the testimony of Claude Farrère, Pierre Héricourt, le Comte de Saint-Aulaire, Admiral Joubert, all of whom—except Joubert—denied any bombing whatsoever.
72. *International Herald Tribune* (hereafter, *IHT*), 14 March 1967; *Le Monde,* 17 March 1967.
73. *NYT,* Amsterdam; *IHT,* 14 March 1967.
74. *IHT,* 14 March 1967.
75. *Le Monde,* 17 March 1967.
76. *Ibid.,* 18 March 1967.
77. Two years later, on 29 March 1969, the Spanish Supreme Court overturned the decision of the Tribunal of Public Order, and ruled that Father Arbeloa was guilty of insults to the National Movement and sentenced him to six months imprisonment (*IHT,* 30-31 March 1969, Reuters).
78. *Le Figaro Littéraire,* 18-24 December 1967, p. 13; Ojanguren y Celaya, "Páginas de mi vida," ms.
79. "Homage to Guernica," by William P. Lineberry, *New Leader,* 24 April 1967, pp. 16-17. Augusto Unceta, the ex-mayor, was owner of an arms factory. According to Lineberry, in 1966

"when Guernica celebrated the sixth centennial of its founding in 1366, Unceta . . . in his official capacity (and reportedly under pressure from the capital) . . . dutifully presented Generalissimo Francisco Franco, whose German allies had reduced the town to rubble, with a diamond-studded medal commemorating the anniversary. Unceta subsequently refused reappointment to another term as mayor, some say because of the trouble over the award and the pressure brought against him and his family by the local people."

80. *L'Espresso,* 18 June 1967, pp. 8-18.
81. *STVY,* pp. 274-275.
82. *Ibid.,* pp. 276-281.
83. *Ibid.,* p. 358.
84. *Guernica: The Official Report,* p. 18.
85. *STVY,* p. 359.
86. *Ibid.,* pp. 356-357. Generally, the Franco people spoke of the "National airforce," and the Republicans used the expression "Nationalist airforce." Bolín, curiously, used the word "National" in his Spanish text and "Nationalist" in his English version.
87. *NYT,* 30 April 1937, p. 8. Carney's dispatch is datelined Durango on 29 April, but the text given is that of the communiqué of 27 April, probably repeated during the day of 28 April. This date coincides with the dates of the two dispatches given by Bolín.
88. See Talón, *op. cit.,* p. 111, quoting an official Nationalist communiqué.
89. *STVY,* p. 357.
90. *HA,* 29 April 1927, p. 1.
91. *GSCW,* p. 279.
92. *Ibid.,* p. 281.
93. *STVY,* p. 359.
94. *Ibid.,* p. 360.
95. *New York Times Book Review,* 1 October 1967.
96. *STVY,* p. 280.
97. *Franco, A Biographical History,* p. 246.
98. *Ibid.*
99. *Ibid.,* pp. 246-247.
100. *Ibid.*
101. *New Statesman,* 29 December 1967. "Their Man in Madrid," by Herbert R. Southworth, p. 907.
102. *Ibid.,* 26 January 1968, p. 110.
103. *Times,* 26 June 1969.
104. *La Quinzaine Littéraire,* 16-30 November 1969, p. 22.
105. *Ibid.,* 1-15 January 1970, p. 20.
106. This basic anti-Republican prejudice on the part of Crozier can be seen in his account of the end of the siege of Santa María de la Cabeza, in Jaén Province. According to Crozier, it ended with "the overrunning of the improvised fortress by the Republicans, and the slaughter of the defenders" (*op. cit.,* p. 233). However, in reality, the vanquished were treated with a generosity rare in the Spanish Civil War, and certainly nothing like it can be found in the accounts of Nationalist treatment of Republican prisoners. See *Epopeya de la guardia civil en el santuario de la Virgen de la Cabeza.* Also La Cierva, *Historia ilustrada,* II, 207. Crozier perhaps obtained his impression of a "slaughter" from Hugh Thomas, who wrote concerning the surrender of the sanctuary, "For a while slaughter was general" (*op. cit.* p. 423). In Thomas's book, this account followed that of Guernica, and the English historian doubtless credited the Republicans with this atrocity in order to keep things in balance.
107. *Franco: A Biographical History,* p. 247.
108. *Franco, historia y biografía,* T.I., pp. 359-360. The false story of the end of the siege of Santa María de la Cabeza was also translated unchanged (p. 338).
109. *Franco: The Man and his Nation,* p. 277.
110. *Ibid.,* p. 293 n. 39.
111. *Ibid.,* p. 277.
112. *Ibid.,* p. 293 n. 39.
113. *Ibid.,* p. 277.
114. *Op. cit.,* p. 107.

115. *ED*, 30 April 1937, p. 1.

116. *Op. cit.*, p. 277. Feeling doubtful about the information fed to Hills, I wrote to the embassy of the German Federal Republic in Paris to obtain von Funck's address. I was informed that he was deceased (letter dated 19 October 1972, signed by Lt. Colonel Kuhnt). However, shortly after the publication of this book in French in Paris in February 1975, I received a letter from the Spanish historian Angel Viñas informing me that he had talked with von Funck about Guernica, and had indeed a letter from him on the subject, dated 19 June 1973. The information given me in 1972 concerning von Funck's death was inexact. Von Funck told Viñas that the information concerning Guernica and von Funck as published by Hills was false. Von Funck was the military attaché; he had nothing whatsoever to do with air force matters. He did not think that Franco would ever have convoked him to discuss the bombing of Guernica; it would have been incorrect for him to have been called, and incorrect for him to have gone. In the letter to Vinas, von Funck wrote: "What Hills says about 'Colonel Funck' is from the beginning to the end pure nonsense." *"ist von A bis Z blanker Unsinn."* This testimony from von Funck should end all discussion on this detail of the controversy.

117. Talón, *op. cit.*, p. 108.

118. Hills, *op. cit.*, p. 293 n. 39.

119. *La intervención de Alemania en favor de Franco en las operaciones del territorio vasco*, pp. 22-25. The dead are listed for the greater part by name.

120. *New Statesman*, 29 December 1967. "Their Man in Madrid," by Herbert R. Southworth, p. 907.

121. *Ibid.*, 5 January 1968, letter from George Hills, p. 13.

122. *Op. cit.*, p. 278.

123. *La Nación*, 29 April 1937.

124. *Op. cit.*, p. 293n.

125. *Ibid.*, p. 277.

126. *Ibid.*, p. 293n.

127. *GSCW*, pp. 404, 424-425.

128. *Der spanische Bürgerkrieg in Augenzeugenberichten*, pp. 268-272. The Cowles and Galland references are from Thomas, *Der spanische Bürgerkrieg*, p. 327. Duval's testimony is from his book, *Entwicklung und Lehren des Kriegen in Spanien*, p. 118 ff.

129. R. de la Cierva, *Importancia histórica e historiográfica de la guerre española*, cover flyleaf.

130. *Crónica de la guerra española*, no. 62, IV. Thomas, pp. 26-30; Labauria, pp. 33-38; Steer, p. 39; Lojendio, p. 26; Martínez Esparza, pp. 38-44; Ansaldo, pp. 43, 46; Bolín, pp. 45-46; Galland, pp. 44-45; Dahms, pp. 30-32. The texts of Galland and Dahms are from their Spanish translations; that of Thomas from the Spanish-language (Ruedo Ibérico) edition, published in Paris. These fascicules were published by Editorial Codex, Buenos Aires.

131. *Crónica de la guerra española*, no. 62, IV, pp. 47-48.

132. *Ibid.*, pp. 25-26.

133. *Corresponsal en España*, p. 194.

134. *Ibid.*, p. 282. The editor wrote in a preface, p. xii: "We have preferred to leave untouched the abundant partial errors of the book and its at times dramatic lack of perspective."

135. *Comentarios a mil imágenes de la guerra civil española*. Picasso's painting, p. 362. This book also contains a photograph of Picasso, "un malagueño universal," p. 371. Photographs of Guernica, pp. 369-370.

136. *"¿Qué pasa?"*, 7 October 1967, quoted in *Oficina de Prensa Euzkadi*, no. 4, 904, p. 1, supplement to *ED*, no. 497.

137. *España en llamas, 1936:* Galland, p. 341; Onaindia, p. 339; Labauria, p. 342; Cleugh, p. 338; Kemp, p. 338; documents of Basque clergy, with Thomas's comment, p. 340; Talón, p. 195; editorial comment (also Talón?), p. 341.

138. Martínez Bande, *Vizcaya*, p. 146.

139. *Los que no perdieron la guerra*, pp. 123-124.

140. *Op. cit.*, p. 341.

141. *Picasso: His Life and Work*, pp. 309, 317.

142. *Síntesis histórica de la guerra de liberación, 1936-1939*, p. 82. The basic work was

done by Colonel of the General Staff Juan Priego López aided by Admiral Indalecio Nuñez Iglesias, Artillery Colonel Jose Manuel Martínez Bande, and Aviation Major Luis de Marimón Riera.

143. *Le Monde*, 29 October 1969, p. 2, article signed "C. L."

144. *Ibid.*

145. *Ibid.*; J. P. Sartre, preface to Gisèle Halimi, *Le procès de Burgos*, p. xxvii. Efforts of the government to interfere with the commemorative masses for Echebarrieta held widely throughout the Basque country caused indignation among the clergy and the villagers.

146. *Le Monde*, 20 October 1969, p. 2.

147. *Ibid.*, 4-5 August 1968. Manzanas had a years-long reputation of torturing political prisoners (Sartre, in Halimi, *op. cit.*, p. xxvii). Elosegi wrote: "I personally knew Commissioner Manzanas. . . . He was a cynical, amoral man. He conducted his interrogations surrounded by shouting and insulting policemen. He always threatened to kill with his own hands men who were so weak a breath could have knocked them over. Manzanas treated as a whore any woman who fell into his hands" (*Quiero morir por algo*, pp. 31-32).

148. *L'Humanité*, 6, 8 August 1968; *IHT*, 7 August 1968; *Le Monde* 8 August 1968. The decree on banditism and terrorism, of 21 September 1960, permitted certain political crimes to be judged as "military rebellion" by military courts. It had been abrogated on 2 December 1963. See Salaberri, *El proceso de Euskadi en Burgos*, pp. 19-76; Halimi, *op. cit.*, pp. 255-261, article by Juan Ignacio Sarda Antón, lawyer at the Barcelona bar.

149. *Le Monde*, 22 November 1968.

150. *IHT*, 30 November-1 December 1968.

151. *Le Monde*, 14 December 1968.

152. *IHT*, 14-15 December 1968.

153. *Ibid.*, 26 December; also: *Le Figaro*, 23, 27 December; *L'Humanité*, 23 December; *Le Monde*, 24 December, all 1968.

154. *L'Humanité*, *Le Figaro*, 2 December 1968.

155. *L'Humanité*, 25, 28, 31 December; *Le Monde*, 28 December 1968.

156. *Le Figaro*, 21 December; *IHT*, 24 December, 1968.

157. *IHT*, 13 (*NYT* dispatch), 14 January; *Le Monde*, 15 January; *L'Humanite*, 16 January, 1969.

158. *IHT*, 16, 18-19 January; *L'Humanité*, 18 January 1969.

159. *IHT*, *L'Humanité*, 15 January 1969.

160. *Le Monde*, 18 January; *IHT*, 18 January, 1969.

161. *L'Humanité*, 22 January 1969.

162. *IHT*, 22 January; *Le Monde*, 23 January, 1969.

163. *IHT* (UPI), 25-26 January; *Le Monde*, 26-27 January; *Le Figaro*, 25-27, pp. 94-95.

164. *IHT*, 6 February; *Le Monde*, 7, 12, 19, 21 February; *ED*, January-February, pp., 1, 5—all 1969.

165. *Le Monde*, 23-24 March; *IHT*, 22-23 March 1969. The decree had originally been for three months.

166. Salaberri, *op. cit.*, pp. 94-95; Halimi, *op. cit.*, pp. 237, 245, 248; *ED*, March-April 1969, p. 5, citing *La Voz de España*, San Sebastián daily.

167. *Le Monde*, 9 April (Reuters dispatch), 13-14 April (Reuters, AFP) 1969. *ED*, March-April 1969, p. 5, cast doubt on the statement that the men had died exactly as the police pretended.

168. *Le Monde*, 16 April 1969.

169. *Ibid.*, 12 April (Reuters); *ED*, March-April 1969, p. 5.

170. Salaberri, *op. cit.*, pp. 96-97; Halimi, *op. cit.*, pp. 235-237, 237-239, 250-251. The three men captured were Jesús Abrisqueta Corta, Víctor Arana Bilbao, and Mario Onaindia Nachiondo.

171. *L'Humanité*, 12 April; *Le Monde*, 13-14 April; *ED*, March-April, p. 5—all 1969.

172. Salaberri, *op. cit.*, p. 97; Halimi, *op. cit.*, pp. 240-243, 245-246, 251-254. These were Juana Dorronsoro Ceberio, Enrique Venancio Guesalaga Larreta, Juan Echave Garitacelaya (a priest), and Eduardo Uriarte Romero. The latter was accused of complicity in the killing of Manzanas.

173. *Le Monde*, 20-21 April 1969.

174. *IHT*, 23 April 1969, AP dispatch.
175. *Le Monde*, 22 April 1969.
176. *Le Monde*, 25, 29 (UPI, Reuters) April; *IHT* 25, 28 April (*NYT* dispatches); *Le Figaro*, 28 April (UPI, AFP), 1969.
177. *Le Monde*, 27-28 April 1969.
178. *Ibid.*, 2 May 1969.
179. *Ibid.*, 13 May 1969.
180. *Le Figaro*, 17 May; *L'Humanité*, 17 May; *ED*, May-June, 1969, p. 7. This killing seems to have been a police error. The victim was a Nationalist war veteran, and damages of one million pesetas were paid to the widow. See *ED*, November-December 1969, p. 5.
181. *ED*, May-June, p. 5; *L'Humanité*, 2 June, 1969.
182. *IHT*, 4 June; Le Monde, 4 June, 1969.
183. *IHT* (Reuters); *L'Humanité*, *Combat*—all 13 June, 1969.
184. *Le Monde*, 28 June 1969.
185. *L'Humanité*, 19 July 1969 (AFP).
186. *Le Monde*, 2 August 1969 (AFP).
187. *L'Humanité*, 7 July; *Le Monde*, 13-14 July: 20 August, 1969. The illegal propaganda consisted of tracts protesting against the imprisoning of Basque priests. This trial was held before the military court of Burgos.
188. Le Monde, 8 August 1969.
189. *IHT*, 25 August; *Le Monde*, 26 August, 1969.
190. *Le Monde*, 27 August 1969.
191. *IHT*, 6 October 1969 (Reuters). One of the condemned men was José María Dorronsoro, who was later tried in the Burgos trial. See Halimi, *op. cit.*, pp. 239-240. On 12 November, he was again sentenced, this time to three years and three months and various fines.
192. *L'Humanité*, 13 October 1969 (AFP).
193. *Le Monde*, 17 October 1969 (AFP, AP).
194. *Lc Monde*, 25-26 October 1969.
195. *L'Humanité*, 21 October; *Le Monde*, 26-27 October 1969.
196. *Le Monde*, 29 October; *Le Figaro*, 29 October 1969.
197. *L'Humanité*, 27 November 1969. Dorronsoro Ceberio was also to appear in the Burgos trial.
198. *L'Humanité*, 15 December 1969 (AFP). This trial was held at the Burgos military court.
199. *ED*, January-February 1970, p. 7, citing *U.G.T.*, *Boletín de la U.G.T. de España en Exilio.*
200. *Le Monde*, 4 December 1969 (AFP).
201. *Le Monde*, 29 October 1969, article signed "C. L."
202. *NYT*, 5 September; *Le Monde*, 5 September 1969.
203. Letter from Merry del Val to *Life Magazine*, 24 January 1969, p. 16A. The editors of *Life* forcefully rejected the arguments of the ambassador.
204. Manfred Merkes, *Die deutsche Politik im spanischen Bürgerkrieg, 1936-1939*, p. 397.
205. *Ibid.* Merkes says the final draft was finished before 8 March 1940. The work was done by the Kriegswissenschaftlichen Abteilung der Luftwaffe, Arbeitsgruppe Spanienkrieg.
206. *Ibid.*, pp. 397-398. The work is entitled: "Bericht über einen vierwochigen Aufenthalt in Spanien, 13.4-9.5 1937." Merkes's original was in the Militärgeschichtliches Forschungsamt Dokumentenzentrale: II H 796/1. In 1973 the Jaenecke report was presented by the German historian Hans-Henning Abendroth as the final word on the Guernica problem. He argued that although bombs of the Condor Legion, which obviously missed their targets, were decisive in the destruction of Guernica, there was no intention on the part of the German pilots to destroy the town. The raid was not a terror bombing; it was a strategic attack intended to cut off the retreat road of the Basque troops (*Hitler in der spanischen Arena: Die deutsch-spanischen Beziehungen in Spannungsfeld der europäischen Interessenpolitik vom Ausbruch des Bürgerkrieges bis zum Ausbruch des Weltkrieges, 1936-1939*, pp. 159-160). Abendroth later elaborated on this argument in the *Times Literary Supplement* (25 July 1975, p. 841), insisting in spite of the mass of opposing evidence that "no incendiary bombs were used in the raid."
207. *Die deutsche Politik im spanischen Bürgerkrieg, 1936-1939*, p. 398. Merkes's source was the "Auswertung Rügen," 2, 69 (MGFA, DZ: E 772).

208. *Ibid*. The source is "Bericht des Kommandeurs der Pioniere VII, Oberst Meise, vom 21 März 1938 an das OKH uber seine Reise nach Spanien, 20.1-28.2.1938" (MGFA, DZ: II H 3 (E), p. 3, quoted by Wohlfeil, *Vierteljahrshefte für Zeitgeschichte* (1968), 2, 115).

209. *Die deutsche Politik im spanischen Bürgerkrieg, 1936-1939*, p. 398. Merkes's source is von Beust's contribution to Study 1 of the "Projektes Karlsruhe," entitled "Die deutsche Luftwaffe im spanischen Krieg" (Legion Condor) (F. A. Spanienfeldzug I 1; MGFA, DZ: LW101/1).

210. *Ibid*.

211. *Ibid*., p. 397.

212. *Le Monde*, 24 October 1969.

213. *Le Monde*, 14 November 1969; *IHT*, 10 November 1969. Max Aub wrote as follows in a letter to Luis Quintanilla, 23 January, 1970: "As cultural attaché to the Spanish embassy in Paris and subcommissioner of the Spanish pavilion in the 1937 Exposition, I ordered a painting—or a fresco—from Picasso for the entrance of the building, conceived and built by the architects Lacasa and Sert. I delivered one hundred and fifty thousand francs for the costs of painting the mural and with the precise condition that when the exposition was finished the artist would remain the sole and absolute owner of the painting and that he could do with it whatever he wished. The past, present and future Spanish governments have nothing whatsoever to do with 'Guernica.' " Aub suggested that the receipt signed by Picasso for the money involved could be found in the papers left in Geneva by Luis Araquistain, who was Spanish ambassador in Paris at the time. Talón in his book seems unaware that Picasso refused to hand over the painting to the Franco government (*op. cit.*, p. 229).

214. According to Jesus Ynfante, Alfredo Sanchez Bella and his two brothers Florencio and Ismael are "militants" of the Opus Dei (*La prodigiosa aventura del Opus Dei*, pp. 353, XXVII).

215. *L'Humanite*, 1 December 1969.

216. *Arriba*, 31 January 1970. La Cierva's role was also to try to influence what foreign historians were writing on modern Spanish history. See not only the *Arriba* interview but also La Cierva's article in *El Alcázar*, 15 January 1972, "La historia vuelve a su cauce."

217. La Cierva wrote that "Ramón Salas and I have discovered documents on the organization of commandos for the destruction of towns and cities, belonging to the separatist Basque army. . . ." He said that these groups burned Amorebieta, but, if true, it hardly proves that they burned Guernica. He also referred to Major Bustán and the project mentioned by Víctor de Frutos to burn the old town of Bilbao.

218. *Arriba*, 31 January 1970. La Cierva had first spoken of Talón's book in *El Alcázar*, 26 April 1969 (Talón, *op. cit.*, p. 7).

219. *Jane's All the World's Aircraft* (1937), said that the He 51 fighter had a range of 431 miles, with an auxiliary tank (p. 178c) and that the Ju 52 bomber had a range of up to 930 miles (p. 185c). Another authority wrote that the He 111 bomber had a range of 930 miles (*Aircraft in Profile*, profile no. 15, p. 3).

220. *Indice*, April 1969, p. 18.

221. La Cierva was referring to the exchange of polemical letters between Brian Crozier and Herbert R. Southworth in *La Quinzaine* Littéraire, 1-15 January 1970, pp. 20-21.

222. *El Pensamiento Navarro*, 15 February 1970.

223. See text in Book I, chap. 2, n. 8.

224. *El Pensamiento Navarro*, 15 February 1970.

225. See *GSCW*, p. 950.

226. *El Pensamiento Navarro*, 15 February 1970.

227. *Ibid*.

228. *Ibid*.

229. *Ibid*., 20 February 1970.

230. *Ibid*. The references to Guernica in *Conspiración y guerra civil* can be found on pp. 860-863, 876-877. The sudden releasing by the censorship of this book—containing the chief elements of the new "revisionist" story on Guernica—is surely linked with the Pérez Embid-La Cierva campaign.

231. *Historia y Vida*, April 1970, pp. 107-108.

232. R. de la Cierva y de Hoces, *Leyenda y tragedia de las brigadas internacionales*, 2d ed., pp. 105-107. These references to Frutos and Guernica had previously been published in *El*

Alcázar in 1969, and then in a 1969 pamphlet entitled *La leyenda de las brigadas internacionales*. For our study, this 1970 reissue is more significant.

233. Víctor de Frutos, *Los que no perdieron la guerra*, p. 123.

234. *Op. cit.*, p. 280.

235. Letters to the author have met with a refusal. Letters to the University of Madrid have remained unanswered. The secrecy around this doctoral dissertation is difficult to understand. It has recently been suggested that the dissertation may never have been presented.

236. *Historia ilustrada de la guerra civil española*, II, 158, where La Cierva writes: "The young and brilliant journalist Vicente Talón has undertaken an exhaustive investigation which probably will clear up many details of the bombing of Guernica."

237. The chief value of this book lies in the illustrations. It is not, as its title suggests, a "history" of the war, but a compilation of articles on certain phases of the war, most of them previously published.

238. *Historia ilustrada*, II, 149.

239. *Ibid.*, p. 158.

240. *Ibid.*, pp. 150, 154. Ricardo de la Cierva had timidly denounced "the old story of Guernica (Bolín version)" in *El Alcázar*, 10 February 1968, p. 11. Luis Bolín had collaborated with Juan de la Cierva, uncle of R. de la Cierva, in the plot to secure an airplane for Franco's eventual trip from the Canaries to Morocco. Bolín, rather than La Cierva, was in charge of that historically important flight because he was not so well known as was the inventor of the autogyro, and there was less danger of his being identified en route, and possibly alerting the Republican authorities to the conspiracy (Bolín, *STVY*, pp. 12-13). Bolín achieved notoriety because of his role in this adventure; Juan de la Cierva died in an accident in England, about the time of Guernica. Did this succession of events worsen rather than improve relations between the two families?

241. *Historia ilustrada*, II, 150, quoting from *España: los años vitales*, p. 275.

242. *Ibid.*, p. 152, quoting *ABC*, Seville.

243. *Ibid.*, pp. 152, 154.

244. *Ibid.*, p. 154.

245. *ED*, 27 May 1937, p. 1; 10 June 1937, p. 1. This letter was published in full in *La Vanguardia* of Barcelona, and then published in a small one-page flyer. This was in the Spanish language and obviously intended for distribution in Spain itself, perhaps in the Rebel zone.

246. *Historia ilustrada*, II, 152.

247. *ED*, 10 June 1937, p. 1. This chronology points to the conclusion that the initiative for the letter came from Isabelle Blume, and that the Basques used it much later.

248. *Historia ilustrada*, II, 152, 154.

249. Joseba Elosegi, *op. cit.*, p. 183.

250. *Historia ilustrada*, II, 154.

251. *Ibid.*, p. 163.

252. Merkes, *Die deutsche Politik im spanischen Bürgerkrieg, 1936-1939*, p. 261.

253. *GSCW*, p. 405. Faupel's confidential communication to Berlin was dated 7 July 1937. Merkes points out that Arranz's visit on 24 June was four days after the fall of Bilbao (*Die deutsche Politik . . .*, pp. 261-262). Also Glenn T. Harper, *German Economic Policy in Spain during the Spanish Civil War, 1936-1939*, p. 70. It is interesting to note that Captain Francisco arranz Monasterio was the aeronautical engineer sent to Berlin with Bernhardt and Langenheim on 24 July 1936 (Merkes, *Die deutsche Politik im spanischen Bürgerkrieg, 1936-1939*, p. 28; Viñas, *La Alemania nazi y el 18 de julio*, p. 394).

254. *GSCW*, pp. 423-424.

255. *Ibid.*, p. 404.

256. *Ibid.*, p. 424.

257. *Die deutsche Politik im spanischen Bürgerkrieg, 1936-1939*, p. 261.

258. *Op. cit.*, p. 293.

259. *GSCW*, p. 424. This is von Mackensen's memorandum of 20 July, in which he reported that Faupel had told him "that as early as several months ago he had submitted the matter to the Führer in person but that the latter, after consultation with Field Marshal von Blomberg, had refused to interfere in a question of military personnel." See also Harper, *op. cit.*, p. 70.

260. *GSCW*, p. 434n. According to Merkes, Göring blamed "Faupel and the Party" for the quarrel between Faupel and Sperrle. See *Die deutsche Politik im spanischen Bürgerkrieg, 1936-1939*, p. 262. See also Harper, *op. cit.*, p. 70n.

261. *GSCW*, p. 434n; Merkes, *Die deutsche Politik im spanischen Bürgerkrieg, 1936-1939*, pp. 262, 264. Merkes dates Stohrer's nomination as of 30 August.

262. *GSCW*, p. 950; Merkes, *Die deutsche Politik* . . . , p. 334.

263. Merkes, *Die deutsche Politik* . . ., p. 262.

264. *Ibid.*, p. 101.

265. *Ibid.*, p. 262. *GSCW*, p. 434n, p. 950. Jesús Salas Larrazábal says that Sperrle was head of the Condor Legion on 11 October, but that Volkmann took over "in October" (*La guerra de españa desde el aire*, pp. 261, 285).

266. *Historia ilustrada*, II, 154.

267. *Ibid.*, p. 155.

268. *Crónica de la guerra española*, 62, IV, 3d cover page.

269. *Bibliografía sobre la guerra de España (1936-1939) y sus antecedentes*, p. 311.

270. *Searchlight on Spain*, 2d impression (1938), pp. 194-198.

271. R. de la Cierva, *Cien libros básicos sobre la guerra de España*, pp. 154-157.

272. *STVY*, p. 358.

273. *Historia ilustrada*, II, 158-159.

274. *Ibid.*, p. 548 n. 197.

275. *Arriba*, 30 January 1970, article by Pedro Pascual.

276. The Madrid weekly *SP* published extracts from Talón's book, pp. 33-46, on 28 June 1970 and announced that the book had just appeared.

277. *Arriba*, 30 January 1970.

278. *Arde Guernica*, p. 46.

279. *Ibid.*, p. 57.

280. *Ibid.*, p. 280.

281. *Ibid.*, pp. 53-54.

282. *Ibid.*, p. 115. See text accompanying nn. 90, 91, Book I, chap. 4.

283. *Ibid.*, p. 40.

284. *Ibid.*, pp. 65-72.

285. *Ibid.*, pp. 3-5

286. *Ibid.*, p. vi. Talón suggests that Steer's pro-Basque sentiments, coupled with anti-Spanish feelings, were attributable to the fact that his first wife's name was Margarita Herrero (*ibid.*, p. 241).

287. *Ibid.*, pp. 40-42, 46.

288. *Ibid.*, pp. 107-108.

289. *Ibid.*, p. 142.

290. *Ibid.*, p. 108. German document reads "east of Guernica" (*ibid.*, p. 264).

291. *Ibid.* See document reproduced pp. 264-265.

292. *HA*, 28 April 1937, p. 7.

293. *Arde Guernica*, p. 109n.

294. *Ibid.*, pp. 125-126.

295. *Ibid.*, p. 138.

296. *Ibid.*, pp. 115-117.

297. *Ibid.*, pp. 110-111.

298. *Ibid.*, p. 206.

299. *Ibid.*, pp. 117-118.

300. *Ibid.*, p. 131. Talón also wrote: "It was the Germans who by their own desire and will took the decision for the bombing, surpassing in this manner the areas of competence which had been assigned to them" (*ibid.*, p. 121).

301. *Ibid.*, pp. 112-113.

302. *GSCW*, pp. 283-284.

303. *Op. cit.*, p. 212.

304. *Ibid.*, pp. 161, 163.

305. *Ibid.*, p. 255.

306. *Ibid.*, p. 261.
307. *Ibid.*, p. 241, n. 2.
308. *Ibid.*, p. 254.
309. *Ibid.*, p. 261.
310. See interview of J. C. Clemente with R. de la Cierva in *Diario de Barcelona*, 19 December 1971, where La Cierva says: "The director of anti-Spanish propaganda, Herbert Rutledge Southworth, can tell you, if he does not wish to lie, as is his habit."
311. *Op. cit.*, p. 394.
312. *Ibid.*, p. 190.
313. *Gudari*, no. 61, 1972.
314. *Op. cit.*, pp. 262-263.
315. *Crossing the Line*, pp. 26-27.
316. *Op. cit.*, p. 261.
317. *Ibid.*, p. 280.
318. *Ibid.*, p. 296.
319. *Ibid.*, p. 259.
320. *Ibid.*, p. 156. Talón has not learned the first rule of journalism—that is, to spell the name correctly. Most of the non-Spanish names in the book are incorrectly written.
321. Private information. This act obviously served as a brake on the distribution of the book. It is difficult not to conclude that when the decision was finally taken to publish the book, it was also decided not to encourage its circulation.
322. *El Alcázar*, 14 July 1970. This ultra-right-wing organ was subsidized by the Spanish ministry of the army.
323. *Pueblo*, 25 July 1970, Revista II. Talón worked for this newspaper.
324. *El Correo Español-El Pueblo Vasco*, 16 August 1970.
325. *Nuevo Diario*, 30 August 1970, article signed Bernabeu.
326. *Diario Vasco*, 6 September 1970, article signed J. B.
327. Article signed José María Ruiz Gallardón. Bautista Sánchez was a witness vouched for by Jaime del Burgo (Talón, *op. cit.*, pp. 116-117; Del Burgo, *op. cit.*, p. 863).
328. *Le Monde*, 30 January; *ED*, January-February 1970, p. 7.
329. *Le Monde*, 18 February 1970.
330. *Ibid.*, 3 February 1970.
331. *Ibid.*, 21 February 1970, AP dispatch.
332. *ED*, May-June 1970, p. 3.
333. *IHT*, 24 April 1970, AP dispatch.
334. *Le Monde*, 12 May 1970.
335. *Ibid.*, 14 May 1970.
336. *Ibid.*, 4 June 1970.
337. *Le Monde, Le Figaro*, 8 June 1970.
338. *IHT*, 8 June 1970.
339. *Le Monde*, 25 June 1970, AFP, Reuters.
340. *IHT*, 9 July, Reuters; *Le Monde*, 9 July, AFP; 11 July, AFP, 1970.
341. *Le Monde*, 22 July 1970, AFP.
342. *Ibid.*, 20-21 September 1970.
343. Elosegi, *op. cit.*, pp. 145-146. Elosegi's company left the burning town on the morning of April 27 (pp. 157-158).
344. *Ibid.*, pp. 197-200.
345. *Ibid.*, p. 216.
346. *Ibid.*, p. 256.
347. *Ibid.*, pp. 37, 40.
348. *L'Humanité*, 26 September 1970. For the Burgos trial, see Salaberri, *op. cit.*
349. *Vizcaya*, pp. 107-109.
350. *Ibid.*, p. 105 n. 160.
351. *Ibid.*, p. 106 n. 162. The reference is to Belforte, *La guerra civile in Spagna*, III, 148. This citation has been discussed earlier in this chapter. It gives no date for the attack on the bridge.

352. *¿Así fue? Enigmas de la guerra civil española*, pp. 310-311.

353. *Ibid.*, pp. 309-310.

354. *Ibid.*, p. 307.

355. *Ibid.*, p. 310.

356. *Ibid.*, p. 308. This quotation is from *Historia y Vida*, and not from the later *Historia ilustrada de la guerra civil española*.

357. *LAE*, 8 June 1972, "La guerra de España," p. 799.

358. *LAE*, 18 May 1972, "La guerra de España," p. 775.

359. Martínez Bande, *La intervención comunista en la guerra de España, 1936-1939*, p. 23.

360. *LAE*, 18 May 1972, "La guerra de España," p. 773. The interview is by Mariano del Mazo.

361. *El Alcázar*, 14 July 1970.

362. *LAE*, 18 May 1972, "La guerra de España," pp. 773-774.

363. Cárdenas Rodríguez, *op. cit.*, pp. 10, 29-30.

364. A thirty-six-page pamphlet entitled *Durango* was published with text in Castilian, French, and English, apparently in Bilbao, and therefore in 1937; *Durango, ville martyre: ce que furent les bombardements de la ville de Durango par les avions allemands*, preface by Martin-Chauffier, was published in Paris, doubtless in 1937, by the Comité Franco-Espagnol; a pamphlet entitled *Durango* was published in Prague in 1937 by a pro-Republican committee.

365. *LAE*, 18 May 1937, "La guerra de España," p. 774.

366. Elosegi, *op. cit.*, pp. 13-14. This book was written by Elosegi for his family; he expected to die at the San Sebastián frontón. For a slighting reference to Elosegi by La Cierva, see *El Alcázar*, 8 January 1927, "La quinta ventana."

367. *Op. cit.*, pp. 145, 151.

368. *Ibid.*, p. 184. Nevertheless, the figure does represent the impression that Elosegi retained of his night of horror in Guernica.

369. *Ibid.*, p. 167.

370. *Ibid.*, pp. 144-158.

371. *Gudari*, no. 62, 1972, p. 8.

372. *National Review*, 5 January 1973, pp. 27-28.

373. *Ibid.*, p. 28.

374. *Ibid.*, pp. 28-29.

375. *Ibid.*

376. *Ibid.*, p. 27.

377. *Human Events*, February 1973.

378. *Washington Post*, 1 April 1973, C 2. Senator Frank Church of Idaho had Beitia's article reprinted in the *Congressional Record*, Appendix, 10 April 1973.

379. *Die Welt*, 11 January 1973, "Welt des Buches," p. II.

380. *Frankfurter Allgemeine*, 17 January 1973. This article was used as the basis of an attack on *Die Welt* and its position on Guernica by *Der Spiegel* (29 January 1973). The German magazine charged that *Die Welt*, a constant defender of United States policy in Vietnam, irked by reactions to the Christmas bombing of Hanoi, such as that of *Le Monde*, which had entitled a protest: "GUERNICA! GUERNICA! GUERNICA!" sought to defuse the Guernica story.

381. *Die Zeit*, 30 January 1937, p. 7. Another refutation of the article in *Die Welt* was given in *Der Widerstandskämpfer*, of Vienna (January-March 1973, pp. 43-45). The evidence produced against Hart in this anti-Nazi publication came from the *Frankfurter Allgemeine*, from Steer's first dispatch, and from the declarations of Onaindia and Yoldi, as reproduced in Kirsch's book. According to this article, the neo-Nazi publications *Deutschen Nachrichten* and *Deutsche Wochenzeitung*, 5 February 1973, also republished Hart's work.

382. Pariset "entered Guernica when the ruins were still smoking. He talked with people, investigated" (*ABC*, 8 February 1973, p. 30, article by Montes).

383. *Il Tempo*, 5 February 1973. Another headline read: "GUERNICA WAS DESTROYED BY REDS AND NOT BY HITLER AIRCRAFT."

384. *ABC*, 8 February 1973, p. 30.

385. *ABC*, 17 March 1973, p. 30. The American news agency UPI sent out a dispatch on Unceta's letter (*IHT*, 19 March 1973).

386. *Francisco Franco: Un siglo de España*, no. 26, p. 612.

387. *Ibid.*, p. 616.

388. *Ibid.*, pp. 612, 616.

389. *Ibid.*, p. 616.

390. Trythall wrote: "Franco, not being concerned with the details of the campaign, was very likely not even informed" (*Franco*, p. 120).

391. *Francisco Franco: Un siglo de España*, p. 616.

392. *Economist*, 5 May 1973, p. 4. Crozier backslid again in the *Times Literary Supplement*, 25 April 1975, p. 457, in a letter in which he insisted that the fact that the Casa de Juntas, the famous tree, and some surrounding buildings had been spared proved that the fire was started on the ground. "No amount of eye witness accounts, polemics, exegesis or analysis of contemporary documents can dispose of this single decisive fact."

393. *Ibid.*, 19 May 1973, p. 4.

394. *Ibid.*, 26 May 1973.

395. *National Review*, 16 March 1973, p. 290.

396. *Ibid.*, 31 August 1937, pp. 936-942.

397. *Saturday Review/World*, 20 November 1973.

398. *Arde Guernica* (Madrid: G. del Toro, 1973). Talón had changed publishers between editions.

399. *Ibid.* (1970), p. 8.

400. *Ibid.*, p. 52.

401. *Ibid.* (1973), p. 74.

402. *Ibid.* (1970), p. 280.

403. *Ibid.* (1973), p. 364.

404. *Ibid.* (1970), pp. 52-53.

405. *Ibid.* (1973), p. 76.

406. *Ibid.*, pp. 377-381.

407. *Historia del ejército popular de la república*, II, 1436 n. 47.

408. *Ibid.*, pp. 1391-1392.

409. *Ibid.*, p. 1386. Salas was citing Talón (*op. cit.*, pp. 141-142), who quoted an official German message. There may well have been more planes available by 26 April.

410. *Op. cit.*, pp. 238-241; *Times*, 29 April 1937.

411. *Op. cit.*, p. 239.

412. *Op. cit.*, 1386.

413. *Ibid.*, p. 1390.

414. *Ibid.*, p. 1387.

415. *Mundo*, 5 April 1975, pp. 26-29, article by Massimo Olmi.

416. It would be unjust to leave the impression that the work of Ricardo de la Cierva is not appreciated in certain university circles, especially in England and in the United States. La Cierva was invited to a study group at Oxford in 1970 (*Arriba*, 30 January 1970, interview of Pascual with La Cierva) and asked to contribute to a scholarly work edited by the Oxford professor Raymond Carr (Carr, ed., *The Republic and the Civil War in Spain*, "The Nationalist Army in the Spanish Civil War" by Ricardo de la Cierva y de Hoces, pp. 188-212). He was invited to the United States to attend the Madison Workshop on Modern Spain, organized by Professor Stanley G. Payne, at the University of Wisconsin, in 1971 (*Newsletter of the Society for Spanish and Portuguese Historical Studies*, Vol. 1, no. 6, 15 October 1971, p. 7). The curious feature of these honors bestowed on the employee of the Spanish propaganda ministry is that nowhere was La Cierva's official work mentioned. He was presented to the readers of Carr's book as "Professor of the History of Ideas at the University of Madrid and Director of the Centre of the Contemporary History of Spain" (Carr, *op. cit.*, p. 257), and to the scholars at the Madison Workshop as being "of the University of Madrid, director of the Study Unit on the Spanish Civil War." (*Newsletter . . .*, p. 7). The jackets of his two volume *Historia ilustrada*, reproduce blurbs from Professor Carr, Professor Payne, and Professor Malefakis, of the University of Michigan. La Cierva saluted Payne's historical assault on the Spanish Republic, *The Spanish Revolution*, with an article headlined, "Una obra maestra de Stanley Payne" (*El Alcázar*, 12 November 1972). Payne wrote a review of La Cierva's *Historia de la guerra civil*,

Vol. I, for a learned quarterly in the United States, and concluded that "it constitutes a major contribution to the historiography of the Spanish Republic that must be carefully studied by all future scholars." More surprising was Payne's assertion that this functionary of the Ministry of Information "is no propagandist" (*The American Historical Review* (April 1973), pp. 454-456). What is the central theme of La Cierva and the Neo-Franquista school in their civil war studies? It is that the Spanish Right was forced by the errors of the Spanish Republic to take to arms, that the military uprising was justified. It is essentially this idea that unites around La Cierva, in the United States, Payne, and in England, Carr (Robinson, Trythall). The outstanding challenges to the theses of the Neo-Franquista school thus far have come, aside from the work of Gabriel Jackson, from two young English scholars, Paul Preston and Martin Blinkhorn. For Preston, see, *Journal of Contemporary History*, 7 (July-October 1972), 80-114, "Alfonsist Monarchism and the Coming of the Spanish Civil War"; *European Studies Review* (1974), 4, "The 'moderate' Right and the Undermining of the Second Republic in Spain, 1931-1933." For Blinkhorn, see, *Journal of Contemporary History*, 7 (July-October 1972), 65-88, "Carlism and the Spanish Crisis of the 1930s"; *European Studies Review* (1973), 1, "Anglo-American Historians and the Second Spanish Republic: The Emergence of a New Orthodoxy."

BOOK III

Chapter 1
Steer, Holburn, Botto, and the Havas Agency

1. These attacks on Steer bore long-lasting results. Allen Guttmann, whose sympathies are evidently with the Republican cause, nevertheless described Steer's "account of the bombing" as being "inaccurate" (*The Wound in the Heart*, p. 106).

2. Steer wrote a book on the Italo-Ethiopian War, *Caesar in Abyssinia*, published in London in 1936, and, as already noted, another book on Ethiopia, *Sealed and Delivered*. For other books by Steer, see in text.

3. All the falsehoods of Nationalist propaganda were propagated by Sencourt: the allegedly false elections of 1936 (p. 70), the presence of Béla Kun in Barcelona in the spring of 1936 (p. 70), the forged Communist plot documents (p. 90), the denial of the reports of the Badajoz massacre (p. 146), the gallant siege of the Alcázar of Toledo (pp. 157-162).

4. Letter from W. R. A. Easthope, editor of the *Times Archives*, 6 January 1969.

5. *Times*, 6 May 1937.

6. Phillip Knightley asserts that "Steer later said that *The Times*, which was already deeply into its appeasement-of-Germany stance, was very unhappy with the story [Steer's first dispatch on Guernica], but felt obliged to run it" (*The First Casualty*, proof sheets, p. 204). Also: "*The Times* printed Steer's second story with even more reluctance than it had displayed over his first account" (*ibid.*, p. 207). Knightley's assertions are apparently based on statements that Steer made to a reporter who was in Bilbao with him. But it is well to remember that Steer was a touchy person (as shown by his attitude toward Holburn), and he had the right to be, when we observe how so many uninformed persons called him a liar or an idiot about his Guernica dispatches. I would ask these questions: If the *Times* felt unhappy with Steer's first dispatch, why was it printed in such a prominent place? If the *Times* printed Steer's second dispatch with reluctance, why did it also give the dispatch favorable editorial support?

7. K. W. Watkins, *England Divided*, p. 100. This letter was addressed to H. G. Daniels, the newspaper's correspondent in Geneva.

8. *History of* The Times, II, 907.

9. *Times*, 2 January 1945.

10. *The First Casualty*, proofs, p. 207.

11. These letters have been placed at my disposition by Phillip Knightley.

12. See C. E. Lucas Phillips, *The Spanish Pimpernel*, p. 34.

13. Letter, the *Times* to De Caux, 13 June 1936.

14. *Times,* 2 January 1945.

15. *History of* The Times, II, 907.

16. Holburn worked with the *Times* from 1934 to 1955. He was editor of the *Glasgow Herald* from 1955 to 1965.

17. Interview, Southworth with Holburn, November 1968.

18. Letter, Holburn to Southworth, 24 January 1969.

19. *Ibid.*

20. *Ibid.* Holburn correctly gauged that an admission of the bombing, passed through the Insurgent censorship and published in the *Times,* was extremely important. In the course of our interview, he said that if he had not been able to include that information, he would not have sent the telegram.

21. It is difficult to fix Holburn's dates in Spain with exactness. The editor of *The Times Archives* wrote on 5 May 1969: "Holburn's service in Spain dated from February 14, 1937. We can find no record of when he left, but we can say that he was still there on June 20. We think that his departure must have followed Philby's taking over, which we can confirm as May 24." Holburn writes: "I can say pretty definitely that I crossed the frontier from Spain, on my last exit, on June 21, 1937. I entered Spain for the first time on February 19, 1937. . . . If I didn't leave Spain until June 21, Philby cannot have taken over from me on May 24" (letter Holburn to Southworth, 24 September 1969).

22. Letter, Holburn to Southworth, 24 January 1969. "I did not ask *The Times* to replace me. I was due to be replaced, and to return to Berlin, when *The Times* found a suitable man to be correspondent with the Franco forces on a permanent basis. So I understood, and certainly no one was posted to the job I had vacated in Berlin." Ebbutt, head of the Berlin office of the *Times,* was expelled in October 1937, and his assistant, Holburn, took over (Gannon, *op. cit.,* pp. 121-122). In Gannon's opinion, Ebbutt's expulsion was due in part to the fact that the Germans were "maddened by *The Times'* article on Guernica" (*ibid.,* p. 123).

23. Bolín remembered Philby as a "decent chap who inspired confidence in his reports because he was so objective" (*The Philby Conspiracy,* p. 74). Philby was a member of the Anglo-German Fellowship, before going to Spain (*ibid.,* pp. 70-71; also Cookridge, *The Third Man,* pp. 35-47).

24. *STVY,* p. 279. Bolín's misinformation was later picked up by Talón (*op. cit.,* p. 259) and by R. de la Cierva (*LAE,* 18 May 1972, "Guerra de España, p. 774).

25. Letter, Holburn to Southworth, 24 January 1969. "Having read my Guernica dispatch for the first time since it was written, it strikes me as being a bit of a hotch potch. Perhaps with the censor in mind, I was trying to be too clever."

26. Records of Auteuil Cemetery. Botto was born 24 December 1895 and died 13 February 1952.

27. PRO, FO 371/21291, W 8472, folios 273-274. Telegram from Sir Eric Phipps. Phipps referred to the story in *Le Jour,* credited to Havas, and to that in *Le Temps,* not attributed to Havas, as the basis for his original information.

28. *Ibid.* We must remark that although Sir Eric was aware of how the Havas-Botto dispatch was being used by the Nazi press to attack the *Times* and the English press in general, both the French and the English press were unexplicably quiet on this detail.

29. AN, 5 AR 272, "Affaire 'Destruction de Guernica' " file.

30. *AN,* 5 AR 271, d'Hospital file.

31. *Ibid.,* Havas memorandum dated 2 November 1937. D'Hospital had cabled that he saw no Italian troops in Majorca.

32. AN, 5 AR 272, Botto file, Havas memorandum dated 4 December 1937.

33. Interview Dussauge-Berniard.

34. AN, 5 AR 271, d'Hospital file, telegram, Havas to d'Hospital, 31 January 1937.

35. Interview Southworth-d'Hospital. Havas had a Spanish stringer in Salamanca, Julio Romero García (AN, 5 AR 272, Romero file, letter, Havas to Romero, 19 April 1937). At one time, Manuel Aznar, a well-known Spanish journalist, worked for Havas (AN, 5 AR 271, d'Hospital file).

36. Interview Southworth-Couderc.

37. AN, 5 AR 272, Botto file. See Botto's "Balance of the results in 1937 for the two

opposing armies," sent to Paris, dated 13 January 1938. "Eibar falls, then Durango. These two towns are but a heap of ruins. They were burned before the departure of the Reds." This statement does honor neither to Botto's ability as a reporter nor to his memory. The Nationalists never claimed that Durango was burned. In fact, as shown previously in this work, Durango was the prize Nationalist exhibit as a town destroyed by bombing and shelling but never burned. Unfortunately for our study, Botto wrote little about Guernica in this report: "Guernica, completely devastated, has sufficiently retained the attention of the world for me to say nothing more at this time." This "balance sheet" was stamped on each page by the Nationalist censor and may have been written merely to curry favor with the Press Office.

38. AN, 5 AR 272, Botto file.

39. *Ibid.,* Botto file, Havas memorandum, 8 March 1937.

40. AN, 5 AR 272, Botto file.

41. *Ibid.,* Havas memorandum, 4 December 1937.

42. Interview, Southworth-Couderc.

43. *PG,* 8 May 1937.

44. AN, 5 AR 272, Botto file, Havas memorandum, 4 December 1937.

45. In fact, nothing in the Havas files indicates that Botto's telegram on Guernica contained either incorrect or false information. The primary proof comes from the English diplomatic files.

46. *Op. cit.,* p. 88.

47. See Southworth, *op. cit.,* pp. 38-40, 47, 199, 223.

48. *Op. cit.,* p. 91. "When I set out from Vitoria on June 19th . . ."

49. AN, 5 AR 272, Botto file. Letter from Havas to Botto, 11 June 1937. This made Botto's salary five thousand francs a month, almost three times what he had made in Paris. This was a small sum compared to his expenses. For example, he paid, at this time, twenty-one thousand francs a month to rent an automobile (*ibid.,* Havas note, 20 May 1937). The pay raise took effect on 1 June.

50. AN, 5 AR 272, Botto file, letter, Botto to Havas, 13 June 1937.

51. AN, 5 AR 271, d'Hospital file. Havas note, 24 June 1937, stated that d'Hospital "accepts to return to Spain. He could be in Hendaye on July 1." D'Hospital was also paid a higher salary than Botto.

52. Interview, Southworth-d'Hospital. In France, Havas dispatches were never signed, a fact that caused displeasure among the correspondents. However, articles were at times signed in the Canadian and Latin American press.

53. AN, 5 AR 272, Botto file. This Havas memorandum is dated 27 November and constitutes an accumulation of grievances against Botto.

54. *Ibid.*

55. *Ibid.* Botto's telegram was dated 23 November 1937.

56. *Ibid.* Botto's telegram was timed 13h45. At 20h that same day d'Hospital informed Paris that Botto's telegram "was written slowly, each expression being weighed, worked over, reshaped by Franco's diplomatic cabinet at San Sebastián." Havas also consulted Léon Bassée, director of the agency's political service, and Bret, correspondent in London (Havas memorandum, 27 November 1937). A Havas "Note of the Management," concerning Botto's telegram read: "It would be well to advise M. Botto to be more prudent."

57. This telegram was also to be datelined "Hendaye" (AN, 5 AR 272, Botto file).

58. *Ibid.* Botto's telegram and Bret's dispatch were both dated 25 November.

59. *Le Jour,* 29 November 1937 (AN, 5 AR 272, Botto file). Havas did not appreciate having its correspondent used by elements of the Nationalist zone for partisan infighting. Nor was it flattered to have its reporter used for a task later given to a correspondent of *Le Jour,* known for its pro-Franco sympathies. This dispatch, aside from linking the mediation proposal to a restoration of the monarchy, also made the mediation conditional on "guaranty of personal security for the leaders of the Valencia government" and "respect for certain provincial statutes concerning Catalonia." All three conditions were unreal in view of the political situation in November 1937.

60. AN, 5 AR 272, Botto file, Havas report, 27 November 1937.

61. *Ibid.,* Havas memorandum, 1 December 1937, recording d'Hospital's telephone call to Paris from Hendaye.

62. AN, 5 AR 272, Botto file, Havas memorandum, 4 December 1937, illegible signature.

The agency's attitude toward Botto had completely changed. "We can be sure that Botto is discredited in the eyes of the Nationalists; in this case, it is to Havas' advantage to recall him" (ibid.).

63. *Ibid.*, note to Perrin from Meynot. D'Hospital was also to handle the expense account from then on. This same day, 10 December 1937, a letter was addressed to Botto, informing him of the changes and saying that if he preferred to return to work in Paris, the Havas management would understand his reasons. Botto accepted the new situation.

64. *Ibid.*, also *AF,* 3 February 1937.

65. AN, 5 AR 272, Botto file, Havas memorandum, 9 February 1938, reporting on Botto's telephone call from Hendaye. Botto was told that, after all, he had been in a theater of war for a year and that it was normal that he be replaced. "On the other hand, it must be said," he was apparently told, "that his copy is generally less fit for publication than that of our other collaborators" (illegible signature).

66. *Ibid.* Vincent remained in Spain until the end of the civil war. He was the son-in-law of Maurice Legendre, a French hispanic scholar, outspokenly for Franco. He was later killed in South America.

67. *Ibid.*, telegram, 23 March 1938.

68. *Ibid.* The telegram, 24 March 1938, was sent by Amato, director of the Fabra News Agency, with which Havas had worked before the civil war. Havas replied the same day that d'Hospital, bureau chief, could make any necessary visits to Nationalist authorities. According to German sources, Fabra had been on the payroll of the French embassy in Madrid before the civil war, and from February 1935 on had also been subsidized by the German embassy, with the result that soon half of its foreign news came from the DNB (Viñas, *La Alemania nazi y el 18 de julio,* pp. 160-170).

69. *Ibid.*, telegram, 26 March 1938.

70. *Ibid.*, telegram to Havas from d'Hospital, 25 March 1938, from Hendaye.

71. *Ibid.*, funeral announcement.

72. *Ibid.*, letter, Mme. Botto to Havas, 5 May 1938.

73. *Ibid.*, "Note for the management," Havas, 6 July 1938. "On May 20, I sent someone to his house to check on the reality of this illness; in fact, M. Botto was in bed."

74. *Ibid.*

75. *Ibid.*, illegible signature.

76. *Ibid.*

77. *Ibid.*, letter from Dr. J. Cochy de Moncan.

78. *Ibid.*

79. *Ibid.*, "M. Botto is extremely nervous," wrote Dr. Cochy de Moncan.

80. *Ibid.*, letter from M. Guillet, 30 April 1938.

81. *Ibid.*, "Note de la direction."

82. AN, 5 AR 271, d'Hospital file. "Rapport sur les services Havas," 30 June 1938, by d'Hospital. D'Hospital wrote: "I hope this is the last time I shall speak of this subject and I should like to think that M. Botto has an excuse, the only one allowable, that of having lost his mental balance." In 1968 d'Hospital resolutely refused to discuss Botto's conduct. See also AN, 5 AR 272, Botto file, Havas memorandum, 6 July 1938.

83. AN, 5 AR 272, Botto file.

84. *Ibid.*, letter Fis to Perrin, 3 August 1938. Botto's initiatives and indiscretions can be said to have affected his work. We have already seen that after Botto sent the false telegram from Hendaye in the fall of 1937, he had difficulty in crossing the frontier into France. This may have happened on still another occasion. "There was a woman in San Sebastián for whom Botto spent without thinking. . . . For the moment she is in St.-Jean-de-Luz, at the Hotel X, where her bills are made in Botto's name. At one time in Spain she was suspected of espionage and because of this, Botto, himself under observation, could not cross into France, for the Commandancia militar had refused him a pass."

85. *Ibid.* The chauffeur sought out Fis to denounce Botto, whom he blamed for having arranged matters so that the chauffeur could not reenter Nationalist Spain. He also seemed angry with Botto for the latter's indiscretions, which, the chauffeur thought, had not only cost Botto his own job but had cost the chauffeur his job too. The owner of a bar in Hendaye wrote

to Havas on 26 August 1938 concerning money that he claimed he had loaned to Botto and which had not been repaid.

86. AN, 5 AR 272, Botto file.

87. *Ibid.* "I am certain that very soon you will be convinced that I have never acted but in the interests of the Agency and that all the principal accusations which weigh against me will vanish, one after the other." The precise nature of these "accusations" are unknown, and they were proferred verbally to Botto.

88. *Ibid.*

89. After the end of World War II, Héricourt was accused of collaboration by the French Resistance; he remained in Spain until his death.

90. Interview, Southworth-Couderc. Did Botto really go back to Spain? D'Hospital had written to Paris on 30 June 1938: "M. Botto has let it be known in Spain that he expected to return very shortly, sent on a semi-official mission by the Quai d'Orsay. On the other hand, certain people have informed me that Botto was supposed to come back for some firm of other. I have been too long a time the victim of his bluffing to believe a word of it" (AN, 5 AR 271, d'Hospital file).

91. Jean-Hérold-Paquis, *Des illusions . . . désillusions (15 Aout 1944-15 Août 1945)*, pp. 19-21.

92. AN, 5 AR 272, "Affaire, 'Destruction de Guernica' " file. Botto's telegram was immediately forwarded to South America without censoring. This is evident from the text published in *La Nación* on 3 May. It is a faithful translation of the original telegram, lacking only the final sentence.

93. Letters, Chadé to Southworth, 5 June, 7 August 1969.

94. AN, 5 AR 272, "Affaire, 'Destruction de Guernica' " file.

95. After several years of research, I have never found any newsmen who went into Guernica in the first days of the Insurgent occupation and who backed up Botto's story, except Massot and Dourec—and also of course the Italian and German reporters. Nevertheless, Jerrold immediately exaggerated the number of such correspondents. He wrote of "the correspondents of the Havas Agency, of *The Times,* and of several other newspapers," and elsewhere referred to "other neutral journalists" (*Tablet,* 5 June 1937, p. 801). Jerrold's statement, which unjustifiably exaggerated the number of pro-Botto witnesses, was frequently quoted, notably by Lunn, *Spanish Rehearsal* (1937), p. 268, and by Bolín, thirty years later, *Spain: The Vital Years,* p. 278. Knoblaugh made a reference to a "joint statement of disinterested correspondents" (*Correspondent in Spain,* p. 176), and Father Thorning improved on this, writing of "The Havas Agency and a committee of international correspondents" (*Why the Press Failed on Spain!* p. 10). Sencourt then attributed the experiences related and the opinions expressed in Botto's article to "a number of foreign journalists" (*Spain's Ordeal,* p. 245). Foss and Gerahty went on to increase the number of such witnesses, stating that "no less than twenty-one foreign journalists had been able to see themselves [that] the town had been destroyed by fire by the retreating forces of the Madrid government on April 26th" (*Spanish Arena,* p. 439). This idea of some international investigatory body underwriting the Nationalist theses on Guernica was also held in France, where, in 1937, Vice-Admiral Joubert asserted that Maritain's version of what had happened at Guernica was contradicted by "the international verification asked for by General Mola himself" (*La guerre d'Espagne et le catholicisme,* p. 32). Raymond Recouly considered the Botto telegram to represent the opinions of "journalists belonging to different nations" (*Gringoire,* 7 May 1937, p. 2). The Italians Bollati and del Bono wrote of "loyal foreign journalists" (*La guerra di Spagna, sino alla liberazione di Gijón,* p. 228). For the American Richard Pattee, Botto was a "group of foreign correspondents" (*This Is Spain,* p. 230). The Havas-Botto message was seldom invoked in Spain itself, although Queipo de Llano immediately after its publication attributed it to a "group of journalists" (*HA,* 6 May 1937). See also Book II, Part 1, chap. 3, n. 104.

96. AN, 5 AR 272, "Affaire 'Destruction de Guernica' " file. This is the title on the original folder.

97. Pierre Fréderix, in his book *Un siècle de chasse aux nouvelles. De l'Agence d'Informations Havas à l'Agence France-Presse,* wrote: "After 1930, Havas-Informations was a deficit operation" (p. 400). He also noted that after the economic crisis of 1929, Havas' publicity

income fell along with the drop in the sale of news (ibid., p. 393). "The [news] deficit passed from eight hundred thousand francs for 1934, to one million two hundred and fifty thousand francs for 1935. The Agency spent almost a million francs to cover the war in Ethiopia" (ibid., p. 399n). This author pleaded the case for the Havas management, who frequently seemed to be more businessmen than journalists. "How was it possible," he asked, "that the Havas Agency not suffer the effects of eight years of crisis?" (ibid., p. 412).

98. "This two-headed corporation [Havas] associated the deficit of its information branch with the extensive profits of its department of publicity, without admitting that the profits of the second compensated the losses of the first, but handling the publicity of the daily press was so remunerative only because the news was sold so cheaply" (Paul-Louis Bret, Au feu des événements. Mémóires d'un journaliste, p. 44). Bret was head of the London bureau of Havas during the time Guernica was destroyed. A severe indictment of the Havas agency was made in 1955 by the French Socialist leader, one-time president of France, Vincent Auriol. After noting that Havas controlled, on the one hand, the news published in the press, and, on the other, the publicity that made possible the press profits, he charged: "By these two powerful means, the Havas agency was able to put pressure on the 'capital,' and, from that vantage point, on the management of the newspapers. The agency oriented the newspapers' policies. It often favored corruption. Rare were the press organs that escaped from its tight embrace" (Hier-demain, II, 308-309). These critical attitudes toward the Havas administration were not shared by Fréderix or by the authors of Histoire générale de la presse française.

99. Fréderix, op. cit., p. 373.

100. Houssaye was still general manager of the agency in 1937, during the period of the Guernica incident. Fréderix wrote that Houssaye and André Meynot were the heads of the "services étrangers" of Havas-Informations, but his chronology is not too clear (ibid., p. 375). Jean Rollin was inspector general of the foreign services at the same time (ibid., p. 374). Botto's letter of resignation was addressed to Meynot, but the noncommittal certificate given to Botto by the agency, dated 17 October 1938, was signed by Houssaye (AN, 5 AR 272, Botto file). An earlier certificate, prepared for Botto's use with the Non-Intervention Committee, dated 24 May 1937, was signed by Meynot, "one of the managing directors" (ibid.).

101. Fréderix, op. cit., p. 373. "The Havas Agency, the contract specified, did not intend to realize any profit in the future, any more than it was realizing any profit in the present, or had realized a profit in the past, on the sums which were entrusted to it by the government for the diffusion of French thought" (ibid., pp. 373-374). But "diffusion of French thought" became "new services realized in the national interest since 1931" on page 412 of Fréderix's book. See also Histoire générale de la presse française, III, 466.

102. Fréderix, op. cit., p. 414. This contract was signed on 11 July 1938.

103. AN, 5 AR 272, "Affaire, 'Destruction de Guernica' " file, telegram dated 4 May 1937.

104. Ibid. This dossier contains a teletype copy of the completely revised dispatch.

105. Ibid., Havas note dated 6 May 1937, illegible signature. "Léon Bassée, for a long time director of the political service of Havas, and, after 1938, member of the board, retired in 1941" (Fréderix, op. cit., p. 422). Bassée was the person queried in November 1937, when Botto sent his false information about English mediation.

106. Dumaine, Le Quai d'Orsay, p. 59.

107. AN, 5 AR 272, Botto file. Botto sent this information "à titre documentaire," for the news concerned France and was not, technically, in his jurisdiction.

108. I know of no exhaustive study of Delbos's policy. William Shirer, in his book The Collapse of the Third Republic, writes that the vacillating position of Delbos limited French aid to the Spanish Republic from the first days of the military revolt (pp. 282-287). Jacques Debû-Bridel confirms Delbos's firm opposition to any help for the Spanish Republic (L'Agonie de la troisième république, p. 380). See also Greene, Crisis and Decline, p. 80.

109. Delbos had found in a Muscovite Museum of the Revolution a room dedicated to Communist activities in Spain, such as radical publications, photographs of communist leaders, scenes of strikes and riots. Delbos deduced from this exhibition that the Soviet Union expected a not too distant success across the Pyrenees from France (L'Expérience rouge [1933], p. 185). The sociological conclusion that conditions in Spain made a revolution probable was easily converted by Franco propagandists into a blueprint for a Soviet-supported uprising. Luis

Carreras remarked on "the clairvoyant observations" of Delbos (*Grandeur chrétienne de l'Espagne,* p. 68n), and Robert Sencourt cited him as an anti-Communist witness in the same class with G. M. Godden and Jacques Bardoux (*op. cit.,* p. 84). Antonio José Gutiérrez considered Delbos's remarks as "unimpeachable evidence" of a Soviet plot (*op. cit.,* p. 193), and Vicente Marrero thought them to be proof of Soviet intervention in Spain (*op. cit.,* p. 216).

110. Shirer credits Léger with the idea of "non-intervention" (p. 286), and writes of the "nervous permanent officials, led by Alexis Léger" (*ibid.*). On March 15, 1938, when Paul-Boncour was foreign minister, at the historic meeting of the cabinet, Léger was firmly against any help for the Spanish Republic (*ibid.,* p. 322). The minutes of this meeting are quoted in Gamelin, *Servir,* II, 322-328, and partly requoted by Juan García Durán, "Foreign Intervention on the Sea" (*Spaanse Burgeroorlog en zijn gevolgen,* p. 37). This position by Léger is confirmed by Pike (*Les francais et la guerre d'Espagne,* p. 296). Jacques Dumaine wrote: "Some people affirm . . . that the minister of foreign affairs is but nominally the head of the Quai d'Orsay . . . and that if the apparent head of the Quai d'Orsay is called Pierre Laval, Flandin, Yvon Delbos, Paul-Boncour or Georges Bonnet, these reign but do not govern: the real minister is called Léger" (*Le Quai d'Orsay,* p. 49).

111. *Op. cit.,* p. 188. A chapter of this book is entitled "Le Quai d'Orsay et l'Agence Havas."

112. *Les Fossoyeurs,* p. 412. The reference to Guernica is repeated in the *Histoire générale de la presse française,* but the references to the Italian planes in Oranie, and to the Italian submarines in the Mediterranean at the time of the Nyon conference are left out (p. 486).

Chapter 2
The Dead and the Dying

1. *Times,* 28 April 1937.
2. *Ibid.* Steer wrote in *The Tree of Gernika,* p. 236: "Monday was the weekly market day of Gernika, when the town existed. At about four-thirty the market, in summer, was at its fullest. The civil war had not made great difference to the Gernika farmers who brought in their animals and produce from the rich valley." However, a pro-Franco Basque reasoned with me in a conversation that few farmers would have wanted to sell on 26 April for the soon to be worthless Republican money. Against this reasoning can be placed that of an anti-Franco Basque, who argued from his own experience that the peasant sold but also bought. The market was a center of exchanges. Steer also pointed out that the influx of refugees and the presence of "two Basque battalions, who had plenty of pesetas to spend" increased the mercantile interest of the market.
3. *Morning Post, Daily Herald,* 28 April 1937.
4. *DE,* 28 April 1937.
5. *DE,* 1 May 1937.
6. *Eyewitness,* p. 94. We have already seen the testimony of the Cuban editor, who on arriving in France declared: "it was market day and there were many peasants in town."
7. PRO, FO 271/21291, W 8661, folio 236.
8. *ED,* 27 May 1937, p. 1; Montserrat, *Le drame d'un peuple incompris,* 2d ed., p. 83.
9. Montserrat, *op. cit.,* 2d ed., p. 79; Onaindia, *Hombre de paz en la guerra,* pp. 238-239.
10. Montserrat, *op. cit.,* 2d ed., p. 85. This witness, a soldier who in 1938 for obvious reasons wished to remain anonymous, was severely wounded in the bombing.
11. *ED,* 27 May 1937, p. 1.
12. *Spain's Ordeal,* p. 237.
13. *Guernica: The Official Report,* p. 1.
14. *Ibid.,* p. 3.
15. *Ibid.,* p. 24.
16. *Informe sobre la situación de las provincias vascongadas bajo el dominio rojo-separatista,* p. 202. The witness for this report on Guernica was himself a refugee in Guernica.
17. *Corriere della Sera,* 1 May 1937.
18. *La Stampa,* 30 April 1937.

19. *Tablet*, 24 September 1938, p. 389.
20. *STVY*, p. 274.
21. *The Spanish Civil War*, p. 537.
22. *La guerre civile d'Espagne*, p. 190.
23. *Franco: The Man and His Nation*, p. 277.
24. *Arde Guernica*, p. 76.
25. *Ibid.*, pp. 68-69 n. 9.
26. *Quiero morir por algo*, p. 151.
27. *Vizcaya*, pp. 103-104, 106.
28. *Guernica: The Official Report*, p. 14.
29. Cárdenas Rodríguez, *Texto taquigráfico de la conferencia por el arquitecto general de regiones devastadas . . . el día 3 de julio de 1940*, pp. 29-30. According to this study, which excluded Bilbao, 401 buildings in the province were totally destroyed; the total value of the damage to buildings, public and private, was calculated to be 35 million pesetas.
30. *Times*, 28 April 1937.
31. *Ibid.*, 6 May 1937.
32. *The Tree of Gernika*, p. 244.
33. *Morning Post, Daily Herald*, 28 April 1937.
34. *DE*, 28 April 1937.
35. *Ibid.*, 29 April 1937.
36. *Ibid.*, 11 May 1937.
37. *Op. cit.*, pp. 97-98.
38. *El Liberal*, Bilbao, 30 April 1937, quoted by Talón, *op. cit.*, p. 66 n. 6.
39. *Ce Soir*, 28 April 1937.
40. *Ibid.*, 29 April 1937.
41. *"Salud camarada!"* p. 294.
42. *News Chronicle*, 29 April 1937.
43. *L'Oeuvre*, 28 April 1937.
44. *Washington Post*, 28 April 1937.
45. *New York American*, 28 April 1937.
46. PRO, FO 371/21291, W 8661, folio 236.
47. "Paginas de mi vida," unpublished manuscript by Angel de Ojanguren y Celaya.
48. *NYT*, AP from Hendaye, 28 April 1937. A cablegram from the same agency the following day quoted the Basque delegation in Valencia as saying that thousands had been killed in recent aerial bombardments on the Basque front; of these, eight hundred in Guernica (*NYT*, 29 April 1937, p. 4). This figure of eight hundred "men, women and children . . . reported killed" was used by the North American Committee to Aid Spanish Democracy in a protest against the bombing released on 9 May (*NYT*, 10 May 1937).
49. *Guernica*, n.p., English-language edition of Basque publication; *ED*, 13 May 1937, p. 1. In the pamphlet text, it is more expressly stated that 592 persons had died in Bilbao hospitals. The French translation in *Euzko Deya* is less precise, but nevertheless would seem to refer also to the deaths in Bilbao hospitals. Talón credits Liezaola with stating that there were 690 deaths in the Guernica bombing, giving as his reference the *Boletín Español de Información* of Valencia, 16 May 1937 (*op. cit.*, p. 66n). The texts published by the Basques on this matter were probably more reliable.
50. *Guernica*, n.p.
51. *De Guernica a Nueva York, pasando por Berlin*, p. 27. These pages of the Spanish text are not found in the English-language translation (*Escape via Berlin* [New York] ; *Freedom Was Flesh and Blood* [London]).
52. Martínez Bande, *Vizcaya*, p. 108n.
53. *Montreal Daily Star*, 30 April 1937, UP dispatch.
54. Montserrat, *op. cit.*, 2d ed., pp. 82-83.
55. *ED*, 27 May 1937, p. 2. The four nurses spoke on 22 May before the World Committee of Women against Fascism.
56. *Times*, 11 June 1937.
57. *Crónica de la guerra española*, fasc. 62, cover 3, IV. However, this precise figure is not found in any of the texts of Labauria's speech used in this study.

58. Talón, *op. cit.*, p. 65.

59. *Searchlight on Spain*, p. 189. In December 1938 the duchess fought a by-election, provoked by her resignation to protest government policy on Spain. Monks was her press aide in the campaign. She lost by a narrow margin (Monks, *op. cit.*, pp. 110-112).

60. *En defensa de la verdad*, pp. 95, 114.

61. *Tablet*, 5 June 1937, p. 801. Jerrold must have seen the *faille* here, and he did not include these phrases in his American article.

62. *Spanish Rehearsal*, pp. 225-229.

63. *Op. cit.*, p. 241.

64. Moral, *Address*, p. 8.

65. *Why the Press Failed on Spain!* pp. 9-10.

66. *Columbia*, July 1937, p. 21. "Atrocities Made to Order," by Wilfrid Parsons, S. J.

67. *The Spanish War and Lying Propaganda*, p. 28.

68. *The March of a Nation*, pp. 279-281.

69. *Spain: The Truth at Last*, p. 15.

70. *Guernica: The Official Report*, p. 54.

71. *Ibid.*, p. 15.

72. *Ibid.*, pp. 41-42.

73. *Ibid.*, pp. 51-53. The dates given here concerning "the corpses found in the various shelters in Guernica" are from 4 May to 29 May. This work must have continued for some time for Talón cites an entry in a Guernica death register concerning the Hospital Asilo Calzada, dated December 1937 (*op. cit.*, p. 69). This avowal of almost a hundred dead in the air attack on Guernica was curiously related by one diehard Nationalist sympathizer, Dr. Halliday Sutherland, who noted that the commission found that the town was bombed on 26 April, that there were fewer than a hundred casualties, but that the town "was actually destroyed by the Reds within it" (*Spanish Journey*, pp. 113-114). It would seem a more reasonable interpretation on the part of a practicing Christian and a practicing physician to have organized his facts in a different order—to wit: although the Reds destroyed the town, the Nationalists, who bombed it, were responsible for almost a hundred deaths.

74. *Ibid.*, p. 8.

75. *Ibid.*, pp. 51-54.

76. *Ibid.*, p. 24.

77. *The Spanish Arena*, pp. 439-440.

78. *This Is Spain*, p. 231.

79. *Mine Were of Trouble*, pp. 88-89.

80. *Die deutsche Politik gegenüber dem spanischen Bürgerkrieg*, p. 176.

81. *The Spanish Civil War* (1961), p. 419.

82. *Ibid.* (1965), p. 537.

83. *Die Ersten und die Letzten*, p. 42.

84. *Spanish Fury*, p. 162.

85. *Der spanische Bürgerkrieg*, p. 176.

86. *Op. cit.*, pp. 190-191.

87. *Op. cit.*, p. 277.

88. *Franco: A Biographical History*, pp. 246-247.

89. *Historia militar de la guerra de España*, p. 406.

90. *Operaciones militares de la guerra de España*, pp. 281-282.

91. *Cruzada*, VII, drawing facing p. 322.

92. *Centinela del occidente*, p. 292.

93. *Guerra de liberación*, p. 201.

94. *General Mola*, p. 316.

95. *La guerra en el aire*, p. 207.

96. *La guerra de liberación nacional*, "La campaña en el norte," pp. 259-314.

97. *Ibid.*, "La aviación en nuestra guerra," pp. 353-386.

98. *Historia de España*, VI, *Época contemporánea* (1962), p. 222.

99. *Ibid.* (1968), p. 257. Seco Serrano writes: "The burning and the destruction of the famous locality, because of its venerable historical significance, will have a profound repercussion in all the enlightened circles of the world." Was it the "burning and the destruction of

the famous locality" that caused the repercussion, or was it the realization that many people had been killed in the holocaust?

100. *Comentarios a mil imágenes de la guerra civil española*, p. 369.
101. *Memorias*, p. 53.
102. *La guerra española de 1936*, pp. 254-255.
103. *La guerra civil española*, p. 215.
104. *Franco, el hombre y su nación*, pp. 280-281, 297.
105. *Legionario en España*, pp. 114-115.
106. *Furia española*, pp. 130-131.
107. *STVY*, pp. 275, 358. Bolín's admission of the bombing is found in a reference that came either from *Guernica: The Official Report* or the Herrán Report. In this paragraph Bolín says that the bombing took place on 25 April.
108. *Diálogos para otra España*, p. 280.
109. Gil Mugarza, *España en llamas* (1936), p. 340-341.
110. *Arriba*, 30 January 1970, article by Pedro Pascual.
111. *Guernica: The Official Report*, p. 15.
112. *Historia y Vida*, April 1970, p. 107.
113. *Historia ilustrada*, II, 154.
114. *Guernica: The Official Report*, p. 15.
115. *El Alcázar*, 14 July 1970.
116. *Op. cit.*, pp. 65-79.
117. *Ibid.*, p. 68n.
118. *Ibid.*, p. 72.
119. Vila-San-Juan, *Así fue? Enigmas de la guerra civil española*, p. 307.
120. *Vizcaya*, p. 108.
121. *LAE*, 18 May 1972, "La guerra de España," p. 772.
122. *Ibid.*, pp. 773-774.
123. *Francisco Franco: Un siglo de España*, no. 26, p. 616.
124. *Pueblo*, 6 November 1973, interview by Luis Garmet.
125. *Historia del ejército popular de la República*, II, 1387.
126. *Guernica: The Official Report*, pp. 8, 24.
127. *Ibid.*, pp. 24, 51.
128. *Ibid.*, pp. 51-54.
129. Gil Mugarza, *op. cit.*, p. 340.
130. *Arde Guernica*, pp. 67-68.
131. *Ibid.*, p. 68.
132. *Ibid.*, p. 68.
133. *Op. cit.*, p. 146.
134. *Guernica: The Official Report*, pp. 51-54. Thirty-eight of the fifty persons enumerated here died in the shelters. They *may* have died from the flames, but all but two of the bodies came from the Santa María shelter or from the Calzada Asylum shelter. The commissioners said that there were no traces of fire at the Calzada Asylum (p. 8), and that the Santa María shelter was bombed. The twelve other persons died from various causes such as exploding shells, machine-gun wounds, and some from heart attacks. These latter were presumably the result of the bombing.
135. *Le Petit Parisien*, 30 April 1937.
136. *Op. cit.*, p. 239.
137. *Militär Wochenblatt*, 25 June 1937, col. 3206. Colonel von Xylander wrote frequently about the Spanish Civil War for *Militär Wochenblatt* from 18 November 1936 to 21 April 1939. He also contributed a continuation, lacking in the original, for the German edition of Joaquin Arrarás's life of Franco.
138. Cárdenas Rodríguez, *op. cit.*, p. 26.
139. *Op. cit.*, p. 71.
140. *Vizcaya*, p. 108.
141. *Op. cit.*, p. 35 n. 4.
142. *La Intervención de Alemania en favor de Franco en las operaciones del territorio*

vasco, pp. 22-25. This publication is not dated, but mention is made of an event that took place on 13 May 1937 (pp. 36-37).

143. *Op. cit.,* p. 65. Talón finds these figures of 1,654 dead and 889 wounded to be "completely disproportionate," and accuses the Basques and their friends of exaggerating the numbers of the dead, but he nowhere refers to the minization of these same numbers by the Nationalists. Some months before the publication of Talón's book, in the *Arriba* interview, La Cierva advanced on no basis whatsoever the figure of "not even a dozen" for the Guernica dead. Talón had read this interview and he referred to it in his book (pp. 52-53), but he did not mention this precise and significant detail. Yet La Cierva's figure of, let us say, eleven dead, is far more "disproportionate" compared with Talón's own figure of "not more than two hundred" than is the figure of 1,654 dead. La Cierva's estimate is eighteen times less than Talón's; the figure of 1,654 is but eight and a half times more, and even Basaldua's figure of 3,000 exaggerates Talón's figure of "not more than two hundred" less than La Cierva's number minimizes it.

144. *DE,* 11 May 1937; *Eyewitness,* p. 98. Monks had cabled to his newspaper on 27 April: "Hundreds of bodies had been found in the debris. . . . At least two hundred others were riddled with machine-gun bullets as they fled to the hills" (*DE,* 28 April 1937).

145. Payne, *The Civil War in Spain, 1936-1939,* p. 225.

146. *Op. cit.,* pp. 148-150.

147. *Ibid.,* p. 156.

148. *La Intervención de Alemania en favor de Franco en las operaciones del territorio vasco,* pp. 22-24.

149. *Op. cit.,* p. 171 n. 12.

150. Payne, *The Civil War in Spain, 1936-1939,* p. 225.

151. *Op. cit.,* p. 157.

152. *Correio da Manhã,* 28 April 1937.

153. When the American journalist Williams talked with Talón in Madrid late in 1973, he had the impression that Talón had raised his figure for the dead to "between two hundred and ten and two hundred and fifty" (*Saturday Review/World,* 20 November 1973, p. 68); rumors that Talón wanted to give a higher figure for the dead had been coming out of Madrid for more than a year. However, if this was so, his revision was not permitted, and his second edition appeared with the figures for the dead unchanged since 1970.

154. *Vizcaya,* p. 108 n. 165.

Chapter 3
How Was Guernica Destroyed? By Whom? Why?

1. Martínez Bande, *Vizcaya,* pp. 107-108.

2. *La guerra de España desde el aire,* 2d ed., pp. 190-191. Salas Larrazábal repeated this idea in greater detail in *LAE,* no. 39. However, whereas the 7 May telegram said that Guernica was being used by Republican units in flight, Salas Larrazábal wrote that the attack was ordered to prevent the use of the bridge by reserves coming up. In a book published early in 1976, Gordon Thomas and Max Morgan-Witts state that, according to a private diary kept by Wolfram, Freiherr von Richthofen, chief of staff of the Condor Legion at the time of the Guernica bombing, he met with Juan Vigon, Mola's chief of staff, shortly after eleven o'clock on the morning of April 26. "The two men . . . discussed the military situation. Then, without reference to higher authority, a Spaniard from Madrid and a German from Silesia settled the fate of the Basque's spiritual home" (*The Day Guernica Died,* pp. 197-198). This scene may have taken place, but unfortunately von Richthofen's diary fails to confirm either the meeting or the decisions allegedly taken there (Maier, *Guernica 26.4.1937,* pp. 69-74). The Thomas/ Morgan-Witts book is totally lacking in scholarly precision. Moreover, a version recently published in Barcelona, highly censored but nevertheless actively touted in Spain by G. Thomas, withdraws from Vigón the blame given him in the English text (*El día en que murió Guernica,* p. 126). History changed according to the whims of the market cannot be accepted by serious historians.

3. Dahms, *Der spanische Bürgerkrieg, 1936-1939*, p. 319. n. 10; *Historia y Vida*, April 1970, p. 107, "El bombardeo de Guernica," by R. de la Cierva.

4. *The Tree of Gernika*, p. 161.

5. J. B. S. Haldane, *A.R.P.*, pp. 47-48. Haldane thought the bombing to be "at the same time an act of terrorism . . . and a technical exercise for the German air force."

6. Jones, *A Diary with Letters*, p. 337. The reference in Jones's diary is dated 7 May 1937.

7. *De Guernica a Nueva York pasando por Berlín*, 3d ed., p. 26.

8. HA, 30 April 1937. Queipo had said essentially the same thing the day before (*ibid.*, 29 April 1937), as did another Nationalist spokesman on 29 April (*ibid.*, 30 April 1937).

9. *Tablet*, 5 June 1937, pp. 801-802.

10. *Spanish Rehearsal*, pp. 266-269.

11. *Guernica: The Official Report*, p. 13.

12. *Spain's Ordeal*, p. 247.

13. *This Is Spain*, p. 231.

14. *STVY*, p. 275.

15. *La Nación*, 1 May 1937.

16. *Why the Press failed on Spain!* p. 10.

17. *The Spanish War and Lying Propaganda*, p. 29.

18. *Correspondent in Spain*, p. 176.

19. *The March of a Nation*, p. 283.

20. *Spanish Arena*, p. 439.

21. *Observer*, 22 August 1937, p. 19.

22. *Guernica: The Official Report*, p. vi.

23. *Address*, p. 23.

24. *Daily Telegraph*, 19 February 1938.

25. *L'Espagne de Franco* (1938), p. 32; (1939), p. 37.

26. *La Renaissance de L'Espagne*, p. 197.

27. *World War in Spain*, p. 72; *Spain, 1923-1948: Civil War and World War*, p. 60.

28. *Histoire de la guerre d'Espagne*, p. 299.

29. *Leçons de la guerre d'Espagne*, p. 149.

30. *This Is Spain*, p. 231.

31. *Franco: A Biographical History*, p. 246.

32. *Airpower*, p. 228.

33. *La persécution religueuse en Espagne*, p. 135.

34. *Sentido y causas de la tragedia española*, p. 168.

35. *AF*, 29 July 1938.

36. *The Spanish Civil War*, p. 421.

37. *La Guerre civile d'Espagne*, p. 191.

38. *Franco: The Man and His Nation*, p. 277.

39. *Spanish Fury*, p. 163.

40. *The Spanish Republic and the Civil War*, p. 381.

41. *Arriba*, 31 January 1970, article by Pedro Pascual.

42. *El Pensamiento Navarro*, 15 February 1937.

43. *Historia y Vida*, April 1970, p. 107.

44. *Historia ilustrada*, II, 154-155.

45. *El Pensamiento Navarro*, 20 February 1970.

46. *Arde Guernica*, p. 131.

47. *Vizcaya*, pp. 112-113.

48. *Op. cit.*, p. 1435 n. 43; p. 1436 n. 45.

49. *Die deutsche Politik im spanischen Bürgerkrieg, 1936-1939*, pp. 397-398.

50. *Franco: A Biography*, p. 119. La Cierva (*Francisco Franco: Un siglo de España*, p. 616) quoted Trythall: "Franco, not being concerned with the details of the campaign, was very likely not even informed" (p. 120) as being disculpatory of the Spanish command. But the phrase does not leave the Spanish military blameless. La Cierva does not cite the other lines quoted in the text here.

51. *Vizcaya*, p. 113.

52. *ABC,* 22 July, p. 4; 23 July, pp. 3, 6; 24 July, p. 7; 25 July, pp. 5, 10; 26 July, pp. 6, 7, 10; 27 July, p. 12. See also Southworth, *Le mythe de la croisade de Franco,* pp. 177-179.

53. Whitaker, *We Cannot Escape History,* pp. 113-114; Southworth, *op. cit.,* pp. 188-189.

54. Francisco Franco, *Marreucos: Diario de una bandera,* p. 177. After recounting this incident, Franco remarked, "This is not the first heroic deed of the young legionary." This incident has been deleted from the later editions of the book, during and since the civil war.

55. *The Tree of Gernika,* p. 214.

56. *Vizcaya,* p. 80; also n. 118.

57. *Ibid.,* p. 23 n. 14.

58. *Ibid.,* p. 113, n. 177.

59. Madariaga accepted the validity of the spurious Communist documents employed against the Republic by the Rebels and sent to the Foreign Office by del Moral. He also accepted the Franquista version of the Badajoz massacre. See *Spain,* pp. 472, 378; Southworth, *op. cit.,* pp. 121, 217.

60. *Daily Herald,* 29 April 1937.

61. See Book II, part 2.

62. *Tablet,* 1 May 1937, p. 621.

63. *Op. cit.,* p. 261. The French Catholic writer Paul Vovard argued that Mola's responsibility for the attack on Guernica was the most "likely" (*Le martyre de Guernica,* p. 42). Why did Mola's secretary, José María Iribarren, who wrote the first biography of the general right after his death, and another one in 1938, never mention the destruction of Guernica, although it was the most talked-of event of the Bilbao campaign? See Iribarren, *Con el general Mola* (1937); *Mola* (1938).

64. Oyarzun, *Historia del carlismo,* pp. 77-83, 99-102, 393-400.

65. Von Richthofen was worried by the problem of Bilbao. In his "official" diary, he wrote two days before the attack on Guernica, "Must we completely destroy Bilbao?" (communication from Angel Viñas).

66. *Tablet,* 5 June 1937, p. 801.

67. *La Nación,* 2 May 1937. Zumalacárregui, the Carlist general, was killed in the first siege of Bilbao.

68. *Evening Standard,* 4 May 1937.

69. *New York American,* 30 April 1937.

70. *NYT,* 30 April 1937.

71. *Times,* 29 April 1937.

72. *Glasgow Herald,* 30 April 1937.

73. Toynbee, *Survey of International Affairs, 1937,* II, 71. Patricio P. Escobal, who was imprisoned in the Basque country, noted in his diary on 7 January 1938 that his prison doctor, Mendieta, who knew Guernica and its region well, told him that the only purpose of the bombing "was to spread terror behind the lines" (*Death Row: Spain 1936,* p. 229).

74. Steer, *op. cit.,* p. 150.

75. PRO, FO 371/22621, W 1725, folio 242.

76. *Tablet,* 24 September 1938, p. 389.

77. It was natural that most of the pilots of the Condor Legion became Luftwaffe pilots during World War II, and it was natural that those who survived the latter war either fled like Galland to a foreign country or tried to continue their careers in the new Federal German Republic. A few years ago I met the German air attaché in Paris, who had no hesitation in saying that he had fought in the Condor Legion—but after Guernica. There are certainly in West Germany today men who bombed Guernica, and probably among them are men in high places. West Germany has been conspiratorially silent about Guernica, as is testified to by the general ignorance concerning Merkes's revelations. On the contrary, East Germany has been aggressively vocal on the subject of the Condor Legion and Guernica. In a handsome publication of 1970, *Pasaremos,* there are references to the men who carried out the bombing. An article asserts that a short wave transmitter, doubtless situated in Republican Spain, called "29.8," broadcast to Germany "the names of the Brown air pirates who on April 26, 1937, carried out the abominable mass murder of the children of Guernica" (p. 250). The names broadcast are not given in the book. However, it is stated that Heinz Trettner, of the Condor Legion, was among

those who bombed Guernica. In 1967 he was inspector general of the West German Luftwaffe (pp. 18, 329). Hannes Trautloft, another Condor veteran, was at the same time commander of the Luftwaffe-Group South (p. 327, photograph). Trautloft and Trettner were both identified as having participated in the bombing of Guernica by the East Berlin newspaper *National Zeitung*, 18 July 1966, according to Talón. Talón added that Trettner had been decorated by American General Lemnitzer with the Legion of Merit, during the postwar years (*op. cit.*, pp. 145-146 n. 15). This note disappeared from Talón's second edition, but the caption of a photograph of Trautloft identified the pilot as one of the men who bombed Guernica (*op. cit.* [1973], photograph between pp. 193 and 194). Jesús Salas Larrazábal writes that Trautloft was one of the pilots who accompanied the first He 51s, which arrived at Cadiz on 6 August 1936 (*La guerra de España desde el aire*, pp. 87, 89). Salas also states that Trautloft had returned to Germany and took part in an air show in Switzerland in July 1937 (*Ibid.*, p. 212). Thomas and Morgan-Witts affirm that Trettner did not participate in the bombing of Guernica. However, since he was Sperrle's adjutant at the time of the raid, it is difficult to understand why these writers consider him blameless in the destruction of the town. Among the German aviators who, according to Thomas and Morgan-Witts, did take part in the attack on Guernica were Hans-Henning, Freiherr von Beust; von Knauer, E. von Dellmensingen Krafft, Franz von Lutzow, Rudolf von Moreau, Knuppel, and Wandel. Those still alive and interviewed by the writers insisted on the accidental nature of the destruction of Guernica. There is nothing in their testimony to explain the murderous swoops of the planes, chasing the fleeing people of Guernica.

Chapter 4
The Existence and the Persistence of the Controversy

1. When Pierre Susini, French representative to the North Vietnamese government, was mortally wounded by an American bomb that struck his residence in Hanoi in 1972, the American secretary of state suggested that the building had been hit by North Vietnamese antiaircraft projectiles. This untenable position was quickly abandoned.

2. Talón, *Arde Guernica*, p. 118; Escobal, *Death Row: Spain 1936*, p. 261.

3. *El Pensamiento Navarro*, 15 February 1937.

4. *Historia ilustrada*, II, 150.

5. *Ibid.*, p. 152.

6. *El Pensamiento Navarro*, 20 February 1937, p. 8.

7. *Conspiración y guerra civil*, p. 110.

8. *Vizcaya*, p. 109.

9. See Book I, chap. 3, text accompanying n. 20-26.

10. *The Unpopular Front*, p. 2.

11. *In Franco's Spain*, pp. 216-217. For other activities of Bolín in England, see text referred to by n. 13, Book III, chap. 1.

12. Communication from the Reverend Father Luis María de Lojendio, Mitred Abbot of the Valley of the Fallen, 2 August 1972: Foreign Press Service in the Spanish National Army, 1936-1939.

1. Foreign Press offices in Seville, Cáceres and Salamanca, successively: Don Luis Antonio Bolín. Foreign Press office in Talavera de la Reina: Don Pablo Merry del Val. Foreign Press office in Toledo: Don Jacobo Pellizeus. Foreign Press office in Avila: Don Luis María de Lojendio. Don Luis Antonio Bolín also directed the foreign press services on the fronts during the offensives of Málaga and Guadalajara. In these offensives the Information service for the foreign press was handled by Don Luis María de Lojendio. Don Gonzalo Aguilera, Cavalry Captain, also served on the fronts as Press officer.

2. This service lasted until the Spring of 1937. The offices of Talavera de la Reina, Toledo and Avila were suppressed. For the Bilbao campaign a foreign Press office was opened in Vitoria. Don Luis Antonio Bolín, Don Gonzalo Aguilera and Don Jacobo

Pellizeus left the service. Don Manuel de Lámbarri y Yanguas, lieutenant colonel, later colonel, took on the direction of the foreign journalists on the fighting fronts. Information for the foreign press was organized as an independent service. A group of press officers was organized on the fronts. The central foreign Press offices, of Salamanca and Burgos, were reorganized. A foreign Press office was opened in San Sebastián and another one in San Juan de Luz.

3. From April 1937, until the end of the war, the foreign Press service was organized in the following form: Don Jesús Pabón y Suarez de Urbina, Chief of the Exterior service of the Delegation of the State for Press and Propaganda. Don Manuel de Lámbarri, chief of the foreign Press service on the fronts. Don Luis María de Lojendio, Press officer in the general headquarters of the Generalísimo and in the command post in the field Campaign. Official informant for the foreign Press, Don Pablo Merry del Val, chief, successively, of the foreign Press offices of Salamanca and Burgos. Press officers on the fronts: Don Miguel Barella, Don Ernesto Giró, Don Enrique Marsans, Don Pedro Giró, Don Juan Antonio Marfá, Don Ignacio Lamadrid, Don Rafael Rifá y Puget, Don Pedro Chastel, Don Juan Bautista Sendra, Don Gerardo Jacob, Don Antonio Beaurier. In the foreign Press office of San Sebastián were: Don Miguel Barella, Don Roberto de Satorres and Don Miguel B. Sanz, and in the Press office of San Juan de Luz, Don Santiago Soler.

This list shows that Bolín left the service immediately after the Guernica incident, and that his place as head of the foreign press office in Salamanca was taken by Pablo Merry del Val. It is to be noted that the name of Rosales (Rosalles) does not appear in this communication. The status of the press officers was changed officially on 19 July 1937 (San Román Colino, *Legislación del gobierno nacional, segundo semestre, 1937*, p. 66). Phillip Knightley has written me that he has been told in Spain, by persons allied with the Bolín family, that Bolín fell into disgrace with Franco because of his inept handling of the propaganda concerning Guernica.

13. *Rouge et or*, p. x.

14. *Ibid.*, p. 13.

15. *Ibid.*, p. 47.

16. *Ibid.*, p. 60.

17. *Ibid.*, pp. 73-74.

18. *Looking for Trouble*, pp. 33, 77.

19. Segàla, *Trincee di Spagna*, p. 102.

20. AN, 5 AR 272, Botto file.

21. *STVY*, p. 300. Bolín might have been in intelligence work, which Sir Percival Phillips thought his true forte. According to McCullagh, Phillips said that Bolín told the newspapermen "very often that he holds an important post in G.H.Q." (*op. cit.*, p. 116).

22. *STVY*, p. 302.

23. Bolín wrote: "Sir Martin Melvin, the proprietor of the *Universe*, was told by Mr. Neville Chamberlain that had it not been for the Catholics he might have had to blockade the Nationalists and intervene against them" (*STVY*, p. 3). Bolín also tells us that to stop possible American aid to the Spanish Republicans, Eileen O'Brien, an Irish Catholic propagandist, "personally spoke on the telephone to every Catholic bishop in the United States and begged them to request their parish priests to ask members of their congregations to telegraph in protest to President Roosevelt. As a result of her efforts more than a million telegrams were received at the White House, and the munitions never reached their destination" (*ibid.*, pp. 3-4).

24. *Cuadernos bibliográficos de la guerra de España (1936-1939)*, Series 1, Fasc. 1, *Folletos*, p. xv.

25. *Op. cit.*, p. xv.

26. *Spain: The Unpopular Front*, p. 26.

27. *Ibid.*, p. 22.

28. *Spanish Rehearsal*, p. 29.

29. *Spain: Impressions and Reflections*, pp. 16-17.

30. *Ibid.*, p. 19.

31. *Ibid.*, p. 20.

32. *Tablet,* 5 June 1937, p. 801.
33. *L'Espagne de Franco* (1938), p. 33; (1939), p. 38.
34. *Why the Press Failed on Spain!* p. 9.
35. *The March of a Nation,* p. 280.
36. *Spanish Arena,* p. 438.
37. *Correspondent in Spain,* p. 176.
38. *This Is Spain,* p. 227.
39. *Der spanische Bürgerkrieg* (1936-1939), p. 319.
40. *La guerra española de 1936,* p. 254.
41. *Spanish Fury,* p. 163.
42. *Spain in Eclipse,* p. 3.
43. *Mine Were of Trouble,* p. 89.
44. *España en llamas,* p. 341.
45. *Op. cit.,* p. 110.
46. *Ibid.,* p. 215.
47. *National Review,* 5 January 1973, p. 29.
48. *Guernica.* N.p., n.d., n.e. There are editions in Basque and English, Basque and French, and probably in Basque and Castilian. 63 unnumbered pages.
49. *Foreign Wings over the Basque Country* (London: The Friends of Spain, 1937), 52 pages.
50. *Guernica. La main mise hitlérienne sur le Pays Basque,* Paris, Comité International de Coordination et d'Information pour l'Aide à l'Espagne republicaine, 1937 (?), 11 pages. *La destruction de Guernica* (Paris: Comité Franco-espagnol, 1937 (?)), 23 pages.
51. *Op. cit.,* p. 11.
52. Msgr. Ramón Echarren, aide to Cardinal Enrique y Tarrancón, quoted in *Valeurs actuelles,* September 1972, p. 37.

BIBLIOGRAPHY

Bibliography

This bibliography mentions all the sources that have been used for the preparation of this work. I have the impression that bibliographies excessively compartmentalized are more of a bother than an aid for the reader, and for that reason I have sought to limit as much as possible the divisions in this list. The bibliography is therefore arranged as follows:

I. Unpublished material: A. official documents; B. private documents; C. books in manuscript.

II. Published material: A. official documents; B. books and pamphlets; C. periodicals.

I. UNPUBLISHED MATERIAL.

A. Official Documents.

The unpublished official documents used in this study came from England, France, the United States, and the German Federal Republic. The principal source has been London, where the thirty-year rule has opened the archives twenty years earlier than in the rest of Europe (except for captured German and Italian documents). The Foreign Office files of 1936, 1937, and 1938, and the Non-Intervention Committee papers, available in the Public Record Office at London, gave me indispensable information concerning the diplomatic activity provoked by the destruction of Guernica. Without the documentation of the Public Record Office, I should never have been able to write the chapter on diplomatic maneuvers around

Guernica. The archives of the Quai d'Orsay are closed to researchers until fifty years after the event of Guernica—that is to say, until 1987. What is irritating for the historian is that he does not know if there exist in the French archives any documents concerning Guernica more significant than the official selection already published. It seems that some French diplomatic archives were burned in 1940; other French diplomatic papers were found half burned in Warsaw at the end of World War II. French secrecy concerning diplomatic documents is maintained to such a point that the files of the Non-Intervention Committee, which can be freely consulted in London, are kept under lock and key in Paris, and the investigator is told that he must wait until fifty years have passed before consulting them—that is, until 1986, 1987, 1988, and 1989.

Some unpublished documents of the United States dealing with the period have been found in Washington. It is minor documentation, and underlines the fact that the United States did not really play an active role in the diplomatic skirmishing around Guernica; the United States did not belong to either the League of Nations or the Non-Intervention Committee.

Some German documents concerning the Condor Legion have been made available by the Bundesarchiv-Militärarchiv im Freiburg-Brisgau, West Germany. Among these were "Die Kämpfe im Norden," Akte II L 14/2, and "Die Kämpfe im Norden," Akte Br. II L 14/3. However, I have been informed that most of the documents dealing with the Condor Legion were destroyed in the air raids of World War II.

B. Private Documents.

The most significant private documents used in this work are the files of the Havas News Agency, now in the National Archives in Paris. The chapter concerning the working conditions of the foreign correspondents in Rebel Spain was in great part based on these papers. An interesting sidelight on the Guernica controversy by Rabbi Stephen Wise came from the Special Collections section of the Brandeis University library, in Waltham, Massachusetts.

C. Books in Manuscript

Some chapters from the unpublished book of *mémoires* of Canon Alberto de Onaindia have been consulted. Since then the book has been published. I have also been allowed to see parts of *Páginas de mi vida,* by Angel Ojanguren y Celaya.

II. PUBLISHED MATERIAL

A. Official Documents.

Akten zur deutschen auswärtigen Politik, 1918-1945. Serie D. (1937-1945), Band III. *Deutschland und der spanische Bürgerkrieg, 1936-1939.* Baden-Baden: Imprimerie Nationale, 1951.

Congressional Record. House of Representatives, May 1937. Washington, D.C.: U.S.G.P.O., 1937.
Congressional Record. Senate, May 1937. Washington, D.C.: U.S.G.P.O., 1937.
Dez anos de política externa (1936-1947). Vol. IV. Lisbon: Ministerio dos Negocios Estrangeiros, 1965.
Documents diplomatiques français, 1932-1939. 2ème série, Vol. V. Paris: Imprimerie Nationale, 1970.
Documents on German Foreign Policy, 1918-1945. Series D (1937-1945). Vol. III. *Germany and the Spanish Civil War, 1936-1939.* Washington, D.C.: U.S.G.P.O., 1951.
Foreign Relations of the United States. Diplomatic Papers, 1937. Vol. I. Washington, D.C.: U.S.G.P.O., 1954.
Parliamentary Debates. House of Commons. Official Report in the Second Session of the Thirty-Seventh Parliament of the United Kingdom of Great Britain and Northern Ireland. 5th series, Vol. 7 of session 1936-1937. London: H.M.S.O., 1937.

B. Books and Pamphlets.

Abendroth, Hans-Henning. *Hitler in der spanischen Arena. Die deutsch-spanischen Beziehungen im Spannungsfeld der europäischen Interessenpolitik vom Ausbruch des Bürgerkrieges bis zum Ausbruch des Weltkrieges 1936-1939.* Paderborn: Fernand Schonigh, 1973.
Acier, Marcel. *In Spanish Trenches.* New York: Modern Age Books, 1937.
Address given by the Marquis del Moral to Members of the House of Commons on Wednesday, May 26th, 1937. London(?): Privately Printed, 1937(?).
Aguirre y Lecube, José Antonio de. *Cinco conferencias pronunciadas en un viaje por América.* Buenos Aires: Vasca Ekin, 1944.
———. *De Guernica a Nueva York, pasando por Berlín.* 3d. edition. Buenos Aires: Vasca Ekin, 1944.
Aircraft in Profile, 1-30. Garden City, N.Y.: Doubleday and Company, 1965.
Alderete, Ramón de. . . . . *Y estos Borbones nos quieren gobernar.* Paris: 1974.
Altabella Gracia, Pedro. *El catolicismo de los nacionalistas vascos.* Madrid: Editora Nacional, 1939.
"Anónimo". *La república española.* Madrid: Librería San Martín, 1933.
"Anonymous". *The Spanish Republic.* London: Eyre & Spottiswoode, 1933.
Ansaldo, Juan Antonio. *¿Para que . . . ?* Buenos Aires: Vasca Ekin, 1951.
Les archives de l'agence Havas (Branche Information) conservées aux Archives Nationales (5 AR). Inventaire par Isabelle Brot. Paris: S.E.V.P.E.N., 1969.
Arenillas, José María. *Euzkadi, la cuestión nacional y la revolución socialista,* suplemento del no. 168 de *La Batalla,* Paris.
Arrarás, Joaquín. *Franco.* Hamburg: Hoffmann und Camps, 1939.
——— (lit. ed.). *Historia de la cruzada española.* Vols. I, II, VII. Madrid: Ediciones Españolas, 1939, 1940, 1943.
Arrarás, Joaquín, and Luis Jordana. *El sitio del Alcázar.* Saragossa: "Heraldo de Aragón," 1937.
Atholl, Duchess of. *Searchlight on Spain.* London: Penguin, 1938.
Auphan, L. F. *Diez días en el norte de España conquistado por Franco.* San Sebastián: Librería Internacional. 1937.
Auriol, Vincent. *Hier . . . demain.* Paris: Charlot, 1955.
Avon, The Rt. Hon. The Earl of. *The Eden Memoirs: Facing the Dictators.* London: Cassell, 1962.
Aznar, Manuel. *The Alcázar will not surrender.* New York: A Group of Friends of Spain, 1957(?).
———. *Historia militar de la guerra de España.* Madrid: Idea, 1940.
———. *Historia militar de la guerra de España.* Vol. II. Madrid: Editora Nacional, 1961.
Bardèche, Maurice, and Robert Brasillach. *Histoire de la guerre d'Espagne.* Paris: Plon, 1939.
Barea, Arturo. *The Clash.* London: Faber and Faber, 1946.
Basaldúa, Pedro de. *En defensa de la verdad.* Buenos Aires: Vasca Ekin, 1956.
Bauer, Eddy. *Rouge et or.* Paris: Attinger, 1938.

Bayle, Constantino.*¿Qué pasa en Espana?* Salamanca: Delegación del Estado para Prensa y Propaganda, 1937.
"Belforte, Francesco" (J. Biondi Morra). *La guerra civile in Spagna.* Vol. III. Varese-Milan: Istituto per gli Studi di Politica Internazionale, 1939.
Berger, John. *Success and Failure of Picasso.* London: Penguin, 1966.
Bernanos, Georges. *Les enfants humiliés.* Paris: Gallimard, 1953.
―――. *Les grands cimetierès sous la lune.* Paris: Plon, 1938.
Bertrán y Musitu, José. *Experiencias de los servicios de información del nordeste de España (S.I.F.N.E.) durante la guerra.* Madrid: Espasa-Calpe, 1940.
Bessie, Alvah, ed. *The Heart of Spain.* New York: Veterans of the Abraham Lincoln Brigade, 1952.
Beumelberg, Werner. *Kampf um Spanien: Die Geschichte der Legion Condor.* Oldenburg: Stalling, 1940.
Bley, Wulf, ed. *Das Buch der Spanienflieger: Die Feuertaufe der neuen deutschen Luftwaffe.* Leipzig: Hase und Koehler, 1939.
Bodin, Louis, and Jean Touchard. *Front Populaire 1936.* Paris: Colin, 1961.
Bolín, Luis. *España: Los años vitales.* Madrid: Espasa-Calpe, 1967.
―――. *Spain: The Vital Years.* London: Cassell, 1967.
Bollati, Ambrogio, and Giulio Del Bono. *La guerra di Spagna, sino alla liberazione di Gijon.* Turìn: Einaudi, 1937.
Bowers, Claude. *My Mission to Spain.* New York: Simon and Schuster, 1954.
Brasillach, Robert. *Notre avant-guerre.* Paris: Plon, 1950.
Bret, Paul-Louis. *Au feu des événements. Mémoires d'un journaliste, Londres-Alger, 1929-1944.* Paris: Plon, 1955.
Brongersma, Dr. E. *Voorproef in Spanje, 1919-1939.* Utrecht-Brussels: Spectrum, 1946.
Bryant, Arthur. *Humanity in Politics.* London: Hutchinson, 1938.
Burgo, Jaime del. *Conspiración y guerra civil.* Madrid: Alfaguara, 1970.
Cárdenas Rodríguez, Gonzalo de. *Texto taquigráfico de la conferencia por el arquitecto general de regiones devastadas [. . .] el dia 3 de julio de 1940.* Madrid: Dirección general de Regiones devastadas y Reparaciones, 1940.
Cardozo, Harold G. *The March of a Nation.* London: Eyre & Spottiswoode, 1937.
Carr, Raymond, ed. *The Republic and the Civil War in Spain.* London: Macmillan, 1971.
Carreras, Luis. *Grandeur chrétienne de l'Espagne.* Paris: Sorlot, 1939.
Carro, Venancio. *La verdad sobre la guerra española.* Zamora: Tip. Comercial, 1937.
Casado, Segismundo. *The Last Days of Madrid.* London: Davies, 1939.
Cassagnau, Robert. *A l'est de Saint-Sébastien.* Paris: France-Empire, 1966.
Cierva, Ricardo de la. *Bibliografía sobre la guerra de España (1936-1939) y sus antecedentes.* Barcelona: Ariel, 1968.
―――. *Cien libros básicos sobre la guerra de España.* Madrid: Publicaciones Españolas, 1966.
―――. *Historia de la guerra civil española.* Vol. I. Madrid: San Martín, 1969.
―――. *Historia ilustrada de la guerra civil española.* Vol. II. Madrid: Danae, 1970.
―――. *Importancia histórica e historiográfica de la guerra española.* Madrid: Ateneo, 1967.
―――. *Leyenda y tragedia de las brigadas internacionales.* Madrid: Prensa Española, 1969.
Le clergé basque. Paris: Peyre, 1938.
El clero vasco, fiel al gobierno, se dirige al Sumo Pontífice, para hacer constar que la vandálica destrucción de Durango y Guernica se debió exclusivamente a la acción de los aviones alemanes. Madrid-Valencia: Ediciones Españolas, 1937.
El clero y los católicos vasco-separatistas y el movimiento nacional. Madrid: Centro de Información Católica Internacional, 1940.
Cleugh, James. *Furia española.* Barcelona: Juventud, 1964.
―――. *Spanish Fury.* London: Harrap, 1962.
Clonmore, Lord. *Pope Pius XI and World Peace.* London: Hale, 1937.
Cockburn, Claud. *Crossing the Line.* London: MacGibbon and Kee, 1959.
Code, Joseph B. *The Spanish War and Lying Propaganda.* New York: Paulist Press, 1938.
Coles, S. F. A. *Franco of Spain.* London: Spearman, 1955.
Controversy on Spain between G. A. Gwynne, C. H., Editor of the "Morning Post," and A. Ramos Oliveira, Spanish Writer. London: United Editorial, 1938.

Cookridge, E. H. *The Third Man*. New York: Putnam-Medallion, 1968.
Corman, Mathieu. *Brûleurs d'idoles*. Paris-Ostend: Tribord, 1937.
———. *"Salud camarada!" Cing mois sur les fronts d'Espagne*. Paris-Ostend: Tribord, 1937.
Cotta, Michèle. "Le Frontisme et 'La Flèche' de 1934 à 1936." Mémoire de l'Institut d'Études Politiques. Paris, 1959. Typescript.
Coutrot, Aline. *Un courant de la pensée catholique. L'hebdomadaire "Sept" (Mars 1934-Août 1937)*. Paris: Cerf, 1961.
Cowles, Virginia. *Looking for Trouble*. London: Hamilton, 1941.
The Crime of Guernica. New York: Spanish Information Bureau, 1937.
Croft, Henry Page. *My Life of Strife*. London: Hutchinson, 1954.
———. *Spain: The Truth at Last*. Bournemouth: Bournemouth Guardian, 1937.
Crozier, Brian. *Franco: A Biographical History*. London: Eyre & Spottiswoode, 1967.
———. *Franco: Historia y Biografía*. Vol. I. Madrid: Novelas y Cuentos, 1969.
Cuadernos bibliográficos de la guerra de España (1936-1939). Serie I, Fasc. I, *Folletos*. Madrid: Universidad de Madrid, 1966.
Dahms, Hellmuth Günther. *Der spanische Bürgerkrieg, 1936-1939*. Tübingen: Wunderlich, 1962.
———. *La guerra española de 1936*. Madrid: Rialp, 1966.
Dautun, Yves. *Valence sous la botte rouge*. Paris: Baudinière, 1937.
Davis, Frances. *My Shadow in the Sun*. New York: Carrick and Evans, 1940.
Debû-Bridel, Jacques. *L'agonie de la troisième République*. Paris: Editions du Bateau Ivre, 1948.
Delbos, Yvon. *L'expérience rouge*. Paris: Au sans pareil, 1933.
Delmer, Sefton. *Trail Sinister*. Vol. I. London: Secker and Warburg, 1961.
La destruction de Guernica. Paris: Comité Franco-Espagñol, 1937.
La destrucción de Guernica. Valencia (?): Servicio Espanol de Informacion, 1937 (?).
Diaz de Villegas, José. *Guerra de liberación (La fuerza de la razón)*. Barcelona: AHR, 1957.
Dumaine, Jacques. *Quai d'Orsay, 1945-1951*. Paris: Julliard, 1955.
Durango. Bilbao: 1937.
Durango, ville martyre: Ce que furent les bombardements de la ville de Durango par les avions allemands. Paris: Comité Franco-Espagnol, 1937.
Duval, General. *Les Espagnols et la guerre d'Espagne*. Paris: Plon, 1939.
———. *Les leçons de la guerre d'Espagne*. Paris: Plon, 1938.
Elosegi, Joseba. *Quiero morir por algo*. Bordeaux: Delmas, Anai Artes, 1971.
Eluard, Paul. *Cours naturel*. Paris: Sagittaire, 1938.
La epopeya de la guardia civil en el Santuario de la Virgen de la Cabeza, 18-VIII-1937, en su XXV aniversario. Madrid (?): Gráficas de Huérfanos de la Guardia Civil, 1962.
Estelrich, Juan. *La persecución religiosa en España*. Buenos Aires: Difusión, 1937.
———. *La persecution religieuse en Espagne*. Paris: Plon, 1937.
———. *La persecuzione religiosa in Spagna*. Milan: Mondadori, 1937.
———. *Prigoana religioasä in Spagna*. Bucharest: "Cugetarea," 1937.
Estier, Claude. *La gauche hebdomadaire, 1914-1962*. Paris: Colin, 1962.
Faldella, Emilio. *Venti mesi di guerra in Spagna*. Florence: Le Monnier, 1939.
"Farrère, Claude" (Charles Bargone). *Visite aux Espagnols (Hiver 1937)*. Paris: Flammarion, 1937.
Fernández Etxeberria, M. *De Euzkadi nación a España ficción*. Carácas: "Ami-Vasco," n.d.
Foltz, Charles, Jr. *The Masquerade in Spain*. Boston: Houghton Mifflin, 1948.
Foreign Journalists under Franco's Terror. London: United Editorial, 1937.
Foreign Office List and Diplomatic and Consular Year Book for 1937. London: Harrison and Sons, 1937.
Foreign Wings over the Basque Country. London: The Friends of Spain, 1937.
Forell, Fritz von, *Mölders und seiner Männer*. Graz: Steirische Verlaganstalt, 1941.
Foss, William, and Cecil Gerahty. *Arena spagnola*. Milan: Mondadori, 1938.
———. *Die spanische Arena*. Stuttgart-Berlin: Rowohlt, 1938.
———. *The Spanish Arena*. London: Gifford, 1938.
Franceschi, Gustavo J. *En el humo del incendio*. Buenos Aires: Difusión, 1938.
———. *El movimiento español y el criterio católico*. Buenos Aires: Difusión, 1937.

Franco, Francisco. *Diario de una bandera.* Madrid: Aguado, 1956.
———. *Marruecos: Diario de una bandera.* Madrid: Pueyo, 1922.
———. *Marruecos: Diario de una bandera.* Seville: La Novela del Sábado, 1939.
———. *Palabras del Caudillo.* Ediciones FE, 1938.
———. *Textos de doctrina política.* Madrid: Publicaciones Españolas, 1951.
Fraser, J. Alban. *Spain's Pilgrimage of Grace.* Glasgow: Burns, 1937.
Frédérix, Pierre. *Un siècle de chasse aux nouvelles. De L'Agence d'Information Havas à l'Agence France-Presse (1835-1957).* Paris: Flammarion, 1959.
Frutos, Victor de. *Los que no perdieron la guerra.* Buenos Aires: Oberón, 1967.
Führing, Hellmuth. *Wir funken für Franco.* Gutersloh: Bertelsmann, 1939.
Fuller, J. F. C. *The Conquest of Red Spain.* London: Burns Oates and Washbourne, 1937.
———. *The First of the League Wars.* London: Eyre & Spottiswoode, 1936.
Galinsoga, Luis de, *Centinela de occidente.* Barcelona: AHR, 1956.
Galland, Adolf. *Die Ersten und die Letzten.* Darmstadt: Schneekluth, 1953.
———. *Memorias: "Los primeros y los últimos."* Barcelona: AHR, 1955.
Gannon, Franklin Reid. *The British Press and Germany, 1936-1939.* London: Oxford, 1971.
García de Castro, Rafael G. *La tragedia espiritual de Vizcaya.* Granada: Prieto, 1938.
García Venero, Maximiano. *Falange en la guerra de España: La unificación y Hedilla.* Paris: Ruedo Ibérico, 1967.
———. *Historia del nacionalismo vasco.* Madrid: Editora Nacional, 1945.
Gay, Vicente. *Estampas rojas y caballeros blancos.* Burgos: Hijos de S. Rodríguez, 1937.
———. *Madre Roma.* Barcelona: Bosch, 1935.
———. *La revolución nacional socialista.* Barcelona: Bosch, 1934.
George, Margaret. *The Warped Vision.* Pittsburgh: University of Pittsburgh Press, 1965.
Georges-Roux (Georges Roux). *La guerra civil de España.* Madrid: Cid, 1964.
———. *La guerre civile d'Espagne.* Paris: Fayard, 1963.
Gerahty, Cecil. *The Road to Madrid.* London: Hutchinson, 1937.
Gibson, Ian. *The Death of Lorca.* London: Allan, 1973.
Gilbert, G. M. *Nuremberg Diary.* New York: Farrar, Strauss, 1961.
Gil Mugarza, Bernardo. *España en llamas.* Barcelona: Acervo, 1968.
Gomá, Isidro. *Por Dios y por España.* Barcelona: Casulleras, 1940.
Gomá, José. *La guerra en el aire.* Barcelona: AHR, 1958.
Gómez, Carlos A. *La guerra de España.* Vol. I. Buenos Aires: Círculo Militar-Biblioteca del Oficial, 1939.
Great Britain, Foreign Office. *Index to General Correspondence, 1937.* Nendeln, Lichtenstein: Kraus-Thomson, 1969.
Greene, Nathanael. *Crisis and Decline. The French Socialist Party in the Popular Front Era.* Ithaca: N.Y.: Cornell University Press, 1969.
Guernica. Bilbao, 1937.
Guernica: Being the Official Report of a Commission Appointed by the Spanish Nationalist Government to Investigate the Causes of the Destruction of Guernica on April 26-28, 1937. London: Eyre & Spottiswoode, 1938.
Guernica. La mainmise hitlérienne sur le Pays basque. Paris: Comité International de Coordination et d'Information pour l'Aide à l'Espagne républicaine, 1937.
La guerra de liberación nacional. Saragossa: Universidad de Zaragoza, 1961.
Gutiérrez, Antonio José. *Sentido y causas de la tragedia española.* San Sebastián: Editora Internacional, 1942.
Gutiérrez de la Higuera y Velázquez, Alfonso, and Luis Molins Correa. *Historia de la revolución española. Tercera guerra de independencia.* Cádiz-Madrid: Cerón, 1940.
Guttmann, Allen. *The Wound in the Heart.* New York: Free Press of Glencoe, 1962.
Haldane, J. B. S. *A.R.P.* London: Gollancz, 1938.
Halimi, Gisèle. *Le procès de Burgos.* Paris: Gallimard, 1971.
Hanighen, Frank C., ed. *Nothing but Danger.* New York: National Travel Club, 1939.
Harper, Glenn T. *German Economic Policy in Spain during the Spanish Civil War, 1936-1939.* The Hague-Paris: Mouton, 1967.
Hart, Merwin K. *America, Look at Spain!* New York: Kenedy, 1939.
Héricourt, Pierre. *Pourquoi Franco a vaincu.* Paris: Baudiniere, 1939.
———. *(Pourquoi Franco vaincra.* Paris: Baudinière, 1936.

———. *Pourquoi mentir? L'Aide franco-soviétique à l'Espagne rouge.* Paris: Baudinière, 1937.

———. *Les Soviets et la France: Fournisseurs de la révolution espagnole.* Paris: Baudinière, 1938.

Hérold-Paquis, Jean. *Des illusions . . . désillusions (14 Août 1944-15 Août 1945).* Paris: Bourgoin, 1948.

Hills, George. *Franco: El hombre y su nación.* Madrid: San Martín, 1969.

———. *Franco: the Man and His Nation.* London: Hale, 1967.

Histoire générale de la presse française. Vol. III. Paris: Presses Universitaires de France, 1972.

The History of The Times. *The 150th Anniversary and Beyond, 1912-1948.* Vol. II. London: Office of *The Times,* 1952.

Hodgson, Sir Robert. *Franco frente a Hitler.* Barcelona: AHR, 1954.

———. *Spain Resurgent.* London: Hutchinson, 1953.

Hoehn, Matthew. *Catholic Authors: Contemporary Biographical Sketches, 1930-1947.* Newark: St. Mary's Abbey, 1948.

Hoyos, Max. *Pedros y Pablos: Fliegen, erleben, kampfen in Spanien.* Munich: Bruckmann, 1941.

Informe sobre la situación de las provincias vascongadas bajo el dominio rojo-separatista. Valladolid: Universidad de Valladolid, 1938.

La intervención de Alemania en favor de Franco en las operaciones del territorio vasco. Documentos relativos a la guerra civil, no. 4. Bilbao: Gobierno Provisional de Euzkadi, 1937.

Jackson, Gabriel. *La Republica española y la guerra civil, 1931-1939.* Mexico, D. F.: Grijalbo, 1967.

———. *The Spanish Republic and the Civil War, 1931-1939.* Princeton: Princeton University Press, 1965.

Jacquelin, André. *Espagne et liberté.* Paris: Kérénac, 1939, 1945.

Jane's All the World's Aircraft, 1937. London: Sampson Law, Marton, December 1937.

Jerrold, Douglas. *Britain and Europe, 1900-1940.* London: Collins, 1941.

———. *Georgian Adventure.* London: Collins, 1937.

———. *The Issues in Spain.* New York: American Review, 1937.

———. *Spain: Impressions and Reflections.* Reprint. *The Nineteenth Century and After,* April 1937.

Jones, Thomas. *A Diary with Letters.* London: Oxford, 1954.

Joubert, H. *L'Espagne de Franco.* Paris: Sorlot, 1938.

———. *La guerre d'Espagne et le catholicisme (Réponse à M. Jacques Maritain).* Paris: S.G.I.E., 1937.

Kemp, Peter. *Legionario en España.* Barcelona: Caralt, 1959.

———. *Mine Were of Trouble.* London: Cassell, 1957.

Kesten, Hermann. *The Children of Guernica.* New York: Alliance, 1939.

———. *Les enfants de Guernica.* Paris: Calmann-Lévy, 1954.

———. *Die Kinder von Gernika.* Amsterdam: Allert de Lange, 1939.

———. *Die Kinder von Gernika.* Hamburg: Rowohlt, 1955.

Kirsch, Hans-Christian, ed. *Der spanische Bürgerkrieg in Augenzeugenberichten.* Dusseldorf: Rauch, 1967.

Kleine-Ahlbrandt, William Laird. *The Policy of Simmering: A Study of British Policy during the Spanish Civil War, 1936-1939.* The Hague: Nijhoff, 1962.

Knickerbocker, H. R. *Is Tomorrow Hitler's?* New York: Penguin, 1942.

———. *The Siege of Alcazar.* Philadelphia: McKay, 1936.

Knightley, Phillip. *The First Casualty.* London: Deutsch, 1975.

Knoblaugh, H. Edward. *Correspondent in Spain.* London-New York: Sheed and Ward, 1937.

———. *Corresponsal en España.* Madrid: Uriarte, 1967.

Koestler, Arthur. *The Invisible Writing.* London: Collins, 1954.

———. *Spanish Testament.* London: Gollancz, 1937.

Layna Serrano, Francisco. *El palacio del Infantado en Guadalajara.* Madrid: Servicio de Defensa del Tesoro Artístico Nacional, 1941.

"Lizarra, A. de" (José María de Irujo). *Los vascos y la república española.* Buenos Aires: Vasca Ekin, 1944.

Lojendio, Luis María de. *Operaciones militares de la guerra de España.* Barcelona: Montaner y Simón, 1940.

Loveday, Arthur F. *Spain, 1923-1948: Civil War and World War*. Ashcott: Boswell, 1949.
———. *World War in Spain*. London: Murray, 1939.
Lunn, Arnold. *Revolutionary Socialism in Theory and Practice*. London: Right Book Club, 1939.
———. *Spain and the Christian Front*. New York: Paulist Press, 1937.
———. *Spain: The Unpopular Front*. London: Catholic Truth Society, 1937.
———. *Spanish Rehearsal*. London: Hutchinson, 1937.
McCullagh, Francis. *In Franco's Spain*. London: Burns Oates and Washbourne, 1937.
McNeill-Moss, Geoffrey. *The Epic of the Alcazar*. London: Rich and Cowan, 1937.
———. *The Siege of Alcazar*. New York: Knopf, 1937.
Madariaga, Salvador de. *Spain*. London: Cape, 1942.
Maier, Klaus A. *Guernica, 26.4.1937. Die Deutsche Intervention in Spanien und der "Fall Guernica."* Freiburg: Rombach, 1975.
Maritain, Jacques, *Questions de conscience*. Paris: Desclée de Brouwer, 1938.
———. *Raison et raisons*. Paris: Eglof, 1947.
Marlowe, John. *Late Victorian*. London: Cresset, 1967.
Marrero, Vicente. *La guerra española y el trust de cerebros*. Madrid: Punta Europe, 1961.
Martin, Claude. *Franco: Soldado y estadista*. Madrid: Uriarte, 1965.
———. *Franco: Soldat et chef d'état*. Paris: Quatre Fils Aymon, 1959.
Martínez Bande, José Manuel. *La intervención comunista en la guerra de España*. Madrid: Servicio Informativo Español, 1965.
———. *Vizcaya*. Madrid: San Martín, 1971.
Mattioli, Guido. *L'Aviazione legionaria in Spagna*. Rome: L'Aviazione, 1938.
———. *L'Aviazione legionaria in Spagna*. Rome: L'Aviazione, 1940.
Mauriac, Francois. *Mémoires politiques*. Paris: Grasset, 1967.
Maurras, Charles. *Vers l'Espagne de Franco*. Paris: Editions du Livre Moderne, 1943.
Mayeur, Françoise. *L'Aube: Étude d'un journal d'opinion*. Paris, 1966.
Mendizábal, Alfredo. *Aux origines d'une tragédie*. Paris: Desclée de Brouwer, 1937.
Menéndez-Reigada, Ignacio G. *Acerca de la "guerra santa": Contestación a M. J. Maritain*. Salamanca: Comercial Salmantina, 1937.
———. *La guerra nacional española ante la moral y el derecho*. Bilbao: Editora Nacional, 1937.
Merkes, Manfred. *Die deutsche Politik gegenüber dem spanischen Bürgerkrieg, 1936-1939*. Bonn: Röhrscheid, 1961.
———. *Die deutsche Politik im spanischen Bürgerkrieg, 1936-1939*. Bonn: Röhrscheid, 1969.
Mévil, Jacques. *Un amour défendu*. Paris: La Nef de Paris, 1957.
———. *Sang d'Espagne*. Grenoble: "Delphina," 1942.
Monks, Noel. *Eyewitness*. London: Muller, 1955.
Montero Moreno, Antonio. *Historia de la persecución religiosa en España, 1936-1939*. Madrid: Editorial Católica, 1961.
"Montserrat, Victor" (Dr. Tarragó). *Le drame d'un peuple incompris: La guerre au Pays basque*. Paris: Peyre, 1937.
Mora, Constancia de la. *In Place of Splendor*. New York: Knopf, 1939.
Morgan-Witts, Max, and Gordon Thomas. *The Day Guernica Died*. London: Hodder and Stoughton, 1976.
Mottin, Jean. *Histoire politique de la presse, 1944-1949*. Paris: Editions "Bilans Hebdomadaires," 1949.
Onaindia, Alberto de. *Experiencias del exilio*. Buenos Aires: Vasca Ekin, 1974.
———. *Hombre de paz en la guerra*. Buenos Aires: Vasca Ekin, 1973.
Oudard, Georges. *Chemises noires, brunes, vertes en Espagne*. Paris: Plon, 1938.
Oyarzun, Román. *Historia del Carlismo*. Bilbao: FE, 1939.
Packard, Reynolds, and Eleanor Packard. *Balcony Empire*. London: Chatto and Windus, 1943.
Page, Bruce, David Leitch, and Phillip Knightley. *The Philby Conspiracy*. Garden City, N.Y.: Doubleday, 1968.
Pasaremos. Berlin: Deutscher Militärverlag, 1970.
Pascual, Pedro. *Proceso a una guerra*. Madrid: Editora Nacional, 1974.
Pascual de Orkoya, Juan. *La verdad sobre la destrucción de Gernika. Réplica a Monseñor Gustavo J. Franceschi*. Buenos Aires: Sebastián de Amorrortu, 1937.
Pattee, Richard. *This is Spain*. Milwaukee: Bruce, 1951.
Payne, Robert, ed. *The Civil War in Spain, 1936-1939*. New York: Putnam's, 1962.

Peers, E. Allison. *Spain in Eclipse, 1937-1943*. London: Methuen, 1943.
Pemán, José María. *Comentarios a mil imágenes de la guerra civil española*. Barcelona: AHR, 1967.
Penrose, Roland. *Picasso: His Life and Work*. London: Penguin, 1967.
El pequeño libro pardo del general. Paris: Ruedo Ibèrico, 1972.
"Pertinax" (Andre Giraud). *The Gravediggers of France*. Garden City, N.Y.: Doubleday, 1944.
Phillips, C. E. Lucas. *The Spanish Pimpernel*. London: Heinemann, 1960.
Piazzoni, Sandro. *Las tropas Flechas Negras en la guerra de España (1937-1939)*. Barcelona: Juventud, 1941.
Picasso, Pablo. *Songes et mensonges de Franco*. Paris, 1937.
Pike, David Wingeate. *Conjecture, Propaganda, and Deceit and the Spanish Civil War*. Stanford: Calif.: Institute of International Studies, 1968.
———. *Les français et la guerre d'Espagne*. Paris: Presses Universitaires de France, 1975.
———. *La presse francaise a la veille de la second guerre mondials*. Paris: Richelieu, 1973.
Portela, Artur. *Nas trincheiras de Espanha*. Lisbon: Pereira, 1937.
Pradera, Victor. *El Estado nuevo*. Madrid: Cultura Española, 1935.
———. *El Estado nuevo*. Burgos: Editorial Española, 1937.
———. *El Estado nuevo*. Madrid: Cultura Española, 1941.
———. *The New State*. London: Sands, 1939.
A Preliminary Official Report on the Atrocities Committed in Southern Spain in July and August, 1936, by the Communist Forces of the Madrid Government. London: Eyre & Spottiswoode, 1936.
Prieto, Indalecio. *Cómo y por qué salí del Ministerio de Defensa nacional*. México, D. F.: Impresos y Papeles, 1940.
———. *Convulsiones de España*. I. México, D.F.: Oasis, 1967.
La reconstrucción de España. Madrid: Publicaciones Españolas, 1947.
Rémond, René. *Les catholiques, le communisme et les crises, 1929-1939*. Paris: Colin, 1960.
Riotte, Jean. *Arriba España! . . . Espagne, éveille-toi!* Tarbes: Imprimerie des Orphelins-Apprentis, 1936.
Rispoli, Tullio. *La Spagna dei Legionari*. Roma: Cremonese Editore, 1942.
Rogers, F. Theo. *Spain: A Tragic Journey*. New York: Macaulay, 1937.
Rojas, Carlos. *Diálogos para otra España*. Barcelona: Ariel, 1966.
Das Rotbuch über Spanien. Berlin: Nibelungen, 1937.
Saint-Aulaire, Comte de. *La renaissance de l'Espagne*. Paris: Plon, 1938.
Salaberri, Kepa. *El proceso de Euskadi en Burgos. Sumarísimo 51/69*. Paris: Ruedo Ibérico, 1971.
Salas Larrazábal, Jesús. *La guerra de España desde el aire*. 2d ed. Barcelona: Ariel, 1972.
Salas Larrazábal, Ramón. *Historia del ejército popular de la República*. Vol. II. Madrid: Editora Nacional, 1973.
Salmon, André. *Souvenirs sans fin*. Vol. III. Paris: Gallimard, 1961.
Salvador, Tomás. *La guerra de España en sus fotografías*. Barcelona: Marte, 1966.
San Román Colino, José P. *Legislación del gobierno nacional. 1936, segundo semestre*. Avila: SHADE, 1937.
———. *Legislación del gobierno nacional. 1937, primer semestre*. Avila: SHADE, 1937.
Sauvage, Marcel. *La corrida*. Paris: Denoël, 1938.
The Second and Third Official Reports on the Communist Atrocities. London: Eyre & Spottiswoode, 1937.
Seco Serrano, Carlos. *Historia de España. Gran historia general de los pueblos hispanos*. Vol. VI, *Época contemporánea*. Barcelona: Gallach, 1962; 2d ed. 1968.
Segàla, Renzo. *Trincee di Spagna*. Milan: Fratelli Treves, 1938.
Seldes, George. *The Catholic Crisis*. New York: Messmer, 1939.
———. *Lords of the Press*. New York: Messmer, 1938.
"Sencourt, Robert" (Robert Esmonde Gordon George). *Spain's Ordeal*. New York: Longmans, 1938.
Shirer, William R. *The Collapse of the Third Republic*. New York: Simon and Schuster, 1969.
Sierra Bustamante, Ramón. *Euzkadi*. Madrid: Editora Nacional, 1941.
Síntesis histórica de la guerra de liberación, 1936-1939. Madrid: Servicio Histórico Militar, 1968.

Smeth, Maria de, *Viva Espana! Arriba Espana!* Berlin: Nibelungen Verlag, 1937.
Somebody Had to Do Something. Los Angeles: James Lardner Memorial Fund, 1939.
Sorrentino, Lamberti. *Questa Spagna.* Rome: Edizioni "Roma," 1939.
Southworth, Herbert Rutledge. *Le mythe de la croisade de Franco.* Paris: Ruedo Ibérico, 1964.
De Spaanse burgeroorlog en zijn gevolgen. Leiden: Universitaire Pers Leiden, 1973.
Spain at War, 18th July, 1936-18th July, 1937. London: Burns Oates and Washbourne, 1937.
Stackelberg, Karl-Georg von. *Legion Condor: Deutsche Freiwillige in Spanien.* Berlin: Verlag die Heimbucherei, 1939.
Steer, George L. *El arbol de Guernica.* Buenos Aires: Gudari, 1963.
———. *Caesar in Abyssinia.* London: Hodder and Stoughton, 1936.
———. *Sealed and Delivered.* London: Hodder and Stoughton, 1942.
———. *The Tree of Gernika.* London: Hodder and Stoughton, 1938.
Sutherland, Halliday. *Spanish Journey.* London: Hollis and Carter, 1949.
Talón, Vicente. *Arde Guernica.* Madrid: San Martín, 1970.
———. *Arde Guernica.* Madrid: G. del Toro, 1973.
Tangye, Nigel. *Red, White and Spain.* London: Rich and Cowan, 1937.
Taylor, F. Jay. *The United States and the Spanish Civil War.* New York: Bookman Associates, 1956.
Téry, Simone. *Front de la liberte.* Paris: Editions Sociales Internationales, 1938.
Thomas, Gordon, and Max Morgan-Witts. *El día en que murió Guernica.* Barcelona: Plaza & Janes, 1976.
Thomas, Hugh. *La guerra civil española.* Paris: Ruedo Ibérico, 1962.
———. *The Spanish Civil War.* London: Eyre & Spottiswoode, 1961.
———. *The Spanish Civil War.* London: Penguin, 1965.
Thompson, Sir Geoffrey. *Front-Line Diplomat.* London: Hutchinson, 1959.
Thorning, Joseph F. *Why the Press Failed on Spain!* New York: International Catholic Truth Society, 1937.
Toynbee, Arnold J. *Survey of International Affairs, 1937.* Vol. II. London: Oxford, 1938.
La tragédie espagnole: Conférence donnée au Théatre des Ambassadeurs, le mercredi 27 avril 1938, par M. Henry Lémery . . . MM. le général Duval . . . le général Jouart . . . le général Joubert. Paris: Supplement de la *Revue des Ambassadeurs,* 1938.
Trythall, J. W. D. *Franco: A Biography.* London: Hart-Davis, 1970.
Vegas Latapié, E. *El pensamiento político de Calvo Sotelo.* Madrid: Cultura Española, 1941.
Vigón, Jorge. *General Mola (el conspirador).* Barcelona: AHR, 1957.
Vila-San-Juan, José Luis. *¿Así fué? Enigmas de la guerra civil española.* Barcelona: Nauta, 1971.
Viñas, Angel. *La Alemania nazi y el 18 de julio.* Madrid: Alianza Editorial, 1974.
Vovard, Paul. *Le martyre de Guernica.* Paris: La Jeune République, 1938.
Watkins, K. W. *Britain Divided.* London: Nelson, 1963.
Weaver, Denis. *Front Page Europe.* London: Cresset, 1943.
Weber, Eugen. *L'Action Francaise.* Paris: Stock, 1964.
Whitaker, John T. *We Cannot Escape History.* New York: Macmillan, 1943.
Williams, Al. *Airpower.* New York: Coward-McCann, 1940.
Wilson, Arnold. *More Thoughts and Talks.* London: Right Book Club, 1939.
———. *Thoughts and Talks.* London: Right Book Club, 1938.
Yeats-Brown, Francis. *European Jungle.* London: Eyre & Spottiswoode, 1939.
Ynfante, Jesús. *La prodigiosa aventura del Opus Dei.* Paris: Ruedo Ibérico, 1970.

C. Periodicals

ABC. Madrid, 1970, 1973.
ABC. Seville. 1936, 1937.
L'Action Française. Paris, 1937, 1938.
La Actualidad Española. Madrid, 1972.
Aeroplane. London, 1937.
Aftonbladet. Stockholm, 1937.
El Alcázar. Madrid, 1968, 1970, 1972.
American Historical Review. 1973.
American Review. New York, 1937.

Arriba. Madrid, 1970.
L'Aube. Paris, 1937.
Berliner Lokal-Anzeiger. Berlin, 1937.
Boletín Oficial del Estado. Madrid, 1939.
Boston Evening Transcript. 1937.
Bulletin of Spanish Studies. Liverpool, 1937.
Bulletin Périodique de la Presse Italienne. Paris, 1937.
Candide. Paris, 1937.
Catholic Herald. London, April-May 1937.
Catholic Mind. New York, January 1937.
Catholic Times. London, April-May 1937.
Ce Soir. Paris, April-May 1937.
Chicago Daily News. April-May 1937.
Chicago Daily Tribune. August 1936, April-May 1937.
Columbia. New York, 1937.
Combat. Paris, 1969.
O Commercio do Porto. Oporto, 1937.
Continental Daily Mail. Paris, 1937.
Correio da Manhã. Rio de Janeiro, 1937.
El Correo Español-El Pueblo Vasco. San Sebastián, 1970.
Corriere della Sera. Milan, 1937.
La Croix. Paris, 1937.
Crónica de la Guerra Española. Buenos Aires, 1967.
Daily Herald. London, 1937.
Daily Mail. London, 1937.
Daily News. New York, 1937.
Daily Telegraph. London, 1937, 1938.
Daily Worker. London, 1937.
La Dépêche. Lille, 1937.
La Dépêche. Toulouse, 1937.
La Dépêche Algerienne. Algiers, 1937.
Diario de Barcelona. 1971.
Diario de Noticias. Lisbon, 1937.
Diario Vasco. San Sebastián, 1970.
L'Echo d'Alger. Algiers, 1937.
L'Echo de Paris. Paris, 1937.
Economist. London, 1973.
Ejército. Madrid, 1957.
L'Émancipation Nationale. Paris, 1937.
L'Espresso. Milan, 1967.
Esprit. Paris, 1937.
Études. Paris, 1937.
Euzko Deya. Paris, 1936-1939, 1969-1970.
Evening News. London, 1937.
Evening Standard. London, 1937.
L'Excelsior. Paris, 1937.
L'Express du Midi. Toulouse, 1937.
Le Figaro. Paris, 1937, 1968-1970.
Le Figaro Littéraire. Paris, 1967.
La Flèche. Paris, 1937.
La France de Bordeaux et du Sud-Ouest. Bordeaux, 1937.
Francisco Franco: Un siglo de España. Madrid, 1973.
Frankfurter Allgemeine Zeitung. Frankfort, 1973.
Gazette. Montreal, 1937.
Glasgow Herald. 1937.
Gringoire. Paris, 1937.
Gudari. 1972.
Hamburger Fremdenblatt. 1937.

Heraldo de Aragón. Saragossa, 1937.
Historia y Vida. Barcelona, 1970.
Human Events. Washington, D.C., 1973.
L'Humanité. Paris, 1937, 1968-1970.
L'Illustration. Paris, 1937.
L'Independance Belge. Brussels, 1937.
Indice. Madrid, 1969.
Índice Histórico Español. Barcelona, 1967.
International Herald Tribune. Paris, 1967-1970.
L'Intransigeant. Paris, 1937.
Je Suis Partout. Paris, 1937.
Le Journal. Paris, 1937.
Journal de Genève. Geneva, 1937.
Journal des Débats Politiques et Littéraires. Paris, 1937.
Journal des Nations. Geneva, 1937.
Journal of Contemporary History. London, 1972.
Kölnische Volkszeitung und Handelsblatt. Cologne, 1937.
Kölnische Zeitung. Cologne, 1937.
La Liberté du Sud-Ouest. Bordeaux, 1937.
La Libre Belgique. Brussels, 1937.
Life. New York, 1969.
London Mercury. 1937.
Manchester Guardian. 1937, 1938.
Le Matin. Paris, 1937.
Il Messagero. Rome, 1937.
La Métropole. Antwerp, 1937.
Militär Wochenblatt. Berlin, 1937.
Le Monde. Paris, 1967-1970.
Montreal Daily Star. 1937.
Morning Post. London, 1937.
La Nación. Buenos Aires, 1937.
National Review. New York, 1973.
Neue Zürcher Nachrichten. Zurich, 1937.
Neue Zürcher Zeitung. Zurich, 1937.
New Leader. New York, 1967.
New Statesman. London, 1967-1968.
New York American. New York, 1937.
New York Herald Tribune. 1937.
New York Herald Tribune. Paris, 1936.
New York Times, Amsterdam, 1967.
New York Times, New York, 1937, 1969.
New York Times Book Review. 1967.
News Chronicle. London, 1937.
Newsletter of the Society for Spanish and Portuguese Historical Studies. Austin, Texas, 1971.
Nieuwe Rotterdamsche Courant. Rotterdam, 1937.
The Nineteenth Century and After. London, 1937.
Nouvelle Revue Française. Paris, 1937.
Le Nouvelliste de Bretagne. Rennes, 1937.
Nuevo Diario. Madrid, 1970.
Observer. London, 1937.
Occident. Paris, 1937, 1938.
L'Oeuvre. Paris, 1937.
Oficina Prensa Euzkadi. Paris, 1967.
L'Ordre. Paris, 1937.
L'Osservatore Romano. Vatican City, 1937.
Paris-Midi. Paris, 1937.
Paris-Soir. Paris, 1937.
El Pensamiento Navarro. Pamplona, 1970.

Le Petit Journal. Paris, 1937.
Le Petit Marocain. Casablanca, 1936, 1937.
Le Petit Marseillais. Marseille, 1937.
Le Petit Parisien. Paris, 1937.
La Petite Gironde. Bordeaux, 1937.
Le Populaire. Paris, 1937.
La Prensa. Buenos Aires, 1936, 1937.
La Presse. Montreal, 1937.
Pueblo. Madrid, 1970.
La Quinzaine Littéraire. Paris, 1969, 1970.
La Revue Catholique des Faits et des Idées. Brussels, 1937.
Saturday Review/World. New York, 1973.
O Seculo. Lisbon, 1937.
Sept. Paris, 1937.
SP. Madrid, 1970.
Spain. London, 1937, 1938.
Spectator. London, 1937.
Der Spiegel. Hamburg, 1973.
La Stampa. Turin, 1937.
Standard and Times. Philadelphia, 1937.
Star. London, 1937.
Sun News. Sydney, 1937.
Sunday Times. London, 1937.
Tablet. London, 1937.
Il Telegrafo. Leghorn, 1937.
Il Tempo. Rome, 1973.
Le Temps. Paris, 1937.
Times. London, 1937, 1969.
Toronto Daily Star. 1937.
La Tribuna. Rome, 1937.
Tribune de Genève. Geneva, 1937.
Universe. London, 1937.
Valeurs Actuelles. Paris, 1972.
La Vanguardia. Barcelona, 1937.
Vértice. San Sebastián, 1937.
La Vie Catholique. Paris, 1937.
Vierteljahrshefte für Zeitgeschichte, Stuttgart, 1968.
La Vigie Marocaine. Casablanca, 1937.
Washington Post. 1937, 1973.
Der Widerstandskämpfer. Vienna, 1973.
Die Zeit. Hamburg, 1973.

Index